TRENDS IN SOVIET THEORETICAL LINGUISTICS

FOUNDATIONS OF LANGUAGE
SUPPLEMENTARY SERIES

VOLUME 18

TRENDS IN SOVIET THEORETICAL LINGUISTICS

Edited by

F. KIEFER

D. REIDEL PUBLISHING COMPANY

DORDRECHT-HOLLAND / BOSTON-U.S.A.

First printing: December 1973

Library of Congress Catalog Card Number 72–95890

ISBN 90 277 0274 8

Published by D. Reidel Publishing Company,
P.O. Box 17, Dordrecht, Holland

Sold and distributed in the U.S.A., Canada, and Mexico
by D. Reidel Publishing Company, Inc.
306 Dartmouth Street, Boston,
Mass. 02116, U.S.A.

Printed in The Netherlands by D. Reidel, Dordrecht

TABLE OF CONTENTS

INTRODUCTION

0. Theoretical linguistics is a term not very often used in Soviet Linguistics. The terms 'structural linguistics', 'mathematical linguistics', 'applied linguistics' (which, incidentally, has another meaning here than in other parts of the world) all may cover theoretical work in linguistics. In older days serious theoretical work was done under the heading 'machine translation'. Very often the need for a special term for theoretically oriented studies in linguistics does not even arise.

Does this mean that there is no real theoretical linguistics in the Soviet Union? This would be, of course, a completely false conclusion. Some linguists tend to identify theoretical linguistics with generative grammar. Though it might be true – and I am myself very much inclined to subscribe to this view – that generative grammar has been the most fruitful linguistic theory up to now, this does not justify, however, the above identification. Incidentally, as we shall see later on, generative grammar has not been left unnoticed in the Soviet Union either. There are different trends within theoretical linguistics, one of which is generative grammar. While generative grammar (though one can worry about the content of this notion for many internal and external reasons) seems to be the mean theoretical trend in the United States and in Western Europe, it represents only one of the main trends in Soviet linguistics.

Soviet linguistics has often been criticized as being uninterested in theoretical investigations. It must be admitted that in view of the immense output of Soviet linguistics, theoretically oriented works constitute only a relatively small portion of this output. However, two further points should be noted. First, the boundaries between theoretical and non-theoretical work are not always very clear. Second, much of the theoretical work requires appropriate linguistic material to work with. This material is furnished by data-oriented linguists. (I am not quite sure if theoretically oriented vs data-oriented is the right opposition, it should be clear, however, what I mean here.)

Terminological difficulties and methodological differences would very often make works in Soviet linguistics hard to understand for an 'outsider'. One would have the feeling that the theoretical background is unclear and one would look in vain for the claims made in a paper. One would also feel some uneasiness about the line of argumentation and about the haziness of presentation. No doubt, our feelings are very often justified. We must not forget, however, that Soviet linguistics has its own tradition (as has German or French linguistics, for that matter; is it easy, for instance, for a linguist used to the generative terminology and methodology to grasp a French or a German study which makes use of 'traditional' terminology and methodology?) and this tradition cannot be neglected, not even in theoretically oriented works. This cannot be an excuse, of course, and it is not always the reader who should be blamed if he fails to understand something. I am sure that in the present volume, too, the reader will find quite a few real puzzles to worry about.

The present book has come about due to chance and to choice factors. Not all linguists whom I would very much have liked to be represented here were able to contribute. That much about the chance part. As to the choice part, my choice, as almost every choice, has been arbitrary. I have chosen to include here roughly five 'trends' in Soviet theoretical linguistics:

(1) semantics (represented here by Apresjan, Iordanskaja, Martem'janov, Mel'čuk, Padučeva and Žolkovskij),

(2) applicative generative grammar (represented here by Šaumjan and Soboleva),

(3) generative grammar (represented here by Erelt, Õim and Rätsep),

(4) structural typology (represented here by Nedyalkov, Silnitsky and Khrakovsky),

(5) mathematical linguistics (represented here by Gladkij and Lecomtsev).

1. The papers on semantics show clearly that we would seek here in vain a homogeneous trend, though it is often referred to as 'Moscow school of semantics'. This term is misleading, however. Most of the Moscow semanticians follow their own conception as to the role of semantics in grammar, as to the means of semantic description, and as to the relationship between syntax and semantics. Very often they use different notational conventions. To put all this together it is rather hard to find a common denominator in the works by the members of the Moscow group. Let us consider the works by Padučeva and those by Mel'čuk, for example. What is at stake here is much more than a difference in interest. Padučeva, for instance, seems to be more interested in the semantics of logical forms (quantified expressions, negation, etc.) than Mel'čuk, while Mel'čuk's main interest seems to be – at least for the time being – the dictionary part of an overall semantic description. The methodological differences seem to be more important, however. Padučeva follows a methodology which could be termed logical analysis. What she says at the beginning of her paper (in this volume) about quantifiers may sound familiar to everybody: "Contemporary thinking has it that

a description of the meaning of a sentence requires reference to its deep structure" which "is close to its notation in one or another logical language. Quantifiers in particular should be included among the lexemes of deep structure language". The main concern of her paper is to show that "certain transformations are applicable or inapplicable to a sentence depending on what sort of quantifier appears in the deep structure". Mel'čuk, on the other hand, puts forward a general linguistic model with an explicit formulation of the methodology followed. The 'Meaning⇔Text' model is singled out by the fact that "it does not seek to generate grammatically correct (or meaningful, etc.) texts, but merely to match, ideally, *any* given meaning with all synonymous texts having this meaning, and conversely, to match *any* given text with all the meanings this text can have". So far substantial work has only been done with respect to the dictionary part of the model. The notion of 'dictionary' is conceived rather broadly and has a dynamic character. We find a formulation of this concept of a dictionary in a paper written jointly by Apresjan, Mel'čuk, and Žolkovskij: "The dictionary is based on the following principle: it must be fully sufficient for a smooth, idiomatic, and flexible expression of a given meaning, that is to say, it must display in an explicit and logical form whatever information may be necessary for the correct choice and usage of words and phrases to convey a given idea in a given speech context". (In F. Kiefer (ed.), 'Semantics and Lexicography: Towards a New Type of Unilingual Dictionary', *Studies in Syntax and Semantics*, D. Reidel Publ. Co., Dordrecht, 1969, p. 1.) This view about the role of the dictionary in linguistic description is rather pretentious, of course. Nobody has written such a dictionary as yet but the authors do work in this direction as is exemplified by the description of a set of dictionary entries in the paper which is included in this volume.

Iordanskaja's article exhibits still another approach to semantics. In many respects she comes rather close to the Apresjan-Mel'čuk-Žolkovskij approach. In the descriptive definitions given for a set of Russian words denoting emotions situational contexts as well as the speaker's attitudes and beliefs are taken into consideration. That the methodology followed in this paper seems to be a little bit outdated can be explained by the fact that the paper was written several years ago (1969).

Apresjan's paper deals with one of his favorite topics: with questions of synonymy, more precisely, with lexical synonymy. He advances a new theory of synonymy making use of a set of different criteria. The author, then, investigates the differences which lexically synonymous lexemes may exhibit. This study is written more or less in the structural semantics vein which, however, nobody working in semantics should neglect quite independently of the approach he is advocating.

Martem'janov's grammar consists of three systems. The first system, called valency grammar is a sort of case-grammar where predicative words are described in terms of valencies (roughly: cases). This grammar is conceived in order to express the abstract relationship between lexical elements of a (simple) sentence. The second system, called valency-junctive grammar, is constructed in order to describe relations between word groups (including sentences). The third system, called valency-junctive-emphasis grammar, is to provide a means for the description of logical emphasis (and perhaps, topicalization, in general). What is meant by grammar here can perhaps better be termed logical syntax since Martem'janov's grammar takes only into consideration abstract semantic relations. I think we come close to the truth by saying that what we have here is a sort of three-level generative semantics.

2. The two papers in applicative generative grammar extend the by now well-known methodology to two new areas: to semantics (Šaumjan) and to word formation (Soboleva).

For Šaumjan meaning description means to provide rules of translation. More precisely, the author states that "The meaning of a linguistic unit is the class of linguistic units which serve as its translations... To give the meaning of a given linguistic unit is to give the rules for translating this linguistic unit into other linguistic units". And then he goes on to say: "This is obviously not the only possible solution of the problem of meaning but it seems that only such a solution is fruitful for a semantic study of language within the framework of generative grammar". In order to arrive at a semantic theory of natural language and not just of a particular natural language one has to base this theory – an evident conclusion in Šaumjan's model – on the genotype grammar which is an abstract (possibly universal) grammar of natural language. As genotype grammar can be mapped into a phenotype grammar by means of language specific rules, so can the semantic description of a particular language be obtained by transforming genotype semantics into phenotype semantics. Another aspect of the Šaumjanian method is its purely deductive character. As Šaumjan puts it "The method we will use to construct the genotype language (in semantics – F.K.) is a particular instance of the hypothetico-deductive method used by the modern theoretical sciences". The elements of the deductive system, referred to as abstract objects, are not always interpretable in a given 'empirical' context. But this derives from the nature of the discrepancies between formal and 'natural' systems and need not be – according to Šaumjan – flaws in the theory.

In Šaumjan's genotype semantics we can spot, among other things, some of Fillmore's cases (agentive, instrumental, affective, locative, objective) and a series of, by now, well-known operators which are built in into a modified predicate calculus. Šaumjan constructs his formal semantic theory in the usual way: he starts out from elementary formulae (axioms) and then he applies semantic rules (rules of inference, rules of derivation). The general line of argumentation and the way this formal theory of semantics is constructed is very similar to Šaumjan's previous works.

The derivational structure of the Russian lexicon is treated in Soboleva's paper. Soboleva thinks that there is at least one aspect of lexical structure "that may lend itself to generative description (in terms of Šaumjan's model – F.K.). This aspect is the derivational structure of a lexicon". What is really meant here by description is a genotype morphology applicable to any natural language. In order to describe the derivational structure of Russian, special correspondence rules are needed which interpret the abstract genotype objects in terms of actually occurring (phenotype) objects. Apart from the morphological structure Soboleva provides a general semantic description of the derivational types. This description is given in terms of such categories as 'process', 'substance', 'quality', etc. Due to the methods chosen nothing is said here about idiosyncrasies in meaning and in morphological structure, nor about the related problem of productivity. Furthermore, derivation is considered as a purely lexical phenomenon.

3. Chomskyan type of generative grammar (where 'Chomskyan' should be taken to mean not-Šaumjanian and nothing else; it includes, therefore, among other things, generative semantics as well as case grammar) has gained ground principally in Estonia. A small group of linguists at the Tartu University has been working in the generative framework for some years. These linguists make use of this framework in tackling various problems of Estonian grammar as well as in their inquiries into the semantics of natural language. The present volume contains three papers written by members of the Tartu group.

Mati Erelt tackles problems of the comparative and superlative sentences in Estonian. His approach is mainly generative semantic: the structures in question are described in purely semantic terms. Although the author considers only the simplest structures he arrives at some general conclusions which might be of interest not only to linguists who are interested in Estonian grammar but also to those who are interested in general theoretical questions. Erelt argues, for instance, that "it seems more sensible to us at the present moment to give up the rigid requirement of identity of semantic representations for paraphrases and to replace it by a more general and at the same time milder requirement of equivalence of semantic representations".

Õim's study treats the problem of presuppositions. He criticizes previous work on presuppositions by saying that "attention has mainly been directed towards the logical properties of this notion, not towards its function". Sentences are to be analyzed – according to Õim – in terms of sequences of messages (elementary propositions), some of which may be presuppositions. These messages are not necessarily linearly ordered. Õim concludes (on the basis of this fact and of some other properties of messages) that the predicate-argument representations of semantic structures practised, for example, by generative semanticians, cannot be adequate.

Rätsep's paper is an interesting study about how certain situations interact with sentence structures where "situation" is interpreted as "a certain state or action in reality and an idea or generalization of it". The "communicative situation" is only one of the possible situations. The paper is mainly concerned with a set of highly abstract situations, called "deep situations". The author analyzes different predicates in terms of these deep situations which seem to involve Fillmore's cases as well as the presuppositions and other meaning elements (possibly features) of the predicate. Rätsep himself, too, admits that his system is related to that of Fillmore. Toward the end of his paper he says: "Such a situation analysis is rather close to the views presented in the so-called case grammar theory. ...The difference is that deep structures are not considered as relations between logical predicates and arguments, but as so-called deep situations... Situation components therefore are much more detailed units than Fillmore's arguments and their cases".

This may suffice to show in what directions the thoughts of the Tartu linguists go. I leave it to the reader to judge to what extent the claims made in their works are substantiated and borne out by the facts.

4. Structural typology has long since been a favored field of research in the Soviet Union. As to the essence of structural typology let me quote B. Uspenskij, one of the most outstanding scholars in this field: "...it seems fully warranted to take the structure of a language as a starting point in typological linguistic comparison – otherwise one compares isolated phenomena which *per se* (...) may not be informative. If the various structures are described in adequate terms and based upon identical assumptions (...), then the comparison of these structures is the subject of structural typology". (B. Uspenskij, *Principles of Structural Typology*, p. 12.)

The two papers on typology should be understood against this background. Nedyalkov and Silnitsky discuss the typology of causatives (causatives formed by a regular and productive means). The paper goes much beyond a simple taxonomy, however. Apart from the morphological classification of causatives, the authors discuss the semantics of the causatives in some detail as well. It is clear that here a purely taxonomic approach would fall short. There is, as the authors point out, for instance, a difference between factitive and permissive causation. These two aspects of causation are, however, not independent of each other. The paper brings out rather clearly what is universal and what is language specific in the causatives though this difference is not always stated explicitly.

The structures discussed in Khrakovsky's paper are defined in the following way: "What will be described here are derived structures in which the concrete lexically expressed agent does not occupy the position of the subject. In other words, the correspondence agent-subject is disturbed in these structures. We shall call such derived surface structures passive constructions". The author proposes a calculus for obtaining the possible passive constructions. After this he proceeds in describing the typology of passive constructions. The classification given in this paper is novel in various aspects. The main novelty is the semantic-syntactic nature of the classification. The traditional definition of passive constructions takes also morphological features into account. In the section on meaning the author makes some inquiries into the intricate question as to what extent the active and the corresponding passive are synonyms. Typology is only one of the topics discussed in this paper. It is perhaps for this reason that no universals with respect to passives are established, although a general characterization of passive constructions is given.

5. Mathematical linguistics has attracted quite a few Soviet mathematicians from the very outset. The first Soviet contribution to this field, which led to lively discussions in the Soviet Union and in many other countries, was Kulagina's famous set theoretic model. Much of the later work in mathematical linguistics has been based on the assumptions made in Kulagina's paper. As has often been pointed out, Kulagina's model is a sort of formalized distributional analysis and it does not go much beyond well-established structuralist methods. (From a purely formal point of view Kulagina's grammar is weakly equivalent to a context-free phrase structure grammar.) Moreover, it takes the set of grammatical sentences for granted, they are given 'from outside'. Later works in Soviet mathematical linguistics (outside the Soviet Union, too, many mathematicians – but for some reason not so many linguists – got interested in Kulagina's model in the early sixties and even later) have provided many refinements of and improvements on this model.

Gladkij's paper has been influenced to some extent by previous works in mathematical linguistics and especially by the works of Kulagina and her followers. The topic discussed in Gladkij's paper itself has received some attention in the Kulagina 'school'. Though sharing many methodological aspects with Kulagina-type mathematical linguistics, Gladkij takes another starting point. In fact, he criticizes Kulagina by saying that "The set of grammatically correct sentences of a language is in fact infinite, so that any procedure for which this set is basic requires infinite examination and is therefore ineffective". He goes on to say "In contrast to this, the present work proposes a system of basic notions, all of whose components are predicates determined on a finite set and are therefore describable by means of finite tables". The starting point for a formal explanation of the notions 'case' and 'gender' is this: "...each case is a set of noun-forms which are in some sense governed identically by other words, while each gender is a set of nouns which in some sense identically govern other words". From this it follows that Gladkij confines himself to the morphological properties of nouns. Although the author discusses some semantic properties of the notions 'case' and 'gender' as well, these are restricted to 'grammatical meaning'.

Lecomtsev's paper bears testimony to the fact that glossematics has still not lost its attractiveness and influence among Soviet scholars. The deductive system (called D-Syntax) outlined in this article is based on such notions as paradigmatic and syntagmatic relations, distinctive features, etc. The main novelty in this system is the assignment of bundles of distinctive features to the elements of D-Syntax.

6. The title of the present collection does not suggest more and not less than it is intended to. I could have called the collection 'Current Trends in Soviet Theoretical Linguistics' or the like. Apart from the fact that the term 'current trend' has often been used (and misused), this title would suggest a certain comprehensiveness and completeness which is *not* intended. Not all trends in Soviet theoretical linguistics are represented here, though – and here enters my subjective evaluation into picture – I think that the most important ones have been included. The ones which are mentioned here have raised most of the theoretical discussions and they have been most internationally acknowledged. And let me add to this a purely personal factor: I know these trends best. There are things I like and things I dislike in them, but I find them all interesting and instructive. I wish I could be more specific on this point but space limitation prevents me from doing this (a good excuse!). Let me also note that the term 'theoretical linguistics' suggests already that we have to do with contemporary linguistics.

It is perhaps not too pretentious to claim that this collection is the most up-to-date one on Soviet (theoretical) linguistics. Most papers were written especially for this volume, others are revised and expanded versions of ear-lier publications in Russian. The translations were checked by the authors. Since the review articles in 'Current Trends in Linguistics' (Vol. 1, Th. A. Sebeok (ed.), Soviet and East European Linguistics, Mouton and Co., The Hague, 1963) much work has been done in Soviet theoretical linguistics and I think that many of the critical remarks which we encounter in the articles of the aforementioned volume have lost their force by now. The more recent reviews published in the 'Georgetown University Monographs' (22nd An-nual Round Table, No. 24, Georgetown Univ. Press, Washington D.C. 1971, pp. 227–301) are not very informative since most of the really inter-esting work has been left unnoticed in them.

Mariedal/Stockholm/Summer 1973

V. P. NEDYALKOV AND G. G. SILNITSKY

THE TYPOLOGY OF MORPHOLOGICAL AND LEXICAL CAUSATIVES*

1. The subject of this paper is the *typology of the causative opposition V_i:V_j*, where V_i designates the constant s_j (i.e., some state), and V_j designates cs_j (i.e., a state, but one which has already been caused). The verbs V_i are *non-causatives*, and the verbs V_j are their *causatives*. V_i and V_j are connected by a *semantic derivation* relation: V_j is 'formed' from V_i by adding an additional meaning c.

The symbols used in this paper refer to the notion of the causative situation. The immediate constituents of a causative situation (*CS*) consist of at least two microsituations which are connected to each other by the *relation of causation* (*c*). Causative relations will in this paper be considered to be synonymous to relations of cause and effect.

The causing/causal micro-situation will be known as the *antecedent*, and the caused micro-situation the *consequent* of a *CS*. Thus, in the example of a *CS My vernulis', tak kak pogoda isportilas'* 'We returned because the weather got worse', *isportilas' pogoda* 'the weather got worse' expresses the antecedent, and *My vernulis'* 'We returned' the consequent, of the *CS*.

The relation of causation c is a constant of the *CS*. This constant is a determinative component of the causative macro-situation, since it organizes this situation. In addition to this determinative component, a *CS* contains at least four more constants: the *agent/ actor*, or the subject of the antecedent of the *CS* (r_i), the causal/causing state (s_i), the *patient*, or subject of the consequent of the *CS* (r_j), and the caused state (s_j).

Your	action	made	him	leave
Tvoj	postupok	zastavil	ego	ujti
r_i	s_i	c	r_j	s_j

antecedent   consequent

macro-situation (*CS*)

The causative situation can be written in a string of symbols:

$$CS = [r_i \, s_i] \quad c\,[r_j s_j].$$

Note. The examples below are given (1) in ordinary orthography, (2) in transcription (sometimes simplified), (3) in transliteration, (4) a combination of (2) and (3). This circumstance is connected with the source where a given example was obtained. These irregularities do not interfere with the illustration of the basic ideas of the paper.

2. V_i and V_j form various types of *formal oppositions*, of which the following are the most important.

* This is a revised version of a paper which was first published in *Tipologija kauzativnyx konstrukcij (Morfologičeskij kauzativ)* (Kholodovič, ed.), Izdatel'stvo Nauka, Leningrad 1969, pp. 20–50.

2.1. *Directed* or *derivational oppositions.* Here one of the members of the opposition is *formally* derived from the other, which is demonstrated by the fact that this member of the opposition has an additional derivational morpheme. Thus, the stem of one of the verbs here is inserted into the stem of the other. From the point of view of the direction of the derivation, two subtypes can be discerned.

2.1.1. The member of the opposition that is causative in meaning is formally marked by means of a *causative* morpheme, i.e., $V_i \rightarrow V_j$. Thus, the directions of the semantic and formal derivations coincide, e.g., Bashkir *hyn-* ('become broken') $\rightarrow$ *hyn-dyr-* ('make broken') and – with the same meanings – Indonesian *patah* $\rightarrow$ *me-matah-kan*; Yukaghir *salƁa* $\rightarrow$ *salƁa-re*; Kamchadal *k'ol-* $\rightarrow$ *ən-k'ol-*; Kurdish (Sorani dialect) *śk* $\rightarrow$ *śk-and-*.

2.1.2. The member of the opposition that is non-causative in meaning is formally marked by means of an *anticausative* morpheme, i.e., $V_i \leftarrow V_j$. Thus, the directions of the semantic and formal derivations here are opposed to each other, for example, Russian *lomat'-sja* ('become broken') $\leftarrow$ *lomat'* ('make broken') and – with the same meanings – Swahili *vunj-ik-a* $\leftarrow$ *vunj-a*, Arabic *ta-kassara* $\leftarrow$ *kassara*, Korean *kkɔkk-ɔ-čži-* $\leftarrow$ *-kkɔkk*.

2.2. *Non-directed oppositions.* In this type of opposition it is not formally obvious which member is to be treated as the underlying one and which as the derived, that is, we have $V_i \leftrightarrow V_j$. This type can be subdivided into *conversive* and *correlative* oppositions.

2.2.1. *Conversive oppositions.* Here the members of the opposition have the same stems. This type of opposition is in turn subdivided into *paradigmatic* and *syntagmatic* oppositions.

2.2.1.1. *Paradigmatic oppositions.* Here the members of the opposition differ in their paradigms, namely: (1) in their forms of agreement with the subject in person and number, e.g., Ancient Greek καί-ω 'I make (it) burn' $\leftrightarrow$ καί-ομαι 'I burn', καί-ει '(he) burns' $\leftrightarrow$ καί-εται '(it) burns', (2) in the alternation of subjective and subjective-objective agreement by means of (a) a change in the number of person markers, e.g., Abkhazian i^1-*blueit*^{2} 'it^1-burns^2' $\leftrightarrow$ $\leftrightarrow i^1$-z^2-*blueit*^{3} 'I^2-it^1-burn^3', i^1-aa^2-*blueit*^{3} 'we^2-it^1-burn^3/set fire to', (b) a substitution of one person marker for another, for example, Chukot *jyr'et-g'i* 'it became filled', filled up $\leftrightarrow$ *jyr'en-nin* 'he-it-filled'; (3) in the means with which temporal forms are constructed, e.g., Bambara [*sebe*^{1}] *jeni*^{2}-*na*^{3} '[the paper^1] burned^{2,3}' $\leftrightarrow$ [n'fa^1] *ya*^{2} [*sebe*^{3}] *jeni*^{4} '[my^1 father^1]

burned[2,4] [the paper[3]]'; (4) in the positional gradation of the inflexion, e.g., Japanese *jak-e* 'burn' ↔*jak-e, jak-a, jak-i, jak-u, jak-o* 'burn make burn'.

2.2.1.2. Syntagmatic oppositions. Causative and non-causative meanings are determined solely by the environment of the verb, for example, English [*water*] *boil-s* → [*my mother*] *boil-s* [*the water*]. Verbs of the type Ossetic *sudzyn* 'burn', 'burn/set fire to'; Lezghin *kun* 'burn', 'burn/incinerate', Ancient Chinese *wang* 'perish', 'destroy', etc., belong to this type.

Note. The syntagmatic marker, which is the only one present in this opposition, is also present as a complementary marker in causative constructions made up of verbs belonging to the other formal oppositions. Thus, all non-syntagmatic markers can, from a certain point of view, be considered superfluous, since the syntactic environment of verbs of the type described above generally indicates its causative or non-causative meaning quite clearly.

2.2.2. Correlative oppositions. Here the stems of both members intersect, i.e., besides the coinciding part they contain elements which differentiate them. This type of opposition can be subdivided into two subtypes.

2.2.2.1. Correlative root oppositions. Here the members of the opposition are distinguished by the partial non-coincidence of their root morphemes, e.g., Lithuanian *lūž-ti* 'break, become broken'↔*lauž-ti* 'break' and, with the same meanings, Nganasan *čaŋxuaʻ*↔*čambiʻ-*.

2.2.2.2. Correlative affixal oppositions. Here the members of the opposition have different alternating affixes. Affixes which function as causatives (cf. 2.1.1.) or anticausatives (cf. 2.1.2.) correlate especially often; cf., for example, Georgian *duɣ-s* 'boils' → *a-duɣ-eb-s* 'boils, makes boil' (*-a- – eb- –* is the causative confix), *i-ček-eb-a* 'hatches, comes out of the shell' ← *ček-s* 'hatches, makes hatch' (*i- – -eb* is the anticausative confix) on the one hand and the correlation of these morphemes *i-ɣ-eb-a* 'comes open'↔*a-ɣ-eb-s* 'opens, makes open' on the other; cf. also Swahili on the one hand: *-chek-a* 'laugh' → *chek-esh-a* 'make laugh' (*-esh-* is the causative suffix), *-vunj-ik-a* 'break, become broken'←*-vunj-a* 'break, make broken' (*-ik-* is the anticausative suffix) and *chem-k-a* 'boil, come to a boil'↔*chem-sh-a* 'boil, bring to a boil', on the other.

2.3. Suppletive oppositions. The members of the opposition differ in the complete non-coincidence of their root morphemes: Russian *umeret'* –

ubit', English *to die – to kill*, German *sterben – töten*, etc. In a suppletive opposition the members of the opposition, which have in fact no morphemes in common (other than functional ones), have no base in common for morphological comparison.

3. It is probable that a formal derivation that is semantically determined by means of causative morphemes[1] will generally be more common than one which is semantically undetermined. As far as we are able to determine on the basis of special literature on the subject, the formation of semantic causative oppositions where the formal derivation has the reverse direction, so common in the Slavic and certain other languages, has on the whole a narrower distribution. For example, the anticausative type of derivation either has a much weaker representation or is completely absent in Chukot, Eskimo, Nanain, Finnish, Yakut, Telugu, Piro, Gilyak, Yukaghir, Guarani, Kwakiute, Tunico, Wiyot, and others.

The converse and correlative types of formal oppositions, the first of which was very common in ancient Chinese and still is so in modern English, also seem to have a limited distribution in different languages and a limited productivity within individual languages.

4. The types of oppositions listed above can be combined, and some of these combinations are given below.

4.1. The combination of types 2.1.1 and (1) from 2.2.1.1. For example: Mari *šol-eš* 'burns' → *šol-t-a* 'burns/make burn' (-*t*- is the causative suffix, and -*eš* and -*a* are 3p.sg. endings of the first and second conjugations, respectively).

4.2. The combination of types 2.1.1 and 2a from 2.2.1.1. For example: Abkhazian i^1-*šueit*^{2} 'it^1-boils^2' → i^1-*sy*^{2}-*r*-*šueit*^{3} 'I^2-it^1-boil/bring to a boil^3' (r- is a causative morpheme).

4.3. The combination of types 2.1.1. and 2b from 2.2.1.1. For example: Chukot *pykir-g'i* 'he arrived' → *ry-pkir-en-nin* 'he-him-brought' (ry- – -en (<-et-) is the causative confix).

4.4. The combination of types 2.1.1 and (3) from 2.2.1.1. For example:

---

[1] There is reason to assume that the majority of languages and language groups have causative morphemes or exhibit traces of them. This can be demonstrated on the basis of material taken from a large number of languages, e.g., Ainu, many American Indian languages, Bantu, Basque, the Dravidian, Indo-European, Ibero-Caucasian, and Sino-Tibetan languages, Korean, Mongolian, the Mont-Khmer, Indonesian, Paleo-Asiatic, Paleo-African, Semitic, Tungus-Manchurian and Turkish languages, Eskimo and Japanese.

Malayalam *katt-unnu* 'I burn', 'you (sg) burn', 'he burns', etc., → *katt-i-ykunnu* 'I burn/make burn', 'you (sg) burn', etc. (-*i*- is the causative suffix; -*unnu* and (*y*)*kkunnu* are present tense suffixes of the weak and strong conjugations, respectively).

4.5. The combination of types 2.1.1 and (4) from 2.2.1.1. For example: Japanese *varaᒋvᒋ-é, varaᒋvᒋ-a, varaᒋvᒋ-i, varaᒋvᒋ-u, varaᒋvᒋo* 'laugh' → → *varav-a-s-e* 'make laugh' (-*s*- is the causative suffix).

4.6. The combination of types 2.1.1 and 2.2.2.1. For example: Finnish *pala-* 'burn' → *pol-tta-* 'burn, make burn' (-*tta*- is the causative suffix).

4.7. The combination of types 2.1.2 and (2b) from 2.2.1.1. For example: Chukot *pela-nen* 'he-him-left' → *pela-t-g'ə* 'he stayed' (-*t*- is the anticausative suffix).

4.8. The combination of types 2.1.2, (1) from 2.2.1.1 and 2.2.2.1. For example: Albanian *dieg-n* 'he burns, incinerates' → *digj-e-t* 'he burns' (-*e*- is the anticausative suffix).

5. When both means of derivation and means of correlation are combined in a single concrete formal opposition, the latter is considered to be directed (cf. for example 4.6, 4.8) – the derived member is marked in a more complex manner.

6. The constants s_j and c may be expressed not only by one, but also by two words, if these form a whole semantic *analytic unit* in which c is expressed by an empty causative verb.

We find an analytic parallel to type 2.1.1 in, for example, the English *to laugh* → *to make laugh* and – with the same meanings – in the Estonian *naerma* → *naerma ajama*; Vietnamese *cu·ŏ·i* → *lam cu·ŏ·i*; Kurdish (Sorani) *pêkenîn* → *we-pêkenîn hênan*; Khmer *saəc* → *thvə: aoy saəc*. Here the second members of the oppositions are represented by *analytic causatives*.

The Tajik *tamom šudan* 'end' ↔ *tamom kardan* 'finish' and the Tāti *xÿrd birən* 'become broken' ↔ *xÿrd sæxtæn* 'break' are analytic parallels to correlations of the type 2.2.2.2.

Analytic oppositions can replace synthetic ones in certain temporal forms; cf. oppositions of the type 2.2.2.2 in Pushtu *mat-iž-i* 'becomes broken, breaks' ↔ *mat-av-i* 'breaks', but *mat šu* 'has broken, become broken' ↔ *mat kər* 'broke'.

Note. In a number of languages there are transitional cases where the causative morpheme can function both as a causative affix and as an empty causative verb. This is the case in Avarian with a causative morpheme that has originated from the verb *ɣabi-ze* 'to do' (cf. *la-ze* 'know' → *la-z-abi-ze* or *la-ze ɣabi-ze*, which are respectively a synthetic and an analytic causative meaning 'teach, instruct').[2]

7. The formal devices listed above do not as a rule have as their only or even most important function the expression of causative oppositions, but also serve other purposes (on the polysemy of causative and anticausative morphemes see 22 and 23). For instance, all paradigmatic means serve to differentiate large groups of transitive and intransitive verbs and are usually only in a relatively small number of cases the only markers differentiating the members of causative oppositions.

8. The pairs of verbs given above to illustrate various formal oppositions can have different oppositions in different temporal forms, persons and/or numbers: in some cases it will be a derivation, in others a correlation; cf. Eskimo *tagi-quq* 'he arrives, comes' → *tagi-ta-qa* 'he-him-brings' (-ta- is a causative suffix of the present and immediate past tenses, *-quq* and *-qa* are endings of subtype *b* from 2.2.1.1), *tagi-ma-q* 'he came' → *magi-si-ma* 'he-him-brought' (*-ma-* is the past tense suffix, *-si-* is the causative suffix of the distant past), but: *tagi-na-quq* 'now-he-comes' ↔ *tagi-na-qa* 'now-he-him-brings' (-na- is the suffix of the immediate future; *na < ta + na*); *tagi-ly-quq* 'he will come' ↔ *tagi-ly-qa* 'he-him-will bring' (-*ly*- is the future suffix), Georgian *duɣ-s* 'boils' → *a-duɣ-eb-s* 'boils, brings to a boil', but *i-duɣ-eb-s* 'will boil' ↔ *a-duɣ-eb-s* 'will bring to a boil' (coincides with the present tense form). Thus, the general picture of the formal relations of a specific pair V_i and V_j can in different tenses, persons and numbers be very complicated.

9. There are other, more complex and less regular means for expressing semantic causative oppositions. We shall cite some cases where a semantic causative opposition cannot be expressed in certain languages solely by means of an intransitive non-causative and a transitive causative.

The causative opposition 'burn-burn/make burn' is expressed in Khantin by two *transitive* verbs: *tut-ny*[1] *te-t-y*[2] 'burns', literally: *by the fire*[1] *is consumed*[2] (the transitive verb is in a passive form)[3] → *tut-a ta-pyt* 'to make

---

[2] See A. A. Bokarev, *Sintaksis avarskogo jazyka*, M.-L., 1949, p. 59.

[3] The meaning of 'to burn' is expressed in a similar manner in a number of other languages, where this means of expression is also the only one; cf. Ket *bok*[1] *dyp*[2], Masai *enkima*[1] *ei-nos-ita*[2] literally: fire[1] eats[2].

burn', literally: *to the fire feed* (the causative is from the transitive verb *te* 'eat', *-pyt-* is a causative suffix).

The causative opposition '(come to a) boil – (bring to a) boil' (tea) is expressed in Chukot by a suppletive opposition (with an incorporation) both members of which are *intransitive* verbs; cf.: *čaj itit-g'i* 'the tea came to a boil' – *yt-len čaj-pat-g'ə* 'he boiled the tea, brought the tea to a boil' literally: he tea-boiled. The noun *čaj* (tea) is not used as a direct object with the transitive verb *ypat-yk* 'boil'.

In Latin, the causative member of the opposition 'laugh – make laugh' is expressed by an analytic construction which governs the optional dative case: *rideo* 'I laugh' → *risum [alicui] moveo* 'I make laugh', literally: I elicit laughter [from someone].

10. The causative member of an opposition which is formally marked by means of a *causative affix* will be said to be either a *morphological* or a *lexical* causative.

The non-causative member of an opposition which is formally marked by means of an *anticausative* affix will be said to be an *anticausative*.

Causatives which are members of suppletive and correlative-root oppositions, and also causatives having corresponding anticausatives, will be said to be lexical.

Causatives formed by a regular and productive means will be called *morphological*. *Lexical* causatives are such as are formed by a non-productive means.

Causatives found in syntagmatic and paradigmatic oppositions will be said to be *conversives*. Conversives are in turn subdivided into: congruentive (see type 2.2.1.1, (1) and (2)), conjugative (see type 2.2.1.1, (3)), positional (see type 2.2.1.1, (4)) and syntagmative (see 2.2.1.2) conversives.

11. Let us consider causative affixes from a distributional point of view, noting first of all that they are usually in immediate contact with the root morpheme of the underlying verb.

Causative affixes display certain tendencies when used with intransitive (V^{in}) and transitive (V^{tr}) verbs.

11.1. It can be established that causative affixes are more productive in combination with V^{in} than with V^{tr}. There are languages in which, with certain exceptions, causative affixes combine only with V^{in}: Arabic, Blackfoot, Gothic, Indonesian, Estonian, Klamath, Goos, Takelma and others. It seems that there is no language in which causative affixes are attached only to V^{tr}.

Thus, if there are causative affixes in a language which serve to form V_j from V^{tr} (such as Georgian *çer-s* 'he writes' → *a-çer-in-eb-s* 'he makes him write'), then this language also has causative affixes which serve to form V_j from V^{in} (Georgian *šrom-ob-s* 'he works' → *a-šrom-eb-s* 'he makes him work', *duɣ-s* 'boils' → *a-duɣ-eb-s* 'brings to a boil'). This is the case in Abkhazian, Georgian, Hungarian, Zulu, Mongolian, Nanaian, Sanskrit, Turkish, Finnish, Japanese, Gilyak, Evenki, Aymara, Kechua and Yukaghir. The reverse assertion does not hold.

11.2. Causative affixes usually combine only or mainly with V^{in} in languages which also have causative empty verbs (which combine only or also with V^{tr}), as for example in Arabic, Armenian, Khmer, Chukot, Guarani and Tāti.[4]

11.3. If a language has several causative affixes, the means for deriving V_j from V^{in} are more varied than those for forming V_j from V^{tr}. In ancient Telugu, for example, V_j are derived from V^{in} by means of five suffixes (*-pu*, *-cu*, *-ncu*, *-ccu*, *-incu*), and from V^{tr} by means of two (*-incu*, *-(i)pincu*).[5] In Yakut, V_j are derived from V^{in} by means of four suffixes (*-ar*, *-yar*, *-t*, *-tar*) and from V^{tr} by means of two (*-tar*, *-t*)[6]. Hungarian has nine (*-l*, *-al*, (*el*), *-lal* (*lal*), *-t*, *-it*, *-dít*, *-aszt*, (*-eszt*), *-at* (*-et*), *-tat* (*-tet*)) and two suffixes (*-at*, (*-et*), *-tat* *-(tet)*), respectively,[7] and in Komi we have two (*-t*, *-öd*)[8] and one (*-öd*). This fact indicates that the derivation of V_j from V^{tr} is secondary and evidently appeared later than the formation of V_j from V^{in}. We should note in this connection that situations which reflect V_j formed from V^{in} (of the type 'burn/make burn') are much more frequent than situations which show V_j to be derived from V^{tr} (of the type 'order to burn').

11.4. Affixes which tend to form V_j from V^{tr} often have a more complicated structure (since they are combinations or reduplications of more simple affixes) than affixes which tend to form V_j from V^{in}. We can propose the following implication: if there are productive complex affixes among

[4] See A. S. Markarjan, *Sostavnye glagoly armjanskogo jazyka*. Author's abstract of his doctoral dissertation, Erevan, 1966, pp. 70–80; Ju. A. Gorgoniev, *Kategorija glagola v sovremennom kxmerskom jazyke*. M., 1963, pp. 84–95; A. L. Grjunberg, *Jazyk severo-azerbajdžanskix tatov*. M.-L., 1963, pp. 56–58, 104–105; J. Platzmann, *Grammatik der Brasilianischen Sprache*, Leipzig, 1874, SS. 139–145.
[5] Bh. Krishnamurti, *Telugu Verbal Bases: A Comparative and Descriptive Study*, Berkeley, 1961, pp. 194–202.
[6] L. N. Xaritonov, *Zalogovye formy glagola v jakutskom jazyke*, M.-L., 1963, pp. 53–58.
[7] K. E. Majtinskaja, *Vengerskij jazyk*, II. M., 1959, pp. 96–102.
[8] V. I. Lytkin, *Ponuditel'nyj zalog v permskix jazykax*. Uč. zap. Udmurtskogo NII IELJa, vyp. 18, Iževsk, 1957, p. 111.

the causative affixes, then by means of them V_j can also (or only) be derived from V^{tr}.

11.5. There are also causative affixes which combine with both V^{in} and V^{tr}. Here we encounter the following cases. (1) One and the same affix is used to form V_j from V^{in} and from V^{tr}; cf. Kechua *huañu-* 'die' → *huañu-chi* 'kill' (V_j from V^{in}), *jacha-* 'to know' → *jacha-chi-* 'to learn' (V_j from V^{tr}).[9] (2) There are a few affixes which form V_j from V^{in} and V^{tr} in accordance with usage and morphonological motivations. In these cases there is also an affix (or affixes) which combines only with V^{in} (as, for example, in Hungarian and Mongolian). (3) One of the affixes generally combines with V^{in}, whereas the other usually combines with V^{tr}, as, for example, in Georgian: *duɣ-s* 'boils, comes to a boil' → *a-duɣ-eb-s* 'boils, brings to a boil' (V_j from V^{in}); compare *çer-s* 'writes' → *a-çer-in-eb-s* 'makes write' (V_j from V^{tr}).

12. Now let us consider some cases of *secondary causative derivation*, where causative verbs are derived by adding a causative morpheme to an already causative verb. We shall indicate such a verb with the symbol V_e. Here we must distinguish between two types of derivational strings.

12.1. $V_i(=V^{in}) \to V_j \to V_e$.

(1) From the point of view of selecting the second causative affix, we can distinguish the following cases: (a) the same affix is added again in its entirety (Keshua *huañu-* 'die' → *huañu-chi* – 'kill' → *huañu-chi-chi-* 'command to kill'), (b) a new affix is added (Turkish *öl-* 'die' → *öl-dür-* 'kill' → *öl-dür-t* 'command to kill'), (c) only those elements of the second affix (if it is a confix) are added which do not coincide with the first affix (Georgian *duɣ-s* 'boils' → *a-duɣ-eb-s* 'boils, brings to a boil' → *a-duɣ-eb-in-eb-s* 'orders to bring to a boil'. Cf.: *çer-s* 'writes' → *a-çer-in-eb-s* 'orders to write').

(2) From the point of view of the possibilities for deriving V_e three basic cases can be distinguished: (a) the V_e is formed (see the examples above), (b) the V_e is not formed (in Abkhazian, for example, a causative cannot contain more than one causative prefix – the V_j *a-r-š-ra* 'bring to a boil' can be derived from the V^{in} *a-š-ra* 'boil, come to a boil', but the meaning of the V_e 'order to boil' can only be expressed by a periphrastic form, although it is theoretically possible in this language to form causatives from V^{tr}; cf.: *a-š'-ra* 'kill' → *a-r-š'-ra* 'force to kill'), (c) the V_e is derived only

---

[9] See E. W. Middendorf, *Das Runa Simi oder die Keshua-Sprache*, Leipzig, 1890, pp. 148, 174.

from V_j with certain causative affixes (for example, in Burjat Mongolian the following derivational chain is possible: *zogso* 'stop, come to a stop', → →*zogs-oo* 'stop, bring to a stop' → *zogs-oo-lgo* 'make, induce smb to stop smb/sth'. After the causative suffix -uul-, however, no second causative suffix can be applied: *bajarla* 'be glad' → *bajarl-uul* 'gladden, make glad'; the meaning 'command to make glad, gladden' can only be rendered periphrastically).

12.2. $V_i (= V^{tr}) \rightarrow V_j \rightarrow V_e$. V_e are found relatively seldom in such derivational chains. We find them, for example, in languages such as Chuvash, Yakut and Mansi[10], e.g., *junty-* 'sew' → *junty-lt-* 'ask to sew' → *junty-lt-a-pt* 'ask (through smb.) smb. to sew' (see also 27.).

13. The following *causation types* can be distinguished.

(1) *Factitive ~ permissive* (respectively *prohibitive*) *causation*. With respect to factitive causation, the only or primary source of changes on the referential plane is the causing subject (r_i): *Ja velel emu prijti* 'I ordered him to come', *ja pozval ego* 'I invited him', *ja zakryl dver'* 'I closed the door', *ja ispugal ego* 'I frightened him'. In permissive causation the primary source of these changes is the caused subject (r_j), and the role of the causing subject (r_i) is reduced to permitting or obstructing the changes: *ja [ne] razrešil emu prijti* 'I [did not] allow(ed) him to come', *ja [ne] vpustil ego* 'I [did not] let him in', *on [ne] dal dveri zakryt'sja* 'he [did not] let the door close'. In other words, if in factitive causation r_j *does something* so that r_j will 'fulfill' s_j, then in permissive causation r_j either (a) *does something* or (b) *does not do anything* to prevent r_j from fulfilling s_j.

These two basic meanings, illustrated above with Russian examples, conceal a wide range of particular types of causation peculiar to various causative morphemes – from the physical reduction of the caused object (r_j) to a given state (s_j) by the causing subject (r_i) and from the most categorial incitement to action to a simple failure to prevent an action due to ignorance, inattention, carelessness or the inability to obstruct it.

(2) *Distant ~ contact causation*. In the case of distant causation there is a mediated relation between the causing subject and the caused state in which a greater or lesser independence of the caused subject is actualized in its initiation (or failure to make an initiation) of the states s_j. This mediation often appears in an actualization of a certain time interval between the causing (s_i) and caused (s_j) states. Permissive causation is according to this

[10] See: §27, this article; L. N. Xaritonov, *Zalogovye formy...*, pp. 59–60; E. I. Rombandeeva, *Kauzativnye glagoly v sovremennom mansijskom jazyke*. Author's abstract of her candidate's thesis, L., 1964, pp. 5–9, respectively.

definition always distant. The subject of the caused state (r_j) in the case of factitive distant causation is usually animate: *ja prikazal emu ujti* (I ordered him to leave).

The characteristics mentioned above are absent in the case of contact causation. Factitive contact causation can have either an animate (a) or an inanimate (b) r_j: (a) *ja ispugal ego* 'I frightened him', (b) *ja otkryl dver'* 'I opened the door'.

Contact causation tends to be found more often than distant causation in typical, recurrent situations.

Distant causation, unlike contact causation, is often connected with the *actualization of various means of bringing about a causing state* (s_i) *by the subject*. For example, Gilyak *pold'* 'to fall' has the derivatives *vol-u-d'* with the contant meaning 'fell, throw down' and *pol-gu-d'* with the distant meaning 'do something so that someone will fall' (*by pushing, tripping, backheeling, not saying anything about the slippery spot, not giving support, purposely or because of ignorance that smb. was falling*, etc.); cf. Evenki *ju-* 'come out', *ju-v-* 'bring, lead out' (contact causation) and *ju-vkén-* 'force (order, allow, request, not hinder, etc.) to come out' (distant causation).[11]

We should be aware of the fact that in a number of concrete instances we will encounter certain difficulties in defining the type of causative meaning on the basis of the given criteria, due to the large number of heterogeneous factors (linguistic and extralinguistic) which affect the nature of a causation.

14. Let us consider the *relationship between factitive and permissive meanings* expressed by causative morphemes.

14.1. If a causative morpheme in any language can express permissiveness, it can usually also express factitivity (as, for example, in Adugei, Aymara, Blackfoot, Georgian, Kechua, Nanaian, Evenki, Japanese, Gilyak, Turkish and Mongolian languages, etc.). The reverse situation is always found (for example, permissiveness is not found in Arabic, Basque, Zulu, Indonesian and Takelma). Here is meant the theoretical possibility of expressing these two meanings with a causative morpheme, not their actual presence in all causatives and in any context. Whether one or the other of these meanings is activated depends on a whole series of factors (see 14.3).

Thus, in this case the causative meaning of a morpheme is in and of itself *global*, if we can permit ourselves such an expression. That is, it cannot be divided into the partial meanings of permissiveness and factitivity in the

---

[11] Cf. 'contact' – 'distant' causation as understood by A. G. Šanidze ('Glagol'nyje kategorii akta i kontakta na primerax gruzinskogo jazyka', *Izv. AN SSSR*, t. V, vyp. 2. 1946, pp. 165–172).

same way that the meaning of the category of number divides into singular, plural, etc.

There are, however, cases in which both basic causative meanings are distributed among different causative morphemes. This is the case, for example, with empty causative verbs in French, which are unlike, for example, the German empty causative verb; compare the French *faire venir* 'tell to come, invite', *laisser venir* 'allow to come', on the one hand, and the German *lassen* with both its causative meanings – *kommen lassen* 'tell to come, invite' and, more seldom, 'allow to come'.

14.2. If a language has a causative morpheme which expresses permissiveness, this morpheme usually combines with a larger group of verbal stems in this meaning than in its second meaning, factitivity, which is implied by the first. This is due to the fact that there is a range of actions which can be permitted (in reality or in the imagination, i.e., because one has not known about them or failed to notice them, because one has waited for them to begin, etc.), but which cannot be directly caused, e.g. Gilyak *kru-gu-d'* 'wait for the dawn, until it dawns', from *kru-d'* 'to dawn'.

14.3. In various languages where the causative morphemes have a global meaning (for example, in Georgian and Gilyak) we find certain *general contextual* (and *situational*) *conditions for the actualization of permissive or factitive meanings* connected with the communicative directionality of the sentence, the 'pleasant' or 'unpleasant' nature of the caused state, the presence of negation, a reflexive direct object, etc. The conditions listed above can of course be combined. Let us consider a few instances.

(1) An imperative situation with a speaker $= r_j$ and without negation in the V_j usually expresses a permissive meaning. This is explained by the simple fact that a person does not usually request that he be forced to do something. For example: Gilyak $Ymyka^1$, $n'ax^2$ mry-gu-ja^3 'Mother[1], let[3] me[2] go swimming[3]' (-gu- is the causative suffix); cf. Georgian *deda m-a-cur-av-e*, which means the same thing (*m*- = 'me', *a*- is a causative prefix).

(2) An imperative situation with a speaker $= r_j$ and with negation in the V_j usually expresses a factitive meaning, namely, a rejection of factitivity. This is explained by the simple fact that we do not usually request that we be not allowed to do something. For example, Gilyak Ta^1 $n'ax^2$ $orbot$-ku-ja^3 'Do not[1] make[3] me[2] work[3]'; cf. Georgian $Šen^1$ me^2 ar^3 m^2-a-mu-$šav$-o^3 [You[1] (sg.)], do not[3] make[3] me[2] work' (*a*- is a causative prefix).

(3) If a caused state is an action which is 'pleasant' for its subject, the causative morpheme usually expresses permissiveness, e.g., Gilyak hy^1 $umgu^2$

p'olaax[3] *ena-vorx*[4] *lay-gu-d'*[5] 'This[1] woman[2] let[5] her[3] daughter[3] go to visit[5] in[4] another[4] village[4]'.

(4) If a caused state is an action which is 'unpleasant' for its subject and if there is no special indication in the context that the subject of the caused state desires to perform this action, the causative usually expresses factitivity, e.g. Gilyak *Ymyk*[1] *n'ax* *tir*[3] *p'uv-gu-d*[4] "Father[1] told[4] me[2] (or 'asked[4] me[2]') to saw[4] the firewood[3]''.

(5) In cases where the subject of the causing action coincides denotatively with the object of the caused action, the V_j generally has a permissive meaning. Verbs which designate 'unpleasant' actions that cause the subject of the causation some sort of harm are often used in this form. A negation is often used in such cases, e.g., Gilyak *Ola*[1] *n'nafkax*[2] *p'sa-gu-d'*[3] 'The son[1] allowed[3] his[2] comrade to beat[3] him[3]' (because he was weaker than his friend or did not offer any resistance); cf. Georgian *Švilma*[1] *amxanags*[2] *tavi*[3] *a-cem-in-a*[4] 'The son[1] allowed[4] his comrade[2] to beat[4] him[3]' (*a- - -in* is a causative confix).

15. The meaning of *assistance* or *help* stands somewhat apart from the factitive and permissive meanings, but of these two it is closer to the latter. This meaning is characteristic of the causative affixes in Zulu (where a V_j cannot express permissiveness proper, i.e., permission, consent) and Georgian (which also has permissive and factitive meanings): Georgian *Švili*[1] *çerils*[2] *çer-s*[3] 'The son[1] is writing[3] a letter[2]' → *Mama*[1]*švils*[2] *çerils*[3] *a-çer-in-eb-s*[4] 'Father[1] tells/allows/*helps*[4] his son[2] write[4] a letter[3]'.

In certain languages the assistive meaning is rendered by special affixes. In Kechua, for example, the suffix *-isi-* (*-usi*) denotes *help, cooperation, sympathy*: *llank'-isi-* 'to help smb in his work' (cf. *llank'a* 'work' → *llank'a-chi* 'tell to work').[12]

It is characteristic of the relationship between the assistive and other causative meanings that in Aymara the morpheme *ya* (*aa*), which designates factitivity and permissiveness, is part of the morpheme meaning 'to help' *jaya* (*jaa*).[13]

If it is simply the joint nature of an action rather than the achievement of a definite result that is accentuated in an assistive meaning, then this meaning can also be expressed by a reciprocal morpheme, as for example in Yakut: *Kini*[1] *miexe*[2] *ot*[3] *tieji*[4]*-s*[5]*-te* 'He[1] helped[5] me[2] bring, drive[4] the hay[3]' (*-s-* is a reciprocal morpheme).[14]

[12] E. W. Middendorf, *Das Runa Simi...*, p. 191.
[13] E. W. Middendorf, *Die Aimara-Sprache*, Leipzig, 1891, p. 148.
[14] L. N. Xaritonov, *Zagolovye formy...*, p. 21.

16. According to how the causative meanings they express are combined, causative affixes can be divided into those which express:

(a) only factitivity (for example, Armenian, Estonian, Takelma), (b) factitivity and permissiveness (Abkhazian, Aymara, Kechua, Gilyak), (c) factitivity and assistiveness (Zulu), (d) factitivity, permissiveness and assistiveness (Georgian, Japanese), (e) only assistiveness (Kechua, Aymara).

17. It seems possible to distinguish groups of languages according to how the meanings expressed by causative affixes are related, on the one hand, and how these affixes combine with V^{in} and V^{tr}, on the other.

Judging by their grammars, the presence of assistive and factitive meanings is compatible with the presence of causatives derived from V^{in} and V^{tr} in Avarian, Aymara, Georgian, Kechua, Lezghin, Mongolian languages, Nanaian, Gilyak, Turkish languages, Evenki and Japanese.

The presence of causatives formed from V^{in} and V^{tr} is only compatible with factitive (and assistive) meanings in the Bantu languages, e.g., Zulu and Swahili.

Causatives formed [almost] exclusively from V^{in} are only compatible with factitive meanings in Armenian, Arabic, Gothic, Indonesian, Estonian, Coos, Takelma, Wappo.

The following probable implication can be formulated: if a language has only affixes which derive causatives from V^{in}, it is unlikely that these affixes will have a permissive meaning.

18. Individual languages display a relative determination of the types of meanings expressed by causative morphemes by their combinability with V^{in} and V^{tr}.

V_j derived from V^{tr} generally express distant causation.

V_j derived from V^{in} can be subdivided into two types. If a causative morpheme forms V_j only from V^{in}, it usually expresses contact causation.

In these cases distant causation is usually expressed by combinations with empty causative verbs (if the given language has such verbs and they can combine with V^{in}): cf. Chukot ekvet-g'i 'he set off' → r-ekvet-ev-nin 'an affixive causative from a V^{in}) 'he sent him off', but ekvet-y-jgut ryn-nin 'he made him leave, set off' (an analytic causative from a V^{in}).

If in a given language a causative morpheme can combine with V^{tr}, then in combination with V^{in} it expresses distant causation more often than morphemes which only combine with V^{in}, cf. the meanings of Gilyak V_j with the suffix -u- (forms V_j only from V^{in}) and the suffix -gu- ∼ -ku- (forms V_j from both V^{in} and V^{tr}): lyrkt' 'sail, float' → lyrk-u-d' 'sail, float (a raft, boat)' (contact causation); lyrk-ku-d' 'let (not hinder, etc.) sail' (distant causation). Cf. also the Batsbien suffixes -d- (forms V_j mainly from V^{in}) and -it- (forms V_j from V^{in} and V^{tr}).

19. Morphemes which combine with both V^{tr} and V^{in} are subdivided into two groups according to whether the caused subject is marked for animateness (morphemes that combine only with V^{in} do not seem to subdivide on the basis of this feature):

(1) causative morphemes not marked for animateness of the caused subject; cf. Chuvash *kus* 'move, shift' → *kus-tar* 'shift' (contact causation) → *kus-tar-tar* 'force to move, shift' (distant causation).

(2) causative morphemes marked for animateness of the caused subject; cf. the Eskimo suffix *-sqa-*, for example, V_j from V^{tr}: *ga[ʁ]-* 'cook' → *gaʁy-sqa* 'ask (allow, force) to cook', V_j from V^{in}: *aʁla* 'go' → *alʁi-sqʁa* 'tell to go'; the suffix in Eskimo which is unmarked with respect to an animate caused subject is *-ta-*; cf. the following V_j formed from V^{in}: *aʁla-* 'go' → →*aʁla-ta-* 'lead', 'carry', *ajyma-* 'break, get broken' → *ajyma-ta* 'break'.

The Chukot analytic causative is also marked for the feature 'animate caused subject'.[15]

20. The majority of causative morphemes which are attached to V^{in} expressing certain consciously performed actions (such as working, dancing, fishing, serving, for example) constitute an exception to the tendency described above (see 18.) in languages which, besides these morphemes, have others which combine only or mainly with V^{tr}; cf., for example, V_j from V^{in} of these two types in Georgian, which are derived by means of the confix a-~-eb, which generally form V_j from V^{in}: *trialeb-s* 'turns, spins' → *a-trialeb-s* 'spins' and *tevza-ob-s* 'fishes' → *a-tevzav-eb-s* 'forces to fish', Cf. V_j from V^{tr} formed by means of the confix a-~-in-eb, which mainly combines with V^{tr}: *çer-s* 'writes' → *a-çer-in-eb-s* 'makes write'.

As for V^{in} designating states, involuntary actions or movements, that is, those meaning for example 'fall', 'laugh', 'become saturated', 'boil', 'come', 'sleep',[16] the morphological V_j formed from them have a tendency to lose the distant causative meaning of an indirectly caused action (*if, of course,*

---

[15] See: P. I. Inenlikaj, V. P. Nedyalkov, and A. A. Kholodovič, 'Kauzativ v čukotskom jazyke', in: *Tipologija Kauzativnyx Konstrukcij*, p. 266.

[16] A number of languages tend to differentiate causative affixes in conformity with various groups of V^{in}. In Mongolian, for example, causatives with the suffix -aa- are mainly formed from verbs designating involuntary actions (for example, *xatax* 'dry, become dry' → *xata-aa-x* 'make dry', *sonox* 'perish' → *son-oo-x* 'destroy'), and the suffix -uul- comes mainly from primary verbs of active action (*javax* 'go' → *jav-uul-ax* 'allow or force to go'. See G. D. Sanžeev, *Sravnitel'naja grammatika mongol'skix jazykov, Glagol.* M., 1963, p. 23.

they ever had such meanings) and to preserve or take on the contact-factitive meanings which are for example characteristic of the Russian causative equivalents of the non-causatives given above, namely: *'ronjat''* (drop), (or *'valit''* (bring, throw down)), *'smešit''* (make laugh), *'nasytit''* (saturate), *'kipjatit''* (bring to a boil), *'privesti'* (bring), *'usypit''*, (lull to sleep), *'uložit' spat''* (put to bed).[17] In Georgian, for example, the contact-factitive meanings 'lull to sleep' and 'put to bed' are allotted to the causative *a-ʒin-eb-s*, but not the distant meaning 'tell, allow, make sleep'. This is explained by the fact that the first meaning corresponds to a more frequent situation than the second. In such cases distant causation is expressed periphrastically.

V_j with contact-factitive meanings are usually given by dictionaries. As a rule, lexical causatives have such a meaning. That contact-factitive meanings are allotted to lexical causatives is apparently to a large extent determined by the fact that it is contact causation that is connected with the most often recurring, typical situations.

21. If a causative morpheme is unproductive in relation to transitives, forming from them a relatively small (closed) group of trivalent causatives (see 11.1), among the latter are usually found causatives from verbs denoting abstract action, which provide causative oppositions such as 'see – show' (Chukot *l'uk → ry-l'u-ŋet-yk*, Arabic *ra'ā → 'arā*, Batsbien *dag → dag-d*, Indonesian *me-lihat → mem-per-lihat-kan*, Hausa *gani → ganad da*), 'remember – remind' (Chukot *ket'ok → ry-két'o-ŋat-yk*, Arabic *zakara → zakkara*, Armenian *hišel → hiš-eçn-el*), 'understand – explain' (Tadžik *faxmidan → faxm-on-dan*, Arabic *fahima → 'a-fhama*, Hausa *fanimta → fanimtad da*), and also from a few verbs of concrete action denoting the consumption of food. These verbs provide, for example, causative oppositions such as 'drink water – give to drink' (Chukot *pylyk → ry-lpy-ŋat-yk*, Indonesian *minum → me-minum-kan*, Armenian *kem-el → kem-ecn-el*, Tadžik *nušidan → nuš-on-dan*, Hausa *sha → sha da*), 'eat – feed' (Armenian *ut-el → ut-eçn-el*, Tadžik *xurdan → xur-on-dan*, Hausa *chi → chi da*), 'suck – suckle' (Kurdish (Kurmandži dialect) *metin → mej-and-in*).

---

[17] The absence in grammars of a distant-causative meaning for morphological causatives is often treated quite simply as the total absence (or loss) of a causative meaning, as a consequence of which V_j are treated like ordinary transitives. It is obviously very difficult to agree with this view (see for example: L. N. Xaritonov, *Zagolovye formy...*, p. 62; K. S. Sakryl, *Affiksacija v abxazskom jazyke*, Abgosizdat, 1961, p. 55; A. Z. Rozenfel'd, 'O zalogax tadžikskogo glagola', *Izv. Otd. Obšč. nauk AN TadžSSR*, vyp. 9, Stalinabad, 1951, p. 117; K. E. Majtinskaja, *Vengerskij jazyk*, č. II. M., 1959, p. 99; V. M. Ollikainen, 'Glagol'nye suffiksy s zalogovym značeniem v sovremennom finskom literaturnom jazyke'. Author's abstract of a candidate dissertation, M., 1955, p. 14; K. Tschenkeli, *Einführung in die georgische Sprache*, Bd. I, Zürich, 1958, p. 325.

The semantic peculiarities of verbs of the type given above favor their primary (in comparison with other transitives) causativation.

In this connection, it does not seem to be a coincidence that among the few causative combinations of the German verb *geben* with an infinitive we also find combinations such as *zu verstehen geben* 'give to understand' and *zu trinken geben* 'give to drink'.

Causatives of the above type have semantic 'supermorphs', as is evident from the translations into English. The presence of 'supermorphs' is explained here by the contact-factitive meanings of these causatives (cf. Russian *ob' jasnit'* 'explain', *kormit'* 'feed', *pokazat'* 'show', etc.). The corresponding distant meanings (for example, '*zastavit'*, *pozvolit' est'* ' 'force, allow to eat') do not have 'supermorphs'.

22. *The polysemy of causative morphemes* is not limited to the range of causative meanings described above, but also embraces a number of other meanings, non-causative or not only causative, which in differing degrees in different languages combine with causative meanings proper. The causative meanings are usually more common than the non-causative ones.

Meanings expressed by morphemes which serve to render causativity apparently do not on the whole extend beyond certain semantic bounds.[18] The realization of one or another meaning of a morpheme which is causative in its basic meaning is often determined by the meaning of the underlying verb.

The following preliminary classification of these meanings can be proposed.

(I) The meanings of derived verbs connected with an increase in the original syntactic valence by one unit.

(1) *Causative meanings proper.* For example, Hungarian *ég-ni* 'burn' → → *ég-et-ni* 'burn, incinerate'; Manchurian *feku-*'jump' → *feku-bu-*'tell to jump'.

Note. As a special subtype of this meaning we introduce a type where r_j does not assume the state s_i in reality, but only in *the mind* of r_i. For example: Arabic *kazaba* 'be a liar' → *kazzaba* 'consider smb a liar' (cf. the

---

[18] Of course, cases where the meanings of a causative have had an individual development are not taken into account. We should not lose sight of the fact that in connection with the development of a lexicon (especially in literary languages) there occurs an 'aging' of causatives which appears in a gradual loss of the semantic correlation between the members of morphological oppositions and in an increase in the specific gravity of verbs standing outside these oppositions. The degree of causative 'aging' in different languages is evidently indicative of the relative age of this category and the degree of its activity. In this respect we can compare, for example, the strong 'aging' of the Finnish causative and the 'youth' of that in Gilyak.

usual causative meaning of the verb, which is also formed by doubling the root consonant: *ḥazira* 'beware of, be careful of' → *ḥazzara* 'force to beware of', that is, 'warn'); Dakota *śic'* '*a* 'be bad' → *yu-śic'* '*a* 'express a low opinion of smb' (cf. *waśte* 'be good' → *yu-waśte* 'make smth, smb good')[19]. Causatives which we have classified as conversives can also have this meaning (see 2.2.1).

(2) *Comitative-causative meanings* appear for the most part in derivatives from verbs signifying movement or actions undertaken jointly. The derivative indicates that the performance by the subject of a given action r_i causes a similar action on the part of r_j; cf., for example, the corresponding pairs of verbs meaning (a) 'talk – talk with smb': Chukot *vetgavyk* → *ry-vetgav-at-yk*, Zulu *khuluma* → *khulum-isa*, Siuslawan *wa'a-yax* → *wa*ᵃ*-yax-a*ᵘ*n*;[20] (b) 'walk (come) – lead (bring), carry (bring)' (i.e., 'walk (come) with smb, smth'); Chukot *pykiryk* → *ry-pkir-et-yk*, Yukaghir *u-* → *u-se-*, Zulu *hamba* → *hamb-isa*, Indonesian *datang* → *men-datang-kan*, Miwok *ýn-* → *'unu-nuku-*.[21]

Note. Certain languages with *morphological causatives* (Adygei, Aymara, Guarani, Jebero, Kechua, Crow and others) also have verbal affixes with a comitative meaning. The comitative in Guarani means 'I do myself and force another to do'; cf. the following examples, where the causative is designated by the prefix *mo-* and the comitative by the prefix *ro-*: *a-çô* 'I go' → → *a-i-mo-ndo* (<*a-i-mo-çô*) 'I send' – *a-ra-co* (<*a-ro-co*) 'I lead' 'I carry'; *a-gebir* 'I return' → *a-mo-gebir* 'I make return', – *a-ro-gebir* [*aoba*] 'I return [the clothing]', i.e., 'I bring it'.[22] Examples from Adygei *ar*¹ *guš'ə'aγe*² 'that one, he¹ talked²' → *ar*¹ *aš'*² *de*³-*guš'ə'aγe*⁴ 'that one¹ talked⁴ with³ him²'; *ar*¹ *ma*²-*kIo*³ 'he¹,² goes³' → *ar*¹ *aš'*² *dé*³-*kIo*⁴ 'he¹ goes⁴ together³ with³ him²'.[23]

(3) *Antireflexive-causative meanings* are found in derivatives which indicate that an action is being performed by the subject not upon himself (the states 'dressed', 'combed' etc. are caused, which the object under normal circumstances produces upon himself); cf. the corresponding pairs of verbs meaning (a) 'to put one's shoes on – to put on smb's shoes for smb': Chukot *plagtyk* → *ry-plagt-at-yk*, Korean *sin* → *sin-gi*; (b) 'comb o.s. – comb smb': Klamath *sli-čiqa* → *his-lči·qa*,[24] Tübatulabal *i·'ciug* → *i·'ci'ug-an*;[25] (c) 'put

[19] See R. S. Riggs, *Dakota Grammar*, Washington, 1893, p. 20.
[20] L. Frachtenberg, *Siuslawan. Handbook of American Indian Languages*, part 2, Washington, 1922, p. 482.
[21] S. Broadbent, *The Southern Sierra Miwok Language*, Berkeley, 1964, pp. 58, 78, 81.
[22] J. Platzmann, *Grammatik...*, p. 140.
[23] G. V. Rogava and Z. I. Keraševa, *Grammatika adygejskoto jazyka*, Krasnodar, 1966, p. 269.
[24] M. Barker, *Klamath Grammar*, Berkeley, 1964, p. 113.
[25] Ch. Voegelin, *Tübatulabal Grammar*, Berkeley, 1935, p. 104.

smth on o.s. (dress o.s.) – put smth on smb (dress smb)': Chukot *jypyk* →
→ *ry-jpy-ŋat-yk*, Tadžik *pušidan* → *puš-on-dan*.

(4) Derivatives which indicate that the subject uses an instrument to perform a given action (as if 'forcing' it to act) have an *instrumental-caus-
ative* meaning, for example: Chukot *ten'ek* 'wash' → *ry-ten'é-v-yk* 'wash
with something'; Indonesian *gosok* 'rub, wipe' → *gosok-kan* 'rub with
smth'.

(5) Derivatives which indicate that an affected object partly performs the
same action as the subject have an *affective-causative meaning*, e.g., Chukot
kergatyk 'become light' → *ry-kerga-v-yk* 'light up, illuminate' (i.e., itself be
bright and make smth else bright); Georgian *brq̇çin-av-s* 'shines' → *a-brq̇çin-
eb-s* 'illuminates'.

(6) An *addressive* meaning is found in derivatives which indicate that an
action is performed for the person who is the object, e.g., Indonesian *membeli*
'buy' → *membeli-kan* 'buy for smb'; Chukot *raŋŋatyk* 'move a yaranga (skin
tent)' → *ry-raŋŋavatyk* 'move a yaranga for smb'.

Note. Apparently *only languages with morphological causatives* (Aymara,
Abkhazian, Blackfoot, Georgian, Dakota, Zulu, Kabardian, Kechua, Crow,
Miwok, Wiyot and others) also have affixes with a special addressive meaning
indicating the person for whom (or to the detriment of whom) an action is
performed (cf. the meaning of *dativus commodi*)[26], e.g., Tübatulabal *vĭc-* 'be
ripe, ready' → *wĭc'-in* 'prepare food' (causative) → *wĭci-i'n-an-* 'prepare food
for smb' (addressive from the causative).[27, 28]

(7) Derivatives which indicate an affixed object towards which a given
action is directed have an *affective (antiabsolute) meaning*. Cf. for example
the corresponding pairs of verbs meaning 'work – treat, process': Chukot
migčiretyk → *ry-migčire-v-yk*, Georgian *mušaobs* → *a-mušavebs*, Zulu *seσenza*
→ *seσenz-isa*, Indonesian *be-kerdja* → *me-ngerdja-kan*.

Combinations of causative and non-causative (or not purely causative)
meanings in a single derivative are also possible.[29]

(II) The meanings of derived verbs connected with a preservation of the
original syntactic valence.

(8) *Intensity or iterativeness*; cf.: Zulu *enza* 'work' → *enz-isa* (a) 'work

---

[26] In Caucasian studies this category is called the 'version' (A. G. Šanidze), while in foreign
grammars the terms 'the addressive', 'the benefactive', 'the dative', 'the indirective', 'the
interest' are common.

[27] Voegelin, *op. cit.*, p. 102.

[28] See also (1) I. O. Gecadze and V. P. Nedyalkov. 'Morfologičeskij kauzativ v abxazskom
jazyke', in: *Tipologija kauzativnyx konstrukcij*, pp. 73–74, (2) I. O. Gecadze, V. P. Nedyalkov, and A. A. Kholodovič, 'Morfologičeskij kauzativ v gruzinskom jazyke', in:
Tipologija kauzativnyx konstrukcij, pp. 146–147.

[29] *Ibid.* (2), p. 136.

persistently' (if there is no direct object), (b) *'force* to work' (if there is a direct object); Swahili *chanja* 'chop smth[9] (firewood) → *chanj-isha* (a) 'chop *energetically'* (if there is only one complement of the type 'firewood', etc.), (b) *'force* smb to chop smth' (if there is a second complement which designates the executor of the action); cf. also Armenian *petet-el* 'turn, rotate' → → *petet-eçn-el* 'turn intensively'.

(9) *Several objects*; cf.: Shoshone *ayi* 'receive' → *aya^ʿ-ni* 'receive *several* objects' (cf. *šaqeq* 'is warm' → *šaqi-ni* 'warm this up!');[30] Miwok *so·p* 'hit smb' → *so·pu'-nY* 'hit *several* people' (cf. *'yw·y-* 'eat' → *ywy-nY* 'feed').[31]

Note. It is apparently no coincidence that in some languages synchronically primary V^{tr} (and even V^{in}) designating actions which are *iterative by nature* and seemingly composed of a set of similar actions contain a causative morpheme, e.g., Abkhazian *a-r-x-ra* 'mow', *a-r-šəa-ra* 'weed', *a-r-ša-ra* 'tie'; Georgian *i-c-in-i-* 'laugh'.[32]

The Ainu suffix -jar- is interesting in this connection, since it syncretically designates both causativity and a plurality of objects. This suffix is used instead of four disjunctive causative suffixes when it is necessary to emphasize the number of the caused objects, e.g., *kor* 'have' → *kor-e* 'make to have', that is, 'give', but *kor-jar* 'make many to have', that is, 'give *to many.'*[33]

(III) The meanings of derived verbs connected with a reduction in the original syntactic valence.

(10) *Reciprocity (several subjects* perform an action upon each other); cf. Piro *-xepha* 'look for lice on smb', 'delouse' (V^{tr}) → *xepha-kaka-* (a) 'delouse *each other'* (if the subject is in the plural[34] and there is no direct object); (b) *'force* smb to delouse smb' (if there is a direct object); cf. also *ximle-* 'boil, come to a boil' → *ximle-kaka-* 'bring to a boil'.[35]

(11) The *Passive* and the other 'intransitive' meanings which usually accompany it (see 23) are realized if a V_j lacks a direct object, as a result of which the action is transferred to the subject; cf. Evenki *kol-* 'drink' → *kol-u* (a) literally: 'be watered, given to drink', (b) 'give to drink'; Karakalpak *soq-tyr-dym* (a) 'I was beaten up (by smb)', (b) 'I *told* (smb) to beat';

---

[30] A. L. Kroeber and G. W. Grace, *The Sparkman Grammar of Luiseño*, Berkeley, 1960, p. 138.

[31] S. Broadbent, *op. cit.*, p. 76.

[32] See A. S. Čikobava, *Čansko-megrel'sko-gruzinskij sravnitel'nyj slovar'* Tbilisi, 1938, p. 382.

[33] See A. A. Kholodovič, *Ajnskij jazyk*, to be published.

[34] It is interesting to note in this respect that the suffix *-kaka-* also forms the *collective plural* of nouns designating people and large animals (see E. Matteson, *The Piro (Arawakan) Language*, Berkeley, 1965, p. 108).

[35] *Ibid.*, pp. 39, 41, 82.

Moxa nu^1-ca^2-$ezeta^3$ 'I^1 was beaten^{2,3} (by smb)'; cf. the V_j with the same prefix nu^1-ca^2-imu^3 'I^1 force^2 to sleep^{3,36}.

Manchurian is especially characteristic in this respect. There the morpheme bu (traceable to a verb meaning 'give') expresses the so-called causative-passive voice. It is not the form of the verb or the subject that indicates which meaning – causative or 'passive' – is to be realized, but the form of the complement; cf.: Bi^1 $gele$-$xé^2$ 'I^1 was, became frightened^{2}' →
→ Bi^1 $indé^2$ $gele$-bu-xe^3 'I^1 was^3 frightened^3 by him^{2}' or 'I^1 allowed^3 him^2 to frighten^3 (me)' and Bi^1 $imbe^2$ $gele$-bu-xe^3 'I^1 made^3 him^2 be frightened^{3}' (= 'I frightened him').[37]

Note. Similar phenomena can be found in analytic causative constructions. Cf. the following Chinese example, where the empty causative verb $kiao$ has a deleted reflexive direct object: Ta^1 $kiao^2$ $jênkia^3$ [pa^4 $t'a^5$] $chotsoule^6$ 'He^1 was^6 seized^6 by them^{3}', literally: he^1 allowed^2 them^3 (because he blundered) to seize^6 him^{4,5}.[38]

It is characteristic that among the examples cited in various grammars on the use of causatives to express the passive, verbs designating various negative actions dominate: 'steal', 'deceive', 'seize', 'curse', 'frighten', etc. It is not out of place here to compare with this fact the way in which the passive is formed in certain languages by means of empty verbs in whose independent meanings one finds evidence that these verbs originally combined with verbs designating actions which are unpleasant for the subject; cf. Burmese $khan$ 'undergo, endure', 'experience', Malayalam $petuka$ 'suffer', Chinese pei 'undergo, endure suffer'.[39]

It is significant in this respect that the Thai empty verb tuk 'endure, suffer', which forms the passive, combines mainly with verbs denoting actions which are unpleasant for the subject, e.g., tuk $kian$ 'be beaten up', tuk kat 'be bitten', etc.[40]

The situation is similar in Chinese, where "the passive construction always designates something unpleasant or unexpected – accidents, injuries, anything that was unfavorable or to the detriment of the person designated as the subject"; cf.: $Women$ pei $jên$ $k'ifule$ 'We were insulted'; Ni pei $t'a$

---

[36] See H. Gabelenz, *Über das Passivum. Eine sprachvergleichende Abhandlung*, Abt. d. K. Sächs. Gesel. d. Wiss., Bd. 8., Leipzig, 1860, pp. 518–519.

[37] I. Zaxarov, *Grammatika man'čžurskogo jazyka*, SPb., 1879, p. 162.

[38] See T. N. Nikitina, *Kauzativnaja i passivnaja konstrukcii v kitajskom jazyke*, Uč. zap. LGU, No. 236, vyp. 6, 1958.

[39] See Naun Maun N'jan, I. A. Orlova, E. V. Puzickij, and N. M. Tagunova, *Birmanskij jazyk*, M., 1963, p. 65; Sekxar, Ju. Ja. Glazov, *Jazyk malajam*, M., 1961, p. 47; Jos. Mullie, *The Structural Principles of the Chinese Language*, vol. II and III, Pei-P'ing, 1937, p. 45.

[40] See L. N. Morev, Ju. Ja. Plam, and M. F. Fomičev, *Tajskij jazyk*, M., 1961, p. 78.

tala 'You were beaten by him'; *Chĭ shĭ Hon San pei jên ta-sĭ* 'It became known that Xe the Third had been murdered (by smb)'.[41]

Verbs of unpleasant actions apparently tend to be used primarily in a passive meaning.[42, 43]

23. Now that we have examined the polysemy of causative morphemes, it is advisable to dwell briefly on the polysemy of anticausative morphemes. Both types of morphemes – causative and anticausative – can provide similar semantic causative oppositions differing only in the direction of the derivation (see 2.1.1 and 2.1.2).

The meanings expressed by *anticausative* (in one of their meanings) *morphemes* when they are combined with V^{tr} do not for the most part go beyond certain semantic bounds. Whether one or the other of these meanings is realized depends (as it does for the meanings which accompany causatives) in a significant number of instances on the meaning of the primary V^{tr}. It is extremely significant that a majority of the meanings of the 'anticausative morphemes' are used in the formation of various semantic oppositions which are more or less similar to the oppositions produced by the various meanings of the 'causative morphemes'.

We can propose the following preliminary classification of the polysemy of anticausative morphemes.[44]

(I) The meanings of derivative verbs connected with a decrease in the original syntactic valence by one unit.

(1) Derivatives which form causative oppositions (cf. the causative meanings in 22, (1)) have a *decausative* meaning; for example: Russian *varit'* 'boil, cook' → *varit'sja* 'be boiling, cooking'; Armenian *ep-el* 'boil, cook' → *ep-v-el* 'be boiling, cooking'; Hungarian *zavar-ni* 'confuse, embarrass' → *zavar-od-ni* 'become embarrassed, confused'; Georgian *xarš-av-s*

---

[41] Van Ljao-i, *Osnovy kitajskoj grammatiki*, M., 1954, p. 127–128.

[42] *Ibid.* (2), p. 148; see also V. P. Nedyalkov, G. A. Otaina, and A. A. Kholodovič, 'Morfologičeskij' i leksičeskij kauzativy v nivxskom jazyke', in: *Tipologija kauzativnyx konstrukcij*, p. 194.

[43] Cf. L. Weisgerber's comment on the necessity of bringing to light extralingual situations, especially which tend to be expressed in the passive (L. Weisgerber, *Die Welt im 'Passive'. Festschrift für Fr. Maurer*, Stuttgart, 1963, p. 58). See also G. Amman's attempt to justify the concept of the 'passive voice' (Leideform) by pointing to the fact that transitives of the type *schlagen* 'beat' are older than transitives of the type *lieben* 'love' and thereby dominate in passive constructions (H. Amman, *Probleme der verbalen Diathese*, Innsbrucker Beiträge zur Kulturwissenschaft, Sonderheft 12, p. 95).

[44] The polysemy of anticausative morphemes is illustrated with examples from 10 languages in which the meanings which accompany the non-causative are unevenly represented. Examples will be given first from Russian, where the polysemy of the anticausative morpheme seems to be best developed. Other languages used for illustration purposes are given in alphabetical order.

'cooks' → *i-xarš-eb-a* 'is boiling, being cooked'; Old Icelandic *hræða* 'fright-'en' → *hræða-sk* 'be frightened'; Khmer *baék* 'open' → *rɔ-baék* 'be opened, open'; Gilyak [*j*] *yl*-d' 'open' → *pʿ-yl*-d' 'be opened, open'; Swahili *vunj-a* 'breaks' → *vunj-ik-a* 'becomes broken, breaks'; Uzbek *jaxšila-moq* 'better, improve' → *jaxšila-n-moq* 'become better, improve'; Evenki *sokor-* 'lose' → → *sokori-v-* 'disappear'.

(2) *Passive* meanings (cf. the passive meanings in 22, (11)); for example: Russian *stroit'* 'build' → *stroit'sja* 'be build'; Armenian *gr-el* 'write' → *gr-v-el* 'be written down, noted'; Hungarian *ver-ni* 'beat, hit' → *ver-ōd-ni* 'be beaten'; Georgian *çer-s* 'writes' → *i-çer-eb-a* 'is written'; Old Icelandic *skeina* 'wound' → *skeina-sk* 'be wounded'; Swahili *it-a* 'calls' → *it-ik-a* 'called, invited'; Uzbek *sakla-moq* 'keep' → *sakla-n-moq* 'be kept'; Evenki *tyré-* 'press' → → *tyr-e-v* 'be pressed, weighed down'.

(3) Derivatives which indicate that an object can be subjected to a given action due to inherent properties of the object have a *passive-potential* meaning; for example, Russian *pit'* 'drink' → *pit'sja* (*legko, xorošo*) '(smth) is easy, good, etc. to drink'; Armenian *kem-el* 'drink' → *kem-v-el* 'easy, etc. to drink'; Hungarian *gyūr-ni* 'crumple' → *gyūr-ōd-ni* 'easily crumpled'; Georgian *svam-s* 'drinks' → *i-sm-ev-a* 'is drunk' (easily, etc), 'can be drunk'; Swahili *l-a* 'eats' → *l-ik-a* 'is edible'.

(4) Derivatives which designate actions of the subject upon himself have a *reflexive* meaning (cf. antireflexive-causative meanings, 22, 3)); for example: Russian *narjažat'* 'dress up, array' → *narjažat'sja* 'dress o.s. up, array o.s.'; Armenian *zardar-el* 'dress up, array' → *zardar-v-el* 'dress o.s. up, array o.s.'; Hungarian *ruház-ni* 'dress' → *ruház-kod-ni* 'dress o.s.'; Georgian *kazm-av-s* 'dresses up, arrays' → *i-kazm-eb-a* 'dresses o.s. up, arrays o.s.'; Old Icelandic *klæða* 'dress' → *klæða-sk* 'dress o.s.'; Gilyak *vetaud'* 'dress' → *pʿ-fetaud'* 'dress o.s.'; *Uzbek kij-moq* 'put on' → *kij-in-moq* 'dress o.s.'.

(5) Derivatives which designate a permissive or factitive causation by the subject of certain actions upon himself have a *reflexive-causative* meaning; for example: Russian *brit'* 'shave' → *brit'sja* 'have o.s. shaved' (in a barber's shop); Armenian *sapr-el* 'shave' → *sapr-v-el* 'have o.s. shaved'; Georgian *pars-av-s* 'shaves' → *i-pars-eb-a* 'is having himself shaved'; Gilyak *omℬd'* 'shave' → *pʿ-omℬd'* 'has o.s. shaved' [45] (see also 24).

(6) Derivatives which indicate that there are *several subjects* (see reciprocal meanings 22, (10)) have a *reciprocal* meaning; for example: Russian *sobirat'* 'collect, gather' → *sobirat'sja* 'gather, come together'; Armenian *hambur-el* 'kiss' → *hambur-v-el* 'kiss each other'; Hungarian *tegez-ni* ''to 'thou' smb'' → → *tegez-ōd-ni* ''to 'thou' each other''; Georgian *krep-s* 'collects, gathers' →

---

[45] These verbs can also function as simple reflexives.

→ *i-kril-eb-a* 'gathers (a crowd, etc)'; Old Icelandic *tala* 'talk to, with' →
→ *tala-sk* 'talk to each other, converse'; Khmer *banh* 'shoot' → *rɔ-banh*
'exchange shots'.

(7) Derivatives which indicate that a subject, having certain inherent
properties, is capable of performing an action have an *absolute-potential*
meaning (cf. antiabsolute meanings 22, (7)); for example: Russian *bodat'*
'butt, ram' → *bodat'sja* 'butts, is apt to butt, has a habit of butting'; Hungarian
gunyol-ni 'jeer, taunt' → *gunyol-od-ni* 'has a habit of jeering, is given to
jeering, is apt to jeer'; Georgian *kben-s* 'bites' → *i-kbin-eb-a* 'bites, has a
habit of biting, is apt to bite'.

(8) Derivatives which designate an action performed by the subject upon
his own unnamed (but implied) objects (cf. 22, 7)) have an *absolute-possessive*
meaning, for example: Russian *pribrat'* 'put in order, tidy up' → *pribrat'sja*
'tidy up everything, put one's things in order'; Gilyak *ivryd'* 'tidy up' →
→ *p'-ivryd'* 'tidy up (in one's home)'.

(II) The meanings of derived verbs connected with a preservation of the
original syntactic valence.

(9) *Iterative* or *intensive* meanings (cf. iterative or intensive meanings in
22, 8)); for example: Russian *njančit'* (*kogo-l.*) 'nurse smb' → *njančit'sja*
(*s kem-l.*) 'fuss over smb'; Georgian *çer-s* 'writes' → *i-çer-eb-a* 'writes often'.

(10) Derivatives which indicate actions of the subject performed by
himself for himself have a *reflexive-addressive* meaning (cf. addressive
meanings 22, (6)); for example: Russian *zapasat'* (*čto-l.*) 'store, stock smth'
→ *zapasat'sja* (*čem-l.*) 'stock up, provide o.s. with smth'); Georgian *çer-s*
'writes' → *i-çer-s* 'writes for o.s.'; Old Icelandic *beiða* 'request' → *beiða-sk*
'request for o.s.'; Uzbek *tila-moq* 'ask, request' → *tila-n-moq* 'ask for o.s.,
beg'.

(III) The meanings of derived verbs connected with an increase in the
original syntactic valence by one unit.

(11) *Causative* meanings (cf. passive meanings 22, (11)); for example:
Evenki *ju-* 'go out' → *ju-v-* 'lead, bring out'.

As can be seen from the examples, certain forms can express more than
one meaning.

24. *Reflexive-causative* meanings occupy a special place among the meanings
expressed by anticausative morphemes. The translation of reflexive-causative
verbs into certain languages with causative morphemes (empty verbs or
affixes) can require that both the reflexivity and the causativity be expressed
explicitly. Cf., for example, Russian verbs of this type with their German
equivalents, which are formed by means of an empty causative verb:
sfotografirovat'sja – sich fotografieren lassen, *pobrit'sja* (at the barber's)

– *sich rasieren lassen, uvleč'sja* – *sich hinreissen lassen, soblaznit'sja* – *sich verführen lassen, smjagčit'sja* – *sich erweichen lassen, krestit'sja* – *sich taufen lassen, razvestis'* – *sich scheiden lassen, zapisat'sja* (into the university) – *sich immatrikulieren lassen, postrič'sja* – *sich das Haar schneiden lassen, rukovodstvovat'sja* – *sich leiten lassen,* etc.

It should be noted in this connection that certain languages have special varieties of forms with a causative morpheme to express *reflexive-causative* meanings. In Georgian, for example, a special passive form of causative verbs can be used to express this meaning: *i-çer-s* 'he arrests him' → *a-çer-in-eb-s* 'he tells him to arrest smb.' → *e-çer-in-eb-a* 'he lets himself be arrested by him'.

To express the reflexive-causative (more precisely, the reflexive-permissive) in Chukot, the empty verb of the analytic causative is changed: *Ytlyge*[1] *ekyk*[2] *talajv-y-nén*[3] 'The father[1] beat[3] the son[2]' → *Ytlygé*[1] *ékyk*[2] *talajv*[3]-*y-jgot*[4] *ryn-nin*[5] 'The father[1] forced[4,5] (smb.) to beat[3] his son[2]' (or 'forced his son to beat smb') → *Ytlygyn*[1] *talajv*[2]-*y-jgot*[3] *itg?i*[4] 'The father[1] allowed[3] (smb) to beat[2] him[4]'.

For reflexive-causative verbs which have mainly a permissive meaning, this meaning is sometimes weakened to mean that some (usually unpleasant or involuntary) action is allowed to be performed on the subject *through his own fault* (due to negligence, for example) or due to the objective inability of the subject to prevent the action (cf. 14.3, 5)).[46]

25. It seems appropriate to *compile a diagnostic list of specific semantic causative oppositions* in order to be able to evaluate the degree of explicit causativity in the languages we wish to compare, and also to be able to reveal systematically *the degree to which a given causative opposition is predisposed to expression by one or another type of formal opposition.* Such a list will facilitate the accumulation of the appropriate material from new languages selected for comparison.

Concrete semantic causative oppositions embrace a significant part of the vocabularies of all languages. Some of these oppositions may not be evident to a native speaker of another language, even though in a number of languages they are expressed by means of causative morphemes; cf., for

---

[46] It is interesting that reflexive causatives are illustrated in various grammars with verbs which designate 'unpleasant' actions. In a grammar of Guarani, for example (see J. Platzmann, *Grammatik...*, p. 94), the only example given to illustrate reflexive causatives is *a-ye-juca-ucâr* 'I allow myself to be killed'; in a grammar of Kechua (see E. W. Middendorf, *Das Runa Simi...*, pp. 176–77) 7 out of 11 cited verbs denote 'unpleasant' actions: *k'ami-rka-chi-cy-* 'allow o.s. to be insulted, injured', etc. It is apparently together with just such verbs that the causative construction in Turkish and Mongolian languages expresses the passive (cf. 14.3, 5, and 22, 11 above).

example, the following semantic causative oppositions: (a) *'paxnut'* (smell) – *obonjat'* (smell)' (i.e., to do smth so that something smells, gives off an odor, for the subject of the action) in Chukot – *tekyk → ry-tke-v-yk* and in Finnish *haista → hais-ta-a* (cf. English *to smell* and German *riechen*, which have both these meanings); (b) *zanimat'* (borrow) – *odalživat'* (lend) (i.e., do smth so that smb. borrows) in Abkhazian *a-psax-ra → a-r-psax-rá*; in Swahili *-azim-a → azim-ish-a*.

The verbs in the diagnostic list must of course be given in certain word-combinations to ensure that equivalent items can be compared. The verb meaning 'to burn', for instance, has various equivalents in certain languages, depending on the specific lexical meaning of the subject. The peculiarities of these equivalents can be rendered approximately with the following examples: *sveša gorit* 'the *candle* burns' = *svetit* 'shines'; *ogon'* gorit 'the *fire* burns' = *greet* 'warms'; *pečka gorit* 'the *stove* burns (is lit)' = *topitsja* 'is heated, stoked'; *bumaga* gorit 'the *paper* burns' = *sgoraet* 'burns up' (is consumed by the fire); *dom gorit* 'the *house* is burning' = =*požar!* 'fire!'; *les gorit* 'the forest is burning' = *stixijnoe bedstvie!* 'a natural catastrophe!'

Such a list will help us to discover: (a) the various *combination types of causative and non-causative or 'near-causative' meanings* expressed in various languages by the morphemes treated above; (b) the most *characteristic instances of the non-one-to-one relationship of causatives to their non-causatives*, when, for example, the same semantic starting point provides several derivative causative meanings in different languages (or within the same language); for example: the V_i meaning 'to fall' can have V_j with the meanings 'to drop', 'to everthrow', 'to throw', etc.; the V_i meaning 'to go' can have V_j which mean 'lead', 'convey', 'carry', 'drive', 'send', etc.; the V_i meaning 'to burn' can have V_j which mean 'ignite', 'incinerate', etc. Typically, the spectrum of causative meanings derived from a given semantic point of departure does not extend beyond certain semantic limits.

26. *Individual concrete causative oppositions display varying predispositions to expression by one or another formal opposition.*

Let us consider from this point of view the following four concrete oppositions, which are expressed in Russian by the corresponding pairs of verbs: (1) *smejat'sja* 'laugh' – *smešit'* 'amuse, make laugh', (2) *kipet'* 'boil, come to a boil', – *kipjatit'* 'boil, bring to a boil' (of water, tea), (3) *goret'* 'burn' – *žeč'* 'burn, ignite' (of paper), (4) *perelomit'sja* 'break, get broken in two' – *perelomit'* 'break in two' (of a stick).

Here we can note the following tendencies, which we have discovered through an investigation of over 100 languages.

(1) The probability that a formal opposition with a *causative* morpheme (see 2.1.1) will appear decreases from the first causative opposition to the fourth.

(2) The probability that a formal opposition with an *anticausative morpheme* will appear (see 2.1.2) increases from the first causative opposition to the fourth.

(3) The probability that *conversive* formal oppositions will appear (i.e., paradigmatic and syntagmatic oppositions, see 2.2 and 2.4) increases from the second causative opposition to the fourth (it was not found at all in the first).

(4) *Suppletive* formal oppositions (see 2.5) are encountered almost exclusively in the second and third causative oppositions, which indicates that there is a greater tendency for the first and fourth semantic oppositions to be expressed by one and the same root morpheme.

The above mentioned tendencies for the expression of given causative oppositions by given formal oppositions are determined by extralingual factors which deserve special consideration.

It seems expedient in this connection to try to solve to more general problem, namely, to research the probable typological determination of certain means of derivation in various languages, to study, if we can be permitted the expression, the 'typological productivity' ('typological valence') of various means of derivation as they are rendered in certain logical relations.[47]

27. The concrete causative oppositions formed by means of causative morphemes may not coincide in different languages. We can note some of the reasons for such a lack of coincidence.

(1) For example, the comitative-causative opposition 'come – bring', which is expressed in Indonesian by means of the causative morpheme *-kan* (*datang → datang-kan*) is nevertheless expressed in Georgian, where the causative morpheme is very productive, by a suppletive, since verbs with meanings of the type 'lead to (bring) – carry to (bring)' are formed from two verbs meaning 'to have' (one verb combines with animate objects, the other with inanimate ones) by means of spatial preverbs; cf., for example: Mas^1 $\check{s}vili^2$ h^3-qav^4-s^4 'He^{1,3} has^4 a son^{2}' → Mas^1 $\check{s}vili^2$ mi^3-h^4-qav-s^5 'He^{14} leads^5 his son^2 out ,away^{3}'; literally 'to him^{1,4} his son^2 is^5 outside^3 (cf.: Mas^1 $\check{s}vili^2$ mo^3-h^4-gav-s^5 He^{1,4} brings^{3,5} (to^3-leads^5) his son^{2}'; cf. the suppletive

[47] For a more detailed account, see V. N. Nedyalkov, *Nekotorye verojatnostnye universalii v glagol'nom slovoobrazovanii*. In the collection *Jazykovye universalii i lingvističeskaja tipologija* (M., 1969).

non-causative $\check{s}vili^1$ mi^2-di-s^3 'The son[1] leaves[2,3] (goes[3] out[2]).[48]

(2) The causative opposition 'tickle (feel tickling) – tickle', which is constructed in a number of languages by means of a causative morpheme (cf., for example, Kechua $culla \rightarrow culla$-$\check{s}hi$, Gilyak $q'om\partial' \rightarrow q'om$-$gu$-$d'$, Chukot $jigy\check{c}g\acute{e}tyk \rightarrow ry$-$jigy\check{c}g\acute{e}$-$v$-$yk$), cannot, for example, be expressed by a formal opposition with a causative morpheme in Georgian or Evenki, since these languages have no underlying intransitive verb meaning 'to feel tickling'.

(3) The causative morphemes of different languages may not coincide in the extent of their meanings. For example, oppositions such as the Gilyak $krud'$ 'dawn' $\rightarrow kru$-gu-d' 'wait until it dawns' have no equivalent in Abkhazian due to the fact that the latter language lacks a causative morpheme with the permissive meaning of 'wait for an action to begin'.[49]

Thus, the semantic fields which concrete causative oppositions and the formal causative oppositions formed by means of causative morphemes cover in various languages are not simply superimposed upon each other, although they may coincide to a significant degree.

28. The semantic relations between verbs having the same root and containing anticausative and/or causative morphemes can be binary, i.e., one V_i can be in a causative relation with two V_j or, conversely, one V_j can be in a causative relation with two V_i (even more complex relations are possible, but we shall not consider these here). The following basic types of oppositions can be found.

(1) *Oppositions with two causatives.* The latter can be *synonymous*, e.g., Chuvash var- (V_j') 'hurl, fling' $\rightarrow var$-an (V_i) 'strike vs' $\rightarrow var$-an-tar (V_j'') 'fling, hurl' or *non-synonymous* causatives, which with respect to the formal relations between the members of the opposition can be divided into at least two subtypes: (a) Mongolian $\check{s}atax$ (V_i) 'burn' $\rightarrow \check{s}at$-aa-x (V_j') 'ignite' $\rightarrow$ $\rightarrow \check{s}at$-aa-lga-x (V_j'') 'let burn up' (through negligence, for example); (b) Gilyak $vyrkt'$ (V_i) '(become) rotten' $\rightarrow vyrk$-u-d' (V_j') 'rot, let smth. rot' $\leftrightarrow vyrk$-ku-d' (V_j'') 'let spoil, get rotten' (through failure to do anything to prevent it, for

---

[48] Verbs of motion in many languages tend to become morphologically isolated. In Chukot, for example, comitative-causatives comprise a majority of the 15 causatives formed with the confix ry------ηat; in Ainu the causative suffix -ke is found in a small group of verbs of motion; in Lezghin the verbs of motion use the suffix -d- (and not -r-); in Abkhazian they are derived by means of special suffix-roots. In Arabic they are formed by means of the preposition bi; in Blackfoot they have a special causative affix (see S. Uhlenbeck, *A Concise Blackfoot Grammar* (Amsterdam, 1938), p. 142.

[49] We can note in this connection that in Eskimo there is a special causative suffix -$nyxsi$- which means 'to wait until that which is denoted by the root morpheme of the verb happens', cf.: $a\mathcal{B}i$- 'get wet' $\rightarrow$ (a) $a\mathcal{B}i$-sta- 'wet, make wet', (b) $a\mathcal{B}i$-$nyxsi$- 'wait until something becomes wet', i.e., let get wet.

example)). As can be seen from the examples, V'_j has a contact-factitive meaning, and V''_j has a distant-causative one.

(2) *Oppositions with two non-causatives.* These oppositions can also be *synonymous* e.g., Abkhazian *a-xua-xa-ra* (V'_i) 'bend, bow down' $\leftrightarrow$ *a-r-xua-ra* (V_j) 'bend' $\rightarrow$ *a-φy-r-xua-ra* (V''_i) 'make bend, bow down' and *non-synonymous*, which with respect to the formal relations between the members of the oppositions can be divided into at least three subtypes: (a) Arabic *džaffa* (V'_i) 'be dry' $\rightarrow$ *džaffafa* (V_j) 'dry' $\rightarrow$ *ta-džaffafa* (V''_i) 'dry up'; (b) Georgian *sosxl-ob-s* (V'_i) 'lives' $\rightarrow$ (*a-sosxl-eb-s* (V_j) 'revive, enliven' $\leftrightarrow$ *sosxl-d-eb-a* 'comes to life, revives' (V''_i)); (c) Chukot (*ajylg-at-yk* (V'_i) 'be afraid of (*bojat'sja*)' $\leftrightarrow$ *ajylg-av-yk* (V''_i) '(*ispugat'sja*) be frightened by') $\rightarrow$ *r-ajylg-av-yk* (V_j) 'frighten'. As can be seen from the examples, V'_i is a static, and V''_i a dynamic (inchoative) intransitive.

29. Now, in a simplified form, let us consider the basic chains of derivational transformations connected with a change in syntactic valency.

Morphological transformations which use only causative affixes can be subdivided into five basic types, which are represented in the following diagram.[50]

Types	valency				
	1	2	3	4	5
I	$R^{in} \rightarrow$ ↘	$R^{in}m_{dis} \rightarrow$	$R^{in}m_{dis}m_{dis}$	–	–
II	–	$R^{in}m_{con} \rightarrow$	$R^{in}m_{con}m_{dis} \rightarrow$	$R^{in}m_{con}m_{dis}$	–
III	–	$R^{tr} \rightarrow$ ↘	$R^{tr}m_{dis} \rightarrow$	$R^{tr}m_{dis}m_{dis}$	–
IV	–	–	$R^{tr}m_{con} \rightarrow$	$R^{tr}m_{con}m_{dis}m_{dis}$	$R^{tr}m_{con}m_{dis}m_{dis}$
V	–	–	$R^{trtr} \rightarrow$	$R^{trtr}m_{dis} \rightarrow$	$R^{trtr}m_{dis}m_{dis}$

Let us examine how these five derivational chains are realized.

Type I is encountered in most languages without the last link, i.e., in the variant $R^{in} \rightarrow R^{in}m_{dis}$. This is the case, for example, in Batsbien, Georgian and Gilyak. Examples: Gilyak *vaxt'-t'* 'become burst' $\rightarrow$ *vaxt'-ku-d'* 'let burst', Georgian *muša-ob-s* 'works' $\rightarrow$ *a-mušav-eb-s* 'he makes him work'.

---

[50] The symbols R^{in}, R^{tr}, R^{trtr} symbolize the roots of intransitive, transitive and transitive verbs with two objects, respectively; m_{con}, m_{dis} are causative affixes with contact-factitive and distant-causative meanings, respectively.

The automatically produced form $R^{in}m_{dis}m_{dis}$ *a-mušav-eb-in-eb-s* 'he tells him to make smb work' is not used.

In general the combination $m_{dis}m_{dis}$, even in languages where it is found in this or other chains, is rather rare, or in any case less common than the combination $m_{con}m_{dis}$.

The following is an example of the full realization of the chain $R^{in} \rightarrow$ $\rightarrow R^{in}m_{dis} \rightarrow R^{in}m_{dis}m_{dis}$: Mansi *rupit-* 'works' $\rightarrow$ *rupit-a-pt-* 'make work' $\rightarrow$ $\rightarrow$ *rupit-a-pt-i-pt-* 'tell smb to make smb work'.

The type II derivational chain is usually found in two variants.

The *first variant* $R^{in} \rightarrow R^{in}m_{con}$ is encountered in languages where the formation of causatives from transitive verbs is generally unproductive (as in Arabic, for example) or where causative affixes are not applied twice to the same verb (as in Abkhazian, for example). Examples: Arabic *galā* 'boil, come to a boil' $\rightarrow$ *'a-glā* 'boil, bring to a boil'; Abkhazian *a-š-ra* 'boil' $\rightarrow$ *a-r-š-ra* 'boil, bring to a boil'.

The *second variant* $R^{in} \rightarrow R^{in}m_{con} \rightarrow R^{in}m_{con}m_{dis}$ is found, for example, in Gilyak (*vaxt'-t'* 'become burst' $\rightarrow$ *vaxt'-u-d'* 'rend, rip, break' $\rightarrow$ *vaxt'-u-gu-d'* 'make, force to rip, break'), Georgian (*duɣ-s* 'boils, comes to a boil' $\rightarrow$ $\rightarrow$ *a-duɣ-eb-s* 'boils, brings to a boil' $\rightarrow$ *a-duɣ-eb-in-eb-s* 'make smb boil sth', Kechua (*huañu-* 'die' $\rightarrow$ *huañu-chi-* 'kill' $\rightarrow$ *huanu-chi-chi* 'tell to kill'), Adygei (*ẑ'o-* 'cook, be cooking, boiling' $\rightarrow$ *ɣa-ẑ'o-* 'cook, boil' $\rightarrow$ *ɣe-ɣa-ẑ'o-* 'make cook').

The whole chain ($R^{in} \rightarrow R^{in}m_{con} \rightarrow R^{in}m_{con}m_{dis} \rightarrow R^{in}m_{con}m_{dis}m_{dis}$) is found in certain languages, for example, in Mansi, Chuvash, and Yakut, although only rarely. For example: Chuvash *lar-* 'sit' $\rightarrow$ *lar-t-* 'seat' $\rightarrow$ *lar-t-tar* 'force to seat' $\rightarrow$ *lar-t-tar-tar* 'tell smb to cause smb to seat smb'.

Type III, like type I, is usually found without the last link, i.e., in the variant $R^{tr} \rightarrow R^{tr}m_{dis}$, e.g.: Gilyak *ršu-d'* 'overtake' $\rightarrow$ *ršu-gu-d'* 'make overtake'; Abkhazian *a-š'-ra* 'kill' $\rightarrow$ *a-r-š'-ra* 'make kill'; Georgian *çer-s* 'writes' $\rightarrow$ *a-çer-in-eb-s* 'makes write'.

The whole chain ($R^{tr} \rightarrow R^{tr}m_{dis} \rightarrow R^{tr}m_{dis}m_{dis}$) is encountered relatively rarely in some languages. For example: Chuvash *selet-* 'sew' $\rightarrow$ *selet-ter-* 'make sew' $\rightarrow$ *selet-ter-tter-* 'make smb (through smb else) sew smth'; Mansi *junty-* 'sew' $\rightarrow$ *junty-lt* 'ask to sew' $\rightarrow$ *junty-lt-apt* 'ask smb (through smb else) to sew smth'.

Type IV is found in two variants.

The *first variant* ($R^{tr} \rightarrow R^{tr}m_{con}$) is encountered in languages where the causative affixes which form $R^{tr}m_{con}$ cannot be repeated, and there are no causative affixes with a distant meaning. For example: Abkhazian *a-psax-ra* 'borrow' $\rightarrow$ *a-r-psax-ra* 'lend', Swahili *-azima* 'borrow' *azim-ish-a* 'lend', Gilyak [*j*]*ama-d'* 'look' $\rightarrow$ [*j*]*ama-gu-d'* 'show', Arabic *'alima* 'know' $\rightarrow$

→'*allama* 'teach', Armenian *ut-el* 'eat' → *ut-eçn-el* 'feed' (see also 11.5, 12 and 21).

The *second variant* ($R^{tr} \to R^{tr}m_{con} \to R^{tr}m_{con}m_{dis}$) is found, for example, in Georgian (*čam-s* 'eats'→*a-čm-ev-s* 'feeds' → *a-čm-ev-in-eb-s* 'make feed'), Batsbien (*dag-* 'see' → *dag-d* 'show' → *dag-d-it-* 'ask to show') and Kechua (*jacha-* 'know' →*jacha-chi-* 'teach' *jacha-chi-chi* 'tell to teach'). We have no examples where the whole chain is realized.

The type V derivational chain is not found in some languages even without the last link (as, for example, in Abkhazian), whereas in Georgian and Mansi, for example, it can occur in the variant $R^{trtr} \to R^{trtr}m_{dis}$, e.g., Mansi *mi-s-te* 'he gave back, up' → *maj-lt-a-s-te* 'he asked to give back', Georgian *mi-s-c-a* 'he gave back, up' → *mi-a-c-em-in-a* 'he made give back'.

We do not have examples where the whole chain is realized. Thus, even if the last links of types IV and V can be realized in some languages, this is apparently rare.

30. Now let us briefly consider the changes in valency connected with derivation. Causatives of the type $R^{in}m_{dis}$ and $R^{in}m_{con}$ generally realize a valency of two (i.e., the valency for a direct object). In this respect they behave like ordinary primary transitive verbs. The causative object has as a rule the same morphological composition as the direct object with primary transitives.[51]

Gilyak is a somewhat curious exception in this last respect, the causative object there having a specific case marker.[52]

As concerns the trivalent causatives ($R^{in}m_{dis}m_{dis}$; $R^{in}m_{con}m_{dis}$; $R^{tr}m_{dis}$), there is a tendency in various languages (e.g., Chuvash, Yukaghir, Finnish) to delete the causative object, i.e., the object which designates the performer of the action. The latter is either clear from the context or is not vitally important. The construction is not interpreted as a syntactic ellipsis and sounds quite complete. Sometimes even native informants (of Yukaghir, for example) refuse to include the causative object in the construction, although semantically it is assumed to have a causative meaning.

The primary direct object in structures produced by all types of causatives does not as a rule change its morphological composition. This is the case in Avarian, Georgian, Zulu, Mongolian, the Turkish languages, Finnish, Japanese, and others.

In structures produced by quadrivalent causatives ($R^{trtr}m_{dis}$) there are usually no causative objects.

Thus, we can state that there is a tendency to delete the object which

---

[51] Gecadze, Nedyalkov, and Kholodovič, *op. cit.*, p. 145.
[52] Nedyalkov, Otaina, and Kholodovič, *op. cit.*, pp. 182, 195.

designates the performer of an action with causatives having a valence higher than two. Quadrivalence is practically never encountered, and quintivalence is apparently impossible due to the bulkiness of the structure that would result.

31. In the table above, each derivational step corresponded to an increase by one unit in syntactic valence. We have seen above that this possibility is far from always realized, and in some cases is not realizable.

We can make one refinement in the question of syntactic valence which is connected with those cases where there is reason to speak of a *preservation of the original syntactic valence*. These are cases encountered very often with verbs of emotion (classified in the table as univalent) and verbs relating to the receiving and taking of smth (classified in the table as bivalent). Cf., for example, in Swahili: *Mtoto*[1] *a-li-mw-ogop-a*[2] *mgeni*[3] 'The baby[1] was frightened[2] by the stranger[3]' (a- is a congruence morpheme for the subject, mw- a congruence morpheme for the object, li- the past tense marker) – *Mgeni*[1] *a-li-mw-ogop-esh-a*[2] *mtoto*[3] 'The stranger[1] frightened[2] the baby[3]' (-esh- is the causative suffix). In such cases, however, it seems more exact to speak not of the full preservation of valence (although there is a direct object in both examples), but of a transformation of valence from syntactically optional to obligatory. Since, however, the reason for fright, just like the reason for any other state, can be expressed by various syntactic forms (cf.: *Giza*[1] *ilipoingia*[2] *mtoto*[3] *a-li-ogop-a*[4] 'When[2] it became[2] dark[1] the baby[3] became frightened[4]'; *Akiona*[1] *mgeni*[2] *mtoto*[3] *a-li-ogop-a*[4] 'When he saw[1] the stranger[2], the baby[3] became frightened[4]', etc.) or can even remain unknown to the speaker, who observes only the outward manifestation of emotion (i.e., there is no mention at all of the cause in the utterance), there is also reason in most cases to look for an increase in valence for verbs of this type, with the reservation that in certain syntactic constructions there can occur an alternation between a construction with several disjunctive syntactic types of optional environments with a non-causative and a construction with one obligatory type of environment (a direct object) with a causative. Of course, far from all specific indications of cause with a V_i can be transformed into the subject in the V_j as was done in the examples above.

Soviet Academy of Sciences, Leningrad

I. A. MEL'ČUK

TOWARDS A LINGUISTIC 'MEANING⇔TEXT' MODEL

SUMMARY. **1.** The proposed model is a translative (=transformative), rather than a generative, system; its purpose consists in establishing correspondences between any given meaning and (ideally) all synonymous texts having this meaning. We assume here that we can formally describe meaning as an invariant of a set of equisignificant texts, that analysis of meaning as such lays outside the model, and that the 'Meaning⇔Text' Model (MTM) is a fragment of the more general model 'Reality⇔(Meaning⇔Text)⇔ ⇔Speech'.
    2. Five levels of utterance representation are used in the MTM: (I) The semantic level – a semantic graph (semantic atoms – *semes* – connected by semantic relations) plus indications of topicalization, etc.; (II) The syntactic level with two sub-levels: (IIa) The deep-syntax representation of a sentence – a deep dependency tree with universal deep-syntax relations plus indications of topicalization, anaphoric relations, and certain constituents (where necessary), (IIb) The surface-syntax representation of the sentence – a surface dependency tree with the specific syntactic relations of the language in question plus the same additional information as in (IIa); (III) The morphological level: (IIIa) The deep-morphology representation of word-forms (the name of the respective lexeme supplied with a full morphological description), (IIIb) The surface-morphology representation of word-forms (a string of morphs and/or morphological operations); (IV) The phonological level; (V) The phonetic/graphic-orthographic level.
    3. The MTM consists of five basic components which establish correspondences between the representations of the above levels. Examples of the rules of each component are given.
    4. Certain linguistic problems connected with the MTM are treated: a new type of dictionary (two dictionary entries are given); word-derivation and the possible formal-semantic relations between linguistic signs (signifié, signifiant, syntactics – information on the combinatorial properties of the sign); and a tentative definition of conversion in English.

In this paper we will proceed from the following hypothesis: a natural language may be viewed as a special kind of (logical) device which provides for the comprehension of a given utterance, i.e., the *perception of its meaning(s)*, or the construction of utterances *which express a given meaning*. Then it should be a device which provides correspondences between meanings and texts, or maps the set of all possible meanings onto the set of all possible texts – and vice versa.

Hypotheses about such devices can be formulated as functional models, or logical systems, describing the mapping 'Meaning⇔Text'. We propose to discuss below one such model.

Here, of course, we can give only a very general description of the model; our exposition will of necessity be sketchy and somewhat dogmatic. The relationship between 'Meaning⇔Text' model and the very closely related

F. Kiefer (ed.), Trends in Soviet Theoretical Linguistics, 33–57. All Rights Reserved.
Copyright © 1973 by D. Reidel Publishing Company, Dordrecht-Holland.

linguistic models proposed by the theories of generative grammars and generative semantics will not be touched upon at all. We will limit ourselves to emphasizing the fact that N. Chomsky's theories and their modern development by M. Halle, C. Fillmore, G. Lakoff, J. McCawley, and many others have significantly influenced the author, who is in addition particularly indebted to A. K. Žolkovskij, with whom he has worked in close contact for several years. Many of our propositions below have been taken from the joint works of A. K. Žolkovskij and the author (most notably, Žolkovskij and Mel'čuk, 1967).

N.B.: Reference will be made only to those publications which have a direct connection with the 'Meaning⟺Text' model described in this paper.

I. PROPERTIES OF THE 'MEANING⟺TEXT' MODELS

The main feature of the 'Meaning⟺Text' model (MTM) consists in the following: it is not a generative, but a translative (=transformative) system; it does not seek to generate grammatically correct (or meaningful, etc.) texts, but merely to match, ideally, *any* given meaning with all symonymous texts having this meaning, and conversely, to match *any* given text with all the meanings this text can have. Here we make the following three assumptions:

(a) We are able to describe the meaning of any utterance in a special semantic language. – Meaning is understood to be an invariant of a set of equisignificant texts (this equisignificance is considered to be intuitively obvious to a native speaker).

(b) The analysis of the meaning itself (the discovery of various semantic anomalies – contradictions, absurdities, trivialities, etc.) goes beyond the MTM as such; a different type of device is needed for this purpose.[1]

(c) The 'Meaning⟺Text' model should be a fragment of the more general and complete model of human (intellectual + linguistic) behaviour: 'Reality⟺Speech', i.e.,

$$\text{'Reality} \underbrace{\Leftrightarrow \text{Meaning}}_{\text{I}} \underbrace{\Leftrightarrow \text{Text}}_{\text{II}} \underbrace{\Leftrightarrow \text{Speech'}}_{\text{III}}.$$

In our opinion, only fragment II is object of linguistics proper; only this fragment is represented in the MTM.

The following limitations have been observed in our work on the MTM:

---

[1] Thus, we meet here with the essential *asymmetry* of texts and meanings: our model should catch all formal, i.e. linguistic, anomalies of a text, but it does not deal with the semantic ones.

(1) The MTM is a *purely functional* model. No attempts have been made to relate it experimentally with psychological or neurological reality; for the time being, therefore, the MTM is nothing more than a logical means for describing observable correspondences between meanings and texts.

(2) The transformation 'meanings ⇔ texts' is described in the MTM only *as a set of correspondences* between the former and the latter. The possible *procedures* for moving from meanings to texts and vice versa will not be treated here at all. In other words, the MTM in its present state models only *competence*, and not *performance*.

(3) Possible 'feedback' between texts and meanings in the process of speaking (changes in the original semantic message under the influence of an already constructed text, etc.) are not taken into account.

(4) Functions of natural language other than the communicative one are not considered at all, which amounts to viewing language as a communication system only, that is, as a 'Meaning⇔Text' transformer.

(5) The extremely important question of how language is acquired and perfected will be left completely untouched.

The MTM has been developed primarily on the basis of Russian linguistic data, which will also be used as illustrative materials in the present paper.

For a general description of the 'Meaning⇔Text' model see Mel'čuk (1970).

II. UTTERANCE REPRESENTATION LEVELS IN THE 'MEANING⇔TEXT' MODEL

In view of the fact that homonymy and synonymy so widely spread in natural languages, highly complicate the direct correspondence between meanings and texts, a number of *representation levels* have been established in the MTM.[2] Five levels for the representation of utterances are distinguished: the semantic, syntactic, morphological, phonological, and phonetic/graphic levels.

(I) *The semantic level: a semantic representation* is assigned to the utterance; see (1) – semantic representation of a set of synonymous Russian utterances exemplified by the sentence:

> *Ivan tverdo obeščal Petru, čto večerom on primet Mariju samym teplym obrazom,*
>
> 'John firmly promised Peter that [this] evening he would receive Mary in a most cordial manner'.

---

[2] In complete accordance with the generally held view: cf. the stratificational grammar of S. Lamb, the Mehrstufiges Generatives System of P. Sgall, and others.

(1)

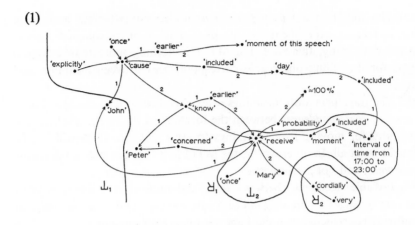

(*N.B.*: This and all subsequent examples do not claim to be semantically precise. They are purely illustrative in nature.)

A possible approximate reading: 'John explicitly caused once [past form of verb is represented by 'earlier than the moment of this speech'] Peter to know that after he, John, would receive Mary, with which reception Peter is concerned, in a moment included in the time interval from 17:00 to 23:00 in the day when it is said, and the reception, which has a probability of nearly 100%, would be very cordial'.

The semantic representation consists of the following two components:

(1) A *semantic graph* gives the meaning of an utterance without distributing it into sentences or words. (Such linguistic features, as the selection of specific words and syntactic constructions, are deliberately not shown at all in the semantic graph.) This is a connected directed graph with no additional restrictions whatsoever.[3]

The nodes of the graph are *semantic units* (SU) which generally represent 'semantic atoms' – meanings which within the given description are considered to be elementary; these meanings are called *semes*. By way of abbreviation, however, we allow 'intermediate' SU's – symbolizing complexes of semes, i.e., whole semantic (sub)graphs. Thus, in (1) the SU '$A \leftarrow$ earlier [than] $\rightarrow B$' is an abbreviation for 'the time of A precedes the time of B', and the SU 'know' is an abbreviation of something like 'have true information about'; it is obvious that 'concerned', 'receive', and 'cordially' are all far from

---

[3] The use of a graph (= network) to represent a semantic content of utterances is by no means a novelty in linguistic analysis. Suffice it to mention here the pioneer paper by K. I. Babickij (*Naučno-texničeskaja Informacija*, 1965, No. 6), the book by W. Hutchins (1971) with further references and many well-known publications in and on the inference and question-answering systems (by Quillian, Bobrow, Simmons, and others).

elementary. A complete analysis into semes would make the graph un-readable.

The arcs of the graph are *semantic relations*, i.e., relations between SU's.

SU's divide into two classes. One type of SU consists of names (of classes) of objects or single objects, in particular, proper names; semantic relation arcs can only enter them. The other type of SU, conventionally called *predicates*, consists of predicates, quantifiers, and logical constants; arcs can also leave them. (*N.B.*: the arrows on the arcs point from predicates to their arguments.)

Predicate semes are never more than two-place; intermediate SU's can have up to five (or even more?) places. The various arcs leaving a single node are numbered: $A \xleftarrow{1}$'cause'$\xrightarrow{2} B$ means that A is the first, and B the second argument of the predicate 'cause' (A is the causer, or the cause; B is the caused, or the result, etc.). How the nodes of a semantic graph are physically distributed on a sheet is of no significance.

(2) *Information about the communicative organization* of an utterance: about the topic (Ⅎ, Fr. thème) – comment (Я, Fr. rhème), about the old – the new, about the psychological value of a particular meaning fragment for the speaker, about emotional emphasis. This information stands in approximately the same relationship to a semantic graph as prosodic phenomena to the string of phonemes which make up a sentence. (In our simplified examples only information about the topic-comment is indicated.)

The division into topic and comment can have successive 'strata'; thus, within the comment of the first stratum in (1), there is a division into $Ⅎ_2 - Я_2$.

(II) *The syntatic level* can be differentiated into two sublevels.

(IIa) *Deep syntax*: the utterance is given as a sequence of sentences; each sentence is assigned a so-called *deep-syntax representation* (DSR); see (2)–(4) – the deep-syntax representations of some synonymous Russian sentences corresponding to semantic graph (1):

(2)

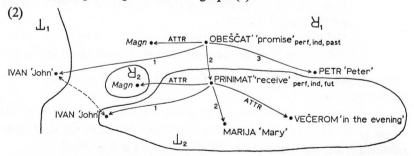

Ivan tverdo obeščal Petru, čto večerom on primet Mariju samym teplym obrazom,

'John firmly promised Peter that this evening he would receive
Mary in the most cordial manner'.

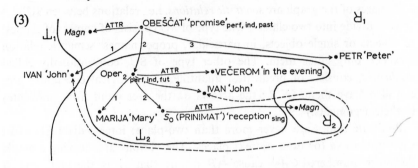

*Ivan tverdo obeščal Petru, čto večerom Marija najdet u nego samyj
teplyj ⟨radušnyj⟩ priem,*
'John firmly promised Peter that this evening Mary would
receive [find] from him a most cordial ⟨hearty⟩ welcome/that
he would welcome Mary most cordially ⟨heartily⟩'.

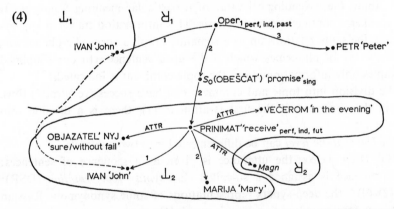

*Ivan dal Petru obeščanie večerom objazatel'no prinjat' Mariju
samym teplym obrazom,*
'John gave Peter his promise that this evening he would without
fail receive Mary in the most cordial manner ⟨most cordially⟩'.

The deep-syntax representation of a sentence consists of the following
five components:

(1) The *deep-syntax structure* of a sentence (DSS) is a dependency tree
whose nodes are *generalized lexemes* and whose branches are *deep syntax
relations*. *N.B.*: the linear order of the DSS nodes is not given!

A generalized lexeme is one of the following objects:

Either it is a full lexeme of the language in question (empty words, strongly governed prepositions and conjunctions, auxiliary verbs in complex forms, etc., are not represented in the DSS);

Or it is a fictive lexeme: for example, the symbol for an indefinite personal subject (≈ Fr. *on*, Ger. *man*), which has no expression in an actual Russian text;

Or it is a whole idiom: e.g., *s'est' sobaku* 'know something backwards and forwards, know one's stuff', *sinij čulok* 'bluestocking', etc.;

Or it is a symbol for a lexical function (see below).

The symbol for a generalized lexeme can have subscripts for the morphological features which have full meaning and are not determined syntactically: number of the noun; aspect, tense, and mood of the verb.

A *lexical function* (LF) **f** is a relation which connects a keyword (or word-group) W – the *argument* of LF – with a set of other words or word-groups $\mathbf{f}(W)$ – the *value* of LF – in such a way that for any W^1 and W^2, if only $\mathbf{f}(W^1)$ and $\mathbf{f}(W^2)$ exist, both $\mathbf{f}(W^1)$ and $\mathbf{f}(W^2)$ hold an identical relationship – with respect to meaning and syntactic role – to W^1 and W^2, respectively; in the majority of cases $\mathbf{f}(W)$ is also different for different W's which means that $\mathbf{f}(W)$ is 'phraseologically bound' by W. We have arrived at about 50 *standard elementary* LF's, that is, those whose number of possible arguments and number of possible values is sufficiently large. *Complex* LF's, which are composed of standard LF's, are also possible. Some examples of LF's: **Syn** (*priglašat'* 'invite') = *zvat'* 'ask, call'; **Syn** (*xudoj* 'thin') = *toščij* 'skinny' [synonym]; $\mathbf{Conv}_{21}$ (*pered* 'in front of') = *szadi* 'in back of', $\mathbf{Conv}_{21}$ (*sledovat'* 'follow') = *predšestvovat'* 'precede' [conversive]; S_0 (*polagat'* 'believe') = *mnenie* 'opinion' [nomen actionis]; **Magn**(*priglašenie* 'invitation') = *nastojčivoe* 'urgent, persistent', **Magn** (*bereč'* 'keep, cherish') = *kak zenicu oka* 'like the apple of one's eye', **Magn** (*xudoj* 'thin') = *kak skelet/ščepka* 'as a skeleton/a lath' [= 'very']; $\mathbf{Oper}_1$ (*prikaz* 'order') = *davat'* 'give', $\mathbf{Oper}_1$ (*mnenie* 'opinion') = *imet'*, *prederživat' sja* 'have, hold' [= 'be the subject of']; $\mathbf{Oper}_2$ (*priglašenie* 'invitation') = *polučat'* 'receive'; $\mathbf{Oper}_2$ (*kontrol'* 'control') = *byt' pod* 'be under' [= 'be the object of']; $\mathbf{Real}_1$ (*obeščanie* 'promise') = *sderžat'* 'keep'; $\mathbf{Real}_2$ (*prikaz* 'order') = *vypolnit'* 'perform, execute' [= 'fulfill, perform, being the subject/the object of']; **Son** (*korova* 'cow') = *myčat'* 'low, moo'; **Son** (*stekla* 'glasses, lenses') = *zvenet'*, *drebezžat'* 'jingle, jar' [typical sound]; etc.

LF's play a very important role in synonymous periphrasing (see below, p. 45), i.e., on the plane of synonymy reduction. Concerning LF's see Mel'čuk (1967c); Mel'čuk and Zholkovskij (1970), pp. 24–32; Zholkovskij and Mel'čuk (1970), pp. 35–60.

A *deep-syntax relation* is one of the following relations:

1, 2, 3, 4, 5 (maybe, 6)–relations which connect a lexeme-predicate with its first, second, third, fourth, fifth (or sixth) arguments, respectively:

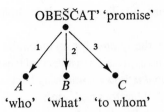

OBEŠČAT' 'promise'

A   B   C
'who' 'what' 'to whom'

ATTR – a relation which connects any entity with its attribute, or modifier (in the broadest sense of the term):

TOČKA 'point', ÈTOT 'this',

PRINIMAT' 'greet', 'receive'   VEČEROM 'in the evening', etc.

COORD – a relation which connects any two coordinated entities:

IVAN 'John'   PETR 'Peter' I 'and' MARIJA 'Mary',

i.e. 'John, Peter, and Mary'.

APPEND – a relation which connects the root of the sentence deep-syntax tree with any so-called 'independent' element (such as parenthetical expression, interjection, address, etc.):

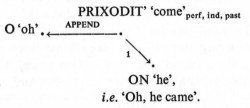

ON 'he',
i.e. 'Oh, he came'.

We presume that these relations are sufficient to be able to describe any syntactic constructions of any language on the deep level.

(2) Information about the communicative organization of the sentence, specifically, indications of the topic and comment, see ⊥ and ʁ in (2)–(4).

(3) Information about coreferentiality of particular phrases; in (2)–(4) the coreferential nodes ('the same John') are connected by a dotted arrow.

(4) Information about constituents – those which cannot be represented in a natural way by a dependency tree (like *old man and women* etc).

(5) Information about meaningful (i.e. not syntactically conditioned) prosodic phenomena, like intonation contours, pauses, junctures, emphatic stresses, and the like.

(IIb) *Surface syntax*: utterances are given as sequences of sentences; each sentence is assigned a surface-syntax representation (SSR); see (5), which is the SSR corresponding to DSR (3), and (6)–(7), which are the SSR's corresponding to DSR (4):

(5)

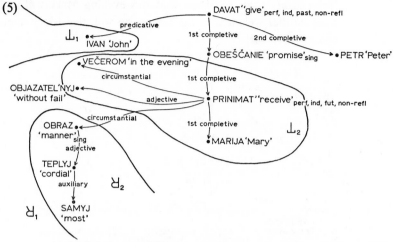

Ivan dal Petru obeščanie večerom objazatel'no prinjat' Mariju samym teplym obrazom,

'John gave Peter his promise that this evening he would without fail welcome Mary in a most cordial manner ⟨most cordially⟩',

(6)

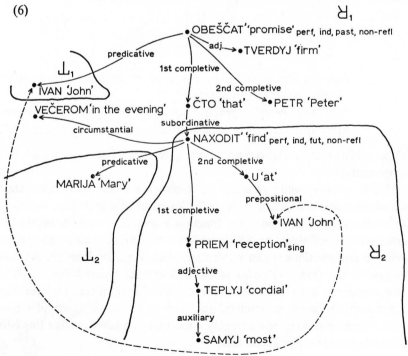

Ivan tverdo obeščal Petru, čto večerom Marija najdet u nego samyj teplyj priem,
'John firmly promised Peter that this evening Mary will find a most cordial welcome at his home / he will give Mary a most cordial welcome',

(7)

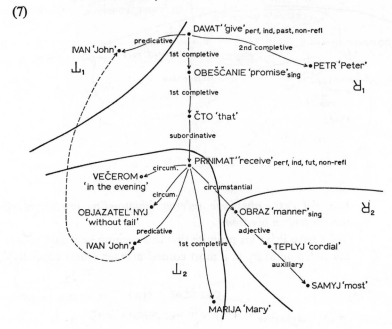

Ivan dal Petru obeščanie, čto večerom on objazatel'no primet Mariju samym teplym obrazom,
'John gave Peter his promise that he would without fail welcome Mary this evening in a most cordial manner ⟨most cordially⟩'.

The surface-syntax representation of a sentence also consists of five components:

(1) The *surface-syntax structure* of a sentence (SSS) is a dependency tree whose nodes are specific *lexemes* (*all* lexemes of the sentences, including the auxiliary, or empty, ones, i.e. function words, and whose branches are *surface-syntax relations*, or SSR's. About 50 SSR's – language-specific syntactic constructions – can be distinguished, e.g., for Russian. As was the case in the DSS, the nodes of the SSS are not ordered linearly. It is done in order to keep apart and not to confound two orders of relations in a sentence: structural, hierarchical relations as such, and those of linear order, which serve as a means (highly important in a language like English) to encode the former in actual text.

(2)–(5) Information about the communicative organization of the sentence, about coreferentiality of nominal and other phrases, about the constituents, and about semantically loaded prosodic features (analogously to the deep-syntax representation).

(III) *The morphological level* also divides into two sub-levels.

(IIIa) *Deep morphology*: utterances are represented as sequences of sentences; each sentence is assigned a sequence of linearly ordered deep-morphological representations (DMR) of word-forms (and indications, which will not be considered here, as to prosodic features or punctuation marks); see (8), which corresponds to surface-syntax representation (5):

(8)   IVAN 'John'$_{sing, nom}$ TVERDYJ 'firm'$_{neut, sing, short}$
OBEŠČAT 'promise'$_{perf, ind, past, non-refl, sing, masc}$
PETR 'Peter'$_{sing, dat}$ ČTO 'that'   MARIJA 'Mary'$_{sing, nom}$
NAXODIT' 'find'$_{perf, ind, fut, non-refl, 3sing}$
U 'at'   ON 'he'$_{sing, gen}$
VEČEROM 'this evening'   SAMYJ 'most'$_{masc, sing, acc}$
TEPLYJ 'cordial'$_{masc, sing, acc}$
PRIEM 'reception'$_{sing, acc}$

A word-form DMR consists of the name of the respective lexeme together with the full morphological description needed to describe unambiguously that particular word-form.

(IIIb) *Surface morphology*: utterances are given as sequences of sentences; each sentence is assigned a sequence of morpheme strings and symbols of morphological operations, each of which describes a word-form, see (9), which corresponds to representation (8):

(9)   {IVAN 'John'} + {sing, nom} {TVERDYJ 'firm'} + {short
neut. sing} {OBEŠČAT' 'promise'} + {perf} + {past} + {masc}
{PETR 'Peter'} + {sing. dat} {ČTO 'that'} {MARIJA 'Mary'} +
+ {sing. nom} {NAXODIT' 'find'} + {perf} + {ind. non-past.
3 sing} {U 'at'} {ON 'he'} + {sing. gen} {SAMYJ 'most'} +
+ {masc. sing. acc} {TEPLYJ 'cordial'} + {masc. sing. acc}
{PRIEM 'reception'} + {sing. acc}.

A morpheme is understood to be a class of morphs (= minimal linguistic signs) having an identical signifié and satisfying sufficiently simple distribution rules.

(IV) *The phonological level*: the phonemic transcription of a sentence with all of its prosodemes indicated.

(V) *The phonetic/graphic level*: the phonetic transcription of a sentence showing all prosodic phenomena, or the spelling of a sentence duly punctuated (*N.B.*: levels (IV) and (V) are not treated in the present paper).

III. THE DESIGN OF THE 'MEANING⇔TEXT' MODEL

Transitions from one level of utterance representation to another are accomplished by the following basic components of the model.

(I) *The semantic component* establishes correspondences between the semantic representation of an utterance and all alternative (=synonymous) sequences of deep-syntax representations of the sentences which make up this utterance.

When moving from meaning to text, the semantic component of the model performs the following operations:

(1) Cuts the semantic graph into subgraphs, each of which corresponds to a sentence.

(2) Selects the corresponding words by means of rules of the type:

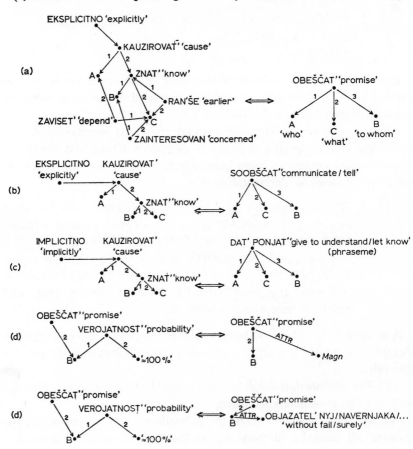

(3) Selects the semantic (i.e., syntactically unconditioned) morphological characteristics of the lexical items by means of rules of the type:

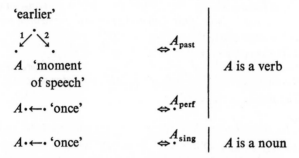

(4) Forms the deep-syntax structure of the sentenses.

(5) Processes the remaining components of the deep-syntax representations.

(6) For each DSS are constructed all its synonymous DSS's such that this synonymy can be described in terms of lexical functions. In other words, an 'algebra' of the transformations on the DSS which contain LF symbols is given.

These transformations can be described by rules of two classes:

Lexical rules (at present there are about 60 of them) are either semantic equivalencies or semantic implications. Examples:

Equivalencies:

(1) $\overset{x}{C} \overset{y}{\Leftrightarrow} \text{Conv}_{21}\,(C).$

The set A also contains the point $x \underset{\text{Conv}_{21}\,(C)}{\Leftrightarrow}$

The point x also belongs to the set A.

(2) $\overset{x}{C} \overset{y}{\underset{c}{\Leftrightarrow}} \text{Adv}_{1\text{B}}\,(C).$

$\qquad\qquad\qquad\qquad\qquad\qquad\qquad\qquad\qquad \text{Adv}_{1\text{B}}\,(C)$

On pospešil vyjti 'He hurried to leave' ⇔ *On pospešno vyšel* 'He hurriedly left'.

(3) $\overset{x}{C} \overset{y}{\Leftrightarrow} S_0\,(C) + \text{Oper}_1\,(S_0\,(C)).$

$\qquad\quad c \qquad\qquad\qquad\qquad\qquad \text{Oper}_1 \quad S_0\,(C)$

On boretsja 'He is struggling' ⇔ *On vedet bor'bu* 'He is waging a struggle'.

(4) $\overset{x}{\text{Real}_2}\,(C) \overset{y}{\Leftrightarrow} \text{Adv}_{1\text{B}}\,(\text{Real}_2\,(C)).$

On posledoval ee sovetu uexat' 'He followed her advice to leave' ⇔ *On uexal po ee sovetu* 'He left on her advice'.

Implications:

(1)   PerfCaus (X) ⇒ PerfIncep (X).

PerfCausFunc₀ (C)   PerfIncepFunc₀ (C)

Petr zapustil motor 'Petr started the motor' ⇒ *Motor zarabotal*
'The motor started'.

(2)   PerfIncep (X) ⇒ X.

PerfIncepFunc₀ (C)   C   Func₀ (C)

Motor zarabotal 'The motor started' ⇒ *Motor rabotaet*
'The motor is running'.

Syntactic rules describe the dependency tree transformations and indicate
what restructuring of the DSS's are necessary when a particular lexical
rule is applied. Thus, in order to operate the lexical rules given above, the
following types of syntactic rules are necessary:

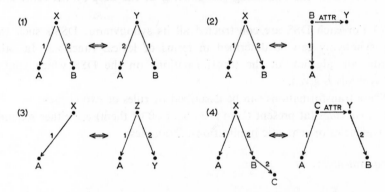

For DSS transformation rules, see Zholkovskij and Mel'čuk (1970),
pp. 60–81.

A special formalism has been devised for describing unordered dependency
tree transformations – so called Δ-grammars (Gladkij and Mel'čuk (1969),
Gladkij and Mel'čuk (1971)).

(II) *The syntactic component* establishes correspondences between the
deep-syntax representation of a sentence and all the deep-morphology
representations which correspond to it. These correspondences are established by two stages.

(IIa) The transition from the deep-syntax representation of a sentence to
all its alternative surface-syntax representations can be conceived of as two
kinds of operations:

(1) DSS⇔SSS transformations. DSS to SSS transformation rules are
used when moving from meaning to text, and these rules again divide into
two classes:

– Lexical rules transform the nodes of the trees.

With the help of the lexicon, they 'compute' the values of the lexical functions, e.g.,

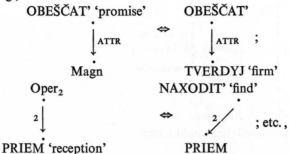

or expand the symbols of the phrasemes into surface-syntax sub-trees, e.g.,

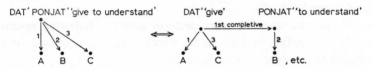

– Syntactic rules transform the tree itself, performing the following operations:

(a) The replacement of a deep relation by a surface one, e.g.,

$$X_{(V)} \quad X_{(V \text{ fin})} \qquad X \qquad X$$

$$1 \downarrow \quad \Leftrightarrow \quad \downarrow \text{predicative;} \quad \downarrow \text{ATTR} \quad \Leftrightarrow \quad \downarrow \text{adjective;}$$

$$Y_{(S)} \qquad Y_{(S)} \qquad Y_{(A)} \qquad Y_{(A)}$$

$$X \qquad X$$

$$\downarrow \text{ATTR} \quad \Leftrightarrow \quad \downarrow \text{quantitative; etc.}$$

$$Y_{(\text{Num})} \qquad Y_{(\text{Num})}$$

(b) The replacement of a deep node by a surface relation:

$$X \qquad X_{(S)} \qquad X_{(S)} \qquad X_{(S)}$$

$$\text{ATTR} \downarrow \qquad \downarrow \qquad \text{ATTR} \downarrow \qquad \downarrow$$
$$\cdot \text{NAME} \quad \Leftrightarrow \quad \text{2nd appositive;} \quad \downarrow Y_{(\text{Num})} \quad \Leftrightarrow \quad \text{approximative}$$
$$2 \downarrow \qquad \qquad \text{ATTR} \downarrow$$

$$Y_{(S)} \qquad Y_{(S)} \qquad \text{PRIBLIZITEL'NO} \qquad Y_{(\text{Num})}$$
$$\qquad \qquad \qquad \text{'approximately'}$$

Množestvo Q, gorod Nansi   *čelovek vosem*
'The set Q', 'The city of Nancy'   'about eight people'

(c) The replacement of a deep relation by a surface node:

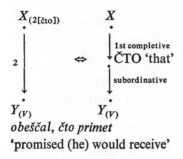

obeščal, čto primet
'promised (he) would receive'

(the notation $X_{(2[\check{c}to])}$ here means "a lexeme whose second deep-syntax valency is filled in the SSS by the conjunction ČTO 'that'; this information is stored in the lexicon").

In addition the syntactic rules perform also the following operation:

(d) The elimination of DSS nodes which occur in anaphoric relations and should not be expressed in the text:

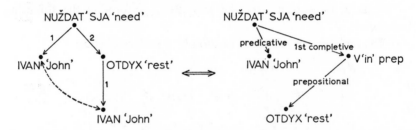

(i.e., *Ivan nuždaetsja v otdyxe* 'John needs rest', but not **Ivan nuždaetsja v svoem otdyxe* 'Jean needs his own rest').

(2) The transfer of information from components (2)–(5) of the deep-syntax representation to the corresponding components of the surface-syntax representation.

(IIb) The transition from the surface-syntax representation of a sentence to all alternative linearly ordered sequences of deep-morphology word-form representations. Here the following operations are performed.

(1) 'SSS morphologization', i.e., the determination of all syntactically conditioned morphological features by means of rules such as:

$$S_{(x)\,y,\,z} \quad S_{(x)\,y,\,z}$$

adj. ⇔	adj.

$$\cdot A \qquad \cdot A_{x,\,y,\,z}$$

(*polnaja tablica* 'complete table')

S (a noun) has no numeral dependent on it (*x, y, z* – gender, number, case; *A* is an adjective)

TABLE I

Pattern of simple noun phrase in Russian

1	2	3	4	5	6	7	8	9	10	11
Coord. conj.	neg. or restr. particle	preposition	quantifier	dem. pronoun	quantity word	poss. adj.	ordinal num. (adj.)	adj.	head	apposition
ili or	*ne* not	*iz* from	*nekotoryx* some of	*ètix* these	*vos'mi* eight	*našix* our	*vtoryx* second	*važnyx* important	*formul* formulae	Z Z

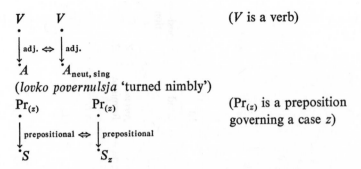

$$\begin{array}{ccc} V & V \\ \bullet & \bullet \\ \Big\downarrow \text{adj.} & \Leftrightarrow & \Big\downarrow \text{adj.} \\ \bullet & \bullet \\ A & A_{\text{neut, sing}} \end{array}$$

(V is a verb)

(lovko povernulsja 'turned nimbly')

$$\begin{array}{ccc} \text{Pr}_{(z)} & & \text{Pr}_{(z)} \\ \bullet & \bullet \\ \Big\downarrow \text{prepositional} & \Leftrightarrow & \Big\downarrow \text{prepositional} \\ \bullet & \bullet \\ S & S_z \end{array}$$

(Pr$_{(z)}$ is a preposition governing a case z)

As a result we obtain deep-morphology representations (DMR's) in the SSS nodes.

(2) 'SSS linearization', i.e., the determination of the linear order of the word-form DMR's (word order) for subtrees of the SSS corresponding to clauses (within a complex sentence) by means of rules of three following types (Mel'čuk, 1967a):

– The determination of word order in the simple phrases in accordance with patterns of the type shown in Table I.

– The determination of the order of simple phrases within derived (full, or compound) phrases.

– The determination of the order of the derived phrases within clauses taking into account topicalization and a number of other intricate mutually interacting factors.

(3) The combination of the DMR strings which correspond to clauses, into a single DMR string for the whole sentence.

(4) The introduction of pronouns into the DMR string (=pronominalization).

(5) The obligatory and optional ellipses carried out on the DMR string.

(III) *The morphological component* establishes – also in two steps – the correspondence between the deep-morphology representations of a word-form and the word-form itself in phonemic transcription.

(IIIa) The transition from a DMR of a word-form to the SMR of this word-form, i.e., to a string of morphemes and morphological operations; this is done by means of rules such as:

$$T_{(S, p)y, z} \Leftrightarrow \{T\}_{(p)} + \{YZ\}.$$

(*T* is a stem; y, z represent number and case; p are combinatorial properties of the stem supplied by the lexicon and called 'syntactics'.)

$$\text{PRIEM 'reception, welcome'}_{(p)\,\text{sing, acc}} \Leftrightarrow \{\text{PRIEM}\}_{(p)} + \\ + \{\text{SING. ACC}\}$$

$T_{(A,\,p)\,x,\,\text{sing, short}} \Leftrightarrow \{T\}_{(p)} + \{\text{SHORT. X. SING}\}$

$\text{TVERDYJ}_{(p)\,\text{neut, sing, short}} \Leftrightarrow \{\text{TVERDYJ}\} +$
$+ \{\text{SHORT. NEUT. SING}\}$

$T_{(V,\,p)\,\text{perf. fut}} \Leftrightarrow \{T\}_{(p)} + \{\text{PERF}\} + \{\text{PRES}\}$

(since the perfective future in Russian is formally constructed like the present).

(IIIb) The transition from the SMR of a word-form to its phonemic transcription; this is performed by means of four groups of rules (Mel'čuk, 1967b, d, 1968; Es'kova *et al.*, 1971):

(1) Morphemo-morphic rules of the type

$\{\text{PRIEM 'welcome'}\}_{(p_1)} \Leftrightarrow /\text{pr,ijom}/_{(p_1)}$,
$\{\text{TVERDYJ 'firm'}\}_{(p_2)} \Leftrightarrow /\text{tv,ord}/_{(p_2)}$,

$\{\text{SING. ACC}\} \Leftrightarrow /\emptyset/$ | either decl. II, masc, inanimate (*dom* 'house') or decl. III, masc/fem (*put'* 'way, road', *noč'* 'night')

$\Leftrightarrow /a/$ | either decl. II, animate (*kota* 'cat') or decl. III, neut. (*vremja* 'time')

$\{\text{SHORT. NEUT. SING}\} \Leftrightarrow /o/$

$\{\text{NAXODIT' 'find'}\} + \{\text{PERF}\} \Leftrightarrow /\text{najd}/$ | *not* past
$\Leftrightarrow /\text{našed}/$ | past and part
$\Leftrightarrow /\text{našod}/$ | past and *not* part

$\{\text{IND. NON-PAST 3 SING}\} \Leftrightarrow /of/$ | conj. I
$\Leftrightarrow /it/$ | conj. II

$\{\text{ON 'he'}\} + \{\text{SING. NOM}\} \Leftrightarrow /on/$

$\{\text{ON 'he'}\} \Leftrightarrow /j/$ | *not* nom | *not* after a preposition
$\Leftrightarrow /n/$ | | after a preposition.

(2) Accentuation rules; perform transformations of the type:

$/\text{pr,ijom} + \emptyset/ \Rightarrow /\text{pr,ijóm} + \emptyset/$
$/\text{tv,ord} + o/ \Rightarrow /\text{tv,órd} + o/$.

(3) Morphonemic rules; perform different kinds of morphologically conditioned phoneme alternations:

$/d/ \Rightarrow /ž/$ ($/\text{tv, órd}/ - /\text{tv, órže}/$) | in certain morphs
$/c/ \Rightarrow /č/$ ($/\text{pt, íca}/ - /\text{pt, íčka}/$) | only, according
$\left.\begin{matrix} /t/ \\ /d/ \end{matrix}\right\} \Rightarrow \Lambda \left(\begin{matrix} /\text{pl, ot} + u/ - /\text{pl, ó} + 1/ \\ /\text{v, od} + ú/ - /\text{v, ó} + 1/ \end{matrix}\right)$ | to syntactics of | these.

(4) Phonological rules; perform morphologically unconditioned phonemic transformations like the following:

$/C_{[\text{voiced}]}\{C_{[\text{-voiced}]}\}/ \Rightarrow /C_{[\text{-voiced}]}\{C_{[\text{-voiced}]}\}/$

IV. *The phonological component* establishes the correspondence between the phonemic and the phonetic transcription of a word-form.

V. *The graphico-orthographic component* establishes the correspondence between the phonemic transcription of a word-form and its spelling. Its rules have the form:

$/X$ja$/ \Leftrightarrow /X/$ А		(/struja/ *струя*)
$/X$ju$/ \Leftrightarrow /X/$ Ю	$/X/$ is not a consonant	(/strujú/ *струю*)
$/X$ji $/ \Leftrightarrow /X/$ И		(/strují/ *струи*)
$/$j$X/ \Leftrightarrow$ Й $/X/$	$/X/$ is not a vowel	(/kraj/ *край*)
$/C,$j$/ \Rightarrow /C/$ Ъ $/$j$/$	$/C/$ is a consonant	(/sv,injá/ *сбинья*)
$/C,$a$/ \Rightarrow /C/$ Я		(/m,áso/ *мясо*)

IV. SOME LINGUISTIC IMPLICATIONS OF THE 'MEANING⇔TEXT' MODEL

Our work on the 'Meaning⇔Text' model has resulted in a number of interesting linguistic problems. We will only mention three of them here (cf. Mel'čuk and Žolkovskij, 1970; p. 40–46).

(1) One of the most important components of the MTM is the *lexicon* which stores all the information (semantic, syntactic, morphological, phonological) about each word necessary for all the components of the model to be able to handle this word correctly. Such a lexicon, or dictionary, known as an *explanatory combinatorial dictionary*, is at present being developed for Russian; see in particular Apresyan *et al.* (1969). Two entries from this type of dictionary are given below by way of illustration (due to lack of space, without any preliminary explanations. We trust the examples will be sufficiently obvious).

1. *OBEŠČAT' 'To promise'*

OBEŠČAT', *obéščan, ju, ješ'*, imperf. 1. *X obeščaet Y Z-u* 'X promises Y to Z' = X explicitly causes Z to know that Y, with which Z is concerned and which depends on X, will occur. Cf. GARANTIROVAT' 'guarantee'; UGROŽAT' 'threaten'.

$1 = X$ who	$2 = Y$ what	$3 = Z$ to whom	
S_{nom}	(1) S_{acc}	S_{dat}	(1) X and Z are persons,
	(2) V_{inf}		(2) If $Y = 2.2$, then $M_1 (Y) = X$
	(3) *čto* + SENT		$[M_1 (Y)$ is the first place, or first actant, of $Y]$.

Ivan obeščal Petru knigu 'Ivan promised Peter a book'; *Ivan obeščal (Petru) dostat' (emu) knigu* 'Ivan promised (Peter) to get (him) ⟨he would get (him)⟩ a book'; *Ivan obeščal, čto kniga budet u Petra zavtra že* 'Ivan promised that Peter would have the book (no later than) tomorrow'.

Syn:
  arch. bookish
    sulit' 'promise';
  colloq. *obeščat'sja*

$Syn_\cap$:
  kljast'sja 'vow';
  zaverjat' 'assure';
  zarekat'sja 'promise not
    to, renounce';
  objazyvat'sja 'pledge
    oneself'

Promise something
in the near future
['tomorrow']
without fulfilling
these promises:
Promise something
instead of doing it:

kormit' $[S_{acc} = Z]$
zavtrakami 'feed
somebody with
(false) hopes'

kormit' obeščanijami
'feed with hopes'

[$Syn_\cap$ stands for an inexact ('semantically intersecting') synonym]

$S_0 = S_2$:
  obeščanie 'a promise'

One cannot rely on
the fulfillment of
that which has been
promised:

*obeščannogo
(govorjat) tri goda
ždut* (proverb) lit.
'you have to wait 3
years for what you've
been promised' =
'words are wind'

Sing = Perf:
  colloq. *poobeščat'*
    'have promised'
$Magn_2^{intens}$:
  tverdo 'firmly'

$Magn_2^{quant} + AntiVer_2$:
zolotye gory//colloq.
naobeščat' $[S_{acc}]$,
naobeščat' s tri koroba
'promise the sun and
the stars, make a lot
of (empty) promises'
[X promises a lot of
Y, but the speaker
does not believe that the
probability of Y is
great]

(2) *X obeščaet Y Z-u* 'X promises Y to Z' = X causes Z to conclude that Y, which is connected with X by cause-and-effect relations, will occur.

$1 = X$	$2 = Y$	$3 = Z$	
S_{nom}	(1) S_{acc} (2) V_{inf} (3) $\check{c}to + $ SENT obligatory	S_{dat} rare	(1) X is not a living being, Z is a person, (2) If $Y = 2.2$, then $M_1(Y) = X$, (3) 2.1:S is a predicate.

Begstvo obeščalo nam spasenie 'Flight promised us salvation', *Den' obeščal byt' teplym* 'The day promised to be warm'.

Syn$_\cap$: *predveščat'* 'portend, foreshadow'; *predskazyvat'* 'foretell, predict'.

A_1 (promise a lot of something good): *mnogoobeščajuščij* 'promising, hopeful'.

2. *OBEŠČANIE* 'A promise'

OBEŠČANIE, *ja*, neut. $S_{0,2}$ *(obeščat' 1)* [the fact that something is being promised and also that which is promised]. Cf. GARANTIJA 'guarantee'; UGROZA 'threat'.

$1 = X$ whose	$2 = Y$ what	$3 = Z$ to whom	
(1) S_{gen} (2) A_{poss}	(1) S_{gen} (2) V_{inf} (3) $\check{c}to + $ SENT	S_{dat} rare	(1) X and Z are persons, (2) If $Y = 2.2$, then $M_1(Y), = X$, (3) $Y = 2.1$, if O. depends on a verb-LF, [*dal obeščanie prixoda* 'gave promise of arrival', etc.], (4) Impossible: 1.1,2 + 2.1.

Obeščanie Petra pridti 'Petr's promise to come'; *moe obeščanie, čto kniga budet zavtra* 'my promise that the book will come tomorrow'; *obeščanie vstreči* 'promise of a meeting'; but **ego obeščanie vstreči* 'his promise of a meeting' is impossible.

Syn$_\cap$:
  bookish *posul* '(lavish) promise'
Syn$_\cap$:
  kljatva 'vow'; *zaverenie* 'assurance'; *slovo* 'word';
  objazatel'stvo 'obligation'; *obet* 'vow'; *zarok* 'pledge'
V_0:
  obeščat' 1 'to promise'
Magn$_1$:
  toržestvennoe 'solemn'
Magn$_2$:
  tverdoe 'firm'

AntiVer_2:

pustoe 'empty'; slang *lipovoe* 'fake, phony'

$\text{AntiMagn} + \text{AntiVer}_2$:

legkomyslennoe 'flippant, frivolous'

$\text{Magn}_2^{\text{quant}} + \text{AntiVer}_2$:

širokoveščatel'nye 'wide, alluring' | *O.* in plural

Oper_1:

davat' $[S_{\text{dat}} - e]$ 'give'

$\text{Liqu}_1 \text{Oper}_1$:

brat' obratno ⟨*nazad*⟩ $[(svoe) - e]$ 'take back'

$\text{Perm}_3 \text{Liqu}_1 \text{Oper}_1$:

osvoboždat $[S_{\text{acc}} = X \text{ ot } -ja]$ 'release from'

Oper_3:

polučat $[ot \ S_{\text{gen}} - e]$ 'receive from'

$\text{Oper}_1(\text{Magnquant} + \text{AntiVer})$:

davat' kuču $[-j]$ 'give a bunch of, a lot of'

Func_2:

sostojat' $[v \ S_{\text{prep}}]$ 'consist in'

Real_1:

vypolnjat', deržat', sderživat' $[(svoe) - e]$ 'keep one's promise' $|D_2$ *(O.)* is
an action of X

not Real_1:

ne vypolnjat', ne deržat', ne sderživat' $[(svoe) - e]$

'not fulfill, keep one's promise' [not do what one promised],

narušat $[(svoe) - e]$ 'break one's promise' [do what one had promised not
to do]

| $D_2(O.)$ is an action of X

Fact_0:

sbyvat'sja 'come true, be realized' | $D_2(O.)$ is not an action of X

(3) Our aim of investigating, within the framework of our work on the
MTM, the relations between meaning and text, i.e. between signifiés and
signifiants of linguistic units, has made it possible to take a new approach
towards problems of word-derivation and treat it against the background
of the universal picture of all the relations possible between words with
respect to their meaning and form. Since both the signifiés ('*A*', '*B*'), and
the signifiants (A, B) of two lexemes can (1) coincide ($=$), (2) be contained
one within the other ($\supset$), (3) intersect ($\cap$) and (4) have no part in common,
we have 17 possible formal-semantic relations (Mel'čuk, 1968).

Both 'classical' facts, i.e., specifically, homonymy ($A = B$, '*A*' $\cap$ '*B*' $= \emptyset$),
absolute synonymy ($A \cap B = \emptyset$, '*A*' $=$ '*B*', 'normal' word-derivation ($A \supset B$,

'A'$\supset$'B') etc., and certain little studied phenomena such as 'contrary word-derivation': $A \supset B$, but 'A'$\subset$'B', are provided for in 'cells' of the deductively derivable system. Examples of contrary derivation:

(1) *radovat'sja* (be glad of) 'experience emotion X' – *radovat'* (make glad of) 'cause to experience emotion X' (and many other similar pairs);

(2) *geolog-ij-a* (geology) 'the science of the Earth...', – *geolog* (geologist) 'a specialist in the science of the Earth...' (and many other pairs);

(3) *A tverž-e B* (*A* is harder than *B*) 'the hardness of *A* exceeds the hardness of *B*' – *A tverd* (*A* is hard) 'the hardness of *A* exceeds the norm established for the objects of the class *A*'. (*N.B.*: *tverže ≠ bolee tverdyj*, i.e. in Russian there exists a difference between 'harder' and 'more hard'): *A bolee tverdyj, čem B*='*A* is hard, and *A* is harder than *B*'; but from *A tverže B* it does not follow that *A* is hard: *A* can be soft, but still harder than *B*.)

At the same time, such relations as *moskvič:moskvička=laborant: laborantka* can of course also be easily described, since *moskvič⊂moskvička*, but 'moskvič' ⊄ 'moskvička' ('moskvič'='a male resident of Moscow', 'moskvička'='a female resident of Moscow'), while *laborant⊂laborant-k-a* and 'laborant'⊂'laborantka' (*laborant*='a technical laboratory worker', *laborantka*='a woman, who is a technical laboratory worker'), etc., as is, in particular, English conversion (see below).

(4) Work on the MTM has led the author to think of a linguistic sign as being *three-dimensional* entity, or an ordered triple $A = \langle A, \text{'}A\text{'}, \sum_A \rangle$, where A is the signifiant, 'A' the signifié, and $\sum_A$ is all information about the combinatorial properties of the sign, which in their totality may be spoken of as *syntactics*, cf. above, page 50. (Information about what part of speech a lexeme is; the gender of nouns, lexical functions, etc. belong to syntactics.) If we consider syntactics as an individual (together with the signifié and signifiant) component of the linguistic sign, we can provide a natural enough formal descriptions of phenomena such as the English *the cook – to cook*, known as conversion. We might define conversion as a linguistic sign whose signifiant is an *operation on the syntactics* of other signs (cf. meaningful alternation: a sign whose signifiant is an operation on the signifiants of other signs).

Examples of conversion:

$K_1 = \langle V \Rightarrow N, \text{'he who...'}, \sum_{K_1} \rangle$ *(to cook – the cook; to bore – the bore)*;
$K_2 = \langle N \Rightarrow V, \text{'cause to act upon...'}, \sum_{K_2} \rangle$ *(the bomb – to bomb; the machine gun – to machine-gun).*

It seems possible to construct a calculus of all conceivable morphological means, or processes, in natural languages.

ACKNOWLEDGEMENTS

The first draft of this paper has been read by and discussed with S. J. Fitialov, A. J. Dikovskij, O. S. Kulagina, N. G. Mixajlova, L. S. Modina, and M. K. Valiev; for helpful comments on the final version I am indebted to Ju. D. Apresjan, L. N. Iordanskaja, N. V. Pertsov, V. J. Rozencvejg, and A. K. Žolkovskij. It is with great pleasure that I acknowledge here their valuable help and sympathetic understanding. Last, but not least, I would like to express my gratitude to Ferenc Kiefer for everything he has done in order to have this paper published in English.

Soviet Academy of Sciences, Moscow

BIBLIOGRAPHY

Apresyan, Ju. D., Mel'čuk, I. A., and Žolkovskij, A. K.: 1969, in F. Kiefer (ed.), 'Semantics and Lexicography: Towards a New Type of Unilingual Dictionary', *Studies in Syntax and Semantics*, Dordrecht, pp. 1–33. (Rev.: 1972, *Language* **48**, No. 3.)

Gladkij, A. V. and Mel'čuk, I. A.: 1969, *Tree Grammars*, International Conference on Computational Linguistics, Stockholm. Preprint No. 1.

Gladkij, A. V. and Mel'čuk, I. A.: 1971, in 'Informacionnye voprosy semiotiki, lingvistiki i avtomaticeskogo perevoda', *Grammatiki derev'ev, I. Opyt formalizacii preobrazovanii sintaksičeskix struktur estestvennogo jazyka*, M., pp. 16–41.

Es'kova, N. A., Mel'čuk, I. A., and Sannikov, V. Z.: 1971, *Formal'naja model' russkoj morfologij. I. Formoobrazovanie suščestvitel'nyx i prilagatel'nyx* (Russian Language Institute, AN S.S.S.R.), M.

Mel'čuk, I. A.: 1967a, *Ordre des mots en synthèse automatique des textes russes*, TA informations, No. 2, pp. 65–84.

Mel'čuk, I. A.: 1967b, *Model' sprjaženija v ispanskom jazyke. Mašinnyj perevod i prikladnaja lingvistika* **10**, 21–53;
also in: *Soviet Papers in Formal Linguistics* (V. Y. Rosencveig, ed.), Vol. I., Atheneum, Frankfurt, 1973.

Mel'čuk, I. A.: 1967c, in 'To Honor Roman Jakobson...', *K voprosu o 'vnešnix različitel'nyx élementax*: semantičeskie parametry i opisanie leksičeskoj sočetaemosti, pp. 1340–1361.

Mel'čuk, I. A.: 1967d, in 'Problemy strukturnoj lingvistiki', *Model' sklonenija vengerskix suščestvitel'nyx*, M., pp. 344–373.

Mel'čuk, I. A.: 1968, *Stroenie jazykovyx znakov i vozmožnye formal'no-smyslovye otnošenija meždu nimi.* – Izvestija AN S.S.S.R, *Literature and Language Series* **27**, 426–438.

Mel'čuk, I. A.: 1970, 'Towards a Functioning Model of Language', in *Progress in Linguistics*, The Hague-Paris, pp. 198–207.

Mel'čuk, I. A. and Žolkovskij, A. K.: 1970, 'Towards a Functioning 'Meaning–Text' Model of Language', *Linguistics*, No. 57, pp. 10–47.

Žolkovskij, A. K. and Mel'čuk, I. A.: 1967, 'O semantičeskom sinteze', *Problemy Kibernetiki* **19**, 177–238.

Žolkovskij, A. K. and Mel'čuk, I. A.: 1970, *Sur la synthèse sémantique*, TA Informations, 1–85 [translation of the preceding article].

V. S. KHRAKOVSKY

PASSIVE CONSTRUCTIONS

(Definition, Calculus, Typology, Meaning)

1. PRELIMINARY REMARKS

The point of departure for this paper is the following statement: all verbs which designate a situation[1] theoretically have, first, semantic actants (participants), and secondly, syntactic actants.[2]

The inventory of participants includes, for example, such universal semantic notions as agent, object, addressee, instrument, starting point, end point, etc. Actants include such universal syntactic notions of the parts of the sentence as the subject and complements.[3]

The distinction between semantic and syntactic notions is not a new one for linguists. Traditional linguistics, in particular Russian linguistics, has in descriptions of the category of voice consistently differentiated between the semantic notions of the 'logical' or 'real' subject and object of an action on the one hand, and the grammatical notions of subject and object, on the other.

The differentiation and contrast of semantic and syntactic notions underlies the modern conception of deep and surface structures – a conception which we share and which has guided us in this paper. In accordance with

---

[1] "Situation is everything that happens, takes place; the names of situations in natural languages can be verbs, prepositions (*do* 'until, before' (precede), *iz-za* 'due to, because of' (cause)), conjunctions (*esli* 'if' (conditionally)), adjectives, many nouns (Fire!, and also love, beginning, honesty, etc.), combinations of words (make a decision, suffer a loss) and whole sentences (It is raining)... Situation is understood here not simply as a fragment of physical reality distinguished on the basis of some sort of extralingual principles, but as a representation of a 'piece' of reality 'carved out' by a given lexical item of a given language" (I. A. Mel'čuk and A. A. Xolodovič, 'K teorii grammatičeskogo zaloga', in *Narody Azii i Afriki*, 1970, No. 4, pp. 111–12).

[2] The term actant is from L. Tesnière. See his *Eléments de syntaxe structurale*, Paris, 1959. In his conception, however, there is no clear-cut distinction between semantic and syntactic actants. A. A. Xolodovič has proposed the use of the term participant instead of the term semantic actant. The use of the term participant to designate semantic notions and the term actant to designate syntactic notions makes it possible to dispense with double-word terms, which is very convenient for practical purposes.

[3] To our knowledge there is no complete theory of participants and actants at the present time. This fact, however, is not essential for the purposes of our investigation. All that is important for us is to differentiate strictly between these two types of notions and to use semantic notions in the description of the content plane of the sentence and syntactic notions in descriptions of the expression plane.

F. Kiefer (ed.), Trends in Soviet Theoretical Linguistics, 59–75. All Rights Reserved.
Copyright © 1973 by D. Reidel Publishing Company, Dordrecht-Holland.

this conception, various surface 'real' syntactic-morphological structures correspond to a single deep semantic structure.[4] Deep semantic structures are in essence situations and their participants, which are written in a predicate-argument form borrowed from symbolic logic. The situation is the predicate, and the participants are the arguments of the predicate. Surface structures are thereby all the actual sentences and combinations of words which describe a single situation.

The opposition of primary and derived syntactic surface structures is also important for us. The primary structure, unlike the derived ones, is isomorphic to the described situation. In the primary structure "syntactic categories (parts of the sentence) correspond to the real functions of substances and signs in a process. The relations between the parts of a sentence 'iconically' reflects the real relations between the elements of a process."[5] In this paper we shall be interested in only one property of the primary surface structure. If the agent is included among the participants, then the concrete, lexically expressed agent occupies the position of the first actant – the subject – in the primary surface structure. In other words, there is a correspondence agent-subject in the primary surface structure which can be said to be the primary diathesis.[6]

2. DEFINITION

We can now define the structures which will be discussed in this paper. What will be described here are derived surface structures in which the concrete lexically expressed agent does not occupy the position of the subject. In other words, the correspondence agent-subject is disturbed in these structures. We shall call such derived surface structures passive constructions.[7] As an example of a passive construction we can take the sentence (1) The school (Sb) is (being) built (Pr) by the workers (C). The corresponding primary active construction is the sentence (0) The workers (Sb) (are)

---

[4] See, for example, D. Langendoen, 'The Accessibility of Deep (Semantic) Structures', *Working Papers in Linguistics*, The Ohio State University, No. 1, 1967; C. J. Fillmore, 'The Case for Case', in *Universals in Linguistic Theory*, New York, 1968; H. E. Brekle, 'Generative Satzsemantik und transformationelle Syntax im System der englischen Nominalkomposition', Internationale Bibliothek für allgemeine Linguistik, Bd. 4, München, 1970.
[5] V. G. Gak, 'K probleme sintaksičeskoj semantiki' in the collection *Invariantnye sintaksičeskie značenija i struktura, predloženija*, M., 1969, pp. 79–80; cf.: R. Jakobson, 'The Quest for the Essence of Language', *Diogenes*, No. 51, 1965.
[6] On the term diathesis see A. A. Xolodović, 'Zalog' in the collection *Kategorija zaloga*, L., 1970.
[7] Cf.: V. S. Xrakovskij, 'Konstrukcii passivnogo zaloga' in the collection *Kategorija zaloga*, L., 1970.

build(ing) (Pr) the school (C).[8] From what has been said it follows that the problem to be solved in this paper belongs to the class of problems text → text.

It should obviously be emphasized that there are also derived syntactic structures in which the correspondence agent-subject is disturbed but which can nevertheless be treated as passive constructions. Here we mean derived structures in which the withdrawal of the agent from subject position is accompanied by the occupation of this position by a participant not designated in the primary structure. Consequently, of the structures of the sentences (1) The house (Sb) is built (Pr) by the neighbor (C) and (2) Circumstances (Sb) force (Pr) the neighbor (C_2) to build (Pr) a house (C_1), which are constructed from the primary sentence (0) The neighbor (Sb) builds, is building (Pr) a house (C_1), we are interested only in the structure of sentence (1). The same participants (agent, object) are designated in this structure as in the primary structure of sentence (0). Consequently, it has a right to be called a passive construction. On the other hand, we shall not consider the structure of sentence (2), because in it the subject position is occupied by a causative agent, i.e., by a participant which is not given in the primary surface structure.[9]

There are also derived structures which, even though they denote the same situation as the primary structure, still cannot be considered to be passive. Here we mean, for example, imperative constructions, examples of which can be seen in the sentences (1) Build (Pr) the school (C)!, (2) Sleep (Pr)! In these constructions the withdrawal of the agent from subject position results in the factual liquidation of this position. In other words, from our point of view only the passive constructions are those in which removing the agent from subject position does not result in the liquidation of this position, but results instead either in that the position is occupied by some other participant or in that it remains unoccupied.

We must also turn our attention to one other fact. We must distinguish between the functional absence of a agent in subject position, which determines the transition from the primary structure to derived passive structures, and the absence on the formal level in the primary structure of an independent unit that can be said to occupy the position of the subject. Let us consider, for example, the following sentences: (1) *Kolje posovetovali vzjat' otpusk* 'Kolja was advised to take a vacation', (2) *Posovetoval Kolje*

---

[8] We shall use the following notation for semantic and syntactic notions: st – situation, Ag – agent, Ob – object, Adr – addressee; Pr – predicate, Sb – subject, C – complement. The numerical indices with the complements serve to distinguish them. Only agentive complements have no index.

[9] Derived structures of type (2), which denote a specific situation different from the situation denoted by structures of types (0) and (1), are usually called causatives. The monograph, *Tipologija kauzativnyx konstrukcij. Morfologičeskij kauzativ*, L., 1969, is devoted to the study of these structures.

vzjat' otpusk, (a on otkazalsja) 'Advised Kolja to take a vacation (but he refused)'. The structure of sentence (1) can be treated as a derived passive construction based on the primary structure of sentence (0) *Ja posovetoval Kolje vzjat' otpusk* 'I advised Kolja to take a vacation'. As for sentence (2), its structure must be regarded as a contextually determined variant of the primary structure of sentence (0) in which there is no formal unit in the position of the subject. It should be noted that the absence of this formal unit in subject position in the primary structure is in certain instances the norm in a number of languages. In such cases there are no grounds for speaking of a transition from the primary to a derived structure. This is precisely the case in, for example, modern literary Arabic, in which there is usually no formal unit in subject position corresponding to the personal pronoun that occupies this position in Russian, e.g., (1) *'arsaltu (Pr) hāḏā l-kitāba (C₁) bi l-'amsi* 'I sent this book yesterday', (2) *'argamūhu (Pr, C) 'alā l-ḫurūǧi (Pr) min al-ǧurfati* 'They forced him to leave the room'.

3. CALCULUS

The agent in passive constructions cannot by definition occupy the subject position. In this case the agent can either occupy the position of another part of the sentence and be thereby designated lexically, or it may not be designated in the structure by a special part of the sentence. Since the agent does not occupy the position of the subject, this position can be filled by some other participant, or it can remain empty.[10] On the basis of these facts we can reach the conclusion that the logically possible number of derived passive constructions that can be formed from each primary structure is determined by the formula $2(n+1)$, where n is the number of possibilities for filling the position of the subject in passive constructions with participants, 1 is the possibility where this position remains unoccupied, and the multiplication by 2 designates two possibilities for the subject, which in passive structures either stands in the position of a special complement, or does not occupy this position and is thereby not designated by a separate part of the sentence dependent on the predicate.

We shall illustrate this formula with examples of uniactant, biactant and triactant primary syntactic constructions. Uniactant constructions are formally written as (0) Sb (Ag)+Pr (st). In accordance with the formula, two passive constructions can be obtained from the uniactant construction: (1) Pr (st), (2) Pr (st)+C (Ag). For example, in certain cases in Russian both

---

[10] If the position of the subject is not filled by a participant, it can either be free or occupied by a form word used to mark the position of the subject in the construction of the sentence.

passive constructions can be obtained: (0) *Ja (Sb) ezdil (Pr)* 'I drove (went)', (1) *Ezženo (Pr)* 'Driven (gone)', (2) *Mnoju (C) ezženo (Pr)* 'Driven (gone) by me'.

Biactant primary constructions, in which the object occupies the position of a complement, are written formally as (0) $Sb(Ag)+Pr(st)+C_1(Ob)$. On the basis of the formula we can obtain four passive constructions: (1) $Pr(st)+ +C_1(Ob)$, (2) $Pr(st)+C_1(Ob)+C(Ag)$, (3) $Sb(Ob)+Pr(st)$, (4) $Sb(Ob)+ +Pr(st)+C(Ag)$. In Russian, all four passive constructions can be obtained in certain cases: (0) *Molnija (Sb) razbila (Pr) stenu (C_1)* 'Lightning destroyed the wall', (1) *Stenu (C_1) razbilo (Pr)* 'The wall was destroyed', (2) *Stenu (C_1) razbilo (Pr) molniej (C)* 'The wall was destroyed by lightning', (3) *Stena (Sb) razbita (Pr)* 'The wall is, has been, destroyed', (4) *Stena (Sb) razbita (Pr) molniej (C)* 'The wall is, has been, destroyed by lightning'.

Triactant primary constructions, in which the object occupies the position of the first complement and the addressee occupies the position of the second, are written formally as (0) $Sb(Ag)+Pr(st)+C_1(Ob)+C_2(Adr)$. In accordance with the formula we can obtain six passive constructions from the triactant construction: (1) $Pr(st)+C_1(Ob)+C_2(Adr)$, (2) $Pr(st)+C_1(Ob)+ +C_2(Adr)+C(Ag)$, (3) $Sb(Ob)+Pr(st)+C_2(Adr)$, (4) $Sb(Ob)+Pr(st)+ +C_2(Adr)+C(Ag)$, (5) $Sb(Adr)+Pr(st)+C_1(Ob)$, (6) $Sb(Adr)+Pr(st)+ +C_1(Ob)+C(Ag)$. In one instance in Russian we can obtain the first, third and fourth passive constructions, and in another case we can get the first and second: (0) *Otec (Sb) podaril (Pr) bratu (C_2) knigu (C_1)* 'Father gave brother a book', (1) *Bratu (C_2) podarili (Pr) knigu (C_1)* 'Brother was given a book', (3) *Kniga (Sb) byla podarena (Pr) bratu (C_2)* 'The book was given to brother', (4) *Kniga (Sb) byla podarena (Pr) bratu (C_2) otcom (C)* 'The book was given to brother by father', (0) *Prepodavatel' (Sb) ukazal (Pr) Maše (C_2) na ošibku (C_1)* 'The teacher showed Maša her mistake', (1) *Maše (C_2) ukazano (Pr) na ošibku (C_1)* 'Maša was shown her mistake', (2) *Maše (C_2) ukazano (Pr) na ošibku (C_1) prepodavatelem (C)* 'Maša was shown her mistake by the teacher'. In English the third, fourth, fifth and sixth passive constructions can be obtained from the triactant construction: (0) He (Sb) gave (Pr) me (C_2) a book (C_1), (3) A book (Sb) was given (Pr) to me (C_2), (4) A book (Sb) was given (Pr) by him (C) to me (C_2), (5) I (Sb) was given (Pr) a book (C_1), (6) I (Sb) was given (Pr) a book (C_1) by him (C).

We must add the following notes to the proposed formula for calculating passive constructions.

(1) Passive constructions with an agentival complement are only found where there are passive constructions without an agentival complement. On the other hand, passive constructions with an agentival complement are not at all obligatory for passive constructions without an agentival complement.

This phenomenon, which is apparently universal, allows us to presume that passive constructions with an agentival complement are genetically secondary and have been generated from passive constructions without an agentival complement.

(2) The occurrence of all the logical possibilities for constructing passive constructions is found quite rarely. In accordance with the formula, from the active biactant construction which is written formally as (0) $Sb(Ag) + Pr(st) + C_1(Ob)$ we can obtain four passive constructions, written formally as (1) $Pr(st) + C_1(Ob)$, (2) $Pr(st) + C_1(Ob) + C(Ag)$, (3) $Sb(Ob) + Pr(st)$, (4) $Sb(Ob) + Pr(st) + C(Ag)$. All four passive sentences can be constructed in Russian from, for example, the primary sentence (0) *Molnija (Sb) razbila (Pr) stenu (C₁)* 'Lightning destroyed the wall': (1) *Stenu (C₁) razbilo (Pr)* 'The wall was destroyed', (2) *Stenu (C₁) razbilo (Pr) molniej (C)* 'The wall was destroyed by lightning, (3) *Stena (Sb) byla razbita (Pr)* 'The wall was destroyed', (4) *Stena (Sb) byla razbita (Pr) molniej (C)* 'The wall was destroyed by lightning'. The number of realizable logical possibilities decreases if instead of the word *molnija* (lightning) we put the word *rabočij* (worker) in subject position in the primary sentence. Cf.: (1) *Stenu (C₁) razbili (Pr)* 'The wall was destroyed', (3) *Stena (Sb) byla razbita (Pr)* 'The wall was destroyed', (4) *Stena (Sb) byla razbita (Pr) rabočim (C)* 'The wall was destroyed by the worker'. The second logical possibility is not found in this particular case.

(3) A single logical possibility can be realized by means of formally different constructions which represent one syntactic invariant. Thus, the sentences (1) *Stenu (C₁) razbilo (Pr)* and (2) *Stenu (C₁) razbili (Pr)* are formal variants of the syntactic invariant: $Pr(st) + C_1(Ob)$. These variants are in a relation of complementary distribution. The first variant is used when there is a non-personal agent in subject position, the second when there is a personal agent in this position in the active construction. In addition, there are cases where formally different constructions function as equals, freely interchangeable realizations of a single syntactic invariant. For example, if the active construction $Sb(Ag) + Pr(st) + C_1(Ob)$ is represented by the sentence (0) *Komandir (Sb) prikazal (Pr) soldatam (C₁) streljat' (Pr)* 'The commander ordered the soldiers to shoot', the passive construction $Pr(st) + C_1(Ob)$ can be realized as two formally distinct, but at the same time equal variants: (1) *Soldatam (C₁) prikazali (Pr) streljat' (Pr)* 'The soldiers were ordered to shoot', (2) *Soldatam (C₁) bylo prikazano (Pr) streljat' (Pr)* 'The soldiers were ordered to shoot'.

Derived passive constructions differ from the primary active construction in a number of respects.

(1) Passive constructions differ from the active construction in the number

and kind of sentence parts in them. To illustrate, let us contrast the biactant active construction (0) Sb(Ag)+Pr(st)+C_1(Ob) – *Pulja (Sb) ubila (Pr) bojca (C_1)* 'The bullet killed the soldier' – with its passive variants: (1) Pr(st)+C_1(Ob) – *Bojca (C_1) ubilo (Pr)* 'The soldier was killed' – (2) Pr(st)+ +C_1+C(Ag) – *Bojca (C_1) ubilo (Pr) pulej (C)* 'The soldier was killed by a bullet' – (3) Sb(Ob)+Pr(st) – *Boec (Sb) byl ubit (Pr)* 'The soldier was killed' – (4) Sb(Ob)+Pr(st)+C(Ag) – *Boec (Sb) ubit (Pr) pulej (C)* 'The soldier was killed by a bullet'. Derivative (1) lacks the subject (*pulja*) found in construction (0). Derivative (2) does not differ from construction (0) with respect to the number of sentence parts in it, but instead of the Sb(Ag) (*pulja*) of construction (0), in the derivative we find C(Ag) (*pulej* 'by the bullet'), which is not structurally obligatory. In derivative (3) the complement found in construction (0) is lacking, and the object stands in subject position (*boec*). Derivative (4) does not differ as to number of sentence parts from construction (0), but the subject and the complement in the construction and in the derivative designated different participants: Sb(Ag) (*pulja* 'bullet') and C(Ob) (*bojca* 'soldier') in the construction and Sb(Ob) (*boec*) and C(Ag) (*pulej* 'by a bullet') in the derivative. The complement in the derivative here is not structurally obligatory.

(2) In passive constructions there are formal operators of constructional derivation. Formal derivational operators are often introduced into verbal predicates. The function of these operators is fulfilled by either (a) a morphological operation, or (b) an additive morpheme, or (c) a form word. Morphological operations and additive morphemes can be called morphological operators, and form words can be said to be analytical operators. Some examples: in literary Arabic the morphological operation whereby the stem-formative verbal affix is changed serves as the formal operator of the passive transformation (*ḳ-a-t-a-l/a* 'he killed' *ḳ-u-t-i-l/a* 'he has been/was killed' – as a result of the morphological operation the transfix *a-a* is replaced by the transfix *u-i*). In a number of Turkish languages an L-suffix added to the stem serves as a passive transformation operator (*jar-* 'broke' → *jar-yl* 'was broken'). In Khmer the passive transformation operator is the form word *tro: w* (*slap* 'he killed' → *tro: w slap* 'he has been/was killed'). A restriction of the paradigm of verbal forms used in the active construction to 3 p. sg. or 3 p. pl. forms can also function as a formal passive transformation operator. The position of the subject in such a case is either unoccupied or filled by a form word which indicates that the lexically designated agent has been removed from this position. Some illustrations: in Russian, the 3 p. pl. form of the verb functions as a formal operator if the subject position in the active construction was filled by a personal subject, while the 3 p.sg. form (neuter in the past tense) has this role if the position of the subject was occupied by a non-

personal agent. (Cf.: *Vrag (Sb) ranil (Pr) soldata (C₁)* 'The enemy wounded the soldier' → *Soldata (C₁) ranili (Pr)* 'The soldier was wounded', *Pulja (Sb) ranila (Pr) soldata (C₁)* 'The bullet wounded the soldier' → *Soldata (C₁) ranilo (Pr)* 'The soldier was wounded'). In both cases the position of the subject has remained empty. This is not the case in German, where the form word *man* fills the position of the subject. Cf.: Der Arbeiter (Sb) baut (Pr) ein Haus (C₁) → Man (Sb) baut (Pr) ein Haus (C₁).

(3) In active constructions the agent is designated on the concrete lexical level by means of a noun in subject position. In the case of passive constructions, the agent is regularly designated on the abstract grammatical level and only optionally on the concrete lexical level. Let us clarify this idea. From our point of view, passive derivations are isomorphic to causative derivations. As has already been demonstrated in a number of publications,[11] derived causative verbs, unlike underlying non-causative verbs, denote not only concrete situations, but also abstract causation, which is understood as anything that can be described with the words "to act in such a way that some agent will be in some state". For example, the Chuvash causative *vyr-tar* differs from the underlying verb *vyr* in that besides the concrete state 'reap' (grain), it also designates an abstract causation, the formal marker of which is the operator suffix *-tar*. Similarly, the Chuvash passive *vyr-an* 'be reaped' differs from the same underlying verb *vyr* in that besides the concrete situation, it also denotes an abstract agent, whose formal marker is the operator suffix *-an*. Consequently, in passive constructions without an agentival complement the agent is designated on the abstract grammatical level, while in constructions with an agentival complement the agent is designated twice: once on the abstract grammatical level and once on the concrete lexical level in the agentival complement.

Our comparison of passive constructions with their active construction allows us to emphasize the following two points: (1) To be able to interpret passive constructions, one is forced to distinguish between the agent as designated on the concrete lexical and the abstract grammatical levels. (2) In certain passive constructions we find a sentence part called the agentival complement which is absent from the active construction. Consequently, we have grounds for making the following two assertions: (1) We must distinguish between the primary-lexical and secondary-grammatical designations of the participants. The primary-lexical designations are used in both the primary construction and the derived constructions. The secondary-grammatical designations are used only in the derived constructions.

---

[11] See the monograph *Tipologija kauzativnyx konstrukcij. Morfologičeskij kauzativ*, L., 1969; see also our article 'Derivacionnye otnošenija v sintaksise' in the collection *Invariantnye sintaksičeskie značenija i struktura predloženija*, M., 1969.

(4) We must also distinguish between primary and secondary syntactic notions in the inventory of syntactic notions of parts of the sentence. Primary sentence parts can appear in both the primary construction and in the derived constructions, whereas secondary parts of the sentence (e.g., agentival complements, causative complements) can only appear in derived constructions.[12]

4. TYPOLOGY

On the expression plane there is a limited number of formal means for constructing passive constructions. This fact makes it possible to suggest a fairly economic typological classification of these constructions.

Two types of passive constructions can be distinguished on the sentence part level: (a) constructions in which the position of the subject is empty, e.g., (1) *Knigu (C₁) otpravili (Pr)* 'The book was sent', (2) *Bojca (C) ranilo (Pr) oskolkom (C)* 'The soldier was wounded by a shell-fragment', (b) constructions in which the position of the subject is filled, e.g., (1) *Kniga (Sb) byla otpravlena (Pr)* 'The book was sent', (2) *Boec (Sb) byl ranen (Pr) oskolkom (C)* 'The soldier was wounded by a shell-fragment'.

In derived structures of type (a) the forms of all the sentence parts except the predicate does not change in relation to the primary construction. As for the predicate, it is either one of the forms used in the primary construction or a form not used in the primary construction. The position of the subject is either empty or filled by a form word which marks the removal of the concrete agent from subject position and thereby indicates that this position cannot be filled by any other lexically expressed participant.

Since in constructions of type (a) there are two possibilities for the predicate and two possibilities for the position of the subject, there are logically four variants of the form of constructions of this type: (a1) the position of the subject is empty, the predicate is a form used in the primary construction, e.g., (1) (Polish) *Ludzie (Sb) posłali (Pr) Stefana (C₁) na front* 'People sent Stefan to the front' → *Stefana (C₁) posłali (Pr) na front* 'Stefan was sent to the front', (2) *Burja (Sb) povalila (Pr) derevo (C₁)* 'The storm knocked over the tree' → *Burej (C) povalilo (Pr) derevo (C₁)* 'The tree was knocked over by the storm', (2a) the position of the subject is empty, the predicate is a form not found in the primary construction, e.g., (1) (Polish) *Ludzie (Sb) posłali (Pr) Stefana (C₁) na front* 'People sent Stefan to the front' → *Stefana (C₁) posłano (Pr) na front* 'Stefan was sent to the front', (2) (Lithuanian) *Čia*

---

[12] See the comparison of deep and surface structures in V. G. Gak's paper 'K probleme sintaksičeskoj semantiki' in the collection *Invariantnye sintaksičeskie značenija i struktura predloženija*, M., 1969.

lankutojai (Sb) klausosi (Pr) muzikos (C_1) 'Here visitors listen to music' →
→ *Čia lankutoju (C) klausomasi (Pr) muzikos (C_1)* 'Here music is listened to
by visitors', (a3) the position of the subject is filled by a form word, and the
predicate is a form which is used in the primary construction, e.g., (1) *Il (Sb)
vend (Pr) la maison (C_1)* → *On (Sb) vend (Pr) la maison (C_1)*. We know of
no examples of a passive construction of type (a3) with an agentival complement. (a4) the position of the subject is filled by a form word, and the predicate
is a form not used in the primary construction, e.g., (1) *Er (Sb) tanzt (Pr)* →
→ *Es (Sb) wird getanzt (Pr)*. No examples of a passive construction of
type (a4) with an agentival complement are known to us.

Now let us consider derivative constructions of type (b). It is fully obvious
that these derivative constructions cannot be obtained from a uniactant primary construction (there are no participants in uniactant primary constructions which could fill the position of the subject), and consequently, we can
speak of constructing derivative structures of type (b) only in relation to
primary structures having two or more actants.

In derived constructions of type (b) we have the same two possibilities
for the form of the predicate. The subject in these constructions either
retains the same form as in the primary construction or it changes it. Thus,
derived constructions of this kind have four possible morphological
forms: (b1) the subject has the same form as in the primary construction,
the predicate is represented by a form used in the primary construction, e.g.,
(1) (Old Chinese) *jên² (Sb) hsien¹ fa² (Pr) chih² mu⁴ (C_1)* 'A man first cuts
a straight tree' → *chih² mu⁴ (Sb) hsien¹ fa² (Pr)* 'A straight tree is cut first',
(2) (Old Chinese) *jên² (Sb) sha¹ (Pr) hu³ (C_1)* 'The man kills the tiger' → *hu³
(Sb) sha¹ (Pr) yü¹ jên² (C)* 'The tiger is killed by the man', (b2) the subject
has the same form as in the primary construction, the predicate is a form
not used in the primary construction, e.g., (1) *Sosed (Sb) postroil (Pr) banju
(C_1)* 'The neighbor has built a sauna' → *Banja (Sb) byla postroena (Pr)*
'The sauna was built', (2) *Sosed (Sb) postroil (Pr) banju (C_1)* 'The neighbor
has built a sauna' → *Banja (Sb) byla postroena (Pr) sosedom (C)* 'The sauna
was built by the neighbor', (b3) the subject has a different form than in the
primary construction, the predicate is a form used in the primary construction,
e.g., (1) (Lakh) *Jusuplul (Sb) kIva darvag (C_1) k'uvk'unu mašan lovssun
bur (Pr)* 'Jusup bought cheaply two bags' → *KIva darvag (Sb) k'uvk'unu
mašan lovssun bur (Pr)* 'Two bags (Sb) have been bought (Pr) cheaply'.
We know of no examples of a passive construction of type (b3) with an
agentival complement. (b4) the subject has a different form than in the primary
construction, and the predicate is a form not found in the primary construction, e.g., (1) (Tush) *stakov (Sb) ujstx (C_1) larķĭ (Pr)* 'The man clipped the
sheep → *ujstx (Sb) daḥ larķbalĭ (Pr)* 'The sheep has been clipped'. We know

of no examples of a passive construction of type (b4) with an agentival complement.

It will be useful to compare the above typological classification of constructions which we have defined as passive with the definitions given these constructions by traditional linguistics. Constructions of type (a1)(1), (a3) (1) are usually treated as indefinite-personal. In the opinion of some linguists, the action in them is performed by an indeterminate number of persons, which is their distinguishing characteristic and differentiates them from primary two-member personal sentences, where a definite number of persons is always expressed.[13] This assertion we find unsubstantiated. We think it more correct to consider that verbal form in such sentences does not express the number of persons and the opposition singular/plural, which is relevant for the verbal forms in primary personal constructions, is neutralized in these types of derived constructions. A formal argument in favor of this interpretation is the fact that in certain languages there are synonymous indefinite-personal sentences which differ from each other in verb forms of different numbers. This is the case, for example, in Polish, where the sentences (1) *Stefana (C$_1$) posłali (Pr) na front*, (2) *Stefana (C$_1$) się posłało (Pr) na front* 'Stefan was sent to the front' are synonymous, although the verbal predicate in the first sentence is in the 3 p.pl., whereas in the second it is in the 3 p.sg. with the pronominal form *się*.[14]

Constructions of type (a1)(2) are usually defined as impersonal on the grounds that the active agent (expressed or not expressed lexically) in them is not a person. The action which this agent performs is spontaneous and unpremeditated.

As for constructions of type (a2), their status has caused a lively discussion. The polemical point is the fact that in constructions of this type the predicate is a passive verbal form which governs the noun in the accusative which stands in direct complement position. The combination of a passive form of the verb in predicate position and a noun in direct complement position does not fit into the traditional theory of voice, where "passive forms... can be defined as verbal forms with which a direct complement cannot be used, i.e., as forms which explicitly express the intransitivity of the verb".[15]

The status of constructions of type (a4) are also being discussed. These constructions are very common in German, and a considerable number of works have dealt with them. Although the predicate position in these con-

[13] See S. I. Sjatkovskij, 'Neopredelenno-ličnye predloženija v sovremennyx slavjanskix jazykax' in the collection *Slavjanskaja filologija*, No. 5, M., 1963.
[14] See in this connection I. P. Raspopov, *Stroenie prostogo predloženija v sovremennom russkom jazyke*, M., 1970.
[15] G. G. Sil'nickij, 'Zalog i valentnost'' in the collection *Kategorija zaloga*, L., 1970, pp. 57–8.

structions is filled by a passive form of the verb, they are said to have lost their passive meaning, so that in this case a formally passive form (the impersonal passive) is actually active and has approximately the same meaning as the indefinite-personal construction with *man*.[16]

Constructions of types (b1) and (b3) are usually not treated by traditional linguistics in discussions of voice and the semantic classification of sentences. The reasons for this fact are quite obvious. The predicate position in these constructions is filled by the same verb form as in the primary construction, but for the traditional theory of voice the question of two different voice constructions can only arise in a case where there is an opposition of two morphologically different verb forms.

Constructions of type (b2) are the only ones which traditional linguistics recognizes as passive. As for constructions of type (b4), they are found only in certain languages having an ergative structure, where they have been described by some research papers as constructions with a medial verb.[17]

The above comparison shows that the range of constructions which we have defined as passive is significantly broader than that of traditional linguistics. The reason for this lies in the fact that the traditional headings and our classification of constructions have been conducted on different bases. The basis of our classification is semantic-syntactic. All constructions in which a concrete lexically designated agent does not stand in subject position are passive. No other features are taken into account in our definition of passive constructions.

The traditional definition of passive constructions is based on semantic-syntactic and morphological features. Simplifying somewhat the real state of things, we can say that passive constructions in traditional linguistics are those constructions in which (1) the object is in subject position and (2) a special 'passive' form of the verb occupies the position of the predicate.

As for the definition of indefinite-personal and impersonal constructions, it is purely semantic, because it proceeds from the specific semantic features of the agent. In indefinite-personal sentences the agent is an indefinite person, whereas in definite personal sentences it is a definite person. In impersonal sentences the agent is a non-person, whereas in personal sentences it is a person.

The feature upon which our definition is based proved to be common to all these constructions, regarded as being so different in traditional linguistics. This feature is very essential. The semantic-syntactic proximity, and in a

---

[16] See K. V. Školina 'Predloženija s *man* i bezličnye predloženija so skazuemym, vyražennym 'odnočlennym passivom' v nemeckom jazyke' in the collection *Voprosy germanskoj filologii*, issue II, LGU, 1969.
[17] See, for example, Ju. D. Dešeriev, *Bacbijskij jazyk*, M., 1953.

number of cases the equivalence of these constructions noted by various linguists, is based on it. Relatively recently T.B. Alisova emphasized this fact:

... transitive indefinite-personal and impersonal constructions in one language... often correspond to personal passive structures in another. Passive and impersonal constructions in a language are often positional variants for the expression of a single semantic-communicative content, which is defined as "the removal of the actor or source of action from the central position of the subject".[18]

5. MEANING

Now let us consider the problem of the nature of the semantic information transmitted by derived passive constructions. We shall be interested in two aspects of this problem: (1) whether the derived passive constructions and the primary active construction are synonymous, (2) whether the derived passive constructions are synonymous with each other. In solving this problem, we shall use the notion of levels of synonymy and shall proceed from the assumption that "synonymy is always relative"[19] and that absolute synonyms in language, if and when they are found among syntactic constructions, are to be considered exceptional.[20]

We shall assume that the absolute synonymy of syntactic constructions, and thereby their contextual interchangeability, are present if these constructions are synonymous: (1) on the level of lexicographic interpretation of the verb, which occupies the predicate position, (2) on the lexeme level, (3) on the grammatical meaning level, (4) on the level of the logical accentuation (topicalization).[21] The absence of synonymy on any one of these levels changes the constructions under comparison into relative synonyms.

In this approach it can be stated that the active and all passive constructions are synonymous on the level of the lexicographic interpretation of the verbal word, whose forms occupy the predicate position in these constructions.[22]

---

[18] T. B. Alisova, 'Semantiko-kommunikativnyj substrat bezličnyx predloženij' in the collection *Invariantnye sintaksičeskie značenija i struktura predloženija*, M., 1969, p. 34.
[19] E. V. Padučeva, *Meždunarodnaja konferencija po semiotike v Pol'še*, NTI, series 2, 1967, No. 2, p. 36.
[20] In the opinion of J. Jelinek, there are no absolute synonyms in language, "since transformations rather have to do with regular structure changes which are accompanied by certain predicable changes in meaning". See J. Jelinek, 'Jazykovoj aspekt transformacionnyx pravil' in *Sbornik perevodov po voprosam informacionnoj teorii i praktiki*, M., 1970, No. 16, pp. 55–56.
[21] The levels of synonymy are not enumerated in random order. The synonymy on each level presupposes synonymy on all preceding ones.
[22] I. A. Mel'čuk has noted this fact. In his words: "... an active verb and its corresponding passive verb do not, trictly speaking, differ in meaning – they have the same signifie:

The problem is somewhat more complex on the lexeme level. Here the primary active structure and the passive construction with an agentival complement (a 'long passive') are synonymous, since they have the same set of lexemes. H. Schuchardt formulated approximately the same point of view on the relationship between these constructions, and its correctness has been emphasized by J. Kuryłowicz, I. A. Mel'čuk, T. B. Alisova, and others. In J. Kuryłowicz's words:

full (three-member) passive constructions – 'the soldier was killed by the enemy', 'the fallow is being plowed by the peasant', etc. – ... do not differ at all with respect to their content from the corresponding active constructions: 'The enemy killed the soldier', 'the peasants plow the fallow'. These two constructions differ only in respect to stylistic nuance.[23]

On the lexeme level, passive constructions without an agentival complement ('short passives') are not synonymous to the primary active construction. If the agent in the primary construction is expressed concretely lexically, the agent in short passive constructions is designated abstractly, grammatically. This fact involves their contextual (situational) conditionality. They are used in the following types of contexts: (1) the concrete agent is evident for the communicants, and there is therefore no reason to name it, (2) the concrete agent is not known to the speaker, so it cannot be named, (3) the concrete agent is known to the speaker, but for some reason he does not want to name it for the listener, (4) the agent is not named because for the speaker it is important to transmit information about the other participants. The characteristics of short passive constructions as compared with the active construction have been noted by various linguists.[24] B. Ju. Norman, who has described them in some detail, writes:

The short "grammatical" passive, with its emphasized action verb and its object and its displaced "actual performer of the action" (agent) is apparently a totally special specific means in the logic of language for the qualitative and quantitative transformation of the structure of the phrase.[25]

It is quite obvious that on the lexeme level short passive constructions

---

Latin *pater hostem occidit* and *a patre hostis occiditur* denote exactly the same situation (we ignore for the moment differences in logical and psychological 'emphasis'". I. A. Mel'čuk, *K ponjatiju slovoobrazovanija*, Izv. OLJa AN S.S.S.R., 1967, 4, p. 360. See also J. J. Katz and P. M. Postal, *An Integrated Theory of Linguistic Descriptions*, Cambridge, Mass., 1964; J. Katz and E. Martin., 'The Synonymy of Actives and Passives', *Philosophical Review* LXXVI, 1967.

[23] Ju. J. Kurilovič, *Ergativnost' i stadial'nost' v jazyke*, Izv. OLJa, 1946, issue 5, pp. 387–88.
[24] See, for example, Kurilovič, *ibid.*; A. V. Isačenko, *Grammatičeskij stroj russkogo jazyka v sopostavlenii so slavackim* II, Bratislava, 1960; H. Brinkmann, *Die deutsche Sprache*, Düsseldorf, 1962.
[25] B. Ju. Norman, 'Vozvratnye konstrukcii v sovremennom bolgarskom literaturnom jazyke', Author's abstract of his doctoral dissertation, Minsk, 1969, p. 7.

are non-synonymous not only to the active construction, but also to the long passive construction. On this same level, however, all short passive constructions are synonymous to each other.

We find a different state of affairs on the level of grammatical meanings, where short passive constructions are generally non-synonymous with each other. To illustrate this point, let us consider the three Russian passive constructions: (1) *Soldata (C₁) ubili (Pr)* 'The soldier was killed', (2) *Soldata (C₁) ubilo (Pr)* 'The soldier was killed', (3) *Soldat (Sb) byl ubit (Pr)* 'The soldier was killed'. These constructions, which have the same set of lexemes, have the same meaning for the grammatical verbal categories of tense and aspect. At the same time, each of these constructions designates a specific bit of grammatical information. Thus, in construction (1) we find an active personal agent, whereas construction (2) has an active non-personal agent. In addition, the action denoted in construction (2) is usually an unpremeditated, 'unpleasant' one. The opposition between the personal and non-personal agent, characteristic for structures (1) and (2), is cancelled in construction (3). In other words, this construction can be interpreted as having either a personal or non-personal agent. At the same time, it stands in opposition to constructions (1) and (2), since its verbal predicate designates the result of a process, something which the predicates in constructions (1) and (2) do not do. The German passive constructions: (1) *Man (Sb) tanzt (Pr)* and (2) *Es (Sb) wird getanzt (Pr)* also differ with respect to their grammatical meanings. Construction (2), unlike construction (1), designates the repeated, usual nature of the action.[26]

As for primary active constructions of the type *Rabočie strojat školu* 'The workers build the school' and the long passive construction *Škola stroitsja rabočimi* 'The school is being built by the workers', they are synonymous on the level of grammatical meanings, since they transmit the same grammatical information.

On the level of logical emphasis, however, these two constructions are not synonymous, either. In the words of R. Jakobson,

... the active and passive forms of the sentence 'The robbers killed the peasant' and 'The peasant was killed by the robbers' differ with respect to how the action is presented (in connection with the distribution of logical accents, these sentences may in a text prove to be uninterchangeable: if a preceding text was about robbers, only the first variant is possible – if it was about peasants, only the second is possible).[27]

[26] See K. V. Školina, 'Predloženija s *man* i bezličnye predloženija so skazyemym, vyražennym 'odnočlennyum' passivom v nemeckom jazyke' in the collection *Voprosy germanskoj filologii*, issue II, LGU, 1969.

[27] E. V. Padučeva, *Meždunarodnaja konferencija po semiotike v Pol'še*, NTI, series 2, 1967, pp. 36–37. It is essential to note that the cited phrases 'The robbers killed the peasant' and 'The peasant was killed by the robbers' are not synonyms even on the level of grammatical

Thus, long passive constructions are used when the object is evident from the context. If the object is evident from the context and the agent is unknown and is introduced for the first time, the object fills the position of topic-subject, and the agent is placed in comment complement position.

The use of long passive constructions is limited stylistically. They are found exclusively in the written language, above all in scientific technical literature. It is also important to note that unlike short constructions, only certian languages have long constructions.[28] The research that has been done thus far on classical and modern European languages tells us that long passive constructions developed later in these languages than short ones.[29] If we acknowledge that such is the general law for the appearance of long passive constructions in language, then we can speak of the presence of a genetic two-stage derivational chain: primary active construction → short passive construction → long passive construction. Proceeding from this fact, we can conclude that short passive constructions cannot be treated as a reduced variant of long passive structures, although such a viewpoint is quite widespread.[30]

Since short passive constructions, as a rule, are non-synonymous as early as on the level of grammatical meanings, the question of their synonymy on the level of logical accentuation is automatically removed. It is also important to mention that they are very often used in different styles of speech. For example, in Russian it is possible to form both indefinite-personal passive constructions (of the type *školu strojat* 'The school is being built') and personal passive constructions (of the type *škola stroitsja* 'The school is being built') with many verbs, but personal passive constructions are a feature of the literary-scientific style, whereas indefinite-personal passive constructions are usual in the spoken language.[31]

Our final conclusion can be summarized as follows: Active and passive constructions are generally relative, rather than absolute, synonyms, which is why they are not freely interchangeable in a given context. Due to just the fact that these constructions, like any paraphrases, are not absolute synonyms, they all have a right to exist in the syntactic system of language.

---

meanings, since their verbal predicates communicate different grammatical information. The form 'was killed' denotes a state which has come about as a result of an action, whereas the form 'killed' designates only the action.

[28] J. Kuryłowicz emphasizes this point in his paper *Ergativnost' i stadial'nost' v jazyke*, Izv. OLJa AN S.S.S.R., 1946, issue 5.

[29] See, for example: E. Neu, *Das hethitische Mediopassiv und seine indogermanische Grundlagen*, Wiesbaden, 1968; K. H. Schmidt, *Zum Agens beim Passiv*, IF, Bd. 68, H.I., 1963.

[30] See, for example, H. Brinkmann, *Die deutsche Sprache*, Düsseldorf, 1962.

[31] On this see, for example: S. I. Sjatkovskij, 'Neopredelenno-ličnye predloženija v sovremennyx slavjanskix jazykax', in the collection *Slavjanskaja filologija*, No. 5, M., 1963.

Absolute synonyms communicate identical information, so that they are unnecessary in practice and are found in language only as exceptions.

One more conclusion – a negative one: There is no specific passive meaning. This meaning, which has traditionally been attributed to the verb in passive constructions, but has never been intelligently defined, is the fruit of honest scientific errors. As we have argued in this paper, all the differences between passive and active constructions and among passive constructions themselves which make these constructions relative synonyms can be described without referring to this notorious passive meaning.

The identifying characteristic of passive constructions is not to be found in the presence of a passive meaning, but in the fact that unlike active constructions, the lexically designated agent in them does not stand in the central grammatical position of the first actant – the subject. As early as the second half of the past century the Russian linguist A. V. Popov astutely noticed this property of passive structures, thereby defining their significance in the system of syntactic constructions: ... the essence of the passive lies not in the fact that "one thing undergoes an action of another", but in the fact that in passive constructions the action is presented as a fact, as a manifestation of an action in which the agent of the action is wholly or to a significant degree ignored.[32]

Soviet Academy of Sciences, Leningrad

[32] A. V. Popov, *Sintaksičeskie issledovanija*, Voronež, 1881, p. 174.

P. A. SOBOLEVA

DERIVATIONAL STRUCTURE OF
THE RUSSIAN LEXICON

The principal object of linguistic studies has always been the grammatical systems of natural languages because the systematic character of grammatical rules has never caused any doubt. As far as language lexicons are concerned, no one can contend that an entire lexicon of any language has been described satisfactorily in a structural, generative or any other systematic way (semantic fields, componential studies of separate word-groups[1] are but a beginning of a systematic approach to the study of lexicons).

What aspects of a lexicon can be subjected to a structural or generative treatment is still a puzzle. However, there is at least one aspect of lexicon arrangement that may lend itself to generative description. This aspect is the derivational structure of a lexicon.

The purpose of this paper is: (a) to show the possibility of a generative approach to the study of an entire lexicon; (b) to show how this approach helps to order the object of study in a new way.

To fulfil this task we shall use the applicative generative model.[2]

The applicative generative model, an artificial semiotic system simulating natural languages, was advanced as an attempt to overcome a fundamental difficulty inherent in the current conception of generative grammar. [3]

According to Chomsky, a natural language grammar is a device for generating all the grammatical sequences of the language. In the mathematico-

---

[1] See for example, E. N. Bendix, *Componential Analyses of General Vocabulary*, Bloomington, Indiana University Research Center in Anthropology, Folklore and Literature (Publication 40), 1966.
[2] See С. К. Шаумян, *Порождающая Лингвистическая Модель на Базе Принципа Двуступенчатости*, Вопросы языкознания № 2, 1963. С. К. Шаумян и П. А. Соболева, *Аппликативная Порождающая Модель и Исчисление Трансформаций в Русском Языке*, Москва, 1963 (English translation, *Foreign Developments in Machine Translation and Information Processing*, No. 162, Joint Publications Research Service, Washington, U.S., Dept. of Commerce, 1964.) С. К. Шаумян, *Структурная Лингвистика*, Москва, 1965 (English edition: S. K. Šaumjan, *Principles of Structural Linguistics*, Mouton, 1970). S. K. Šaumjan, *Outline of the Applicational Generative Model for the Description of Languages*, Foundations of Language, No. 1, 1965. S. K. Šaumjan and P. A. Soboleva, *Transformations as a Semantic Tool of Studying Natural Languages*, Foundations of Language, No. 1, 1965. С. К. Шаумян и П. А. Соболева, *Основания Порождающей Грамматики Русского Языка*, Москва, 1968, etc.
[3] See S. K. Šaumjan, *Linguistic Models as Artificial Languages Simulating Natural Languages*, Estratto da Linguaggi nella società e nella tecnica, Edizioni di Comunità, Milano, 1970.

F. Kiefer (ed.), Trends in Soviet Theoretical Linguistics, 77–103. *All Rights Reserved.*
Copyright © *1973 by D. Reidel Publishing Company, Dordrecht-Holland.*

logical sense, the word 'generating' means specifying all possible sentences
of the language through mathematical rules.[4]

Such a device might be possible if natural languages were well-defined
mathematical objects. But a natural language is a highly involved system
which defies direct mathematical description, and therefore no practicable
device for generating natural language sentences can be constructed.

Though we cannot generate the sentences of a natural language, we can
generate those of an artificial language simulating a natural language or
natural languages. This artificial language is, in effect, a linguistic model,
a theoretical construct, an idealisation of natural languages for studying
their inner structure.

The use of an artificial language to study the phenomena of natural
languages involves splitting the concept grammar into two concepts, namely
genotype grammar, which is a device for generating the sentences of an artificial language simulating natural languages and phenotype grammar – a set
of rules of correspondence between the sentences of the artificial language
and those of natural languages. Accordingly, we call the artificial language
generated by the former genotype language; the natural languages, whose
relation to the genotype language is described by the phenotype grammar
may be termed phenotype languages.

A fundamental difference between genotype and phenotype grammar is
that genotype grammar specifies a mathematically well-defined language,
whereas the language or languages specified by phenotype grammar are not
well-defined mathematically. Hence the mathematical nature of the rules of
the former and the empirical nature of the rules of the latter.

Explicit distinction between genotype and phenotype languages and between genotype and phenotype grammars is the two-level principle introduced into the theory of linguistic models by S. K. Šaumjan.

The applicational generative model is the first model based on the two-
level principle. It is a genotype grammar which generates a genotype language called the relator language.[5] The relator language consists of relator
words and relator phrases. In the present paper we shall deal only with
the relator words.

Generation of the relator words of the applicative genotype language
is a calculus of functions having the form R_iX, where X is the argument, R_i
is a function and R_iX is the value of the function. R_i has the following
values: R_1, a verbilizing function; R_2, a nominalizing function; R_3, an adjec-
tivizing function, and R_4, an adverbializing function. X equals O or R_iX. O

[4] N. Chomsky, *Syntactic Structures*, The Hague, 1957, p. 13.
[5] At present a new version of the genotype language has been developed (see S. K. Šaumjan, *The Genotype Language and Formal Semantics*, present volume, p. 251)

simulates an amorphous word-root deprived of grammatical functions. R_i may also be called an operator, X – an operand and R_iX – an R-image of X. R-words of the applicative model are analogues of words in natural languages.

R-words with one relator simulate primary underived[6] words, e.g.

R_1O – *(he) runs, (I) read* (finite form);

R_2O – *(a) box, (the) cat, sand*;

R_3O – *yellow, clumsy, keen*;

R_4O – *here, now, yesterday.*

R-words with two relators simulate derived words, e.g.:

R_2R_1O – *(a) runner, movement* – i.e. verbal nouns;

R_1R_2O – *becloud, amalgamate* – i.e. denominative verbs etc.

R-words with three relators simulate words of the second degree of derivation, e.g.:

$R_2R_3R_2O$ – *homelessness, corpuscularity*;

$R_3R_3R_1O$ – *unreadable, unloving*, etc.

R-words with four relators simulate words of the third degree of derivation, for example

$R_2R_3R_2R_1O$ – *editorialist, impressionability* etc.

R-words with n relators simulate words of n-1th degree of derivation.

The principal operation in this system is the operation of application which is defined as the operation of joining the function to its argument. Every instance of application is called a derivational step.

Placing R-words of the artificial language in correspondence with words of natural language implies viewing the underlying word as the argument, the derived word as the value of the function and the derivational formant as the function itself.

Owing to the transparency of their structures the R-words of the genotype language can easily be arranged in classes. Classes of R-words are called R-structures.

In modelling the derivational organization of a lexicon it is expedient to use two types of R-structures:

(1) Classes of R-words with identical first relators (counting from the root O). There are four such classes: $\{R_i^n R_1 O\}$, $\{R_i^n R_2 O\}$, $\{R_i^n R_3 O\}$, $\{R_i^n R_4 O\}$ $(n \geqslant O)$. R_i indicates any relator of the four, i.e. $R_1 \vee R_2 \vee R_3 \vee R_4$, R_n^i is the abbreviation of R_i applied n times. $\{\ \ \}$ is an indication of a class of R-words.

(2) Classes of R-words with two identical final relators. There are sixteen such classes: $\{R_1 R_1 R_i^m O\}$, $\{R_1 R_2 R_i^m O\}$, $\{R_1 R_3 R_i^m O\}$, $\{R_1 R_4 R_i^m O\}$,

---

[6] When we speak of primary underived words we mean only their present synchronic status.

$\{R_2R_1R_i^mO\}$, $\{R_2R_2R_i^mO\}$ etc., $(m \geqslant O)$, where R_i^m is the abbreviation of R_i applied m times.

R-structures of the first type are placed in correspondence with word-families such as *read, reader, readable, reading, unreadable* etc., $\{R_i^nR_1O\}$, *white, whiteness, (the) white, whiten* etc., $\{R_i^nR_3O\}$.

R-structures of the second type are placed in correspondence with word-series, i.e. words with identical derivational formants, such as *humidity* (R_2R_3O), *permissibility* $(R_2R_3R_1O)$, *atomicity* $(R_2R_3R_2O)$, *justifiability* $(R_2R_3R_1R_3O)$ *spheroidicity* $(R_2R_3R_2R_2O)$, etc., all belonging to the class $\{R_2R_3R_i^mO\}$.

The R-structure apparatus by which derivational groups of words such as word-families and word-series can be simulated (or modelled), enables description of the derivational level of a language in terms of larger units than those used conventionally for this purpose, i.e. derivational patterns. Derivational patterns are the smallest units of the derivational system and their inventory[7] is a necessary but a preliminary step in presenting the entire derivational level of a language.

Only through such units as word-families and word-series can the hierarchical ordering of the derivational structure of a lexicon be clearly seen.

We shall now dwell on the units relevant to our study of a lexicon. According to the two-level principle mentioned above we split all the units into two categories: genotype units and phenotype units.

The *elementary unit* of the derivational system is a *derivational step*, corresponding to the operation of application at the genotype level (within the applicative grammar) and to joining the derivational formant (or class of formants) to the underlying form (or class of forms), on the phenotype level.

The concept 'derivational step', is a dynamic reformulation of synchronic derivational relations, i.e. the relations between underlying and derived words.

According to the relation between the value of a function and its argument (derived and underlying words) all derivational steps are subdivided into two categories – transpositional: R_1R_2X, R_1R_3X, R_1R_4X, R_2R_1X, R_2R_3X, R_2R_4X, R_3R_1X etc., altogether twelve, and identificational: R_1R_1X, R_2R_2X, R_3R_3X, R_4R_4X. The derivational step R_iO, which generates primitive words from roots may be referred equally to both categories.

A transpositional derivational step transposes a word to another grammatical class, e.g. кипятить – кипячение (R_2R_1X), *head – behead* (R_1R_2X),

---

[7] See, for example, an excellent study of derivational patterns in H. Marchand, *The Categories and Types of Present-Day English Word-formation*, A Synchronic-Diachronic Approach, Wiesbaden, 1960.

riche – enricher $(R_1 R_3 X)$. An identificational step leaves the word within the same grammatical class, e.g. *кипятить – вскипятить* $(R_1 R_1 X)$ *readable – unreadable* $(R_3 R_3 X)$, *Mann – Männchen* $(R_2 R_2 X)$.

The list of derivational steps given above is universal for languages which distinguish between four principal functional word classes (verb, noun, adjective and adverb). However, not all the steps are equally realizable in different languages. The realization of universal derivational steps in natural languages can be the object of a typological study.

In the content plane each derivational step is characterised by a general derivational meaning which can be stated in terms of relations between four abstract semantic categories: process (R_1), substance (R_2), quality (R_3), quality of process or of quality (R_4). Thus, the meaning of $R_1 R_2 X$ can be described as relation of process to substance, or rather 'process pertaining to substance', the meaning of $R_2 R_1 X$ as 'substance pertaining to process', the meaning of $R_2 R_3 X$ as 'substance pertaining to quality', $R_3 R_3 X$ as 'quality pertaining to quality' etc. – altogether sixteen combinations of categories and therefore sixteen general derivational meanings.

General derivational meanings are realized in a set of concrete derivational meanings independent of the means of derivation (suffixation, prefixation, conversion etc.) and of the richness or poverty of derivational patterns at the disposal of the given language. For example, the derivational step $R_2 R_1 X$ corresponds to the following set of concrete derivational meanings, whatever the derivational means:

(1) Action (instance of an action): *pugna* (Lat.), *creusage, joute* (Fr.), *Laufen, Knicks* (Ger.), *movement, jerk* (Engl.), *чтение, прыжок* (Russ.)

(2) Agent (instrument) of an action: *umbraculum* (Lat.), *fouleur, fouloir* (Fr.), *Flieger, Kocher* (Ger.), *poker, guard* (Engl.), *сцепщик, задвижка* (Russ.)

(3) Place of an action: *aratio* (Lat.), *foulerie, résidence* (Fr.), *Formerei, Gießerei* (Ger.), *forgery, smoker* (Engl.), *раздевалка, ожидальня* (Russ').

(4) Object of an action (often with a shade of result): *spectaculum* (Lat.), *exposition, transponent* (Fr.), *employee, catch* (Eng.), *находка, приёмыш* (Russ.)

(5) Result of an action: *naratio* (Lat.), *partage, extenuation* (Fr.), *Malerei, Folge* (Ger.), *cut, building* (Engl.), *царапина, выводок* (Russ.)

Correlation between derivational meanings, both general and concrete, and the sixteen derivational steps pertains to the sphera of language universals.

Though in the content plane the derivational step corresponds to a universal set of meanings, in the expression plane it corresponds to a specific set of derivational patterns for every language. For example, in Russian the universal derivational step R_1R_2X corresponds to twelve derivational patterns:

N^8-a-flex (завтрак-а-л), N-и-flex (шпион-и-л), N-ствова-flex (шеф-ствова-л), N-нича-flex (столяр-нича-л,) N-е-flex (звер-е-л), N-ова-flex (стекл-ова-л), pref-N-и-flex (об-лес-и-л), pref-N-flex-ся (о-степен-и-л-ся), N-и-flex-ся (пузыр-и-л-ся), pref-N-е-flex (о-звер-е-л), N-а-flex (хлыст-а-л), N-е-flex (скорб-е-л).

But in English the same derivational step corresponds to only five derivational patterns: N-∅-flex (coat-ed), N-ize-flex (colon-ize-d), N-ate-flex (vaccin-ate-d), N-ify-flex (gas-ifi-d), and pref-N-flex (be-cloud-ed).

The derivational meanings pertaining to this step are the same and do not depend on the variety of patterns either in Russian or in English. They depend on the nature of the derivational step, R_1R_2X in this case, and the semantic category of the underlying word. If the underlying noun denotes an agent, the derived verb will mean 'act like N' (шефствовать, to doctor), if it denotes an instrument the derived verb will mean 'act with the help of' (утюжить, to hammer), if the underlying noun means the object of an action, the derived verb may mean 'give, or add, deprive of' (хомутать, потрошить, to amalgamate, to skin). If the underlying noun has a locative category the derivative will mean 'place in, put into' (складировать, hospitalize) etc.[9]

Although there is a tendency for every pattern to attract certain definite meanings associated with the derivational step the distribution of derivational meanings among derivational patterns is not rigorous. Theoretically any pattern may realize any derivational meaning characteristic of the derivational step. E.g. говорильня does not mean 'place of the action', but the action itself, вытрезвитель is neither an agent nor an instrument, but a place, украшение is both an action and an instrument etc.

Thus, on the one hand each derivational step corresponds to a universal set of concrete derivational meanings, on the other hand in every language it corresponds to a definite set of derivational patterns, thus establishing a many-to-many-relation between derivational meanings and derivational patterns.

The invariant of this relation is the derivational step.

The secondary unit of the derivational level is the *derivational structure of a word*, which is defined as *a sequence of derivational steps* generating an

---

[8] *N* denotes a noun stem.
[9] Cf. a promising description of derivational meanings pertaining to what we call the derivational step R_3R_2X by Magnus Liung, *English Denominal Adjectives*; a generative study of the semantics of a group of high-frequency denominal adjectives in English, Acta Universitatis Gothoburgensis, Lund, 1970. The derivational meanings established by Magnus Liung are unquestionably universal in nature.

R-word at the genotype level and a class of phenotype words at the phenotype level. Phenotype words corresponding to a genotype R-word can be grouped in many fashions: identity of root or identity of any (or several) of their derivational affixes. One possible grouping, convenient for our purpose, is identity of final derivational formants. We call a group of words with identical derivational structure and identical final derivational formants an L-class of words. Thus, correspondences are established between R-words and L-classes in the above interpretation of the term. For example, the genotype word R_2R_1O corresponds in Russian to forty six L-classes of nouns: *чтение, свержение..., писатель, открыватель..., агитация, ратификация..., сажальщик, рисовальщик..., читальня, купальня..., нуждаемость, сопротивляемость..., било, точило..., галдёж, грабёж...* etc. The genotype word $R_2R_1R_1O$ corresponds to twenty one L-classes of nouns: *написание, отозвание..., измеритель, завоеватель..., демобилизация, реорганизация..., насыпальщик, разрезальщик..., слетанность, сработанность...,* etc. The set of derivational steps, generating the R-word $R_1R_3R_2O$ at the phenotype level generates four L-classes of verbs: *босячил, левачил..., стеклянел, паршивел..., нормализировал, централизировал..., нервничал, вольничал.* The set of derivational steps, generating the genotype word $R_2R_3R_2R_1R_1O$ corresponds to an L-class, consisting of one word *допризывник (звал-призвал-призыв-допризывный-допризывник).*

There is an inverse dependence between the complexity of an R-word, i.e. the number of derivational steps required to generate it, and the number of L-classes it simulates in the phenotype language.

Note: There is no isomorphism between the derivational structure of a word, objectivized by relator-notation, and its morphemic composition (at least in fusional languages). Cp:

redd-en em-bold-en	R_1R_3O
быстр-о на-бел-о	R_4R_3O
bak-er-ess murder-ess	$R_2R_2R_1O$
за-сол-ка де-картел-из-ация	$R_2R_1R_1R_2O,$

where a different number of derivational morphemes corresponds to the same number of derivational steps, and

irrit-ate	R_1O
irrit-able	R_3R_1O
пилот-аж	$R_2R_1R_2O$
тип-аж	R_2R_2O
floor-ing (a kind of stroke)	$R_2R_1R_2O$
floor-ing (material)	R_2R_2O
москов-ский	R_3R_2O
тоболь-ский	$R_3R_2R_2O,$

where on equal number of derivational morphemes corresponds to a different number of derivational steps.

The absense of isomorphism between the morphemic composition of words and their derivational structure is due to a number of reasons. Some of these are:

(1) Discontinuous formants (*ac-climat-ise* R_1R_2O, *про-худ-ил-ся* R_1R_3O);

(2) Zero derivation (*a run* R_2R_1O, *to floor* R_1R_2O, *синь* R_2R_3O, *перевоз* $R_2R_1R_1O$);

(3) Fusion at the morpheme boundaries, e.g. morpheme clipping (*murder* → *murder-er* → *murder-ess* $R_2R_2R_1O$, where *-er-* is clipped off, cp. *bak-er-ess* $R_2R_2R_1O$, where it is not; *пилот* → *пилот-ировал* → *пилот-аж* $R_2R_1R_2O$ where *-ирова-* is clipped off, cp. *пилот-ирова-ние* $R_2R_1R_2O$, where it is not) and superposition of morphemes (*Тобол* → *Тоболь-ск* → *Тоболь-ский* $R_3R_2R_2O$, where – *ский* R_3 is superimposed on -*ск-* $\emptyset$ R_2).

(4) Change of affixes as a means of derivation, as opposed to their agglutination (*irritate* R_1O – *irrit-able* R_3R_1O, *demonstr-ate* R_1O – *demonstr-able* R_3R_1O, cp. *hydrate*, *read* R_1O – *hydrat-able*, *read-able* R_3R_1O) etc.

Thus the derivational structure of a word, which is a construct objectivized by a relator notation of derivational steps should be strictly distinguished from and never confused with its morphemic composition, that is its actually observed separable morphemes.

The units next in rank of derivational level are *word-families* and *word-series*.

A *word-family* is a class of derivational structures with identical first derivational step. At the genotype level it corresponds to an R-structure of the first type[10] (genotype word-family). At the phenotype level it corresponds to a set of words with identical root-morphemes. This set of words falls into subsets, called L-structures (phenotype word-families).

Examples of genotype and phenotype word-families are given in Table I and Figures 1–5.

Each line in Table I contains words of identical derivational structure. The identical derivational step is R_2O.

To picture the structure of genotype word-families we use oriented graphs

TABLE I

Examples of genotype and phenotype word families.

Genotype Word-family (R-structure $\{R_i^n R_2O\}$	Phenotype word-families (L-structures)				
R_2O	дудка	луг	мышь	протез	столяр ...
R_1R_2O	дудел	залужил: залуживал	мышковал	протезиро- вал	столярни- чал ...
R_2R_2O	дудочка	луговина лужайка	мышка мышонок	протезист	столярка ...
R_3R_2O	дудчатый	луговой	мышастый мыший мышиный	протезный	столяр- ный ...
$R_2R_1R_2O$	дударь	залужение	мышкование	протезиро- вание	столярни- чанье ...

[10] See page 79.

with conventionally directed branches, a vertical branch corresponding to R_2, a branch slanting left and down, to R_1, a branch slating right and down, to R_3, and a horizontal right-bound branch, to R_4.

Figure 1 is the graph of the R-structure given in Table I.

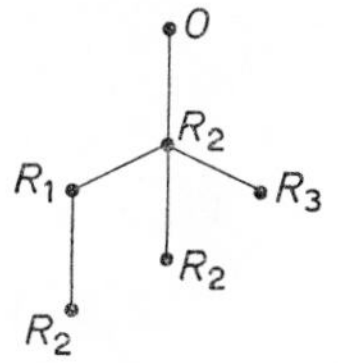

Fig. 1.

Figures 2–5 show genotype word-families which simulate dozens of phenotype word-families in Russian.

The R-structure in Figure 2 models such Russian word-families as

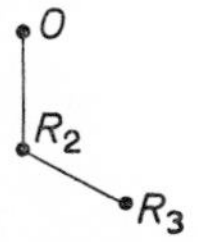

Fig. 2.

R_2O	R_3R_2O
аберрация	аберрационный
абразивы	абразивный
авангард	авангардный
абордаж	абордажный
аборт	абортивный
авантаж	авантажный
август	августовский
аврал	авральный
автобус	автобусный
	etc.

Here and in the following instead of table-form we simply list phenotype word-families underneath their graphs. The order of R-classes beneath the graphs is taken as follows:

R_1X R_2X R_3X R_4X

The head-word of the word family is printed in italics.

Such is the arrangement of word-families accepted in the derivational dictionary, compiled by the Dept. of Structural Linguistics of the Institute of Russian (ed. by S. K. Šaumjan, E.L. Ginzburg, and P. A. Soboleva; in preparation).

Some exerpts from the dictionary are given below:

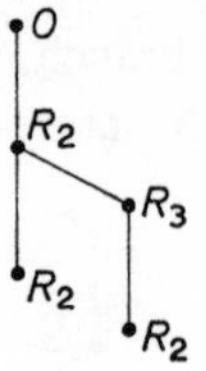

Fig. 3.

R_2O
бровь
R_2R_2O
бровка

$R_2R_3R_2O$
надбровье

R_3R_2O
безбровый

бровастый
бровный

надбровный

R_2O
дно
R_2R_2O
днище
донце
донышко
$R_2R_3R_2O$
бездна
поддон

R_3R_2O
бездонный
донный
поддонный

R_2O
овраг
R_2R_2O
овражек
$R_2R_3R_2O$
приовражье

R_3R_2O
овражистый
овражный
приовражный

R_2O
озеро
R_2R_2O
озерко
озерцо
$R_2R_3R_2O$
приозёрье

R_3R_2O
заозёрный
озерный
приозёрный

etc.

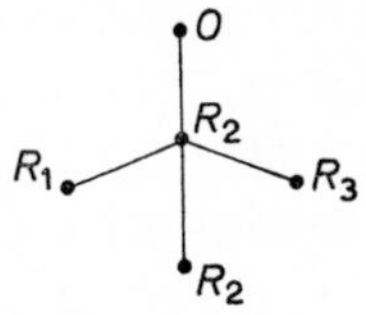

Fig. 4.

R_1R_2O	R_2O	R_3R_2O
актёрствовал	*актёр*	актёрский
	R_2R_2O	
	актёрка	
	актрисса	

R_1R_2O	R_2O	R_3R_2O
атаманил	*атаман*	атаманский
	R_2R_2O	
	атаманство	
	атаманша	

R_1R_2O	R_2O	R_3R_2O
бабничал	*баба*	бабий
обабился	R_2R_2O	бабин
	бабёнка	бабский
	бабища	
	бабник	

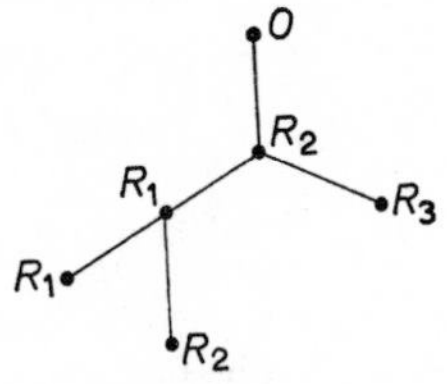

Fig. 5.

R_1R_2O	R_2O	R_3R_2O
бугрился	*бугор*	бугорчатый
	R_2R_2O	бугристый
	бугорок	

etc.

R_1R_2O
асфальтировал
$R_1R_1R_2O$
заасфальтировал

R_2O
асфальт
$R_2R_1R_2O$
асфальтирование

R_3R_2O
асфальтный

R_1R_2O
фиглярил
фиглярничал
фиглярствовал
$R_1R_1R_2O$
сфиглярил
сфиглярничал

R_2O
фигляр

R_1R_2O
фиглярство

R_3R_2O
фиглярский

R_1R_2O
бальзамировал
$R_1R_1R_2O$
набальзамировал

R_2O
бальзам
$R_2R_1R_2O$
бальзамирование

R_3R_2O
бальзамный
бальзамический

R_1R_2O
гипсовал
$R_1R_1R_2O$
загипсовал

R_2O
гипс
R_2R_1O
гипсование

R_3R_2O
гипсовый

etc.

Figures 6–8 show some typical deverbal word-families:

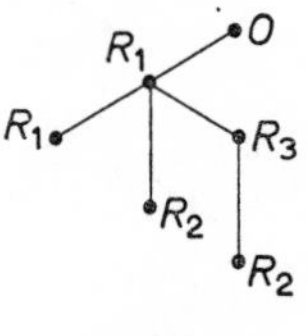

Fig. 6.

R_1O
брюзжал
R_1R_1O
побрюзжал
пробрюзжал
разбрюзжался

R_2R_1O
брюзжание
брюзга

$R_2R_3R_1O$
брюзгливость

R_3R_1O
брюзгливый

R_1O
внушил/внушал
R_1R_1O
внушался

R_2R_1O
внушение
$R_2R_3R_1O$
внушительность

R_3R_1O
внушительный

R_1O
возбудил/возбуждал

R_1R_1O
возбуждался

R_2R_1O
возбудитель
возбуждение
$R_2R_3R_1O$
возбудимость
возбуждаемость
возбужденность

R_3R_1O
возбудимый
возбуждающий
возбужденный

R_1O
возмутил/возмущал
R_1R_1O
возмутился/
возмущался
etc.

R_2R_1O
возмущение
$R_2R_3R_1O$
возмутительность
невозмутимость

R_3R_1O
возмутительный
возмущенный
невозмутимый

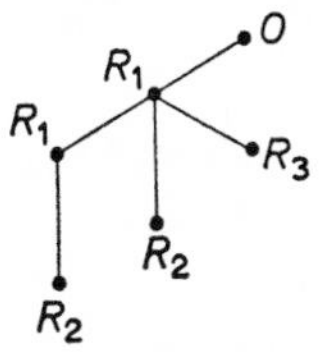

Fig. 7.

R_1O
выл
R_1R_1O
взвыл
завыл/завывал
подвыл/подвывал

R_2R_1O
вой
$R_2R_1R_1O$
вытье
завывание
подвывание

R_3R_1O
завывающий

R_1O
зевал/зевнул
R_1R_1O
зазевал
зазевался
назевался
позевал

R_2R_1O
зевака
зеванье
зевок
зевота
$R_2R_1R_1O$
позёвывание

R_3R_1O
зевательный

$R_1 O$
   мигал/мигнул
$R_1 R_1 O$
   замигал
   перемигнулся
   подмигнул/
   подмигивал

$R_2 R_1 O$
   мигалка
   мигание
$R_2 R_1 R_1 O$
   подмигивание

$R_3 R_1 O$
   мигательный
   немигающий

$R_1 O$
   скрипел/скрипнул
$R_1 R_1 O$
   заскрипел
   поскрипел/
   поскрипывал
   проскрипел
   etc.

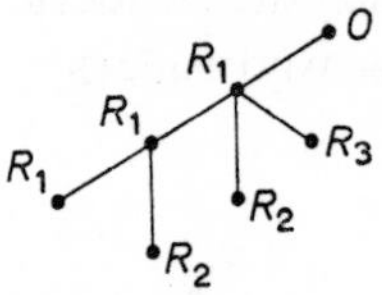

$R_2 R_1 O$
   скрип
   скрипение
$R_2 R_1 R_1 O$
   поскрипывание

$R_3 R_1 O$
   скрипучий

Fig. 8.

$R_1 O$
   воплотил/воплощал[11]
   воплотился/
   воплощался
$R_1 R_1 O$
   перевоплотил/
   перевоплощал
$R_1 R_1 R_1 O$
   перевоплотился/
   перевоплощался

$R_2 R_1 O$
   воплощение
$R_2 R_1 R_1 O$
   перевоплощение

$R_3 R_1 O$
   воплощенный

$R_1 O$
   дислоцировал
$R_1 R_1 O$
   дислоцировался
   передислоцировал

$R_2 R_1 O$
   дислокация
$R_2 R_1 R_1 O$
   передислокация

$R_3 R_1 O$
   дислокационный

[11] Relations between *плоть* and *воплощал* are etymological rather than derivational.

$R_1 R_1 R_1 O$
передислоцировался

$R_1 O$	$R_2 R_1 O$	$R_3 R_1 O$
корчевал	корчевание	корчевальный
$R_1 R_1 O$	корчеватель	
выкорчевал/	корчёвка	
выкорчевывал	$R_2 R_1 R_1 O$	
корчевался	выкорчёвка	
накорчевал	выкорчёвывание	
раскорчевал	раскорчевка	
$R_1 R_1 R_1 O$	раскорчёвывание	
выкорчёвывался		

$R_1 O$	$R_2 R_1 O$	$R_3 R_1 O$
крал	кража	краденый
$R_1 R_1 O$	$R_1 R_2 R_1 O$	
выкрал/выкрадывал	обкрадывание	
крался		
накрал/накрадывал		
обокрал		
перекрал		
раскрал/раскрадывал		
$R_1 R_1 R_1 O$		
выкрадывался		
накрадывался		
обкрадывался		
раскрадывался		
etc.		

Graphs in figures 9–11 show some very typical deadjectival word-families.

Fig. 9.

$R_2 R_3 O$	$R_3 O$	$R_4 R_3 O$
безалаберность	*безалаберный*	безалаберно
безалаберщина		

внезапность	*внезапный*	внезапно
имманентность	*имманентный*	имманентно
пристальность	*пристальный*	пристально etc.

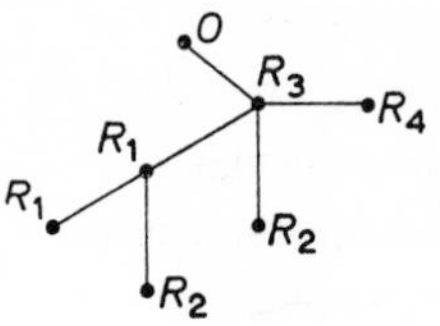

Fig. 10.

$R_1 R_3 O$ актуализировал	$R_2 R_3 O$ актуальность	$R_3 O$ *актуальный*	$R_4 R_3 O$ актуально
$R_1 R_1 R_3 O$ актуализировался	$R_2 R_1 R_3 O$ актуализация		
$R_1 R_3 O$ убыстрил/ убыстрял	$R_2 R_3 O$ быстрота	$R_3 O$ *быстрый*	$R_4 R_3 O$ быстро
$R_1 R_1 R_3 O$ убыстрился/ убыстрялся	$R_2 R_1 R_3 O$ убыстрение		
$R_1 R_3 O$ важничал	$R_2 R_3 O$ важность	$R_3 O$ *важный*	$R_4 R_3 O$ важно
$R_1 R_1 R_3 O$ заважничал поважничал	$R_2 R_1 R_3 O$ важничанье		
$R_1 R_3 O$ глупел глупил оглупил	$R_2 R_3 O$ глупость	$R_3 O$ *глупый*	$R_4 R_3 O$ глупо
	$R_2 R_1 R_3 O$ оглупление		
$R_1 R_1 R_3 O$ наглупил поглупел etc.			

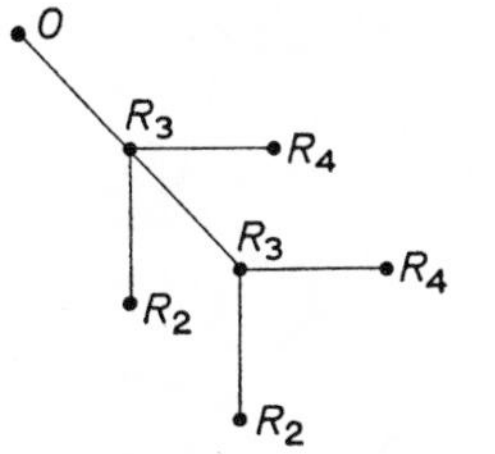

Fig. 11.

R_2R_3O	R_3O	R_4R_3O
аккуратность	*аккуратный*	аккуратно
$R_2R_3R_3O$	R_3R_3O	$R_4R_3R_3O$
неаккуратность	неаккуратный	неаккуратно
R_2R_3O	R_3O	R_4R_3O
вежливость	*вежливый*	вежливо
невежа		
$R_2R_3R_3O$	R_3R_3O	$R_4R_3R_3O$
невежливость	невежливый	невежливо
R_2R_3O	R_3O	R_4R_3O
заурядность	*заурядный*	заурядно
$R_2R_3R_3O$	R_3R_3O	$R_4R_3R_3O$
незаурядность	незаурядный	незаурядно
R_2R_2O	R_3O	R_4R_3O
известность	*известный*	известно
$R_2R_3R_3O$	R_3R_3O	$R_4R_3R_3O$
неизвестность	безвестный	безвестно
	неизвестный	неизвестно
		etc.

There is an inverse dependence between the complexity of genotype *R*-structures and the number of phenotype word-families they simulate. *R*-structures of complexity one to six (meaning that they consist of from one to six *R*-words each) possess high modelling capacity. *R*-structures of complexity over 9 or 10 are individual, i.e. they model single phenotype word-families. For example, the genotype word-family shown in Figure 12 is individual. Its complexity is 14. This *R*-structure simulates the generation of ninety three words derived from the adjective *сухой* (counting verbs differing in aspect as one word rather than two: *засушил/засушивал,*

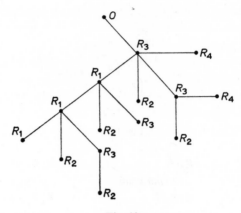

Fig. 12.

пересушил/пересушивал, просушил/просушивал etc.). *R*-structures of high complexity (up to 20) and small modelling capacity consist of substructures which coincide with *R*-structures of low complexity and high modelling capacity.

In the derivational dictionary mentioned above the *R*-structures modelling phenotype word-families are presented in order of increasing complexity and decreasing modelling capacity. Each graph is followed by a list of the word-families it models, as illustrated above.

The dictionary consists of four sections: deverbal word families $\{R_i^n R_1 O\}$, denominal word families $\{R_i^n R_2 O\}$, deadjectival word families $\{R_i^n R_3 O\}$ and deadverbal word families $\{R_i^n R_4 O\}$. Each section is closed by an *R*-structure, which is the set-theoretical sum of all the *R*-structures in the section. We call this *R*-structure a genotype macro-family. It may also be called an 'ideal *R*-structure'. It is 'ideal' because it does not model a separately taken phenotype-word family but a whole field of word-families. All 'real *R*-structures', i.e. those simulating phenotype word-families, are substructures of the 'ideal' one. Figures 13, 14, 15 and 16 are ideal *R*-structures which model all the

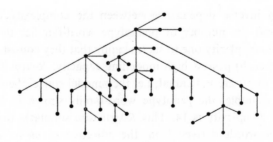

Fig. 13.

deverbal, deadjectival, denominal, and deadverbal word-families of Russian. They are the set-theoretical sums of all 'real' *R*-structures modelling corresponding phenotype word-families in Russian.

As is evident from Figure 13–16 the most complex in structure is the deverbal macro-family (55 *R*-words). The deadjectival and denominal macro-families are second in complexity (50 *R*-words respectively). The least complex, as might have been expected, is the deadverbal macro-family (16 *R*-words).

Fig. 14.

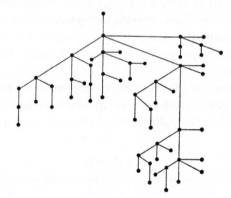

Fig. 15.

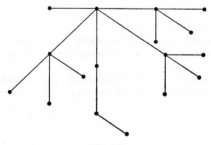

Fig. 16.

The above data will no doubt be useful for typological studies, e.g., for comparing the generative capacities of verbs, nouns, adjectives and adverbs in different languages.

It was said above that apart from the word-family another tertiary unit of the derivational level following the derivational structure of a word in rank is the word-series.

Like the concepts discussed previously, the concept word-series is split into two concepts: genotype word-series and phenotype word-series.

Word-series is defined as a class of word-structures having identical final derivationals steps. At the genotype level it corresponds to an R-structure of the second type[12] (genotype word-series). At the phenotype level it corresponds to a set of words with identical derivational formants.

This set consists of a number of subsets called L-structures (phenotype word-series).

Examples of a genotype and phenotype word-series are given in Table II.

Each line in Table II contains a class of words with identical derivational structures (an L-class).

To represent the structure of genotype word-series we use the same kind of graphs as we used to represent the structure of genotype word-families.

The graph in Figure 17 corresponds to the word-series given in Table II.

The modelling capacity of genotype word-series like that of genotype word-structures and genotype word-families, is inversely dependent on their complexity.

Genotype word-series (R-structures of the second type) of complexity between 1 and 3 R-words can model up to 50 phenotype word-series in Russian. Word-series of complexity over 5 or 6, as a rule, simulate individual

TABLE II

Examples of a genotype word-series and phenotype word-series.

Genotype word-series (R-structure $\{R_1R_3R_i{}^mO\}$)	Phenotype word-series (L-structures)			
R_1R_3O	подличал	неитрализовал	сушил	чернел
	нагличал	вульгализировал	синил	белел
	. . . .	. . . .	. . . .	. . . .
	нервничал	централизовал	слюнявил	деревенел
$R_1R_3R_2O$	роскошничал	нормализовал	грязнил	стекленел
	. . . .	. . . .	. . . .	. . . .

[12] See page 80.

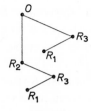

Fig. 17.

phenotype word families. Figure 18 is a graph of fairly high complexity (12 R-words). It models only one phenotype word-series, namely, the L-structure-*ени, -ни*-flex.

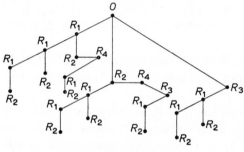

Fig. 18.

Table III contains L-classes of words corresponding to the nodes of the graph.

Other examples of word-series can be found in P. A. Soboleva, *Investigation of a Word-Building System on the basis of the Applicational Generative Model*.[13] A complete inventory of Russian word-series is presented in C. K.

TABLE III

L-classes of words corresponding to the nodes of Figure 18.

R-word	L-class		
(1) R_2R_1O	чтение,	свержение,	наступление ...
(2) $R_2R_1R_1O$	написание,	покачивание,	застегивание ...
(3) $R_2R_1R_2O$	соление,	газирование,	приземление ...
(4) $R_2R_1R_3O$	сушение,	свежевание,	озеленение ...
(5) $R_2R_1R_1R_1O$	выталкивание,	выпрыгивание,	выдергивание ...
(6) $R_2R_1R_1R_2O$	выпиливание,	размораживание,	выруливание ...
(7) $R_2R_1R_1R_3O$	подсушивание,	забеливание,	подсинивание ...
(8) $R_2R_1R_4R_2R_1O$	обеззараживание,		
(9) $R_2R_1R_3R_4R_2O$	обескровливание,		

[13] Semiotica II, 1970, 1.

Шаумян and П. А. Соболева, *Основания Порождающей Грамматики Русского Языка.*[14] In this book the word-series are presented hierarchically, beginning with complex structures and ending up with simple ones.[15]

Each hierarchy opens with an 'ideal' R-structure of a macro-series, this being a set-theoretical sum of all 'real' R-structures, i.e. R-structures which simulate at least one phenotype word-series (L-structure). All 'real' R-structures are substructures of the 'ideal' ones.

Russian, like any other language distinguishing between 16 'ideal' macro series:

$$\{R_1R_1R_i^mO\}, \quad \{R_1R_2R_i^mO\}, \quad \{R_1R_3R_i^mO\}, \quad \{R_1R_4R_i^mO\},$$
$$\{R_2R_1R_i^mO\}, \quad \{R_2R_2R_i^mO\}, \quad \{R_2R_3R_i^mO\}, \quad \{R_2R_4R_i^mO\},$$
$$\{R_3R_1R_i^mO\}, \quad \{R_3R_2R_i^mO\}, \quad \{R_3R_3R_i^mO\}, \quad \{R_3R_4R_i^mO\},$$
$$\{R_4R_1R_i^mO\}, \quad \{R_4R_2R_i^mO\}, \quad \{R_4R_3R_i^mO\}, \quad \{R_4R_4R_i^mO\},$$

where $m \geqslant 0$.

(To these we must add the four formulas R_1O, R_2O, R_3O, R_4O which can be regarded as word series only theoretically because they simulate underived words.)

Figure 19 shows a hierarchy (incomplete, for the sake of brevity) of word-series of Russian deverbal nouns. It opens with the 'ideal' R-structure $\{R_2R_1R_i^mO\}$. All its substructures are 'real' because they model phenotype word-series.

The largest units of the derivational level are macro-families and macro-series – 'ideal' R-structures, obtained by adding up all the 'real' R-structures.

The derivational structure of a lexicon may be regarded as a hierarchy of the units discussed above. There are two aspects of this hierarchy:

(a) Inclusion of lower-rank units in higher-rank units. The system of such inclusions has been shown above: derivational step $\supseteq$ derivational structure of a word $\supseteq$ word-family (word-series) $\supseteq$ macro-familiy (macro series).

(b) Arrangement of units (derivational structures, word-families and word-series within the same rank according to complexity).

The degree of complexity for units of different ranks is defined as follows:

The complexity of derivational structure of a phenotype word is measured by the number of relators in its corresponding R-word. For example, the complexity of derivational structure of *пилотаж* or *асфальтирование* is three ($R_2R_1R_2O$), that of *деполяризация* is five ($R_2R_1R_1R_3R_2O$).

---

[14] Издательство 'Наука', Москва, 1968, Part I.
[15] This book as well as the paper mentioned above (Semiotica II, 1, 1970) reflected a different approach to perfective and imperfective verb-pairs. Verbs characterized by what is known as 'secondary imperfectivation', e.g. *перечитывал, замораживал, пересушивал* were regarded as the next cycle of word generation as compared with their perfective counterparts: *перечитал, заморозил, пересушил,* Hence, the more complex word-series than those in this paper.

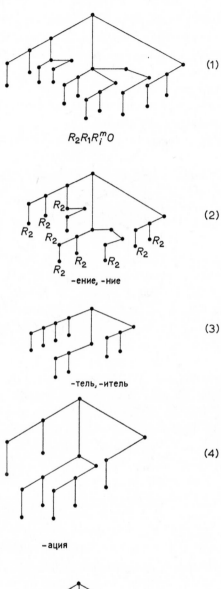

$R_2 R_1 R_i^m O$ (1)

-ение, -ние   (2)

-тель, -итель   (3)

-ация   (4)

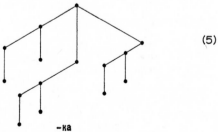

-ка   (5)

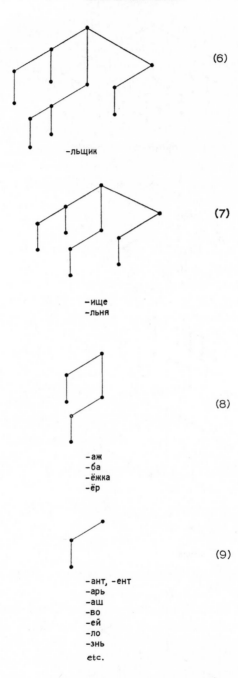

(6)

−льщик

(7)

−ище
−льня

(8)

−аж
−ба
−ёжка
−ёр

(9)

−ант, −ент
−арь
−аш
−во
−ей
−ло
−знь

etc.

Fig. 19.

The complexity of a phenotype word-family is measured by the number of R-words constituting its corresponding R-structure. For example, the complexity of the word-family shown in Figure 2 equals two, in Figure 3 and 4 – four, in Figure 5, 6 and 7 – five, in Figure 8 – six, in Figure 12 – fourteen, etc.

The complexity of a word-series is also measured by the number of the R-words of the corresponding R-structure. For example, the complexity of the 'real' word-series shown in Figure 19 is as follows: nine (-ение), seven (-тель, -ация), six (-ка), five (-льщик), four (-ище, -льня), two (-аж, -ба etc.) and one (-ач, -арь, -аш, etc.) Both aspects of the hierarchy must be observed in describing the derivational structure of any lexicon.

Having obtained the genotype images ('ideal' R-structures) of all the sixteen macro-series, it becomes possible to obtain the genotype images of the entire class of nouns $\{R_2 R_i^n O\}$, verbs $\{R_1 R_i^n O\}$, adjectives $\{R_3 R_i^n O\}$ and adverbs $\{R_4 R_i^n O\}$ of any language.

The genotype image of the noun is obtained as a result of adding up the four macro-series $\{R_2 R_1 R_i^m O\}$, $\{R_2 R_2 R_i^m O\}$, $\{R_2 R_3 R_i^m O\}$ and $\{R_2 R_4 R_i^m O\}$. Figure 20 shows the genotype image of the Russian noun $\{R_2 R_i^n O\}$ obtained in this way.

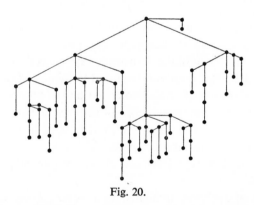

Fig. 20.

The genotype images of the adjective $\{R_3 R_i^n O\}$, verb $\{R_1 R_i^n O\}$ and adverb $\{R_4 R_i^n O\}$ are obtained in a similar way. Like macro-families they are also 'ideal' R-structures.

Unlike deverbal, deadjectival, denominal, and deadverbal sections of Russian lexicon (macro-families) the derivative complexity of the principal parts of speech is distributed in an almost reverse order. The most complex is the noun, second in complexity is the adjective, third – the adverb and the last is the Russian verb.[16]

---

[16] See their graphic representations in Semiotica II, 1970, 1, pp. 75–76.

The entire image of the derivational structure of Russian lexicon can be obtained by adding up either the genotype images of the noun $\{R_1 R_i^n O\}$, verb $\{R_2 R_i^n O\}$, adjective $\{R_3 R_i^n O\}$ and adverb $\{R_4 R_i^n O\}$ or by adding up the genotype images of macro-families $\{R_i^n R_1 O\}$, $\{R_i^n R_2 O\}$. $\{R_i^n R_3 O\}$ and $\{R_i^n R_4 O\}$. The result should be the same[17].

In conclusion we must say that the relator-language of the applicational generative model helps to solve some crucial questions of derivatology, e.g. semantic and formal identification of derivational morphemes, direction of derivation, etc. However, this subject deserves special consideration and is treated in another paper.[18]

SUMMARY

(1) By a linguistic model we mean an artificial semiotic system simulating natural languages. An artificial semiotic system is a well-defined mathematical object used for the study of natural languages, which are not well-defined objects in the mathematical sense.

The object of study in this paper is the derivational structure of Russian lexicon. The means of study is the relator language of the applicational generative model.

The derivational structure of Russian lexicon is described in terms of units split into genotype and phenotype concepts.

(2) The elementary unit of the derivational system is the derivational step, which is defined on the genotype level as the joining of a function to its argument (the operation of application) and on the phenotype level as the joining of a class of formants to a class of underlying words.

(3) The secondary unit of the derivational level is the derivational structure of a word which is defined as a finite set of derivational steps generating an R-word on the genotype level and classes of phenotype words on the phenotype level.

The number of L-classes simulated by a genotype R-word is inversely dependent upon the number of relators in the R-word.

(4) There are two tertiary units: word-families and word-series. A word-family is defined as a finite set of derivational structures with identical first derivational steps. A word-series is defined as a finite set of derivational structures with identical final derivational steps. Both units are split into

---

[17] See the graphic representation of the derivational structure of the Russian lexicon in Semiotica II, 1970, 1, p. 76, obtained by adding up the genotype images of the Russian noun, verb, adjective and adverb.

[18] See P. A. Soboleva, *моделирование словообразованиц, проблеми структурной линг-вистики*, 1971, Москва 1972, pp. 165–212.

genotype and phenotype counterparts with a one-to-many correspondence between them.

There is also an inverse dependence between the complexity of tertiary genotype units, which are called R-structures (R-families and R-series) and the number of R-families and R-series they simulate.

(5) The largest units of the derivational level are macro-families and macro-series. In languages with four principal word-classes: nouns, verbs, adjectives and adverbs there are four macro-families – $\{R_i^n R_2 O\}$, $\{R_i^n R_1 O\}$, $\{R_i^n R_3 O\}$, $\{R_i^n R_4 O\}$ and sixteen macro-series – $\{R_2 R_1 R_i^m O\}$, $\{R_2 R_2 R_i^m O\}$, $\{R_2 R_3 R_i^m O\}$, $\{R_2 R_4 R_i^m O\}$, $\{R_1 R_2 R_i^m O\}$, $\{R_1 R_1 R_i^m O\}$, $\{R_1 R_3 R_i^m O\}$, $\{R_1 R_4 R_i^m O\}$, etc. A macro-family (macro-series) is a set-theoretical sum of all the R-structures simulating phenotype word-families (word-series) of a given type.

(6) By hierarchical organization of the derivational level we mean:

(a) Inclusion of lower-rank units in higher-rank units. Above, the system of such inclusions has been shown through the hierarchy: derivational step $\supseteq$ $\supseteq$ derivational structure $\supseteq$ word-family (word-series) $\supseteq$ macro-family (macro-series);

(b) Organization of the units within the same rank according to their degree of complexity, either from simple to complex, as was shown through the ordering of word families, or from complex to simple, as was shown through the ordering of word-series.

(7) Analysis of genotype macro-families shows that the greatest variety of derivational structures is generated by the Russian verb, (hence its generative capacity is the greatest), second in this respect is the adjective, third – the noun, and fourth – the adverb.

(8) Analysis of genotype macro-series and their set-theoretical sums – genotype images of the Russian noun, verb, adjective and adverb shows that the Russian noun has the greatest variety of generated structures. Second in this capacity is the adjective, third, the adverb and last, the verb (see Semiotica II, 1970, N1).

Soviet Academy of Sciences, Moscow

H. RÄTSEP

ON DEEP SITUATIONS AND SENTENCE PATTERNS

(1) The study of semantics in modern linguistics has recently made progress both in depth and in breadth. At the same time, its point of departure has often consisted of some mere isolated facts drawn from concrete language matter on the basis of which, and for the interpretation of which, attempts have made to create new theoretical conceptions. Due to certain circumstances, the points of view presented in the present article have a somewhat different origin. We have proceeded from the analysis of a rather extensive material on Estonian sentences. Only the gradual development of the analysis has brought us to the conclusions presented here.

Our first aim was to fix the formal patterns of the Estonian simple sentences by proceeding from the verb and verbal government structures as the central elements of the sentence (details: Rätsep, 1969). The gradual generalization and classification of numerous sentence patterns and elements recurring in them inevitably lead us to a more extensive consideration of semantics. A different sentence pattern usually corresponds to each meaning of a polysemic verb, while the opposite is not always obligatory, i.e. a different lexical meaning need not correspond to each sentence pattern. It has sometimes been said that a different structural meaning corresponds to each sentence pattern.

In the final analysis it was revealed that a conclusive description of the material and interpretation of the results is possible only when the so-called deep situations which form the basis for sentence patterns and which also group them are taken into account. Such an approach was conditioned by a reliance upon the extensive material of one specific language and by the directing influence of the ideas and concepts of generative grammar.

(2) Thus, a closer examination of the structure of the Estonian sentence has brought us to the conclusion that besides a purely formal characterization, formal sentence patterns, an essential role is played in the formation of sentences by the meanings of words and by the abstract situations which form the basis for them (and through them the basis for the sentence as a whole).

We understand a situation to be a certain state or action in reality and an idea or generalization of it; certain objects participate in this situation and the situation has certain relevant features.

Natural languages take into account and present information about various kinds of situations.

F. Kiefer (ed.), Trends in Soviet Theoretical Linguistics, 105–122. *All Rights Reserved.*
Copyright © 1973 by D. Reidel Publishing Company, Dordrecht-Holland.

First of all, the text provides information about the *communicative situation* in which the text is conveyed. The communicative situation is a state which is conditioned by the particular message being transmitted. In Estonian, the essential relations seem to be those which exist between such components of the communicative situation as the source of the message (the person from whom the message originates), the informer (the person conveying the message), the recipient, the object of the message (the person or object spoken about), the location of the informer and the receiver, and also the relations between these components and the agent of the action presented in the message. Certain grammatical forms and lexical elements provide information about these relations.

We have explained elsewhere (Rätsep, 1971) that a certain feature in the communicative situation is characteristic of the so-called obviative mood and intermediary imperative in Estonian. Namely, the fact that the source of the message and the informer are different persons. For example, let us compare sentences (1) and (2) with sentences (3) and (4).

(1)   Ma minevat täna õhtul professori juurde.
        'I am said to be going to the professor tonight'.
(2)   Ma mingu täna õhtul professori juurde.
        'I have been told to go to the professor tonight'.
(3)   Ma lähen täna õhtul professori juurde.
        'I am going to the professor tonight'.
(4)   Mine täna õhtul professori juurde!
        'Go to the professor tonight!'

In the first sentence the verb is in the so-called obviative mood and here the message does not come from the speaker, the informer himself (from me), but from a certain third person, while in the third sentence the speaker (I) is the source of the message. In the second sentence the verb is in the so-called intermediary imperative (by the way, the intermediary imperative is as yet absent from the verb paradigms in Estonian grammar books) and denotes the fact that the order has not come from the informer himself. The source of the order is a third person. In the fourth sentence, the speaker, informer and the source of the order are identical. In general, we may state that in all moods except the obviative and the intermediary imperative the source of the message and the informer are identical in Estonian.

On the basis of such an analysis we have reached the conclusion that it would be reasonable to join the obviative mood and the so-called intermediary imperative of Estonian into one category form – the intermediary manner of communication or indirectal. The indirectal would thus be opposed to the other category form of the manner of communication – the direct manner of communication or directal – on the basis of the fact that the informer is not identical with the source of the message. All other traditional moods would belong to the directal. The intermediary manner of communication consists of two moods: the indicative (earlier called the obviative mood) and the imperative (the so-called intermediary imperative). The category of the manner of communication is not the only one directly connected with the communicative situation. The differentiation of separate forms of the category of person is also directly connected with the information about the communicative situation.

Concrete sentences often provide information about *concrete action situations*. This is obvious in sentences (5), (6).

(5)   Peeter sõitis eile rongiga Tallinna.
        'Yesterday Peter went to Tallinn by train?

(6)   See raamat on mul juba olemas.
        'I have got that book already.'

Each language has its own means of expressing situations concretely. In the Estonian language an essential role is played by the pronouns, proper nouns, means for the topicalization of the time and place, etc. while the whole context (linguistic or extralinguistic) surrounding the sentence may also refer to the concrete situation.

If we 'detopicalize' the sentence presenting a concrete action situation, i.e., if we eliminate from the sentence everything that refers to concrete single objects and refer to concepts only, the result is an *abstract action situation* which all languages have means for rendering. For instance, sentences (7) and (8) present abstract action situations.

(7)   Üliõpilased õpivad ülikoolides.
        'Students study at universities.'

(8)   Koer on koduloom.
        'The dog is a domestic animal.'

(3) In the present paper we shall offer one more situation type which, in principle, is also abstract but is considerably more general than the preceding ones. We shall name abstract situations of this type *deep situations*. Deep situations are directly connected with the structure of languages. They form the basis for the meaning of words and sentences and for surface structure sentence patterns.

We shall deal below with deep situations represented by the verb stems only. The only reason for doing this is that we have been studying sentence patterns with a verb as the central element.

When we establish a sentence pattern in Estonian where *elama* 'live' in the meaning given in sentences (9)–(12) is the central verb

(9)   Kirjanik elas mere ääres.
         'The writer lived by the seaside.'

(10)   Kirjanikke elab pealinnades.
         'Some writers live in capital cities.'

(11)   Diogenes elas vaadis.
         'Diogenes lived in a tub.'

(12)   Eideke elas alumisel korrusel.
         'The old woman lived on the ground floor.'

we get

$$\frac{\{\text{N}+\text{nom.}\sim\text{N}+\text{part.}\}\ \text{V Loc}}{\text{V}=\text{elama 9}, \ldots,}$$

where N – noun, nom. – nominative, part. – partitive, V – verb, Loc – a substitution class referring to the static place where one finds oneself, $\sim$ denotes substitution relations between two elements in the sentence pattern (details: Rätsep, 1969).

When we begin to generalize these concrete sentences, having in mind the sentence pattern and considering 'living' in the meaning that occurs in these sentences to be the central element, we reach a very general situation which can form the basis for all such cases of living. The essential components in such a situation are the dweller who lives somewhere and the residence – the place where somebody lives. Thus, first we obtain the situation LIVING as the basis for *elama 9*, the relevant components of which are DWELLER and RESIDENCE:

LIVING {DWELLER, RESIDENCE}

(capital letters are always used to designate names of situations and components).

But such a generalization is probably not sufficient, since one element of the sentence – the verb – is actually preserved in a less general form. Here again one should proceed in a more general direction. This is indicated already by the sentence pattern, where the members of V (i.e. a certain verb class) comprise not only *elama 9*, but also, e.g. *asuma 9* (in sentences (12), (13), *elunema* (in sentences (14), (15), *elutsema* (in sentences (16), (17)).

(12)   Perenaine asus eraldi korteris.
         'The landlady lived in a separate flat.'

(13)   Indiaanlased asuvad ürgmetsades.
         'Indians live in primeval forests.'

(14)   Ürginimesed elunesid koobastes.
           'Primitive men lived in caves.'

(15)   Põgenikud elunesid suurte puude all.
           'The fugitives lived under big trees.'

(16)   Theodor elutses osmikus.
           'Theodor lived in a hut.'

(17)   Kunstnik elutses köögis.
           'The artist lived in a kitchen.'

To put it briefly, we must generalize the action and state itself just as we
did with the components of the situation. The result is a still more general
situation which covers a whole class of situations, which we shall call a
deep situation. In the case of the verbs given above, the deep situation is
obviously the situation that denotes location in a certain place. Its essential
components are the resident, the person who resides somewhere and the
place itself – where the person resides. We could represent the deep situation
in the following way

LOCATION {RESIDENT, PLACE}.

It seems that it is possible to reach such a deep situation for all verbs.
In addition, it is obvious that the number of such deep situations is considerably smaller than the number of the meanings of the verbs.
In the following we shall attempt to draw some more general conclusions,
taking into consideration what has been said above.

There must be a certain action or state whose generalization is an abstract
situation – corresponding to each lexical meaning. Such a deep situation
does not exist in an isolated form but is either directly or indirectly connected with various levels of the formation of sentences and, as will be seen
later, it plays an important role in the fixation of sentence patterns.

Deep situation itself is a notion of a certain very general action or state
and in the present case, it is the central, determining concept. Components
of such situations are concepts which in the case of this deep situation are
essential, relevant, and whose peculiarity is determined by their function in
the situation (action, state).

As the components of deep situation are general notions, they should be
considered to be classes of notions which may have many members. The
residents may be quite different, but they are all joined into one class by the
fact that in the given deep situation they play the role of the person residing
somewhere. The same applies to the members of the class of residence.

It follows from the above comments that a given deep situation need not be the basis for one word, it usually forms the basis for a whole group of words, since we have to do with a generalized action or state.

Deep situation itself does not become evident in the same way as all the words for which it forms the basis. It seems that all situation components need not be expressed and in some cases cannot be expressed in a concrete sentence. In this sense, deep situation is more complete than the sentence. What is expressed in a sentence and what is not is determined by the rules of the sentence patterns of the respective language and the will of the speaker.

For example, let us try to find deep situations for the verbs *andma 19* 'give' and *ulatama 2* 'pass, hand', which occur in sentences (18)–(21),

(18)   Poiss andis õpetajale raamatu lugeda.
         'The boy gave the teacher a book to read.'

(19)   Vaba käega andis külaline arve ametniku kätte.
         'With his free hand the guest gave the bill to the clerk.'

(20)   Poiss ulatas õpetajale oma raamatu.
         'The boy handed his book to the teacher.'

(21)   Mees ulatas kepi üle plangu sõbrale.
         'The man handed the stick over the fence to his friend.'

In the case of sentences (18), (19) the deep situation seems to be

GIVING {GIVER, RECEIVER, OBJECT OF GIVING,
        INSTRUMENT, PLACE, POINT OF
        DEPARTURE, DESTINATION, HINDRANCE,
        AIM},

where GIVER is the person who gives; RECEIVER – the person who in the course of giving gets something from the GIVER; OBJECT OF GIVING – what the GIVER gives to the RECEIVER; INSTRUMENT – part of the body or an instrument by means of which the GIVER gives the OBJECT OF GIVING to the RECEIVER; PLACE – the place where both the GIVER and RECEIVER are located; POINT OF DEPARTURE – the place where the GIVER or/and the OBJECT OF GIVING are situated; DESTINATION – the place where the RECEIVER is located; HINDRANCE – the hindrance, over or through which the giving takes place; AIM – a secondary action or state in the name of which GIVING takes place.

As we can see, not all situation components are expressed in sentences (18) and (19), but they may be expressed there in certain combinations and forms – according to the will of the speaker. The form is determined by the sentence pattern, not the deep situation.

When we carry out the same procedure of generalization on the verb *ulatama 2*, the preliminary situation is as follows

HANDING{HANDER-OVER, RECEIVER, OBJECT OF
HANDING, INSTRUMENT, PLACE, POINT
OF DEPARTURE, DESTINATION,
HINDRANCE, AIM}

Since the grade of generalization of such a situation is too low, we must find a more general counterpart to it. It seems that the deep situation of GIVING is best suited for the purpose. Thus, we may substitute the more general GIVING for the detailed and more concrete HANDING.

Variations may occur in a deep situation. Situation variants differ as regards which situation components are essential in the case of a certain concrete action and which are not. A direct result of this is a variation in the meaning of the corresponding word. In the case of *andma 19* and *ulatama 2*, the main difference lies in the fact that in the latter case the difference in the location of GIVER and RECEIVER is essential. This is referred to by the components POINT OF DEPARTURE AND DESTINA-TION, while in the case of *andma 19*, RECEIVER and his location (DES-TINATION) are more essential – the action is directed at them.

The most complete variant of a deep situation is regarded as the main variant of this deep situation, and by proceeding from it we can describe the differences between other variants.

The representation of the deep situation in surface structure takes place according to the rules of the given language. By virtue of these rules, some components may under certain conditions never be realized, others must always be realized, while some of the components may coincide in a certain surface structure element.

The comparison of the deep situations thus obtained and the division of them into groups on the basis of similar features in them, perhaps even some kind of fixation of archesituations, seems to constitute a different problem.

Quite obviously, no similarity can be detected between the deep situations LOCATION and GIVING presented above. A certain similarity may well be observed between the deep situations GIVING, CARRYING and IN-FORMATION. Let us compare the components of these situations.

GIVING {GIVER, RECEIVER, OBJECT OF GIVING,
INSTRUMENT, PLACE, POINT OF

DEPARTURE, DESTINATION, HINDRANCE,
AIM}
INFORMATION {INFORMER, RECEIVER, TEXT,
OBJECT OF INFORMATION,
INSTRUMENT, CODE, PLACE, POINT
OF DEPARTURE, DESTINATION,
HINDRANCE}
CARRYING {CARRIER, RECEIVER, OBJECT OF
CARRYING, INSTRUMENT, PLACE, POINT
OF DEPARTURE, DESTINATION, WAY,
AIM}

The deep situation of GIVING has been explained above.

In the deep situation INFORMATION, information is conveyed from INFORMER to RECEIVER, whereas TEXT is the material rendered and OBJECT OF INFORMATION is what (whom) the information is about. INSTRUMENT may be either a technical instrument or, for example, the human voice, CODE is a certain system of signs. PLACE denotes the area where INFORMER and RECEIVER are located, POINT OF DEPARTURE is the area of the location of INFORMER and DESTINATION is the area of the location of RECEIVER. HINDRANCE is an obstacle in the way of the transmission of the message.

The information situation forms the basis for verbs of saying. Details from the point of view of situation analysis are given in Rätsep (1973), where 'action situation' is still used instead of 'deep situation'.

In the case of CARRYING, an object – OBJECT OF CARRYING is carried (taken) from one place (POINT OF DEPARTURE) to another (DESTINATION) to somebody (RECEIVER) by CARRIER, while it is essential for CARRIER or/and INSTRUMENT to move together with OBJECT OF CARRYING. Therefore, POINT OF DEPARTURE is here the original location of OBJECT OF CARRYING, CARRIER and IN-STRUMENT, while DESTINATION is their final place of location. IN-STRUMENT is usually a vehicle. WAY is a way or area along which the carrying takes place. AIM is a secondary action or state for the sake of which CARRYING is performed and in which OBJECT OF CARRYING participates after the carrying.

The deep situation CARRYING is the basis for the verbs of the type *viima, tooma, vedama*, as in sentences (22)–(24).

(22)   Ma viisin haigele haiglasse apelsine.
         'I took some oranges to a patient in the hospital.'

(23)   Ma toon sulle apelsine.

'I shall bring some oranges to you.'

(24)   Jaan vedas vilja kuivatisse kuivama.
'John transported the grain to the drying-room (to dry).'

If we compare the deep situations of GIVING, INFORMATION and CARRYING, we can see that they have rather much in common. In all of them there is an object (be it an object, person or information) whose location is changed, while in all three cases the change is connected with two persons and an instrument (a vehicle) which directly changes the location of the object. Nothing new is created in this action (no new object or quality), only the location changes (sometimes the owner together with it, too). We could create a still more generalized archesituation for these deep situations. TRANSFERING would cover GIVING, CARRYING and INFORMA-TION, and in addition several other deep situations such as, for example, TAKING.

This archesituation together with its components could be represented in the following way.

TRANSFERING {TRANSFERER, RECEIVER, OBJECT
               OF TRANSFERING, INSTRUMENT,
               LOCATION, POINT OF DEPARTURE,
               DESTINATION}

where TRANSFERER is the person who transfers OBJECT OF TRANS-FERING from POINT OF DEPARTURE to DESTINATION to RE-CEIVER by means of an INSTRUMENT (part of the body, vehicle, etc.). PLACE is the area in the limits of which the transfer occurs.

Such an archesituation of TRANSFERING is easily comparable with the situation of LOCATION if we generalize the latter deep situation into an archesituation covering several other deep situations as, for instance, SITTING, STANDING, etc.

It turns out that not all components of deep situations belong to the components of the archesituation. Components of a deep situation fall into general components that are also present in the archesituation and specific components which are characteristic (only or first and foremost) of this deep situation and are absent from the archesituation.

The situation MOVING will be presented as the third local archesituation.

MOVING {MOVER, POINT OF DEPARTURE,
          DESTINATION, PLACE, INSTRUMENT}

where MOVER is the person who moves from POINT OF DEPARTURE to DESTINATION by means of the INSTRUMENT or without it, PLACE is the area in the limits of which the moving happens.

All verbs of motion belong to this archesituation, e.g. *minema* 'go', *lendama* 'fly', *ujuma* 'swim', *kukkuma* 'fall', *tõusma* 'rise', *veerema* 'roll', etc.

It seems to be reasonable to suggest that the final establishment of archesituations is possible only through an analysis of large amounts of language material.

On the other hand, we cannot leave unmentioned, even in the case of the archesituations under treatment, that certain relations in language and speech originate in archesituations or deep situations.

Several relations of dependence between the words in the sentence may thus be traced back to the relations between the components of the deep situation and the concept of situation itself. For instance, the dependence on the verb *ulatama* in the sentence *Poiss ulatas õpetajale raamatu* 'The boy handed a book to the teacher' certainly represents certain relations occurring in the deep situation.

Naturally, this does not apply to all relations of dependence in the sentence. Each word in the sentence has its own deep situation with its own situation components. Thus, each lexical word in the sentence may represent both the situation component and the concept of situation. In each simple sentence one notion of situation is central while others are subjected to it. For example, in sentence (25)

(25)   Õpetajale raamatut ulatav poiss seisis akna juures.
        'The boy who was handing a book to the teacher was standing
        at the window.'

the words *ulatav* and *poiss* play a certain role in the representation of the components of two deep situations simultaneously. *Poiss* is the expression of TRANSFERER of the deep situation TRANSFERING and that of RESIDENT of the deep situation LOCATION in surface structure. *Ulatav* is at the same time the representation of the situation notion TRANS-FERING and of a certain component of the situation BOY in the sentence.

From the above deep situations it should be clear that causality originates in the corresponding deep situations. Several other deep situation pairs similar to MOVING and TRANSFERING could be presented here, e.g. ORIGINATION and CREATION, CHANGE (intrans.) and CHANGE (trans.).

(4) What is the relationship between the meaning of the verb and the deep situation? Obviously the level on which the meanings of words are formed, is higher than the deep situation level, i.e., it is somewhat closer to surface structure.

In surface structure the deep situation is realized as a sentence, word combination or a separate word. Therefore, the expression of the central notion of the deep situation on the level of word meaning and higher may be rather different in different cases.

Depending on the language, the components of the deep situation may be expressed in separate words which are dependent on the central word of the sentence. In such a case the meaning of the central word of the sentence or word combination is general and closest to the notion of deep situation.

But some of the components of the deep situation may also be represented in the word representing the notion of deep situation as one element of the meaning of the word. At the same time, this component of the deep situation is often made concrete, i.e., the component is not represented as a general notion but as a certain member of the notion class. We shall offer one example. How is the deep situation

COVERING {COVERER, OBJECT OF COVERING,
　　　　　　　MATERIAL FOR COVERING, INSTRUMENT
　　　　　　　FOR COVERING, PLACE OF COVERER,
　　　　　　　PLACE TO BE COVERED ON OBJECT OF
　　　　　　　COVERING}

realized in Estonian?

The realizations of this deep situation on the level of word meaning are numerous, depending on which notions from among the situation components (as members of the notion classes) are chosen and on the way in which the latter are realized in the semantics of the words.

When we realize the deep situation notion COVERING in the meaning of the word *katma* we evidently encounter a situation where the central word of the sentence renders only the deep situation notion, while the components of the deep situation notion are expressed in the sentences in separate words depending on that central word. For example, in sentence (26)

(26)　　　Ema kattis laua laudlinaga.
　　　　　'Mother covered the table with a table-cloth.'

ema 'mother' represents COVERER, *kattis* 'covered' COVERING, *laua* 'the table' OBJECT OF COVERING and *laudlinaga* 'with a table-cloth' MATERIAL FOR COVERING. In sentences (27) and (28)

(27)　　　Meister kattis kastikese väljastpoolt kullaga.
　　　　　'The craftsman coated the outer side of the box with gold.'

(28)　　　Meister kattis kastikese töökojas kullaga.
　　　　　'The craftsman coated the box with gold in the workshop.'

meister 'the craftsman' represents COVERER, *kattis* 'coated' COVERING, *kastikese* 'the box' OBJECT OF COVERING, *kullaga* 'with gold' MA-TERIAL FOR COVERING; in sentence (27) *väljastpoolt* 'from the outside' PLACE TO BE COVERED ON OBJECT OF COVERING and in sentence (28) *töökojas* 'in the workshop' PLACE OF COVERER. In sentences

(29)   Pintsel kattis puupinna värviga.
         'The paint-brush coated the wood surface with paint.'

(30)   Ema käed katsid lapse tekiga.
         'Mother's hands covered the child with a blanket.'

pintsel 'the paint-brush' and *käed* 'hands' represent INSTRUMENT FOR COVERING.

The Estonian language allows (in some cases) certain deep situation components to be realized in a concrete form (i.e., not general notions but some of their concrete members) in the word which also represents the situation notion. Let us compare, for example, sentences (31)–(33) with the ones above

(31)   Meister kuldas kastikese väljastpoolt.
         'The craftsman gilded the outer side of the box.'

(32)   Meister kuldas kastikese töökojas.
         'The craftsman gilded the box in the workshop.'

(33)   Pintsel värvis puupinna.
         'The paint-brush painted the wood surface.'

In the latter cases certain concrete representatives of the situation component MATERIAL FOR COVERING (GOLD, PAINT) have been added to the meaning which represents the deep situation notion itself, and the result is that we get the quite new word meanings 'to gild', 'to paint'. Certain derivation processes in the construction of the form of words also represent such a semantical operation.

In the case of Estonian the same procedure may be performed on some members of the situation component INSTRUMENT FOR COVERING. For example, in sentence (34)

(34)   Meister pintseldas pinna värviga.
         'The craftsman brushed the surface with paint.'

the concrete member of the situation component INSTRUMENT FOR COVERING – PAINT-BRUSH (PINTSEL) – has been added to the meaning representing the situation COVERING. The result is a new meaning 'pintseldama – to brush.'

Still, it should be emphasized that the expression of the situation component in the form of an element of the meaning of the central word need not be revealed in the form of the word; it need not be clear that the word is a derivative. This is already a question of the composition of the vocabulary of the language concerned.

It is in these possibilities for realizing situation components where the peculiarities of a given language become evident, and this phenomenon can be described rather concretely. We merely have to ascertain for which situation components and in which range such an addition of meanings is possible.

The above examples refer to the fact that the meaning of the word presupposes the existence of a deep situation. The meaning of the word may consist of elements, one of which corresponds to the general notion of situation, while others correspond to the situation components.

Depending on the language, components of the deep situation may be represented in surface structure as separate words alongside with the word representing the situation notion. In this case the meaning of the latter (word) is of a general character and closest to the notion of deep situation. If a situation component is expressed in the same word together with the central notion, the meaning of such a word is considerably more special and detailed, since the added component does not usually represent only a class of notions, but a single notion as well. On the other hand, the more complicated the meaning of the word as regards its composition, the more independent such a word is in the sentence, and the clearer the meaning of the word even when taken separately. If the central word expresses the notion of deep situation only, its meaning is usually vague and becomes clear only in the sentence, where situation components are also represented. Such a word is often polysemic, i.e., its basis may be formed by several deep situations. They can be differentiated only on the basis of a concrete sentence, since it is there that situation components become evident. For example, the meaning of such Estonian verbs as *saama*, 'get, become, receive', *pidama* 'be forced to, keep', *andma* 'give', etc. is not clear outside the sentence. Their meaning becomes evident only in the sentence, where the deep situation (their basis) is clear.

(5) Two factors play an important role in the manifestation of deep situations in surface structure: the will of the speaker and the structure of the language.

First of all, the chosen semantic deep situations are represented on the level of word stems, word meanings are formed, and the question of which lexical units will express this or that component of the deep situation is decided. Only here does it become clear when the expressions of situation components in surface structure are optional and when they are obligatory. The occurrence of optional elements is determined by the will of the speaker.

The formation of words is accompanied by the appearance of the characteristic features of the part of speech, as the differences concerning parts of speech do not become evident in deep situations – they are phenomena which lie closer to the surface. Actually, even the basis of nouns is formed by deep situations which denote certain general actions or states. Whether the central notion in the language is expressed by the noun or the verb, depends on the will of the speaker, on the one hand, and on the structure of the respective language, on the other. Thus, in the Estonian language the deep situation LOCATION presented above is the basis for both the sentence *Kirjanik peatub hotellis* 'The writer stays in the hotel' and such word combinations as *kirjaniku peatumine hotellis* 'the writer's stay in the hotel', *hotellis peatuv kirjanik* 'the writer staying in the hotel', *hotellis peatuja* 'the stayer in the hotel', *peatus hotellis* 'the stay in the hotel', etc. Derivation is also directly connected with the formation of the meanings of words and the appearance of the characteristic features of the parts of speech.

In the sentence, each lexical word is an expression of the central notion of a certain deep situation. Still, in the Estonian simple sentence all other elements are subjected to the centre of the sentence – the verb. Only after the formal accumulation of the elements of the sentence around the centre of the sentence, the verb, do the lexical units acquire the syntactic relations and functions of sentence parts. Lexical units are joined into word combinations according to the thought to be expressed and the structure of the language. Now the concrete language elements acquire a definite grammatical form according to the sentence pattern characteristic of the central verb and the word combination patterns. Context also has a considerable influence, as do the context rules valid for the given language. These rules may allow the omission of some elements, etc.

Let us take a concrete example. Let us observe the formation of the sentence *Juhataja tühjendas laeka paberitest* 'The director emptied the drawer of papers' in Estonian. In this sentence the central word is the verb *tühjendama* 'empty' and its basis may be suggested as the deep situation

CHANGING (transitive) {CHANGER, OBJECT OF
                CHANGING, RESULT, INSTRUMENT,
                PLACE}

where CHANGER is the person who changes, OBJECT OF CHANGING is what is being changed, RESULT – what or like what the OBJECT OF CHANGING is changed to, INSTRUMENT – by means of what CHANGER changes and PLACE – the place where the CHANGER,

INSTRUMENT and OBJECT OF CHANGING are located during the process of changing.

In the course of the concrete expression of this deep situation in Estonian one concrete member TÜHI (EMPTY) of the component RESULT is added to the expression of the central notion CHANGING of the situation and the word meaning 'tühjendama – to empty' is the result. Such an operation is possible in the semantics of the Estonian language. The rules of the Estonian language also allow such a combination to be rendered by a definite formal derivative. But in Estonian there is another possibility: the central notion of the deep situation acquires a general meaning 'muutma – change' and the concrete meaning of the component RESULT is 'tühi – empty'. It is also a rule in Estonian that the real carrier of the meaning 'muutma – change' in such a connection cannot be the verb *muutma* but the verb *tegema* 'do'. So the synonym of the sentence presented above is *Juhataja tegi laeka paberitest tühjaks* 'The director made the chest empty of papers'. Let us now return to the first variant. The equivalent of the meaning 'tühjendama – to empty' in the form of the central word of the sentence is the verb *tühjendama*. Other components of the deep situation are represented on the word level as follows: CHANGER – *juhataja* 'director', OBJECT OF CHANGING – *laegas* 'drawer'. The components INSTRUMENT and LOCATION are not represented in the given sentence due to the wish of the author of the sentence and not because of language rules.

Which component is represented by the word *paberitest* 'of papers' in the sentence? Here we come across quite a characteristic phenomenon in Estonian. The word *paberitest* in this sentence actually represents the component of the deep situation which is the basis for the meaning 'tühi – empty'. We could provisionally consider the word to be the expression of the component ABSENTEE. This becomes quite clear from the fact that the same *paberitest* is also the representative of the component ABSENTEE in the word combination *paberitest tühi* 'empty as to papers' where the central word is *tühi* and it represents an independent deep situation. In the sentence under observation the meaning 'tühi – empty' is included in the meaning 'tühjendama – to empty'. This meaning 'tühi – empty' requires that the component of its basis situation be expressed by the noun in the elative case, this time as a secondary part of the sentence belonging to the verb. Thus, different elements of the meaning of the verb may require different secondary parts of the sentence to the verb, whereas the syntactic subordination relations are determined by the verb as a whole.

Let us now turn to the form of the above sentence. The verb *tühjendama*, the basis of whose meaning is the deep situation CHANGE (we denote it as *tühjendama 1*) presupposes the following sentence pattern:

$$N^1 + \text{nom. V } N^2 + \text{ngp. } (N^3 + \text{el.}) (N^4 + \text{kom.}) \text{ (Loc)}$$
$$N^4 + \text{nom. V} + 3.\text{p. } N^2 + \text{ngp. } (N^3 + \text{el.}) \text{ (Loc)},$$

where N^1+nom. is a noun in the nominative which represents CHANGER,
V – the verb *tühjendama 1* in a certain finite form, V+3.p. – *tühjendama 1*
in the 3rd person only, N^2+ngp. – a noun in the nominative, genitive or
partitive (depending on other factors) which represents OBJECT OF
CHANGING, N^3+el. – a noun in the elative representing ABSENTEE,
N^4+kom. – a noun in the comitative and N^4+nom. – the same noun in
the nominative; they both represent INSTRUMENT while N^4+nom. is the
subject of the sentence; Loc is a substitution class referring to the place
of location (that has been mentioned above) and representing PLACE.
Elements in brackets are optional. Taking the previous example for our
basis, we get the following examples of main variants:

(35)   Juhataja tühjendas laeka. (N^1 + nom. V N^2 + ngp.)
       'The director emptied the chest.'

(36)   Juhataja tühjendas laeka paberitest.
       (N^1 + nom. V N^2 + ngp. N^3 + el.)
       'The director emptied the chest (as to papers).'

(37)   Juhataja tühjendas laeka oma käega.
       (N^1 + nom. V N^2 + ngp. N^4 + kom.)
       'The director emptied the chest with his own hand.'

(38)   Juhataja tühjendas laeka kabinetis.
       (N^1 + nom. V N^2 + ngp. Loc)
       'The director emptied the chest in (his) study.'

(39)   Juhataja tühjendas laeka paberitest oma käega.
       (N^1 + nom. V N^2 + ngp. N^3 + el. N^4 + kom.)
       'The director emptied the chest (as to papers) with his own hand.'

(40)   Juhataja tühjendas laeka kabinetis oma käega.
       (N^1 + nom. V N^2 + ngp. Loc N^4 + kom.)
       'The director emptied the chest in his study with his own hand.'

(41)   Juhataja tühjendas kabinetis laeka paberitest.
       (N^1 + nom. V Loc N^2 + ngp. N^3 + el.)
       'The director emptied the chest (as to papers) in his study.'

(42)   Juhataja tühjendas kabinetis laeka paberitest oma käega.
       (N^1 + nom. V Loc N^2 + ngp. N^3 + el. N^4 + kom.)

'The director emptied the chest (as to papers) in his study with his own hand.'

(43) Käsi tühjendas laeka.
      $(N^4 + \text{nom. V} + \text{3.p. } N^2 + \text{ngp.})$
      'A hand emptied the chest.'

(44) Käsi tühjendas laeka paberitest.
      $(N^4 + \text{nom. V} + \text{3.p. } N^2 + \text{ngp. } N^3 + \text{el.})$
      'A hand emptied the chest (as to papers).'

(45) Käsi tühjendas kabinetis laeka.
      $(N^4 + \text{nom. V} + \text{3.p. Loc } N^2 + \text{ngp.})$
      'A hand emptied the chest in the study.'

(46) Käsi tühjendas kabinetis laeka paberitest.
      $(N^4 + \text{nom. V} + \text{3.p. Loc } N^2 + \text{ngp. } N^3 + \text{el.})$
      'A hand emptied the chest (as to papers) in the study.'

The word order (which is free in Estonian to a certain extent) has not been taken into account in the present sentence pattern. To a certain extent, the word order rules rely on just such sentence patterns. Sentence patterns of this type (with the verb as the central element) establish only the form of sentence elements whose form is directly determined by the meaning of the verb and the deep situation that forms its basis.

Such a sentence pattern may be characteristic of one or several verbs. These verbs may, but need not be, close in meaning. For instance, the sentence pattern of *tühjendama 1* is also characteristic of the verbs *desinfitseerima* 'to desinfect', *vabastama 4* 'to free', *vallandama 3* 'to dismiss'. The reason for heterogeneity usually lies in the fact that components of the deep situation are sometimes expressed in the meaning of the central verb. Thus the sentence patterns of the verb do not reflect only deep situations but also the later stages of the formation of the meaning of the verb.

Thus, deep situations are a certain general basis for the formation of sentences. To what extent the function of one or other situation component determines the grammatical form of the word corresponding to it in the sentence is a question that needs to be studied further on the basis of extensive material. Certain more detailed relations seem to exist.

Such a situation analysis is rather close to the views presented in the so-called case grammar theory (Fillmore, 1968, 1969). The difference is that deep structures are not considered as relations between logical predicates and arguments, but as so-called deep situations, i.e., abstract actions and states generalized from concrete situations. Situation components therefore are much more detailed units than Fillmore's arguments and their cases.

They are notion classes fixed on the basis of a certain function in the given deep situation. Different deep situations comprise different components. Natural languages are more complicated than logical systems. The predicate, two or three arguments and some ten cases are not sufficient for their description.

Tartu University

BIBLIOGRAPHY

Fillmore, Ch. J.: 1968, 'The Case for Case', in *Universals in Linguistic Theory*, New York.
Fillmore, Ch. J.: 1969, 'Types of Lexical Information', in *Studies in Syntax and Semantics. Foundations of Language Supplementary Series* 10, Dordrecht.
Rätsep, H.: 1969, 'On the Form of Government Structure Types of Estonian Simple Verbs', *Annual Meeting of the Research Group for Generative Grammar*, Tartu.
Rätsep, H.: 1971, 'Kas kaudne kõneviis on kõneviis? Verbivormide situatsioonianalüüsi', *Keel ja Struktuur* 5, Tartu.
Rätsep, H.: 1973, 'Government Structure Types of the Verbs of Saying and Action Situations', in *Generative Grammar in Europe* (ed. by F. Kiefer and N. Ruwet), Reidel, Dordrecht-Holland.

HALDUR ÕIM

PRESUPPOSITIONS AND THE ORDERING OF MESSAGES

(1) In (Õim, 1972) I suggested how the functioning of language could be described in linguistic semantics; more precisely, how the act of predication, which is taken to be the basic act underlying the communicative function of language, could be described. In the present paper I want to develop one certain point of this approach which was only briefly touched upon in the paper mentioned above, namely the treatment of actual sentences within the framework of the given approach. At the same time I want to show how a certain explication to one of the most discussed notions of present-day semantics – the notion of presupposition – quite naturally follows from this treatment.

There are few notions more popular in the literature on semantics than the notion of presupposition. One may suppose that the extraordinary interest investigators have shown in this notion somehow reflects the importance of the notion in the functioning of language.

But what is the role of presupposition in the functioning of language? How exactly do the phenomena represented by this notion participate in the activities we carry out by means of language? This is not at all clear. Consequently, the appropriate way to handle the presupposition relation in the semantic descriptions of sentences is also quite obscure. For instance, this relation has been connected with the notion of selection restrictions and with the 'appropriateness conditions' of the corresponding sentences; it has been proposed to treat this relation as a primitive predicate to be contained directly in the semantic representations of the corresponding sentences; and it has been treated as a logical relation between sentences, alongside such relations as entailment and implication.

Attention has mainly been directed towards the logical properties of this notion, not towards its function. This in its turn seems to result from a general striving within generative semantics towards logic; from an inclination to consider language as a certain logical system and nothing more. But such an approach, it seems to me, is too abstract for linguistics. The requirements presented by it are too general. In the context of this approach we are unable to understand or handle in any definite way many facts of language, among them the facts connected with presupposition. In solving concrete problems a situation often arises where many solutions to a problem are logically possible and we are unable to prove the superiority of one solution above the others.

F. Kiefer (ed.), Trends in Soviet Theoretical Linguistics, 123–134. All Rights Reserved.
Copyright © 1973 by D. Reidel Publishing Company, Dordrecht-Holland.

As I have said, in the present paper I want to offer a definitely new treatment of some of the phenomena connected with presupposition, departing from a general approach to semantics in which attention is primarily directed towards the functional aspect of language.

(2) As stated above, the general approach from which I will depart here is described elsewhere (Õim, 1972). Here I will present only the main points of this approach that are significant with respect to the present discussion.

The specific context from the point of view of which I want to discuss the problems of semantics is the context of communication. As I see it, language is above all man's instrument of communication It is this function, first of all, that has shaped the structure and logical properties of language and, accordingly, it is just this function that we should depart from in investigating them. Such a proposal is not very original in itself, of course. The important question however, is, how to specify the notion of communication in linguistics. How useful the corresponding approach will be depends on the definition of this notion.

In the most general terms, I am treating communication as the transformation of particular structures (by the hearer) under the influence of the received messages. And sentences, which we have to describe in linguistics, are the units of this process. It is from this fact that they derive their role as basic units in any language.

What does this 'transforming' concretely consist in, considered on the level of individual sentences? Communication carried out by means of natural language, is, as a rule, about something – about certain objects, persons, places, events, etc. The recipient (the hearer), when he receives a message, should be able to identify the corresponding objects which the message is about – i.e. he should have certain descriptions of these objects in his memory. And receiving a message that tells some new information about them means, from the point of view of the recipient, that he has to modify the corresponding descriptions in a certain way Thus, the semantic description of a sentence, taken from this point of view, should specify at least the following points: (1) what 'objects' the sentence is about, i.e. to the knowledge of which it contributes something; (2) what constitutes the hearer's previous knowledge of each of these objects; (3) what new information about each of these objects the hearer receives from the given sentence and, accordingly, what modifications are to be carried out in the descriptions of these objects.

It should be pointed out that such an 'information processing approach' is generally accepted in computational linguistics (see, e.g., Quillian, 1969; Schwarcz, 1969), but in linguistics proper it has been generally assumed that the linguistic information by itself does not suffice for specifying points (1)–

(3) in the case of a concrete sentence. This is a confusion, I think. The problem is quite parallel, e.g., to that of specifying the truth conditions of sentences: just as specifying the conditions upon which the truth of a sentence depends is quite different from saying whether a concrete sentence is really true or not, specifying points (1)–(3) in the abstract, or logical, sense is also quite different from deciding in a concrete case what the recipient really knows about the corresponding 'objects', what new knowledge he practically can derive from the sentence, etc. Exactly as we can specify abstractly for every individual predicate its truth conditions and from these derive the ones of complex expressions, so it should be possible to determine for every individual predicate, as a part of the description of its meaning, the modifications it carries out in its arguments, when asserted, and to determine the processing of actual sentences departing from the rules associated with individual predicates contained in them. The treatment of single predicates is described in some detail in (Õim, 1972). To give here only a rough example, let us take such a verb as *to awake* If it is asserted about some x that x awoke, x should previously have been identified as having been asleep (in addition to other facts that *to awake* requires from its subject – such as being animate, etc); i.e., x's description should contain the information 'x is asleep'. And the assertion of the predicate *to awake* changes this description into the one where on the place of this information stands 'x is awake'.

I will not try to describe here what the descriptions of such arguments would look like and how their processing should be represented formally, since this is of no principial importance for the treatment of the problems I am interested in here. Some considerations about the nature of the needed formalism will be presented below. Here, I will assume that every predicate represents certain rules for transforming its arguments in a definite way and that the assertion of a predicate means applying these rules. I will concentrate my attention on the question of how the representation of an actual sentence can be built up from the representations of the individual predicates contained in it.

(3) In (Õim, 1972) I emphasized two points in the treatment of actual sentences: first, that in the case of a concrete sentence all the logically possible ways of interpreting it as a message should be described (and not only the most typical or usual one); and second, that in every such interpretation the corresponding sentence breaks up into a number of single messages, and these messages are always ordered in a certain way with respect to each other.

The reason for analysing sentences into elementary messages and for ordering them into a definite sequence lies in the fact that this order represents the order of processing the corresponding arguments in certain elementary steps. For instance, if we take the sentence *The boy hit the ball* and choose among its possible interpretations the interpretation that may be explicitly paraphrased as 'What the boy hit was the ball', then it can be said to represent the following sequence of messages:

(1)   There was a boy.
(2)   The boy did something.
(3)   What the boy did was that he hit something.
(4)   What the boy hit was the ball.

As can easily be seen, proposition (4) presupposes propositions (1)–(3): in fact, this is just the basis upon which they are established. Thus, it is here that the role of presuppositions reveals itself: when we have a certain assertion (as, for instance, (4)), then the role of presuppositions is to provide the information that should be previously known to the recipient in order for him to understand the given assertion; i.e., to provide the information upon which the given assertion will operate. Taken by themselves, presuppositions are nothing but certain messages (=assertions); but they are messages that logically precede (have preceded) the assertion under consideration, and it is only with respect to this assertion that they are presuppositions.

G. Lakoff (1970) has observed that among the presuppositions of a sentence there often exists a definite hierarchical ordering: a given sentence immediately presupposes certain sentences, which represent its first-order presuppositions; these in turn (immediately) presuppose certain other sentences, which represent the second-order presuppositions of the original sentence, and so on. Lakoff has also offered some tests by means of which the first-order presuppositions of a sentence can be distinguished from its higher order presuppositions. First of all, there are constructions called 'qualifications':

(5)   Few men have stopped beating their wives, if any at all have.

'Few men have stopped beating their wives', taken by itself, presupposes that some men have stopped beating their wives, but (5) as a whole does not presuppose it: the qualifying phrase 'if any at all have' has cancelled out this presupposition. Now, the important fact about such qualifying phrases is that they can cancel out only first-order presuppositions, not second or higher order presuppositions. The sentence (6), where the qualifying phrase is made to cancel out a non-first-order presupposition, is quite strange:

(6)   Few men have stopped beating their wives, if any have ever beaten them at all.

Since I am treating presuppositions as previous messages about the corresponding objects, the hierarchies of presuppositions, as established by Lakoff, should logically be the same thing as the sequences of messages which I mentioned above. And it is not difficult to see that they are indeed identical. Moreover, by dealing with the hierarchies of presuppositions it can be shown that the treatment of actual sentences by means of such ordered interpretations as I am offering here is not an artificially established procedure but rather represents the typical way sentences are interpreted in actual communication. Consider the following example:

(7)   The boy hit the ball,
       (a) if anyone hit it at all.
       (b) if he hit anything at all.
       (c) if he did anything at all to the ball.

The sentence (clause) (7) can be followed by any of the qualifying phrases (a)–(c), which means that 'Someone hit the ball', 'The boy hit something' and 'The boy did something to the ball' represent first-order presuppositions of the sentence 'The boy hit the ball'. But, of course, not all at once and in one and the same sense. We cannot add the phrases (a)–(c) to the sentence (7) all at once. Each of these phrases determines a certain interpretation of the sentence (7); and, accordingly, each of the presuppositions corresponding to the phrases (a)–(c) is an immediate presupposition only for one particular interpretation of this sentence. The difference between these interpretations lies in the different orderings of the material contained in this sentence. For instance, the phrase (a) is appropriate, if the sentence (7) is interpreted as 'The one who hit the ball was the boy'; the phrase (b), if (7) is interpreted as 'What the boy hit was the ball', etc.

Note also that each of the phrases (a)–(c) determines a certain possibility for locating emphasis in the sentence (7): for instance, in the case of (a) only *the boy* can be emphatically stressed, not *hit* or *the ball*. As the function of emphasis in such cases is to indicate where the new, lastly asserted information in the corresponding sentence lies, it can be said that in actual communication sentences are always interpreted *in the way that becomes evident in the case of emphasis*: the role of emphasis is not to introduce order into the semantic material contained in a sentence; the order is always there – the role of emphasis is only to indicate this order when it differs from some basic or neutral order in a definite way.

Thus, as is evident from the given context, the relation of presupposition is a kind of order-establishing relation. Morgan (1969) reaches practically the same conclusion:

the relationship between unuttered presuppositions and the sentence with which they are connected is exactly the same as that between a left-conjoined sentence and the conjuncts that follow. By all indications, presuppositions are somehow conjoined to the left of the performative.

The only trouble with such a characterization is that in the usual conception of generative semantics such a left-to-right ordering has no clear theoretical significance: of course, we can write the corresponding propositions in this order, but what will this mean? On the other hand, in the present model the order has an unequivocal significance: this is the order in which the corresponding messages are processed.

Let us now consider in more detail what an ordered semantic treatment of actual sentences consists in. As has been stated earlier the present approach is based on the treatment of individual predicates as presenting definite rules for modifying the information presented by their arguments. In the treatment of an actual sentence every predicate (predicative structure) contained in the sentence should be processed according to the rules that the predicate represents. I.e., in the semantic description of a sentence to every predicate contained in it there corresponds its own message; as a whole, the sentence seems to be a program offered to the recipient for computing new descriptions of certain objects in his memory.

Let us take the following sentence for closer examination:

(8)   The boy took a book from the table.

As has been stated above, the full description of such a sentence consists, first, in determining all the different possibilities of using it as a concrete message and, second, in describing each of these interpretations separately. The sentence (8) apparently represents at least the following different messages.[1]

(9)   Where the boy took a book from was the table.
(10)   What the boy took from the table was a book.
(11)   The one who took a book from the table was the boy.
         etc.

Let us take one of these interpretations and try to establish the sequence of

---

[1] I do not want to consider here the problem of how this should be decided when all the possible interpretations of a sentence are specified. I think some of the general criteria for such a decision can be found by dealing with the second half of the problem: when a certain combination of the material contained in the sentence will determine a different way of processing this material, in comparison with other combinations, and when not. As to the form of the sentences used here for presenting the interpretations, this has been chosen with the intention that from this it could be explicitly seen what the immediately asserted unit of the corresponding sentence is. Note that sentences of this type have been analysed in detail in Halliday (1967).

messages which correspond to it. Let this be the interpretation (10). In establishing the 'previous' messages corresponding to it we can make use of some well-known criteria used in establishing the presuppositions of a sentence, first of all the following one: if B follows logically both from A and the negation of A, then B is a presupposition of A. Thus, we have to take sentence (10) and to establish all the sentences that represent its presuppositions, after which we take these latter sentences and establish their presuppositions, and so on. And in establishing the proper order among these sentences we can use the 'if at all' test (and other tests of this type). The final outcome of such an analysis should be the string of messages that has logically preceded the given message.[2]

Operating as described above we establish in the given case the following sequence of messages:

(a)   There was a boy$_i$.
(b)   The boy$_i$ did something.
(c)   What the boy$_i$ did was that he took something from somewhere.
(d)   There was a table$_j$.
(e)   Where the boy$_i$ took something from was the table$_j$.
(f$=10$)   What the boy$_i$ took from the table$_j$ was a book.

For instance, it is easy to see that both from (f) and from its negation 'What the boy$_i$ took from the table$_j$ was not a book' it follows logically that the boy$_i$ took something from the table$_j$ ($=$e). That this presupposition is an immediate one is revealed by the fact that sentence (12) is possible:

(12)   What the boy$_i$ took from the table$_j$ was a book, if he$_i$ took anything from the table$_j$ at all.

On the other hand, (f) also clearly presupposes, e.g., the sentence (d) – i.e. that there was a certain table. But the strangeness of the sentence (13) shows that this is not a first-order presupposition of (f):

(13)   What the boy$_i$ took from the table$_j$ was a book, if there was a table at all.

Instead, (14) reveals that (d) is an immediate presupposition of (e):

(14)   Where the boy$_i$ took something from was a table, if there was a table at all.

Note that in the above sequence there are messages 'There was a boy$_i$.' and 'There was a table$_j$.' that explicitly introduce the corresponding objects (the

---

[2] I emphasize here the word 'logically'. As has been stated already, this is only a logical description of how the communication has proceeded. No claim is made as to how the corresponding information in reality has reached the hearer.

boy$_i$ and the table$_j$) into the discourse, but there is no message in this sequence that asserts the existence of the third object mentioned in the sentence (10) – the corresponding book. Although it follows from (10) that such
a book should exist, this is not presupposed by (10). From the negation
'What the boy$_i$ took from the table$_j$ was not a book' nothing can be concluded
about the existence of a particular book.

As the above list shows, the sequence of messages which correspond to a
sentence is generally not strictly linear. The sequence starts with a certain
'line' (here, the 'boy$_i$-line'), but as the sequence proceeds, certain new 'lines'
may appear. For instance, in the given case the message (d) introduces a
new line – the 'table$_j$-line', which in the next message (e) joins the former
'boy$_i$-line'. If in the sentence (10) there were more NP's in the nonassertive
position than just the NP's *the boy$_i$* and *the table$_j$*, then there would also be
more such 'lines'; and if, for instance, *the table$_j$* had some attributes,
its 'line' would also be longer.

Bearing in mind that we want the sequence (a)–(f) to be a logical description of how all the information contained in (10) can be carried to a
recipient, it is natural to ask whether the messages (a)–(f) exhaust the information a recipient can logically derive from (10). Of course, this is not
the case. Beside the facts presented in (a)–(f), as the recipient understands
it he should also derive the following information from (10):

(g)   The book really existed.
(h)   The book was (previously) on the table$_j$.
(i)   (After the fulfilment of the act described in (10)) the book was
        not on the table$_j$.

It is also evident why these messages remained outside of the earlier list. We
constructed that list on the basis of the presupposition-relation, and although
(g)–(i) follow logically from (10), they are not presuppositions of this sentence. What this means is the trivial fact that there are other logical relations,
besides the relation of presupposition, which are also involved in interpreting
the sentences in communication.

Nevertheless, this fact does not contradict the idea of a linear treatment
of sentences. It only means that we should not rely strictly on the relation
of presupposition when we establis the sequences of messages which correspond to actual sentences.

The semantic relation involved in the given case is apparently what has
been called implication (in its weaker sense).[3] Since it is clear that the mes-

---

[3] See (Karttunen, 1970a, 1970b). The relation is defined as follows: A implies B if and
only if, whenever A is true, B is also true. It has also been called semi-entailment, as
Karttunen reports (Karttunen, 1970b).

sages (g)–(i) have a quite definite influence upon the information that ulti-mately will hold about the objects mentioned in the sentence (10), we have to include them in the sequence of messages which correspond to this sen-tence. But since they are not presuppositions, they cannot precede the assertion proper of the sentence, but should follow it; i.e., the operations represented by them will be carried out only after the assertion proper has itself been processed. Such a treatment is in full agreement with the properties of the relation under consideration, in particular, with the fact that when the sentence (10) is negated, the messages (g)–(i) no longer follow from it. As the negation of (10) means (among other things) that the operations corre-sponding to its assertion proper (f) will not be carried out, it is natural that the given messages cannot be processed either.

(4) Let us now turn to the questions raised in Section 2. How will the given treatment answer these questions?

First, what 'objects' is sentence (10) about? There are three objects whose existence is explicitly asserted in the sequence (a)–(i): the boy, the table and the book. The hearer receives a certain amount of information from the given sentence about each of them. He has to create a description for each of these objects and to modify it, according to how the new information is provided in the sequence.

I do not want to say that only the descriptions of those 'objects' whose existence is explicitly asserted in the corresponding sequence can result from a sentence, but this is clearly one of the criteria. What other criteria should be used is not very clear yet and I will leave this question out of consideration here. (Some of the needed criteria can surely be found if we deal with the anaphora: what types of 'objects' we can refer back to in the course of communication; but this question also needs special study.)

The main point that such a sequence of elementary messages is thought to explicate is related to the questions (2) and (3) above, i.e. how the infor-mation carried by a sentence is added to the descriptions of the corresponding objects. Through the sequence (a)–(i) it is not difficult to follow how the information is gathered in the case of each of the mentioned objects, that is, how every new message adds something to the previously given material. (It must only be taken into account that we conventionally took all the words in the analysed sentence to be elementary; in order to get the complete picture of what is actually going on we should analyse every word into elementary predicates and process every such predicate separately.) In this connection it is important to draw attention to the form of the sentences which present the messages. As has been stated above this form has been chosen, first of all, because it unambiguously reveals the assertion proper of the corresponding sentence. But this form deserves attention in yet another respect. Namely, when we look at the sentences (c), (e) and (f), we observe that the common structure of these sentences is such that the first half the sentence *(What the boy$_i$ did, Where the boy$_i$ took something from, What the boy$_i$ took from the table$_j$)* 'picks out', or 'identifies', a certain variable, while the other half of the corresponding sentence *(he$_i$ took something from somewhere, the table$_j$, a book)* supplies the concrete value to be given to the corresponding variable. This apparently suggests that communication should generally be treated as a process where concrete values are substituted for the corresponding, previously identified variable. Every single message presents an operation of substituting a concrete value for a certain variable. The sequence of messages (a)–(i) represents the sequence of such substitutions which corresponds to the whole sentence (10).

Of course, the 'concreteness' of every such value to be substituted in a concrete case is quite relative. The value may itself have certain aspects that need concretization. But the important fact is that communication can be treated as proceeding through just such a gradual determination of more and more concrete values. In the above case, for example, a certain individual, the boy, is first introduced in (a), and in the second message one aspect of this individual is selected with respect to which the meaning of the word *the boy* itself is not determined and, accordingly with respect to which it is possible to add certain new information – that the boy is involved in a definite activity. The information about this activity is then made more concrete in (c) by saying that the activity consisted in the boy's taking something from somewhere, but, as we see, two new variables appear which in their turn must be concretized: what it was the boy took and where he took it from; and so on.

Furthermore, it must be noted that in the course of the given sequence only one aspect or variable of the concept 'the boy' receives a concrete value. We come to know something only about the activity the given boy was involved in. But many other variables remain unconcretized. We do not know anything, e.g., about his characteristics as a person: how old he is, or how tall, or what kind of character he has, etc. As the communication about the boy proceeds, all these aspects can be given a concrete value. What I want to emphasize is that from the point of view of the present approach there is no difference between the way such variables are connected with the concept of a person and, e.g., the way the 'who', 'what' and 'from where' variables are connected with the concept of taking. In both cases we have to do with certain variables to which concrete values can be (or should be) given in communication. And the former are logically as inseparable from the concept of a person as the latter are from that of taking: just as we cannot imagine a concrete instance of taking without someone who is performing the act of taking, without something that is taken and without some place from where it is taken, we cannot also imagine a concrete person without a definite age, a definite height, a definite character, etc. And, of course, the concept of person is not any exceptional phenomenon in this respect, e.g., in the case of a thing we speak exactly in the same way of its size, shape, weight, etc, or in the case of a motion of its direction, speed, etc.[4]

This brings us to the problem of the form in which the semantic descriptions of sentences should be given in order for these descriptions to satisfy the requirements presented by the described approach. There is quite little I can say about this question here.

The question of the form of the semantic representations of sentences, as understood in the above sense, actually breaks into two questions: (1) what form should the identifying (or argument) structures have that are modified in the course of processing the corresponding messages, and (2) what should the form of sentences as wholes be – the form that could determine the process of modifying, step by step, the corresponding identifying structures. It should be quite clear that the usual phrase structure trees, as they are used in generative semantics, do not suit our purposes. One need only try to imagine, e.g., the tree corresponding to the sentence (8) (or (10)) which we analysed: how could we possibly read out from such a tree the information represented by the sequence (a)–(i)? In my previous paper (Õim, 1972) I have used a form of representation where the presuppositions about a certain object are attached in the form of relative clauses to the index that represents this object and where the processing of the whole tree proceeds from the bottom up. For instance, according to this procedure, the sentence 'The one who hit the ball was the boy' receives the following representation

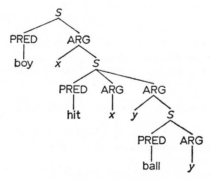

'There was a ball. Someone hit the ball. The one who hit the ball was the boy.'

---

[4] For a little fuller treatment of these questions see Õim, (1971).

It is not difficult to see, however, that such a form of representation is suitable only for the simplest cases. When we take into account the remarks made above about the possible treatment of communication, it becomes especially clear that the simple predicate-argument structures do not offer any adequate means for representing this process. The foregoing discussion suggests instead that something of the so-called attribute-value type of representations would be much better suited to our purposes. It is not a coincidence, I think, that just this form of representation has been used in so many systems of computational linguistics. If we look for some linguistically acceptable formalism that would correspond to this form of representation, we find that among the ones used so far in linguistics Fillmore's case structures come closest to it. The notion of case need only be considerably extended, to be able to include also attributes of the above type (such as 'size', 'shape', 'color' etc. in the case of a thing, or 'age', 'sex', etc. in the case of a person). In the case of such attribute-value structures it would be possible to explicate quite easily the fact that communication consists in substituting concrete values for the variables (attributes) contained in the corresponding concepts and, in particular, the fact that the meanings of most words can be described as structures where the values of certain variables are already given, whereas those of certain others are not and can be supplied in communication.

Tartu University

BIBLIOGRAPHY

Halliday, M. A. K.: 1967, 'Notes on Transitivity and Theme in English II', *Journal in Linguistics*, No. 2.
Karttunen, L.: 1970a, 'Implicative Verbs', *Language*, No. 6.
Karttunen, L.: 1970b, 'Some Observations on Factivity', Paper presented at the 45th Annual Meeting of the Linguistic Society of America in Washington, D.C., December 29, 1970.
Lakoff, G.: 1970, *Linguistics and Natural Logic*, Studies in Generative Semantics No. 1, Phonetics Laboratory, University of Michigan.
Morgan, J.: 1969, 'On the Treatment of Presupposition in Transformational Grammar', *Papers from the Fifth Regional Meeting of the Chicago Linguistic Society*, Chicago, Illinois, pp. 167–177.
Quillian, M. R.: 1969, 'The Teachable Language Comprehender: A Simulation Program and Theory of Language', *Communications of the ACM* 12, 459–476.
Schwarcz, R. M.: 1969, 'Towards a Computational Formalization of Natural Language Semantics', International Conference on Computational Linguistics, Stockholm, Preprint No. 29.
Õim, H.: 1971, 'Predicates, Nouns and Referring Structures', *Abstracts of the Annual Meeting of the Research Group for Generative Grammar*, Tartu State University, Dept. of Estonian Language.
Õim, H.: 1972, in F. Kiefer and N. Ruwet (eds.), 'On the Semantic Treatment of Predicative Expressions', *Generative Grammar in Europe*, D. Reidel Publ. Co., Dordrecht, Holland.

MATI ERELT

SOME REMARKS ON COMPARATIVE
AND SUPERLATIVE SENTENCES IN ESTONIAN

0. GENERAL

Previous studies of the Estonian language have in their descriptions of comparison mainly stressed its morphological side, rather than the syntactic and semantic aspects of comparative and superlative constructions. In this paper we shall try to compensate somehow for this drawback. However, we do not claim to give an exhaustive description of the Estonian system of comparison. We confine ourselves to a mere semantic description of a few sentences of the simplest type.

The general theoretical framework for the following analysis is generative semantics, which we accept, more or less, in the shape presented in the works of McCawley (1967, 1968), Lakoff (1970), and others; the only modifications we expose it to stem from the ideas advanced in Fillmore's case grammar.

We think of grammar as a mechanism which begins its work from the generation of sentences in the form of their semantic representations, or semantic underlying structures. These are presented in terms of semantic elementary predicates which semantically mark elementary relations or properties. Since these predicates are units of the semantic metalanguage, we shall distinguish them from the words of the language described by using capital-letter writing. Elementary predicates are connected with each other in the structure by means of referential indices. Arguments are connected with elementary predicates through definite semantic relationships, called case relationships. Formally we present cases in the same manner as Fillmore, i.e. we record them in semantic representations as independent constituents. Generally, we use the symbols $C_1, ..., C_n$ to represent cases. A case symbol is combined in the structure with the corresponding noun phrase marking the argument and with the symbol K, which denotes formal markers of the case. In order to avoid an excessive use of symbols, we present structures without the symbols PRED and NP, the latter of which marks an argument. Of all cases and their morphological markers, we present only those that are relevant for the description of comparison. We shall not make a separate issue of the derivation of the syntactic structures of sentences. It may be noted that they are derived from the semantic representations of sentences by means of transformations which produce definite combinations

F. Kiefer (ed.), Trends in Soviet Theoretical Linguistics, 135–147. All Rights Reserved.
Copyright © 1973 by D. Reidel Publishing Company, Dordrecht-Holland.

of elementary predicates and then replace the resulting complex predicates
with concrete lexical units.

1. SEMANTIC STRUCTURE OF THE COMPARATIVE
SENTENCE: THE BASIC COMPONENTS.

(1.1) Let us analyse sentences where two concrete objects are compared
with respect to the degree (intensity) of a property, i.e. sentences such as

(1)   *Ants on pikem kui Mart*
         'Ants is taller than Mart',
(2)   *Mart on lühem kui Ants*
         'Mart is shorter than Ants'.

To find out which elementary predicates are needed to represent the semantic
structure of the comparative sentence let us consider what semantically
elementary conclusions can be drawn from it. Sentence (1) allows us to draw
three principal conclusions. First, sentence (1) expresses the fact that both the
object compared, *Ants*, and the standard of comparison, *Mart*, have the
property *height*. This property is expressed by a definite predicate. As the
sentence contains two such objects, the sentence structure must contain two
occurrences of the predicate as well. From the viewpoint of the description
of comparison, the break-up of the predicate is immaterial, so below we
shall assume this predicate to be elementary. We are giving it a conventional
shape 'PIKK' ('tall'), bearing in mind the well-known fact that in certain
contexts the adjective *pikk* may appear in a purely dimensional sense.
Consider, e.g., the sentences

(3)   *Ants on 2 meetrit pikk*
         'Ants is 2 meters tall',
(4)   *Kui pikk Ants on?*
         'How tall is Ants?'.

In order to discriminate this dimensional predicate from the adjective *pikk*
as an implicitly comparative word, we have placed the latter between
apostrophes. Second, sentence (1) implies that both objects have the stated
property to a certain extent which is known to the speaker. In other words,
the objects *Ants* and *Mart* both have a value on the height scale. This kind
of information could be formally presented by simply adding a new argument to the predicate marking the given dimension. Suppose that such an
argument is one connected with the predicate through a special case relationship, QUANTITY. Let this be marked by the symbol Q. The elementary
predicate marking the dimension of height, then, is a two-place predicate
one argument of which is a noun phrase which marks some concrete object

(*Ants* or *Mart* in sentence (1)); and the other argument is a noun phrase which marks the quantity of height of the object and stands in case relationship Q with the predicate. Giving the height quantities corresponding to *Ants* and *Mart* by the symbols q_1 and q_2, we may represent the two occurrences in sentence (1) of the predicate marking the dimension of height as follows:

(5a)   'PIKK' $(x_1 : Ants) \underset{Q\ \ Q}{(q_1)}$,

(5b)   'PIKK' $(x_2 : Mart) \underset{Q\ \ Q}{(q_2)}$.

Third, sentence (1) means that q_1 exceeds q_2. Let this relationship be represented by a two-place comparative elementary predicate

(6)   ROHKEM (q_1, q_2),

where *rohkem* means 'more'. The comparative predicate (6) may be realised in Estonian not only in the form of the adverb *rohkem*, but also as the adverb *enam* 'more', the verb *ületama* 'exceed', the preposition *üle* 'above, over' and also as the adjective *suurem* 'greater'. At any rate, *rohkem* is the best word to convey the purely quantitative idea implied by the predicate (6), while both the verb *ületama* and the comparative adjective *suurem* first and foremost express concrete spatial relations between objects, the abstract intensity relation coming into account only as an accessory meaning. (This is not to suggest, however, that the abstract intensity relationship cannot be reduced to a place relationship in the underlying structure.) Of course the notation here, as for all elementary predicates, is rather arbitrary. Instead of ROHKEM we could as well use the $>$ sign of mathematics, but since everywhere else we make use of concrete Estonian words and not abstract symbols, we shall stick to the same practise here, for the sake of uniformity. As regards the comparison conjunction *kui* 'than', there is no need to treat it as part of an abstract comparative predicate. It is rather better suited for a case marker in the sentence structure.

Now we have sufficient information as to what the semantic elements are that the semantic representation of sentence (1) is make up of, and we may present it in the shape (7):

(7)   ROHKEM $((q_1 (\text{'PIKK'}(x_1 : Ants) \underset{Q\ \ Q}{(q_1)})) K)$
$\underset{C_1}{}$
$((q_2 (\text{'PIKK'}(x_2 : Mart) \underset{Q\ \ Q}{(q_2)})) \underset{C_2}{K})$.
$\underset{C_2}{}$

Along with the elementary predicate ROHKEM we shall introduce the elementary predicate

(8)   VÄHEM (q_2, q_1)

(where *vähem* means 'less') which will be needed for the representation of semantic underlying structures of sentences like

(2)   *Mart on lühem kui Ants.*

See structure (9):

(9)   VÄHEM $((q_2(\text{'PIKK'}(x_2: Mart)(q_2)))\ K)$
           C$_1$ $\phantom{(\text{'PIKK'}(x_2: Mart))}$Q Q C$_1$
           $((q_1(\text{'PIKK'}(x_1: Ants)(q_1)))\ K).$
           C$_2$ $\phantom{(\text{'PIKK'}(x_1: Ants))}$Q Q C$_2$

(1.2) Now let us consider how comparative predicates are related to their arguments. No particular difficulties seem to crop up when the case of the argument marking the object *compared* is to be determined. That which is compared, e.g. in the syntactic structure of sentence (1) the argument *Ants* of the predicate *pikem*, is obviously in the OBJECTIVE, i.e. semantically in the most neutral case of Fillmore's (1968) case system. At least intuition tells us that for the moment such a supposition is the most acceptable.

But what is the case of the other argument? There are several papers where the proximity of comparative constructions to locative constructions has been pointed out in respect to both form and content, and rather con-convincing arguments have been forwarded in support of the view that on a deep enough level of analysis, comparative constructions have essentially the same structure as a certain type of locative constructions (see, e.g., Campbell and Wales, 1969).

As for the semantic side of the matter, it is really hard not to notice a certain similarity between these two types of constructions. To be sure, comparison is most obviously connected with spatial images in the case of so-called space adjectives. But even when the adjective gives no direct reference to any known space dimension, as in the sentences

(10)   *Urve on ilusam kui Virve*
           'Urve is more beautiful than Virve',
(11)   *Tänapäeva automootorid on võimsamad kui varem*
           'The car engines of today are more powerful than before',

there still is reason to believe that the difference between the intensity degrees of the properties of objects is interpreted somehow in spatial terms. As an indication of this, consider the fact that the two last sentences can be para-phrased so as to make the adjective *suur* 'great' appear in the comparative form:

(12)   *Urve ilu on suurem kui Virve ilu*
           'Urve's beauty is greater than Virve's',

(13)   *Tänapäeval on automootorite vôimsus suurem kui varem*
         'Today the power of car engines is greater than before'.

The proximity of comparative constructions to locative ones is also suggested
by data from studies of aphasia: it has been found out that damages in the
occipital lobe of the brain that cause disturbances in spatial orientation and
thus inhibit the understanding of sentences expressing spatial relations like-
wise cause disturbances in the understanding of comparative sentences
(Luria, 1962; Bein, 1957).

Evidently the concept of *place* in linguistics has to be handled as being
much more abstract than is usually done. It need not necessarily be associated
in our mind with the concept of physical space; such treatment of space is,
from the viewpoint of man's mental life, more a particular case than a
general rule. As far as comparative sentences are concerned, it can obviously
be maintained that the case for the second argument of the comparative
predicate, i.e. the argument marking the *standard of comparison*, is some
kind of local case. In our opinion, in the given occasion we are concerned
with the same case which we find, for example, in the noun *aken* 'window'
in the sentence (14) or *maa* 'the country' in the sentence (15):

(14)   *Varblane lendab aknast eemale*
         'The sparrow is flying away from the window',
(15)   *Ma sôitsin maalt linna*
         'I came from the country to town'.

A noun occurring in this case expresses *starting-point*[1], and we call the
corresponding case ABLATIVE. ABLATIVE is a deep case relationship
which need not be (and in Estonian comparative sentences actually is not)
realized in the ablative form in the surface structure. In comparative sentences an argument in the ablative case in the underlying structure appears
on the surface either in the elative, which is a typical case for Estonian comparison, as in the sentences

(16)   *Ants on Mardist pikem*
         'Ants is taller than Mart',
(17)   *Mart on Antsust lühem*
         'Mart is shorter than Ants',

---

[1] Campbell and Wales (1969), too, seem to have taken the position that the standard of
comparison in comparative sentences is to be understood as starting-point. According to
them, a modifier of place connected by means of a suffix of comparison or by the adverb
more should be marked by the following set of features: (+directional, −spatio-temporal,
−to).

or in the nominative, being in the latter instance linked to the predicate by the conjunction of comparison *kui* (sentences (1) and (2)). We regard the conjunction *kui* here as a formal marker of ABLATIVE on a par with case endings and particles. Such a treatment may possibly be an oversimplification; but at least as far as the description of comparison goes it does not cause any contradictions.

Thus, maintaining that the cases of the comparative predicate are OBJECTIVE and ABLATIVE, we could give sentence (1) *Ants on pikem kui Mart* on a certain level of its syntactic derivation the following structure:

(18)   *pikem*   ($(x_1: Ants)$ $(\emptyset)$)   ($(x_2: Mart)$ $(-lt)$).
          OBJ   K K   OBJ   ABL   K K   ABL

The symbols $\emptyset$ and *-lt* denote the typical markers of the cases: $\emptyset$ means the absence of morphological markers. *-lt* is the ending of the (surface) ablative. Transformations will later on replace *-lt* with by either the conjunction of comparison or the elative ending *-st*.

Returning now to the semantic representation of the comparative sentence, it is no doubt clear that the cases required by the comparative form of a particular adjective from its arguments will in that representation become case relationships of the arguments of the elementary predicates ROHKEM and VÄHEM. After all, it is just these predicates that are directly applied to express comparativity. The adjectives themselves or the corresponding dimensional predicates add nothing from this point of view; they rather demand some totally different case relationships from their own arguments. As the cases of the arguments $x_1: Ants$ and $x_2: Mart$ of the predicate 'PIKK' are immaterial from the viewpoint of the description of comparison, we are simply leaving them unmarked in the semantic representation of sentence (1), and the structure takes the shape

(19)   ROHKEM   ($(q_1('PIKK'(x_1: Ants)(q_1)))$ $(\emptyset)$)
              OBJ   Q Q   K K OBJ
          ($(q_2('PIKK'(x_2: Mart)(q_2)))$ $(-lt)$).
          ABL   Q Q   K K ABL

(1.3) Structure (19) corresponds to the comparative sentence (1) expressing the 'superiority' of one object to another in the intensity of some property, height in the given case. The treatment of the situation in reverse in sentence (2) *Mart on lühem kui Ants* is represented (with due consideration to the cases of the arguments) by the underlying semantic structure

(20)   VÄHEM   ($(q_2('PIKK'(x_2: Mart)(q_2)))$ $(\emptyset)$)
              OBJ   Q Q   K K OBJ
          ($(q_1('PIKK'(x_1: Ants)(q_1)))$ $(-lt)$).
          ABL   Q Q   K K ABL

But sentences (1) and (2) actually represent one and the same objective situation. In view of the conception that paraphrases always have an identical underlying semantic structure, it should also be identical for these two sentences; this in turn means that there should be some third predicate which would be semantically more elementary than the predicate ROHKEM and VÄHEM. Yet it is very difficult to find such an elementary predicate as the difference between sentences (1) and (2) is not in the cases of the topicalized arguments (in the sense of Fillmore (1968)) but in the arguments themselves. Unlike, e.g., the sentences

(21)   *Jüri ostis Jaanilt raamatu*
        'Jüri bought a book from Jaan',

(22)   *Jaan müüs Jürile raamatu*
        'Jaan sold Jüri a book',

or sentences in the Active/Passive Voice, in both (1) and (2) the argument in one and the same case, viz. OBJECTIVE, is topicalized.

It seems more sensible to us at the present moment to give up the rigid requirement of identity of semantic representations for paraphrases and to replace it by a more general and at the same time milder requirement of equivalence of semantic representations. The latter would mean that on certain occasions the paraphrase relationship can be regarded as a relationship between sentences whose underlying structures contain different elementary predicates.

We regard comparative predicates such as *pikem – lühem* and the like as so-called converse predicates whose properties are given by the equation

(23) $x_1 \text{ PRED } x_2 = x_2 \text{ PRED}^{-1} x_1$.

Equation (23) shows that converse predicates express one and the same semantic relation between the arguments (x_1 and x_2) but differ in the topicalization of the different arguments.

Taking into account cases of arguments, it appears expedient to discriminate between two types of conversives. The first type is made up of such conversives as meet the equation

(24) $(x_1) \text{ PRED } (x_2) = (x_2) \text{ PRED}^{-1} (x_1)$.
        $\underset{C_1\,C_1}{} \quad \underset{C_2\,C_2}{} \quad \underset{C_2\,C_2}{} \quad \underset{C_1\,C_1}{}$

Examples of this type are *ostma* 'buy' – *müüma* 'sell', active vs. passive predicates, etc. Paraphrases with such predicates arise from identical underlying structures. The other type of conversives we consider to be those predicates whose topicalized arguments are in one and the same case, i.e. those that meet the equation

(25) (x_1) PRED (x_2) $=$ (x_2) PRED^{-1} (x_1).
 $c_1 c_1$ $c_2 c_2$ $c_1 c_1$ $\phantom{PRED^{-1}}$ $c_2 c_2$

The comparative predicates *pikem – lühem, vanem* 'older' – *noorem* 'younger' and the like belong to this group. The conversiveness of this kind of predicates proceeds from the conversiveness of their inherent elementary predicates ROHKEM and VÄHEM, which is indicated by the equation

(26)   ROHKEM $($ $($ x_1 $)$, $($ x_2 $)$ $)$ = VÄHEM$($ $($ x_2 $)$,
 OBJ OBJ ABL ABL OBJ OBJ

 $($ x_1 $)$ $)$.
 ABL ABL

(1.4) Structures (19) and (20) correspond to comparative sentences with so-called *relative* adjectives (to use Katz' (1967) term). Sentences applying the positive degree forms of relative adjectives contain an implicit comparison with the average (or normal) member of the class of objects with respect to a given property; so from the semantic point of view the positive forms of relative adjectives are more complex than their comparative forms. (This fact was pointed out already by Sapir (1949); later, it has been mentioned by Fillmore (1965), and others.) Thus in the sentence

(27)   *Mees on pikk*
         'The man is tall'

it is declared that the height of the man in question exceeds that of an average member of the class of men. Relative adjectives form pairs of antonyms (*pikk – lühike, kallis* 'dear' – *odav* 'cheap', *ilus* 'beautiful' – *inetu* 'ugly', etc.) indicating two opposite poles on the intensity scale of a property (*pikkus* 'height', *hind* 'price', *ilu* 'beauty', etc.). The poles are separated by the point corresponding to the average quantity of the property and by a certain area of indeterminancy on either side of that point. In relative adjectives we are concerned with contrary antonyms, which means that the negation of one member of an antonym pair is not equal to the affirmation of the other one:

(28)   *Mees on pikk* $\neq$ *Mees ei ole lühike*
         'The man is tall' $\neq$ 'The man is not short',

(29)   *Mees ei ole pikk* $\neq$ *Mees on lühike*
         'The man is not tall' $\neq$ 'The man is short'.

The group of relative adjectives is contrasted to that of absolute adjectives (*haige* 'ill', *terve* 'well', *lahtine* 'open', *kinnine* 'closed', *katkine* 'broken', etc.). With absolute adjectives the intensity scale is determined by just one member of an antonym pair (for *haige – terve*, e.g., this member is *haige*) whereas the other member simply defines the end-point of the scale (*terve*). Absolute adjectives form pairs of contradictory antonyms where the negation of one member is equal to the affirmation of the other:

(30)   *Mees on haige = Mees ei ole terve*
         'The man is ill = The man is not well',

(31)   *Mees ei ole haige = Mees on terve*
         'The man is not ill = The man is well'.

Unlike relative adjectives, sentences which apply the positive degree forms of absolute adjectives, such as the sentence

(32)   *Mees on haige,*

contain no implicit comparison, and the comparative forms are semantically secondary with reference to the positive ones.

In comparative sentences with absolute adjectives the pertinent adjective itself serves as the conventional elementary predicate marking a property. For instance, for

(33)   *Ants on haigem kui Mart*
         'Ants is worse than Mart',

HAIGE can be regarded as the elementary predicate. A support for this is that the sentence can be paraphrased into

(34)   *Ants on rohkem haige kui Mart.*

For both the semantic representation is (35).

(35)   ROHKEM ($(q_1(\text{HAIGE}(x_1:Ants)(q_1)))(\emptyset)$)
                          OBJ   Q Q K K OBJ
                   ($(q_2(\text{HAIGE}(x_2:Mart)(q_2)))(-lt)$).
                          ABL   Q Q K K ABL

The predicate HAIGE also shows up in the semantic representation of the sentence

(36)   *Mart on tervem kui Ants*
         'Mart is better than Ants',

since the paraphrase of the latter is

(37)   *Mart on vähem haige kui Ants*

and not the sentence

(38)   *Mart on rohkem terve kui Ants.*

The semantic representation here can be given as (39).

(39) VÄHEM ($(q_2(\text{HAIGE}(x_2:Mart)(q_2)))$ (∅))
           OBJ   Q Q   K K OBJ
      ($(q_1(\text{HAIGE}(x_1:Ants)(q_1)))$ (-lt)).
       ABL   Q Q K K ABL

2. SUPERLATIVE

In order to get a clear-cut idea of the superlative in Estonian, let us first consider an important kind of comparative sentence where one (or several) of the members of a clearly defined group of objects is opposed to the other members of that group. Thereby the place (position as to the quantity) of some object(s) is defined within the group of objects. Comparative sentences of the type just mentioned have been briefly treated by Noreen (1923), but he goes no further than a description of a specific case of this comparison type. Namely, Noreen deals with such sentences where the position of an object is defined in relation to *all* the other members of the group of objects, i.e. sentences like

(40) *Ants on pikem kui kôik teised poisid vôistkonnas*
      'Ants is taller than all the other boys on the team',

(41) *Mart on lühem kui kôik teised poisid vôistkonnas*
      'Mart is shorter than all the other boys on the team'.

Noreen calls such comparison 'definitive gradus superior'; but since exactly the same type of comparison also occurs with 'diminutive' gradation ('gradus inferior' in Noreen's terminology), it would perhaps have been more appropriate to use the general term 'definitive gradus differentiae' to combine both instances.

In fact, the comparison type under discussion covers a considerably wider area than in Noreen's treatment. Besides the above case, where the position of an object is defined in relation to all the other members of the group, there are cases where an object is compared to *many*, a *few*, etc., other members of the group. E.g., see the following sentences:

(42) *Ants on pikem kui môned teised poisid vôistkonnas*
      'Ants is taller than some of the other boys on the team',

(43) *Ants on pikem kui mitmed teised poisid vôistkonnas*
      'Ants is taller than several other boys on the team',

(44) *Ants on pikem kui paljud teised poisid vôistkonnas*
      'Ants is taller than many other boys on the team',

(45) *Ants on pikem kui enamik (suurem osa) teisi poisse vôistkonnas*
'Ants is taller than most (the greater part) of the other boys on the team',

(46) *Ants on pikem kui see (too) teine poiss vôistkonnas*
'Ants is taller than this (that) other boy on the team',

(47) *Ants on pikem kui need teised poisid vôistkonnas*
'Ants is taller than these other boys on the team', etc.

Kôik 'all', as well as *môned* 'some', *mitmed* 'several', *paljud* 'many', *enamik* 'most (of)', *see* 'this', *too* 'that', *need* 'these', etc., are linguistic quantifiers. Surely one can find more of them than has been listed here, and the number of the subtypes of the comparison type grows accordingly.

That comparison takes place inside a group is indicated by the words *teised* and *ülejäänud* 'the rest'. If the group consists of only two objects – as can be concluded from sentence (46) – the corresponding entity is the singular form *teine* 'other'.

What do the underlying semantic structures of sentences such as these which express comparison inside a group look like? Let us try and describe sentence (45) *Ants on pikem kui enamik teisi poisse vôistkonnas*.

Let X be a given area of individuals, a set of objects with the elements $x_1, x_2, ..., x_n$. Let one of the characteristic properties of the listed objects be that they are boys, and the other one – that their 'typical location' is a team. This means that any object x_i of the set X meets

(48) $POISS(x_i)$ & $LOC(x_i, z(VÕISTKOND(z)))$

where LOC denotes an abstract Locative predicate. That predicate takes two arguments and serves to express the location of something in somewhere (or to belonging to a group), which is indicated by the referential index z and defined by the predicate VÕISTKOND 'team'. Let the object x_1 be named *Ants*, i.e. in our denotation system $x_1 : Ants$. Let us split the set X into two subsets: a one-element-set, $\{x_1\}$, and its complementary set, $X - \{x_1\}$. The latter is the set whose members form 'the rest' with reference to the set $\{x_1\}$. The statement that the object x_1, named *Ants* and incorporated in the set $\{x_1\}$, is taller than most of the objects of the set $X - \{x_1\}$, can be represented as

(49) $ROHKEM($ $($ $q_1('PIKK'$ $($ $\underset{x_1 \in \{x_1\}}{x_1}$ $: Ants(POISS(x_1)$
$_{OBJ}$

 & $LOC(x_1, z(VÕISTKOND(z))))))$ $(q_1)))$ $(\emptyset)$ $)$
$_{Q\ Q\ K\ K\ OBJ}$

$(IGA(q_i)$ $('PIKK'(ENAMIK$ $\underset{x_i \in X - \{x_i\}}{(x_i}$ $(POISS$
$_{ABL}$

(49) (x_i) & $LOC(x_i, z(VÕISTKOND(z)))))$ $(q_i)))$
                                                        Q   Q
                         $(-lt)$),
                         K   K   ABL

where IGA means 'every'. This happens to be just the desired representation
of sentence (45).

Let us now return to the type of sentences examined by Noreen, i.e.
sentences with the quantifying predicate *kôik*. That the superlative sentence

(50)   *Ants on kôige pikem poiss vôistkonnas*
         'Ants is the tallest boy on the team'

is a paraphrase of sentence (40) *Ants on pikem kui kôik teised poisid vôistkonnas* is beyond all doubt. Noreen here speaks of two different ways of
expressing one and the same comparison type: the exclusive way, i.e. by
means of the comparative, and the inclusive way, i.e. by means of the superlative. From the semantic point of view superlative sentences are in no way
opposed to comparative ones, as has unfortunately been implied or stated
in a number of grammars. Superlative sentences constitute a definite subtype of comparative sentences. From the point of view of content, the characteristic features of the superlative are the inside-of-class nature of comparison
and the contraposition of one or several members of a class to all the rest
of its members. But formally it is characterized in Estonian first of all through
the use of a special suffix or the use of *kôige* 'the most'. Such formal features,
as we know, are far from being characteristic of all languages, and Estonian,
too, could do without them. It may very well be that it is just this special
form of the superlative that has caused the erroneous opinion that the superlative as compared to the comparative always expresses a 'higher degree'.
Even the term *superlative* as such must be meant to denote, above all, the
corresponding form, since nobody calls (40) a superlative sentence although
in essence it is not different from sentence (50). The whole triade positive,
comparative, superlative is a system only in the morphological, and not
in the semantical, sense. As a matter of fact, this is not particularly new.
The same assertion has been made by Jespersen (1933), Noreen (1923),
Sapir (1949), and a few others. May we quote Jespersen (1933, p. 35), for
instance:

There is a good deal of loose thinking with regard to the degrees of comparison, chiefly because people are accustomed to look upon the three grades strong, stronger, strongest as
standing in the relation 1-2-3 (or 1-2-4), whereas the truth is that the superlative does not
mean more than the comparative, but means the same from a different point of view (*A* is
stronger than *B*, *C*, and *D*=*A* is the strongest of *A*, *B*, *C*, and *D*) and the positive does not
mean less than the comparative.

As a semantic equivalent of the ternary morphological system, only a system of absolute degrees of comparison is conceivable. We are not denying the possible occurrence in Estonian of certain instances of the absolute comparative or absolute superlative; but before one can say something definine about them one must investigate these matters more thoroughly.

The semantic representation corresponding to the superlative sentence (50) and its comparative paraphrase (40) can thus be presented as follows:

(51)   ROHKEM ($(q_1($'PIKK' $(x_1:$ $Ants($POISS(x_1)
          OBJ $x_1 \in \{x_1\}$

          & LOC$(x_1, z($VÕISTKOND$(z)))))$ $(q_1)))$ $(\emptyset)$)
                                                        Q Q K K   OBJ

          $($IGA(q_i) ('PIKK'(KÕIK $(x_i$ (POISS
          ABL $x_i \in X - \{x_i\}$

          (x_i) & LOC$(x_i, z($VÕISTKOND$(z)))))$ $(q_i)))$
                                                        Q Q

          $(-lt)$)   .
          K K   ABL

Tartu University

BIBLIOGRAPHY

Campbell, R. N. and Wales, R. J.: 1969, 'Comparative Structures in English', *Journal of Linguistics* 5, 215–251.

Fillmore, Ch.: 1965, 'Entailment Rules in a Semantic Theory', The Ohio State Univ., POLA Reports No. 10, 60–82.

Fillmore, Ch.: 1968, in E. Bach and R. T. Harms (eds.), 'The Case for Case', *Universals in Linguistic Theory*, New York, pp. 1–88.

Jespersen, O.: 1933, *The System of Grammar*, London, Copenhagen.

Katz, J. J.: 1967, 'Recent Issues in Semantic Theory', *Foundations of Language* 3, 124–194.

Lakoff, G.: 1970, 'Linguistics and Natural Logic', *Studies in Generative Semantics*, The Univ. of Michigan, No. 1.

McCawly, J. D.: 1967, 'Meaning and the Description of Language', *Kotoba no Uchū* 2, No. 9–11.

McCawley, J. D.: 1968, 'Lexical Insertion in a Transformational Grammar without Deep Structure', Papers from the Fourth Regional Meeting of the Chicago Linguistic Society, pp. 71–80.

Noreen, A.: 1923, *Einführung in die Wissenschaftliche Betrachtung der Sprache*, Halle, Saale.

Sapir, E.: 1949, in D. G. Mandelbaum (ed.), 'Grading: A Study in Semantics', *Selected Writings of Edward Sapir*, Berkely, Los Angeles, pp. 124–149.

Бейн, Э. С.: 1957, 'О Некоторых Особенностях Смысловой Структуры Слова и Грамматического Строя Речи Сенсорной Афазии', *Вопросы психологии*, No. 4, pp. 92–101.

Лурия, А. Р.: 1962, *Высшие корковые функции человека*, Москва.

E. V. PADUČEVA

ON THE LOGICAL ANALYSIS OF RUSSIAN
QUANTIFIER ADJECTIVES

§1. QUANTIFIERS IN DEEP STRUCTURES

Contemporary thinking has it that a description of the meaning of a sentence requires reference to its deep structure [1], and, as experience has shown, the deep structure of a sentence is close to its notation in one or another logical language [2]. Quantifiers in particular should be included among the lexemes of deep structure language. For example, the important difference in meaning of sentences (1) and (2) below can be attributed to a difference in quantifiers[1]:

(1)   *Starye ljudi velikodušny*
        'Old people are generous'
        $(\forall \text{ man}_x) (\text{OLD (man}_x) \rightarrow \text{GENEROUS (man}_x))$;
(2)   *Hekotorye starye ljudi velikodušny*
        'Some old people are generous'
        $(\exists \text{ man}_x) (\text{OLD (man}_x) \& \text{GENEROUS (man}_x))$.

Certain transformations are applicable or inapplicable to a sentence depending on what sort of quantifier appears in the deep structure. In sentence (2), with the existential quantifier, the attribute can be detached into a separate assertion, but in sentence (1), the deep structure of which contains the universal quantifier, such a transformation is impossible:

(1′)   *Ljudi stary i velikodušny*
        'People are old and generous'.
(2′)   *Nekotorye ljudi stary i velikodušny*
        'Certain people are old and generous';

The meaning of a sentence is essentially dependent not only on the inventory of quantifiers in its deep structure, but also on their syntactic position. Examples:

---

[1] For the logical representation of sentences in natural language see, for example, [12]. Certain aspects of the representations cited which are not connected with quantifiers do not claim to be definitive.

F. Kiefer (ed.), *Trends in Soviet Theoretical Linguistics*, 149–171. *All Rights Reserved.*
Copyright © 1973 by D. Reidel Publishing Company, Dordrecht-Holland.

(3)(a) *Vozmožno, on ne zametil kakoj-nibuď ošibki*
'It is possible that he didn't notice some mistake'
POSSIBLE (($\exists$ mistake$_x$) $\neg$ NOTICED (he, mistake$_x$));

(b) *Vozmožno, on ne zametil nikakoj ošibki*
'It is possible that he didn't notice any sort of mistake whatsoever'
POSSIBLE (($\exists$ mistake$_x$) NOTICED (he, mistake$_x$));

(4)(a) *Vse škoľ niki ne znajut zakona Oma*
'All pupils are ignorant of Ohm's law'
($\forall$ student$_x$) $\neg$ KNOWS (student$_x$, Ohm's law);

(b) *Ne vse škoľniki znajut zakon Oma*
'Not all of the pupils know Ohm's law'
$\neg$ ($\forall$ student$_x$) KNOWS (student$_x$, Ohm's law);

(5)(a) *Kto by ni prišel, ona menja pozovet*
'No matter who comes, she will invite me'
($\forall$ person$_x$) (COMES (person$_x$) $\rightarrow$ WILL INVITE (she, I));

(b) *Esli vse pridut, ona menja pozovet*
'If everybody comes she will invite me'
($\forall$ man$_x$) COMES (person$_x$) $\rightarrow$ WILL INVITE (she, I);

(6)(a) *Nemnogie sčastlivcy pobyvali na každoj vystavke*
'A few lucky people have been to every exhibition'
($\exists$ few lucky man$_x$) ($\forall$ exhibition$_y$) VISITED (lucky man$_x$, exhibition$_y$);

(b) *Na každoj vystavke pobyvali nemnogie sčastlivcy*
'There were a few lucky people at every exhibition'
($\forall$ exhibition$_x$) ($\exists$ few lucky man$_y$) VISITED (lucky man$_x$, exhibition$_y$).

The parentheses in the formula determine the relation of subordination on the set of its autonomous symbols. If we construct a formula of predicate calculus according to S.C. Kleene [3, pp. 69–70], that is, include each of the arguments of predicate, connective or operator in parentheses (assuming here with A. Church [4] that quantifiers are two-place operators), then the system of parentheses thus obtained unambiguously determines the relation of subordination. According to this subordination, the difference between sentences (a) and (b) in examples (3)–(6) consists in the fact that in (a) the quantifier Я subordinates some operator (negation, connective, quantifier), while in (b), the inverse is true – this operator subordinates Я. For example (the parentheses are arranged in conformity with Kleene's rule):

(5a) = ∀ (person$_x$) (COMES (person$_x$) ⟶ (WILL INVITE (she, I)) =

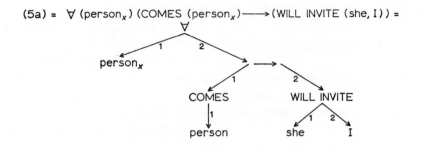

(5b) = (∀ (person$_x$) COMES (person$_x$)) ⟶ (WILL INVITE (she, I)) =

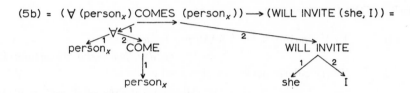

Marking the arrows makes it possible to show which place of the predicate or operator a given lexeme occupies.

In what follows we will be dealing with deep structures represented in the form of labelled trees of subordination (dependency trees); see this sort of representation of deep structures in [9].

A lexeme subordinated to a quantifier by arrow 2 is the vertex of a subtree which is called the *scope* of the quantifier.

The syntactic usage of quantifiers which characterizes formulas (1)–(6) can be called *predicative*. Of the quantifier words and constructions in Russian, we can consider *kakov (kakoj) by ni byl* to be predicative equivalent for ∀, and *suščestvuet* (exists), and *najdetsja* (can be found) to be predicative equivalent for ∃. Thus, sentences in which these words correspond to quantifiers have a surface structure which is close to their deep structure. All of the other quantifier words and constructions in the sentences of natural language (including constructions with implied quantifiers, as in example (1)) must be obtained as results of synonimity transformations.

§2. A GENERAL OUTLINE OF THE TRANSFORMATIONAL DESCRIPTION OF QUANTIFIER WORDS

Let us list the fundamental types of transformations capable of generating all or at least an important part of the surface structures of sentences with quantifier words.

I. Adjectivization of the quantifiers; examples:

(1)   *Kakaja by ni byla zadača, Petja rešit ee ⇒*
                              ⇒ Petja rešit ljubuju zadaču
       'No matter what the problem, Peter can solve it ⇒
                              ⇒ Peter can solve any problem'
(2)   *Est' vešči, kotorye znajut vse ⇒*
       ⇒ Nekotorye vešči znajut vse
       'There are things that are known by all ⇒
                              ⇒ Certain things are known by all'.

II. The substitution VSJAKIJ ⇒ VSE (every ⇒ all); VSJAKIJ ⇒ ⇒KAŽDYJ (every ⇒ each); examples:

(3)   *Vsjakij požiloj čelovek legko prostužaetsja ⇒*
                       ⇒ Vse požilye ljudi legko prostužajutsja
       'Every elderly person catches cold easily ⇒
                              ⇒ All elderly people catch cold easily);
(4)   *Vsjakij pioner dolžen byt' čestnym ⇒*
                       ⇒ Každyj pioner dolžen byt' čestnym
       'Every pioneer should be honest ⇒
                              ⇒ Each pioneer should be honest'.

III. The substitution VSJAKIE DVA ⇒ VSE any two ⇒ all examples:

(5)   *Vsjakie dva prjamyx ugla ravny meždu soboj ⇒*
                       ⇒ Vse prjamye ugly ravny meždu soboj
       'Any two right angles are equal to each other ⇒
                              ⇒ All right angles are equal'.

IV. The introduction of the implied quantifier of generality; examples:

(6)   *Vsjakij požiloj čelovek legko prostužaetsja ⇒*
                       ⇒ Požiloj čelovek legko prostužaetsja
       'Any elderly person will easily catch cold easily ⇒
                              ⇒ An elderly person will catch cold easily'.

V. The introduction of the implied existential quantifier; example:

(6)   *K Pete prišel odin požiloj čelovek ⇒*
                       ⇒ K Pete prišel požiloj čelovek
       'A certain elderly person came to Petja's ⇒
                              ⇒ An elderly person came to Petja's'.

There are a number of transformations which apply not specifically to quantifiers, but it is convenient to include them into the list for the sake of completeness, see transformations VI–VIII.

VI. The introduction of a sentence-determinant with a quantifier verb:

(7)   *Suščestvuet srednjaja linija trapecii* ⇒
                    ⇒ (8) *U trapecii suščestvuet srednjaja linija*
         'There exists a median of a trapezium ⇒
                    ⇒ (8) *lit.* For a trapezium there exists a median.

VII. The introduction of synonyms for the quantifier verbs:

(8)⇒(9) *U trapecii umeetsja srednjaja linija.*

VIII. The introduction of conversives for the quantifier verbs:

(9)⇒(10) *Trapecija imeet srednjuju liniju*
         'A trapezium has a median'.

IX. The tautological doubling of the quantifier words:

(11)   *U každogo čeloveka imejutsja nedostatki* ⇒
                    ⇒ *U každogo čeloveka imejutsja kakie-nibuď nedostatki*
         'Everyone has shortcomings ⇒
                    ⇒Everyone has some sort of shortcomings'.

X. The introduction of desemanticized quantifier temporal adverbs:

(12)   *Summa vsjakix dvux posledovateľnyx čisel nečetna* ⇒
                    ⇒ *Summa dvux posledovateľnyx čisel vsegda nečetna*
         'The sun of any two consecutive numbers is odd ⇒
                    ⇒The sum of two consecutive numbers is always odd'.

XI. Automatic transformations of quantifiers in a context of negation:

(13)   *Vsjakij čelovek ne ljubit uniženij* ⇒
                    ⇒ *Ni odin čelovek ne ljubit uniženij*
         '*lit.* Everyone does not like to be humiliated ⇒
                    ⇒ *lit.* No one does like to be humiliated';
(14)   *On vsegda ne možet vo-vremja ostanoviť sja* ⇒
                    ⇒ *On nikogda ne možet vo-vremja ostanoviť sja*
         'He is always unable to stop in time ⇒
                    ⇒ He is never able to stop in time'.

In the present essay we will mainly treat the adjectivization of quantifiers (see papers [6], [7], [8], [9], [10] devoted to adjectival quantifiers).

Our research material includes, in the first place, mathematical texts, in which the semantic possibilities of quantifiers are utilized rather fully. Those phenomena which cannot be considered facts of the literary language but are peculiarities of mathematical jargon were not taken into consideration. For ease of comprehension, the illustrative material is often based on an ordinary, rather than a mathematical, dictionary.

Remarks. It is natural to suppose that the language of deep structures should meet the condition of minimality, i.e., a single deep structure should correspond to all synonymous sentences in the language. Our language is not minimal; namely, there are synonymity relations which are determined by the following transformations of deep structures into one another (every transformation is an equivalence of the predicate calculus):

(1)(a) $\forall x \neg \mathfrak{A}(x) \Leftrightarrow \neg \exists x \mathfrak{A}(x)$;

(b) $\exists x \neg \mathfrak{A}(x) \Leftrightarrow \neg \forall x \mathfrak{A}(x)$

($\mathfrak{A}(x)$ is an arbitrary formula containing x);

(2) $\forall x (\mathfrak{A}(x) \to \mathfrak{B}) \Leftrightarrow (\exists x \mathfrak{A}(x) \to \mathfrak{B})$;

(3) $\forall x \mathfrak{A}(x) \,\&\, \forall y \mathfrak{A}(y) \Leftrightarrow \forall z (\mathfrak{A}(z) \,\&\, \mathfrak{B}(z))$

(x, y and z are variables of one and the same sort);

(4) $\forall x (B \nabla \mathfrak{A}(x)) \Leftrightarrow B \nabla \forall x \mathfrak{A}(x)$

(∇ is the connective copula $\&$, $\vee$ or $\to$: B does not contain x);

(5) $\rtimes' x \, \rtimes'' \mathfrak{A}(x, y) \Leftrightarrow \rtimes'' y \, \rtimes' x \mathfrak{A}(x, y)$

($\rtimes'$ and $\rtimes''$ are either both universal or both existential quantifiers.

It is assumed that transformations I–XI leave the translation of a sentence into logical language unchanged within the equivalence described by relations (1)–(5).

§3. PREDICATIVE QUANTIFIERS AND QUANTIFIER ADJECTIVES

The adjectivization transformation consists in: (a) replacing the predicative quantifier with an adjectival one, i.e., a quantifier adjective; (b) eliminating the subquantifier occurrence of the variable and subordinating the quantifier adjective to the first of the non-subquantifier occurrences of this variable. For example:

(1)

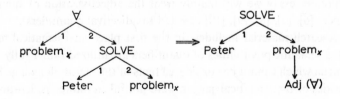

Kakova by ni byla zadača, Petja rešit ee ⇒

⇒ *Petja rešit ljubuju zadaču*

'No matter what the problem, Peter will solve it ⇒

⇒ Peter will solve any problem';

(2)

Est' vešči, kotorye sleduet znat' ⇒ ⇒*Nekotorye vešči sleduet znat'*

'There are things that one should know ⇒

⇒ One should know certain things'.

Adjectivization is possible only under certain conditions. If the deep structure does not satisfy these conditions, applying quantifier adjectivization to such a structure will lead either to a violation of grammaticality or to a change in the meaning of the sentence caused by the change in the scope of the quantifier. Cf. sentences (1), (2), where the transformation is applicable, and sentences (3), (4), where it is not:

(3)   *Kakova by ni byla zadača, najdetsja kto-nibud', kto ee rešit*
'No matter what the problem, someone can always be found who can solve it' ≠
Najdetsja kto-nibud', kto rešit ljubuju zadaču
'Someone can always be found who can solve any problem'

(4)   *Kakova by ni byla zadača, esli Petja v sostojanii ee rešit', ja proigral pari*
'No matter what the problem, if Petja is able to solve it, I have lost the bet' ≠
Esli Petja v sostojanii rešit' ljubuju zadaču, ja proigral pari.
'If Peter is able to solve every problem, I have lost the bet'.

Thus, the primary task in connection with the adjectivization transformation consists in understanding the mechanism which determines the scope of quantifier when manifested by adjectives.

Remark. The deep structure of a sentence can change if the sentence is uttered with special phrase accents. However, we are going to treat sentences only in their preferred interpretation (according to Chomsky [1]), that is, as being read with normal intonation. In fact, when dealing with the written language, we can assume that a meaning whose expression requires unnatural intonation is unsuccessfully expressed by a particular sentence, since it can always be expressed by another sentence (usually by merely rearranging the words) in which this meaning is rendered with natural intonation. Thus, for the sentence *Xuliganit Petja* (It is Peter who behaves like a hooligan) the natural interpretation has the logical emphasis on *Petja*. This sentence can be given a different meaning if the word *xuliganit* is emphasized; but this meaning corresponds to the preferred interpretation of the sentence *Petja xuliganit*. Another example. The sentence *Beskonečno mnogo toček ležit meždu ljubymi dvumja točkami prjamoj* (There is an infinite number of points which are situated between any two points of a straight line) is false in its preferred interpretation. It can be read as true; but this meaning is the preferred interpretation for another sentence – *Meždu ljubymi dvumja točkami prjamoj ležit beskonečno mnogo toček.*[2]

We should emphasize that adjectivization consists in merely replacing a predicative quantifier with an adjectival one and subordinating it to a noun. If in order to obtain a satisfactory result we must in addition, for example, rearrange the words, then the transformation can be considered to be inapplicable to the given structure and applicable to the structure in which the words are permuted.

The adjectival equivalents for the universal and existential quantifiers are cited in Table I. The existential quantifier can be considered a particular instance of the numerical quantifier – there exist *at least two, there exists exactly one, more than one, several, infinitely many*, etc. (this is written $\exists_{\geqslant 2}$, $\exists_1$, $\exists_{>1}$ $\exists_\infty$). In fact, the word *exists* (suščestvuet) is understood as 'there exists at least one'.

TABLE I

Adjectivized quantifiers in a general context

Adj ($\forall$)	*vsjakij, ljuboj* (only in sing.)
Adj ($\exists$)	*po krajnej mere odin, xot' odin, xotja by odin*
Adj ($\exists_{>1}$)	*nekotorye* (only in pl.)
Adj ($\exists_{\geqslant 2}$)	*po krajnej mere dva* (similarly with the other numerals and adverbs)

Quantifier adjectives are divided into those which can be used in a random context and those which are used only in marked contexts or which express

---

[2] There are infinitively many points between any two points of a straight line.

some sort of additional meaning. The former are given in Table I, and the others will be shown after the kinds of relevant contexts are found out.

§4. Auxiliary notions

The adjectivization transformation is applied to a predicative quantifier appearing in a structure where possibly some other kinds of transformations have already been applied to some other lexemes – for example transformations, which introduce attributes, homogeneous parts of the sentence, terms formed from predicates (of the type *storona* ⟨*treugol'nika*⟩ (side of a triangle) from the predicate '*x javljaetsja storonoj y*' (*x* is a side of *y*)), etc., see [11]; this can in particular be a structure in which the adjectivization transformation has already been applied to the other quantifiers. Thus, this structure no longer corresponds to the formula of predicate calculus.

We will need the concepts below for what follows. A *predicate* will be said to be any element of a structure which has a verb or an adjective as its equivalent in natural language – for example, ∃, but not ∀ and not ESLI(IF). The *predication* of predicate *P* is defined as a subtree which includes predicate *P* and those nodes which are semantically subordinate to it (i.e., subordinate either immediately or through coordinative conjunctions). For example, in the structure of the sentence *Petja' i Vanja znajut čeloveka, kotoryj ženilsja na zuluske* (Peter and John know a man who married a Zulu) the predication of the predicate ZNAET (KNOWS) is as shown below:

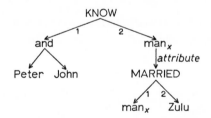

In addition, let us introduce the notion of an expanded predication. The *expanded predication* of predicate *P* in a tree *D* is the subtree which includes *P* and all the nodes which are semantically subordinate to *P* whether immediately or through nouns (more precisely, only nouns which are names of objects, such as *storona* treugol'nika ⟨a side of a triangle⟩, but not those which are names of facts, such as *ravenstvo* ⟨treugol'nikov⟩) (equality) ⟨of triangles⟩. For example, the whole sentence (1) is the expanded predication of the predicate ZENILSJA:

(1)   *Syn prijatelja Petja ženilsja*
        'The son of Petja's friend got married'.

A linear order can be described in a natural way for every predication. Let us describe a linear order on the expanded predication, also. The concept of expanded predication arises in a sentence whose structure is potentially transformable into a structure where the nodes which are indirectly subordinated to the predicate become its immediate dependents and are arranged in the order shown in examples (1)–(3):

(1)   *Syn prijatelja Peti ženilsja* ⇒
                              ⇒ **U Peti u prijatelja syn ženilsja;*

(2)   *Petja znaet biografiju Puškina*
        'Peter knows Pushkin's biography' ⇒
                              ⇒ **U Puškina Petja znaet biografiju;*

(3)   *Syn Peti znaet biografiju Puškina*
        'Peter's son knows Pushkin's biography' ⇒
                              ⇒ **U Peti u Puškina syn znaet biografiju.*

We will consider the linear order for an expanded predication to be the one in which the elements of the predication would be distributed as a result of such a transformation.

Further, the *kernel of the scope of* quantifier K will be defined as the full subtree of the predicate which it is possible to reach from Я by proceeding along the arrows only though the quantifiers. For example, in structure (4), the kernel of the scope of quantifier ∀ is the full subtree of the predicate PRINADLEŽIT (BELONGS):

(4)   *Vsjakaja točka prinadležit nekotoroj prjamoj*
        'Every point belongs to some straight line'

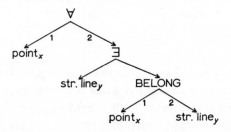

One more secondary notion – the notion of the *plural term*. This is any term which designates a plural object; for example, a term which is coordinated – *Petja i Vanja* (Peter and John), *nekotoraja prjamaja a i nekotroaja prjamaja b* (some straight line *a* and some straight line *b*), or a term which includes Adj (∀) or Adj ($\exists_n$), where $n = 2, 3, \ldots$, e.g., *ljuboj čelovek* (any person), *po krajnej mere dve točki* (at least two points).

§5. CONDITIONS FOR APPLICATION OF THE QUANTIFIER ADJECTIVIZATION TRANSFORMATION

A necessary condition for the adjectivization of quantifier Я in structure D is that (1) the vertex of the scope of Я in D is a predicate; (2) the first occurrence of the subquantifier term belongs to the expanded predication of this predicate. Examples of sentences where conditions (1) and (2) are not met and adjectivization is impossible:

(1)   *Kakova by ni byla prjamaja, čerez vsjakuju točku proxodit edinstvennaja prjamaja, kotoraja ej perpendikuljarna*
'No matter what the straight line, there is only one straight line passing through a given point which is perpendicular to it' $\neq$
Čerez vsjakuju točku proxodit edinstvennaja prjamaja, kotoraja perpendikuljarna vsjakoj prjamoi
'For every point there exists exactly one straight line which is perpendicular to every straight line'.

(2)   *Kakov by ni byl čelovek, esli on bolen, ego nado poslat'k vraču*
'No matter what the person, if he is sick, he must be sent to the doctor') $\neq$
**Esli vajskij čelovek bolen, ego nado poslat'k vraču.*

In sentence (1) the vertex of the quantifier scope is not a predicate but a quantifier, in (2) it is a conjunction. Examples (3) and (4) from §3 are of the same kind.

If conditions (1) and (2) for some quantifier Я in structure D are fulfilled and neither situation I nor situation II takes place (see below), then Я can be adjectivized with the help of a general equivalent from Table I. Examples:

(3)   *Najdetsja čelovek, kotoryj znaet Petju Ivanova*
'Someone will be found who knows Peter Ivanov' $\Rightarrow$
        $\Rightarrow$ *Po krajnej mere odin čelovek znaet Petju Ivanova*
'At least one person knows Peter Ivanov';

(4)   *Kakov by ni byl golodnyj, ni odin sytyj ego ne pojmet*
'*lit.* Whatever the hungry man, not a one who is full will catch him' $\Rightarrow$ *Ni odin sytyj ne pjmet ni odnogo golodnogo*
No man who is full will catch a man who is hungry'
(*ni odin* $\Leftarrow$ *ljuboj* by virtue of the automatic transformations in a context of negation);

(5)   *Kakov by ni byl zulus, ego otec i mat' javljajutsja zulusami*
'Whatever the Zulu, his father and mother are Zulus' $\Rightarrow$
        $\Rightarrow$ *Otec i mat' vsjakogo zulusa javljajutsja zulusami*;

(6)   *Suščestvujut takie ljudi, čto ix nedostatki javljajutsja prjamym prodolženiem ix dostoinstv*
        'There are people whose faults are a direct extension of their virtues' ⇒
        ⇒ *Nedostatski nekotoryx ljudej javljajutsja prjamym prodolženiem ix dostoinstv.*

If situations I or II arises in the structure, adjectivization is realized in a more complicated manner.

Situation I. Quantifier Ʞ is ∀ or $\exists_n$ (with operator variable X), and Ʞ subordinates the predicate in whose expanded predication the term y with the dependent Adj($\exists$) appears, no matter, singular or plural. In such a predication, the additional contextual meaning 'each of' is connected with the term X, and the meaning 'generally speaking, its own for each x', x'', ..., $\in X$' is connected with term y; that is, the meaning of *distributivity* is contained in the predication, and when the quantifier is adjectivized, it should not be lost.

(A) Let the term X be located in an expanded predication to the left of term y[3]; then if we adjectivize Ʞ with the help of a general equivalent from Table I, the implicit meaning of *distributivity* automatically appears in the predication. Examples:

(7)   *Kakov by ni byl voditel', on sobljudaet nekotorye pravila dviženija*
        'No matter what the driver, he observes certain traffic rules' ⇒
        ⇒ *Vsjakij voditel' sobljudaet nekotorye pravila dviženija*
        'Every driver follows certain traffic rules';

(8)   *Kakov by ni byl aspekt problemy, on razrabatyvaetsja po krajnej mere odnim sotrudnikom*
        'No matter what the aspect of the problem, it is worked out by at leat one of the scientists' ⇒
        ⇒ *Ljuboj aspekt problemy razrabatyvaetsja po krajnej mere odnim sotrudnikom.*

(B) Adjectivization of quantifier Ʞ is also possible in a case where a way can be found to express explicitly the meaning of distributivity in the predication. For this it is sufficient to replace Adj($\exists$) in term y, i.e., the general adjectival equivalent for $\exists$, with a special equivalent with the meaning 'Adj ($\exists$), its own' (see Table II). In this case the relative linear order of terms X and y is unimportant. Examples:

(9)   *Kakov by ni byl čelovek, po krajnej mere odnu ošibku on soveršil*
        'No matter what a man is like, he has made at least one mistake' ⇒
        ⇒ *Kakuju-nibud' ošibku soveršil ljuboj čelovek;*

---

[3] Here and from now on, by the occurrence of a term in a predication will be meant its first occurrence.

(10)   *Kakova by ni byla kandidatura, po krajnej mere odnim nedostat-*
       kom ona budet obladat'
       'No matter what the candidature, at least one shortcoming it will
       have' ⇒
       ⇒ *Kakim-nibud' nedostatkom budet obladat' ljubaja kandidatura*;
(11)   *Kakova by ni byla rabota, po krajnej mere odin čelovek dolžen byl*
       ee proverit'
       'No matter what the work is like, at least one man should have
       checked it' ⇒ *Kto-nibud' dolžen byl proverit' ljubuju rabotu.*

TABLE II

Special adjectival equivalents for ∃

	Situation I
'Adj (∃), own'	*kakoj-nibud'*
'Adj (∃$_{>1}$), own'	*kakie-nibud'*
'Adj (∃$_{>2}$), own'	—

	Situation II
'Adj (∃), the same'	*odin i tot že, kakoj-nibud'odin i tot že, nekotoryj odin i tot že, kakoj-to odin i tot že*
'Adj (∃$_{>1}$), the same'	*odin i te že, kakie nibud'odin i te že, etc.*
'Adj (∃$_2$), the same'	*odin i te že dva*

As can be seen from Table II, for the numerical quantifiers, besides ∃$_{>1}$, there
are no special equivalents with the meaning 'Adj (∃), own', For this reason,
in sentence (12), for example, it is impossible to express distributivity if the
order of the terms is unchanged, and adjectivization is impossible:

(12)   *Kakova by ni byla zadača, po krajnej mere dvum ljudjam ona*
       ponravitsja
       'No matter what the problem, at least two persons will like it' ≠
       Po krajnej mere dvum ljudjam ponravitsja ljubaja zadača
       'At least two persons will like every problem'.

Situation II. Quantifier Я is ∃ (in particular, ∃$_n$) with a variable *x*, and Я
subordinates a predicate in the expanded predication of which a certain
plural term *Y* appears. In such a predication, the additional contextual
meaning 'the same for all *y'*, *y''*, …, ∈ *Y'* is connected with the term *x*, and the

additional meaning 'all' is connected with term Y; that is, the meaning of *collectivity* is contained in the predication, and it should not be lost when quantifier Ӿ is adjectivized.

(A) Let term x be located in an expanded predication to the left of the plural term Y; then if we adjectivize x with the help of a general equivalent from Table I, the meaning of collectivity will automatically appear in the predication; examples:

(13)   *Po krajnej mere odin čelovek možet rešit' ljubuju zadaču*
       'At least one person can solve any problem';

(14)   *Nekotorye pravila dviženija sobljudajutsja vsjakim voditelem*
       'Certain traffic rules are observed by all drivers';

(15)   *Nekotorye devočki ljubjat i Petju, i Vanju*
       'There are some girls who like both Peter and John'.

(B) Adjectivization of quantifier Ӿ is also possible in a case where a way of expressing explicitly the meaning of collectivity can be found. For this it is sufficient to adjectivize Ӿ not with the help of a general equivalent, but through a special equivalent with the meaning 'Adj ($\exists$), the same' (see Table II). Again, the relative order of the terms x and Y is in this case unimportant. Examples:

(16)   *I Petju, i Vanju ljubjat nekotorye odni i te že devočki*
       'Some girls like both Peter and John';

(17)   *Nekotorym odnim i tem že nedostatkom obladaet ljubaja kandi-datura*
       'All candidatures have a certain common shortcoming';

(18)   *Vsjakij porjadočnyj čelovek sobljudaet nekotorye odni i te že pravila povedenija*
       'There are some rules of behaviour observed by all respectable people';

(19)   *Po krajnej mere dva pokolenija soveršajut nekotorye odni i te že ošibki*
       'At least two generations are making the same mistakes'.

Remark 1. The combinations *xot' odin, po krajnej mere odin* (at least one), which are interpreted in Table I as Adj ($\exists$) (see example (a)), are understood in some contexts as 'Adj ($\exists$) own' (see example (b)), and in some contexts are ambiguous (see example (c)), in such a way that, in contrast to the examples from the Remark in §3, none of the interpretations is preferable:

(a)   *Xotja by odna probka podxodit k ljuboj butylke*
       'There must be one cork that fits all the bottles';

(b) *Xot' odna ošibka soderžitsja v ljubom tekste*
     'Any text will contain at least one mistake`;
(c) *Xot' odnu zadaču rešit vsjakij*
     'Everyone will be able to solve at least one problem; There must be one problem which everybody is able to solve'.

These constructions need further analysis.

Remark 2. It is possible that the word *kakoj-nibud'* (any) is more correctly interpreted not as having the meaning 'Adj($\exists$), own', but as a word with the meaning Adj($\exists$), permissible, however, only in the context of some subordinating operator. In fact, the use of *kakoj-nibud'* in sentences of the type

(a) **Ja pročel kakuju-nibud' knigu*

results in ungrammaticality, but in a context with the subordinating ESLI (if), VOZMOŽNO (it is possible); NEVERNO (it is not true; it is not the case) such a usage is possible [12]:

(b) *Kogda kakoj-nibud' čelovek pytaetsja Petju obmanut', Petja krasneet*
     'When anyone tries to trick Peter, Peter blushes';
(c) *Možet byt', Petja soveršil kakuju-nibud' ošibku*
     'It is possible that Peter has made some kind of mistake'.

In such a case, sentences (9)–(11) should be understood as containing $\exists$, which is subordinated to $\forall$, simply due to the assumption of their grammaticality.

The word *nekotoryj* 'some, a certain' (in the singular) is analogous to the word *kakoj-nibud'* in the sense that it can be used as Adj ($\exists$) only in a context with the subordinating operators $\forall$, ESLI, VOZMOŽNO, NEVERNO. etc. Unlike *kakoj-nibud'*, however, *nekotoryj* has a second meaning, as is seen in sentence (d):

(d) *Petja xočet, čtoby vy speli nekotoryj romans*
     'Peter wants you to sing a certain romance' = definite, but not communicated to the addresse.

Due to the presence of this second meaning, sentences with *nekotoryj* without a subordinating operator are not ungrammatical, but replacing *nekotoryj* with *kakoj-nibud'* in examples (9)–(11) results in a change in meaning.

§6. THE TRANSFORMATIONS VSJAKIJ $\Rightarrow$ VSE, VSJAKIJ $\Rightarrow$ KAŽDYJ

If the meaning of distributivity or collectivity is already expressed in the predication in one way or another, then adjectives which are 'colored' by this context can function as adjectival equivalents for $\forall$. See Table III.

TABLE III

Contextual adjectival equivalents for ∀

Context of distributivity	Adj(∀) – *každyj*
Context of collectivity	Adj(∀) – *vse*

Violation of the contextual restrictions described in Table III usually makes the sentence ungrammatical. See examples (1), (2):

(1)   **Oba dviženija presledovali svoi celi (oba ⇒ každoe iz)*;
(2)   **Každyj is dvux studentov predložil odno i to že rešenie (kàždyj iz dvux ⇒ oba).*

Compare, however, sentence (3), where use of the word *každyj* in a context of collectivity does not seem incorrect (cf. also sentence (6) from §1).

(3)   *V Každoj iz pjati formul soderžitsja odna i ta že ošibka*
        'Each of the five formulae contains the same mistake'.

The division of quantifier adjectives into those which explicitly express the idea of distributivity/collectivity (Table II) and those which are possible only in the appropriate context (Table III) is to a certain degree arbitrary. The difference is simply that since contextual restrictions can be violated, the presence of the adjective *každyj(vse)* in a sentence does not unambiguously point to distributivity (collectivity), but only makes such an interpretation more probable.

Thus, in the ambiguous sentence (b) from Remark 1 §5, the use of contextually colored universal quantifiers makes the one interpretation considerably more probable than the other:

(4)   *Xot' odnu zadaču rešit každyj* (*xot' odnu*, most probably, = 'Adj(∃), own');
(5)   *Xot' odnu zadaču rešat vse* (*xot' odnu*, most probably, = 'Adj (∃), the same').

The opposite interpretation, however, is not entirely excluded. Let us look at sentences (6) and (7):

(6)   *V každoj formule soderžitsja nekotoraja ošibka*
        'Each formula contains some mistake'.
(7)   *Kakie protivopostavlenija predstavleny v každom iz trex klassov?*
        'What oppositions occur in each of the three classes?'

The word *nekotoryj* is ambiguous (see Remark 2 from §5), but in sentence (6) it is most likely to be understood as Adj (∃), so that the meaning of distributivity occurs in the predication. As a matter of fact, if there were no meaning of distributivity it would be more natural to say not *v každoj formule* (in each/every formula), but *vo vsex formulax* (in all the formulae). The second interpretation, however, is generally possible also.

Sentence (7) is also ambiguous – it can mean either that the oppositions occurring simultaneously in all the classes, or those which, occur in at least one, are to be shown. The second interpretation, however, is to be preferred, since in the case of the first it would be most natural to say not *v každoj*, but ⟨*odnovremenno*⟩ *vo vsex*.

Distributivity and amalgamation can also be contextually independent meanings accompanying the idea of plurality. For example:

(8)   *Vsjakij pioner dolžen byt' čestnym* ⇒

⇒ *Vse pionery dolžny byt' čestnymi*

(9)   *Vsjakij pioner dolžen byt' čestnym* ⇒

⇒ *Každyj pioner dolžen byt' čestnym.*

The difference in meaning here is quite small, so that the transformations are accepted as synonymous.

§7. Remarks

Remark 1. It is clear from all that has been said thus far that only a quantifier adjective which appears in the expanded predication of some predicate which is used predicatively can result from adjectivization. Sentences with quantifier adjectives included in an attributive construction are obtained by replacing a predicative construction which already contain quantifier adjectives with an attributive phrase. Examples:

(a)   *Zadači, predlagaemye vsem, dolžny byt' prostymi*
'The problems assigned to everyone should be simple ones' ⇐

⇐ *Esli zadači predlagajutsja vsem, oni dolžny byt' prostymi*;

(b)   *Zadača, kem-libo rešennaja, ne goditsja dlja konkursa*
'A problem which someone or other has solved will not do in the competition' ⇐

⇐ *Esli zadača kem-libo rešena, ona ne goditsja dlja konkursa*;

(c)   *Dva ugla, smažnye s odnim i tem že uglom, ravny meždu soboj*
'Two angles which are adjacent to the same angle are equal to each other' ⇐

⇐ *Esli dva ugla smežny s odnim i tem že uglom, to oni ravny meždu soboj.*

Remark 2. The notion of expanded predications needs to be elaborated upon, because in certain contexts the vertex of the scope of a quantifier adjective appearing in an expanded predication of a predicate P is not P, but a predicate corresponding to one of the intermediate nouns; for example, the predicate BYT' PUSTYM MNOŽESTOVM (to be an empty set) is not included in the scope of the quantifier corresponding to the adjective *vsex* in sentence (a), and the predicate NAZYVAT'SJA FAVORIT OM (to be called a favorite) is not included in the scope of the quantifier corresponding to the adjective *kakoj-nibud'* in example (b), although the subordinating nouns appear in the expanded predication of these predicates:

(a)   *Obščaja čast' vsex množestv javljaetsja pustym množestvom*
'The part which all sets have in common is an empty set'
$(\forall x) ((\forall \text{ set}_y) (\text{PART}(x, \text{set}_y) \rightarrow \text{EMPTY SET}(x))$;

(b)   *Ljubimec kakogo-libo vysokopostavlennogo lica nazyvaetsja favoritom*
'The favorite of any sort of high-ranking person is called a minion'
$(\forall x) ((\exists \text{ high ranking person}_y) \text{ FAVORIT}(x, \text{ person}_y) \rightarrow$
$\Rightarrow \text{MINION}(x))$.

Remark 3. The meanings of collectivity and distributivity can occur simultaneously in a single predication:

(a)   *U vsjakogo kvadrata nekotoryj otrezok raven ljuboj storone*
'An intercept of any square is equal to any of its sides';
The intercept is its own for every square, but the same for all of its sides;

(b)   *U vsjakogo raznostoronnego treygol'nika kakaja-nibud' storona men'še vsex drugix*
'A certain side of any scalene triangle is shorter than all the others'
The side is its own for each triangle, but one and the same for all the sides.

Sentence (c) also provides an interesting example of the combination of distributivity and collectivity:

(c)   *Vsjakie tri točki prinadležat kakoj-nibud' odnoj i toj že ploskosti*
'Any three points belong to some ⟨one and the same⟩ plane'.
The plane is the same for all the three points, but its own for every set of three points.

The consecutive stages of synthesizing this sentence from its deep structure are as follows:

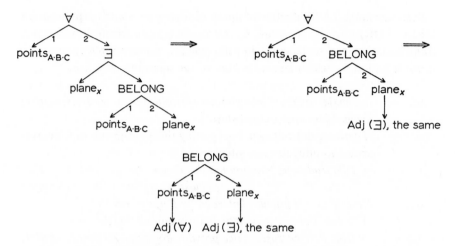

The meaning of collectivity is expressed explicitly, while the meaning of distributivity is indicated only by the word order.

The fact that quantifiers in one sentence must agree with respect to distributivity/collectivity can be an obstacle to combining simple sentences into a complex one:

(d)   *Každyj iz detej igraet na kakom-libo muzykaľnom instrumente i izučaet odin i tot že inostrannyj jazyk;

(e)   *Každyj čelovek, soveršivšij kakoe-nibuď prestuplenie, budet podvergnut odnomu i tomu že nakazaniju.

Remark 4. There are syntactic transformations that can translate a structure in which conditions (1) and (2) from §5 for a given quantifier are not fulfilled into a synonymous structure where they are fulfilled:

Transformation I. The introduction of the predicates TAKOV (SUCH), OBLADAET SVOJSTVOM (HAS THE QUALITY). Cf. sentence (a), which illustrates such a transformation, and sentence (b), in which the preliminary application of this transformation makes the adjectivization of the quantifier possible:

(a)   *Kogda Petja bolen, on legko razdražaetsja*
         'When Peter is ill, he is easily irritated' ⇒
                   ⇒ *Petja takov, čto kogda on bolen, on legko razdražaetsja;*

(b)   *Kakov by ni byl čelovek, kogda on bolen, on legko razdražaetsja*
         'Regardless of what a person is like, when he is ill he is easily irritated' ⇒
                   ⇒ *Vsjakij čelovek obladaet tem svojstvom, čto kogda on bolen, on legko razdražaetsja.*

Transformation II. Introduction of a prepositional group with the preposition DLJA (FOR) into the structure. Cf. sentences (c)–(e), which illustrate this transformation, and sentence (f), in which the preliminary application of this transformation makes an adjectivization of the quantifier possible:

(c)   *Imejutsja trudnosti interpretacii slovosočetanija, cootvetstvujuščie trudnostjam interpretacii slova*
       'There are difficulties in interpreting the word-group which correspond to difficulties in interpreting the word' ⇒
       ⇒ *Dlja trudnostej interpretacii slova imejutsja sootvetstvujuščie im trudnosti interpretacii slovosočetanija;*

(d)   *Ne suščestvuet pravila, kotorogo by Petja ne narušal*
       'The rule doesn't exist that Petja wouldn't break' ⇒
       ⇒ *Dlja Peti ne suščestvuet pravila, kotorogo by on ne narušal;*

(c)   *Našlas' sinjaja kartočka, parnaja k želtoj*
       'The blue card that was the twin to the yellow one was found' ⇒
       ⇒ *Dlja želtoj kartočki našlas' sinjaja ⟨kartočka⟩, parnaja k nej;*

(f)   *Kakovo by ni bylo čislo x, suščestvuet čislo y, kotoroe bol'še čisla x*
       'Regardless of what number x is, there is a number y larger than number x' ⇒
       ⇒ *Kakovo by ni bylo čislo x, dlja čisla x suščestvuet čislo y, kotoroe bol'še ego* ⇒
       ⇒ *Dlja ljubogo čisla x suščestvuet čislo y, kotoroe bol'še ego.*

Transformations I and II result in the setting off of a given term into a kind of supersubject (the term is from [13]). This term has one additional occurrence in the transformed sentence comparing with the original one.

There are, practically speaking, no restrictions on applying transformation I (once) to any term of a sentence (if we discount the fact that it is difficult for natural language to tolerate any however complex hierarchy of grades of logical emphasis). In contrast, transformation II is possible only for a limited class of predicates, cf. the irregular phrase from mathematical jargon: **Dlja ljubogo čisla x libo x bol'še nulja, libo x men'še nulja.*

§6. APPARENT COUNTEREXAMPLES

In sentences (1) and (2) quantifiers are adjectivized for which conditions (1) and (2) from §5 are not fulfilled:

(1)   *Vsjakaja ženščina zlo, no dvaždy v žizni ona byvaet prekrasnoj*
       'Every woman is evil, but twice in her life she is beautiful'

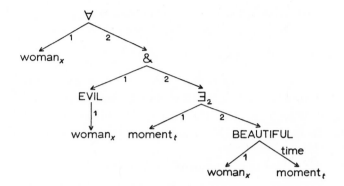

(2)   *Esli kto-nibud' ošibetsja, my ego popravim*
       'If anyone makes a mistake, we will correct him'

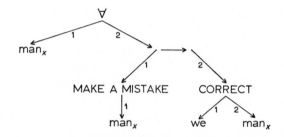

Cf. other sentences of the same type:

(3)   *Ob ètom dumaet každyj čelovek osobenno esli emu 18 let*
       'This is something every person thinks about, especially if he is
       18';

(4)   *Každaja storona treygol'nika men'še summy dvux drugix storon,
       no ona bol'še ix raznosti*
       'Each side of a triangle is smaller than the sum of the other two
       sides, but it is greater than their difference';

(5)   *Nekotorye babočki prekrasny, no uvidet' ix trudno*
       'Some butterflies are beautiful, but it is difficult to see them';

(6)   *Petja xočet pojmat' kakuju-nibud' rybku, a Vanja xočet ee s' ' est'*
       'Peter wants to catch a fish and John wants to eat it'.

To analyze sentences (1)–(6), it seems most natural to postulate transformations forming an expansion of a logical language, namely forming a language
in which the scope of the quantifiers does not include all the occurrences of
the subquantifier variable:

(a) $\lambda x(\mathfrak{A}(x)\ \&\ \mathfrak{B}(x)) \Leftrightarrow \lambda x\mathfrak{A}(x)\ \&\ \mathfrak{B}(x);$

(b) $\forall x(\mathfrak{A}(x) \rightarrow \mathfrak{B}(x)) \Leftrightarrow \exists x\mathfrak{A}(x) \rightarrow \mathfrak{B}(x)$

(cf. transformation (2) from §2).

If there were no free variables in the logical language used (which is but natural when logical language is used for semantic purposes cf. A. Church [4], transformations (a) and (b) will be mutually conversible: the initial formula can be reconstructed on the basis of the anaphorical relations between variables connectives.

Sentences (1)–(6) can be considered to have been obtained with the help of the same quantifier adjectivization transformation, but from the structures to which transformations (a) and (b) were applied beforehand.

If a structure contains occurrences of the subquantifier variable of quantifier λ which do not enter into its scope we will say that this scope is *conditional*.

Remarks. Sentences (1), (3), and (4) contradict W. Quine's thesis [14] that a pronoun cannot have as its antecedent a nominal group that includes the universal quantifier. The treatment of sentence (2) does not coincide with that proposed by H. Reichenbach [15] and developed by E. Charney [16] to the effect that the word *kakoj-nibud'* (any) in contexts such as (2) is to be understood as a free variable marker. We think it more natural to consider *kakoj-nubud'* in example (2), as well as in all of the examples from §5, to be the adjectival equivalent of the existential quantifier.

§8. CONCLUSIONS

Hence, we can conclude that the scope of a quantifier expressed with a quantifier adjective can be established with the help of the following three mechanisms:

(1) The predicate of an expanded predication containing a subordinating noun is always the vertex of the kernel of the scope (possibly a conditional one) for a quantifier adjective.

(2) Transition from the kernel of the scope to the scope itself (possibly conditional), i.e., the order of the quantifiers having the same kernel of the scope is determined by the meanings of distributivity or collectivity in the predication.

(3) Transition from a conditional scope to a non-conditional one is determined by anaphorical relations.

It has been asserted in works [8] and [11] that the quantifier adjectives of a simple sentence are connected with each other by a relation of subordination (analogous in meaning to subordination of quantifiers in deep structure determined by their linear order). In the first place, however, there are exceptions to this rule (examples (9)–(11) and (18), (19) from §5); secondly, and more important, the postulation of a new relationship between words which is not reducible to any type known thus far can hardly be considered satisfying. At the same time, the strange relations between quantifier adjectives can be reduced to the typologically quite normal linguistic phenomenon namely the following: a meaning that is usually just a redundant companion to a basic semantic opposition in some marked context proves to be the principal manifestation of this opposition in some other context. Namely, a semantic opposition consisting in subordination of quantifiers develops (in a case where several quantifiers have variables assembled in the same predication) into an opposition of distributivity and collectivity. (Cf. numerous analogous examples on the phonological level, cf. [17].)

Soviet Academy of Sciences, Moscow

BIBLIOGRAPHY

[1] N. Chomsky, *Aspects in the Theory of Syntax*, Cambridge, Mass. 1965.
[2] A. V. Kuznetzov, E. V. Padučeva, and N. M. Ermolaeva, 'Ob informatzionnom jazyke dlja geometrii i algoritme perevoda s estestvennogo jasyka na informatzionnyj i obratno', in *Lingvističeskie issledovanija po mašinnomu perevodu*, Moskva 1961.
[3] S. C. Kleene, *Vvedenie v metamatematiku*, Moskva 1957.
[4] A. Church, *Vvedenie v matematičeskuju logiku*, T. 1, Moskva 1960.
[5] A. K. Žolkovskij and I. A. Mel'čuk, 'O semantičeskom sinteze', in *Problemy kibernetiki*, No. 19, Moskva 1967.
[6] G. Carden, 'English Quantifiers', *Mathematical Linguistics and Automatic Translation*, Report N NSF-20, Cambridge, Mass. 1968.
[7] R. S. Jackendoff, 'Quantifiers in English', *Foundations of Language* IV (1968), 422.
[8] G. Lakoff, 'Linguistics and Natural Logic', *Studies in Generative Semantics*, No. 1, 1970.
[9] B. H. Partee, 'Negation, Conjunction and Quantifiers: Syntax vs Semantics', *Foundations of Language* 6 (1970), 153–165.
[10] G. S. Tzejtin, 'Jazyk matematičeskoj logiki kak sredstvo issledovanija semantiki estesvennogo jazyka', in *Problemy prikladnoj lingvistiki*, Tezisy mežvuzovskoj konferentzii. P. II, Moskva 1969.
[11] E. V. Padučeva, 'Semantičeskij analiz estestvennogo jazyka pri perevode na jazyki matematičeskoj logiki', in *Trudy III Vsesojunznoj konferentzii po informatzionno-poiskovym sistemam i avtomatičeskoj obrabotke naučno-texničeskoj informatzii*, Moskva 1967.
[12] O. N. Seliverstova, 'Opyt semantičeskogo analiza slov tipa *vse* i tipa *kto-nibud'*, *Voprosy jazykoznanija*, 1964, No. 4.
[13] Ju. S. Martem'janov, 'Aktual'noe členenie frazy', in *Problemy prikladnoj lingvistiki, Tezisy mežvuzovskoj konferentzii*, p. II, M., 1969.
[14] W. O. Quine, 'Logic as a Source of Syntactical Insight', in *The Structure of Language and its Mathematical Aspects*, Providence 1961.
[15] H. Reichenbach, *Elements of Symbolic Logic*, N.Y. 1948.

[16] E. K. Charney, *On the Semantical Interpretation of Linguistic Elements that Function Structurally*, 1st International Conference on MT of Languages and Applied Language Analysis, Teddington 1961.
[17] R. Jakobson and M. Halle, *Fundamentals of Language*, 's-Gravenhage 1956.

JU. D. APRESJAN

SYNONYMY AND SYNONYMS*

The purpose of the present paper is to suggest several modifications of the theory of lexical synonyms. The groundwerk for this has to a significant degree been laid by the practical work of compiling synonym dictionaries [1], in the course of which an abundant body of new material was systematized, and by theoretical studies in the field of semantics [2], which have made it possible to look at synonyms from a new point of view.

1. MEANS OF EXPRESSING SYNONYMY

All natural languages have means of synonymous expression, i.e., different ways of expressing the same content. One can list here:

(1) Purely syntactic transformations, whereby the syntactic relations between the words, the word order, and the derivational or inflexional status of the words in the transformed expression may change, while its lexical morphemes remain constant. Examples are: *Ja ne xoču, čtoby on uxodil* (I don't want him to leave) – *Ja xoču, čtoby on ne uxodil* (I want him to stay), *Ja verju v ego čestnost'* (I believe in his honesty) – *Ja verju, čto on česten* (I

---

* This is an extended and revised version of a paper originally published in Russian, *Voprosy jazykoznanija* 4 (1969), 75–91.
[1] A number of synonym dictionaries have been published in the last 10–12 years; cf. H. Bénac, *Dictionnaire de synonymes conforme au Dictionnaire de l'Académie française*, Paris, 1956; *Webster's Dictionary of Synonyms*, Springfield, 1957; Z. E. Aleksandrova, *Slovar' sinonimov russkogo jazyka*, M., 1968. Cf. also J. Filipec's monograph on Czech synonyms (Josef Filipec, *Česká synonyma z hlediska stylistiky a lexicologie*, Praha 1961). Dozens of articles containing a large and to a considerable degree new body of factual material have been published on various questions of synonymy in connection with the compilation of an "explanatory" dictionary of Russian synonyms. See, for example, *Očerki po sinonimike sovremennogo russkogo literaturnogo jazyka*, M-L, 1966; *Leksičeskaja sinonimija*, M., 1967.
[2] We particularly have in mind the theory of synonymous transformations of linguistic expressions. See: Z. S. Harris, 'Transformational Theory', *Language* 41, 1965; A. K. Žolkovskij and I. A. Mel'čuk, 'Ob odnom sposobe i instrumentax semantičeskogo sinteza', *Haučno-texničeskaja informacija*, 1965, 6; K. J. Babitskij, 'O sintaksičeskoj sinonimii predloženij v estestvennyx jazykax', *Naučno texničeskaja informacija* 6, 1965; U. Weinreich, 'Explorations in Semantic Theory', *Current trends in linguistics* III, Theoretical foundations, London-The Hague-Paris, 1966; J. F. Staal, 'Some Semantic Relations Between Sentoids', *Foundations of language. International Journal of Language and Philosophy* 3, 1, 1967; H. Hiž, 'Computable and Uncomputable Elements of Syntax', *Transformations and Discourse Analysis Papers* 69, University of Pennsylvania, 1967; A. K. Žolkovskij and I. A. Mel'čuk, 'O semantičeskom sinteze', *Problemy kibernetiki* 19, 1967.

F. Kiefer (ed.), Trends in Soviet Theoretical Linguistics, 173–199. All Rights Reserved.
Copyright © 1973 by D. Reidel Publishing Company, Dordrecht-Holland.

believe that he is honest), *Ja predlagaju vam ujti* (I advise you to leave) – *Ja predlagaju, čtoby vy ušli,* (I suggest that you leave), *On proverjaet semena na vsxožest'* (He is checking the seed for its germinating ability) – *On proverjaet vsxožest' semjan* (He is checking the germinating ability of the seed), *On pokajalsja mne vo vsem* (He confessed everything to me – *On pokajalsja peredo mnoj vo vsem,* etc.

(2) Lexical transformations based on the substitution of a given word by (a) its conversive, cf. *Butylka vmeščaet tri litra* (The bottle holds three liters – *V butylku vxodit tri litra, On otstaet ot sestry v razvitii* (He lags behind his sister in development) – *Sestra operežaet ego v razvitii* (His sister has surpassed him in development), *On skoree prožekter, čem mečtatel'* (He's more of a schemer than a dreamer – *On he skol'ko mečtatel', skol'ko prožekter*[3] (He's not so much a dreamer as a schemer); (b) its antonym: *somnevat'sja* (to doubt) – *ne byt' uverennym* (to be unsure, not to be sure), *otsutstvovat'* (to be absent) – *ne prisutstvovat'* (not to be present), *Vse pomnjat* (Everybody remembers) – *Nikto ne zabyl* (Nobody has forgotten) *načinat' sobljudat' pravila* (to begin to observe the rules) – *perestavat' narušat' pravila* (to stop violating the rules); (c) a generic term with a modifier: *karty* (cards) – *kartočnaja igra* (card game), *igra v karty* (game of cards), *lingvistika* (linguistics) – *lingvističeskaja nauka* (the linguistic science) *gotika* (Gothic) – *gotičeskaja arxitektura* (Gothic architecture), *šeptat'* (to whisper) – *govorit' šepotom* (to speak in a whisper); (d) a derived word: *On pomogaet mne* (He helps me) – *On okazyvaet mne pomošč* (He gives me help) – *Ja pol'zujus' ego pomošč'ju* (I enjoy his assistance) – *On moj pomoščnik* (He is my helper); *Eti objazannosti tjagotjat ego* (These duties irk him) – *Eti objazannosti tjagostny emu* (These duties are irksome to him) – *Eti objazannosti emu v tjagost'* (These duties are a burden for him); *On skryl svoj ot"ezd* (He kept his departure secret) – *On uexal tajno* (He left secretly); (e) a word in a given semantic relation to the initial word: *On carstvoval 30 let* (He reigned for 30 years) – *On prosidel na prestole 30 let* (He occupied the throne for 30 years) (throne = "instrument of reigning"), *On poxoronen za selom* (He is buried outside the village) – Ego *mogila-za selom* (His grave is outside the village) (grave = "place where people are buried"), *On ušel po moemu sovetu* (He left on my advice) – *On posledoval moemu sovetu ujti* (He followed my suggestion that he leave) (to follow advice = "to execute the requirement of the situation 'advice'")[4];

[3] Ch. Bally (*Traité de stylistique francaise*, 2-eme éd. Paris, p. 141) as far back as 1921 pointed out expressions of the type *avoir le droit* "to have the right" and *être légitime* "to be legitimate" as a source of synonymy (Cf. He had a right to protest – His protest was legitimate). Cf. also O. Espersen, *The Philosophy of Grammar*. London, New York, 1924, ch. XII; Z. S. Harris, 'Discourse Analysis'. *Language* 28, 1, 1952.

[4] The productive means of forming synonymous expressions given in points (2a)–(2e) have been studied and formalized in the works of A. K. Žolkovskij and I. A. Mel'čuk

f) its semantic code: *obessmyslivat'* – *lišat' smysla* (make absurd), *vyparyvat'* – *uničtožat' parom* (destroy with steam), and the more complex and interesting instances of the type *Krome nego nikto ne prišel* (No one came besides him) – *On byl edinstvennym, kto prišel* (He was the only one who came), *Ja ždu ot vas iskrennego raskajanija* (I expect sincere repentance from you) – *Vy dolžny iskrenne raskajat'sja* (You should repent sincerely), *Ego ždali v subbotu* (He was expected on Saturday) – *On dolžen byl priexat' v subbotu* (He was due to arrive on Saturday), *Včera on zakončil perevozku veščej s dači* (Yesterday he finished moving his things from the cottage) – *Včera on perevez s dači poslednie vešči* (Yesterday he moved the last things from the cottage); g) its lexical synonym: *Rasstojanie meždu nimi umenšilos' /sokrašilos'/) vdvoe* (The distance between them was reduced (cut) by half).

The above mentioned means of expressing synonymy relations comprise in their totality *synonymy in the broad sense* and are the subject of the theory of semantically invariant transformations. Since *lexical synonyms in the narrow sense* (point (g)) are one of the sources of synonymy in the broad sense, they should also be studied from the point of view of their role in semantically invariant transformations of linguistic expressions.

2. A DEFINITION OF LEXICAL SYNONYMS IN THE NARROW SENSE

Lexical synonyms are usually defined as words which designate the same thing but emphasize different aspects of it, or as words which have the same meaning but differ in its finer shades. Without going into unnecessary, detail we shall note two general features of such definitions. First, none of them can be considered to be exact, because they contain terms ("aspect of a thing", "shade of meaning") which have no clear content. Secondly, in the majority of definitions, emphasis is laid not on the general semantic properties of synonyms, but on the differences between them[5].

If we want to formulate a definition of synonyms based on an effective comparison of their meanings, we must have at our disposal an explanatory

---

(see footnote 2). Some of the means mentioned in points (1) and (2d) are described in detail in the author's book *Eksperimental'noe issledovanie semantiki russkogo glagola*, M., 1967. Derivation as a source of lexical synonymy has always attracted the attention of linguists; see, for example: Ch. Bally, *ibid.*, §85; A. M. Peškovskij, 'Glagol'nost'' kak vyrazitel'noe sredstvo', in *Metodika rodnogo jazyka, lingvistika, stilistika, poetika*, L., 1925; G. O. Vinokur, 'Glagol ili imja'?, *Russkaja reč, Novaja serija* III, L., 1928; S. I. Ožegov, 'O strukture frazeologii', *Leksikografičeskij sbornik* 2, M., 1957, p. 44; L. Zawadowski, *Constructions grammaticales et formes périphrastiques*, Krakow-Wrocław-Warszawa, 1959, p. 114; A. P. Evgen'eva, 'Osnovnye voprosy leksičeskoj sinonimiki', *Očerki*, p. 7.
[5] Cf. A. B. Šapiro, 'Nekotorye voprosy teorii sinonimov', *Dokl. i soobšč. In-ta jazykoznanija AN SSSR* 8, 1955, p. 72.

dictionary meeting a number of important requirements. Some of them concern the logical structure of the definition, others specify the semantic language whose phrases or sentences serve as definitions of particular meanings, still others refer to the structure of the defined expression.

The conditions which the *definitions* should satisfy are as follows: (1) they should not be circular, (2) the meaning of the defined and the defining expressions should be identical: if $A = $ 'BC', then 'BC' must be necessary and sufficient for A. Note in particular that if "BC" is necessary for A, but not sufficient (in fact, $A = $ 'BCD') then there will be no formal grounds to preclude the treatment of A and A' ($A' = $ 'BC') as purely synonymous. If on the other hand 'BCD' is sufficient for A, but not entirely necessary (in fact, $A = $ "BC"), then the actually synonymous words A and A' ($= $ 'BC') may be treated as having different meanings.

Now let us consider the conditions which the *defining language* (the semantic metalanguage) must satisfy [6]. The first of them concerns its vocabulary and can be formulated as follows: each word in the vocabulary of the semantic language should express exactly one meaning, and each meaning should be expressed by exactly one word of the semantic language, irrespective of the definition in which it occurs (meanings and their names should be in a one-to-one correspondence). For example, if some part of the meaning of the adjective *korotkij* (short) is defined by means of the word 'nebol'šoj' (small), the latter should figure in the definitions of the adjectives *uzkij* (narrow), *nizkij* (low), *tonkij* (thin), *legkij* (light), etc., rather than the words 'malyj' (little), 'neznačitel'nyj' (insignificant), and so on, as is usual in current explanatory dictionaries. On the other hand, if the expression 'v poperečnike' (in diameter, across) is included in the definitions of the adjectives *uzkij* (narrow) and *širokij* (broad), which may be applied to two-dimensional objects, it should not occur in the definitions of *tonkij* (thin) and *tolstyj* (thick, fat), which in their principal meaning cannot be applied to less than three-dimensional objects; otherwise the expression turns out to have two different senses, as is clear from the current lexicographic practice: 'v širinu' (wide, in width) for the first pair of adjectives and 'v sečenii' (in cross-section) for the second. In other words, in the dictionary of the semantic language there should be neither synonymy, nor homonymy of the names of meanings. If this condition is not fulfilled, it will be impossible to state the semantic identities and differences of the words of a natural language in an explicit form.

A similar condition should be imposed on the syntax of the semantic language. Meanings may differ from one another not only in the nature of

---

[6] The author takes up this and the related questions in detail in the papers 'Tolkovanie leksičeskix značesnij kak problema teoretičeskoj semantiki' (*Izvestija AN SSSR, serija literatury i jazyka* 1, 1969; 'O jazyke dlja opisanija znacenij slov' (*Ibid.* 5, 1969).

their semantic constituents but also in the types of their syntactic organization. Consider the elementary meanings 'ne' (not) and 'načinat' (to start). They are the semantic constituents of the phrase *ne načina' (rabotat')* (not to start (to work)) in which *ne* syntactically depends on *načinat'*:

ne načinat' (rabotat').

The same two constituents make up the meaning of the verb *perestavat'* (to stop), but their syntactic structure is different:

perestavat' (rabobat') = "načinat' ne (rabotat)",

where the negation modifies not the verb *načinat'*, but the infinitive which it governs. It is precisely this syntactic difference that accounts for the semantic difference between *načinat' ne rabotat'* and *perestavat' rabotat'*. It follows, therefore, that to give an exact formulation of the meaning of a word one should state unambiguously the syntactic structure of its constituents. This is achieved through a dependency syntax in which every dependency tying up two constituents (presentable in the final analysis as configurations of elementary meanings) is specified as to its ordinal number with regard to the main constituent and its semantic interpretation (Sub(ject), Obj(ect), Adr(esse), Instr(ument), Loc(us) and so on).

Observance of these two conditions on the semantic language provides a foundation for a formal comparison of the definitions with a view to discovering their semantic identities and differences. Otherwise, statements as to the greater or lesser "similarity of meanings" and the synonymy between words become, strictly speaking, pointless.

The last set of conditions we should consider concerns the *structure* of the *defined expression*. Before we formulate these conditions, let us analyze the material which makes them necessary in the first place. In all explanatory dictionaries of Russian *reputacija* (reputation, name) is defined through *mnenie* (opinion, view); cf. *reputacija-"sozdav šeesja obščee mnenie o dostoinstvax i nedostatkax kogo-čego-l"* (the general opinion about the virtues and shortcomings of smb. or smth.). This formulation is not fully correct, since it treats reputation as a type of opinion. In reality, *reputacija and mnenie* exhibit an interesting difference in voice which can be reduced to the difference between the verbal forms (or verbs) *sčitat'sja* (be considered, reputed) and *sčitat'* (consider): *NN sčitaetsja u nix xorošim* (Among them, NN is reputed to be good) = *NN imeet u nix xorošuju reputaciju* (NN has a good reputation among them), but *Oni sčitajut NN xorošim* (They consider NN to be good) = = *Oni imejut ob NN xorošee mnenie* (They have a high opinion of NN). Consequently, *reputacija* and *mnenie* are (near) conversives: *reputacija A u X-ov*

(A's reputation among the X's) $\simeq$ *mnenie X-ov ob A* (The X's opinion of A). Here, as in many other (but not all) cases of conversion (*davat'* (give) and *polučat'* (receive), *stroit'* (to build) and *stroit'sja* (to be build), etc.), it is in principle impossible to achieve a state of things where each of the converse terms will have a definition of its own, logically independent of the other. Due to the semantic asymmetry of conversives in natural languages, the definition assigned to the primary word (i.e., the word which designates the 'direct' relation) is extended to both words. Nonetheless, since conversives are not synonyms, the difference between them should be fixed in some way. Since this difference cannot be expressed in the text of the definitions, there is only one way left – to express it through some difference in the structure of the defined units. It cannot be expressed so long as the definiendum is a single word, but the situation changes as soon as we take for definiendum a whole expression containing the given word in the syntactically nuclear position and variables for the other elements of the phrase to which it corresponds, for instance, *reputacija A u X-ov* $\cong$ "what the X-s think of A".

Thus, we have examined the conditions which should be imposed on the definitions, the semantic language in which they are formulated, and the defined expressions, to make possible a rigourous study of the synonymic relations between words. Now let us turn to the definition of lexical synonyms proper.

If we consider lexical synonyms within the framework of the theory of semantically invariant transformations (and we are pursuing just this goal), the current notion of lexical synonymy will have to be refined in several respects. We stated above that in the majority of definitions of lexical synonyms, emphasis is laid not on their general semantic features, but on the differences between them. However, only those lexical synonyms whose meanings coincide completely can participate in semantically invariant transformations. Therefore, in the large class of words and (semantically indivisible) phraseological units which are usually said to be synonymous, it is necessary to set apart a more or less narrow subclass, the elements of which have absolutely identical definition in the sense specified above. We shall call such elements *lexical synonyms* in the narrow sense of the word, as distinct from *quasisynonyms*, which exhibit an important but incomplete coincidence of meanings.

However, this is not a sufficient condition of synonymy. As we have seen above, there are words with precisely the same lexical meaning (cf. *stroit'* – *stroit'sja*) which nevertheless will not be granted the status of lexical synonyms within any reasonable theoretical framework, because they exhibit fundamental syntactic differences. Consider the words *stroit'* and *stroit'sja* (or, for that matter, *mnenie* and *reputacija*). They are syntactically bivalent; the difference between them consists in the fact that the first valence of the word *stroit'* is subjectival and the second valence is objectival, whereas for the word *stroit'sja* the first valence is objectival and the second is subjectival[7]. It follows from this example that the preliminary steps to determining synonymy should include not only a comparison of the formal definitions of words, but also the fixation and comparison of their valency structures. Two words which have the same definition are not yet synonyms if their valency structures are different, in that the valencies of the same name (subjectival, objectival and so on) have different numbers. Only those words which have the same valency structure can pass the test of synonymy.

Now let us turn to the last group of facts whose interpretation has a direct bearing on the definition of lexical synonyms. The conditions of identical lexical meaning and identical valency structure are satisfied not only by pairs of words like *kidat' – brosat'* (throw), but also by the pairs of syntactic derivatives of the type *podderživat' – podderžka* (to support – support), *ravnyj – ravenstvo* (equal – equality), and so on. It is apparently pointless to regard such pairs as lexical synonyms. The latter are an irregular, purely lexical category; they cannot be built anew after a certain pattern but function in any natural language as ready-made units. In contradistinction to this, derivatives are a regular, to a certain extent a grammatical category. Since such pairs as *ravnyj – ravenstvo* are in principle describable as regular formations they should be treated as such, regardless of the fact that they differ from the more familiar typs of derivatives in that they have the same lexical meaning – a feature that does indeed make them akin to synonyms.

It would seem at first glance that the effect we are looking for – the expulsion of syntactic derivatives from the domain of lexical synonyms proper – can be achieved by requiring that the latter belong to the same part of speech; derivatives are naturally allowed to belong to different parts of speech. Consider, however, the following rare but interesting instances: *stoit – kak tol'ko* (as soon as) (*Stoit emu vojti – Kak tol'ko on vxodit* (As soon as he comes in)), *odin* (alone) – *tol'ko* (only) (*Ja skažu ob etom odnomu Petru – Ja skažu ob etom tol'ko Petru* (I shall tell only Peter about it)). Here *stoit* is a verb and *kak tol'ko* is a conjunction, *odin* is an adjective and *tol'ko* is a particle. The parts of speech are thus different, yet to treat all these instances as cases of (say, suppletive) derivation would be stretching the facts: the regular derivational models of Russsian do not allow the formation of conjunctions from verbs or of particles from adjectives (or the other way round). To postulate a new category intermediate between syntactic derivation and lexical synonyms would be just as unresonable, because the corresponding facts are rather scarce. The treatment of such pairs as lexical synonyms

---

[7] The valencies are numbered in decreasing order of obligatoriness.

seems to reflect linguistic intuition better than anything else, and we shall try to provide formal grounds for it.

In analyzing the sentences *Stoit emu vojti – Kak tol'ko on vxodit*, or *Ja skažu ob etom odnomu Petru – Ja skažu ob etom tol'ko Petru* we note that the words which we would like to treat as synonymous play the same role in their respective syntactic structures. To be more exact, the syntactic trees of the corresponding sentences do not differ in anything but the part of speech affiliation of the words under consideration, cf. Figure 1.

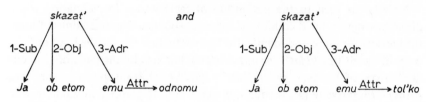

Fig. 1

In the light of such examples, one is tempted to think that the distinguishing feature of synonyms is their ability to fulfil the same syntactic function with regard to the same nodes in at least one syntactic tree. This is tantamount to saying that synonyms are partially interchangeable. But interchangeability as a criterion of lexical synonymy is untenable for two reasons: on the one hand, there are words with precisely the same meaning which nevertheless can never be substituted for one another owing to the fact that their selectional restrictions are entirely different; on the other hand, there are certain types of derivatives which in certain types of trees fulfil the same syntactic functions and thus are capable of partial interchangeability (cf. *umnyj* (clever) – *umnica* (clever one) in such sentences as *Kakoj ty umnyj!* – *Kakoj ty umnica!* (How clever you are!)). The criterion of interchangeability assigns to lexical synonyms the property of superficial syntactic similarity; but we should like to see the essence of lexical synonyms in their deep semantic and syntactic identity.

To solve this difficulty, we shall have to resort to the notion of the scheme of a syntactic tree. By the scheme of a syntactic tree we understand the structure of dependencies with variable nodes but with the numerical order and the semantic interpretation of depencies specified. We shall achieve all our purposes by requiring that synonyms be substitutable in any schemes of syntactic trees in which at least one of them can occur (in other words, we require that synonyms be capable of serving as the same nodes in the same schemes of syntactic trees).

Thus, to set up the relation of lexical synonymy between two words (or semantically indivisible phraseological units) *A* and *B* it is necessary and sufficient that they (1) have the same definition, (2) have the same set of syntactic valencies, such that valencies with the same number have the same semantic interpretation, and vice versa, (3) be capable of replacing one another in any schemes of syntactic trees in which at least one of them can serve as a node.

Note that this definition does not require that synonyms have the same or partially coincident selectional restrictions (power of combinability). Neither does it predetermine anything about their stylistic and other related properties which may naturally be very different[8].

There is a widely held view to the effect that there are no 'exact' or 'absolute' synonyms in natural languages. The vagueness of these terms prevents us from evaluating the truth of the judgement. It is possible to state, however, that if we understand exact synonyms in the sense defined above there are quite a few of them in natural languages. By way of illustration we shall briefly survey a number of language processes which give rise to semantically exact synonyms.

3. The Sources of Lexical Synonyms

Any literary language exhibits a tendency to get rid of units which are functionally similar[9]. However, different layers of vocabulary respond to this tendency in different degrees. It is most prominent among the principal meanings of native words or completely assimilated loans of long standing, preferably non-derived, which are stylistically neutral and have a wide range of use. In this layer of vocabulary the processes of semantic differentiation are constantly at work; they are responsible for the reduction of exact synonyms and the rise of quasisynonyms. The relatively rare cases of exact lexical synonymy found here may be illustrated by the following examples: *brosat'* – *kidat'* (throw), *gasit'* – *tušit'* (extinguish), *gljadet'* – *smotret'* (look), *est'* – *kušat'* (eat), *metit'(sja)* – *celit'(sja)* (aim), *prekraščat'sja* – *perestavat'* (stop), *spešit'* – *toropit'sja* (hurry); *bezumie* – *sumašestvie* (madness), *bitva* – *sraženie* (battle), *zabastovka* – *stačka* (strike), *osminog* – *sprut* (octopus), *podlinnik* – *original* (original); *gromadnyj* – *ogromnyj* (tremendous), *suxoščavyj* – *xudoščavyj* (rather lean); *vezde* – *vsjudu* (everywhere), *vpopyxax* – *vtoropjax* (in a hurry), *edva* – *ele* (with difficulty), *edva* – *čut'* (barely) etc.

In all the other layers of vocabulary the effect of the above mentioned tendency is to a considerable extent neutralized or mitigated by various

---

[8] In the present paper we shall not concern ourselves with the problem of the possible stylistic and emotive distinctions between lexical synonyms.

[9] See M. V. Panov, 'Russkij jazyk', in *Jazyki narodov SSSR* I, Moskva, 1966, p. 55.

processes of innovation (the rise of new meanings, word formation, recent borrowing, emotive innovation, and so on). Normalization which manifests itself in semantic differentiation lags a little behind innovation; the less stable vocabulary units possessing the above-mentioned properties are therefore able to resist the tendency towards semantic differentiation much more successfully. It is precisely in this sphere that exact lexical synonymy springs into being and functions in language not as an exotic by-product of linguistic change but as a regular and stable phenomenon. Cf. the following examples:

(1) Relatively recent loans and native words, especially of terminological character: *avtonomija – samoupravlenie* (autonomy, self-rule), *akkuzativ – vinitel'nyj* (accusative) *aplodirovat' – rukopleskat'* (applaud), *argument – dovod* (argument) *duel' - poedinok* (duel), *kompensirovat' – vozmeščat'* (compensate, reimburse), *koncentrirovat' – sosredotočivat'* (concentrate), *lingvistika – jazykoznanie* (linguistics), *identičnyj – toždestvennyj* (identical), *fundament – osnovanie* (foundation, basis), *kannibal – ljudoed* (cannibal).

(2) Words derived from the same root: *brosat' – sbrasyvat'* (bomby) (toss, drop (bombs)), *rvat' – vzryvat'* (most) (blow up (a bridge)), *menjat' – razmenjat'* (den'gi) (change (money)), *zakalka – zakalivanie* (hardening, tempering), *osnova – osnovanie* (basis), *bolezn' – zabolevanie* (sickness), *rešitel'nyj – rešajuščij (boj)* (decisive (battle)), *poxožij – sxodnyj* (similar, like), *celikom – vsecelo* (entirely), *vsjudu – povsjudu* (everywhere), *vo-vremja – svoevremenno* (in time, timely), *vidimo – po-vidimomu* (evidently)[10].

(3) A word and a phraseological unit or two phraseological units: *bezdel' ničat' – bit' bakluši* (loaf around), *pobeždat' – brat' verx* (win, gain the upper hand), *zagnat' v ugol – priperet' k stene* (corner smb.) *byt' na veršok ot (gibeli) – byt' na kraju (gibeli)* (be a hair's breadth from/on the edge of/ruin), *vo vsju ivanovskuju – blagim matom* (at the top (of one's voice)), *v mgnovenie oka – glazom ne uspel morgnut' (kak)* (in the twinkling of an eye).

(4) Words in emotive meanings: *vkatit'/vlepit'/(vygovor)* (give smb. a chewing out), *valandat'sja – kanitelit'sja* (mess, fool around), *pustomelja – pustozvon -pustobrex,* (blabbermouth, windbag) *axineja – beliberda – galimat'ja* (balderdash, gobbledygook, tommyrot), *bezgolovyj – bezmozglyj* (scatter-brained), *bezdna(del) – beda skol'ko (del)*[11] (a heap of (things to do)).

(5) Words in transferred and figurative meanings: *mčat'sja – nestis' – letet'*

---

[10] An abundance of synonyms formed from the same root, especially among verbs, seems to be a typological feature of synonymy in Russian; see A. E. Evgen'eva, *O nekotoryx osobennostjax leksičeskoj sinonimii russkogo jazyka*, "Leksičeskaja sinonimija...", p. 67.
[11] J. Vendreyes (in his *Langage*) was one of the first linguists to have called attention to the ease with which 'affective' words contract synonymic relations with one another. Similar observations will be found in A. B. Šapiro's paper (*op. cit.* 75) and a number of later publications.

(rush, tear along, fly) *vyxodit'* – *polučat'sja* (turn out, prove to be) (*Iz nego vyjdet /polučitsja/ xorošij sprinter*) (He'll turn out to be a good sprinter/We'll get a good sprinter out of him/), *idti* – *teč'* (come, flow) (of blood from a wound), *vypadat'* – *vylezat'* (of wool, hair) (come, fall out, wear), *bit'* – *streljat'* (shoot (at entrenchements)), *duša* – *serdce* (soul, heart), *nauka* – *urok (na vsju žiz'n')* (lesson).

(6) Words in so-called phraseologically bound meanings: *Sozdaetsja/ skladyvaetsja/(vpečatlenie)* ((An impression) arises/is formed/), *(Veter) stix/ulegsja/* ((The wind) has quieted down/subsided/), *(Doroga) beret/ zabiraet/ vlevo* ((The road) goes/takes off/to the left), *(Vino) udarjaet/brosaetsja/ v golovu* ((The wine) rushes to your head), *vpadat'/prixodit'/ (v otčaianie)* (give way to (despair), *stavit'/brat'/čto-l. (pod kontrol')* (take (control of)), *doslovnyj/bukval'nyj/(perevod)* (word-for-word (translation)), *nesmetnye/ nesčetnye/ (polčišča)* (incalculable/countless/(hordes)) *zakljatyj/zlejšij/(vrag)* (sworn/most bitter/ (enemy), *beskonečnaja/bezmernaja/(blagodarnost'* (infinite/boundless/(gratitude))[12].

Exact lexical synonymy occurs in all of the above instances, i.e., the formal definitions fully coincide and the syntactic identity of the corresponding units in the sense specified in (2) and (3) is total[13]. Even in this situation however, synonyms can show interesting differences in their semantic, lexical, and morpho-syntactic combinability (selectional restrictions).

4. TYPES OF SELECTIONAL RESTRICTIONS

By a *semantic* selectional restriction of a word in a given sense we shall mean a limitation in its use that can be formulated in terms of a particular semantic feature or features of other words with which it is syntactically combined. Thus, animate nouns, and such nouns only, can function as the subject of the

---

[12] Lexical synonyms of the majority of the groups listed here have been subjected to a detailed linguistic analysis only in the last 10–15 years. It is not surprising, therefore, that many of them are not found even in a work as complete and as carefully compiled as Z. E. Aleksandrova's synonym dictionary (see footnote 1). For example: *gran'* – *različie* (distinction, difference) (*Stirajutsja grani (različija) meždu umstvennym i fizičeskim trudom*) (The differences between intellectual and physical labor are being erased) *vypadat'* – *vydavat'sja* (occur, turn out to be (about a fine day)), *padat'* – *ložit'sja* (fall to (of responsibility)), *brat'* – *povoračivat'* (*vlevo*) (take, turn (to the left) (of a road)), *ispytyvat' (vlijanie)* – *naxo'ditsja (pod vlijaniem)* (see above), *byt'* – *stojat'* (*u vlasti*) (be (in power)), *zapasat'sja* – *vooružat'sja (terpeniem)* (arm o.s. (with patience)), *neoproveržimyj* – *neotrazimyj (dovod)* (irrefutable (argument)), *vporu* – *oo merke* (to measure).

[13] Linguists are far from unanimous in their treatment of such words. The words *tušit'* – *gasit'*, *kidat'* – *brosat'* are considered synonyms; *zabastovka* – *stačka* (strike) *lingvistika-jazykoznanie* are sometimes called synonyms, sometimes doublets; *zakalka* – *zakalivanie*, *vsjudu* – *povsjudu* are qualified either as synonyms or as word variants. This differentiation seems to us to be simply a matter of terminology; it deprives of a clear content not only the term 'synonym', but also the terms 'doublet' and 'variant'.

expression *byt' vinovnikom* (be the cause of an undesirable state of things); cf. *On byl vinovnikom vsex ee bed* (He was to blame for all her troubles), but not *Etot slučaj byl vinovnikom vsex ee bed* (This event was to blame for all her troubles), in contrast to the nearly synonymous expression *byt pričinoj* (be the cause of), which allows of such a combination. It follows from this definition that if the words A and B form a syntagm (A B or A B) and if X is a semantic selectional restriction of A, then X makes part of the meaning of B, and not of A.

By a *lexical* selectional restriction of a word in a given sense we shall mean a limitation in its use which cannot be formulated otherwise than by listing all the words with which it can combine syntactically. It is immaterial here whether they have common semantic features or not. The word *general'nyj* (general) in the meaning "most important in some hierarchy" combines idiomatically with a limited group of nouns whose meanings are not generalizable (cf. *general'nyj sekretar'* (general secretary), *general'nyj prokuror* (public procurator of the Supreme Court), *general'nyj štab* (general staff)). In contrast to this, the meanings of the nouns which can combine with its synonym *verxovnyj* (supreme) allow of a generalization, cf. *verxovnyj glavnokomandujuščij* (commander-in-chief), *Verxovnyj Sovet* (Supreme Soviet), *Verxovnyj Sud* (Supreme Court) with the common semantic feature 'vlast' (power). Nonetheless, this is also a case of a lexical, rather than semantic selectional restriction, since the adjective *verxovnyj* cannot combine freely with *any* noun whose meaning includes the feature 'power' (cf. the unacceptable phrase **verxovnyj komandir* (supreme officer)). Consequently, to describe the selectional restrictions of *verxovnyj* we should make up a list of nouns with which it can combine.

By a *morpho-syntactic* selectional restriction of a given word in a given sense we shall mean a limitation in its use which can be formulated in terms of the classes of word-forms with which it co-occurs syntactically either as the subordinate or as the subordinating member of the syntagm. Among the classes of word-forms we conventionally include prepositional forms (e.g., a noun in the instrumental case with the preposition *pered*, and the like) and the class S, i.e. the class of sentences. As in the preceding two cases, the morpho-syntactic selectional restrictions of (quasi)synonyms may be different; cf. *kosit' (glaza na kogo-l.)* (look askance at smb.) and *kosit'sja (glazami na kogo-l)*, *tjanut' (ruku k zvonku)* (reach for the bell) and *tjanut'sja (rukoj k zvonku)* and other verbs of this group.

The notion of a semantic selectional restriction raises an important theoretical problem – that of the difference between combinability and meaning. Three classes of instances may be set up.

(1) A definite peculiarity in the use of a word can be described only as a feature of its meaning. Consider the verb *dostavat'* (reach for, take out, get) in the phrases (a) *On dostal košel'ok iz karmana* [*knigu s polki*] (He took the purse out of his pocket [a book from the shelf]), *On dostal iz karmana ruku ubitoj obez'jany* (He got out of his pocket the hand of the killed monkey); (b) *On dostal ruku iz karmana* [*nogu iz sapoga*] (He took his hand out of his pocket [his leg out of the boot]), *On dostal nožku stola iz vody* (He drew the leg of the table out of the water). The phrases in the second set seem to be unacceptable, and one might be tempted to conclude that this effect is due to the violation of a selectional restriction: *dostavat'* cannot combine with the name of a non-displaceable object which denotes an organic part of an integral whole. The following obvious consideration, however, refutes this decision: we cannot mark every noun in the dictionary as to whether it denotes a displaceable object or not. Displaceability is not a semantic component of the lexical meaning of the nouns in question (cf. *ruka, noga, nožka*), but a property of the corresponding *physical objects* in the extralinguistic situation, which are displaceable or non-displaceable, as the case may be. Note in particular that the phrases in the second set are unacceptable only if we proceed from the (rather natural) assumption that ruka, noga, nozka are not, in the given situations, parts of dismembered bodies; but once we think of them as separated from the human body or the body of the table (shocking though the situation may seem) the corresponding phrases immediately become correct. Thus, since the component 'displaceability' cannot be included in the lexical meanings of the nouns there is only one possible decision left – to assign it to the meaning of the verb *dostavat'*: *dostavat'* A iz/s B = "vynimat' or snimat' A iz/s B; A is displaceable and is not an organic part of any physical object".

(2) A definite peculiarity in the use of a word can be described only as a feature of its combinability. Consider the verb *uxudšat'sja* (become worse) in the phrases (a) *Ego zrenie* [*povedenie*] *uxudšaetsja* (His eyesight [behaviour] is getting worse) and (b) *Pjotr* [*Marja*] *uxudšaetsja* (Peter [Mary] is getting worse). The phrases in the second set are again unacceptable, but this time it is entirely due to the violation of a semantic selectional restriction: *uxudšat'sja* does not take as its subject the names of persons. Note that *uxušat'sja* means just "stanovit'sja xuže" (become worse), and the meaning "stanovit' sja xuže" is definitely combinable with the names of people; cf. *Pjotr* [*Mar'ja*] *stanovitsja zuže* which is a perfectly acceptable Russian sentence. Any semantic explanation of the non-combinability of *uxudšat'sja* with the names of people would be less adequate than this.

(3) A definite peculiarity in the use of a word can be accounted for in both ways (non – uniqueness of semantic descriptions). Consider the words *svora*

(pack), *staja* (flock), *tabun* (herd of horses) and the like. The semantic decision would be to describe them as quasisynonyms, with the following differences in meaning: *svora*="sovokupnost' sobak..." (a set of dogs...), *staja*="sovokupnost' volkov ili ptic..." (a set of wolves of birds...), *tabun* "sovokupnost' lošadej..." (a set of horses...), and so on. Then, to account for the instances like *svora sobak* (a pack of dogs), *staja volkov* (a pack of wolves), *tabun lošadej* (a herd of horses) we shall have to postulate the follow-

ing non-additive rule of meaning addition: if for a given syntagm $\overset{\overset{i}{\frown}}{A\ X}$ (for certain A-s and X-s and certain types of syntactic relations between them) the replacement of A by its definition from the dictionary results in the structure $\overset{\overset{j}{\frown}\overset{i}{\frown}}{B\ X}\ X$, then this structure should be simplified to $\overset{\overset{i}{\frown}}{B\ X}$. We cannot do without such a rule because undoubtedly such word-groups as *tabun lošadej* do not mean "sovokupnost' lošadej lošadej". Now let us turn to the other alternative. The combinability decision would be to regard the words *tabun, svora, staja* as pure synonyms with the common meaning "sovokupnost'" and entirely different selectional restrictions. Then to account for the fact that phrases like *Tabun mčalsja prjamo na nas* (The herd of horses was heading right for us) are uniquely understood to mean "Sovokupnost' lošadej mčalas' prjamo na nas", we shall have to postulate at least two different meanings for each such word: "sovokupnost'" for instances like *tabun lošadej* and "sovokupnost' lošadej" for instances like *Tabun mčalsja prjamo na nas*. As can be seen, the second conclusion, although it implies the necessity of splitting a single vocabulary unit into two different ones, does not presuppose the use of an extra rule; on the other hand, the first decision does not imply the splitting of vocabulary units but does require the use of an extra rule. We shall not dwell here on the criteria for the choice of the more appropriate alternative but shall emphasize once again that theoretically both are possible because their explanatory power is precisely the same.

Selectional restrictions can in principle be violated, e.g. for stylistic purposes. The semantic theory should not only make provision for such cases but it should also specify for each of them what the resulting stylistic effect or trope is. One would expect for example, that the difference between semantically non-motivated and semantically motivated selectional restrictions may turn out to be relevant. Semantically non-motivated or purely selectional restrictions are not immediately deducible from any semantic component of the lexeme in question, whereas semantically motivated selectional restrictions are immediate projections of a definite element of meaning onto combinability. In a very tentative way it may be suggested that the violation of the former for stylistic purposes produces various humourous effects, cf. *Pjotr vyšel zamuž* (*vyjti zamuž* (marry) takes as its subject the name of a female; when humourously applied to a man, instead of the selectionally correct word *ženit'sja* (marry), the expression may imply that Peter was too effeminate, or that his wife was abnormally masculine, and so on). The violation of the latter usually results in a trope, mostly in the semantic error known as metaphor. A typical instance is the phrase *ušibat'sja ob etot zapax* (hit oneself on this smell): the verb *ušibat'sja* means "to experience pain as a result of a sharp contact with a dense body" and as such takes the name of a *dense* physical body for the object – a requirement the word *zapax* does not satisfy.

Besides the type of selectional restrictions (semantic, lexical, and morphosyntactic) lexical synonyms may differ from each other in the degree of non-coincidence of selectional restrictions (combinability), and in each of the three cases we may have (1) full coincidence of combinability, (2) inclusion of combinability, (3) intersection of combinability, (4) full non-coincidence of combinability. All in all there are 12 types of elementary combinability differences between lexical synonyms. We shall take them up in more detail.

5. Types of Combinability Differences Between Lexical Synonyms

5.1. *Full Coincidence of Combinability*

Full coincidence of semantic and morpho-syntactic combinability occurs mainly in the types of synonymy mentioned above on pages 182 and 183 (points (1) through (3)) and may be illustrated by the pairs of words *kidat'* – *brosat'*, *aplodirovat* – *rukopleskat'*, *menjat'* – *razmenivat'*, *zagnat' v ugol* – *priperet' k stene*, *bezumie* – *sumašestvie*, *argument* – *dovod*, *sxodnyj* – *sxožij*, *vezde* – *vsjudu*, *edva* – *s trudom*. Full coincidence of lexical combinability, which characterizes mainly the synonymy of phraseologically bound meanings (point (6) on p. 183), is a relatively rare phenomenon, since the rules of lexical combinability, at least, in a synchronic description of language, are largely unmotivated. The adjectives *bespardonnyj* (impudent), *bezzastenčivyj* (brazen), *bessovestnyj* (bare-faced), *naglyj* (insolent) can serve as one of the very few examples: in the meaning of "high degree" all of them can combine with the nouns *lož'* (lie), *obman* (fraud), *vran'e* (lying) and the corresponding names for the agent (*lžec* (liar), *obmanščik* (fraud), *vrun* (liar)).

The three remaining types of differences occur mainly in the cases mentioned on pages 182–183 (points (4) through (6)).

5.2. *Inclusion of Combinability*

5.2.1. *Semantic combinability.* The verb *dostigat'* in the meaning "be equal or almost equal to" combines with nouns and numerals denoting both definite and indefinite size, while its synonym *doxodit' do* (amount to) is confined in its use to the nouns and numerals of the first group only, cf. *dostigat' 40 gradusov* (be slightly under 40 degrees Centigrade), *dostigat' 10 metrov* (be as high as ten metres), *dostigat' rosta čeloveka* (be almost as tall as a man), *dostigat' vysoty doma* (be almost as high as a house), but only *doxodit' do 40 gradusov, doxodit' do 10 metrov*. One can say *lakirovannyj* (laquered) of shoes (*lakirovannye botinki [sandalii]* (laquered shoes [sandals])) and furniture (*lakirovannyj stol [knižnyj škaf]* (laquered table [bookcase])); *lakovyj*, its exact equivalent in meaning, goes only with the names of shoes (*lakovye botinki*, but not *lakovyj stol). The verb *arendovat'* (lease) can combine with nouns denoting living quarters (*kvartiru* (apartment), *dom* (house)) and land (*zemel'nyj učastok* (plot of ground), *les s pašnej* (forest with field)), whereas its synonym *snimat'* combines only with the names of living quarters. *Edva, kak tol'ko* (hardly, as soon as) combine with both perfective and imperfective verbs (i.e., with the semantic features perfectiveness and imperfectiveness), but their synonym *stóit* can combine only with perfective verbs (i.e., only with the feature of perfectiveness): *Edva/kak tol'ko/on otošel, koster pogas = Stoilo emu otojti, kak koster pogas* (As soon as he left the fire went out), but only *Edva/kak tol'ko/on otxodil, koster gas* (not **Stoilo emu otxodit', kak koster gas*).

5.2.2. *Lexical combinability*. The nouns *osnova* and *osnovanie* (base, basis, foundation) in the meaning "that on which something is based" can be subordinated to the verbs *byt'* (be), *služit'* (serve), *obrazovyvat'* (form, make up), *sostavljat'* (comprise), *ležat'* (lie), *imet'* (have), *klast'* (lay): *byt' /služit'/ osnovoj/osnovaniem/(gipotezy)* (be/serve/as the basis/foundation/(of a hypothesis)), *obrazovyvat'/sostavljat'/osnovu/osnovanie/(gipotezy)* (make up/comprise/the basis/foundation/(of a hypothesis), *imet' v osnove/v osnovanii/ (fakty)* (have (facts) at the base/basis/)) *ležat' v osnove/v osnovanii/(gipotezy)* (underlie (the hypothesis)), *klast' (fakty) v osnovu/v osnovanie/(gipotezy)* (proceed from facts in making a hypothesis). The lexical combinability of their synonyms *baza* (base) and *fundament* (foundation) is considerably narrower: they can be subordinated only to the first four verbs; **Ležat' v fundamente/v baze/(gipotezy)' *imet' (fakty) v fundamente/v baze/, *klast' (fakty) v fundament/v bazu/(gipotezy)* are unacceptable. *Absoljutnyj* as an intensifier may be used more or less freely with a wide range of nouns, cf. *absoljutnaja svoboda [temnota, uverennost']* (absolute freedom [darkness, certainty]), *absoljutnaja protivopoložnost'* (something that is diametrically opposite), whereas its synonym *diametral'nyj* (diametrical) combines only with the noun *protivopoložnost'*. *Prud prudi, zavalis'* in the meaning of "very much" may be said of money, books, crockery and the like, cf. *Deneg [knig, posudy] – prud prudi/zavalis'/*. Contrary to this, the synonymous expression *kury ne kljujut* is normally used only of money, cf. *Deneg – kury ne kljujut.*

5.2.3. *Morpho-syntactic combinability.* The verb *kazat'sja* subordinates a clause (*Mne kažetsja, čto ty ošibsja* (It seems to me that you have made a mistake)), a predicative noun or adjective in the instrumental case (*On kažetsja (mne) dobrym/dobrjakom/*(He seems (to me) to be a kind person)) and an adjective in the comparative degree (*Eta doroga kažetsja (mne) koroče* (This road seems (to me) to be shorter)). Its colloquial synonym *sdavat'sja* can normally be used only in the first of the above mentioned constructions, cf. *Mne sdaetsja, čto ty ošibsja* (It seems to me that you have made a mistake). The adverb *tol'ko* in the meaning "nothing but" can combine equally well with nouns and with verbs, cf. *My objazany tol'ko emu* (We are indebted only to him), *On deržalsja tol'ko siloj duxa* (He held on only thanks to his moral strength), *Fiziki-teoretiki tol'ko dumajut, a fiziki-praktiki tol'ko eksperimentirujut* (Physics theoreticians do nothing but think, and experimentators do nothing but experiment). Unlike it, the adverb *edinstvenno* (solely) in precisely the same meaning combines only with nouns. A similar distinction can be observed in the behaviour of the adverbs *namnogo* and *gorazdo* (by far); the former modifies both, graded verbs and adjectives in the comparative degree (cf. *namnogo operedil sopernika* (left his rival far behind), *namnogo men'še* (considerably smaller), while the latter can be used only in the second type of construction.

The verbs *prekraščat'* and *perestavat'* (stop, leave off) can subordinate an infinitive. Although this construction is somewhat archaic for *prekraščat'*, it is still not marked as such in modern explanatory dictionaries; cf. *prekratit'/perestat'/zanimat'sja* (stop studying), *prekratite/perestan'te/šumet'* (stop making noise!). In addition, the verb *prekraščat'* is capable of subordinating a noun – a construction absolutely unacceptable for its synonym; cf. *prekraščat'* (but not **perestavat'*) *soprotivlenie (strel'bu, perepisku)* (discontinue/cease/resistance, shooting, correspondence). Special mention should be made of those instances where one of the synonyms tends to be restricted in its use to negative, interrogative, exclamatory or other modal constructions, whereas the other synonym has a greater syntactic freedom. One can quote *odin – edinyj* (one, single), *umnyj – dalekij* (clever), *ponimat' – smyslit'* (understand), *pojavljat'sja – brat'sja ("načinat' byt' u kogo-l.")* (appear, begin (to have)), *ponimai' – brat' v tolk* (understand, figure out); cf. *Ni odnogo/edinogo/pjatnyška net* (There is not a single/the least little/spot), *Paren' ne očen' umnyj/dalekij/* (The guy's not too bright), *Mnogo ty ponimaeš'/smycliš'/v étom*! (A lot you understand about this!), *Čto ty v etom* *ponimaeš'/smysliš'*? (What do you know about this?), *Ničego ty v etom ne ponimaeš'/ne smysliš'/*(You don't understand anything about this), *Otkuda pojavilis'/vzjalis'/u nego den'gi*? (Where did he get money from?), *On nikak ne mog ponjat'/vzjat' v tolk/, čto ot nego trebuetsja* (He couldn't figure out what it was he was expected to do) and the incorrectness of **On vse smyslit* (correct: *On vse ponimaet*), **Edinoe pjatnyško est'* (correct: *Odno pjatniško est'*), **U nego vzjalis' den'gi* (correct: *U nego pojavilis' den'gi*) etc.

5.3. *Intersection of Combinability*

5.3.1. *Semantic combinability.* One can say *končat'sja* (be over) of any rational activity (*Boj končilsja* (The battle is over), *Zanjatija končilis'* (Classes were over)) or a natural phenomenon such as rain, snow or wind (*Buran končilsja* (The storm was over), *Groza končilas'* (The thunderstorm was over)), but not of an emotional state (cf. the unacceptability of **Zlost' končilas'* (Anger was over), **Obida končilas'* (The feeling of offence, the soreness was over)). On the other hand, one can say *proxodit'*, in precisely the same meaning, of a natural phenomenon *(Buran prošel, Dožd' prošel)* or an emotional state *(Gnev prošel, Obida prošla, Smuščenie prošlo)*, but not of a rational activity (cf. the unacceptability of **Boj prošel*). *Uničtožat'* (do away with) can take as its object the name of an emotion (usually with the implication of uncertainty, cf. *nadeždy* (hopes), *somnenija* (doubts), *straxi* (fears)), or the name of a social system (*gosudarstvennyj apparat* (state apparatus), *sistemu eksploatacii* (the system of exploitation)), but it does not combine with nouns denoting various types of lagging behind; unlike it, its synonym *likvidirovat'* (liquidate) freely combines with the third group of nouns (cf. *likvidirovat' otstavanie* (do away with backwardness), is quite common with the nouns of the second group *(likvidirovat' gosudarstvennyj apparat, likvidirovat' sistemu eksploatacii)*, but cannot be applied to the nouns of the first group (cf. the unacceptability of **likvidirovat' nadeždy [straxi]*). The nouns *sozdatel'* and *avtor* in the sense of "one who has created something" subordinate with identical ease names of (a) works of art and (b) developed ideas *(sozdatel'/avtor/kartiny [muzyki, romana], sozdatel'/avtor/proekta [teorii])*. Besides this, the first synonym can take as its complement the name of an organization or mechanism; cf. *sozdatel' armii [kolxoza partii, orkestra]* (creator of an army [kolchoz, party, orchestra]), *sozdatel' mašiny [samoleta, prisposoblenija]* (creator/inventor/ of a machine [aircraft, contrivance]), whereas **avtor armii [orkestra], *avtor mašiny [prisposoblenija]* are impossible in standard Russian. Only the second word, in its turn, is capable of subordinating nouns with the meaning of an idea; cf. *avtor* (but not **sozdatel'*) *gipotezy [zamysla, idei]* (author of the hypothesis [scheme, idea]).

5.3.2. *Lexical combinability.* The verbs *podvergat'sja* and *naxodit'sja (pod)* in the meaning "be under the influence of that which is designated by the dependent noun" can take as a complement the nouns *vlijanie* (influence), *davlenie* (pressure), *dejstvie* (action, effect); only the former, however, can freely combine with the word *presledovanie* (persecution) and only the latter combines with the word *vlast'* (power); cf. *podvergat'sja vlijaniju [davleniju]* (be subject to the influence [pressure] of), *naxodit'sja pod vlijaniem [pod davleniem]* (be under the influence of [under pressure]), but *podvergat'sja presledovanijam* (be persecuted) and *naxodit'sja pod vlast'ju* (be under the power of), **naxoditsja pod presledovanijami* and **podvergatsja vlasti* being unacceptable. The verbs *vpadat'* and *prixodit'* in the meaning "to begin to be in the state indicated by the dependent noun" combine equally well with the nouns *bešenstvo* (rage) and *jarost'* (fury) *(vpadat'/prixodit'/v bešenstvo [v jarost'])* (become furious/fly into a rage/). Only the former, however, can take the verbal position in the word-combinations *vpadat' v trans* (fall into a trance), *vpadat' v zabyt'e* (lapse into oblivion), *vpadat' v xandru* (be blue), and only the latter can take the verbal position in the combinations *prixodit' v vosxiščenie [v izumlenie]* (go into raptures [be wonderstruck]). The adjectives *blizkij* and *skoryj* in the sense "pertaining to something that will begin to occur in a short period of time" can be used equally well in the word-groups *blizkij/skoryj/ot"ezd [-aja razluka]* (impending departure [parting]), but the first of them is preferred in the word-groups *blizkoe buduščee* (the near future), *blizkaja noč'[vesna]* (the approaching night [spring]), while the second is better in the groups *do skorogo svidanija* (see you soon)!, *v skorom vremeni* (before long).

5.3.3. *Morpho-syntactic combinability.* The passive syntactic properties (the ability to function as dependents) of the nouns *katastrofa* and *krušenie* (smashup, wreck) are identical; cf. *privodit' k katastrofe/k krušeniju/*(result in a smashup/a wreck/), *Proizošla katastrofa, Proizošlo krušenie* (A smashup/ a wreck/has taken place). However, they differ from each other considerably in their active syntactic properties: the subjectival valency of the word *katastrofa* is expressed mainly by adjectives, while for the word *krušenie* it is expressed mainly by a noun in the genitive case, cf. *aviacionnaja [železnodorožnaja, avtomobil'naja] katastrofa* (plane [train, car] wreck), but not **katastrofa samoleta [poezda, avtomobilja]*; on the other hand, *krušenie sudna [poezda]* (shipwreck, trainwreck), but not **sudovoe [železnodorožnoe] krušenie*. The common morpho-syntactic feature of the nouns *redaktirovanie* and *redakcija* (editing) is their ability to serve as dependents of the verb, cf. *pristupat' k redaktirovaniju/k redakcii/knigi* (start editing a book), *provodit' redaktirovanie/redakciju/* (edit) and so on. However, only *redakti-*

rovanie can combine with the subjectival instrumental (*redaktirovanie knigi professorom NN* (the editing of the book by prof. NN)), and only *redakcija* can combine with the preposition *pod* in the dominant position (*kniga pod redakciej professora NN* (a book edited by prof. NN)), but not the other way about. Both, *nemnogo* (a little) and *slegka* (slightly) can combine with verbs denoting graded properties or states, cf. *nemnogo/slegka/kartavit* (burr slightly, have a slight burr), *nemnogo/slegka/ustal* (is slightly tired). However, the former is preferred with adjectives in the comparative degree and nouns denoting graded properties (*nemnogo bol'še [molože]* (a little larger [younger])), *nemnogo poet* (a little of a poet), while the latter is preferred with verbs denoting actions (*slegka udarit' [kosnut'sja]* (strike [touch] slightly)).

5.4. Full Non-Coincidence of Combinability

5.4.1. *Semantic combinability.* The most obvious examples are the adjectives *ženatyj, xolostoj, zamužnij, nezamužnij* (married, unmarried). The first two adjectives are used to refer to a male (*Pjotr ženat [xolost]* (Peter is married [unmarried])), while the last two adjectives are used to refer to a female (*Mar'ja zamužem [nezamužem]* (Mary is married [unmarried])). Of the two adjectives meaning "belonging to a species that has been developing under the influence of man", *domašnij* and *kul'turnyj*, the first is preferred in reference to an animal (*domašnie životnye* (domestic animals), *domašnjaja lošad'* (domesticated horse)), while the second is usually applied to plants (*kul'turnyj luk* (cultivated onion), *kul'turnoe rastenie* (cultivated plant)). *Vo ves' opor* (full speed) is usually said of living beings (*Lošad' mčalas' vo ves' opor* (The horse was putting its best foot foremost)), while its synonym *na vsex parax* is normally used in reference to mechanical means of transportation (*Korabl' [poezd] mčalsja na vsex parax* (The ship [the train] was going full speed)).

5.4.2. *Lexical combinability.* The idea that two words may completely coincide in meaning and yet have totally different selectional restrictions is contained in the concept of a "lexical parameter" as defined in the papers of A. K. Žolkovsky and I. A. Mel'čuk. A handy example is furnished by the verbs *povyšatsja* and *usilivat'sja* in the meaning "to become greater". The former combines with the nouns *temperatura* (temperature), *ceny* (prices) in the subject position, while the latter takes for its subject the nouns *groxot* (racket), *davlenie* (pressure), *žar* (heat), *protivorečija* (contradictions); an exchange of subjects between the verbs is impossible. Similar relations hold between the members of the pairs *glavnyj* and *pervyj* (cf. *glavnyj vrač* (head physician) but *pervyj sekretar'* (first secretary)), *okazyvat' vlijanie* (exert influence on) and *proizvodit' vpečatlenie* (make an impression on), *kosjak ryby* (school of fish) and *stado korov* (herd of cows), *General'nyj Prokuror* (Public procurator of the Supreme Court) and *verxovnyj (glavno-komandujuščij)* (Supreme Commander-in-Chief), *splošnaja (kollektivizacija)* (100% collectivization) and *poval'nye (obyski)* (general searches,) etc.[14]

5.4.3. *Morpho-Syntactic combinability.* The verb *utračivat'* ("to cease having") governs the accusative case of the noun, whereas its synonym *lišat'sja* governs the genitive (*utračivat' vlijanie* (lose influence), but *lišat'sja vlijanija*; cf. also *dotragivat'sja (do čego-l.)* and *prikasat'sja (k čemu-l.)* (touch), *vstupat' (v brak)* and *zaključat' (brak)* (enter into matrimony with), *sčitat' (kogo kem)* and *rassmatrivat' (kogo kak kogo)* (consider smb. to be smb./smth.), *kosit' (glaza na kogo-l.)* and *kosit'sja (glazami na kogo-l.)* (look askance at smb.), *vozobladat'* and *pobedit'* (conquer, prevail over) (*Čuvstvo dolga vozobladalo nad straxom* (His sense of duty prevailed over his fear) – *Čuvstvo dolga pobedilo strax* (His sense of duty conquered his fear), *nedomogat'* and *nezdorovit'sja* (be ill, feel unwell) (*On nedomogaet* – *Emu nezdorovitsja* (He's not feeling well)), *žalet'* and *žal'* (pity, feel compassion for) (*On žaleet menja* – *Emu žal' menja* (He feels sorry for me)), *vrjad li/edva li/*(hardly) and *somnitel'no* (it is doubtful) (*Vrjad li/edva li/on pridet* (He will hardly come) – *Somnitel'no, čtoby on prišel* (I doubt that he will come)), *vopreki (protestu)* (despite the protest) and *nesmotrja (na protest)* (in spite of the protest), *kak tol'ko/edva/(on vidit menja)* (as soon as he sees me) and *stóit (emu uvidet menja')*.

6. SOME OTHER QUESTIONS OF THE THEORY OF LEXICAL SYNONYMS

6.1. *Interchangeability*

As is clear from the above remarks, interchangeability is a possible but not a necessary property of lexical synonyms. In cases 1, 2, and 3 the synonyms are interchangeable, at least partly, and in case 4 (full non-coincidence of combinability) they are not. Speaking more precisely, there is complete bilateral interchangeability in the first case (synonyms *A* and *B* can substitute for each other in any context); in the second case there is complete substitutability in one direction and partial substitutability in the other (the word *A* which has a broader range of combinability than its synonym *B*,

---

[14] See Žolkovsky's and Mel'čuk's papers mentioned in footnote 2. V. V. Vinogradov's papers on phraseological collocations and phraseologically bound meanings are also directly related to this theme (see, for example, *Ob osnovnyx tipax frazeologičeskix edinic v russkom jazyke'* sb. 'A. A. Šaxmatov', M., 1947; *Osnovnye tipy leksičeskix značesnij slova*, VJa, 1953, 5).

can be substituted for the latter in any context; unlike it, *B* can replace
A only in certain contexts); in the third case interchangeability is partial
in both directions (synonyms *A* and *B* can be substituted for each other
only in certain contexts). If we take into account the fact that it is not
actually elementary differences that are represented in synonym pairs, but
combinations of differences, the picture becomes even more involved.[15]

The straightforward type of interchangeability discussed above illustrates
the least interesting aspect of the problem. A more interesting case of interchangeability is represented in such instances as *dotragivat'sja (do čego-l.)*
and *prikasat'sja (k čemu-l.)*. Those two synonyms are in complementary
distribution with regard to their morpho-syntactic combinability and thus
are not interchangeable in the straightforward way. However, they can be
substituted for each other if we replace not only the verb itself but also
the objectival prepositional phrase which it governs: not *dotragivat'sja do
čego-l.* → **prikasat'sja do čego-l.*, but *dotragivat'sja do čego-l.* → *prikasat'sja
k čemu-l.* The same principle applies in the more sophisticated instances of
synonyms which are in complementary distribution with regard to their
lexical combinability. Interchangeability is possible if one of the synonyms
occurs in the given text together with its "lexical parameter" (in the sense
of Mel'čuk and Žolkovskij) and if we replace both, the word at issue and
the expression of the lexical parameter. Consider the values of the parameter
Magn ("high degree") when its arguments are the nouns *durak* and *olux*
(fool) which are exact semantic (though not stylistic) synonyms: Magn
(durak) = *kruglyj* ("round"), *nabityj* ("stuffed"), while Magn *(olux)* = *carja
nebesnogo* ("of the heavenly tsar"). The straightforward substitution *kruglyj
durak* → *kruglyj olux results in an unacceptable phrase, but the double
substitution *kruglyj durak* → *olux carja nebesnogo* whereby the value of Magn
is also appropriately changed does carry the day. Cf. also *pri naličii (gazov)*
(when there are gases; *pri* = Loc *(naličie)*) → *v prisutstvii (gazov)* (in the
presence of gases; *v* = Loc *(prisutstvie)*).[16]

It has been argued above that interchangeability, even partial, is not a
necessary property of exact lexical synonyms. We can add now that, on the
other hand, there are interchangeable words and expressions which never-

---

[15] Here we have in mind only the semantic interchangeability of synonyms; since the
selection of a synonym in any specific speech situation is determined by many other
factors besides bare meaning, the freedom of substitution in a concrete text is somewhat
reduced. Cf. G. O. Vinokur's extreme point of view on this question (G. O. Vinokur,
'Problema kul'tury reči', *Russkij jazyk v sovetskoj škole* 5, 1929, p. 85.)

[16] As a matter of fact, what we actually do in both these cases is to replace two synonyms
simultaneously (*do čego-l.* and *k čemu-l.* are synonyms because they have the same
objectival meaning, *kruglyj* and *carja nebesnogo* are also synonyms because they have
the same meaning of high degree).

theless cannot claim the status of exact lexical synonyms. This kind of interchangeability is characteristic of quasisynonyms in contexts where their semantic differences are neutralized (needless to say, there are quasisynonyms with non-neutralizable semantic distinctions).

6.2. *Quasisynonyms and Interchangeability: Neutralization of Meaning Differences*

Quasisynonyms are any two words which satisfy the second and third conditions of synonymy as stated on p. 181 and whose semantic similarity, although not total, is yet greater than or equal to the sum of their semantic differences.[17] If A and B are quasisynonyms, such that $A =$ 'XYZ', and $B =$ 'XY', then neutralization may be effected in one of the following two ways: (a) the given context eliminates 'Z' in A; (b) the given context imparts 'Z' to B. If both quasisynonyms have specific elements of meaning, neutralization is effected in the first way.

The first possibility is often realized in cases of the disjunctive organization of constituents in the semantic structure (tree) of the given meaning. If $A =$ 'XY or Z', $B =$ 'XY', and F is a semantic feature of the context incompatible with the constituent 'Z', then 'Z' will be suppressed in the context of F, with the neutralization of the semantic difference between the generally quasisynonymous words A and B as a result. By way of illustration we shall consider the verbs *ulučšat'sja* and *ispravljat'sja*.

The verb *ulučšat'sja* means "stanovit'sja lučše" (become better), while its quasisynonym *ispravljat'sja* means "stanovit'sja lučše ili stanovit'sja xorošim" (become better or become good).[18] Note that the definitions of *ulučšat'sja* and *ispravljat'sja* contain non-terminative[19] adjectives (adjectives in the comparative degree are always non-terminative); besides this, the definition of *ispravljat'sja* contains (after the disjunction) a terminative adjective.[19]

The following semantically motivated selectional restrictions underlie the

---

[17] This definition is completely formalizable.

[18] Since the disjunction is inclusive, "stanovit'sja lučše" and "stanovit'sja xorošim" are not two different meanings of the verb, but a single meaning; the distinguishing feature of polysemy is the exclusively disjunctive organization of meanings (either A, or B, but not A and B simultaneously).

[19] This distinction was introduced in the author's paper *Ob eksperimental'nom tolkovom slovare russkogo jazyka, Voprosy jazykoznanija*, 1968, No. 4. Terminative adjectives denote qualities which have an utmost limit or a maximum of concentration, cf. the adjectives of colour, some adjectives of form (*kruglyj* (round)), of small size (*korotkij* (short)) and so on. Non-terminative adjectives denote qualities which have no limit or maximum of concentration, cf. the adjectives of large size (*dlinnyj* (long)). Note in particular that one can increase indefinitely the length of a long thing, for example, a solid cylinder, and it will still be called *long*, but one cannot decrease indefinitely the length of a short cylinder, because after a certain lower limit of length is passed the cylinder will be appropriately

use of terminative and non-terminative adjectives. Terminative adjectives can be modified by adverbs denoting the full degree of a quality, cf. *soveršenno kruglyj* (ideally round), *sovsem/vpolne/xorošij* (quite good), the total meaning being that the utmost limit of the corresponding property is achieved. On the other hand they cannot very well be modified by adverbs denoting an insignificant degree of a quality (cf. the unacceptability of **nemnogo xorošij* (a little good), **čut'-čut' xorošij* (a tiny bit good)) because the resulting word-groups are contradictory: *nemnogo* and *čut'-čut'* convey the idea of incompleteness, while *xorošij* conveys the idea of completeness. With the non-terminative adjectives it is the other way round; they can be modified by the adverbs of the first group (cf. *čut'-čut' lučše* (a tiny bit better), *nemnogo lučše* (slightly better), but they do not combine with the adverbs of the first group: the expressions **sovsem lučše* (quite better) or *soveršenno kruglee* (completely rounder) are semantically contradictory (and therefore, in the case at issue, unacceptable), because *sovsem* and *soveršenno* convey the idea of completeness, while *lučše* and *kruglee* convey the idea of incompleteness.

Now let us go back to the verb *ispravljat'sja*. Since its definition contains a non-terminative and a terminative adjective, it can be combined with both types of adverbs. When it is combined with the adverbs of the first group (e.g., *sovsem*), the non-terminative constituent of its meaning, incompatible with the idea of completeness, is suppressed: *sovsem ispravit'sja*="stat' sovsem xorošim" (become quite good). This is the position of maximum semantic contrast for *ispravljat'sja* and *ulučšat'sja*: for the reasons stated above the latter does not combine with *sovsem* at all. Now, when *ispravljat'sja* is combined with the adverbs of the second group (cf. *nemnogo*), the terminative constituent of its meaning, incompatible with the idea of incompleteness, is suppressed: *nemnogo ispravit'sja*="stat' nemnogo lučše" (become a little better). This is a position of semantic neutralization for *ispravit'sja* and *ulučšit'sja*: although they contrast in a number of positions they become semantically equivalent in combination with the adverbs of the second group: *Ego povedenie nemnogo ulučšilos'*=*Ego povedenie nemnogo ispravilos'* (His behaviour has become a little better). Precisely the same semantic relations hold between their antonyms *uxudšat'sja* – *portit'sja* and the causative verbs *ulučšat'* – *ispravljat', uxudšat'* – *portit'*. Other examples are *bombardirovat'* – *bombit, kopat* – *ryt. Bombardirovat'*="to drop bombs or shell from guns", – *bombit'*="to drop bombs". If the subject of these

---

called *thin* and not *short* (it will switch into a different dimension). There are important differences between various types of such adjectives which cannot be elaborated in the framework of the present paper.

actions is an aircraft, then the second constituent of *bombardirovat'* is suppressed and the verbs become interchangeable: *Vražeskie samolety bombili/bombardirovali/gorod dnem i noč'ju* (The enemy planes bombed the city day and night). In the sentence *Gorod bombila aviacija i bombardirovala tjaželaja artillerija* (The city was bombed by aircraft and bombarded by heavy artillery), however, there is an obvious semantic contrast. *Kopat'* and *ryt'* (dig) differ in that *kopat'* means "to dig with a tool" whereas *ryt'* means "to dig with a tool or an organ" (Normally, *Lisa roet* (not *kopaet!*) *noru* (The fox digs a burrow)). To bring about the conditions for neutralization and subsequent interchange it is sufficient to combine the verbs with the name of a tool, cf. *ryt'/kopat'/zastupom [lopatoj] glubokuju jamu* (to dig a deep pit with a shovel [a spade]).

Another type of semantic structure which allows of neutralization at the expense of eliminating one of the semantic constituents of the specific quasisynonym is the structure with probable, but not obligatory constituents. *Prekraščat'sja* and *končat'sja* have the same general meaning of cessation, but *končat'sja* often points to the fact that the action has reached its natural limit. Therefore, when combined with nouns denoting rational activity (*Zanjatie [putešestvie, rabota] prekraščaetsja – končaetsja* (The lesson [the journey, the work] stops – is over)) the verbs are in semantic contrast: lessons, journeys, and work require completion. On the other hand, natural processes do not require completion; therefore in combination with such nouns as *dožd'* (rain), *sneg* (snow) and the like the specific feature of *končat'sja* is eliminated, and the semantic difference between the two quasisynonyms is neutralized: *Dožd' tak že vnezapno prekratilsja/končilsja/, kak i načalsja* (The rain stopped as suddenly as it had begun).

The following example illustrates a somewhat rarer instance of neutralization whereby two quasisynonyms simultaneously drop their specific semantic features. *Rubit'* differs from *kolot'* in that it presupposes the use of an instrument; the process described by *kolot'* is not necessarily carried out with the help of an instrument. One can say *NN kolet led o kamen'* (NN is breaking the ice against a stone), but one can hardly substitute *rubit'* for *kolot'* in such a sentence. In its turn, *kolot'* implies a hard non-viscous object, and there is no such implication in *rubit'*; cf. *rubit' drova [led, mjaso, kapustu]* (to chop wood [ice, meat, cabbage]), but only *kolot' drova [led]*, **kolot' mjaso [kapustu]* being unacceptable in the normal situation (they are acceptable in the situation when meat or cabbage are frozen so hard that they break into pieces at a blow). Neutralization takes place if both conditions are observed, i.e. if the objectival noun denotes a normally hard object and if the action is carried out by means of an instrument, cf. *NN kolol/rubil/drova toporom* (NN chopped wood with an ax).

As has been pointed out above, the second possibility of neutralization consists in the imparting to $A=$'XY' of a specific feature characteristic of its quasisynonym $B=$'XYZ'. This type of neutralization occurs mostly (but not exclusively) in cases of the conjunctive organization of constituents in the semantic structure of the given meaning. Neutralization may be effected in one of the following two ways: (a) 'Z' is attached only to A; then $A=$ $=$'XY'$+$'Z'$=$'XYZ'; (b) 'Z' is attached both, to A and to B; then $A=$'XY'$+$ $+$'Z'$=$'XYZ', and $B=$'XYZ'$+$'Z'$=$'XYZZ'$=$(by a special rule for suppressing tautology) 'XYZ'.

The equation 'XY'$+$'Z'$=$'XYZ' may also mean two things. (1) 'Z' may be represented by a separate word tied up with $A=$'XY' by the same syntactic relation as in the definition of $B=$'XYZ'; (2) 'Z' may be a new semantic constituent of A inserted in the definition of A in the given context by a special rule (such rules are the converse of the rules of elimination or suppression and may be called the rules of semantic enrichment). Only (2) is a case of real neutralization, if by neutralization we mean a process confined to a single word; in (1) neutralization manifests itself in stretches of text longer than a single word. However, it is mostly (1) that occurs in actual speech, and we shall illustrate only this process.

Snačala (first) denotes the first place in any sequence of events: *Snačala NN pošel za pokupkami, potom pobrilsja* (First NN went out to do some shopping, and then he shaved), *Snačala šel dožd', potom grad* (At first it rained, but then there was a hail). The quasisynonymous expressions *pervym delom, pervym dolgom, v pervuju očered'* (in the first place) include the meaning of *snačala* and suggest in addition that the rational agent who is the subject of the corresponding events prefers the given order of events to any other possible order. *Pervym delom/pervym dolgom, v pervuju očered'/ my pojdem za pokupkami, a potom uže sdelaem vse ostal'noe* (First of all we shall do the shopping and then we shall attend to the other things); cf. the unacceptability of **Pervym delom/pervym dolgom/prišel poezd dal'nego sledovanija, a potom – dačnyj* (In the first place, the long distance train arrived, then came the suburban train), or **Pervym delom/pervym dolgom/ NN podumal, čto našel razgadku tajny, no potom uvidel, čto ošibsja* (In the first place NN thought that he had found clue to the mystery, but then he saw that he was in error). Neutralization takes place in the presence of a modal verb with the meaning of 'nužno' (should, necessary) and on condition that the subject of the action is a rational agent: *Snačala/pervym delom, pervym dolgom, v pervuju očered'/nužno pobrit'sja, a potom možno i poest'* (First of all, we should shave, and then we can eat).

A slightly more complicated instance of neutralization is furnished by the pair of verbs *soveršenstvovat' – soveršenstvovat'sja*. *Soveršenstvovat' X=*

="make X more perfect", cf. *soveršenstvovat' mašinu [talant, svoi znanija]* (to perfect a machine [one's talent, one's knowledge]); *soveršenstvovat'sja v X*="become more perfect in X or make X more perfect; X is a property of the subject", cf. *soveršenstvovat'sja v znanijax [v svoem iskusstve, vo francuzskom, v igre na pianino]* (to perfect one's knowledge [one's skill, one's French, one's performance on the piano]). The part "become more perfect" in the definition of *soveršenstvovat'sja* is necessary, because *soveršenstvovat'sja* does not always imply a deliberate effort on the part of the subject but may suggest a natural and uncontrollable growth of one's knowledge or skill. Neutralization takes place on condition that (a) the above mentioned constituent of the meaning of *soveršenstvovat'sja* is eliminated, (b) X is explicitly stated to be a property of the subject. Condition (a) is satisfied if, for example, the verb is modified by an adverb of the type *uporno* (stubbornly) *sistematičeski* (systematically) and the like, denoting a deliberate effort on the part of the subject and therefore incompatible with the idea of incontrollability. Condition (b) is satisfied if, for example, X is prefixed with the reflexive pronoun *svoj* and if *X* denotes a skill or an intellectual accomplishment: *On uporno soveršenstvoval svoe masterstvo – On uporno soveršenstvovalsja v svoem masterstve* (He did his best to perfect his skill).

The problems we have touched upon in the present paper make up only a small and relatively simple part of the fascinating whole called lexical synonymy; but to draw a complete picture of this pivotal semantic phenomenon it is probably the best policy to begin by investigating its simplest manifestations.

Soviet Academy of Sciences, Moscow

A. GLADKIJ

AN ATTEMPT AT THE FORMAL DEFINITION
OF CASE AND GENDER OF THE NOUN*

The development of linguistics has now entered a stage where rigorous logical analysis of its concepts has become possible and necessary. We need not speak of the importance of such an analysis: until the logical structure of a notion is elucidated with sufficient clarity, its use will be impeded in much the same way that reading is made more difficult if the contours of the letters are erased.

Many researchers have recognized the necessity of making linguistic notions more exact. One has occasion, however, to encounter an erroneous view (perhaps not always fully realized by its bearers) according to which the transformation of linguistics into an exact science should be connected exclusively with the creation of new conceptions. Traditional linguistic notions such as the noun, the adjective, case, gender, etc. are, in view of their logical inadequacy, to be either ignored or used in an auxiliary function having no more than an heuristic significance. Such a point of view leads to the conclusion that the introduction of exact concepts and methods into linguistics demands a complete break with tradition. Hence, perhaps, the still rather widely spread opposition of 'traditional' and 'structural' linguistics as two almost different disciplines; and hence the mistrust which many 'traditional' linguists feel towards exact notions and methods, in which they are inclined to see a source of destruction.

If we are to approach the matter seriously, there can, of course, be no discussion of ignoring 'traditional' language science, of refusing the concepts it has developed and which have been used successfully for a very long time. The problem consists first of all in giving JUST THESE NOTIONS a basis which can satisfy contemporary demands on the logical structure of scientific conceptions. The situation here is to a certain degree analogous to one which at one time occurred in geometry. The fundamental ideas of this science had been used for many centuries without any rigorous logic analysis. Such an analysis was made in the past century, but it did not at all mean that the old categories of geometry were 'abolished'; these categories merely came to be clearer and more deeply understood. Just thanks to this, however, geometry passed into a qualitatively new stage in its development

* Originally published in *Mathematical Models of Language* (F. Kiefer, ed.), Athenäum Verlag, 1973, by permission of Språkförlaget Skriptor, Copyright © 1972, Skriptor, Stockholm. The paper has been revised for the present volume. (*Editor's note.*)

and attained an extremely important advance which otherwise would have been impossible and in directions which could not even have been contemplated earlier. In a similar way, the creation of new trends in linguistics demands logical analysis and the systematization of its traditional concepts. More specifically, it is necessary to construct a system of linguistic notions which would include all of the most important traditional concepts in such a way that the base of this system would be made up of a certain complex of basic notions – such a complex should be logically simple and comparatively 'poor', and allow easy viewing but at the same time it should be natural – and we should be able to obtain all other notions from these initial ones strictly formally[1], with only the help of logical constructions. A tendency towards this sort of structure for linguistic theory has existed for some time already; probably its most vivid manifestation is the renowned book by L. Hjelmslev [1]. This book, however, was written before investigations on the formalization of concrete linguistic notions had been extensively developed, and it takes as its subject the general principles of linguistic theory, rather than its actual development. Studies on the formal substantiation of many linguistic concepts have at the present time advanced rather far, and this creates the prerequisites for the actual construction of a system of linguistic notions on the basis of the principles stated above. Nevertheless, the full development of such a system remains a matter for the future even now (although, perhaps, not the very distant future); the concrete task thus far is to construct certain individual systems, and it is in the process of solving this problem that we can hope to establish how a general formalized theory is to be created.

One such individual system is proposed in the present article, which is intended to define the notions of case and gender of the noun. It is not the first system to have such a purpose; the question of the definition of these notions has already been treated several times. The first formal definition of case for the noun is in fact contained in the pioneer work of O. S. Kulagina [4], which marked the beginning of all those studies which have sought to formalize 'traditional' grammatical notions. A definition of case has been proposed by A. N. Kolmogorov and V. A. Uspenskij [5][2]. Different variants of formal definitions of case and gender can be found in the works of S. Marcus [6] (Ch. IV), [7] (Ch. VI) and I. I. Revzin [8] (§§ 40, 45).

---

[1] The word 'formally' here and below means "exactly, definitely, without logical gaps" (and not "without reference to meaning", as the word is often understood in works on linguistics). The only time we depart from this definition of the word is when we use it in the term 'formal coordinational class' (Section 5).

[2] This paper has been a bibliographical rarity for a long time. A somewhat altered presentation of Kolmogorov and Uspenskij's definition can be found in A. A. Zaliznjak's book [2], §§ 2.3, 2.4.

All of the works mentioned above (with the exception of [5], in which certain semantic elements are found among the basic notions), use essentially the same system of basic notions – a system whose basic component is the notion of a grammatically correct sentence. But this concept is hardly simple enough. The set of grammatically correct sentences of a language is in fact infinite, so that any procedure for which this set is basic requires infinite examination and is therefore ineffective. In contrast to this, the present work proposes a system of basic notions, all of whose components are predicates determined on a finite set and are therefore describable by means of finite tables. Using such a system of basic notions would also seem to make it possible to make the definitions more natural and adequate – in other words, this system makes it possible for us to come closer to the formalization of the linguistic intuition which lies at the base of 'ordinary', 'non-formal' concepts of case and gender, that is, the notions of case and gender used in Russian grammatical tradition.

The basic idea of our definitions, which we think coincides with the basic idea of the traditional concepts of case and gender, can be explained as follows: each case is a set of noun forms which are in some sense governed identically by other words, while each gender is a set of nouns which in some sense identically govern other words.

We cannot, of course, expect that our definitions will arrive at exactly that which the grammatical tradition (if there is one) of any given language calls case and gender. On the contrary, the applicability of our definitions to some languages and their unapplicability to others can help elucidate the typological differences between categories which for these languages have traditionally been called by the same name.

The author became interested in the problem treated in the present paper while reading (in manuscript) I. I. Revzin's book [8]. The author was subsequently able, with great benefit for himself, to discuss the problem with A. A. Zaliznjak and I. I. Revzin. A. A. Zaliznjak and I. A. Mel'čuk read one of the first versions of the manuscript; the author has found their criticism to be very helpful. T. I. Šed'ko, who discovered an inaccuracy in the definition of gender given in the original version, made some extremely important comments. The author would like to express his sincere gratitude to these persons. In addition, it must be mentioned that A. A. Zaliznjak[3] independently (and earlier) obtained results similar to our own.

An abbreviated exposition of the material of the present paper has been published in [10].

The preliminary experimental checking of the definitions given here for

[3] Unpublished work.

Russian was conducted by T. I. Šed'ko [11], [12]. The cases and genders distinguished in this experiment basically coincided with the traditional ones.

1. PRELIMINARY EXPLANATIONS

(1) Before presenting the system of initial concepts, it will be useful to give some non-formal explanations concerning the general premises behind our approach to grammatical meanings.

We think that the lexical and grammatical meanings corresponding to the words [4] of a language can be divided into two types. Meanings of the first type are those which are, so to say, internally inherent in the words, that is, those which more or less directly correspond to certain ideas in the consciousness of native speakers of the language and which are associated by the speakers with the words in question. All lexical meanings belong here. The plural of the Russian noun, which corresponds to a rather clear idea of 'plurality', can serve as an example of a grammatical meaning of this type. Meanings of the second type are constructs which arise as a result of a rather complex abstraction and do not directly correspond to any sort of ideas in the consciousness of the speakers of the language (at any rate not of those who have not studied grammar). We are of the conviction that the meanings of the basic cases in modern Russian belong to this type. It is in fact hardly possible, for example, to indicate the definite idea in the consciousness of a native speaker of Russian which is realized in the utterance of each of the word-groups *dovolen synom, vygljadit starikom, rabotaet tokarem, rabotaet lopatoj, vladeet zavodom, zanimaetsja fizikoj, vzvešivaetsja kladovščikom, idet novoj dorogoj, idet bystrym šagom, prenebregaet opasnost'ju' torguet ryboj, nazvala Ivanom, éto bylo nesčast'em, snabžaet toplivom, rasstavljaet rjadami, svistit solov'em, boleet grippom, vysok rostom, živet pod Moskvoj, naxoditsja pod sledstviem, stoit nad obryvom, prjačetsja za derevom, bumaga za ego podnis'ju, spravilsja s protivnikom, razgovarivaet s drugom, poslal s okaziej, buterbrod s syrom* ((he) is satisfied with his son, looks like an old man, works as a lathe operator, works with a spade, owns a factory, is studying physics, is weighted by the storekeeper, takes the new road, walks with quick steps, ignores danger, trades in fish, (she) called him Ivan, (it) was a disaster, supplies with fuel, arranges in rows, whistles like a nightingale, is ill with the flu, is tall, lives near Moscow, is under investigation, stands over the precipice, hides behind the tree, paper against his signature, coped with his opponent, is talking with his friend, sent by smb., cheese sandwich (sandwich with cheese)).

[4] The vagueness of the term 'word' (see below) does not present any important obstacles in the present arguments.

Thus, the meanings 'nominative case', 'genitive case', etc. of the Russian noun most naturally fit into the second type. We also think it correct to place the meanings of the gender of the Russian noun in this group.

The meanings of the first type and the grammatical categories which correspond to them will be said to be INTERNAL, and meanings of the second type and their categories will be called EXTERNAL. In all probability, such a division of grammatical categories basically coincides with the usual division into 'semantic' and 'syntactic'[5].

Now we can pose a question as to the place of internal and external meanings and categories in the system of formal language description. Here we can proceed from the point of view according to which language is a working mechanism and any good description of language is a description of how this mechanism works; ideally, it should allow for reproduction of the operation of the mechanism in all details, i.e., it should be its WORKING MODEL. In such an approach it is reasonable to assume that internal meanings and categories should be organic constituent parts of such a model. Specifically, it is natural to include internal meanings in the semantic notation in 'meaning-text' models, and the rigorous definition of such meanings will be nothing other than an indication of their role in the semantic notation. The external meanings have to be defined on the basis of an analysis of the structure of the language mechanism, or the process of its operation, or the result of this process, that is, speech. We are not obliged here to use all the information we have about language as a mechanism to define each category; on the contrary, it is necessary to try to limit oneself to the smallest possible body of such information – to only that which is actually necessary. In the first place, this makes the definitions simpler and clearer, thus making them more convenient to work with, and secondly and more importantly, it allows us to show what parts of the language mechanism one or another external category is directly connected, that is, we can explain its place in the general system.

We think that what has been stated thus far makes it possible to bring some clarity into the question of the interrelation of two contemporary approaches to the formal description of language: the 'synthetic' approach, which finds its expression in the construction of so-called 'synthetic models' or 'language models proper' – generative grammars and 'meaning-text' models, – and the 'analytic' approach, which is connected with the construction of 'analytical models' or 'research models', and also decoding algorithms. The second approach is more natural for describing external

---

[5] We mean a coincidence in the intuitive reasons for the division rather than a coincidence in its results. Case in Russian is most often classified among the 'semantic', i.e., the internal categories, which in our opinion is incorrect.

meanings and categories, while the first is better for all other purposes. Of course, descriptions of an 'analytic' or 'decoding' nature can be also possible for a part of the internal meanings and categories, since the language mechanism is not obliged to satisfy any sort of requirements of minimality or independence of constituent parts. These definitions can have significance in their practical, as well as in their purely theoretical aspects; nonetheless, such methods should play a subordinate role for the treatment of internal meanings within the framework of the general system at the same time as they should be considered primary in the study of external meanings.

To sum up, we can now say that if we wish to understand the nature of one or another external category (or group of external categories) and want to construct its formal definition (and the present study attempts to do just this), then we will have to take as a basis for all our treatments some system of notions which contains (in, of course, a very clear-cut form) some sort of information about the structure of the language mechanism, or about the process of its operation, or about speech; specifically, this system can contain certain information about internal meanings and/or categories. It is desirable here to attempt to make these basic notions as simple and 'poor' as possible, not, of course, to the detriment of the naturalness of their content. We shall try to hold to just these principles as we formulate our definitions of case, coordinational class, and gender.

(2) The second explanation will have a more special character. It has to do with how we refine the meaning of the notion 'word'. As is well known, such refinement can result in several different concepts (which are not always sufficiently clearly distinguished in linguistic literature or even in the most recent works on formal language description). A. A. Zaliznjak [2] lists the following meanings of the word 'word': (1) "The word as a unit of the external side of text", that is, in reference to the written form of language, simply a string of letters from one break to another. A. A. Zaliznjak calls such an object a SEGMENT. Two segments are considered identical when and only when they coincide graphically[6], independently of their lexical and grammatical meanings; for example *luk* meaning 'vegetable' (onion) and *luk* in the meaning 'weapon' (bow) are identical segments in the same way as *máčty* (mast) in the meaning gen. sg. and *máčty* in the meaning nom. pl.; (2) "The word as a two-sided unit of text (i.e., as a unit having both expression and content)" he calls a WORD-FORM. In other words, a word-form is a segment taken together with its lexical and all its grammatical meanings. When any meanings of two word-forms fail to coincide, these

---

[6] Of course, for the notion graphic coincidence to have an exact meaning, a notation method would have to be established beforehand.

word-forms are considered to be different. Thus, *máčty* in the meaning nom. pl. and *máčty* in the meaning gen. sg. are different word-forms; *luk* in the meaning 'vegetable', nom. sg. is not the same word-form as *luk* in the meaning 'weapon' nom. sg.; (3) "The word as a unit of the dictionary, that is, as a bilateral extra-textual unit of language which arises on the basis of an analysis of all the texts of a given language", is a LEXEME. A lexeme can be equated – cf. [2], § 1.7 – with the set of all word-forms which have the same lexical (in Zaliznjak's terminology, *nominative proper*) meaning.

Segments and word-forms can be divided into CONCRETE and ABSTRACT. A concrete segment is a segment treated together with the place in the text where it is located, in contrast to an abstract segment, which is viewed independently of its place in the text. Concrete segments which coincide graphically but differ in the place they occupy in the text are considered to be REPRESENTATIVES of a single abstract segment (the conditions of segment identity formulated above thus relate to abstract segments). Concrete and abstract word-forms are defined in a similar way.

The notions listed above do not, however, exhaust all the refinements of the word 'word' which might prove to be useful in linguistic theory. Specifically, the following object, which is in a certain sense intermediary between the segment and the word form, seems quite natural; the segment together with its lexical meaning, but without any sort of grammatical meanings. We shall call such an object a LEXICALLY MEANINGFUL SEGMENT. As was the case with segments and word-forms, it is necessary to differentiate between concrete lexically meaningful segments, or those taken together with their place in the text, and abstract ones, those which are treated without reference to their places. We shall as a rule use the following (usual in mathematics) terminology: an abstract lexically meaningful segment will simply be called a lexically meaningful segment, and a concrete segment will be said to be an OCCURRENCE of a lexically meaningful segment in a text (for example, in a sentence). Using this terminology ,we can say that two lexically meaningful segments are identical when and only when they coincide graphically and their lexical meanings coincide. Thus, in the sentence *vyveska nad dver'ju čajnoj perekosilas', a v samoj čajnoj ne bylo ni odnoj čajnoj ložki* (The sign above the door of the tea-house is crooked, and in the tea-house itself there was not a single teaspoon), the first two occurrences of the segment *čajnoj* correspond to the same lexically meaningful segment with the meaning "a type of public house where the customers can drink tea and get simple meals" (S. I. Ožegov, *Slovar' russkogo jazyka*), while the third belongs to a different lexically meaningful segment (with the meaning 'adjective from *čaj*' (tea)).

In the future we will use metonymic phrasing of the type "the lexically meaningful segment *vodá* (water)", having in mind "a lexically meaningful segment the external side of which is the segment *vodá*" (cf. [2], p. 21).

Sets of lexically meaningful segments with the same lexical meaning will be called NEIGHBORHOODS. By the very definition of the concept of lexically meaningful segment, neighborhoods should be mutually disjunct sets.

We shall now adopt the following terminological convention: since the notion of segment will not be used by us in the future, we shall for the sake of brevity agree to call lexically meaningful segments simply SEGMENTS. It is segments in this sense and neighborhoods which constitute the base of our system of basic notions.

(3) To conclude this section, let us make the following observation. A definition of COORDINATIONAL CLASS will precede our definition of gender. The area covered by this concept probably coincides for a number of languages with that of the notion of gender. The category in Russian which has traditionally borne the name 'gender' differs from the coordinational class concept. Since this latter notion is logically clearer and possesses a greater generality than the category of gender in traditional Russian grammar, it seems convenient to treat coordinational class as being the simpler, so to say, 'more primary' basic category. When the notion of coordinational class is defined, we will be able to show the procedure which builds the concept of 'traditional gender' on its foundations (see below, Section 5).

The notion of coordinational class (like the term 'coordinational class' itself) was, I suppose, introduced by A. A. Zaliznjak [3] (cf. also [2], §§ 2.14–2.16). It was he who showed that gender and coordinational class in Russian do not coincide ([3], pp. 26–27; [2], pp. 66–67).

2. BASIC NOTIONS

We consider the following objects, which will function as basic undefined notions, to have been given:

(1) The finite set V, whose elements are interpreted as segments (see the terminological remark at the end of the preceding section) of some natural language. This set will be called the VOCABULARY, and its elements will be called SEGMENTS.

(2) The system of mutually disjunct subsets of set V, which in their aggregate wholly cover this set. These subsets will be said to be NEIGHBORHOODS. Linguistically, each neighborhood is a set of segments having identical lexical meanings (cf. Section 1 (2)), that is, the set of all forms of a single word. Examples of neighborhoods: {*dom, dóma, dómu, dómom, dóme, domá, domóv, domám, domámi, domáx*} (house); {*nóvyj, nóvoe, nóvaja, nóvogo, nóvoj, nóvomu, nóvuju, nóvym, nóvoju, nóvom, nóvye, nóvyx, nóvymi,*

nov, nová, nóvo, nový}[7] (new); {*na*} (on); {*ókolo*} (near); {*óčen'*} (very)[8].

A neighborhood containing segment *x* will usually be called a NEIGHBORHOOD OF SEGMENT *x*.

(3) The subset *S* of set *V*, content-wise interpretable as the set of all nouns of a given language. The set *S* should be a union of some system of neighborhoods. (In other words, a neighborhood is either contained in *S*, or does not intersect with *S*.)

The segments which belong to *S* will be called *S*-SEGMENTS, and the neighborhoods contained in *S* will be said to be *S*-NEIGHBORHOODS.

(4) The binary relation → on the vocabulary, which we will call the RELATION OF POTENTIAL SUBORDINATION (the expression *x* → *y* is read '*x* potentially subordinates *y*').

The expression *x* → *y* means that there exists a grammatically correct simple sentence in the language in question in which some occurrence of segment *x* syntactically directly subordinates some occurrence of segment *y*. We will assume here that the subject is always subordinated to the predicate.

Thus, from the correctness of the sentence

žil na svete staričok malen'kogo rosta

(once upon a time there lived a short little old man) with the arrows of subordination arranged as they are, we conclude that the assertions *žil* → *staričók, žil* → *na, na* → *svéte, staričók* → *rósta, rósta* → *málen'kogo* are true. At the same time, the assertions *rósta* → *málen'koj, na* → *svétom, pod* → *svéte* are false, since in a grammatically correct Russian sentence the segment *rósta* cannot subordinate the segment *málen'koj*, the segment *na* – the segment *svétom*, nor the segment *pod* – the segment *svéte*[9].

Let us make two further remarks on the interpretation of the relation of subordination in Russian: (a) in those cases where the choice of the direction of the arrow seems disputable (*dva stola, dvum stolam* (two tables), *neskol'ko stolov, neskol'kim stolam* (several tables)), we will not fix the relation of potential subordination in either direction (i.e., for example, both of the

---

[7] Thus, we consider the formation of the comparative degrees of the adjective to belong to word formation (cf. [2], §2.23). This is, however, unimportant for our construction.

[8] All examples will be based exclusively on Russian materials. We use an accentuated orthographic notation for the segments in the examples ([2], §0.4), so that the stress is omitted in coherent texts, one-syllable segments, and over *ë* (cf. *ibid.*, §0.5).

[9] Using the notion of a grammatically correct sentence to interpret potential subordination does not contradict the statement made above that this notion is not included among the basic facts of our system. We actually need it only for purposes of ELUCIDATION. Besides, a knowledge of the WHOLE SET of grammatically correct sentences is not required for the practical compilation of a table of potential subordination.

assertions $dva \to stolá$ and $stolá \to dva$ will be considered false). Moreover, we will assume that in combinations such as *dva bol'šix stola, dvux bol'šix stolov* (two large tables), the adjective is subordinated not to the noun, but to the group of noun plus numeral, and on the basis of this assumption we will consider such statements as $stolá \to bol'šix$, $stený \to bol'šix$ to be false; (b) we shall place an 'imaginary copula' which will be considered to be the root of the sentence-tree into sentences of the type *On učitel'* (He is a teacher), *Etot čelovek očen' umen* (This man is very clever) *Vanja sejčas v škole* (Vanja is at school now);specifically, the phrases cited above will be analyzed as follows:

On ε učitel', Etot čelovek ε očen' umen, Vanja sejčas ε v škole

(ε designates the 'imaginary copula'). It is suitable here to include the 'imaginary copula' in the vocabulary V. In accordance with what has been said thus far, we shall consider assertions such as $\varepsilon \to on$, $\varepsilon \to učitel'$, $\varepsilon \to čelovék$, $\varepsilon \to umën$, $\varepsilon \to Vanja$, $\varepsilon \to v$, $\varepsilon \to sejčás$ to be true, and statements such as $učitel' \to on$, $umën \to čelovék$, $v \to Vanja$, $v \to sejčás$ to be false.

(5) The two subsets of S – S_1 and S_2 – which satisfy the condition $S_1 \cup S_2 = S$ and which can be interpreted as a set of nouns in the singular and a set of nouns in the plural, respectively. S_1 and S_2 are not necessarily non-intersecting; the following segments, for example, belong to the intersection $S_1 \cap S_2$: *rýby* (fish), *téni* (shadow), *pal'tó* (overcoat), *sáni* (sledge) (as regards the last example cf. [2], §1.12)[10].

(6) The two ternary relations $D_1(x, y, z)$ and $D_2(x, y, z)$ on the vocabulary, which satisfy the conditions: if $D_1(x, y, z)$, then $y \in S_1$, $x \to y$ and $y \to z$; if $D_2(x, y, z)$, then $y \in S_2$, $x \to y$ and $y \to z$.

The meaning of the expression $D_1(x, y, z)$ consists in the following: there exists a grammatically correct simple sentence in the given language in which some occurrence of the S-segment y, which has the MEANING SINGULAR, is syntactically immediately subordinate to some occurrence of segment x and syntactically immediately subordinates some occurrence of segment z. The expression $D_2(x, y, z)$ is interpreted in exactly the same way, by substituting the plural for the singular.

The following assertions, for example, are true: $D_1(staričók, rosta, málen'kogo)$, $D_1(iz, pal'tó, nóvogo)$ (from, overcoat, new), $D_1(v, pal'tó, nóvom)$ (in, overcoat, new). At the same time, $D_1(v, pal'tó, nóvogo)$ is false in spite of the truth of $v \to pal'tó$ and $pal'tó \to nóvogo$. The proposition $D_1(popadájutsja, rýby, krúpnye)$ (are caught, fish, big) is false regardless of

---

[10] We need the sets S_1 and S_2 only to be able to define coordinational class and geneler.

the fact that $rýby \in S_1$ and there exists a correct sentence

v seti popadajutsja krupnye ryby

(large fish are (being) caught in the net), since neither in this sentence nor in any other where the segment *rýby* subordinates the segment *krúpnye* does the first of these segments have the meaning singular.

Analogously, the propositions $D_2(iz, pal'tó, nóvyx)$, $D_2(v, pal'tó, nóvyx)$ are true, while $D_2(v, pal'tó, nóvymi)$, $D_2(ot, rýby, krúpnye)$ are false[11].

Hence, the basic notions of our system consist of a set of segments with a subset of *S*-segments distinguished in it, a system of neighborhoods, the relation of potential subordination, the sets S_1 and S_2 and the relation of 'double potential subordination' D_1 and D_2, in which the last two components are unnecessary for a definition of case. This means that in order to define the notions of case, coordinated class, and gender, we will need the following information about the language:

(a) We have to know all the segments of the language in question.

(b) For each segment we have to know whether it is a noun form.

(c) For each pair of segments we have to know whether they have identical lexical meaning.

(d) For every two segments x, y we have to know whether x can immediately subordinate y in a grammatically correct simple sentence.[12]

(e) For each *S*-segment we have to know whether it has the meaning singular and whether it can have the meaning plural.

(f) For every three segments x, y, z where y is an *S*-segment we have to know whether a situation is possible where in some grammatically correct simple sentence the occurrence of y has the meaning singular (respectively, plural), is immediately subordinate to the appearance of x, and immediately subordinates the occurrence of z.

No other information is necessary for a definition of the notions of case, coordinated class, and gender. Moreover, points (a)–(d) suffice for a definition of case[13].

To conclude this section, it will be helpful to make the following observation. The arsenal of mathematical resources used thus far is very poor – it

---

[11] The relations D_1 and D_2 will be used only to define coordinated class and gender.

[12] As will be seen from the definitions, this information is in fact needed only for those pairs x, y in which y is an *S*-segment.

[13] Coordinational class and gender could (with respect to Russian, in any case) be defined without referring to the notion of number, i.e., without using point [*e*], and replacing the two relations D_1 and D_2 in point [*f*] by a single 'relation of double potential subordination' (interpreted in the same way as D_1, but without the requirement that y have the meaning of singular). Such a definition, however, would be less natural.

is restricted to the most rudimentary concepts of set theory. Nor will we need a more complex mathematical apparatus in the future. But since the fundamental notions of set theory are more logical than mathematical in their nature, we are justified in saying that our method of defining coordinational classes and case does not significantly draw upon a mathematical apparatus. This also holds to a significant degree for other definitions of these and similar notions that we know of.

3. A DEFINITION OF CASE

(1) Let O be any neighborhood and y be any segment. We shall say that O POTENTIALLY SUBORDINATES y if y is potentially subordinate to at least one segment from O.

For example, a neighborhood of the segment *namereválsja* (intended) potentially subordinates each of the segments *čelovek* (man), *ljúdi* (people), *doč'* (daughter), *ty* (thou), *čitat'* (to read) (since the assertions *namereváetsja* → *čelovek*, *namerevájutsja* → *ljúdi*, *namereválas'* → *doč'*, *namereváeš'sja* → *ty*, *namereváetsja* → *čitat'* are true). A neighborhood of the segment *obladála* ((she) had, possessed) potentially subordinates the segments *slon* (elephant), *sloný*, *kniga* (book), *knígi*, *slonóm*, *slonámi*, *knígój*, *knígami*, and the (single-element) neighborhood of the segment *za* (behind, beyond) potentially subordinates the segments *góru* (mountain), *góry*, *gorój*, *gorámi*.

N_O will designate for the arbitrary neighborhood O the set of all S-segments which are potentially subordinate to this neighborhood. To simplify our notation here, we will agree to designate N_O as N_x for any segment x which belongs to O. For example, instead of 'N_O where $O = \{stená, stené,..., sténax\}$ (wall)' we will simply write $N_{stená}$; instead of 'N_O, where O is the neighborhood of the segment *sidít* (sits)' we will write $N_{sidít}$, and instead of $N_{\{za\}} - N_{za}$.

For example, the set $N_{na}(na = \text{'on'})$ includes the segments *stolý* (tables), *stol, stolé, stoláx, stené, ókna* (windows), etc.; $N_{čérez}(čérez = \text{'through, across'})$ includes *stolý, stol, ókna*, etc.; $N_{pri}(pri = \text{'near, at, by'})$ includes *stolé, stoláx, stené*, etc.; $N_{mešála}(mešála = \text{'(she) stirred, bothered, hindered'})$ includes *sup* (soup), *súpa*[14], *lóžkoj* (spoon), *lóžkami, otcú* (father), *sestrá* (sister), *brat* (brother), etc.; $N_{staráetsja}(staráetsja = \text{tries})$ includes *brat, sestrá, dóžd'* (rain), *pogóda* (weather), *putešéstvie* (trip), etc.; $N_{dom}(dom = \text{'house'})$ includes *sestrý*,

---

[14] *Mešála* → *súpa* because there is, for example, the sentence

ona ne mešala nikakogo supa

(She didn't stir any soup).

otcá, detéj (children), etc.; $N_{ókolo}$ (*ókolo* = 'near') *stený, sten, dóma, domóv, okná,* etc.

The sets N_O which correspond to certain O can be empty ($N_{jedvá}$(*jedvá* = = 'hardly'), $N_{počtí}$(*počtí* = 'almost')).

(2) It is natural to call the set N_O MINIMAL if it is non-empty and there is no non-empty N_O, which is its proper subset. Thus, the set N_{na} is not minimal, since at least $N_{čérez}$(and also N_{pri}) is its proper subset. $N_{mešála}$ is not a minimal set, for $N_{obladáet}$, for example, is its proper subset. At the same time, $N_{čérez}$, $N_{ókolo}$, $N_{staráetsja}$, and N_{dom} are minimal.

THE MINIMAL SETS N_O WILL BE CALLED CASES. If for two different neighborhoods O and O' the sets N_O and $N_{O'}$ coincide, we will not consider N_O and $N_{O'}$ to be different cases, but one and the same case.

Thus, $N_{ókolo} = N_{dom} = N_{króme}$(*króme* = 'besides') is the genitive case; $N_{staráetsja} = N_{móžet}$(*móžet* = 'can') is the nominative; $N_{čérez} = N_{tošnít}$(*tošnít* = 'nauseates') is the accusative.

(3) Obviously, cases do not have to be mutually disjunct sets. The segment *stené*, for example, belongs to N_k(k = 'to, towards') (the dative case) as well as to N_{pri}(the prepositional case); the segment *stolý* belongs to $N_{móžet}$(nominative) as well as to $N_{čérez}$(accusative).

The fact that it is possible for certain S-segments not to fall into any case is somewhat more unexpected. Thus, the segment *lesú* (*les* = forest) seemingly belongs to only one set of the form N_O, namely, N_v(v = in), which is not minimal ($N_{čérez}$, for example, is its proper subset). The same goes for the segments *godú* (year), *mostú* (bridge), and *škafú* (cupboard). For this reason, the so-called second prepositional case is not a case according to the above definition.

Neither will the second genitive case (the genitive partitive), which can be equated with the set $N_{nemnógo}$(*nemnógo* = 'a little') containing the segments *sáxara* (sugar), *sáxaru, čája* (tea), *čáju, knígi, knig, skvorcá* (*skvoréc* = 'starling'), *skvorcóv*, be a case according to the above definition.[15] The set $N_{ókolo}$ (the first genitive case) is in fact a proper subset of the set $N_{nemnógo}$.

Thus, the second prepositional and genitive cases occupy 'a special position' in our formal system. This is evidently not a coincidence, since these cases differ from the 'traditional' six cases at least in that they can be viewed as being internal: the second prepositional case always has the meaning 'place', and the second genitive always means 'a part of a whole'. There are two more important differences: first, they have 'independent'

---

[15] Note that we are being rather coarse in allowing combinations such as *nemnogo knigi (lit. 'a little of book') or *nemnogo skvorca (lit. 'a little/a few of starling'), but we have to deal with these sort of crudities if we are to differentiate grammatical correctness from intelligibility.

forms, which are not homonymous to the forms of the other six cases for only a small number of nouns; secondly, they do not have independent sets of forms for words which coordinate with them – the second prepositional case behaves with respect to coordination just like the first; the second genitive behaves exactly like the first genitive. The second prepositional case, however, is typologically closer to the other cases than is the second genitive. The latter contains another case (the first genitive) as its proper subset, and for this reason its use is, so to say, 'optional': whenever the 'independent' form of the second genitive is used, the form of the first genitive can be used in its stead (instead of *stakan čaju* (a glass of tea) it is possible to say *stakan čaja*); at the same time, for some (albeit for very few) nouns, the second prepositional has no forms which are homonymous to the forms of other cases – we cannot say *v lése* or some such instead of *v lesú* (in the forest).

This difference between the second genitive and the second prepositional cases finds reflection in instances where our definition is naturally altered so that the potential subordination relation is replaced by the relation of double potential subordination (on this relation see footnote 13; to avoid superfluous complications we shall not describe such an alteration in an explicit form) and the second prepositional case is included among the cases. The second genitive, in contrast, will not be a case in this or any other alteration of our construction which we could at this point regard as natural.

(4) The following problem arises in view of the possibility of homonymy between case forms (such homonymy is found in Russian): for a specific occurrence of an S-segment in a sentence on which the syntactic subordination relation is described (that is, is supplied with arrows), determine which case should be assigned to the given occurrence of the segment in the given sentence (a segment can occur in a sentence more than once). Thus, for the (single) occurrence of the segment *dušé* (soul, spirit) in the sentence

> *bylo   jemu   mračno   i   osenne   na   duše*

(he was in a gloomy autumnal mood), the problem consists of determining which of the two cases (dative or prepositional) possible for this segment should be given to it.

A very simple way of solving this problem (in the case of a simple sentence[16]) consists in the following: let the occurrence of the S-segment x be fixed in the sentence, and let there be a segment z which directly subordinates this occurrence and which belongs to the neighborhood O. The segment z, obviously, can be defined in only one way [17]. If $N_{O_1}, ..., N_{O_k}$ are

[16] We limit ourselves to this case due to the fact that our interpretation of the potential subordination relation (see Section 2) is based on a treatment of only simple sentences.
[17] This assertion follows from the fact that a sentence with the syntactic subordination relation described on it is a tree.

all cases which contain x and are contained in N_O, then each of these cases is by definition assigned to the given occurrence of the segment x in the given sentence.

In the example given above, if $x = du\check{s}\acute{e}$, then $z = na$. The segment $du\check{s}\acute{e}$ belongs to two cases – the dative and the prepositional, but only one of them – the prepositional – is contained in the set N_{na} (which also contains the accusative case). Thus, the occurrence of the segment $du\check{s}\acute{e}$ in the given sentence is assigned one case – the prepositional.

Let us consider yet another example. Assume that we have to assign cases to the segments *kóška* (cat) and *lápu* (paw) in the sentence

nesčastnaja koška porezala lapu,

('The poor cat cuts its paw'.) The immediately dominating segment for both of these segments is *porézala* (cut); there is only one case containing the segment *kóška* (cat) – the nominative, and it is contained in the set $N_{por\acute{e}zala}$. The segment *lápu* (paw) also belongs to only one case – the accusative, which is again contained in $N_{por\acute{e}zala}$. Hence, the segment *kóška* is assigned the nominative case, and *lápu* is given the accusative.

(5) Now is a good time to pose two questions: (1) Will the procedure we have just presented assign a case to any occurrence of an S-segment in a simple sentence (which has been supplied with arrows)? (2) Does this procedure guarantee the uniqueness of the case it assigns to an S-segment?

We will immediately receive a negative answer to the first question if we remember that there are S-segments which are not included in any case whatsoever. This question can be asked in a somewhat weaker form so that it refers only to those S-segments which are included in some case. Even in this case the answer will be negative. The segment *čáju* (tea), for example, is included in only the dative case; but in the sentence *on nalil mne stakan čaju* (he poured me a glass of tea), this segment is not assigned the dative case, which means that it is not assigned any case at all, since the dative case is not contained in the set $N_{stak\acute{a}n}$. This fact, of course, fully corresponds to our linguistic intuition, since what we have here is the second genitive case, which is not a case in the sense of our definition.

Turning to the second question – on the uniqueness of the case assigned to a segment – it is easy to see that the answer to it is also negative. Let us consider, for example, the sentence *Oni ne dali plemeni vremeni na razmyšlenie* (They did not give the tribe time to think it over). The segment *plemeni* (tribe) in this sentence is assigned two cases: the genitive and the dative, since they both contain this segment and are contained in the set $N_{d\acute{a}li}$.

At first glance this peculiarity of our procedure might seem to be a shortcoming; this is only partly true, however. From the purely syntactic point of view, for example, the above sentence can be interpreted not only as *oni ne dali plemeni* (*čemu*) *vremeni* (*čego*), but also as *oni ne dali plemeni* (*čego*) *vremeni* (*čemu*); the solution of this homonymy is possible only when we take meaning into consideration[18].

Let us consider two similar examples. In the sentence *on sel za bjuro* (he sat down at the bureau (writing desk)), the segment *bjuró* is assigned two cases – the accusative and the instrumental. It seems most natural to understand this phrase as *on sel za bjuro* (*kuda* – whither), that is, to interpret *bjuró* as a form of the accusative case. Similarly, in the sentence *On postavil jaščik pod trjumo* (He put the box under the cheval-glass), the segment *trjumó* can be interpreted as a form of the accusative case or as a form of the instrumental, and it happens that just these two cases are assigned to this segment by our procedure. (Note that this ambiguity in assigning cases occurs most often with indeclinable nouns.)

Thus, in many instances the ambiguity of our procedure corresponds to a real ambiguity in the selection of case on syntactic criteria. This is not always the case, however. The point is that the case of one or another occurrence of an *S*-segment in a sentence usually also depends on other syntactic factors than just what segment this occurrence is subordinated to. Thus, the segment *plemeni* in the sentence *Oni ne dali plemeni zemli* (They didn't give the tribe any land) will be assigned in accordance with our procedure the genitive and dative cases, and the segment *port'é* (doorman) in the sentence *On beseduet s port'é* (He is conversing with the doorman) is assigned the genitive, accusative and instrumental cases. At the same time, both of these sentences are syntactically non-homonymous, and the segment *plémeni* in the first of them can only be understood as a form of the dative case, while the segment *port'é* in the second example can only be interpreted to be a form of the instrumental. The exact determination of case in the first instance is based on the fact that the segment *zemlí* is assigned only the genitive case, and the verb *dáli* (gave) cannot have two complements in the genitive case; in the second example we utilize the fact that the verb *beséduet* (converses) cannot govern a prepositional group consisting of the preposition *s* and a noun in the genitive or accusative case. Thus, in both instances we must make use of information outside the information we have on potential subordination (which is the base of our definition of case) and on the sub-

---

[18] Cf. the completely analogous sentence *On ne otdal materi dočeri* (He did not surrender the daugther to the mother/the mother to the daughter), where it is impossible to solve the syntactic homonymy even by considering meaning (on the basis of just this one sentence). The probability of encountering such a sentence in actual speech, of course, is small, but this fact can be explained by attempts of speakers to avoid ambiguity.

ordination actually found in a given sentence (which lies at the base of our procedure for assigning a case to an occurrence of a segment in a sentence).

The facts we have just considered lead us to the proposition that either our definition of case or at least the procedure through which we assign cases must be in some respect inadequate. The following remarks can be made on this problem. Ambiguities of the type *On beseduet s port'e* would not have arisen if in our definition of case we had accounted not only for 'immediate' potential subordination, but also for 'indirect' subordination – in, for example, the above-mentioned change in the definition where the potential subordination relation was replaced by the relation of double potential subordination. As far as ambiguities of the type *Oni ne dali plemeni zemli* are concerned, to eliminate them we have to draw upon information on the valencies of the words. It seems quite probable that it would be advisable to account for these valencies in some form or other in our definition of case, also. In general, the definition variant presented here should be regarded as preliminary; additional work is needed to be able to construct a more adequate definition based on the same idea of 'identical government'. In particular, the question of the interrelation between this method of defining case and the ideas of R. O. Jakobson's classical work [9] needs a special treatment. We think it probable – although such an assertion may seem paradoxical - that there is no internal contradiction between our approach to the notion of case and that of R. O. Jakobson; we are unable, however, to dwell on this question here. The assertion we have just made is in any case still just a preliminary hypothesis.

4. A DEFINITION OF COORDINATIONAL CLASS

(1) We will need certain secondary notions to be able to define the coordinated class.

Let all the primary objects described in Section 2 be given, and let k cases $\Pi_1, ..., \Pi_k$ be defined in accordance with the definition in Section 3 (this means ALL the cases thus defined). The numbering of the cases is arbitrary, but will be considered fixed in what follows.

The PARADIGM of an arbitrary S-neighborhood A will be said to be the ordered system of sets $\mathfrak{A} = \langle A^{11}, A^{12}, ..., A^{1k}, A^{21}, A^{22}, ..., A^{2k} \rangle$, where $A^{11} = = A \cap S_1 \cap \Pi_1, A^{12} = A \cap S_1 \cap \Pi_2, ..., A^{1k} = A \cap S_1 \cap \Pi_k, A^{21} = A \cap S_2 \cap \cap \Pi_1, ..., A^{2k} = A \cap S_2 \cap \Pi_k$.

Let us consider, for example, the following S-neighborhoods:

$A_1 = \{dom, dóma, dómu, dómom, dóme, domá, domóv, domám, domámi, domáx\}$;

$\bar{A}_1 = \{ded, déda, dédu, dédom, déde, dédy, dédov, dédam, dédami, dédax\}$
(grandfather);

$A_2 = \{reká, rekí, reké, réku, rekój, rekóju, réki, rek, rékam, rékami, rékax\}$
(river);

$\bar{A}_2 = \{rýba, rýby, rýbe, rýbu, rýboj, rýboju, ryb, rýbam, rýbami, rýbax\}$ (fish);

$A_3 = \{seló, selá, selú, selóm, selé, sëla, sël, sëlam, sëlami, sëlax\}$ (village);

$\bar{A}_3 = \{čudóvišče, čudóvišča, čudóvišču, čudóviščem, čudóvišč, čudóviščam,$
$čudóviščami, čudóviščax\}$ (monster);

$\tilde{A}_3 = \{pal'tó\}$ (overcoat);

$A_4 = \{sáni, sanéj, sanjám, sanjámi, sanjáx\}$ (sledge);

$\bar{A}_4 = \{roditeli, roditelej, roditeljam, roditeljami, roditeljax\}$ [19] (parents);

$A_5 = \{zadíra, zadíry, zadíre, zadíru, zadíroj, zadíroju, zadír, zadíram,$
$zadírami, zadírax\}$ (bully).

We shall proceed from the assumption that the six usual Russian cases are defined, and shall number them in the order commonly used; in other words, Π_1 will designate the nominative case, Π_2 – the genitive, Π_3 – the dative, Π_4 – the accusative, Π_5 – the instrumental, and Π_6 – the prepositional.

We will then obtain the following paradigms for the above neighborhoods [20]:

$A_1 = \langle dom, dóma, dómu, dom, dómom, dóme, domá, domóv, domám, domá,$
$domámi, domáx\rangle$;

$\mathfrak{A}_1 = \langle ded, déda, dédu, déda, dédom, déde, dédy, dédov, dédam, dédov,$
$dédami, dédax\rangle$;

$\mathfrak{A}_2 = \langle reká, rekí, reké, réku, \{rekój, rekóju\}, reké, réki, rek, rékam, réki,$
$rékami, rékax\rangle$;

$\bar{\mathfrak{A}}_2 = \langle rýba, rýby, rýbe, rýbu, \{rýboj, rýboju\}, rýbe, rýby, ryb, rýbam, ryb,$
$rýbami, rýbax\rangle$;

$\mathfrak{A}_3 = \langle seló, selá, selú, seló, selóm, selé, sëla, sël, sëlam, sëla, sëlami, sëlax\rangle$;

$\bar{\mathfrak{A}}_3 = čudóvišče, čudóvišča, čudóvišču, čudóvišče, čudóviščem, čudóvišče,$
$čudóvišča, čudóvišč, čudóviščam, čudóvišč, čudóviščami, čudóviščax\rangle$;

$\tilde{\mathfrak{A}}_3 = pal'tó, pal'tó, pal'tó, pal'tó, pal'tó, pal'tó, pal'tó, pal'tó, pal'tó, pal'tó,$
$pal'tó, pal'tó\rangle$;

---

[19] roditeli here is a (lexically meaningful) segment with the meaning 'father and mother' (as in the word group moi roditeli 'my parents') as distinct from the (lexically meaningful) segment roditeli with the meaning 'pl. of roditel' = father or mother' (as in the word group vse roditeli, prišedšie na voskresnik – ix bylo desjat' (all the parents who came to the Sunday party – there were ten of them). Note that the segment roditeli in the first sense can have both a singular (moi roditeli) and a plural (moi i tvoi roditeli) meaning (cf. moj i tvoj otcy). In certain word combinations the segment roditeli can be regarded both as the plural of roditeli = 'father and mother' and as the plural of roditel' = 'father or mother'; for example, roditeli učenikov vtorogo classa (the parents of the pupils in the second grade).

[20] In writing the ordered groups of sets of segments, we shall, in order to simplify the notation, identify each one-unit set with its single element, i.e., write dom instead of {dom}.

$\mathfrak{A}_4 = \langle$ *sáni, sanéj, sanjám, sáni, sanjámi, sanjáx, sáni, sanéj, sanjám, sáni, sanjámi, sanjáx* $\rangle$;

$\overline{\mathfrak{A}}_4 = \langle$ *rodíteli, rodítelej, rodíteljami, rodítelej, rodíteljami, rodíteljax, rodíteli, rodítelej, rodíteljam, rodítelej, rodíteljami, rodíteljax* $\rangle$;

$\mathfrak{A}_5 = \langle$ *zadíra, zadíry, zadíre, zadíru,* {*zadíroj, zadíroju*}, *zadíre, zadíry, zadír, zadíram, zadír, zadírami, zadírax* $\rangle$.

(2) Let A be an S-neighborhood, $\mathfrak{A} = \langle A^{11}, ..., A^{1k}, A^{21}, ..., A^{2k} \rangle$ be its paradigm, and let B be an arbitrary neighborhood. We will say that the SEGMENT $Z \in B$ agrees with the segment $y \in A^{ij}$ FOR THE NUMBER S_i and THE CASE $\Pi_j (i = 1, 2; j = 1, 2, ..., k)$, if for any neighborhood O for which $N_O = \Pi_j$ there exists a segment $x \in O$ which is such that $D_i(x, y, z)$.

For every pair i, j where $i = 1, 2, j = 1, ..., k$, B^{ij} will designate the set of the segments from B which agree for the number S_i and the case Π_j with the segments occurring in A^{ij}.

For example, let $\overline{\mathfrak{A}} = \langle A^{11}, ..., A^{16}, A^{21}, ..., A^{26} \rangle$ be the paradigm for the neighborhood of the segment *sobáka* (dog), and let B be the neighborhood of the segment *bol'šój* (large, big). Specifically, we have: $A^{11} = \{sobáka\}$, $\Pi_1 = = N_{O_1} = N_{O_2} = N_{O_3} = ...$, there $O_1, O_2, O_3, ...$ are neighborhoods of the segments *uméet* (can, knows how to), *staráetsja, namereváetsja,...* respectively. There are two segments in the neighborhood O_1 which potentially subordinate the segment *sobáka: uméet, uméla.* The single segment Z, which occurs in B and satisfies at least one of the conditions D_1 (*uméet, sobáka, Z*) and D_1(*uméla, sobáka, Z*) is *bol'šája.* (This segment actually satisfies both conditions.) It is easy to ascertain that the same holds for O_2, O_3, and in general for any neighborhood O which is such that $N_O = \Pi_1$: if $x \in O$ and $x \rightarrow sobáka$, then *bol'šája* will be the only segment Z occurring in B and satisfying the condition $D_1(x, sobáka, Z)$, Thus, *bol'šája* is the only segment that agrees with the segment *sobáka* for number S_1 and case Π_1 (the nominative), so that $B^{11} = \{bol'šája\}$. By a quite analogous reason we have, for example, $B^{15} = \{bol'šój, bol'šóju\}$, $B^{21} = \{bo'lšíe\}$.

Due to the possibility of homonymy in case forms, we cannot define B^{ij} as simply the set of segments from B which are potentially subordinate to the segments from A^{ij}. We also have to consider the segments which SUBORDINATE the segments from A^{ij}, which makes it possible to single out those instances where a segment from A^{ij} is really used in the meaning of a jth case. Thus, if we take the neighborhood of the segment *móre* (sea) as A and the neighborhood of the segment *bol'šój* as B, then the set of segments from B which are potentially subordinate to the segments from A^{11} will include, in addition to the segment *bol'šóe*, the segment *bol'šóm*, which agrees with the segment *móre* for the prepositional but not the nominative case.

Now let A be any S-neighborhood, $\mathfrak{A} = \langle A^{11}, ..., A^{1k}, A^{21}, ..., A^{2k} \rangle$ is its paradigm, and B is an arbitrary neighborhood. We will define the sets $B^{11},..., B^{1k}, B^{21},..., B^{2k}$ in the manner indicated above. If B^{ij} is not empty for any i, for which A^{ij} is not empty, we will call the ordered system of sets $\mathfrak{B} = \langle B^{11},..., B^{1k}, B^{21},..., B^{2k} \rangle$ a COORDINATIONAL SYSTEM (CS) RELATIVE TO NEIGHBORHOOD B WHICH HAS BEEN GENERATED BY PARADIGM $\mathfrak{A}$.

Let us consider, for example, the neighborhood $B = \{$*nóvyj, nóvoe, nóvaja, nóvogo, nóvoj, nóvuju, nóvym, nóvoju, nóvom, nóvye, nóvyx, nóvymi, nov, nová, nóvo, nóvy*$\}$.

The paradigms $A_1, \bar{A}_1, ..., A_5$ treated above generate the following CS, respectively, for this neighborhood:

$\mathfrak{B}_1 = \langle$*nóvyj, nóvogo, nóvomu, nóvyj, nóvym, nóvom, nóvye, nóvyx, nóvym, nóvye, nóvymi, nóvyx*$\rangle$;

$\overline{\mathfrak{B}}_1 = \langle$*nóvyj, nóvogo, nóvomu, nóvogo, nóvym, nóvom, nóvye, nóvyx, nóvym, nóvyx, nóvymi, nóvyx*$\rangle$;

$\mathfrak{B}_2 = \langle$*nóvaja, nóvoj, nóvoj, nóvuju, $\{$nóvoj, nóvuju$\}$, nóvoj, nóvye, nóvyx, nóvym, nóvye, nóvymi, nóvyx*$\rangle$;

$\overline{\mathfrak{B}}_2 = \langle$*nóvaja, nóvoj, nóvoj, nóvuju, $\{$nóvoj, nóvoju$\}$, nóvoj, nóvye, nóvyx, nóvym, nóvyx, nóvymi, nóvyx*$\rangle$;

$\mathfrak{B}_3 = \langle$*nóvoe, nóvogo, nóvomu, nóvoe, nóvym, nóyom, nóvye, nóvyx, nóvym, nóvye, nóvymi, nóvyx*$\rangle$;

$\overline{\mathfrak{B}}_3 = \langle$*nóvoe, nóvogo, nóvomu, nóvoe, nóvym, nóvom, nóvye, nóvyx, nóvym, nóvyx, nóvymi, nóvyx*$\rangle$;

$\widetilde{\mathfrak{B}}_3 = \mathfrak{B}_3$;

$\mathfrak{B}_4 = \langle$*nóvye, nóvyx, nóvym, nóvye, nóvymi, nóvyx, nóvye, nóvyx, nóvym, nóvye, nóvymi, nóvyx*$\rangle$;

$\overline{\mathfrak{B}}_4 = \langle$*nóvye, nóvyx, nóvym, nóvyx, nóvymi, nóvyx, nóvye, nóvyx, nóvym, nóvyx, nóvymi, nóvyx*$\rangle$;

$\mathfrak{B}_5 = \langle \{$*nóvyj, nóvaja*$\}, \{$*nóvogo, nóvoj*$\}, \{$*nóvomu, nóvoj*$\}, \{$*nóvogo, nóvuju*$\}, \{$*nóvym, nóvoj, nóvoju*$\}, \{$*nóvom, nóvoj*$\}, nóvye, nóvyx, nóvym, nóvyx, nóv'ymi, nóvyx* $\rangle$.

As for the neighborhood $C = \{$*mnógie, mnógix, mnógim, mnógimi*$\}$, none of the above paradigms can generate a coordinated system for it; if we define, say, C_1^{ij} for paradigm $\mathfrak{A}_1$ in the same way as we defined B^{ij}, the sets C_1^{11}, $C_1^{12},..., C_1^{16}$ will be empty.

Neither will any of the paradigms $\mathfrak{A}_1, \overline{\mathfrak{A}}_1, ..., \mathfrak{A}_5$ generate a CS with respect to the one-unit neighborhood $D = \{$*čitat'*$\}$ (to read) (we find it convenient to relate the infinitive and personal forms of the verb to different neighborhoods), since any segment which is included in the neighborhoods $A_1, \bar{A}_1, ..., A_5$ cannot potentially subordinate the segment *čitat'* (so that if we define, for example, the sets D_1^{ij} for $\mathfrak{A}_1$ in the same way as we defined B^{ij}, all D_1^{ij} will be empty). However, the paradigm $\mathfrak{A}' = \langle$ *stáránie, stáránija, stárániju, staránie, starániem, staránii, staránija, staránij, staránijam, staránija, staránijami, staránijax* $\rangle$ (effort) generates with respect to D the coordinational system $\mathfrak{D}' = \langle$ *čitát', čitát', čitát', čitát', čitát', čitát', čitát', čitát', čitát', čitát', čitát', čitát'* $\rangle$.

With respect to the neighborhood $F = \{$*otéc, otcá, otcú, otcóm, otcé, otcý, otcóv, otcám, otcámi, otcáx*$\}$, each of the paradigms $A_1, \bar{A}_1, ..., A_5, A'$ generates one and the same CS $\mathfrak{F} = \langle \{$*otcá, otcóv*$\}, \{$*otcá, otcóv*$\}, \{$*otcá, otcóv*$\}, \{$*otcá, otcóv*$\}, \{$*otcá, otcóv*$\}, \{$*otcá, otcóv*$\}, \{$*otcá, otcóv*$\}, \{$*otcá, otcóv*$\}, \{$*otcá, otcóv*$\}, \{$*otcá, otcóv*$\}, \{$*otcá, otcóv*$\}, \{$*otcá, otcóv*$\} \rangle$.

We will call a neighborhood COORDINABLE if with respect to it the paradigm of each S-neighborhood (except 'defective paradigms', which do not contain all cases) generates a CS which contains at least two different sets. Neighborhood B in our example is coordinable, while C, D, and F are not.

(3) Now let B be any coordinable neighborhood, and let $\mathfrak{B} = \langle B^{11}, ..., B^{1k}, B^{21}, ..., B^{2k} \rangle$ be some ordered system of subsets of set B. $R_{\mathfrak{B}}$ will represent the union of all S-neighborhoods whose paradigms generate a coordinational system equal to $\mathfrak{B}$ with respect to B. (If $\mathfrak{B}$ is not generated as a CS relative to B by any paradigms, then $R_{\mathfrak{B}}$ is empty.)

In the example just taken up it is apparently possible to assume that $R_{\mathfrak{B}_1}$, $R_{\mathfrak{B}_2}$ and $R_{\mathfrak{B}_3}$ are sets of inanimate nouns, masculine, feminine, and neuter, respectively; $R_{\bar{\mathfrak{B}}_1}$, $R_{\bar{\mathfrak{B}}_2}$ and $R_{\bar{\mathfrak{B}}_3}$ are animate masculine, feminine and neuter nouns, respectively; $R_{\mathfrak{B}_4}$ and $R_{\bar{\mathfrak{B}}_4}$ are sets of inanimate and animate *pluralia tantum*, respectively; and $R_{\mathfrak{B}_5}$ is a set of nouns of 'common gender'.[21]

The set $R_{\mathfrak{B}}$ will be said to be MINIMAL if it is non-empty and if no non-empty $R_{\mathfrak{C}}$ is a proper subset of $R_{\mathfrak{B}}$. The sets $R_{\mathfrak{B}_1}, R_{\bar{\mathfrak{B}}_1}, ..., R_{\mathfrak{B}_5}$ treated above are apparently minimal.

We will call the minimal set $R_{\mathfrak{B}}$ the COORDINATIONAL CLASS (CC) DETERMINED BY SET B. If for two different systems $\mathfrak{B}$ and $\mathfrak{C}$ the sets $R_{\mathfrak{B}}$ and $R_{\mathfrak{C}}$ coincide, we shall assume that these sets are not two different CC's, but one and the same CC. Thus, $R_{\mathfrak{B}_1}$ coincides with the CC defined by the set $\langle$*bélyj, bélogo, bélomu, bélyj, bélym, bélom, bélye, bélyx, bélym, bélye, bélymi, bélyx*$\rangle$ (white).

Hence, we can assume that there are at least nine CC's in Russian: $R_{\mathfrak{B}_1}$, $R_{\bar{\mathfrak{B}}_1}, R_{\mathfrak{B}_2}, R_{\bar{\mathfrak{B}}_2}, R_{\mathfrak{B}_3}, R_{\bar{\mathfrak{B}}_3}, R_{\mathfrak{B}_4}, R_{\bar{\mathfrak{B}}_4}, R_{\mathfrak{B}_5}$. It seems plausible to assume that there are no other CC's [unless we take into account nouns with incomplete para-

---

[21] We proceed from the assumption here that all nouns have plural forms. If we assume that certain nouns do not have plural forms, the picture changes: the classes $R_{\mathfrak{B}_1}, R_{\bar{\mathfrak{B}}_1}, R_{\mathfrak{B}_2}$ $R_{\bar{\mathfrak{B}}_2}, R_{\mathfrak{B}_3}, R_{\bar{\mathfrak{B}}_3}$ will include only nouns which have forms of both numbers, and the *singularia tantum* will comprise separate classes (for example, *singularia tantum* of the neuter gender will make up a class which corresponds to the ordered system of sets $\{$*nóvoe, nóvogo, nóvomu, nóvoe, nóvym, nóvom*, $\emptyset, \emptyset, \emptyset, \emptyset, \emptyset, \emptyset\}$, where $\emptyset$ is an empty set.

digms (see below, (5)) and words such as *šimpanzé* (chimpanzee) (see [2], p. 67].

(4) It seems expedient to introduce some new notions to help us explain the place of 'common gender' (coordinational class $R_{\mathfrak{B}_5}$) in our system.

Let R be some CC. $\varDelta$ will designate the set of all ordered systems $\mathfrak{B}$ for which $R = R_{\mathfrak{B}}$. Let $\varDelta = \{\mathfrak{B}_1, ..., \mathfrak{B}_t\}$, where for every $l = 1, ..., t$ $\mathfrak{B}_l = \langle B_l^{11}, ..., B_l^{1k}, ..., B_l^{2k} \rangle$. Let $B_1^{11} \cup B_2^{11} \cup ... \cup B_t^{11} = \delta^{11}, ..., B_1^{2k} \cup ... \cup B_t^{2k} = \delta^{2k}$. The ordered system $\delta = \langle \delta^{11}, ... \delta^{1k}, \delta^{21}, ..., \delta^{2k} \rangle$ will be called the FULL COORDINATIONAL SYSTEM (FCS) corresponding to the coordinational class R.

For example, the full coordinational system for the coordinational class $R_{\mathfrak{B}_1}$ (see above) will have the form $\langle \delta_1^{11}, \delta_1^{11}, ..., \delta_1^{26} \rangle$, where $\delta_1^{11} = \{$*nóvyj, bol'šój, krásnyj* (red), ...$\}$, $\delta_1^{12} = \{$*nóvogo, bol'šógo, krásnogo*...$\}$, etc.

We shall also say that the CC R''' is a JUNCTURE of the two CC's R' and R'' if the fully coordinational systems $\mathfrak{B} = \langle B^{11}, ..., B^{2k} \rangle$, $\mathfrak{C} = \langle C^{11}, ..., C^{2k} \rangle$, $\mathfrak{D} = \langle D^{11}, ..., D^{2k} \rangle$ correspond to the classes R', R'' and R''', respectively, and if two conditions are fulfilled for any $i = 1, 2, j = 1, ..., k$: (1) $D^{ij} = B^{ij} \cup C^{ij}$; (2) for each element of the set $R_{\mathfrak{D}} \cap S_i \cap \Pi_j$ in B^{ij} as well as in C^{ij} segments can be found which are potentially subordinate to it.[22] The class $R_{\mathfrak{B}_5}$ in our example is the juncture of $R_{\overline{\mathfrak{B}}_1}$ and $R_{\overline{\mathfrak{B}}_2}$.

From a linguistical point of view the fact that $R_{\mathfrak{D}}$ is the juncture of $R_{\mathfrak{B}}$ and $R_{\mathfrak{C}}$ means that the nouns from $R_{\mathfrak{D}}$ can agree with the words subordinate to them either according to the rules which are operative for $R_{\mathfrak{B}}$, or according to the rules which are operative for $R_{\mathfrak{C}}$.[23]

We will now say that the CC R'' DOMINATES the CC R' if $R' \neq R''$ and R' is the juncture of R'' with some other CC.[24]

The CC $R_{\mathfrak{B}}$ will be said to be PRIMARY if there exists no CC which dominates $R_{\mathfrak{B}}$. In our example, $R_{\overline{\mathfrak{B}}_1}$ and $R_{\overline{\mathfrak{B}}_2}$ dominate $R_{\mathfrak{B}_5}$; all CC's except $R_{\mathfrak{B}_5}$ are primary.

Finally, a set that is the union of some primary RC and all the CC's which it dominates will be called a REDUCED COORDINATIONAL CLASS (RCC).

We obtain eight RCC's in our examples:

(1) $R_{\mathfrak{B}_1}$ ('masculine inanimate gender');
(2) $R_{\overline{\mathfrak{B}}_1} \cup R_{B_5}$ ('masculine animate gender');
(3) $R_{\mathfrak{B}_2}$ ('feminine inanimate gender');

---

[22] We could analogically define the juncture of more than two CC's.

[23] The notion of juncture is a refinement of A. A. Zaliznjak's notion of 'crossing coordinational class' ([2], §2.15). It would, of course, be possible to 'separate' each of the (lexically meaningful) segments of the type *zadíra* into two segments having the meanings 'masculine' and 'feminime', respectively (as is done in the second chapter of [2]), in which case there would be no coordinational class R_{B_5}.

[24] In order to obtain more generality, we should foresee a case where R' would be a juncture of more than two CC's, one of which would be R'' (see footnote 22), but for the sake of simplicity we will limit ourselves to junctures of two CC's.

(4) $R_{\overline{\mathfrak{B}}_2} \cup R_{B_5}$ ('feminine animate gender');

(5) $R_{\mathfrak{B}_3}$ ('neuter inanimate gender');

(6) $R_{\overline{\mathfrak{B}}_3}$ ('neuter animate gender');

(7) $R_{\mathfrak{B}_4}$ ('twin inanimate gender');

(8) $R_{\overline{\mathfrak{B}}_4}$ ('twin animate gender')[25].

(5) For the sake of simplicity we have not treated nouns with incomplete paradigms – i.e., those for which there are empty sets among the sets of A^{ij}. If, using the definition of dominance formulated above, we attempt to take such nouns into consideration, they will be classified in a special RCC. In order to obtain a natural interpretation of nouns with incomplete paradigms, it seems useful to introduce certain changes into our definitions of dominance and RCC which, however, will not affect these notions in instances where the paradigms of all the nouns are complete.

Let $\delta = \langle \delta^{11}, ..., \delta^{1k}, \delta^{21}, ..., \delta^{2k} \rangle$ and let $\bar{\delta} = \langle \bar{\delta}^{11}, ..., \bar{\delta}^{1k}, \bar{\delta}^{21}, ..., \bar{\delta}^{2k} \rangle$ be two full coordinational systems. We shall say that $\bar{\delta}$ is a CONTRACTION of δ if for any i, j ($i = 1, 2; 1, ..., k$) for which $\bar{\delta}^{ij}$ is non-empty, the equality $\bar{\delta}^{ij} = \delta^{ij}$ occurs.

Now, to change the definition in the preceding section, let us say that the CC R'' DOMINATES the CC R' if $R' \neq R''$ and either R' is a juncture of R'' with some other CC, or the FCS which corresponds to R' is a contraction of the FCS corresponding to R''. For example, the neighbourhoods $\{ \check{s}\check{c}ec \}$ and $\{ drovec \}$ (diminutive forms from $\check{s}\check{c}\acute{i}$ (cole soup) and $drov\acute{a}$ (firewood) having only a genitive case), as is easy to see, form a CC. The FCS $\langle \varepsilon^{11}, ..., \varepsilon^{16}, \varepsilon^{21}, ..., \varepsilon^{26} \rangle$ in which $\varepsilon^{12} = \varepsilon^{22} = \{ bol'\check{s}\acute{i}x, n\acute{o}v\acute{y}x, kr\acute{a}snyx... \}$ and the other sets are empty, will correspond to this CC. This FCS will be a contraction for the FCS's which correspond to the coordinational classes $R_{\mathfrak{B}_4}$ and $R_{\overline{\mathfrak{B}}_4}$. The CC $\{ \check{s}\check{c}ec, drov\acute{e}c \}$ will be contained in the seventh and eighth RCC's.

Furthermore, if we allow that certain nouns do not have plural forms (cf.

---

[25] The term 'twin gender' is borrowed from A. A. Zaliznjak ([2], §2.19). True, Zaliznjak does not distinguish a 'twin animate gender', which seems to us to be a fully natural formation, even though it consists of a very few neighborhoods. Besides the neighborhood of the segment *rodíteli* it includes, for example, the neighborhoods of the segments *suprúgi* (spouses), *ljubóvniki* (lovers), *vljublënnye* (lovers), *narečënnye* (the betrothed), each of which segments has one or two 'lexically homonymous' segments – for example, besides the segment *suprúgi* (husband and wife) we have the segment *suprúgi* (pl. of *suprúg* (husband)) and the segment *suprugi* (pl. of *suprúga* (wife)), and the neutralization of this homonymy is possible in certain contexts (cf. footnote 19). As for the neighborhoods of the segments *bélye* (white) and *čërnye* (black) as the names of sides in chess, etc. ([2], p. 78), homonymy occurs here, also: in the meaning 'white/black chessmen' these segments fall into the 'twin inanimate gender', but in the meaning 'the player who plays the white/black pieces', they belong to the 'twin animate'; cf. Zaliznjak's examples: *Beri sebe belye, a ja voz'mu černye* (You take white and I'll take black); *On vynudil belyx sdat'sja* (He forced White to surrender).

footnote 21), then the FCS which corresponds to such a noun will be a contraction of the FCS corresponding to one of the coordinational classes $R_{\mathfrak{B}_1}$, $R_{\mathfrak{B}_2}$, $R_{\mathfrak{B}_3}$, so that the *singularia tantum* will be naturally distributed to the first, third and fifth RCC's, respectively. (For example, if we assume that the paradigm of the neighbourhood of the segment *molokó* (milk) has the form ⟨*molokó, moloká, molokú, molokó, molokóm, moloké, ∅, ∅, ∅, ∅, ∅, ∅*⟩, then this neighborhood, even though it does not occur in the CC $R_{\mathfrak{B}_3}$, will still be contained in the fifth RCC.)

Finally, let us note the following: In our treatment of the nouns which we assigned to the seventh and eighth RCC's, we proceeded from A. A. Zaliznjak's point of view, according to which they have singular forms which are homonymous to the corresponding plural forms. This view seems to us to be far more convincing than the traditional one, which consists in denying the existence of singular forms for these nouns. The applicability of our procedure for distinguishing CC's and RCC's does not, of course, depend on how we look upon the nature of the *pluralia tantum*, although if this view is changed the results of the procedure will also change. Namely, if we accept the traditional viewpoint (according to which, for example, the paradigm of the neighborhood of *sáni* (sledge) will have the form ⟨*∅, ∅, ∅, ∅, ∅, ∅, sáni, sanéj, sanjám, sáni, sanjámi, sanjáx*⟩), the coordinational classes $R_{\mathfrak{B}_4}$ and $R_{\bar{\mathfrak{B}}_4}$ will not form separate RCC's, but will be included in others – $R_{\mathfrak{B}_4}$ will be contained in the first, third and fifth RCC's (in each of them), and $R_{\bar{\mathfrak{B}}_4}$ will be in the second, fourth and sixth; thus, we obtain a system of RCC's which corresponds to the traditional Russian gender system [26].

(6) Our definitions do not exclude the possibility of 'gender synonymy', so that we can pose the question of finding a procedure for assigning RCC's to the S-segments in a sentence – on the analogy of the procedure of (4) in the preceding section. We naturally proceed from the assumption here that the basic information includes not only the relation of syntactic subordination in a sentence, but also an indication of the number – singular or plural – assigned to a particular occurrence of an S-segment.

[26] A. A. Zaliznjak notes ([2], p. 76), that such a gender system is unsatisfactory even with regard to the traditional view of *pluralia tantum*. This, however, is connected with the fact that he refutes one other premise which figures inexplicitly in the traditional construction of the gender system and which consists in the condition that only 'direct' agreement is accounted for. We, on the other hand, have retained this premise in our constructions. Accounting for 'indirect' agreement would result in a significant complication of our definitions and at the same time (in contrast to the construction of the case system – cf. the end of Section 3), would hardly give us any serious gain in naturalness. (For Russian it seems we can note only one instance where some benefit might be derived: the nouns *ščec, drovec* will not, in the 'untraditional' interpretation, occur in the seventh and eighth RCC's simultaneously, but will occur only in the seventh, due to constructions such as *ja videl nekotorye iz tex drovec...* (I saw some of those firewoods ...). This instance, however, is rather isolated, and the naturalness of such a change is open to discussion.

Such a procedure can have the following form. Assume that some occurrence of the S-segment x is fixed in a simple sentence with a syntactic subordination relation described on it, and let this occurrence be given the meaning of singular or plural (only one of these meanings)[27]. For simplicity we shall limit ourselves to cases where two conditions are fulfilled: (1) the S-segment x belongs to some coordinational class R, which is the only such class; (2) the procedure from (4) of the preceding section assigns this segment x some case Π_j, which is the only such case. Now let us assume that (a) $Q_1, \ldots, Q_n$ are all those RCC's which contain R, and that $\delta_1 = \langle \delta_1^{11}, \ldots, \delta_1^{2k} \rangle, \ldots, \delta_s = \langle \delta_n^{11}, \ldots, \delta^{2k} \rangle$ are the FCS's corresponding to them (more precisely, the FCS's corresponding to primary CC, which determine these RCC's); (b) u is the segment whose occurrence immediately subordinates x; (c) $u_1, \ldots, u_n$ are all the segments whose occurrences in a given sentence are immediately subordinated to the given occurrence of x and which at the same time agree with x for the number S_i and the case Π_j, where $i = 1$, if the given occurrence of x is assigned the meaning of singular, and $i = 2$, if the given occurrence of x is assigned the meaning of plural. The segment u is necessarily present – in view of condition (2); at the same time, the segments $u_1, \ldots, u_n$ may also be absent. Now we will by definition assign the given occurrence x some of the RCC's from among $Q_1, \ldots, Q_n$ in the following manner: if the segments $u_1, \ldots, u_n$ are absent, then the given occurrence is assigned all the RCC's $Q_1, \ldots, Q_n$; otherwise it is assigned those and only those RCC's Q_e from among $Q_1, \ldots, Q_n$ for which at least one of the segments $u_1, \ldots, u_n$ belongs to δ_e^{11}.

Assume, for example, that we wish to assign RCC's to (the single) occurrence of the segment $x = zabijáka$ (bully) in the sentence *étot zabijaka postojanno deretsja* (this bully is always fighting), where the segment *zabijáka* is assigned the meaning of the singular. The segment *zabijáka* belongs (apparently) only to the single CC $R_{\mathfrak{B}_5}$ (see above), and the procedure of point (4) of the preceding section assigns this segment the only case Π_1 (the nominative), so that conditions (1) and (2) are fulfilled. We have $u = derëtsja$ (fights), $n = 1$, $u_1 = étot$ (this) (as can easily be checked, the segment *étot* agrees with the segment *zabijáka* for the singular and for the nominative case). There are (apparently) two RCC's which contain $R_{\mathfrak{B}_5}$: the second and the fourth (see above, the end of point (4)). If $\delta_2 = \langle \delta_2^{11}, \ldots, \delta_2^{26} \rangle$, $\delta_4 = \langle \delta_4^{11}, \ldots, \delta_4^{26} \rangle$ are the corresponding FCS's, then the segment *étot* obviously belongs to δ_2^{11} and does not belong to δ_2^{14}. The given occurrence of the segment *zabijáka* is therefore assigned one RCC – the second ('masculine animate gender'). If we consider the sentence:

---

[27] Here, of course, it is natural to demand that the meaning of singular (plural) be assigned to the given occurrence of x only under the condition that x belongs to S_1 (respectively S_2).

zabijaka postojanno deretsja,

where the occurrence of the segment *zabijáka* is also assigned the meaning of
the singular, then our procedure will assign this occurrence two RCC's – the
second and the fourth (since now the segments $u_1, ..., u_n$ are absent).

It is easy to extend the procedure to a more general case, where the segment x occurs in several CC's $R_1, ..., R_t$ and the procedure of point (4)
of the preceding section assigns this occurrence several cases: $\Pi_{i_1}, ..., \Pi_{i_n}$. In
such a case it is natural to proceed as follows: for each pair R_h, $\Pi_{i_g} (h =$
$= 1, ..., t; g = 1, ..., r)$ apply the procedure described above, and by definition
assign the given occurrence of x all the RCC's obtained by this procedure
for all such pairs.

(7) Note that in all of the examples in this section we used the traditional
conception according to which an S-neighborhood includes both singular
and plural forms. If we assume that the singular and plural forms of the
noun belong to different neighborhoods [28], then the coordinational classes
for Russian will, of course, have another form. (At the same time, this will
not affect the cases!)

5. A DEFINITION OF GENDER

(1) The RCC's we have obtained for Russian are regarded by traditional
grammar as 'secondary' formations produced by the categories of gender
and animation. It is appropriate here to pose the question of the place of
these categories in our system.

The category of animation (in Russian, at any rate) is an internal category,
so that it is hardly advisable to attempt to define it with our basic notions. As
for the category of gender, we shall attempt to formulate a definition for it
which seems to us to adequately reflect its essence, which consists, roughly
speaking, in the following: gender is structured like a coordinational class, but
the role that cases play in the definition of CC's belongs, so to say, to the
'formal cases' in a definition of gender; somewhat more precisely, if two
case-number forms coincide for a given noun, and if they have the same
segments in agreement with them (for example, the nominative and accusative
singular forms of animate masculine and neuter nouns), then these forms
should, in a definition of gender, 'fuse' into a single form [29]. Rather than
attempt to formulate a definition of gender independently, we think it
simpler and more natural to use the notion of coordinational class which we
have already constructed.

[28] This alternative is discussed in [2] (§2.11) and [3].
[29] The author is indebted for the formulation of this point of view to his discussions with
I. A. Mel'čuk.

(2) Let R be some CC, let $\delta = \langle \delta^{11}, \ldots, \delta^{2k} \rangle$ be its corresponding FCS and let A be some neighborhood contained in R. Let us assume that there exist two sequences of sets from δ: $\delta^{i_1 j_1}, \ldots, \delta^{i_n j_n}$, $\delta^{i'_1 j'_1}, \ldots, \delta^{i_n j_n}$ (it is important to emphasize here that n is the same for both sequences for which the equalities $\delta^{i_1 j_1} = \delta^{i'_1 j'_1}, \ldots, \delta^{i_n j_n} = \delta^{i'_n j'_n}$ take place. We will eliminate all the sets $\delta^{i'_1 j'_1}, \ldots, \delta^{i'_n j'_n}$ from set δ and replace them with asterisks. This operation will be called a CANCELLATION of the FCS δ, and the set obtained as a result of the cancellation and consisting of sets and asterisks will be called a CANCELLED FCS, designated δ'. We will say that neighborhood A is CONJUGATE with the contracted FCS δ'.

If, for example, $\delta_1 = \langle \delta_1^{11}, \ldots, \delta_1^{26} \rangle$ is the FCS which corresponds to the CC $R_{\mathfrak{B}_1}$ (Section 4 (3)), and A_1 is some neighborhood from the $R_{\mathfrak{B}_1}$, then we will have: $\delta^{11} = \delta^{14}$, $\delta^{21} = \delta^{24}$, therefore, if we replace δ^{14} and δ^{24} with asterisks, we produce cancellation of the FCS δ_1, and the neighborhood A_1 will be conjugate with the cancelled FCS $\delta'_1 = \langle \delta_1^{11}, \delta_1^{12}, \delta_1^{13}, *, \delta_1^{15}, \delta_1^{16}, \delta_1^{21}, \delta_1^{22}, \delta_1^{23}, *, \delta_1^{25}, \delta_1^{26} \rangle$.

Now, if instead of δ_1 we take the FCS $\bar{\delta}_1 = \langle \bar{\delta}_1^{11}, \ldots, \bar{\delta}_1^{26} \rangle$, which corresponds to the CC $R_{\bar{\mathfrak{B}}_1}$, and if instead of A_1 we take some neighborhood $\bar{A}_1$ from the $R_{\bar{\mathfrak{B}}_1}$, we will obtain a different system of equalities: $\bar{\delta}_1^{12} = \delta_1^{14}$, $\bar{\delta}_1^{22} = \delta_1^{24}$. As a result of the cancellation of the RCC δE_1, however, we obtain the same cancelled FCS as in the preceding example.

Of course, different ways of cancellation of any one RCC can be possible (for example, it is possible to eliminate $\delta^{i_1 j_1}$ instead of $\delta^{i'_1 j'_1}$; we should also note that our definition does not contain any requirement of 'maximality' on the sequences $\delta^{i_1 j_1}, \ldots, \delta^{i'_1 j'_1} \ldots$, that is, nothing is said of the impossibility of 'further cancellation').

The union of all the neighborhoods which are conjugate with a given cancelled FCS will be called a FORMAL COORDINATIONAL CLASS (FCC). For the sake of generality, it is convenient to assume that every FCS is also a cancelled FCS and that every CC is accordingly an FCC.

It is clear that all the neighborhoods contained in one CC are conjugate with the same FCS's; therefore, every FCC is a union of some CC's.

Returning to the examples in the foregoing section, we are now able to distinguish for Russian the following FCC's (in addition to those which are CC's):

$R_{\mathfrak{B}_1} \cup R_{\bar{\mathfrak{B}}_1}$ – the FCC corresponding to the following cancelled FCS: $\langle \{novyj, krásnyj, \ldots\}, \{nóvogo, krásnogo, \ldots\}, \{nóvomu, krásnomu, \ldots\}, *, \{nóvym, krásnym, \ldots\}, \{nóvom, krásnom\}, \{nóvye, krásnye, \ldots\}, \{nóvyx, krásnyx, \ldots\}, \{nóvym, krásnym, \ldots\}, *, \{nóvymi, krásnymi, \ldots\}, \{nóvyx, krásnyx, \ldots\} \rangle$.

$R_{\mathfrak{B}_2} \cup R_{\bar{\mathfrak{B}}_2}$ – the FCC corresponding to the cancelled FCS: $\langle \{nóvaja,$

krásnaja,...}, {nóvoj, krásnoj,...}, {nóvoj, krásnoj,...}, {nóvuju, krásnuju,...}, {nóvoj, nóvoju, krásnoj, krásnoju,...},{nóvoj, krásnoj,...},{nóvye, krásnye,...}, {nóvyx, krásnyx,...}, {nóvym, krásnym...}, ∗, {nóvymi, krásnymi,...}, {nóvyx, krásnyx,...}}⟩.

$R_{\mathfrak{B}_3} \cup R_{\overline{\mathfrak{B}}_3}$, $R_{\mathfrak{B}_4} \cup R_{\overline{\mathfrak{B}}_4}$ – FCC'S corresponding to cancelled FCS's which the reader can easily construct for himself.

It must be noted that a single FCC can correspond to more than one cancelled FCS. Thus, the FCC $R_{\mathfrak{B}_2} \cup R_{\overline{\mathfrak{B}}_2}$ corresponds, in addition to the cancelled FCS indicated above, to one which is obtained by eliminating the set occupying the third (or sixth) place.

(3) We will call an FCC a GENDER if it is a union of several CC's (in particular if it is itself a CC), and if it is not contained in any other FCC.

We obtain the following genders from our example:

$$R_{\mathfrak{B}_1} \cup R_{\overline{\mathfrak{B}}_1}, \; R_{\mathfrak{B}_2} \cup R_{\overline{\mathfrak{B}}_2}, \; R_{\mathfrak{B}_3} \cup R_{\overline{\mathfrak{B}}_3}, \; R_{\mathfrak{B}_4} \cup R_{\overline{\mathfrak{B}}_4}, \; R_{\mathfrak{B}_5}.$$

Now let us define the juncture of two [30] FCC's in the same way as this was done for the juncture of two CC's (Section 4, point (4)), but instead of the FCS's we will use the corresponding cancelled FCS's, if the asterisks in them occupy the same places; if this condition is not met, we will preliminarily change these cancelled FCS's as follows: Assume, for example, that in the first of the two cancelled FCS's there is the set $\delta^{i'j'}$ in the place with the numbers i', j', and that there is an asterisk in the corresponding place in the second. Then we find these i, j, for which the set with which we 'identified' the set with the numbers i', j' during cancellation stands in the place with the numbers i, j in the second cancelled FCS (there can generally be several such pairs i, j, in which case we select any one of them), and then in the first cancelled FCS we take the set δ^{ij} occupying the same place and replace it with the union $\delta^{ij} \cup \delta^{i'j'}$, and we replace $\delta^{i'j'}$ with an asterisk. We proceed in this manner for every place which has an asterisk in only one system, whereafter we define the juncture by means of the procedure from point (4) of Section 4. Further, we define the contraction of the FCC's in the same way as in point (5) of Section 4, with the difference that we equate an asterisk to an empty set. Finally, we define the domination for the FCC's as this was done for the CC's in point (5) of Section 4 (and not as in point (4)).

A gender which is not dominated by any other gender will be said to be PRIMARY. The set which consists of the union of a primary gender and all of the genders dominated by it will be said to be a REDUCED GENDER.

---

[30] Or more – cf. footnote 22.

In our example the genders $R_{\mathfrak{B}_1} \cup R_{\overline{\mathfrak{B}}_1}$ and $R_{\mathfrak{B}_2} \cup R_{\overline{\mathfrak{B}}_2}$ dominated $R_{\mathfrak{B}_5}$, and we have four reduced genders:

$$R_{\mathfrak{B}_1} \cup R_{\overline{\mathfrak{B}}_1} \cup R_{\mathfrak{B}_5} \quad \text{('masculine')}$$
$$R_{\mathfrak{B}_2} \cup R_{\overline{\mathfrak{B}}_2} \cup R_{\mathfrak{B}_5} \quad \text{('feminine')}$$
$$R_{\mathfrak{B}_3} \cup R_{\overline{\mathfrak{B}}_3} \quad \text{('neuter')}$$
$$R_{\mathfrak{B}_4} \cup R_{\overline{\mathfrak{B}}_4} \quad \text{('twin gender')}$$

It is curious that every gender here is a union of just two RCC's, one of which is contained in the class of all non-animate nouns, and the other in the class of all animate nouns.

(4) It seems plausible that our definition of gender, which has been developed to apply mainly to Russian, is also natural for a number of other languages, including those in which the nouns do not change with respect to case (the definitions in Section 3 should give only one case for such a language). For example, for French are seemingly distinguished two special CC's which consist of masculine and feminine *pluralia tantum*, respectively, together with two more CC's which include nouns of masculine and feminine gender, respectively, with non-homonymous number forms (cf. [2], p. 79), and that an application of the procedures in this section 'joins' both masculine CC's into the one gender and both 'feminine' CC's into the other. In fact, if we use l_1 and l_2, respectively, to designate the set of all possible masculine singular and plural forms, respectively, of the French adjective, then the FCS's corresponding to the coordinational classes R which consist of masculine nouns with non-homonymous number forms, and to $\tilde{R}$, which consist of masculine *pluralia tantum*, will have the following forms, respectively: $L = \langle l_1, l_2 \rangle$, $\tilde{L} = \langle l_2, l_2 \rangle$. Obviously, the FCS $\tilde{L}$ can be cancelled to the cancelled FCS $\tilde{L}' = \langle *, l_2 \rangle$, where the FCC corresponding to this cancelled FCS will coincide with $\tilde{R}$. Thus, $\tilde{R}$ is a contraction of R, and therefore R dominates $\tilde{R}$. Since each of the sets R and $\tilde{R}$ will apparently be a gender where R does not dominate any gender other than $\tilde{R}$ and has no gender dominating it, the set $R \cup R$ proves to be a reduced gender. The reasoning for the feminine gender is similar.

Soviet Academy of Sciences, Novosibirsk

BIBLIOGRAPHY

[1] L. Hjelmslev, *Prolegomena to a Theory of Language*, Baltimore 1953.
[2] A. A. Zaliznjak, *Russkoe imennoe slovoizmenenie*, Moscow 1967.
[3] A. A. K. Zaliznjak, 'Voprosu o grammatičeskix kategorijax roda i oduševlennosti v russkom jazyke, *Voprosy Jazykoznanija* **4** (1964), 25–40.
[4] O. S. Kulagina, 'Ob odnom sposobe opredelenija grammatičeskix ponjatij na baze teorii množestv', *Problemy Kibernetiki*, vypusk 1, Moscow 1958, pp. 203–214.

[5] V. A. K. Uspenskij, 'Opredelenija padeža po A. N. Kolmogorov', Bjulleten' objedi-
nenija po problemam mašinnogo perevoda, vypusk 5, Moscow 1957, pp. 11–18.

[6] S. Marcus, *Introduction mathematique à la linguistique structurale*, Paris 1967.

[7] S. Marcus, *Algebraic Linguistics; Analytical Models*, N. Y.–London 1967.

[8] I. I. Revzin, *Metod modelirovanija i tipologija slavjanskix jazykov*, Moscow 1967.

[9] R. Jakobson, 'Beitrag zur allgemeinen Kasuslehre', *Travaux du Cercle Linguistique
de Prague* 6 (1936), 240–287.

[10] A. V. Gladkij, 'K opredeleniju ponjatij padeža i roda suščestvitel'nogo', *Voprosy
jazykoznanija* 2 (1969), 110–123.

[11] T. I. Šed'ko, 'Proverka formal'nogo opredelenija padeža suščestvitel'nogo na materiale russkogo jazyka', *Naučno-texničeskaja informacija*, ser. 2 (1971), 28–42.

[12] T. I. Sed'ko, 'Proverka formal'nogo opredelenija roda suščestvitel'nogo na materiale
russkogo jazyka', *Naučno-texničeskaja informacija*, ser. 2 (1971), 29–34.

YU.C. LECOMTSEV

ON MODELS FOR A SYNTAX WITH EXPLICITLY
DIFFERENTIATED ELEMENTS (D-SYNTAX)*

1. PRELIMINARY NOTES

The aim of this article is to discuss a formal language for the description of linguistic data and to discuss possible ways of further restricting that formal language. These restrictions should finally lead to the construction of a linguistic theory.

Concerning the characteristics of a D-syntax model, it should be noted that our model is a continuation of the glossamatic variant of the Saussurian trend, partly complemented by Russian and American concepts. The notions of syntagmatic-paradigmatic relations and distinctive features lie at the heart of the concept.

Generally speaking, a model that includes both a syntactic system and the distinctive features by which syntactic elements or subsets of elements can be distinguished seems to have always been considered throughout European thought to be the *signum* together with its *accidentia*.

Ne have to start with an epistemological clarification of terms. First of all, both main categories – that of linguistic object and that of its model – should be taken into account. By the linguistic object primary here is meant the linguistic data together with some hypothetical entities. It is convenient for us to consider the two aspects of a model (or, in other words, the two forms of representation of a model), the non-formal and the formal. The difference between these two kinds of representation is that the latter has a symbolic form, i.e., it is a text in a formal language having many interpretations, while the first is similar to a system of things, i.e., as a system of *real things* with their abundance of qualities and net of interrelations (although the things and interrelations being considered here are rather abstract).

Thus the following scheme is accepted:

	MODEL
LINGUISTIC OBJECT	(1) NON-FORMAL REPRESENTATION
	(2) FORMAL REPRESENTATION

* Originally published in *Mathematical Models of Language* (F. Kiefer, ed.), Athenäum Verlag, 1973, by permission of Språkförlaget Skriptor, Copyright © 1972, Skriptor, Stockholm. This paper has been revised for the present volume. (*Editor's note*.)

Now we are going to explicate the non-formal representation of a D-syntax model, after which the formal representation of the model will be treated in the form of an axiomatic system. Linguistic interpretations will be given at various places in the paper.

2. THE NON-FORMAL REPRESENTATION OF A D-SYNTAX

A D-syntax model is divided into two domains – the differentiation system and the syntax. Only the main characteristics are to be given here to the two domains.

2.1. *The Differentiation System*

Any collection of objects about which one may ask whether they are different and in which way they are different may be regarded as a differentiation system. To be more exact in our calculations, the differences between objects are treat as discrete and explicitly given in the form of distinctive features.

In more exact words: A set of distinctive features or differentors given any subset of differentors is called an *element* and any set of elements such that some elements, at least, do not coincide, i.e. do not consist of the same differentors, is called a *differentiation system* (abbr. DS). Thus in the differentiation theory abstract objects (elements) are dealt with, which are differentiated or partly differentiated by abstract distinctive features (or differentors). Depending on various restrictions to which the systems of explicitly differentiated elements are subject, various kinds of systems can be constructed.

The determination of the possible kinds of such systems belongs to one of the main problems of differentiation theory.

We shall start by pointing out some important types of differentiation systems.

If the alphabet of differentors is infinite, the DS (differentiation system) is also infinite. If the alphabet of differentors is finite the DS is finite except when the differentors are contained in elements which are repeated infinitely. However, in this paper we are going to concentrate only on the cases where the DS are finite.

Given a finite DS, this DS is called *primitive* if (1) for any differentor α and any element x exactly one repetition of α may belong to x; (2) for any differentors α, $\beta \in x$ and β, $\alpha \in y$

$$x = (\alpha_1, \beta_2); \qquad y = (\beta_1, \alpha_2)$$

implies $x = y$, i.e. the difference in position of differentors within elements does not have to be taken into account.

Given a finite set A of differentors, a DS is called *complete*, if any subset in $B(A)$ (Boolean of A) is an element in the DS.

A finite DS is called *non-primitive I* if for some differentors (or for all differentors) the maximal number k of repetitions is defined and those differentors may belong repatedly (not more than k repetitions) to any element in the DS.

A finite DS is called *non-primitive II* if a system of places (in particular a halfordering) within any element is defined such that for $x = (\alpha_1 \beta_2)$, $y = (\beta_1 \alpha_2)$

$$x \not\equiv y.$$

The case of a primitive non-complete DS is typical for our axioms below.

Given a DS, various types of relations and operations may be introduced to investigate it.

A primitive DS may be regarded as a metric space, where the distance (or metric function) d between elements A, B, is defined as the number of differentors belonging to the symmetrical difference of A and B:

$$d(A, B) = n[(A - B) \cup (B - A)].$$

It is obvious that a primitive DS may be regarded as a partially ordered set on basis of inclusion relation ($\subseteq$). E.g. if element $A = (\alpha, \beta)$ and $B = (\alpha, \beta, \gamma)$ then $A \subseteq B$ (in particular $A \subset B$).

The linguistic interpretation of DS's is transparent. A DS may be interpreted, e.g. as a system of phonemes and distinctive features according to Jakobson and Halle (1956).

A DS may be interpreted as a semantical system with semantical features as differentors. But in the latter case some essential details in the semantical mechanism are not yet known. A DS may also be interpreted as a system of grammatical classes where grammatical morphemes are instead of differentors.

2.2. *Syntax*

In the domain of syntax the subject of our study is the compatibility of elements or classes of elements within units (sequences of elements). It may also be formulated as the field of studying the laws of how units are constructed from elements. The units in process of their construction are regarded to be situated in a space of n dimensions. The orientation (direction) of the constructive process must be determined.

In our case the units, i.e. sequences of elements, are situated in one-dimensional space, i.e. on a line. The orientation is from left to right.

The syntax has two different aspects, relational and operational, i.e., we can say that the syntactic elements belong to binary (n-ary) relations of various kinds and describe those relations. Otherwise we can determine on the set of elements some binary (n-ary, in general) operations in such a way that the units belong to the set of results of those operations. In this case they are called synthetical operations (operations of synthesis).

If the operations are determined on the set of syntactic units and the elements belong to the set of results of those operations, the operations are said to be analytical (operations of analysis).

2.2.1. *Distribution.* The notion of distribution seems to be one of the most fundamental in structural linguistics. To say element x is distributed among elements $w, y, z...$, is synonymous to saying x is compatible with $w, y, z, ...$

To formalize the notion of distribution (and that of compatibility) we have used a *distributive law* for concatenation relatively choice operation:

$$(1) \qquad a \cdot (b // c) = (a \cdot b) // (a \cdot c).$$

It runs: the concatenation of an element with a class of elements to be chosen equals the alternative choices between the concatenations of that element with elements of the class. It should be noted that concatenation is analogous to the syntagmatic relation (both-and relation), and choice-operation is analogous to the paradigmatic relation (either- or relation) in L. Hjelmslev's system.

The left part of Equation (1) was called the *generator*, and the right part of the equation was called the *text*.

The procedure of constructing the right part of Equation (1) from the left part was called text-*synthesis*, and the procedure of constructing the left part of Equation (1) from the right part was called *text-analysis*.

2.2.2. *Protoelements and Elements. Positional Schemes.* In a syntax it is important to discriminate between protoelements and elements. Protoelements are primitive symbols of an alphabet. Protoelements together with information about their positions within syntactic units are called syntactic elements. By information about positions is meant the indices $i \in I$, which indicate which place is taken by the protoelement in the general positional scheme of the unit. E.g. if the syllables vardh, varṣ, sparç, svaj, svar in Sanscrit are taken, the general positional scheme for them is:

S_1	P_2	A_3	R_4	DH_5 $Ç_5$ $Ṣ_5$
	V_2			J_{4-5}

where S_1, P_2, $\S_5$, etc. are elements, and S, P, $\S$ etc. are the corresponding protoelements[1]. It is postulated that for any elements a_i, a_j, $a_i \neq a_j$. It is postulated as well that there exists in a language a standard ordering of syntactical elements within a general scheme, which may be called *normal order*.

The normal order can be established on the basis of statistical calculation in real texts or may be chosen voluntarily, e.g., for texts whose word-order is conventionally unstable. On succeeding stages of model construction inversions of the normal order are to be introduced to model real fluctuations in the order of elements (see below on replacement operation).

2.2.3. *Zero elements.* Within a general positional scheme, where columns represent paradigms, whose elements are terms of the choice operation ($//$), and the elements of neighbouring columns are terms of the concatenation ($\cdot$), the construction of a shorter sequence (unit) is represented by using zero elements such that

(1) $\qquad a_i \cdot \mathbf{n}_{i+1} = a_i$
(2) $\qquad \mathbf{n}_i \cdot a_{i+1} = (a_{i+1})_i$

It can be seen that in (2) a shift of index occurs.

E.g. syllables svar and var may be placed into one general positional scheme, in which a zero element ($\emptyset$) is introduced

S	V	A	R
$\emptyset$			

or

$$(S//\emptyset) \cdot V \cdot A \cdot R.$$

The concatenation – choice approach to syntax is closely connected with the notion of a Cartesian product of sets in mathematics. Provided A is an alphabet and I is a set of indices $1, 2, ..., n$, a syntax S may be determined as a subset of $(A \times I)^I$.

The approach discussed above refers directly only to most plain structures in linguistics, e.g. syllabic structure. In order to speak about more complex structures, e.g. the structure of a sentence, the concatenation-choice model has to be expanded by the introduction of a replacement operation (see below).

Let a set S' of concatenation-choice formulas be given

$$F_1, F_2 \dots .$$

[1] The construction of general positional schemes can be carried out algorithmically. See, e.g., the author's article 'Distribucija fonem i generacija slogov', in *Voprosy struktury jazyka*, Moscow, 1964.

Each formula consists of certain components.

The components of a formula may be divided into the three following types:

atoms are terms of the choice operation; e.g. a, b, $(a \cdot b \cdot c)$;

members are such terms of the concatenation that are paradigms, a, b, e.g. $(a//b)$, $(a//b//...//n)$;

structures are expressions including symbols for both operations, e.g. $(a//b) \cdot (c//d)$, F_i.

The operation of replacement ($\rhd$) is an action in which a component x from F_i is put into F_j instead of a component $y (y \in F_j): x \rhd y = x/F_i, F_j, F_j^i/$.

Let us say that atoms are less than members and members are less than structures. Then the following types of replacement are possible:

exchange: $a \rhd a, m \rhd m, s \rhd s$.

shortening: $a \rhd m, a \rhd s, m \rhd s$.

enlargement: $m \rhd a, s \rhd a, s \rhd m$.

The replacement process treated here is collective in character, i.e. replacement performed together with concatenation and choice results in a set of chains, not in a unique chain (or sequence of elements).

In order to produce unique chains we should regard particular structures of the type $(a//a) \cdot (b//b) \cdot (c//c) ...$ and use replacements such that we could never obtain $(x//y)$.

Evidently, when combining the replacement transformations with the syntax, only replacements of the types: exchange and enlargement should be used, since the effect of using shortening replacements can be obtained by exploiting zero elements[2].

2.3. *Differentiation system and Syntax (D-Syntax).*

In D-syntax a syntax is treated whose elements are explicitly differentiated by a certain number of differentors, i.e. any syntactical element corresponds to an element of a DS.

3. AXIOM FOR D-SYNTAX

Axioms for D-syntax are divided into three groups: axioms for DS, axioms for syntax and Transitional Axioms (from a DS to Syntax).

After each list of axioms some comments will be made that are intended to clarify some details. Those comments are to be regarded as a continuation of the preceding sections on the non-formal representations of DS-syntax.

(1) The axioms for DS

---

[2] More detailed account can be found in the author's book *Vvedenije v formal'nyj jazyk livingstik'i* ('An Introduction to a Formal Language for Linguistics'), in press.

D.1. $\forall A \quad A \leqslant A$.

D.2. $\forall A, \forall B \quad A \leqslant B \ \& \ B \leqslant A \Rightarrow A = B$.

D.3. $\forall A, \forall B, \forall C \quad A \leqslant B \ \& \ B \leqslant C \Rightarrow A \leqslant C$.

DEFINITION D.1.

$A \leqslant B \ \& \ \neg (A = B) \sim_{\mathrm{df}} A < B$.

D.4. $\forall A, \forall B, \forall \alpha, \forall \beta \quad A = B \rightleftarrows ((\alpha \in A) \Rightarrow$
$\Rightarrow (\alpha \in \beta)) \ \& \ ((\beta \in B) \Rightarrow (\beta \in A))$.

D.5. $\forall A, \forall B, \forall \alpha, \exists \beta \quad A < B \rightleftarrows ((\alpha \in A) \Rightarrow (\alpha \in B)) \ \& \ (\beta \notin A) \ \& \ (\beta \in B)$.

D.6. $\forall X, \exists A, \exists \chi^* (A \neq \emptyset) \ \& \ \neg (X < A) \Rightarrow \chi^* \in A$.

3.1. *Comments*

(1) Axioms D1–D3 are the axioms of a partially ordered set.

(2) Axioms D4–D6 determine the rules for ascribing differentors to the elements of a DS.

(3) In D6 the symbol χ^* denotes any final set of differentors which can be ascribed to a minimal non-empty element of a DS.

What we have said in (2) should become more claer after we have considered the following example. Given a partially ordered set H which is subject to the axioms D1–DS. E.g., in terms of basical graphs, let set H be

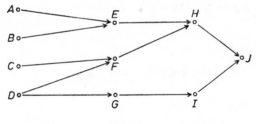

Fig. 1.

According to axioms D4–D6 differentors can be ascribed, for instance, in the following way:

$$A = \chi_1^* \alpha; \qquad B = \chi_2^* \beta;$$
$$C = \chi_3^* \gamma; \qquad D = \chi_4^* \delta;$$
$$E = \chi_1^*; \chi_2^* \alpha \beta \varepsilon; \qquad F = \chi_3^* \chi_4^* \gamma \delta \eta;$$
$$G = \chi_4^* \delta \xi; \qquad H = \chi_1^* \chi_2^* \chi_3^* \chi_4^* \alpha \beta \gamma \delta \varepsilon \eta \iota;$$
$$I = \chi_4^* \alpha \xi \chi; \qquad J = \chi_1^* \chi_2^* \chi_3^* \chi_4^* \alpha \beta \gamma \delta \varepsilon \eta \xi \iota \kappa.$$

It is to be noted that, first, the elements of H in our example as well as elements of any DS, can contain more differentors than those which are obligatory according to the axioms. The differentors that are not ascribed obligatory but are permitted to be according to the axioms may be called *redundant*. Secondly, some differentors that have been asccribed according to the axioms may coincide or be empty. If we are not going to use this possibility of enlarging or reducing some of them, we may speak of *non-minimal* (or *maximal*, in particular) representation. In the opposite case we speak about *non-maximal* (or *minimal*, in particular) representation.

DEFINITION D2. $A\square B$ (A is incomparable with B) $\sim_{df} \neg (A \leqslant B)\ \&\neg (B \leqslant \leqslant A)$.

3.2. *The Axioms of Syntax* 1 (SI)

A finite partially ordered set A^1 of elements, called syntax 1, is given. Syntactic elements are denoted by the small Latin letters $a, b, c,..., z$. Syntax 1 is subject to the following axioms.

SI.1. $\forall a$ $a \leqslant a$.
SI.2. $\forall a, \forall b$ $a \leqslant b\ \&\ b \leqslant a \Rightarrow a = b$.
SI.3. $\forall a, \forall b, \forall c$ $a \leqslant b\ \&\ b \leqslant c \Rightarrow a \leqslant c$.

DEFINITION SI.1.

$$a \leqslant b\ \&\ \neg (a = b) \sim_{df} \quad a < b.$$

DEFINITION SI.2

$$a < b\ \&\ \neg (\exists c, a < c\ \&\ c < b) \sim_{df} a \lessdot b.$$

DEFINITION SI.3

$$\neg (a \leqslant b)\ \&\ \neg (b \leqslant a) \sim_{df} a\ \square\ b.$$

DEFINITION SI.4

$$a\ \square\ b\ \&\ \exists c((a < c\ \&\ b < c) \not\equiv (c < a\ \&\ c < b)) \sim_{df} a\ \boxdot\ b.$$

SI.4. $\forall a, \forall b$ $a \cdot b \Rightarrow a < b$.
SI.5. $\forall a, \forall b$ $a \cdot b = ab$.
SI.6. $\forall a, \forall b, \forall c$ $(a \cdot b) \cdot c = a \cdot (b \cdot c)$.
SI.7. (1) $\forall a, \exists n$ $a \cdot \mathbf{n} \Rightarrow a \cdot \mathbf{n} = a$;
      (2) $\mathbf{n} \cdot a \Rightarrow \mathbf{n} \cdot a = a$.
SI.8. $\forall a, \forall c$ $a // c \Rightarrow a\ \boxdot\ c$.
SI.9. $\forall a, \forall c$ $a // c = (a, c)$.

SI.10. $\forall a, \forall c$ $a//c = c//a$.

SI.11. $\forall a, \forall c, \forall e$ $a//(c//e) = (a//c)//e$.

SI.12. $\forall a, \forall b, \forall c$ $a \cdot (b//c) = (a \cdot b)//(a \cdot c)$.

3.3. Comments.

(1) Axioms SI.1–3 and the following definitions are connected with a partial ordering of syntactic elements.

The interpretation of this partial ordering is quite different from that of the axioms D1–3. In this case one means the relative positions of syntactic elements or, in other words, the inclusion relation among strings, e.g. $c \leqslant d$ if the string $abc \subseteq abcd$ (in D1–3 the inclusion relation among sets was mentioned).

(2) Axioms S1–4 and S1.8 introduce operations which are not wholly determined. The domains of their determination are controlled by order relations ($<$ and $\boxdot$ respectively).

(3) From an algebraic view-point a set with the two binary operations of concatenation ($\cdot$) and choice ($//$) may be regarded as *a half-semi-ring*.[3] I.e. the operations in a half-semi-ring are not wholly determined. But the choice operation departs from an algebraic operation in two respects. Firstly, it is endomorphic, secondly it is many-valued (namely, two-valued).

DEFINITION. An operation is called *endomorphic*, in our terms provided its result coincides with at least one, of the elements of departure.

Many-valued operations have some specific features of their own. The notation for the choice operation $a//c = a$ and $a//c = c$ results in $a = c$, which is generally false. We shall understand the usual notation to be a shortened form of the following notation

$$a//c = (a, c),$$
$$a//c =_l a \quad \text{or} \quad a//c =_a a,$$
$$a//c =_r c \quad \text{or} \quad a//c =_c c,$$
$$a = c \Rightarrow (a//c =_l a) \,\&\, (a//c =_r c) \,\&\, (a//c =_l c) \,\&\, (a//c =_r a).$$

If we have $a//b//c//...//d$ the equality symbols can be marked with numeric indices, e.g. $a_1//b_2//c_3//...//d_n =_k e_k, 1 \leqslant k \leqslant n$.

The indexing of the equality symbols seems to be connected with the idea of Riemann surfaces.

---

[3] Cp. the notion of *ring* in symbolic logic, considered by Alonzo Church. A calculus P_1 is viewed as a ring, where logical equivalence is regarded as an equality relation, logical antiequivalence and conjunction are regarded as binary operations of addition and multiplication, respectively. See A. Church, *Introduction to Mathematical Logic* I, Princeton, 1956, p. 87.

(4) In axiom S1.6 the idea of linguistic distribution (or compatibility) is pronounced. See the section on syntax in Ch.1.

(5) Axiom S1.7 has to do with zero elements (see syntax in 2.2.1.).

In syntax there are many repetitions (inclusions) of the zero symbol of the syntactic alphabet A.

It should be emphasized that zero elements are defined in terms of concatenation only. From the point of view of the choice operation a zero element does not differ from any other element of the syntax.

In particular, it may correspond to the empty element of a DS (if there is one).

(6) There is no non-commutative law for concatenation among the axioms since it is to be deduced from the relational restriction of concatenation in S1.4 ... Moreover, in case $a \cdot b$, the result of $b \cdot a$ is not determined (symbolically: $b \cdot a = 0$). Some theorems follow immediately from D or SI. One of them is given as an example here.

THEOREM D.1. If elements A and B are incomparable, there exist differentors α and β such that α belongs to A and does not belong to B and β belongs to B and does not belong to A.

Proof. According to Definition D.2. $A \square B \sim_{\text{of}} \neg (A \leqslant B) \& \neg (B \leqslant A)$. From axioms D.4.–5. it follows that

$$A \leqslant B \rightleftarrows \forall \alpha, \qquad \alpha \in A \Rightarrow \alpha \in B$$

and

$$B \leqslant A \rightleftarrows \forall \beta, \qquad \beta \in B \Rightarrow \beta \in A .$$

Hence

$$\neg (A \leqslant B) \rightleftarrows \neg (\forall \alpha \; \alpha \in A \Rightarrow \alpha \in B) \rightleftarrows \exists \alpha$$
$$\alpha \in A \& \alpha \notin B.$$

Analogously we can obtain

$$\neg (B \leqslant A) \rightleftarrows \exists \beta \qquad \beta \in B \& \beta \notin A .$$

Thus $A \square B \sim_{\text{df}} \exists \alpha \exists \beta \; (\alpha \in A \& \alpha \notin B) \& (\beta \in B \& \beta \notin A)$.

Replacement transformations in syntax 1.

Any system that is a syntax 1 can be transformed into another system that is also a syntax 1.

Such transformations may be given in the form of a replacement operation.

Any subset of S1, including the terms of both operations ($\cdot$ and $//$) is said to be a formula in S2.

Given all Formulae F_i, the set F of Formulae $(F_1, F_2, ..., F_n)$ is regarded as a set of components which are of three kinds:

atoms, i.e. basic terms of choice operation;

members, i.e. terms of concatenation;

structures, i.e. terms for both operations.

The set $\mathfrak{C}$ of all the components of F is given as $C_j(F_i)$, the notation for a component of the formula F_i.

In $\mathfrak{C}$ an operation, called the replacement operation, is defined between components $C_j(F_i)$, $C_k(F_e)$:

$$S2 \cdot 1 \cdot C_j(F_i) \rhd C_k(F_e) = [C_j]_k(F_e').$$

The theory of replacement transformation is of great importance, especially for the description of the most complicated linguistic structures, e.g. sentence structure, semantic structures. Nevertheless those transformations will not be used in this paper.[4]

4. Transitional axioms

The axioms governing the coordination between D and the S1 axioms are as follows:

$$T1 \cdot \forall a\,(a\in B)\,\exists A\,(A\in DS) \qquad A = \delta(a).$$

In other words the one-valued mapping $\delta: S \Rightarrow DS$ is defined.

If we choose the semantic interpretation, our formal system should be expanded by some additional postulates (see below, Section 5).

4.1. *Some Theorems for D-Syntax*

Only some theorems for D-syntax will be given as an illustration of the possibilities of the axiomatic systems represented in II. Those theorems may be divided into the following groups:

(1) Contrast relation in G;

(2) latent and exposed differentors in the contrast relation;

(3) bag-paradigms.

4.2. *Contrast Relation in G_1.*

DEFINITION 1. A subset P of a partially ordered set H such that for every pair of elements a, $b\,(a\in P,\, b\in P)\, a\,\square\,b$, i.e. a and b are immediately incomparable, is called a *paradigm* in H.

---

[4] It seems to be indispensable to emphasize the fact that syntax is treated in this paper in its most fundamental form, which is at the same time rather oversimplified. In principle, a more complicated form of syntax is possible, e.g. a syntax where the IC principle is postulated and the concept of *signal* is introduced, signal being a formal analogue to elements with grammatical functions as affixes, conjunctions or particles. However, in our first approximation to the subject of matter it is convenient to use a more primitive formalism, which is at once more lucid and does not notably distort linguistic phenomena.

DEFINITION 2. A partially ordered set H, the paradigms of which are ordered, i.e. for every pair of paradigms P_i, $P_j (i \neq j)$, either $P_i < P_j$ or $P_j < P_i$ is true, is called a *protosyntax*.

DEFINITION 3. Any protosyntax regarded in terms of concatenation and choice ($\cdot$ and $//$) is called a *regular generator*.

DEFINITION 4. The set T of all the chains in a partially ordered set H is called a *text*.

Remark. A text is said to be generated by the operations of choice and concatenation. In other words, in the formula

$$(a//b) \cdot (c//d) = (a \cdot c)//(a \cdot d)//(b \cdot c)//(b \cdot d),$$

the left part of the equation is called the generator and the right part of it is called the text.

DEFINITION 5. A paradigm that does not contain the zero element is called *nuclear*.

DEFINITION 6. A regular generator G which includes only one intermediate (neither the first nor the last) nuclear paradigm is called *a regular nuclear generator*.

DEFINITION 7. If in a regular nuclear generation G_1 the elements of the nuclear paradigm are identical with those elements of a DS that are not identical with elements of the other paradigms in G_1, G_1 is called a *disjoint nuclear generator*.

Let a regular disjoint nuclear generator G_1 be given. Let us call the nuclear paradigm of G_1 *medial*, all the paradigms preceding the medial paradigm *initial* and all the paradigms following the medial paradigm *final*. We shall use the following abbreviated symbols: B for the first paradigm, $I - B$ for any initial paradigm that is not the first, M for the medial paradigm, $F - E$ for any final paradigm that is not the last and E for the last paradigm.

LEMMA 1. Given a text T generated by a regular disjoint nuclear generator G_1. There exists a text $T' (T' \subset T)$ generated by another regular disjoint nuclear generator G_1' such that (a) the number of paradigms in G_1' is less by one than that in G_1

$$n(P) - n(P') = 1$$

and (b) G_1' includes a paradigm P^* that is the union of two neighbouring paradigms in G_1

$$P^*(P^* \subset G_r^1) = Pi \cup P_{i+1}(P_i \cdot P_{i+1} \subset G_1).$$

Proof. Let us take from T all the chains having the zero element either at the ith or at the $i+1$th place. For every pair of chains of the type.

$$\ldots ax_i \, \emptyset_{i+1} b \ldots$$
$$\ldots a\emptyset_i \, y_{i+1} b \ldots$$

elements x_i, $y_{i+1}(x_i \in P_i,\ y_{i+1} \in P_{i+1})$ are, according to axiom SI.7 and the definition SI.4, immediately incomparable

$$(x_i \, \Box \, (y_{i+1})_i.$$

i.e. x_i, $(y_{i+1})_i$ belong to the same paradigm now

$$x_i,\ y_i \in P^*(P^* \subset G_1').$$

DEFINITION 8. The generator G_1' regarded in the lemma is to be called the secondary relative G_1.

DEFINITION 9. The immediate incomparability relation in a union of any number of paradigms, as a result of a progressive construction of secondary relative generators G_1, is said to be *secondary*.

DEFINITION 10. A secondary immediate incomparability relation where the environment is identical is called the contrast relation (CR) with identity of environment.

THEOREM 1. *In a regular disjoint nuclear generator the CR (contrast relation) does not include the pairs of elements belonging to the following pairs of paradigms (the types of paradigms are indicated):*

$$(1)\ B,\ F - E; \qquad (2)\ B,\ E; \qquad (3)\ I - B,\ E.$$

The CR includes the types of pairs (1) I, I; (2) M, M; (3) F, F; (4) I, M; (5) M, F.

Proof. (1) First, we have to prove the assertion $\neg(B \Box F - E)$. Let us assume the contrary to be true, i.e. $B \Box F - E$. By definition $B \Box F - E \sim$ $\sim (B \ll M) \to ((F - E) \ll M)$. But the assertion $(F - E) \ll M$ is false. Therefore $\neg(B \Box F - E)$ is true.

(2) Now the assertion $\neg(B \Box E)$ has to be proved. If we assume the contrary to be true we have $B \Box E \sim B \ll M \to E \ll M$, which is false.

(3) The assertion $\neg(I-B\boxdot E)$ has to be proved. $I-B\boxdot E\sim I-B\leqslant M\rightarrow$ $\rightarrow E\leqslant H$, which is false.

Now we have to prove that certain types of pairs belong to the CR.

(1) $I_i\boxdot I_j$.

Let us select from the text T strings with a fixed M in which all F-paradigms are represented by $\emptyset$ and $k-1$ from k initial paradigms are also represented by $\emptyset$.

It is then obvious that any I-paradigm contrasts with any other I-paradigm.

(2) $M\boxdot M$.

Let us select from T all the strings where both k initial paradigms and i final paradigms are represented by $\emptyset$. Any $a\in M$ contrasts with $b\in M$.

(3) $F_i\boxdot F_j$.

Let us choose from T all the strings with a fixed M element where all the initial paradigms are represented by $\emptyset$ and $i-1$ final paradigms are represented by $\emptyset$. Any element $a\in F_i$ contrasts with any $b\in F_j$.

(4) $I_i\boxdot M$ and $M\boxdot F_i$.

Let us select from T all the strings where either all the F paradigms and $k-1$ initial paradigms or all the initial paradigms and $i-1$ final paradigms are represented by $\emptyset$, i.e. strings of the types I_iM and MF_i. Then any element from I_i contrasts with any element of M and any element from F_i contrasts with any element from M.

For the matrix for CR with identity of environment see Figure 2.

	B	$I-B$	M	$F-E$	E
B	1	1	1	0	0
$I-B$	1	1	1	1	0
M	1	1	1	1	1
$F-E$	0	1	1	1	1
E	0	0	1	1	1

Fig. 2.

4.3. *Latent and Exposed Differentors*

According to axiom T.1. there exists a mapping δ from the set S' of syntactic elements into $DS(\delta:S'\Rightarrow DS)$. Let P_i be a paradigm in S. First of all some subsets of mapping δ of the type

$$\delta : P_i \Rightarrow DS$$

are interesting for us. The following principle is to be adopted

$$\delta(P_i \cup P_j) = \delta(P_i) \cup \delta(P_j).$$

In addition to the operations determined by the axioms, we are going to use the operations of set theory, i.e. union, intersection and difference, for the DS.

DEFINITION 11. A differentor $\alpha(\alpha \in DS)$ is said to be *latent* in a CR if for every pair of the element $(a, b) \in CR$

$$\alpha \in \delta(a) \cap \delta(b).$$

DEFINITION 12. Differentor $\alpha(\alpha \in DS)$ is said to be *exposed* in CR if for one pair at least

$$(a, b) \in CR \neg (\alpha \in \delta(a) \cap \delta(b))$$

holds true.

As can be seen from the matrix for the CR (see above), there are paradigms P_i, P_j such that $(x, y) \in CR$ if $x \in P_i$ and $y \in P_j$. Let us call such paradigms P_i, P_j *polar* paradigms. Any paradigm P_k such that for a pair of polar paradigms P_i, P_j.

$$(x, z) \in CR \quad \text{and} \quad (z, y) \in CR,$$

where $x \in P_i, y \in P_j, z \in P_k$, may be called an *intermediate* paradigm between the polar paradigms P_i, P_j.

LEMMA 2. If a differentor α is exposed in a paradigm P_i then α is also exposed in any paradigm $P_i \cup P_k$ such that $P_i \times P_k \subseteq CR$.

Proof. α is exposed in P_i, i.e. there exists such a pair $e, e' \in P_i$ that $\alpha \in \delta(e)$ and $a \notin \delta(e')$. Both cases are possible – either α is latent in P_k or α is exposed in P_k. Byond that α may be excluded from P_k i.e. for every $e^* \in P_k$ $\alpha \notin \delta(e^*)$.

If α is latent in P_k (i.e. latent in the CR within P_k) and exposed in P_i, then α is obviously exposed in $P_k \cup P_i$.

If α is exposed in both P_i and P_k, α is exposed in $P_i \cup P_k$. If α is excluded from P_k, i.e. α is latent in P_k, then obviously α is exposed in $P_i \cup P_k$.

THEOREM 2. If a, b is a pair of elements belonging to the polar paradigms $P_i, P_j (a \in P_i, b \in P_j)$ and α, β are differentors such that $\alpha \in \delta(a)$ and $\beta \in \delta(b)$, then α, β are exposed in the CR within G_1.

Proof. According to the definition of a CR there is in G_1 a paradigm P_k intermediate between P_i and P_j, in particular the medial paradigm is intermediate.

Let us consider the possible cases. The differentor α may be (1) exposed in P_i or (2) latent in P_i.

If α is exposed in P_i, then according to Lemma 1α is exposed in $P_i \cup P_k$.

If α is latent in P_i, then it is either exposed in P_k, or latent in P_k.

If α is exposed in P_k, then, according to Lemma 1, it is exposed in $P_i \cup P_k$.

If α is latent both in P_i and in P_k, then there exists in G_1 a medial paradigm P_m (intermediate between P_i and P_j) such that for every $e \in P_m$

$$\alpha \notin \delta(e).$$

Obviously α is exposed in $P_i \cup P_m$ and α is exposed in $P_k \cup P_m$. Therefore either in Case 1 or in Case 2 the differentor α is exposed in $P_k \cup P_j$. The proof for the differentor β is to be carried out analogously.

Linguistic interpretation. Theorem 2 may be viewed as a formal analogue for N.S. Trubetzkoy's assertion that phonemes that are not opposed immediately (e.g. h and η in German or English) enter the net of oppositions within a phonological system.[5]

4.4. *On Bag-Paradigms*

DEFINITION 13. If in a partially ordered set H there are paradigms P_i, P_j, P_k such that $P_i \lessdot P_j$ and $P_i P_j \boxdot P_k$, the set H is called a *primitive syntax*.

DEFINITION 14. A primitive syntax regarded in terms of operations of choice and concatenation is called a *non-regular generator*.

DEFINITION 15. A paradigm P_k^* in a primitive syntax that is immediately incomparable with a chain of paradigms $P_i P_{i+1} ... P_j$:

$$P_i P_{i+1} ... P_j \boxdot P_k^*$$

is called a *bag-paradigm*.

DEFINITION 16. A chain of paradigms P_{k-1}^* in a primitive syntax consisting of m paradigms such that it is immediately incomparable to another chain of paradigms P_{i-j} consisting of n paradigms ($m < n$) is called a *bag-paradigm chain*.

In terms of operations of concatenation and choice P_k^* is called a bag-

[5] N. S. Trubetzkoy, *Grundzüge der Phonologie*, Praha, 1939, S. 70.

paradigm if

$$(P_i P_{i+1} \ldots P_j)//P_k^*$$

and $P_k \ldots P_1$ is called a bag-paradigm chain if

$$(P_i P_{i+1} \ldots P_j)//(P_k \ldots P_1)$$

when $(1-k) < (j-i)$.

DEFINITIONS 17. A non-regular generator G which includes a nuclear paradigm (see definition) is said to be a *non-regular nuclear generator*.

THEOREM 3. In a non-regular nuclear generator G a bag-paradigm P_k^* ($P_k^* \square P_{i-j}$, P_{i-j} being a chain of n paradigms) belongs to the CR with any paradigm contrasted with P_{i-j}.
Proof. Let us choose from the text T generated by G all those strings in which the chain P_{i-j} is represented by $n-1$ zero elements as well as the strings containing P_k^*. P_k^* contrasts with any paradigm of P_{i-j}. Since the immediate incomparability relation is transitive, P_k^* belongs to the CR with any P_m that contrasts with P_{i-j}.

DEFINITION 18. A bag-paradigm P_k^* in a non-regular generator G is said to be *complete* if P_k^* is immediately incomparable with the longest string of paradigms (containing the most number of paradigms) in G.

THEOREM 4. In a non-regular nuclear generator G including a complete bag-paradigm P_k^* the elements of P_k^* belong to the CR only with elements of the medial paradigm (i.e. the paradigm that does not contain any zero element).
Proof. Paradigm P_k^* occurs in the environment # – # only, and therefore it can contrast either with the longest chain of paradigms that occurs in the same environment or with a unique paradigm P_n (# P_n #). The only paradigm in G which satisfies the condition is the medial paradigm.

Linguistical interpretation. If it is assumed that the verbal predicate of a sentence can never be dropped, then a minor sentence of the type 'Oh!' or 'Hush' (interjections) can be contrasted in identical environment only with the verbal predicate.

5. THE PROBLEM OF APPLYING THE D-SYNTAX MODEL TO SEMANTIC

Our previous attempts were adjusted for a phonological study (i.e. on the expression plane) or for a grammatical study (on the sign-level) rather than for a semantic approach. Semantics, similar though it is in some characteristic aspects to phonology, is subject beyond that, to certain specific laws some of which we can as yet merely suspect. Formal approximation to these laws depends on field-work progress in linguistic semantics. Nevertheless we shall try to trace some possibilities for adjusting a D-syntax model for the description of semantic phenomena. A rather rough approximation can be obtained by taking some additional axioms of the T-group (transitional axioms).

(T.2) $\forall a, b \exists \alpha \, a \cdot b \Rightarrow \alpha \in \delta(a) \,\&\, \alpha \in \delta(b)$.

(T.3) $\forall a, c \, (a \neq c) \, \exists \beta \, a//c \Rightarrow (\beta \in \delta(a) \,\&\, \beta \notin \delta(c)) \not\equiv (\beta \notin \delta(a) \,\&\, \beta \notin \delta(c))$.

(T.2) asserts that neighbouring syntactical elements have at least one differentor in common.

(T.3) assert that every pair of non-identical elements in a paradigm differs by at least one differentor.

(T.4) $\forall n \exists \eta, \quad \eta \in \delta(n)$.

(T.5) $\forall a \exists n \exists \eta \quad (\eta \in \delta(n))$
          $a \cdot n = a^* \Rightarrow \eta \notin \delta(a) \,\&\, \eta \in \delta(a^*)$.

In (T.5) the symbol a^* denotes the fact that the string a is a reduction of the string an.

(T.4) asserts that every zero-element in a syntax contains at least one differentor from DS (or has it as image in mapping from S into DS).

(T.5) asserts that differentors belonging to a zero-element have to be ascribed to neighbouring non-zero-elements.

Thus the zero element is interpreted here as a zero element on the expression plane, but not on the content plane, when the zero-symbol is eliminated.

(T.5) also means that DS elements or δ-mapping can be transformed by syntactic operations. In other words, the extention of D-syntax for semantics causes a reconstruction of Axiom T.1.

However, a syntax with the additional Axioms T.2–5 is still unsatisfactory for semantical description. In order to get a deeper insight into semantic data and to elaborate an appropriate formalism afterwards, at least the following details should be considered.

Let us analyse a sentence, e.g., 'The boat was overturned by the storm on the open sea', from the view-point of how semantic features (differentors) belong to the neighbouring words (cf. Axiom T.2).

Let us assume that the meaning of the word TO BE OVERTURNED is represented by a semantic differentor α. According to Axiom T.2 the word BOAT includes at least one differentor common with the neighbouring word TO BE OVERTURNED. We may assume that the differentor in common for both of the words is α. It is obvious that α in 'boat' is not the same as α in 'to be overturned'. The word 'boat' denotes an *object that may be overturned*. Thus if the word 'to be overturned' contains α, the word *'boat'* contains some *possibility of* α. Similar assertions may be made relative to other words in the sentence above.

Having based our assumption on reasoning of the type just demonstrated, a hypothesis can be put forward that can be formulated as follows.

Any element of a semantic DS (a set of semantical differentors) has differentors of two types.

Every element in a semantical DS includes a nucleus, which contains nuclear differentors, and a periphery, which contains peripheric differentors.[6]

We may assume that neighbouring syntactic elements A and B have a differentor in common that is nuclear in A and peripheric in B or vice versa. Accordingly, syntactic elements belonging to one and the same paradigm differ, at least, by one nuclear differentor.

Symbolically: let α_n, β_n and β_p denote nuclear and peripheric differentors respectively.

(T*2) $\forall a, b \; \exists \beta_n \beta_p \, a \cdot b \Rightarrow (\beta_n \in \delta(a) \; \& \; \beta_p \in \delta(b)) \not\equiv (\beta_p \in \delta(a) \; \& \; \beta_n \in \delta(b)),$

(T*3) $\forall a, c \exists \alpha_n \, a//c \Rightarrow (\alpha_n \in \delta(a) \; \& \; \alpha_n \notin \delta(c)) \not\equiv (\alpha_n \notin \delta(a) \; \& \; \alpha_n \in \delta(c)).$

Obviously, the conception stated above demands further investigation.

6. Summary

In this article a formal system for the description of linguistic data called D-syntax was proposed. It is characteristic for D-syntax that its elements are somehow connected with certain bundles of distinctive features. However, the question of in which a form distinctive features have to be connected with syntactical elements, e.g., what type of a mapping should exist between them, essentially depends on the progress of linguistical investigations.

As an example illustrating possibilities of D-syntax some theorems were deduced concerning the contrast relation, latent and exposed features and the bag-paradigms.

A possible application to semantics was analyzed.

The mathematical domains with which D-syntax is closely connected are partially ordered set theory and half-algebras.

Lomonosov University, Moscow

---

[6] Cf. A. J. Greimas's viewpoint. According to Greimas 'une sémantème' (S) consists of 'un noyau sémique' (N_s) and 'une contextuelle séme' (C_s): $S = N_s + C_s$. A. G. Greimas, *Sémantique Structurale*, Recherche de méthode, Paris, 1966, p. 49.

BIBLIOGRAPHY

Birkhoff, G., *Lattice Theory*, New York, 1948.
Brodda, Benny and Karlgen, Hans, *Relative Positions of Elements in Linguistic Strings*, Smil, Vol. 3, 1964.
Church, A., *Introduction to Mathematical Logic*, Vol. I, Princeton, 1956.
Greimas, A. G., *Sémantique structurale*, Paris, 1966.
Harris, Z. S., *Structural Linguistics*, Chicago-London, 1963.
Hjelmslev, L., *Prolegomena to a Theory of Language*, Baltimore, 1953.
Holt, Jens, *Beiträge zur sprachlichen Innhaltsanalyse*, Innsbruck, 1964.
Jakobson, R. and Halle, M., *Fundamentals of Language*, 's-Gravenhage, 1956.
Lekomcev, Yu. K., *Vvedenije v formalnyj jazyk lingvistiki* (in press).
Lekomcev, Yu. K., *K tipologii razlicenija grammaticeskih klassov Narody Azii i Afriki* **6** (1963).
Lekomcev, Yu. K., 'Elementy teorii različenija', in the volume *Problemy strukturnoj lingvistiki*, Moscow, 1968.
Lekomcev, Yu. K., 'Elementy teorii jazvkovoj sočetajemosti', in the volume *Problemy strukturnoj lingvistiki*, Moscow, 1963.
Lekomcev, Yu. K., 'Towards a Differentiation Theory for Linguistics', in the volume *Studies in General and Oriental Linguistics*, presented to Shiro Hattori, Tokyo, 1970.
Mac-Neille, H. M., 'Partially Ordered Sets', *Trans. Am. Math. Society* **42** (1937).
Saussure, F. de, *Cours de linguistique générale*, Paris, 1922.
Sørensen, H. Ch., *Studies on Case in Russian*, Copenhagen, 1957.
Togeby, Knud, *Structure immanente de la langue Française*, Copenhagen, 1951.
Trubetzkoy, N. S., *Grundzüge der Phonologie*, Praha, 1939.
Ulldall, H. J., *Outline of Glossematics*, Copenhagen, 1957.
Ungeheuer, G., 'Das Fundament binären Phonemklassifikationen', *Studia Linguistica* **8** (1959).
Winter, W., 'Über eine Methode zum Nachweis struktureller Relevanz von Oppositionen distinktiver Merkmale', *Phonetica. Symposion Trubetzkoy*, 1958.

S. K. ŠAUMJAN

THE GENOTYPE LANGUAGE AND FORMAL SEMANTICS

1. The problem of meaning

Let us begin with the notion of the sentence. Definitions of the sentence such as the following are very widespread: "A sentence is a thought expressed in words", or "A sentence is a completed thought expressed in words", or "A sentence is a linguistic unit which expresses a thought", etc. All of these are not definitions of the sentence in the strict sense of the word, but are rather explanations of what we intuitively grasp to be the concept of the sentence. In such definitions of the sentence the question immediately arises of what a thought is and how it is expressed in a sentence.

Thought does not exist in a pure form, but is always enclosed in a linguistic shell, just as value does not exist in a pure form, but is always contained in a commodity shell. Just as the value of a particular commodity can only be found in its relation to other commodities equivalent to it in value, so can the thought contained in a particular sentence be found only in the relation of this sentence to other sentences which are equivalent to it in terms of the thoughts contained in them. Just as the equivalence of various commodities is determined by how they can be exchanged for one another, so is the equivalence of different sentences determined by how one sentence can be substituted for another in a given situation.

Any commodity can be accepted as a standard of value, that is, as an object which directly represents value, and all other commodities will then be regarded as realizations of this value. In the same way, given a class of sentences, any of these sentences can be taken as a standard of a thought, i.e., as a sentence which directly represents the thought, and all the other sentences will in this case be regarded as the linguistic forms of the thought. Take, for example, the sentences:

(1)   The father gives money to his son.
(2)   Money is given by the father to his son.
(3)   The son receives money from his father.
(4)   Money is received by the son from his father.
(5)   The father provides his son with money.
(6)   The son is provided with money by his father.

Any of these six sentences can be taken as the thought standard, that is,

F. Kiefer (ed.), Trends in Soviet Theoretical Linguistics, 251–333. All Rights Reserved.
Copyright © 1973 by D. Reidel Publishing Company, Dordrecht-Holland.

as the direct representation of the thought, and the other five sentences will then be treated as linguistic forms of the thought.

We are now able to answer the question of what a thought is and how it is realized in a sentence as follows:

From the linguistic point of view a thought is any sentence conventionally accepted as the immediate representation of the thought. The realization or embodiment of a thought in a sentence is a periphrasing of the sentence conventionally accepted as the immediate representation of the thought by means of some other sentence. Since any one sentence can be periphrased in many ways, we will say that a single thought is realized in many sentences, which function as its various forms.

Hence, when we assign the relation 'to be the thought standard' to the sentences of a language, we break down all the sentences of the language into classes in each of which one sentence is taken to be the pure thought and the other sentences are regarded as various forms, various realizations of this thought. We will be using below the terms 'sentence meaning standard' and 'sentence content standard' as terms synonymous with 'thought standard'.

We can continue with our analogy between the notions of thought and value. Just as money serves as a general measure of value, so must there be a general measure of meaning. It is reasonable to propose that the simplest sentences grammatically should serve as the universal measure of meaning for a given language. It is precisely this type of sentence that must be taken as the 'thought standard' or 'sentence meaning standard'. For example, of the six sentences given above the first is the simplest grammatically, and it is therefore natural to allot it the role of standard. If we continue in this way we can distinguish in any language a standard sublanguage made up of its grammatically simplest sentences. Thus, we divide all languages into standard sublanguages taken as the immediate representations of thought and derived sublanguages which are regarded as forms of thought or embodiments of thought in a linguistic shell.

Hence, all sentences have a dual nature: they can function either as sentence meaning standards or as linguistic forms which realize the meanings of the sentences. The same can be said of the linguistic units which make up a sentence, i.e., words and morphemes. All linguistic units have a dual nature: they can function either as meaning standards for their given classes of linguistic units or as linguistic forms which realize the meanings of the linguistic units.

On the basis of what has been said above we can define the notion of the meaning of a linguistic unit. The meaning of a linguistic unit is the class of linguistic units which serve as its translations. Thus, the the notion of meaning is reduced to the notion of translateability. To give the meaning of a given linguistic unit is to give the rules for translating this linguistic unit into other linguistic units. This is obviously not the only possible solution of the problem of meaning, but it seems that only such a solution is fruitful for a semantic study of language within the framework of a generative grammar. The present paper is to be regarded a a substantiation of the fruitfulness of such a solution of the problem of meaning.

2. THE SEMANTIC THEORY OF NATURAL LANGUAGES AND THE NOTION OF THE GENOTYPE LANGUAGE

Let us go on to a tentative definition of the semantic theory of language. The semantic theory of language may be defined as a linguistic theory which attempts: (1) to determine the standard sublanguage treated as the immediate representation of thought, (2) to determine the rules for transforming the standard sublanguage into a derived sublanguage considered as a form of thought, as the linguistic shell in which the thought is contained.

Taking the definition of the semantic theory of language just given, it follows that first, each language must have its own semantic theory, and secondly, there exist as many different immediate representations of thought as there are languages.

Let us begin by considering the second consequence of our definition of the semantic theory. The same considerations discussed above in relation to sentences having equivalent meanings in a single language are applicable to the standard sublanguages considered as immediate representations of thought. If we compare sentences with equivalent meanings of different standard sublanguages, the problem of the relationship between thought and its linguistic shell arises once again. Let us compare, for example, the Russian sentence *Ja obučaju detej grammatike* with the Latin and French sentences having equivalent meanings: *Doceo pueros grammaticam* and *J'enseigne la grammaire aux enfants.* Any one of these sentences can be arbitrarily selected as the thought standard, i.e., as the immediate representation of the thought, and the other sentences will then be regarded as linguistic forms of the thought Now we must seek a universal measure of meaning not within an individual language, but on the level of a comparison of the languages of the world. In connection with this it is reasonable to assume that there exists a language not found in direct observation which is expressed by meaning standards; the expression of Russian and other natural languages are to be seen here as various linguistic forms of meaning realization. I call this ideal language the genotype language, and specific natural languages, the pheontype languages.

The genotype language functions as an abstract model of natural languages. In its capacity of abstract model of natural languages, the genotype language must simulate semantic processes in natural languages. Since all natural languages have a standard sublanguage considered as the immediate representation of thought and a derived sublanguage considered as a linguistic shell for thought, a corresponding limitation must also be made in the genotype language. We also distinguish a standard sublanguage and a derived sublanguage in the genotype language. The semantic processes in natural languages are simulated by the rules for transforming the standard sublanguage into the derived sublanguage of the genotype languages.

In connection with what has just been said above, we must generalize the notion of semantic theory in relation to the natural languages of the world. The theory we shall call the semantic theory of natural languages is a theory which simulates the semantic processes in natural languages by means of the genotype language. The semantic theory of natural languages attempts: (1) to determine the standard sublanguage in the genotype language which is regarded as the immediate representation of thought, (2) to determine the rules for transforming the standard sublanguage of the genotype language into its derived sublanguage, regarded as the form of thought, as the linguistic shell of thought.

In connection with the introduction of the notion of the semantic theory of natural languages, we must refute the definition given above of semantic theory for each individual natural language. It is now expedient to speak of the semantic theory of natural languages and the semantic description of each individual natural language in relation to the semantic theory of natural languages. Between the semantic theory of natural languages and the semantic description of individual natural languages there should exist, so to say, an inverse relation: the semantic theory of natural languages is the abstract simulation of specific semantic descriptions; specific semantic descriptions function in turn as specific simulations of the semantic theory. Both the semantic theory and the specific semantic descripions must be perfected in accordance with the progress of scientific research.

Let us note in passing and without going into the philosophic side of the question that the notion of a genotype language makes it possible to consider the conception of linguistic relativity in a new light. The conception of linguistic relativity was most clearly formulated in the works of Sapir and Whorf. The essence of this conception is that the linguistic representations of the world are relative. That language gives a relative picture of the world is an indisputable fact. But this is only one side of the matter. The other side of the matter is that any relative picture of the world contained in the linguistic shell of a particular language must be considered as a projection of some invariant of world pictures. The genotype language functions as such an invariant. Phenotypic languages are various projections of the genotype language. Thus, the relative pictures of the world represented by phenotype, i.e., specific natural languages, also contain something non-relative, an invariant represented by the genotype language.

The semantic theory of natural languages should have a deductive form. As the experience of the author of the present paper has shown, for this purpose it is expedient to use the formal apparatus of the applicative grammar. Hence, the applicative grammar enriched by the rules for transforming the standard sublanguage of the genotype language into its derived sublanguage can function as a semantic theory of natural languages.

The problem we have posed and the solution we have proposed to it lead us to a conclusion of fundamental importance. If we want to ascend from the empirical level to the theoretical level, we will have to consider language not by itself, but in relation to thought. Language and thought make up a many-faceted problem which has fascinated the representatives of various specialities: logicians, psychologists, philosophers. This problem has also fascinated linguists. But for linguists, discussions about the relationship between language and thought have been of a marginal nature. These discussions, however interesting they may have been, have never been thought of as a part of linguistics, but have always been relegated to the area of the so-called philosophy of language. Our treatment of the problem posed above radically changes the picture: it turns out that the relationship between language and thought is not some sort of philosophical problem, but is a central, strictly linguistic problem, one which lies at the very heart of linguistics.

3. How the Genotype Language is Constructed

The genotype language is an hypothesis about the common semiotic basis of the languages of the world. As such an hypothesis the genotype language functions as a system of universal linguistic categories. In this connection the question arises: how are these universal linguistic categories obtained?

We can obtain universal linguistic categories in two ways:

The first way consists in the systematic study of a large number (ideally all) languages of the world and in the selection through generalization of common linguistic categories.

The second method consists in defining the basic properties of the object we call a natural language and deductively inferring from this definition all the consequences that proceed from it.

The first method is widely used in modern linguistics. Interesting results have already been obtained with it, which is evidence of its fruitfulness. But for the construction of an abstract linguistic theory we must select the second method. From the point of view of an abstract linguistic theory a system of universal linguistic categories by itself is neither true nor false: it is merely given by definition. This does not mean, however, that we can be satisfied with any system of universal linguistic categories. The only system that suits us is one that can accurately predict the possible linguistic categories in actual languages. Thus, the whole question lies in the predictive power of the system of universal linguistic categories. If the predictive power of such a system is high, this system will be able to functions as an effective instrument in the study of real natural languages, and it is this which constitutes its justification.

The method we will use to construct the genotype language is a particular instance of the hypothetic-deductive method used by the modern theoretical sciences.

4. THE SIMPLEST FORM OF THE GENOTYPE LANGUAGE

If we abstract from everything in natural languages that can be considered secondary to the process of communication between speaker and listener, we can get three fundamental classes of linguistic objects: (1) names of objects, (2) names of situations, (3) transformers. Let us explain what each of these classes of linguistic objects consists of.

Names of objects are nouns or nominal phrases, e.g. in Russian: *sobaka* 'dog', *bol'šaja sobaka* 'big dog', *bol'šaja moxnataja sobaka* 'big shaggy dog', *bol'šaja moxnataja černaja sobaka* 'big black shaggy dog'. We shall call the name of an object a term.

A situation is either a whole consisting of some object and some property (in the broadest sense of the word) attributed to it, or a whole consisting of objects and a relation between them ascribed to them. The objects included in a situation will be said to be participants of the situation. Situations whose participants are other situations are also permissible. We shall therefore distinguish between simple and complex situations. A simple situation is one which has only objects as its participants. A complex situation is one among whose participants there is at least one situation.

We shall distinguish between concrete and abstract situations. Concrete situations are those whose participants are concrete objects to which are attributed concrete properties or relations. For example, *Sobaka est mjaso* 'The dog eats meat', *Koška pjét moloko* 'The cat is drinking milk', *Mal'čik čitaet knigu* 'The boy is reading a book', *Otec pišet pis'mo* 'Father is writing a letter'. These are examples of concrete situations. Abstract situations are those in which we abstract from the participants, properties and relations of concrete situations. For example, the single abstract situation '*X* performs some action on *Y*' would correspond to the examples of different concrete situations given above.

Sentences will be said to be the names of situations. The names of properties and relations will be called predicates. The names of the participants of a situation will be called the arguments of the predicate.

From the definition of a predicate just given it is obvious that the linguistic notion of a predicate differs from the logical notion, since predicates in logic are not simply properties or relations, but those properties or relations to which truth or falshood can be ascribed.

Linguistic objects which change the linguistic objects of one class into either the linguistic objects of another class or into the linguistic objects of the same class will be called transformers. The classes of transformers are introduced as follows. We regard terms and sentences as the basic classes of linguistic objects, so that besides the two initial classes of linguistic objects we obtain four others:

(1)   transformers of terms into sentences,
(2)   transformers of sentences into terms
(3)   transformers of terms into terms,
(4)   transformers of sentences in to sentences.

These classes can be given in symbolic notation as follows.

A term will be designated with the Greek letter α, and a sentence with the Greek letter β.

The word 'transformer' will be denoted by the Greek letter Δ and we will agree to read the formula ΔXY as: 'the transformer of X into Y'. We now have the six following formulae:

α – 'term'
β – 'sentence'
$\Delta\alpha\beta$ – 'transformer of a term into a sentence'
$\Delta\alpha\alpha$ – 'transformer of a term into a term'
$\Delta\beta\alpha$ – 'transformer of a sentence into a term'
$\Delta\beta\beta$ – 'transformer of a sentence into a sentence'

These formulae will serve as the names of classes of linguistic objects. Now let us bring in the symbolic notation for linguistic objects belonging to the different classes. The symbolic notation for these objects has the form:

eX.

It is read as: the linguistic object X belongs to the class of linguistic objects e.

Different linguistic objects will be denoted either by various capital Latin letters or by the same large Latin letter supplied with different superscripts, e.g. $X, Y, Z...$ or $X^1, X^2, ..., Y^1, Y^2, ..., Z^1, Z^2, ...$ etc.

Let us dwell for a moment on some specific examples of symbolic notation for individual linguistic objects (for the sake of brevity we will use simply 'object' below). Assume we have the formulae αX, αY, αZ or αX^1, αX^2, αX^3. These formulae are read as: 'The object X, which belongs to, the class of terms', 'The object Y, which belongs to the class of terms', etc.

Or: $\Delta\alpha\beta X^1$, $\Delta\alpha\beta X^2$, which are read: 'The object X^1 belonging to the class of transformers of terms into sentences', 'The object X^2 belonging to the class of transformers of terms into sentences', etc.

Before we consider other objects of the genotype language, let us dwell for a moment on the problem of how these objects are to be interpreted. We will distinguish two types of interpretation: abstract interpretation and empirical interpretation. Abstract interpretation is determined solely by the rules for constructing objects. Thus, the interpretation of the objects $\Delta\alpha\beta$, $\Delta\beta\alpha$, $\Delta\alpha\alpha$, $\Delta\beta\beta$ is determined by the rules for constructing them from the objects α, β with the given interpretation. Thus, if we gave α the meaning of term and β the meaning of sentence and Δ the meaning of transformer, it follows that for example $\Delta\alpha\beta$ must be interpreted as 'the transformer of a term into a sentence'. Hence, we have to distinguish between given and derived abstract interpretations.

To be able to explain what the empirical interpretation of objects of the genotype language is, we will have to go into the notion of isomorphism (identity of structure), since this notion is of great importance to the concept of empirical interpretation.

The theory of vibrations is a classic example of description by means of the notion of isomorphism. As is well known, there are various kinds of physical vibrations: mechanical vibrations, acoustical vibrations, electromagnetic vibrations, physiological vibrations of living tissues, etc. But the theory of vibrations studies vibrations independently of the physical nature of the objects which are subject to vibration. Thus, from the point of view of the theory of vibrations, the objects under study are described not by their specific physical nature, but by a certain net of relations expressed in the form of mathematical equations. There is an identity of structure (isomorphism) among the various forms of physical vibrations. It is for just this reason that certain forms of physical vibrations can be transformed into other forms of physical vibrations. Thus, for example, the mechanical vibrations of a phonograph needle are transformed into acoustical vibrations of air particles, and the acoustical vibrations of the air particles are transformed into the physiological vibrations of the eardrum. It follows that there is a structural identity between the surface of a phonograph record, the music produced by the phonograph and the auditory sensations of the human being who apprehends the music.

We can now turn to defining the notion of isomorphism. It is defined as follows: given two classes, K with elements $a, b, c, ...$, and K' with elements $a', b', c', ...$; then if the elements of K can be placed in one-one correspondence with those of K' and if for every relation R between elements of K there is a relation R' between the corresponding elements of K', the two classes are isomorphic.

We can see that the notion of isomorphism as it has just been defined here is a highly abstract notion. As a matter of fact, the notion of isomorphism can be used to identify with each other objects which have profound qualitative differences.

Isomorphism is of fundamental importance for all abstract empirical sciences, since any abstract empirical science defines the empirical objects of its field up to isomorphism.

Using the notion of isomorphism, let us turn to an explanation of empirical interpretation. Let us begin with some concrete examples.

The object $\Delta\alpha\alpha$ is interpreted on the abstract level as the transformer of a term into a term. On the empirical level a term is interpreted in, let us say, Russian, as an adjective in some cases and as an affix in others. Compare, for example, the Russian *malen'kij dom* and *dom-ik* 'little house'. The adjective *malen'kij* 'little' transforms the noun phrase *dom* 'house' into the new noun phrase *malen'kij dom* 'little house' (all nouns in a natural language are, as is well known, particular cases of the noun phrase). From this example we see that there is an isomorphism in Russian between the class of noun phrases 'adjective+noun' and the class of derived nouns 'simple noun+underlying suffix'. This is not all. Transformers of terms into terms can be interpreted in Russian as participles (cf. *gorjaščij dom* 'burning house'), the genitive case of the noun (cf. *dom otca* 'the house of the father', 'father's house'), a noun with preposition (*dom na beregu* 'house on the shore') and a noun in the other oblique cases. Hence, the empirical interpretation of the object $\Delta\alpha\alpha$ makes it possible to discover isomorphism between different types of noun phrases and derived nouns. We obtain similar results from the interpretation of $\Delta\alpha\alpha$ in other languages, for example in English. But since there are no cases in English, we find here isomorphism between noun phrases with various types of prepositional constructions. The empirical interpretation of $\Delta\alpha\alpha$ also allows us to establish isomorphisms between various types of noun phrases in different languages (compare, for example, Russian *dom otca* and English *the house of the father*).

Our example of the empirical interpretation of $\Delta\beta\beta$ reveals two characteristic features of empirical interpretation.

(1) Empirical interpretation assigns abstract objects empirical objects correct up to isomorphism.

(2) Unlike abstract interpretation, which is of a deductive nature (as was shown above, the abstract interpretation of derived abstract objects follows deductively from an interpretation of the initial simple abstract objects), empirical interpretation is given in the form of certain correspondences between the abstract and empirical objects called correspondence rules.

In addition, empirical interpretation is, as we will see below, incomplete: not every abstract object can be put into correspondence with an empirical object. There exist abstract objects which make sense only as elements of deductive systems.

Let us turn to the empirical interpretation of the remaining, above-mentioned objects of the genotype language. The object $\Delta\alpha\beta$ is interpreted as a one-place predicate, since a one-place predicate is nothing other than a transformer of a noun phrase into a sentence. Here we can discover isomorphism not only between classes of Russian phrases of the type *Mal'čik guljaet* 'The boy is walking'; *Otec – učitel'* 'The father is a teacher'; *Den' – xolodnyj* 'The day is a cold one', but in the isomorphic relation to classes of phrases of this type we also find classes of nominative sentences of the type *Noč'* 'It is night'. In nominative sentences the predicate is implicit and is expressed by an appropriate intonation.

The object $\Delta\beta\beta$ is interpreted on the empirical level as modal words, sentence negation, means for transforming narrative sentences into interrogative ones, and all manner of other grammatical means for the transformation of one sentence into another. From this point of view the classes represented by the following sentences are isomorphic. *On zabyl ob ètom'* He forgot about this'; *Kstati, on zabyl ob ètom* 'By the way, he forgot about this'; *Nepravda, čto on zabyl ob ètom* 'It is not true that he forgot about this'; *Zabyl on ob ètom?* 'Did he forget about this?', etc.

The object $\Delta\beta\alpha$ is interpreted on the empirical level as a means for transforming sentences into noun phrases, i.e., as subordinating conjunctions (cf. the phrases *mal'čik guljaet* 'the boy is walking' and *čto mal'čik guljaet* 'that the boy is walking', which are part of isomorphic phrase classes)...

As we have already seen from the examples above, the object α is interpreted on the empirical level as a noun phrase of any degree of complexity As for the object β, it is interpreted on the empirical level as simple or complex sentences.

Let us return to the objects of the genotype language on the abstract level. We have taken two objects as initial objects: α and β. We then introduced the notion of a transformer, designated by the symbol Δ. Since any object of this class can by definition be transformed into either an object of another class or an object of the same class, we constructed four new classes: $\Delta\alpha\beta$, $\Delta\beta\alpha$, $\Delta\alpha\alpha$, $\Delta\beta\beta$.

We now have six classes of objects which are themselves treated as abstract objects. Since we have six classes of objects, we can transform the objects of any given class into either objects of the same class or into objects of any of the five other classes.

Thus, we obtain another 32 classes of transformers. With a total of 38 classes now, we can once again transform any of them into either an object of the other 35 classes or objects of the same class, etc.

We can now give a formal description of the calculus of the classes of objects in the genotype language. In this calculus are given:

(1) The atoms α, β called elementary episemiones.

The object Δ, called a derivator of the episemions.

(2) The rules for constructing the linguistic universals called episemions.

(a) the elementary episemions α, β are episemions.

(b) if p and q are episemions, then Δpq is also an episemion.

Rule (b) can be written in the form of a diagram known as a tree diagram:

$$\frac{p \quad q}{\Delta pq}$$

the horizontal line here denotes consequence, i.e., that Δpq follows from p and q.

The process of constructing episemions can be divided into stages. At the first stage we have the episemions α and β. At the second stage, the episemiones $\Delta\alpha\alpha$, $\Delta\beta\beta$, $\Delta\alpha\beta$, $\Delta\beta\alpha$. At the third stage we have episemions derived from episemions obtained at the first two stages, and so on. At each stage episemions are constructed from the episemions obtained at all preceding stages.

The set of episemions that can be constructed by means of the two rules given above will be known as the episemion system.

All episemions except α and β are transformers. The notion of transformer is relative, since any transformer can function as a transformed element in relation to another transformer. Below we shall agree to call transformers operators and transformed elements operands.

We shall now introduce the following rule into the episemion system: the episemion q follows from the episemion Δpq and the episemion p.

This rule, known as the application operation, or the application of an operator to an operand, can be given in the form of the following tree diagram:

$$\frac{\Delta pq \quad p}{q}$$

Below is a specific instance of application:

$$\frac{\Delta\alpha\beta \quad \alpha}{\beta}$$

This case can be interpreted empirically as follows: a one-place predicate transforms a noun phrase into a sentence.

The episemion calculus given above is a kind of universal scheme for the description of the languages of the world. This scheme grasps many of the essential universal characteristics of the languages of the world. However, the fact that episemions are classes treated as abstract objects, i.e., classes which we discuss like special, independently existing objects, thus ignoring the study of the possible differences between the elements of these classes, brings us to a fundamental difficulty, one that can be illustrated on the basis of the following example. As was shown above, the episemion $\Delta\alpha\alpha$ is interpreted on the empirical level in Russian as the suffix -ik (for example, in the word dom-ik 'little house'), malen'kij (malen'kij dom 'little house'), gorjaščij (gorjaščij dom 'burning house'), otca (dom otca 'father's house'), na beregu (dom na beregu 'house on the shore'), etc. Thus, the words malen'kij 'little', gorjaščij 'burning', otca 'father's', the phrase na beregu 'on the shore' and the suffix -ik are treated simply as grammatically identical elements of a single class. It is obvious, however, that although, say, the word malen'kij 'little', the word otca 'father's' and the word gorjaščij 'burning' function as attributes of the word dom 'house', they stand in different relations to this role: for the word malen'kij 'little' the role of attribute of the noun is primary, that is, inherent to it, whereas for the words otca 'father's' and gorjaščij 'burning' this role is secondary – the word otca is a noun and the word gorjaščij is a verb which has been given the role of an adjective. We can see that the elements which belong to the class are not only identical among themselves, but also have a definite hierarchical relationship to each other the study of which is of great interest for the linguist. We will discover the same thing if we examine the elements of all the other classes; elements of the same class are related hierarchically to each other, and these relations are of great significance for the structure of language. The main difficulty in using episemion calculus in describing the languages of the world is that we cannot use this calculus to study the hierarchical relations between the elements of universal linguistic classes.

In order to overcome this difficulty we will have to go one level lower, that is, to the level of the elements belonging to each episemion. We will have to enumerate these elements, which will be known below as semions.

In the semion calculus are given:

(1) Atoms, which we will call elementary semions.

Elementary semions divide into two groups:

(1) Basic elementary semions: A and B.

(2) Operators: each operator is denoted by the symbol Φ, to which are given the symbols of the various episemions, except α and β. For example: $\Phi_{\varDelta\alpha\beta}$, $\Phi_{\varDelta\alpha\alpha}$, $\Phi_{\varDelta\varDelta\alpha\beta\varDelta\alpha\beta}$ etc.

Each elementary semion has many occurrences. To distinguish the occurrences of the same elementary semion, we will use superscripts, e.g. A, A^1, A^2, ..., B, B^1, B^2, ...,

$$\Phi_{\varDelta\alpha\beta}, \ \Phi^1_{\varDelta\alpha\beta}, \ \Phi^2_{\varDelta\alpha\beta}, \ ..., \ \Phi_{\varDelta\alpha\alpha}, \ \Phi^1_{\varDelta\alpha\alpha}, \ \Phi^2_{\varDelta\alpha\alpha}, \quad \text{etc.}$$

Which episemion each elementary semion belongs to is clear from the lower index it has been given, in the case of operators. As for the elementary semions A and B, A belongs to the episemion α, and B belongs to the episemion β.

(2) Rules for deriving semions.

(a) Elementary semions are semions.

(b) If X is a semion belonging to the episemion pq and Y is a semion belonging to the episemion p, then XY is a semion belonging to the episemion q.

Rule (b) can be given in the form of the following tree diagram:

$$\frac{pqX \qquad pY}{qXY}$$

We will call X an operator, Y an operand and XY the result of the application of X to Y. Rule (b) itself will be known as a semion application rule.

From the point of view of the application operation all elementary semions can be devided into two groups: (1) absolute operands, i.e., A and B; (2) primary operators, i.e., those operators which have semions belonging to the episemions α or β as their operands; (3) secondary operators, i.e., operators which have other operators as their operands.

Now let us give an empirical interpretation of the basic elementary semions. The interpretation of each elementary semion given below will be a partial one, since it only applies to Russian.

Examples of elementary semions:

Absolute Operands

A Nouns which designate common and proper names

B Impersonal sentences (such as *Duet* 'It is blowing')

Primary Operators

$\Phi_{\Delta\alpha\alpha}$ Adjectives or affixes which derive nouns from nouns

$\Phi_{\Delta\alpha\Delta\alpha\alpha}$ Affixes of the oblique cases of nouns which govern other nouns (with or without a preposition), affixes which derive adjectives from nouns.

$\Phi_{\Delta\alpha\beta}$ Personal forms of intransitive verbs.

$\Phi_{\Delta\alpha\Delta\alpha\beta}$ Personal forms of verbs with one complement, copulas.

$\Phi_{\Delta\alpha\Delta\alpha\Delta\alpha\beta}$ Personal forms of transitive verbs with two complements.

$\Phi_{\Delta\beta\alpha}$ The conjunction *čto* 'that'.

$\Phi_{\Delta\beta\beta}$ Negation or interrogative particles.

$\Phi_{\Delta\beta\Delta\beta\beta}$ Subordinating conjunctions connecting two sentences.

Secondary Operators

$\Phi_{\Delta\Delta\alpha\alpha\Delta\alpha\alpha}$ Ad-adjectival adverbs. Affixes which derive adjectives from adjectives.

$\Phi_{\Delta\alpha\Delta\Delta\alpha\alpha\Delta\alpha\alpha}$ Case affixes (with or without a preposition) which transform nouns into attributes of adjectives.

$\Phi_{\Delta\Delta\alpha\beta\alpha}$ Affixes which transform verbs into abstract nouns

$\Phi_{\Delta\Delta\alpha\beta\Delta\alpha\beta}$ Adverbs governing (which are attributes of) intransitive verbs. Affixes which derive intransitive verbs from intransitive verbs.

$\Phi_{\Delta\alpha\Delta\Delta\alpha\beta\Delta\alpha\beta}$ Affixes which derive adverbs from nouns.

The construction of the semions proceeds in stages. At the first stage we have the elementary semions; at the second stage, semions consisting of two elementary semions; at the third stage, semions consisting of three or four elementary semions, and so forth.

The set of all semions that can be constructed is called the genotype language.

Let us now return to the interpretation of the episemions $\Delta\alpha\alpha$ and $\Delta\alpha\beta$ and let us use these examples to show how semion calculus makes it possible to make a more profound classification of the facts of natural languages.

As has been shown above, the episemions we have just mentioned have the following possible interpretations

$\Delta\alpha\alpha$	$\Delta\alpha\beta$
-ik (cf. *dom-ik* 'little house')	*guljaet* 'walks' (cf. *mal'čik guljaet* 'the boy walks, is taking a walk')
malen'kij 'little' (cf. *malen'kij dom* 'little house')	*byl učitel'* 'was a teacher' (cf. *Otec byl učitel* "Father was a teacher'), or
otca 'father's' (cf. *dom otca* 'fa-	*učitel'stvuet* 'is, works as a teacher' (cf.

ther's house')

Otec učitel'stvuet 'Father is, works as a teacher')

byl xolodnyj 'was cold' (cf. *Den' byl xolodnyj* 'The day was (a) cold (one)')

na beregu 'on the shore' (cf. *dom na beregu* 'the house on the shore') *gorjaščij* 'burning' (cf. *gorjaščij dom* 'the burning house')

predicative intonation in nominative sentences of the type *Noč'* 'It is night'.

Let us also take the episemion α. It can be interpreted as:

dom 'house'

dom-ik 'little house'

malen'kij dom 'little house'

dom otca 'father's house'

dom na beregu 'the house on the shore'

gorjaščij dom 'burning house'

guljanie 'walk, walking'

belizna 'whiteness'

On the episemion level the interpretation of each of these episemions was considered to be equal. On the semion level we can now establish hierarchical differences between these interpretations.

If we take the interpretations of the episemion $\Delta\alpha\alpha$, the affix *-ik* and the adjective *malen'kij* 'little' correspond to the elementary semion $\Phi_{\Delta\alpha\alpha}$.

The particle *gorjaščij* 'burning' will correspond to the tree:

$$\frac{\Delta\Delta\alpha\beta\Delta\alpha\alpha\Phi_{\Delta\Delta\alpha\beta\Delta\alpha\alpha} \qquad \Delta\alpha\beta\Phi_{\Delta\alpha\beta}}{\Delta\alpha\alpha\Phi_{\Delta\Delta\alpha\beta\Delta\alpha\alpha}\Phi_{\Delta\alpha\beta}}$$

Since the lower indices of the various elementary semions distinguish a given elementary semion from other elementary semions by unambiguously indicating to which semion it belongs, we can leave out the deductive characteristics (i.e., the episemions written to the left) for the elementary semions in tree diagrams. Since the deductive characteristics of the elementary semions *A* and *B* are also defined unambiguously, they will also be omitted. Thus, the diagram above will now look like:

$$\frac{\Phi_{\Delta\Delta\alpha\beta\Delta\alpha\alpha} \qquad \Phi_{\Delta\alpha\beta}}{\Delta\alpha\alpha\Phi_{\Delta\Delta\alpha\beta\Delta\alpha\alpha}\Phi_{\Delta\alpha\beta}}$$

It goes without saying that the deductive characteristics for the elementary semions are omitted only for the sake of simplifying the notation and must be reconstructed mentally.

If we take *otca* 'father's' and *na beregu* 'on the shore', they correspond to the tree:

$$\frac{\Phi_{\Delta\alpha\Delta\alpha\alpha} \qquad A}{\Delta\alpha\alpha\Phi_{\Delta\alpha\Delta\alpha\alpha}A}$$

Let us turn to the interpretation of the episemion $\Delta\alpha\beta$.

The personal forms of the verb *guljaet* 'walks, takes a walk' or predicative intonation will correspond to the elementary semion. The wordgroup *byl učitel'* 'was a teacher' or the derived personal form of the verb *učitel'stvuet* 'is, works as a teacher' correspond to the tree:

$$\frac{\Phi_{\Delta\alpha\Delta\alpha\beta} \qquad\qquad A}{\Delta\alpha\beta\Phi_{\Delta\alpha\Delta\alpha\beta}A}$$

The word-group *byl xolodnyj* 'was cold' corresponds to the tree:

$$\frac{\Phi_{\Delta\Delta\alpha\alpha\Delta\alpha\beta} \qquad\qquad \Phi_{\Delta\alpha\alpha}}{\Delta\alpha\beta\Phi_{\Delta\alpha\alpha\Delta\alpha\beta}\Phi_{\Delta\alpha\alpha}}$$

Let us consider the interpretations of the episemion α. The word *dom* 'house' corresponds to the semion A. The word *domik* 'little house' and the word-group *'malen'kij dom'* 'little house' correspond to the tree:

$$\frac{\Phi_{\Delta\alpha\alpha} \qquad\qquad A}{\alpha\Phi_{\Delta\alpha\alpha}A}$$

The word *guljanie* 'walking' has the tree:

$$\frac{\Phi_{\Delta\Delta\alpha\beta\alpha} \qquad\qquad \Phi_{\Delta\alpha\beta}}{\alpha\Phi_{\Delta\Delta\alpha\beta\alpha}\Phi_{\Delta\alpha\beta}}$$

The word *belizna* 'whiteness' has the tree:

$$\frac{\Phi_{\Delta\Delta\alpha\alpha} \qquad\qquad \Phi_{\Delta\alpha\alpha}}{\alpha\Phi_{\Delta\Delta\alpha\alpha}\Phi_{\Delta\alpha\alpha}}$$

The word-group *gorjaščij dom* 'burning house' has the tree:

$$\frac{\dfrac{\Phi_{\Delta\Delta\alpha\beta\Delta\alpha\alpha} \qquad\qquad \Phi_{\Delta\alpha\beta}}{\Delta\alpha\alpha\Phi_{\Delta\Delta\alpha\beta\Delta\alpha\alpha}\Phi_{\Delta\alpha\beta}} \qquad\qquad A}{\alpha\Phi_{\Delta\Delta\alpha\beta\Delta\alpha\alpha}\Phi_{\Delta\alpha\beta}A}$$

The word-group *dom otca* 'father's house' and *dom na beregu* 'the house on the shore' have the tree:

$$\frac{\dfrac{\Phi_{\Delta\alpha\Delta\alpha\alpha} \qquad\qquad A^1}{\Delta\alpha\alpha\Phi_{\Delta\alpha\Delta\alpha\alpha}A^1} \qquad\qquad A^2}{\alpha\Phi_{\Delta\alpha\Delta\alpha\alpha}A^1A^2}$$

It can be seen from the above examples that a semion calculus makes it possible to formalize the difference between simple and derived words, the difference, related to this one, between primary and secondary word roles, and also the difference between words and word-groups. Thus, the word *guljat'* 'to walk', for example, is a simple word, and the word *guljanie* 'walk, walking' is a derived word, which is expressed in the different formal notations of these words. At the same time the role of predicate, in which the word *guljaet* 'walks' functions, must be regarded as its primary role, whereas the word *guljanie* 'walk, walking' must be regarded as one of the secondary roles of the word *guljaet*: in this case this word functions as a noun. There is also a difference in the formal notation between the simple word *dom* 'house' and the derived word *domik* 'little house', between the word *dom* and the word-groups *malen'kij dom* 'little house' and *dom otca* 'father's house', etc.

The following important comment must be made on differentiating simple and derived words and words and word-groups in formal notation. We can when necessary give this differentiation a relative character. Thus, for example, when we take up a purely syntactic study of a given specific language, we must partly ignore the morphological structure of the language. In this case we can treat derived words like simple ones and place not only the simple word *guljaet* 'walks' but also the derived words *proguljaet* 'will walk (an animal); will miss', *otguljaet* 'will finish (a leave, vacation); take compensatory leave' etc., into correspondence with the elementary semion $\Phi_{A\alpha\beta}$. On the level of the study of parts of the sentence we can treat the word-group *malen'kij dom* 'little house' like a simple linguistic unit and put it into correspondence with the elementary semion A. Thus, when we speak of simple and derived linguistic units, this difference is absolute only in the global study of language. But when we study separate linguistic levels this difference is relative. We must consider the fact that semion calculus makes it possible to distinguish between simple and derived structures on the one hand, and to give this difference a relative character, on the other, to be one of its essential features. Thus, we are introducing the notion of a reference point into the empirical interpretation of derivability.

As was shown above, any semion consisting of several elementary semions is written in the form of a tree. Notation in the form of trees, however, although very clear, is not always suitable due to its cumbersomeness. To translate a tree into a linear notation we shall formulate semion construction rule (b), using parentheses. Rule (b) can then be given in the form of the following tree:

$$\frac{pqX \qquad\qquad pY}{q(XY)}$$

Now we can replace this tree with the linear notation (XY). On the basis of the above tree, which corresponds to the word-group *gorjaščij dom* 'burning house', we can show how the use of parentheses makes it possible to replace a tree with a linear notation. If we introduce parentheses into the above tree, it will have the following form:

$$\frac{\dfrac{\Phi_{\varDelta\varDelta\alpha\beta\varDelta\alpha\alpha} \qquad\qquad \Phi_{\varDelta\alpha\beta}}{\varDelta\alpha\alpha\left(\Phi_{\varDelta\varDelta\alpha\beta\varDelta\alpha\alpha}\Phi_{\varDelta\alpha\beta}\right) \qquad\qquad A}}{\alpha\left(\left(\Phi_{\varDelta\varDelta\alpha\beta\varDelta\alpha\alpha}\Phi_{\varDelta\alpha\beta}\right)A\right)}$$

We can now replace it with the linear notation $\left(\left(\Phi_{\varDelta\varDelta\alpha\beta\varDelta\alpha\beta}\Phi_{\varDelta\alpha\beta}\right)A\right)$. It is easy to see that we can reconstruct the tree from this linear notation by applying rule (b).

To avoid superfluous parentheses, let it be understood that in a row of elementary semions without parentheses the application operations are to be performed from left to right, so that $XY^1Y^2Y^3Y^4$, for instance, will mean the same as $\left(\left(\left(XY^1\right)Y^2\right)Y^3\right)Y^4$.

If we agree to do this, the semion given above will be written:

$$\Phi_{\varDelta\varDelta\alpha\beta\varDelta\alpha\alpha}\Phi_{\varDelta\alpha\beta}A\,.$$

The possibility of writing semions both as trees and in linear notation leads us to an abstract conception of the semion which is independent of how the semion is represented graphically – as a tree or in linear notation.

The semion, as an abstract object, must be considered to be an invariant with respect to the transformation of the tree representation of a semion into a linear representation and vice versa.

Let us return to episemions and make some remarks on their formal interpretation.

Any episemion $\varDelta pq$ is an abstract object consisting of a left component p and a right component q. Episemions are interpreted as one-place functions whose argument is denoted by their left components p and whose value is denoted by their right components q.

Taking into account the demands of linguistic research, we will find it expedient to introduce a new level of formal interpretation for the episemion $\varDelta pq$ on which the episemion $\varDelta pq$ can be interpreted as a multiplace function according to the following formal rule: divide the episemion $\varDelta pq$ into its components p and q, which are in their turn episemions. If the right component q is equal to α and β, the analysis ends here. But if q is the new episemion $\varDelta p'q'$, then we also analyze it into a left component p' and a right component q'. If the right component is equal to α or β, the process of analyzing the episemion pq ends here. But if the right component q' is the new episemion $\varDelta p''q''$, the process of analyzing the episemion $\varDelta q''p''$ will continue until the right component of one of the episemions obtained in the process of analyzing the original episemion Δpq is equal to α or β. The analysis of the episemion Δpq will then be completed. If this process of analyzing the episemion Δpq is performed in n steps, the episemion Δpq is interpreted as an n-place function.

Let us consider some concrete examples of how this rule is applied.

The analysis of the episemions $\Delta \alpha \beta$, $\Delta \beta \beta$, $\Delta \beta \alpha$ can be performed in one step. These episemions can therefore be interpreted only as one-place functions.

The episemion $\Delta \alpha \Delta \alpha \Delta \alpha \beta$ is broken down in the first step into the left component α and the right component $\Delta \alpha \Delta \alpha \beta$, in the second step into the left component α and the right component $\Delta \alpha \beta$, and in the third step into the left component α and the right component β.

Since the process of analyzing the episemion $\Delta \alpha \Delta \alpha \Delta \alpha \beta$ is performed in three steps, this episemion is to be interpreted as a three-place function.

The episemion $\Delta \Delta \alpha \beta \Delta \alpha \beta$ is broken down in the first step into the left component $\Delta \alpha \beta$ and the right component $\Delta \alpha \beta$, in the second step into the left component α and the right component β. Since the analysis of the episemion $\Delta \Delta \alpha \beta \Delta \alpha \beta$ is performed in two steps, this episemion is to be interpreted as a two-place function.

Semions are also interpreted in accordance with this formal interpretation of episemions.

If the semion X belongs to the episemion e, which is interpreted as an n-place function, then the semion X is also interpreted as an n-place function.

5. THE GENOTYPE LANGUAGE WITH A CASE SYSTEM

In the preceding section we considered the simplest form of the genotype language. The simplest form of the genotype language can serve as a considerably powerful instrument for the study of the natural languages of the world. But it still covers only the most general features of these languages. To be able to delve deeper into the study of natural languages, a successive broadening of the genotype language is necessary. We shall begin by introducing a case system into the genotype language as follows.

Let us return to episemion calculus. In the system of episemions, we will consider α to be a variable that can be replaced by the following constants: a, i, f, l, c, o, which we will call α-constants.

For example, if we take the episemion $\Delta \alpha \beta$, we can replace α with the above constants and obtain $\Delta a \beta$, $\Delta i \beta$, $\Delta f \beta$, $\Delta l \beta$, $\Delta c \beta$, $\Delta o \beta$. We will divide all semions into canonical and non-canonical. An episemion is canonical if it contains several occurrences of α and only different constants can stand in place of the different occurrences of α. For example, from the episemion

$\Delta\alpha\Delta\alpha\Delta\alpha\beta$ we can obtain $\Delta i\Delta o\Delta c\beta$, but not $\Delta i\Delta i\Delta c\beta$ or $\Delta i\Delta o\Delta o\beta$; here we allow for cases where some or all occurrences of α are not replaced, so that we can have $\Delta\alpha\Delta o\Delta c\beta$, $\Delta\alpha\Delta\alpha\Delta c\beta$ or simply $\Delta\alpha\Delta\alpha\Delta\alpha\beta$. We will say that an episemion is non-canonical if at least two occurrences of α are replaced by the same constants. As will be seen below, canonical episemions are the more significant ones.

These constants are interpreted as nouns in various situational roles.

The constant a, known as an agentive, is interpreted as an animate object which produces some action.

The constant i, called an instrumentive, is interpreted as an inanimate object in the broadest sense which serves as the cause of the action or state expressed by the predicate.

The constant f, called an affective, is interpreted as an animate object which is subjugated to the action or is in the state expressed by the predicate.

The constant l, called a locative, is interpreted as an object localized in space or time.

The constant c, called a completive, designates a complement to an empty predicate.

The constant o, called an objective, is interpreted as an object with a neutral role in a situation; the meaning of this role depends entirely on the meaning of the predicate.

A full exposure of the meaning of these interpretations is possible on the basis of the concrete examples which will be given below. Let us agree that nouns in the broad sense, i.e., expressions functioning as the names of objects will be called terms. We now turn to an expanded semion calculus. The following elementary semions are postulated in the expanded semion calculus.

Elementary terms:

$$T_\alpha, \; T_\alpha^1, \; T_\alpha^2, \ldots$$

Any of the above enumerated α-constants can replace α in the lower indices of the elementary terms.

Elementary predicates:

(1) One-place elementary predicates:

$$P_{\Delta\alpha\beta}, \; P_{\Delta\alpha\beta}^1, \; P_{\Delta\alpha\beta}^2, \ldots$$

(2) Two-place elementary predicates:

$$P_{\Delta\alpha\Delta\alpha\beta}, \; P_{\Delta\alpha\Delta\alpha\beta}^1, \; P_{\Delta\alpha\Delta\alpha\beta}^2, \ldots$$

(3) Three-place elementary predicates

$$P_{\Delta\alpha\Delta\alpha\Delta\alpha\beta}, \ P^1_{\Delta\alpha\Delta\alpha\Delta\alpha\beta}, \ P^2_{\Delta\alpha\Delta\alpha\Delta\alpha\beta}, \ \ldots$$

Predicates with more places are also possible, but we shall not be considering them here. We must in any case bear in mind that the semion calculus is open as regards the number of places for the elementary predicates.

If the various occurrences of α in the lower indices of the elementary predicates can be replaced only by different α-constants, such elementary predicates will be called canonical.

To make our notation more compact we will use abbreviations introduced by a definition. These definitions introduce new symbols or expressions found in the calculus itself and give the abbreviations of them that will be used instead of certain episemions or semions. To make the writing of the definitions more convenient we will use arrows, which are to be read as 'is the abbreviation for' or 'is used as an abbreviation instead of'. Our definitions will be:

$$P_\alpha \to P_{\Delta\alpha\beta}$$
$$P_{\alpha\alpha} \to P_{\Delta\alpha\Delta\alpha\beta}$$
$$P_{\alpha\alpha\alpha} \to P_{\Delta\alpha\Delta\alpha\Delta\alpha\beta}$$

In accordance with the formula of combinations of n elements

$$A_n^k = n(n-1)(n-2)\ldots(n-k+1)$$

as a result of substituting the six α-constants we obtain six one-place elementary canonical predicates, 30 two-place elementary canonical predicates and 120 three-place elementary canonical predicates.

Now let us turn to a systematic examination of elementary terms and canonical elementary predicates. Here, of course, we do not intend to go through all of the 156 possible elementary canonical predicates mentioned above, but will instead concentrate our attention on the most important elementary canonical predicates.

The elementary terms T_a, T_a^1, ... will be known as elementary agents.

The elementary canonical predicates in agreement with elementary agents have the form: P_a, P_a^1, ...

Here and below we will understand agreement in the semantic sense, that is, as the correspondence of predicates with a certain meaning to terms with a given meaning.

The generation of sentences with elementary agents is written:

$$\frac{P_a \qquad\qquad T_a}{\beta(P_a T_a)}$$

The sentence $P_a T_a$ can be interpreted as *Mal'čik begaet* 'The boy is running', *Devočka xodit* 'The girl walks', etc.

The elementary terms T_o, T_o^2 are known as elementary objectives. They denote objects in a state or objects which are subjected to an action. The elementary predicates P_o, P_o^1 agree with the elementary objects.

Sentences with elementary objects are generated as follows:

$$\frac{P_o \qquad\qquad T_o}{\beta(P_o T_o)}$$

The sentence $P_o T_o$ is interpreted as *Šar katitsja* 'The ball rolls', *Truba dymit* 'The chimney smokes', *Voda kipit* 'The water is boiling', *Poezd ostanavlivaetsja* 'The train stops', *Bol'no ruke* '(smb's) hand hurts'.

If we compare agentives and objectives, we see that in Russian they are expressed by the nominative case, but an objective can also be expressed by the dative case (and by other cases). In languages with an ergative construction the agentive can be expressed by other cases.

The elementary terms T_f, T_f^1... will be called elementary affectives. Elementary affectives denote animate objects which are in some kind of state or which are subjected to some kind of action. The elementary predicates $P_f P_f^1$ agree with the elementary affectives.

Sentences with elementary affectives are generated as follows:

$$\frac{P_f \qquad\qquad T_f}{\beta(P_f T_f)}$$

The sentences $P_f T_f$ is interpreted as *Bratu xolodno* 'Brother is cold (lit. it is cold to brother)', *Otec spit* 'Father is sleeping', etc.

The elementary terms T_l, T_l^1 ... will be called elementary locatives. Elementary locatives denote spatial, temporal or abstract localization.

The elementary predicates P_l, P_l^1 ... agree with the elementary locatives.

Sentences with elementary locatives are generated as follows:

$$\frac{P_l \qquad\qquad T_l}{\beta(P_l T_l)}$$

The sentence $P_l T_l$ can be interpreted as *V Afrike žarko* 'It is hot in Africa', *Utrom bylo proxladno* 'It was cool this morning'; *Na duše tjaželo* 'The heart aches (lit. in the soul it is heavy)'.

If we change the point of reference of derivability (as was mentioned above), then on the empirical interpretation level predicates can correspond not only to verbs, but also to adjectives and nouns.

Specifically, the sentence $P_a T_a$ can be interpreted as *On-učitel'* 'He is a teacher', *On-rabočij* 'He is a worker', where the predicates *učitel'* 'teacher' and *rabočij* 'worker' correspond to the predicate P_a. The sentence $P_o T_o$ can be interpreted as *Sosna – derevo* 'The pine is a tree', *Kislorod – gaz* 'Oxygen is a gas', where the predicates *derevo* 'tree' and *gaz* 'gas' correspond to the predicate P_o.

The elementary predicates $P_{(a)}, P_{(o)}, P_{(f)}, P_{(l)}$ (with the lower indices in parentheses) are elementary predicates which lack the corresponding arguments, i.e., elementary predicates which coincide on the interpretation level with impersonal sentences. Thus, we can have the following interpretations as impersonal sentences:

$P_{(a)}$ as *Begajut* '(they) run', *Xodjat* '(they) walk';
$P_{(o)}$ as *Katjatsja* '(they) ride', *Dymjat* '(they) smoke';
$P_{(f)}$ as *Xolodno* '(it is) cold', *Spjat* '(they) sleep'
$P_{(l)}$ as *Zdes' žarko* 'it is hot here', *Tam proxladno* 'There it is cool', etc.

The elementary terms $T_i, T_I^1, \ldots$ will be called elementary instrumentives. Elementary instrumentives denote objects or factors which cause the action or state expressed by the corresponding elementary operators.

Let us take, for example, the elementary predicates $P_{oi}, P_{io}^1, \ldots$. Each of these elementary predicates, since it is applied to one of the terms $T_o, T_o^1, \ldots$ generates a predicate which represents the episemion $\Delta i\beta$. The application of this predicate to one of the terms $T_i, T_i^1, \ldots$ gives a sentence. The generation of the given sentence can be shown in the form of the following tree diagram:

$$\frac{\dfrac{P_{oi} \qquad\qquad T_o}{\Delta i\beta\,(P_{oi}T_o) \qquad\qquad T_i}}{\beta\,((P_{oi}T_o)\,T_i)}$$

As a result of applying the elementary operator P_{oi} to the term T_o we obtain the predicate $P_{oi}T_o$, whose application to the term T_i gives the sentence $P_{oi}T_o T_i$; we see that only one-place functions are considered to be predicates proper. But by applying the above formal rule for interpreting one-place functions as multiplace functions, we can broaden the notion of a predicate and consider the operator P_{oi} to be a two-place predicate whose arguments are the terms T_o and T_i. We can obtain three-place predicates in a similar way. For instance, let us take the elementary operators P_{ioa}, $P_{ioa}^1, \ldots$ The application of each of these elementary operators to one of the elementary terms $T_i, T_i^1, \ldots$ gives the operator $P_{ioa}T_i$, whose application to one of the elementary terms $T_o, T_o^1, \ldots$ gives the predicate $P_{ioa}T_i T_o$, whose application to the key-word T_a gives the sentence $P_{ioa}T_i T_o T_a$.

The generation of this sentence can be shown in the following tree diagram:

$$\frac{\dfrac{P_{ioa} \qquad\qquad T_i}{\varDelta o \varDelta \alpha \beta \left(P_{ioa}T_i\right) \qquad\qquad T_o}}{\dfrac{\varDelta \alpha \beta \left(\left(P_{ioa}T_i\right) T_o\right) \qquad\qquad T_a}{\beta \left(\left(\left(P_{ioa}T_i\right) T_o\right) T_a\right)}}$$

We can interpret the elementary operator P_{ioa} as a three-place predicate with the terms T_i, T_o, T_a as its arguments. In basically the same way we can obtain predicates with a larger number of arguments. But they do not find any broad interpretation in natural languages, and for this reason we will not treat them here.

The dual interpretation of operators as transformers of terms into one-place predicates (on the level of one-place functions) and as multiplace predicates with several arguments (on the level of multiplace functions) is of great linguistic significance. The generally accepted interpretation of sentences as structures made up of predicates with one or several actants reflects only one side of the matter. The other side of the matter consists in the fact that the actants are inequal among themselves. For example, if we take the sentence *Mal'čik čitaet knigu* 'The boy is reading the book', it is insufficient to say that the word *čitaet* 'reads' is a predicate with two actants. This is only one side of the matter. The other side of the matter consists in the fact that the word *čitaet* 'reads' is more closely bound to the word *knigu* 'book' than with the word *mal'čik* 'boy', namely, it transforms the word *knigu* 'book' into the predicate *čitaet knigu* 'reads a book'. Hence, it is necessary to distinguish two layers of predicativity: (1) a layer of multiplace predicates, (2) a layer of transformers of nouns into one-place predicates. Both of these layers are in a complementary relationship to each other and must be taken into consideration by any grammar that claims to be an adequate study of the syntactic structure of the sentence.

Let us return to the sentence $P_{oi}T_oT_i$, in which P_{oi} is treated as a two-place predicate. This sentence can be interpreted, for example, as *Sneg zanes dorogu* 'Snow has blocked the road' or *Molnija ubila korovu* 'Lightning killed the cow'. We see that an elementary instrumentive can be expressed in Russian with the nominative case.

We shall now introduce the notion of semantic accent. Semantic accent will be said to be the emphasis of the main term in a sentence. If there are two terms in a sentence, the semantic accent falls on the last term. Thus, in the sentence $P_{oi}T_oT_i$ the semantic accent falls on the term T_i. If there are three terms in a sentence, we will distinguish between a main and a secondary semantic accent. In such a case the main semantic accent falls on the last term, and the secondary semantic accent falls on the next to the last term.

If some two-place predicates differ from each other only in the semantic accent of their arguments, we will say that such predicates are two-place converse predicates. For example, P_{oi}, P_{io} are converse predicates. The sentence $P_{oi}T_oT_i$ can be interpreted as *Doroga zanesena snegom* 'The road is blocked with snow', *Korova ubita molniej* 'The cow has been killed by lightning' or *Korovu ubilo molniej* 'The cow has been, was killed by lightning' (cf. the interpretations of the sentence $P_{oi}T_oT_i$ above).

Let us dwell for a moment on some other examples of two-place converse predicates.

The elementary predicates $P_{oa}, P_{oa}^1, ..., P_{ao}, P_{ao}^2, ...$ function as converse predicates in relation to each other.

The sentence $P_{oa}T_oT_a$ can be interpreted as *Mal'čik podnimaet karandaš* 'The boy lifts the pencil', and the sentence $P_{ao}T_aT_o$ as *Karandaš podnimaetsja mal'čikom* 'The pencil is lifted by the boy'.

The elementary predicates $P_{fa}, P_{fa}^1, ..., P_{af}, P_{af}^1$ can serve as another example of two-place converse predicates.

The sentence $P_{fa}T_fT_a$ can be interpreted as *Syn ljubit mat'* 'The son loves his mother', and the sentence $P_{af}T_aT_f$ as *Mat' ljubima synom* 'The mother is loved by her son'.

The predicates $P_{of}, P_{of}^1, ..., P_{fo}, P_{fo}^1, ...$ are also two-place converse predicates.

The sentence $P_{of}T_oT_f$ can be interpreted as *Otec slušaet muzyku* 'Father is listening to the music', and the sentence $P_{fo}T_fT_o$ as *Muzyka slušaetsja otcom* 'The music is listened to by father'.

Let us turn to the elementary terms $T_c, T_c^1, ...$, which we shall call elementary completives. Completives denote abstract or concrete objects especially used with empty predicates. Completives turn empty predicates into full. For example, the elementary predicates $P_{ca}, P_{ac}, P_{cf}, P_{fc}$ belong to the class of two-place empty predicates.

Let us now consider some examples of sentences with empty elementary predicates and elementary completives.

Let us take the elementary predicate P_{cf} and its converse P_{fc} (in accordance with what has already been said above on converse predicates, we can assume the inverse – that the predicate P_{cf} is the converse of the predicate P_{fc}, which amounts to the same thing). The sentence $P_{cf}T_cT_f$ can be interpreted as *Otec prinimaet vannu* 'Father takes a bath', and the sentence $P_{fc}T_fT_c$ as *Vanna prinimaetsja otcom* 'The bath is taken by father'.

One or both arguments can be omitted from two-place predicates. This is designated by placing the corresponding indices of these predicates in parentheses, e.g. $P_{o(a)}$, $P_{(o)a}$, $P_{f(a)}$, $P_{(f)(a)}$, etc. We thereby obtain sentences such as:

$P_{(o)a}T_a$ *Mal'čik čitaet*
'The boy reads'
$P_{(o)(a)}$ *Čitajut* '(they) read'
$P_{oi}T_oT_i$ *Voda zalivaet luga*
'Water floods the meadow'
$P_{o(i)}T_o$ *Luga zalivaet*
'The meadow floods'

$P_{o(a)}T_o$ *Kniga čitaetsja*
'The book is read'

$P_{(o)i}T_i$ *Zalivaet vodoj*
'Floods with water'
$P_{(o)(i)}$ *Zalivaet* 'Floods'

Let us proceed to three-place elementary predicates. Any detailed study of three-place predicates, as of predicates in general, could be the theme of a special paper. We will limit ourselves here to some isolated examples.

Let us take the elementary predicates P_{ioa}, P_{ioa}^1, ... The sentence $P_{ioa}T_iT_oT_a$ can be interpreted as *Mat' režet kolbasu nožom* 'Mother cuts the sausage with a knife'. The elementary predicates P_{ioa}, P_{ioa}^1, ... which differ from those just cited in that their arguments have been permuted. Thus, the sentence $P_{ioa}T_iT_oT_a$ can be interpreted as *Kolbasa režetsja mater' ju nožom* 'The sausage is cut by mother with a knife'. These predicates, and even other predicates, can be used in a reduced form: $P_{(i)oa}$, $P_{io(a)}$, $P_{(i)o(a)}$ etc.

The sentence $P_{io(a)}T_iT_o$ can be interpreted as *Kolbasa režetsja nožom* 'The sauge is cut with a knife'. The sentence $P_{oi(a)}T_oT_i$ can be interpreted as *Nož režet kolbasu* 'The knife cuts the sausage'. The sentence $P_{o(i)(a)}T_o$ can be interpreted as *Kolbasu režut* '(They) cut the sausage'. The sentence $P_{(o)(i)(a)}$ can be interpreted as *Režut* '(They) cut'.

The notion of conversion can be extended to three-place predicates and multiplace predicates in general. We shall call two multiplace predicates converse if they differ from each other by a permutation of any two arguments. For an example, let us take the elementary predicate P_{foa}.

If we take this predicate to be an initial one, in accordance with the theory of permutations we can obtain six predicates which differ from each other in the order of symbols in their indices: P_{foa}, P_{fao}, P_{ofa}, P_{oaf}, P_{afo}, P_{aof}.

Converse predicates can be given in the form of the following tree:

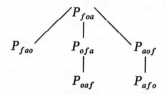

According to our agreement, predicates in adjacent nodes of a tree are to be considered converse.

Now let us transform this tree of converse predicates into a tree of sentences which we shall call converse sentences.

$$P_{foa}T_fT_oT_a$$

$$P_{fao}T_fT_aT_o \qquad P_{ofa}T_oT_fT_a \qquad P_{aof}T_aT_oT_f$$

$$P_{oaf}T_oT_aT_f \qquad P_{afo}T_aT_fT_o$$

If we interpret the sentence $P_{foa}T_fT_oT_a$ as *Brat daet den'gi sestre* 'Borther gives money to sister', the converse of this sentence will be interpreted: $P_{fao}T_fT_aT_o$ as *Den'gi dajutsja bratom sestre* 'The money is given by the brother to the sister', $P_{ofa}T_oT_fT_a$ as *Brat snabžaet sestru den'gami* 'Brother supplies sister with money', $P_{afo}T_aT_fT_o$ as *Sestra polučaet den'gi ot brata* 'The sister receives money from the brother'.

The sentence $P_{oaf}T_oT_aT_f$ will be interpreted as *Sestra snabžaetsja bratom den' gami* 'The sister is supplied with money by the brother', and the sentence $P_{afo}T_aT_fT_o$ as *Den'gi polučajutsja sestroj ot brata* 'Money is received by the sister from her brother'.

6. Depredicators

The genotype language with a case system can be further extended by introducing into it a new kind of elementary operators, which we shall call depredicators. Depredicators will be denoted with the symbol D and the appropriate lower indices, which will be given below.

Depredicators transform predicates either into various types of terms or into operators. Let us examine the basic types of depredicators.

To devise the lower indices for the depredicators, we introduce the Greek letter π as a variable denoting any *n*-place predicate. The formula of the episemion $\varDelta\pi\alpha$ will then be read: the transformer of any predicate π into the term α. If we replace π in this formula with the different episemions that function as the names of predicate classes, we obtain $\varDelta\varDelta\alpha\beta\alpha$, $\varDelta\varDelta\alpha\varDelta\alpha\beta\alpha$, $\varDelta\varDelta\alpha\varDelta\alpha\varDelta\alpha\beta\alpha$ etc.

We can now draw up the following list of the most important depredicators.

$D_{\varDelta\pi\alpha}$ (the operator that transforms any predicate into an agentive): $D_{\varDelta\pi\alpha}P_\pi =$ he who...

P_π	$D_{\varDelta\pi\alpha}P_\pi$
tancuet 'dances'	*tancor* 'dancer'
čitaet 'reads'	*čitatel* ''reader'
lečit 'heals'	*vrač* 'doctor'

ubivaet 'kills'   *ubijca* 'killer, murderer'
obmanyvaet 'deceives'   *obmanščik* 'deceiver, fraud'
učit 'teaches'   *učitel'* 'teacher'
predaet 'betrays'   *predatel'* 'traitor'

$D_{\Delta \pi f}$ (the operator that transforms any predicate into an affective):
$D_{\Delta \pi f} P_\pi$ = he whom... or he who... (is subjected to something)

P_π	$D_{\Delta \pi f} P_\pi$
ljubit 'loves'	*ljubimec* 'favorite, pet'
stradaet 'suffers'	*stradalec* 'sufferer'
učit 'teaches'	*učenik* 'pupil'
arestovyvaet 'arrests'	*arestant* 'prisoner, convict'
ssylaet 'exiles, banishes'	*ssylnyj* 'exile'
lečit 'heals'	*pacient* 'patient'
priglašaet 'invites'	*gost'* 'guest'

$D_{\Delta \pi i}$ (the operator that transforms any predicate into an instrumentive):
$D_{\Delta \pi i} P_\pi$ = that with which...

P_π	$D_{\Delta \pi i} P_\pi$
rubit 'chops'	*topor* 'ax'
režet 'cuts'	*nož* 'knife'
pilit 'saws'	*pila* 'saw'
podmetaet 'sweeps'	*metla, venik* 'broom'
p'et 'drinks'	*stakan, časka, kružka* 'glass, cup, mug'
kosit 'mows'	*kosa* 'scythe'
ubeždaet 'convinces'	*dovod* 'argument'
letaet 'flys'	*samolet* 'airplane'

$D_{\Delta \pi l}$ (the operator that transforms any predicate into a locative): $D_{\Delta \pi l} P_\pi =$
that where...

P_π	$D_{\Delta \pi l} P_\pi$
xranit 'keeps'	*xranilišče* 'storehouse'
spit 'sleeps'	*spal'nja* 'bedroom'
streljaet 'shoots'	*strel'bišče* 'shooting range'
učitsja 'studies'	*učilišče* 'school, college'
citaet 'reads'	*čital'nja* 'reading room'
est 'eats'	*stolovaja* 'dining room'
varit 'cooks'	*kastrjulja* 'saucepan'
žarit 'fries'	*skovoroda* 'skillet'

$D_{\Delta \pi c}$ (the operator that transforms any predicate into a completive):
$D_{\Delta \pi c} P_\pi$ (an abstract notion derived from a predicate)

P_π	$D_{\Delta \pi c} P_\pi$
čitaet 'reads'	*čtenie* 'reading'

guljaet 'walks, strolls'

obščaetsja 'associates'

vstrečaet 'meets'

rabotaet 'works'

pugaetsja 'be frightened'

bežit 'runs'

guljanie 'walking'

obščenie 'intercourse, contact'

vstreča 'meeting'

rabota 'work'

strax 'fear'

beg 'running, race'

$D_{\Delta\pi o}$ (the operator that transforms any predicate into an objective): $D_{\Delta\pi o}P_{\pi}$ = that which... (in the role of object or subject):

P_{π}	$D_{\Delta\pi o}P_{\pi}$
vyigryvaet 'wins'	*vyigrys* 'win, profit'
pokupaet 'buys'	*pokupka* 'purchase'
darit 'gives as a present'	*podarok* 'present'
posylaet 'sends'	*posylka* 'parcel'
lovit 'catches'	*ulov* 'catch'
naxodit 'finds'	*naxodka* 'find'

So far we have considered the depredicators for transforming predicates into various types of key-words. Now let us dwell for a moment on some other types of depredicators.

$D_{\Delta\pi\Delta a\alpha}$ (the operator that transforms any predicate into a participle):

P_{π}	$D_{\Delta\pi\Delta a\alpha}P_{\pi}$
guljaet 'walks'	*guljajuščij* 'walking, that walks'
čitaet 'reads'	*čitajuščij* 'reading', *citaemyj* 'read'
daet 'gives'	*dajuščij* 'giving, that gives'
xranit 'keeps'	*xranjaščij* 'that keeps', *xranimyj* 'kept'

$D_{\Delta\pi\Delta\pi\pi}$ (the operator that transforms any predicate into a verbal adverb):

P_{π}	$D_{\Delta\pi\Delta\pi\pi}P_{\pi}$
guljaet 'walks'	*guljaja* 'walking, while walking, etc.'
čitaet 'reads'	*čitaja* 'reading'
daet 'gives'	*davaja* 'giving'
xranit 'keeps'	*xranja* 'keeping'

To make our depredicator notation more compact, we will introduce certain abbreviations. The formula $X \to Y$ will mean: 'X is an abbreviation used in place of Y'.

$$D_a \to D_{\Delta\pi a}$$
$$D_f \to D_{\Delta\pi f}$$
$$D_i \to D_{\Delta\pi i}$$
$$D_l \to D_{\Delta\pi l}$$
$$D_c \to D_{\Delta\pi c}$$
$$D_o \to D_{\Delta\pi o}.$$

In addition, we will use the following abbreviations:

$$\alpha' \rightarrow \Delta\alpha\alpha$$
$$\alpha'' \rightarrow \Delta\Delta\alpha\alpha\Delta\alpha\alpha$$

etc.

$$\pi' \rightarrow \Delta\pi\pi$$
$$\pi'' \rightarrow \Delta\Delta\pi\pi\Delta\pi\pi.$$

etc.

Whence we obtain the following abbreviations:

$$D_{\alpha'} \rightarrow D_{\Delta\pi\Delta\alpha\alpha}$$
$$D_{\pi'} \rightarrow D_{\Delta\pi\Delta\pi\pi}$$

7. RELATORS AND CONJUCTORS

The extension of the genotype language by means of relators and conjunctors is of primary importance for the study of natural languages.

Relators are a special kind of operators that transform the semions of any class into the semions of the given class. The following relators are the most important ones:

R_{α} the relator for transforming any semion into a term

$R_{\pi'}$ the relator for transforming any semion into a one-place predicate

$R_{\Delta\pi\pi'}$ the relator for transforming any semion into a two-place predicate

$R_{\Delta\pi\Delta\pi\pi}$ the relator for transforming any semion into a three-place predicate

$R_{\alpha'}$ the relator for transforming any semion into the attribute of a term

$R_{\pi''}$ the relator for transforming any semion into the attribute of a one-place predicate

Conjunctors are the operators C, Al, Im. C, called the coordinator, functions as an abstract analogue of the conjunction i 'and' in Russian and the other languages of the world. Al, called the alternator, is an abstract analogue of the conjunction ili 'or'. Im, called the implicator, is an abstract analogue of the conjunction $esli$ 'if'.

The following two remarks must be made regarding conjunctors. First, the meaning of the genotype conjunctors only approximately coincides with the meaning of the conjunctors in mathematical logic. Conjunctors in mathematical logic are strictly defined through the truth functions whereas here we have to do with the possibility of partial interpretation with free notions. The possibility of partial interpretation gives the genotype language a flexibility which is necessary to be able to study specific languages. Secondly, we are considering conjunctors as a pure instance of predicates in the broad sense. Predicates in the broad sense are defined as operators that transform any operand into a sentence.

Now let us examine the formal properties of conjunctors, beginning with coordinators.

A coordinator is a two-place function which can have as its arguments any semions belonging to the same episemion.

Let X and Y be semions belonging to the episemion z, in which case the operator C can be shown in the following tree:

$$\frac{\dfrac{\Delta z \Delta zzC \qquad\qquad zX}{\Delta zzCX \qquad\qquad zY}}{zCXY}$$

The action of a coordinator will be called coordination.

Coordinators are interpreted on the empirical level as coordinating conjunctions. Coordinators can correspond to coordinating conjunctions which connect sentences, or to coordinating conjunctions which connect homogeneous parts of the sentence. The arguments of a coordinator can be permuted with no change in the meaning of the expression, as the following equality shows:

$$CXY = CYX.$$

This equality can be illustrated on the empirical level through the following examples:

otec i syn 'father and son' = *syn i otec* 'son and father'
otec spit, a syn čitaet knigu 'the father is sleeping, and the son is reading a book' = *syn čitaet knigu, a otec spit* 'the son is reading a book, and the father is sleeping'.

Let us consider the formal properties of coordination.

Application and coordination are related asymmetrically by the laws of distributivity, i.e., application is distributive with respect to coordination, but coordination is not distributive with respect to application.

The laws of the distributivity for application with respect to coordination can be shown in the form of the following two equalities:

(1) $\qquad Z(CXY) = C(ZX)(ZY)$

(2) $\qquad (CXY)Z = C(XZ)(YZ).$

The first equality is called the left law of distributivity for application with respect to coordination. The second equality is called the right law of distributivity for application with respect to coordination.

Both of these equalities can be illustrated on the empirical level with the following equalities:

(1)   *Otec i syn rabotajut* 'The father and son work' = *Otec rabotaet i syn rabobaet* 'The father works and the son works'.

(2)   *Sneg padaet i taet* 'The snow falls and melts' = *Sneg padaet i sneg taet* 'The snow falls and the snow melts'.

The left and right laws of distributivity for application with respect to coordination resemble the left and right laws of distributivity for multiplication with respect to addition in algebra, which have the following form:

(1) $a(b + c) = ab + ac$

$(b + c)a = ba + ca.$

Let us turn to alternators. We will call the operation of an alternator alternation. As was stated above, alternators are interpreted as the conjunction *'ili'* 'or'. The properties of alternators are isomorphic to the properties of coordinators, and for this reason application and alternation are connected by laws of distributivity in exactly the same way as application and coordination. The laws of distributivity for application with respect to coordination and alternation can be given in the form of the following two equalities:

(1) $(AlXY) = Al(ZX)(ZY)$

(2) $(AlXY)Z = Al(XZ)(YZ).$

These two equalities can be illustrated on the empirical level with the following equalities:

> *Prišel otec ili syn* (The father or the son came' = *ili prišel otec ili prišel syn* 'Either the father came or the son came'.
> *Otec libo spit, libo bodrstvuet* 'Father is either asleep or awake' = *Libo otec spit, libo otec bodrstvuet* 'Either father is asleep or father is awake'.

As was the case for the arguments of a coordinator, the arguments of an alternator can be permuted without changing the meaning of the expression:

$$AlXY = AlYX$$

Finally, let us consider implicators. Implicators are interpreted as the conjunctions *'esli'* 'if' or *'esli...to'* 'if...then'. Like coordinators and alternators, implicators are two-place functions with sentences as their arguments. In relation to its formal properties implicators differ from coordinators in two respects. First, the arguments of an implicator cannot be permuted without changing the meaning of the expression. Thus, the formulae ImS^1S^1 and ImS^2S^1 have opposite meanings. Secondly, application and implication are not connected to each other by laws of distributivity.

8. A DEFINITION OF FORMAL SEMANTICS

We considered above the rules for constructing the objects of the genotype language – episemions and semions. By applying these rules we can obtain any object of the genotype language. We shall agree to call the rules for constructing episemions and semions the formal syntax of the genotype language.

Now let us pose a new problem: how can we obtain semions with a given meaning?

Since, as has already been mentioned above, meaning does not exist by itself, but is always enclosed in a linguistic shell, to be able to solve this problem we are going to have to distinguish a genotype sublanguage in the genotype language that contains semions which we can agree to use as meaning standards. These meaning standards will be called semantic axioms. We assume that meaning standards should have a simple structure. Moreover, we must give the rules that make it possible to derive from the semantic axioms the semions whose meanings include them in the semantic axioms. Any semions can theoretically be semantic axioms, but we shall agree to take only semions that can serve as sentences.

We shall agree to call the rules for deriving semions from semantic axioms the formal semantics of the genotype language. Thus, an applicative grammar can be divided into two parts: the formal syntax and the formal semantics of the genotype language.

A formal semantics of the genotype language is possible because the genotype language contains synonymous expressions. In connection with this the question arises of whether it is not possible to get along without synonymy in the genotype language if, as was stated above, the expressions of the genotype language are to serve as a universal measure of meaning for natural languages. Can't we go directly from the expressions of the genotype sub-language containing the semantic axioms to the expressions of natural languages?

It appears that we cannot. Many semantic invariants underlying expressions have complex structures which are derivable from more simple structures. Hence, it is not always possible to go from semantic axioms directly to expressions in natural languages. In many cases the transition from semantic axioms to expressions in natural languages is only possible through semions derived from the semantic axioms. Synonymy is an indispensible aspect of the genotype language, and formal semantics is consequently also an indispensible part of the applicative grammar.

Formal semantics is a formal system in which are given:

(1) A finite set of formulae, known as semantic axioms.

(2) A finite set of semantic derivation rules.

Semantic axioms and the formulae derivable from them are assertions of the form:

$$\Vdash X,$$

where X is a semion. The sign $\Vdash$ will be called the sign of assertion. This formula is read: 'The semion X is included in a semantic field'. A semantic field will be said to be a set of semantic axioms and the formulae derivable from them.

Let us agree to omit the sign $\Vdash$ in semantic axioms and the formulae derivable from them.

Semantic derivation rules are formulae of the form:

$$X \Rightarrow Y.$$

The symbol $\Rightarrow$ denotes that the semion X can be replaced by the semion Y. All in all we can have n semantic derivation rules.

We shall say that the semion V is semantically derivable from the semion U if V is either equal to U or is obtained from U as a result of the successive application of semantic derivation rules. We will use the sign $\Vdash$ to denote semantic derivability. The notation

$$U \Vdash V$$

will mean that the semion V is semantically derivable from the semion U.

We shall say that the semion V is directly semantically derivable from the semion U if V is obtained from U as a result of the application of a single semantic derivation rule. To designate direct semantic derivability we will use the sign $\vdash$. The notation

$$U \vdash V$$

will mean that the semion V is semantically directly derivable from the semion U.

If we have n semantic derivation rules, we have n types of direct semantic derivability.

For the sake of brevity, we will say 'semantic rules' instead of 'semantic derivation rules' below.

The characteristic properties of semantic derivability are defined by the following assertions:

(1) $U \Vdash U$ for any semion U;

(2) $U \Vdash V$ & $V \Vdash Z \rightarrow U \Vdash Z$;

(3) $U \Vdash V \rightarrow ZU \Vdash ZV$;

(4) $U \Vdash V \rightarrow UZ \Vdash VZ$;

(5) $U \vdash V \rightarrow U \Vdash V$;

(6) $U \Vdash V$ when and only when it is possible to construct a series of semions:

$$U_0, \ldots, U_m \quad (m \geqslant 0), \quad \text{such that}$$
$$U_0 = U$$
$$U_m = V$$
$$U_{i-1} \vdash U_i \quad (0 < i \leqslant m);$$

(7) $U \Vdash V$ and $V \Vdash U$ when and only when it is possible to construct a series of semions

$$U_0, \ldots, U_m \quad (m \geqslant 0), \quad \text{such that}$$
$$U_0 = U$$
$$U_m = V$$
$$U_{i-1} \vdash U_i \quad \text{and} \quad U_i \vdash U_{i-1} \, (0 < i \leqslant m).$$

The symbol & in these assertions means '...and...', and the symbol $\rightarrow$ means 'if..., then...'. In assertion (3) the symbol Z denotes identical operators for the operands U and V, and the symbol Z in assertion (4) denotes identical operands for the operators U and V.

Semantic derivability defines inclusion with respect to meaning. We will say that the semion V is included with respect to its meaning in the semion U if

$$U \Vdash V.$$

We will say that the semion V is included with respect to its meaning in the semion U and the semion U is included with respect to its meaning in the semion V (i.e., are in a relationship of semantic equivalence, or synonymy) if

$$U \Vdash V \quad \text{and} \quad V \Vdash U.$$

Let us now consider the relation of meaning inclusion and the relation of meaning equivalence from the operational point of view.

We say that the semion V is included with respect to its meaning in the semion U if and only if any object or situation denoted by the semion U can also be denoted by the semion V. We can show this through examples of semions interpreted with Russian expressions. Thus, the expression *sobaka* 'dog' is included with respect to its meaning in the expression

bol'šaja sobaka 'big dog' because the object denoted by the expression
bol'saja sobaka 'big dog' can also be denoted by the expression *sobaka* 'dog'
(a big dog is always a dog). But the reverse does not hold: the expression
bol'šaja sobaka 'big dog' is not included with respect to its meaning in the
expression *sobaka* 'dog', because the object denoted by the expression *sobaka*
'dog' is not necessarily denoted by the expression *bol'šaja sobaka* 'bid dog'
(since the dog is not necessarily big, but can also be small). Another example:
the expression *rubjat derevo* '(they) chop down the tree' is included with
respect to its meaning in the expression *brat rubit derevo* 'brother chops
down the tree', because the situation denoted by the expression *brat rubit
derevo* 'brother chops down the tree' can also be denoted by the expression
rubjat derevo '(they) chop down the tree, the tree is being chopped down'.
But the reverse does not hold: the expression *brat rubit* 'brother chops' is
not included with respect to its meaning in the expression *brat rubit derevo*
'brother chops down the tree', because the situation denoted by the expression *rubjat derevo* '(they) chop down the tree' is not necessarily denoted
by the expression *brat rubit derevo* 'brother chops down the tree', but can
be denoted, for example, by the expressions *otec rubit derevo* 'father chops
down the tree', *krest'janin rubit derevo* 'the peasant chops down the tree',
etc.

We will say that the semion *U* is equivalent with respect to its meaning
to the semion *V* if and only if any object or situation denoted by the semion
U is also denoted by the semion *V*, and conversely, any object or situation
denoted by the semion *V* is also denoted by the semion *U*. On the level
of interpreted semions the expression *jazykoznanie* 'linguistics, lit. language
knowledge' is equivalent with respect to its meaning to the expression
lingvistika 'linguistics', and the expression *brat rubit derevo* 'brother chops
down the tree' is equivalent with respect to its meaning to the expression
derevo rubitsja bratom 'the tree is chopped down by brother'.

Let us agree that meaning inclusion will be called semantic inclusion, and
meaning equivalence will be called semantic equivalence.

9. COMBINATORY OPERATORS

The operators which we will agree to call combinatory operators play an
essential role in semantic rules. Since combinatory operators are used to
transform semions into other, semantically equivalent, semions, we have to
incorporate them into the genotype language[1].

---

[1] The ideas here on the logical aspects of the use of combinatory operators are closely
related to those developed by H. B. Carry in combinatory logic (see H. B. Carry and Feys,
Combinatory Logic, Vol. 1, Amsterdam, 1958).

Let us begin with the conversion operator, which is designated with the symbol Cv_{ik}.

The conversion operator is to be supplied with a numerical index that indicates which two symbols in the index of a multiplace function are to exchange places, e.g. Cv_{12}, Cv_{13}, Cv_{23}, etc.

Hence we obtain, for example, the following equalities:

$$Cv_{12}F_{fa} = F_{af}$$
$$Cv_{12}F_{foa} = F_{ofa}$$
$$Cv_{13}F_{foa} = F_{aof}$$
$$Cv_{23}F_{foa} = F_{fao}.$$

The repeated application of the conversion operator makes it possible to obtain various transformations of the initial function, which we are not going to dwell on here.

The operator W is called the duplicator. If F is a two-place function, then WF is a one-place function connected to the function F by the equality $WFX=FXX$.

The duplicator can be interpreted on the empirical level as, for example, an operator that generates reflexive verbs. Let some predicate P_{fa} be applied to two identical terms: $P_{fa}T_f^1T_a^1$

This formula can then be interpreted, for example, with the phrase *Mal'cik₁ umyvaet mal'čika₁* 'The boy₁ washes the boy₁' (identical upper and lower numerical indices mean that both arguments of the predicate are identical to each other).

Now the equality *Mal'čik umyvaetsja* 'The boy washes (himself'= *Mal'čik umyvaet mal'cika* 'The boy washes the boy' will correspond to the equality $WP_{f,a}T_f^1=P_{fa}T_f^1T_a^1$.

The lower index on the term $T_{f,a}^1$ in the left side of the equality signifies that this term has two roles simultaneously: that of affective and that of agentive. The lower index on this term is obtained through the general rule: if we have the terms T_x^1 and T_y^1, merging them gives the term $T_{x,y}^1$.

The operator B is called the compositor. Let F be some one-place function, and let the argument of function F be the value of some other one-place function G having X as its argument, which can be written:

$$F(GX).$$

Such an expression is sometimes inaccurately called a function from a function. The term 'function from the value of a function' will be correct. By means of the operator B we can obtain instead of two functions F and G one complex function BFG, which is immediately dependent on X. The function BFG is related to the functions F and G by the equality: $BFGX = F(GX)$.

The complex function BFG is obtained as follows: first B is applied to F, as a result of which we obtain the function BF, which has the function G as its argument. Then we apply BF to G and obtain the function BFG, which has X as its argument. When we apply BFG to X we obtain the combination $BFGX$, which is equal to the combination $F(GX)$.

It should be noted that there are four initial components in the first combination: B, F, G, X, and only two in the second: F and (GX). If we reconstruct the parentheses in the first combination in accordance with our agreement on grouping to the left, it will have the form:

$$(((BF)\,G)\,X)$$

or (if we do not restore the outer parentheses): $((BF)\,G)\,X$.

The compositor can be interpreted on the empirical level as an operator that transforms predicates with subordinate object clauses into the construction 'accusative + infinitive'. When we consider the operation of the compositor we must bear in mind that subordinate object clauses can be formed not only by applying conjunctions (for example, the Russian *čto* or the English *that*) to the independent clauses and then applying predicates to the result of this application, but also by directly applying predicates to independent clauses (in which case the independent clause is considered to be one of the arguments of the predicates). Following the first method for forming subordinate object clauses we obtain in English, for example, sentences with the conjunction *that*: *I know that he paints*, and following the second method we obtain sentences without *that* (with the same meaning): *I know he paints*. Let us introduce a formal rule in accordance with which we replace the symbol o in the lower index with the symbol β in cases where an independent clause serves immediately as one of the arguments of these predicates. It is precisely this kind of predicate with a subordinate object clause that the compositor transforms into structures interpreted as 'accusative + infinitive'.

Let F be any predicate, say, $P_{\beta f}$. If we apply this predicate to the sentence $P_a T_a$ we obtain

(1) $P_{\beta f}(P_a T_a)$,

to which the predicate *know he paints* corresponds.

If we apply formula (1) to the term T_f^2 we obtain

(2) $P_{\beta f}(P_a T_a^2)\,T_f^2$,

to which the sentence *I know he paints* corresponds.

Using the compositor, we can now obtain the following two equalities:

(3) $\quad BP_{\beta f}P_a T_a = P_{\beta f}(P_a T_a)$

(4) $\quad BP_{\beta f}P_a T_a T_f = P_{\beta f}(P_a T_a)\,T_f\,.$

The left-hand part of equality (3) corresponds to the phrase *know him to paint*, and its right-hand part corresponds to *I know he paints*.

The sentence *I know him to paint* corresponds to the left-hand part of equality (4), and the phrase *I know he paints* corresponds to its right-hand part.

The operator L will be called the confluentor (the fusion operator). Let F be a two-place function with X as its first argument and the value/meaning of the one-place function G, which also has X as its argument, as its second argument. This can be written:

$$FX(GX).$$

If we apply L to F and LF to G, we obtain the complex one-place function LFG, which is connected to the function F by the equality:

$$LFGX = FX(GX).$$

We see that when we introduce the function LFG a fusion into a single argument takes place between the two identical arguments on which the functions F and G depend.

The confluentor can be interpreted on the empirical level, for instance, as an operator that transforms causative constructions with subordinate object clauses into causative constructions with the structures 'accusative + infinitive'.

Let F be a causative predicate $Ca_{f\beta a}$, the application of which to the term T_f^f and the application of the result of this application to the sentence $P_a T_a^1$ gives the complex semion

$$Ca_{f\beta a}T_f^1(P_a T_a^1),$$

which can be interpreted *Velit mal'čiku, čtoby mal'čik guljal* 'Orders the boy that the boy take a walk'.

By using the confluentor we can obtain the following two equalities:

(1) $\quad LCa_{f\beta a}P_a T_{f,a}^1 = Ca_{f\beta a}T_f^1(P_a T_a^1)$

(2) $\quad LCa_{f\beta a}P_a T_{f,a}^1 T_a^2 = Ca_{f\beta a}T_f^1(P_a T_a^1)\,T_a^2\,.$

The phrase *Velit mal'čiku guljat'* 'Orders the boy to take a walk' corresponds to the left-hand part of equality (1), and the phrase *Velit mal'čiku, čtoby mal'čik guljal* 'Order the boy that the boy take a walk' corresponds to its right-hand part.

The phrase *Mat' velit mal'čiku guljat'* 'Mother orders the boy to take a walk' corresponds to the left-hand part of equality (2), and the phrase *Mat' velit mal'čiku, čtoby mal'čik guljal* 'Mother orders the boy that the boy take a walk' corresponds to its right-hand part.

Using the confluentor, we apply the rule given above for obtaining the lower index for the fusion of identical terms. As in the example with the operator W, the fusion of the terms T_f^1 and T_a^1 gives the term T_{fa}^1.

The operator $K_{(i)}$ is called the operator for introducing a fictive argument. If F is an n-place function, then $K_{(i)}F$ is a function which is related to the function F by the equality:

$$K_{(i)}F_n X^1 \ldots X^i X^{i+1} X^j \ldots X^n = F_n X^1 \ldots X^i X^j \ldots X^n.$$

The lower index on the operator $K_{(i)}$ is a variable which is replaced by a figure indicating after which argument the fictive argument is to be introduced, for example, $K_{(3)}$ means that the fictive argument is to be introduced after the third argument; K_0 means that the fictive argument is to be introduced after the zero argument, i.e., immediately after the function (in other words, the fictive argument is to be placed before the first argument). The fictive argument does not have case indices. Here is an example of a specific equality and its interpretation:

$$K_{(0)}P_f T_{\theta} T_f = P_f T_f.$$

This equality can correspond to the equality *Otec dumaet dumu* 'Father thinks a thought' = *Otec dumaet* 'Father thinks'. The noun *duma* 'thought' is superfluous with the predicate *dumaet* 'thinks' and must therefore be considered a fictive argument with this predicate.

We will call the operator I the identificator. Let X be a semion. The result of applying I to X is then identical to X, which can be expressed by the equality

$$IX = X.$$

The application of I to X can be interpreted as an identical transformation, i.e., a transformation the result of which is that X remains itself. The benefit of this operator will become clear below.

We will call the operator U the permutator. If F is a one-place function with X as its argument, then UF is a function related to the function F by the equality

$$UXF = FX.$$

As a result of applying the operator U to X and UX to F, the function and its argument X exchange roles: X is transformed into a function and F becomes its argument. For example, if we interpret the formula $P_0 T_0$ as *šar katitsja* 'the ball is rolling' and agree that T_0 is the theme and P_0 the rheme (a function which has a term as its argument will be considered a rheme, then the formula $UT_0 P_0$ can be interpreted as *katitsja šar* 'what rolls is the ball', that is, as a sentence in which the rheme and the theme have exchanged roles.

We will call the operator E_i the eliminator. If F_n is an n-argument function, then the operator E_i will be connected with the function F_n by the equality

$$E_i F_n \dots X^{i-1} X^{i+1} \dots X^n = F_n \dots X^{i-1} X^i X^{i+1} \dots X^n .$$

It can be seen from this equality that as a result of applying the operator E_i to the n-place function F_n the argument X^i on this function is eliminated.

The use of the operator E_i can be illustrated with the following example. Assume we have $P_{foa} T_f T_o T_a$, which we will interpret as, say, *otec daet den'gi synu* 'The father gives money to his son', so that by using the operator E_i we can have $E_1 P_{foa} T_o T_a$ *Otec daet den'gi*, 'Father gives money', $E_2 P_{foa} T_f$-T_a *'Otec daet synu'* 'Father gives his son', $E_3 P_{foa} T_f T_o$ *Den'gi dajutsja synu* 'The money is given to the son', $E_1(E_2 P_{foa}) T_a$ *Otec daet* 'Father gives', $E_2(E_3 P_{foa}) T_f$ *synu dajut* '(They) give the son', $E_1(E_3 P_{foa}) T_o$ *Den'gi dajutsja* 'Money is given', $E_1(E_2(E_3 P_{foa}))$ *Dajut* '(They) give'. The operators $E_1 E_2 E_3$ have the property of permutability, so that instead of, say, $E_2(E_3 P_{foa}) T_f$ it is possible to write $E_3(E_2 P_{foa}) T_f$, etc.

The operator U is connected with the operators Cv_{12} and g by the equality

$$UXY = Cv_{12} IXY .$$

This equality is derived as follows:

$$UXY = YX = I(YX) = I(IYX) = IYX = Cv_{12} IXY .$$

We shall distinguish between rules for introducing combinatory operators and rules for eliminating combinatory operators. Let us give a systematic survey of these rules.

Rule for introducing the operator C_{vik}:

$$F_n T^1 \dots T^i \dots T^k \dots T^n \rightarrow Cv_{ik} F_n T^1 \dots T^k \dots T^i \dots T^n .$$

Rule for eliminating the operator Cv_{ij}:

$$Cv_{ij}F_nT^1 \ldots T^i \ldots T^k \ldots T^n \to F_nT^1 \ldots T^k \ldots T^i \ldots T^n.$$

Rule for introducing the operator W:

$$F_2XX \to WF_2X.$$

Rule for eliminating the operator W:

$$WF_2X \to F_2XX.$$

Rule for introducing the operator B:

$$F(GX) \to BFGX.$$

Rule for eliminating the operator B:

$$BFGX \to F(GH).$$

Rule for introducing the operator L:

$$FX_{\iota}GX) \to LFGH.$$

Rule for eliminating the operator L:

$$LFGX \to FX(GX).$$

Rule for introducing the operator $K_{(i)}$:

$$F_nX^1 \ldots X^iX^j \ldots X^n \to K_{(i)}F_nX^1 \ldots X^iX^{i+1}X^j \ldots X^n.$$

Rule for eliminating the operator $K_{(i)}$:

$$K_{(i)}F_nX^1 \ldots X^iX^jX^k \ldots X^n \to F_nX^1 \ldots X^iX^k \ldots X^n.$$

Rule for introducing the operator I:

$$X \to IX.$$

Rule for eliminating the operator I:

$$IX \to X.$$

Rule for introducing the operator U:

$$FX \to UXF.$$

Rule for eliminating the operator U:

$$UXY \to YX.$$

Rule for introducing the operator E_i:

$$F_nX^1 \ldots X^hX^iX^j \ldots X^n \to E_iE_nX^1 \ldots X^hX^j \ldots X^n.$$

Rule for eliminating the operator E_i:

$$E_i F_n X^1 \ldots X^h X^j \ldots X^n \to F_n X^1 \ldots X^h X^i X^j \ldots X^n.$$

Since the rules for introducing and eliminating combinatory operators are determined in conjunction with functions, which are regarded as variables that can be replaced with specific functions of the genotype language, the combinatory operators are not to be assigned specific episemions, but abstract episemion formulas containing variables that can be replaced with specific episemions. For the sake of brevity we will call abstract episemion formulas abstract episemions. Thus, the questions we have just posed, will have to be formulated as follows: What abstract episemions can be assigned to the combinatory operators Cv_{ij}, W, B, L, $K_{(i)}$, I, U, E_i?

Our method for determining which abstract episemion formula is to be assigned to a given combinatory operator consists in the following.

We begin by taking the formula in the left-hand part of the rule for introducing the given combinatory operator and we assign this formula a random abstract episemion z. We regard this formula and the abstract episemion assigned to it as the root of a tree for constructing semions, and we construct the tree by successively breaking this formula down to its elementary components. In the process of constructing the tree we assign each component an abstract episemion in accordance with semion construction rule (b). According to this rule, if a formula X with the abstract episemion z assigned to it breaks down into an operator A and an operand B, then, having assigned the random abstract episemion u to the operand B we have to conclude that the operator A should be assigned the abstract episemion Δuz.

What episemions can be assigned to the combinatory operators Cv_{ij}, W, B, L, $K_{(i)}$, I, U, E_i?

After we have obtained a tree for the formula in the left-hand part of the rule for introducing the combinatory operator, we construct a corresponding tree in the right-hand part of this rule, using the information obtained for the first tree. As a result, we arrive at the determination of what abstract episemion is to be assigned to the corresponding combinatory operator.

We can use a concrete example to show how the above method for determining abstract episemions for combinatory operators is applied. Assume that we want to determine the abstract episemion to be assigned to the combinatory operator B.

In determining the abstract episemion to be assigned to the compositor B we will proceed from the following considerations. Let the expression $F(GX)$ be assigned the abstract episemion z; then, according to semion construction rule (b) it is possible to assume that GX has the abstract episemion v and F has the abstract episemion $\varDelta uz$. This can be shown on the tree:

$$(1) \quad \frac{\varDelta vzF \qquad v(GX)}{zF(GX)}$$

Furthermore, if the expression (GX) has the episemion v, then according to the above semion derivation rule we can assume that X has the episemion v and G has the episemion $\varDelta uv$. Thus, we obtain the tree:

$$(2) \quad \frac{\varDelta vzF \qquad \dfrac{\varDelta uvG \qquad uX}{v(GX)}}{zF(GX)}$$

Now let us construct a tree for the formula $BFGX$. If we assigned the abstract episemion z to the formula $F(GX)$, then we must also assigne this abstract episemion to the formula $BFGX$. We know from tree (1) that the semion X is assigned the abstract episemion u; at the first step in constructing the new tree we will therefore have

$$\frac{\varDelta uzBFG \qquad uX}{zBFGX}$$

We know from tree (1) that the semion G is assigned the abstract episemion $\varDelta uv$; at the second step in constructing the new tree we will therefore, have

$$(3) \quad \frac{\dfrac{\varDelta\varDelta uv\varDelta uzBF \qquad \varDelta uvG}{\varDelta uzBFG} \qquad uX}{zBFGX}$$

We know from tree (2) that the semion F is assigned the abstract episemion $\varDelta vz$; the final step therefore gives us:

$$(4) \quad \frac{\dfrac{\dfrac{\varDelta\varDelta vz\varDelta\varDelta uv\varDelta uzB \qquad \varDelta vzF}{\varDelta\varDelta uv\varDelta uzBF} \qquad \varDelta uvG}{\varDelta uzBFG} \qquad uX}{zBFGX}$$

It can be seen from tree (4) that the combinatory operator B must be assigned the abstract episemion

$$\varDelta\varDelta vz\varDelta\varDelta uv\varDelta uz\,.$$

A similar reasoning determines the abstract episemion to be assigned to the confluentor L. Assume that the expression $FX(GX)$ is assigned the episemion z; then according to semion construction rule (b), if we assume that the expression $G(X)$ has the abstract episemion v, the expression (FX) has the abstract episemion Δvz. Furthermore, if we assume that X has the episemion u, then F must have the episemion $\Delta u \Delta vz$, and G the episemion Δuv. This can all be shown in the form of a tree:

$$(5) \quad \frac{\dfrac{\Delta u \Delta vz F \qquad uX}{\Delta vz\,(FX)} \qquad \dfrac{\Delta uv G \qquad uX}{v\,(GX)}}{zFX\,(GX)}$$

Proceeding from this tree, it is easy to determine the abstract episemion that is to be assigned to the confluentor L. This episemion should have the form: $\Delta \Delta u \Delta vz \Delta \Delta uv \Delta uz$. The operation of the confluentor L can be shown in the following tree:

$$(6) \quad \frac{\dfrac{\dfrac{\Delta \Delta u \Delta vz \Delta \Delta uv \Delta uz L \qquad \Delta u \Delta vz F}{\Delta \Delta uv \Delta uz LF \qquad uvGX}}{\Delta uz LFGX \qquad uX}}{zLFGX}$$

Let us turn to the operator W. Assume that the expression FXX has been assigned the abstract episemion z; then, according to episemion construction rule (b), if we assume that the expression X has the abstract episemion v, the expression FX must have the abstract episemion Δvz. From here it follows that F must have the abstract episemion $\Delta v \Delta vz$. Thus, we obtain the tree:

$$(7) \quad \frac{\dfrac{\Delta v \Delta vz F \qquad vX}{\Delta vz FX} \qquad vX}{zFXX}$$

Proceeding from this tree, it is easy to determine the abstract episemion that is to be assigned to the operator W. This episemion should have the form: $\Delta \Delta v \Delta vz \Delta vz$.

The operation of the operator W can be shown in the following tree:

$$(8) \quad \frac{\dfrac{\Delta \Delta v \Delta vz \Delta vz W \qquad \Delta v \Delta vz F}{\Delta vz WF \qquad vX}}{zWFX}$$

Let us consider the operator U. If we assume that the expression XY has the tree

$$(9) \qquad \frac{\Delta vzX \qquad\qquad vY}{zXY}$$

then proceeding on the basis of this tree the operator U has to be assigned the abstract episemion $\Delta v \Delta \Delta vzz$.

The action of the operator U can be shown in the following tree:

$$(10) \qquad \frac{\dfrac{\Delta v \Delta \Delta vzzU \qquad\qquad vY}{\Delta \Delta vzzUY} \qquad\qquad \Delta vzY}{zUYX}$$

Let us proceed to the operator Cv_{ik}. If F is an n-place function it will be assigned the abstract episemion

$$\Delta z_1 \ldots \Delta z_i \ldots \Delta z_k \ldots z_{n-1}z_n.$$

It follows that the operator Cv_k must be assigned the abstract episemion

$$\Delta \Delta z_1 \ldots \Delta z_i \ldots \Delta z_k \ldots \Delta z_{n-1}z_n \Delta z_1 \ldots \Delta z_k \ldots z_i \ldots \Delta z_{n-1}z_n.$$

Let us take a concrete example. If F_3 is a three-place function, it must be assigned the abstract episemion $\Delta z_1 \Delta z_2 \Delta z_3 U$. Let us construct the tree of this function with its arguments:

$$(11) \qquad \frac{\dfrac{\dfrac{\Delta z_1 \Delta z_2 \Delta z_3 u F_3 \qquad\qquad z_1 X^1}{\Delta z_2 \Delta z_3 u F_3 X^1} \qquad\qquad z_2 X^2}{\Delta z_3 u F_3 X^1 X^2} \qquad\qquad X^3}{u F_3 X^1 X^2 X^3}$$

On the basis of the above general formula of the episemion assigned to the conversion operator Cv_{ik} we can now assign an abstract episemion to a specific conversion operator, if we assume that it has the form Cv_{13} and is applied to the three-place function F_3. In this case the conversion operator Cv_{13} will be assigned the abstract episemion

$$\Delta \Delta z_1 \Delta z_2 \Delta z_3 u \Delta z_3 \Delta z_2 \Delta z_1 u.$$

Let us construct a tree showing the action of the operator Cv_{13} applied to the three-place function F_3:

The operator $K_{(i)}$ is to be assigned an abstract episemion on the basis

$$
(12) \quad \cfrac{\cfrac{\cfrac{\cfrac{\Delta\Delta z_1 \Delta z_2 \Delta z_3 u \Delta z_3 \Delta z_2 \Delta z_1 u C v_{13} \qquad\qquad \Delta z_1 \Delta z_2 \Delta z_3 u F_3}{\Delta z_3 \Delta z_2 \Delta z_1 u C v_{13} F_3 \qquad\qquad z_3 X^3}}{\Delta z_2 \Delta z_1 u C v_{13} F_3 X^3 \qquad\qquad z_2 X^2}}{\Delta z_1 u C v_{13} F_3 X^3 X^2 \qquad\qquad z_1 X^1}}{u C v_{13} F_3 X^3 X^2 X^1}
$$

of the following argument. Let the n-place function F be assigned the episemion $\Delta z_1 ... \Delta z_i \Delta z_j ... \Delta z_{n-1} \Delta z_n$. The function $K_{(i)}$ will then be assigned the abstract episemion

$$\Delta\Delta z_1 ... \Delta z_i \Delta z_j ... \Delta z_{n-1} z_n \Delta z_1 ... \Delta z_i \Delta z_{i+1} \Delta z_j ... \Delta z_{n-1} \Delta z_n.$$

The operator E_i is assigned an abstract episemion as follows: we assume that the n-place function F has the abstract episemion

$$\Delta z_1 ... \Delta z_{i-1} \Delta z_i \Delta z_j ... \Delta z_{n-1} z_n.$$

The operator E should then have the abstract episemion

$$\Delta\Delta z_1 ... \Delta z_{i-1} \Delta z_i \Delta z_j ... \Delta z_{n-1} z_n z_1 ... \Delta z_n \Delta z_j ... z_{n-1} z_n.$$

The operator I should have the abstract episemion Δzz. This is obvious if we assume that the expression X, to which I is applied, has been assigned the abstract episemion z.

To conclude this section we will give a complete list of the combinatory operators treated above together with the episemions assigned them.

$$\Delta\Delta z_1 ... \Delta z_i ... \Delta z_k ... \Delta z_{n-1} z_n \Delta z_1 ... \Delta z_k ... z_i ... \Delta z_{n-1} z_n C v_{ik}$$

$$\Delta\Delta v \Delta vz \Delta vz W$$

$$\Delta\Delta vz \Delta\Delta uv \Delta uz B$$

$$\Delta\Delta u \Delta vz \Delta\Delta uv \Delta uz L$$

$$\Delta\Delta z_1 ... \Delta z_i \Delta z_j ... \Delta z_{n-1} z_n \Delta z_1 ... \Delta z_i \Delta z_{i+1} \Delta z_j ... \Delta z_{n-1} z_n K_{(i)}$$

$$\Delta zz I$$

$$\Delta v \Delta\Delta vzz U$$

$$\Delta\Delta z_1 ... \Delta z_{i-1} \Delta z_i \Delta z_j ... \Delta z_{n-1} z_n \Delta z_1 ... \Delta z_{i-1} \Delta z_j ... \Delta z_{n-1} z E_i.$$

10. THE HYBRID GENOTYPE LANGUAGE

In an extended semion calculus some elementary semions are interpreted as grammatical objects, and other elementary semions are interpreted as lexical objects. If we treat the elementary semions interpreted as lexical objects as lexical variables, we will be able to incorporate into the genotype language lexical constants substituted for the lexical variables. The lexemes of various specific languages are used as lexical constants. By substituting lexical constants for lexical variables we obtain mixed languages, each of which has two components: a grammatical and a lexical. The grammar of the genotype language will be the grammatical component of all the languages obtained in this manner. The set of lexemes of the appropriate natural language (by lexemes here are conventionally meant here words of natural languages considered as roots or amorphous lexical stems) will be the lexical component of each of these languages.

Thus, we obtain hybrid languages (the grammar of the genotype language + the lexical roots or stems of a natural language: the hybrid Russian language, hybrid French, hybrid Vietnamese, etc.). The grammar of the genotype language is the grammatical component of each of these languages.

The hybrid genotype language can be used to give a graphic notation of the process of semantic derivation in natural languages.

11. SEMANTIC AXIOMS

Let us proceed to a treatment of semantic axioms and rules, which for illustration purposes will be interpreted principally on the basis of Russian language materials. It goes without saying that our list of axioms and rules is far from complete. We shall concentrate mostly on simple sentences, and will hardly consider at all the axioms and rules which concern transformations over several sentences. We can add that in general no list of axioms and rules should be considered closed. On the contrary, every formal system should serve as the object of experimentation on an empirical body of material, and depending on the results of this experimentation, a list of semantic axioms and rule can be modified and be enlarged.

The semantic axioms will be given by a generative device which contains:

(1) A set of semions, known as the lexicon of the semantic system. All semions belonging to this lexicon are divided into non-terminal and terminal semions. Terminal semions are those to which no rule of the semantic system can be applied. Non-terminal semions are such to which rules of the semantic system can be applied. Among the non-terminal semions we distinguish the initial semion S, with which the generation of the axioms begins. The notion of a terminal semion is relative: if we hold ourselves to within the genotype language, the elementary semions of the genotype language have to be considered to be terminal; if we turn to the hybrid languages, the corresponding lexemes are regarded as terminal semions. To distinguish between the terminal and non-terminal semions of the genotype

language, we shall denote terminal semions with capital letters supplied with dots above them, and non-terminal semions with these same capital letters, but without the dots. Examples of terminal symbols: $\dot{P}, \dot{P}^1, \dot{P}^2, \dot{T}, \dot{T}^1, \dot{T}^2$. Examples of non-terminal symbols P, P^1, P^2, T, T^1, T^2. Certain symbols, Ng for example, can only function as terminal symbols in the genotype language, and it is not necessary therefore to dot them.

(2) A set of semantic axiom generation rules is presented in two forms. Either:

$$Z \rightarrow (XY),$$

where X is the operator, Y the operand and (XY) the result of applying the operator to the operand Y. The symbol Z is to be considered a simple expression for which the expression (XY) can be substituted. In accordance with this it is understood that if Z belongs to the episemion q and Y belongs to the episemion p, X must belong to the episemion Δpq.

Or:

$$U \rightarrow V.$$

where U is to be considered a simple expression for which the simple expression V can be substituted; it is implied here that if U belongs to the episemion q, V must also belong to the episemion q.

Braces are used when two rules are fused. For example, instead of the two rules

(1) $X \rightarrow Y$
(2) $X \rightarrow Z$

we can write a single rule with braces:

$$X \rightarrow \left\{ \begin{array}{c} Y \\ Z \end{array} \right\}.$$

Let us examine the lexicon of the semantic system developed below. To it belong:

βS – the global symbol for a sentence.

$\beta S'$ – the symbol for a sentence that functions as an argument, also called an 'embedded' sentence.

$\Delta \beta \beta M d$ – the symbol for a one-place modal predicate. The argument of a modal predicate is always an embedded sentence. Modality is understood in the broadest sense as the attitude of the speaker to an utterance. Modality is considered to be an obligatory part of all sentences. Modality can be expressed in natural languages both explicitly and implicitly. For example, in the sentence *Verojatno, poezd opasdyvaet* 'Probably the train is late' the high degree of probability of an event is expressed by means of a parenthetical modal word. In the sentence *Poezd opazdyvaet* 'The train is late', however, the speaker's certainty that the event is indeed taking place is implied.

Under the simple sentence *Poezd opazdyvaet* 'The train is late' is implied a complex sentence of the type *Ja uveren* 'I am sure' or *Ja utverždaju, čto poezd opazdyvaet* 'I assert that the train is late'.

A class of two-place modal operators:

$\Delta\alpha\Delta\beta\beta Af$ – the symbol for a two-place predicate of assertion, for example, *Ja utverždaju, čto poezd opazdyvaet* 'I assert that the train is late'.

$\Delta\alpha\Delta\beta\beta Ng$ – the symbol for a two-place predicate of negation, e.g. *Ja otricaju, čto on videl nas* 'I deny that he saw us'.

$\Delta\alpha\Delta\beta\beta Db$ – the symbol for a two-place predicate of obligation, e.g. *On sčitaet objazatel'nym, čtoby vse prisutstvovali* 'He considers it obligatory that everybody attend'.

$\Delta\alpha\Delta\beta\beta Ps$ – the symbol for a two-place predicate of possibility, e.g. *Ja sčitaju vozmožnym, čtoby nekotorye otsutstvovali* 'I think it possible for some to be absent'.

$\Delta\alpha\Delta\beta\beta Em$ – the symbol for a two-place emotive predicate.

Em is an analogue of emotive verbs such as *ogorčat'* 'grieve', *radovat'* 'gladden', *serdit'* 'anger', *besit'* 'enrage', *vosxiščat'* 'delight' *rasstraivat'* 'confuse'. The first argument of a modal emotive predicate is a key-word, and the second argument is a sentence. For example, *Menja raduet, čto vy zdorovy* 'I am glad that you are healthy/It gladdens me...'; *Brata vosxiščaet to, kak poet sestra* 'Brother is delighted with the way his sister sings/It delights brother...'.

$\Delta\alpha\Delta\beta\beta Fi$ – the symbol for a two-place predicate of fictive action such as *kazat'sja* 'seem', *predstavljat'sja* 'appear', *voobražat'* 'imagine'. As was the case for emotive verbs, the operator of fictive action first operates on a term, than on an embedded sentence. For example, *Mne kažetsja, čto vy ošibaetes'* '*It seems* to me you are mistaken'.

$\Delta\alpha\Delta\beta\beta Mt$ – the symbol for two-place predicates of mental perceptions. *Mt* is an analogue of verbs of the type *dumat'* 'think', *verit'* 'believe', *polagat'* 'suppose', *sčitat'* 'consider'. For example, *Ja dumaju, čto vy ošibaetes'* 'I think you are mistaken'.

$\Delta\alpha\Delta\beta\beta Vl$ – the symbol for two-place predicates of desire and will. *Vl* is an analogue of volative verbs such as *xotet'* 'want', *želat'* 'desire' *predpočitat'* 'prefer', *mečtat'* 'dream about', *stremit'sja* 'strive'. For example, *Mne xočetsja, čtoby on priexal* 'I want him to come'; *Ja predpočitaju, čtoby vy ostalis' doma* 'I prefer you to stay at home'.

ΔαΔββQ – the symbol for two-place predicates of question, e.g. *Ja sprašivaju, kto rešil zadaču* 'I am asking who solved the problem'.

ΔαΔββEx – the symbol for predicates of exclamation, e.g. *Galilej voskliknul, čto zemlja vertitsja* 'Galileo exclaimed that the Earth revolves'.

It follows from the above that our understanding of modality is very broad. Modality includes assertions about the truth of a fact or event, the negation of its realizability, belief in its necessity or possibility, emotional relation to an event, the notion of an event as fictive, desirable, doubtful, etc. It is quite possible that the class of modal predicates can be detailed even more.

ΔαβCa' – is a causative complex consisting of a causative verb together with its object and embedded sentence, i.e., the causator, the object of causation and the caused situation. For example, *Prikazal emu, čtoby on vstal* 'Told, ordered him to stand up'. The application of a causative complex to a term generates a causative sentence.

ΔβΔαβCa" is a causative sub-complex consisting of a causator and an object of the causation, for example, *Prikazal emu* 'Ordered him'. The application of a causative sub-complex to a sentence, then to a term, generates a causative sentence.

ΔβΔαβCa is the causator, namely, *prikazal* 'told, ordered'. The application of the causator to the object of the causation generates the causative sub-complex *Ca"*. The application of the sub-complex *Ca"* to a sentence generates the causative complex *Ca'*. As was indicated above, the final step in the derivation of a causative sentence is the application of the causative complex to a term.

ΔβΔββC – the coordinator or a two-place predicate connecting sentences. The conjunctions *i* 'and', *a* 'and' and other function as analogues of the coordinator in natural languages.

ΔβΔββAl – the alternator, also a two-place predicate that functions as the analogue of conjunctions such as *ili...ili* 'either...or'.

ΔβΔββIm – the implicator, the analogue of the conjunctions *esli...to* 'if...then'.

ΔβΔββLc – the localizator, or a two-place predicate that localizes situations in time or space. *Lc* is the analogue of the words *kogda* 'when', *v to vremja kak* 'at the time that', *posle togo kak* 'after', *pered tem kak* 'before', *tam...gde* 'there...where'.

ΔβΔββCj – the conjunctor, the class of two-place predicates *C*, *Al*, *Im* and *Lc*, which connect sentences.

ΔββCj' – is a conjunctor complex which includes the conjunctor, i.e., one of the coordinative two-place predicates listed above, and the first sentence to which it is applied, e.g.... *a devočka spit* 'and the girl is sleeping', or *my pojdem, ili...* 'we will go or ...', *Esli vy prišlete knigu, to* 'If you send the book then...' *Gde my vstretilis'*, *tam...* 'Where we met, there...'. The application of the conjunctor complex generates the analogue of a complex sentence.

$\Delta\alpha\beta P_k$ – the symbol for a propositional complex consisting of the aspectual operator *As* or the operator of verbs of perception *Pr* and its argument, the embedded sentence *S''*. Unlike *S'*, the embedded sentence *S''* is a pure situation free from modality. The application of the propositional complex P_k to the term *T* generates a sentence.

$\Delta\beta\Delta\alpha\beta As$ – the symbol for the aspectual operator, e.g. *načal* 'began', *prodolžaet* 'continues', whose argument is *S''* – a pure situation. The application of the aspectual operator to the embedded sentence *S''*, for example, *Čitaet brat* 'Brother reads' and then to a term, for example, *brat* 'brother' generates an aspectual sentence of the type **Brat načal, brat čitaet* 'Brother began, brother read'. The symbol *As* is non-terminal.

The class of terminal aspectual operators:

$\Delta\beta\Delta\alpha\beta Ig$ – the ingressive, or the operator for the beginning of an action.

$\Delta\beta\Delta\alpha\beta If$ – the imperfective, or the operator of duration or incompleteness of an action.

$\Delta\beta\Delta\alpha\beta Re$ – the resultative, or the operator for a result of an action

$\Delta\beta\Delta\alpha\beta It$ – the iterative, or the operator for repeated action.

$\Delta\beta\Delta\alpha\beta Tm$ – the terminative, or the operator for a terminated action.

$\Delta\beta\Delta\alpha\beta Pr$ – the symbol for the operator of verbs of perception such as *vidit* 'sees', *slyšit* 'hears, smells'.

Like the operator *As*, the operator *Pr* as the first argument has an embedded sentence *S''*, and a term as the second argument, for example, *Ja slyšu, kak pojut pticy* 'I hear the birds singing'.

$\beta S''$ – the symbol for a pure situation conceived of as being outside modality.

$\Delta\alpha\beta P_x$ – a one-place predicate where *X* denotes the variable that takes on value of the case indices *a, o, i, f, l* and *c*.

αT – a term with any case index.

$\Delta\alpha\Delta\alpha\beta P_{yz}$ – a two-place predicate where *y* and *z* denote variables which take on the following case index values: $z: f, a$ and $y: o, l, i, c$.

This limitation on the conbinability of the cases is caused by the fact that certain standard situations function as axioms. When a standard is selected for a situation one has to take semantic accent into account. Of the various possibilities for the selection of case distribution it seems most natural to assume that the semantic accent falls on animate objects, that is, on the affective and agentive.

Hb – the symbol for a two-place predicate with a possessive meaning that is an analogue of verbs of the type *imet', vladet', obladat'* 'own, have, possess'.

Es – the symbol for a two-place copulative predicate, e.g. *On byl učenym* 'He was a scholar'.

We propose the following rules to generate axioms for a formal semantic system:

(1) $\quad S \rightarrow \begin{Bmatrix} (MdS') \\ (Cj'S) \end{Bmatrix}$

(2) $\quad S' \rightarrow \begin{Bmatrix} (MdS') \\ (Ca'T) \\ (P_kT) \\ S'' \end{Bmatrix}$

(3) $\quad Cj' \rightarrow CjS$

(4) $\quad Md \rightarrow \begin{Bmatrix} (AfT) \\ (NgT) \\ (DbT) \\ (PsT) \\ (QT) \\ (ExT) \\ (EmT) \\ (FiT) \\ (VlT) \\ (MtT) \end{Bmatrix}$

(5.1) $\quad S'' \rightarrow (P_xT)$

(5.2) $\quad x \rightarrow a, f, o, i, l, c$

(6.1) $\quad P_x \rightarrow (P_{yz}T)$

(6.2) $\quad y \rightarrow o, l, i, c, f$

(6.3) $\quad z \rightarrow f, a \quad \text{with} \quad y \neq z$

(7) $\quad Ca' \rightarrow (Ca''S')$

(8) $\quad Ca'' \rightarrow (CaT)$

(9) $\quad Cj \rightarrow \begin{Bmatrix} C \\ Al \\ Im \\ Lc \end{Bmatrix}$

(10) $\quad P_k \rightarrow \begin{Bmatrix} (AsS'') \\ (PrS'') \end{Bmatrix}$

$$(11) \qquad As \rightarrow \begin{cases} Ig \\ If \\ Re \\ It \\ Fm \end{cases}$$

$$(12) \qquad T \rightarrow \dot{T}, \dot{T}^1, \ldots$$

$$(13) \qquad P_a \rightarrow \dot{P}_a, \dot{P}_a^1, \ldots$$

$$(14) \qquad P_f \rightarrow \dot{P}_f, \dot{P}_f^1, \ldots$$

$$(15) \qquad P_o \rightarrow \dot{P}_o, \dot{P}_o^1, \ldots$$

$$(16) \qquad P_i \rightarrow \dot{P}_i, \dot{P}_i, \ldots$$

$$(17) \qquad P_l \rightarrow \dot{P}_l, \dot{P}_l^1, \ldots$$

$$(18) \qquad P_c \rightarrow \dot{P}_c, \dot{P}_c^1, \ldots$$

$$(19) \qquad P_{of} \rightarrow \begin{cases} \dot{P}_{of}, \dot{P}_{of}^1, \ldots \\ Hb \end{cases}$$

$$(20) \qquad P_{lf} \rightarrow \dot{P}_{lf}, \dot{P}_{lf}^1, \ldots$$

$$(21) \qquad P_{if} \rightarrow \dot{P}_{if}, \dot{P}_{if}^1, \ldots$$

$$(22) \qquad P_{fo} \rightarrow \begin{cases} \dot{P}_{fo}, \dot{P}_{fo}^1, \ldots \\ Es \end{cases}$$

$$(23) \qquad P_{oa} \rightarrow \dot{P}_{oa}, \dot{P}_{oa}^1, \ldots$$

$$(24) \qquad P_{la} \rightarrow \dot{P}_{la}, \dot{P}_{la}^1, \ldots$$

$$(25) \qquad P_{ia} \rightarrow \dot{P}_{ia}, \dot{P}_{ia}^1, \ldots$$

$$(26) \qquad P_{ca} \rightarrow \dot{P}_{ca}, \dot{P}_{ca}^1, \ldots$$

$$(27) \qquad P_{fa} \rightarrow \dot{P}_{fa}, \dot{P}_{fa}^1, \ldots$$

Let us take up some examples of semantic axiom generation. A derivation of the axiom X from the initial symbol S will be said to be a series of semions $Y^1, \ldots, Y^n$, such that $Y^1 = S$, $Y^n = X$ and Y^{i+1} is directly derived from Y^i by applying one of the axiom generation rules (for $i = 1, \ldots, n-1$).

All derivations are described in the form of tables consisting of three columns: (1) the number of the line on which one of the members of the series $Y^1, \ldots, Y''$ is written is indicated in the first column. (2) Y^{i+1} is given in the second column. (3) the number of the rules by which is directly derived from Y^i is given in the third column.

We will agree to apply the greatest number of semantic rules possible to a given semion at each step of the derivation.

We will also agree to supply terminal semions of the same kind with upper indices from left to right when we apply rules 11–27. The indices are placed in the last line of the derivation.

Coreferential terms are supplied with identical apostrophes.

Examples of axiom derivations.

Let us derive the axiom $Af\dot{T}(\dot{P}_f\dot{T})$, which functions as the analogue of phrases such as *Ja utverždaju, čto vy zabluždaetes'* 'I assert that you are mistaken'. In a hybrid language this axiom corresponds to the following notation: *utverždat' ja(zabluždat'sja vy)* 'assert I(mistaken you)'. This axiom is obtained from the initial symbol S in six steps:

(1) S

(2) (MdS') rule (1)

(3) $((AfT)\,S'')$ rules (2), (4)

(4) $((AfT)\,(P_xT))$ rule (5.1)

(5) $((AfT)\,(P_fT))$ rule (5.2)

(6) $((Af\dot{T})\,(\dot{P}_f\dot{T}))$ rules (12), (14)

The sixth line of the derivation corresponds to the axiom when the parentheses are removed.

Let us give some examples of more complex derivations.

Let us derive the axiom $Ng\dot{T}^1(P_2(\dot{P}_a\dot{T}^2)\,\dot{T}^3)$, which is an analogue of phrases with negative modality and an embedded sentence with verbs of perception. This axiom corresponds to sentences such as *Ja otricaju, čto vy videli, kak on bežal* 'I negate that you saw him running'. In a hybrid language this phrase is written: *otricat' ja (videt' (bežat' on) vy)* 'negate I(see(run he) you)'.

The axiom is derived as follows:

(1) S

(2) (MdS') rule (1)

(3) $((NgT)\,(P_kT))$ rules (4), (2)

(4) $(Ng\dot{T})\,((P_2S'')\,\dot{T})$ rules (10), (12)

(5) $(Ng\dot{T})\,((Pr\,(P_xT))\,\dot{T}))$ rule (5.1)

(6) $(Ng\dot{T})\,((Pr\,(P_a\dot{T}))\,\dot{T}))$ rules (5.2), (12)

(7) $(Ng\dot{T}^1)\,((Pr\,(\dot{P}_a\dot{T}^2))\,\dot{T}^3))$ rule (13).

The last line of the derivation corresponds to the axiom. After applying the parentheses omission rule the last line assumes the desired form

$$Ng\dot{T}^1\,(Pr\,(\dot{P}_a\dot{T}^2)\,\dot{T}^3).$$

Let us derive the axiom

$$Em\dot{T}^1 (Vl\dot{T}^2 (P_{oa}\dot{T}^3\dot{T}^4))$$

which is an analogue of phrases with dual modality – an 'external' and an 'internal'. This axiom models complex sentences of the type *Menja raduet, čto on xočet, čtoby doč' okončila institut* 'I am glad he wants his daughter to finish the institute'. In a hybrid language this phrase is written: *radovat' ja(xotet' on(končit' institut doč'))* 'gladden I(want he (finish institute daughter))'.

Axioms with dual modality are obtained by means of the following derivation:

(1)	S	
(2)	(MdS')	rule (1)
(3)	$(Md(MdS'))$	rule (2)
(4)	$((EmT)((VlT)S''))$	rules (4), (2)
(5)	$((Em\dot{T})((Vl\dot{T})(P_xT)))$	rules (12), (5.1)
(6)	$((Em\dot{T})((Vl\dot{T})((P_{yz}T)\dot{T})))$	rules (6.1), (12)
(7)	$((Em\dot{T})((Vl\dot{T})((P_{oa}\dot{T})\dot{T})))$	rules (6.2), (6.3), (12)
(8)	$((Em\dot{T}^1)((Vl\dot{T}^2)((\dot{P}_{oa}\dot{T}^3)\dot{T}^4)))$	rules (23).

After the parentheses are omitted the last line of the derivation assumes the form

$$Em\dot{T}^1 (Vl\dot{T}^2 (\dot{P}_{oa}\dot{T}^3\dot{T}^4)).$$

Let us derive the axiom

$$Im((Db\dot{T}^{1'})(P_a\dot{T}^{2''}))(P_{fa}\dot{T}^{3''}\dot{T}^{4'})$$

which functions as the analogue to complex sentences with implication. The axiom also contains a sentence with the modality operator in an embedded sentence. This axiom approximately corresponds to natural language phrases such as *Esli vy somnevaetes', čto on pridet, to (vy) pozvonite emu* 'If you doubt that he's coming, then call him'. In a hybrid language this phrase is written:

Al (*somnevat'sja vy'* 'doubt you') (*pritti on''* 'come he')) (*pozvonit' on'' vy'* 'call he you'). Identical terms are marked with apostrophes.

This axiom, which contains the alternator and modality in an embedded sentence, is obtained through the following derivation:

(1)	S	
(2)	$Cj'S$	rule (1)

(3)	$(CjS)\,S$	rule (3)
(4)	$(Im\,(MdS'))\,S''$	rules (9), (2)
(5)	$(Im\,((DbT)\,S''))\,(P_xT)$	rules (4), (5.1)
(6)	$(Im\,((Db\dot{T})\,(P_xT)))\,((P_{yz}T)\,\dot{T})$	rules (5.1), (6.1), (12)
(7)	$(Im\,((Db\dot{T}')\,P_a\dot{T}'))\,(((P_{fa}\dot{T}'')\,\dot{T}')$	rules (13), (6.2)
(8)	$(Im\,((Db\dot{T}^{1\prime})\,\dot{P}_a\dot{T}^{2\prime\prime})))\,((\dot{P}_{fa}\dot{T}^{3\prime\prime})\,\dot{T}^{4\prime})$	rule (27).

By applying the parentheses omission rule we obtain the desired axiom.

We shall now demonstrate the derivations of some axioms containing causative constructions, for example, an axiom with modality as an operator in an embedded sentence with one causative construction:

$$Ps\dot{T}^1\,(Ca\dot{T}^{2\prime}\,(P_a\dot{T}^{3\prime})\,\dot{T}^4).$$

This axiom corresponds to phrases such as *Ja predpolagaju, čto brat zastavljaet sestru, čtoby sestra rabotala* 'I assume that the brother makes the sister work that brother makes sister that sister work'.

In a hybrid language this phrase is written: *Predpolagaju ja (zastavljat' sestra (rabotat' sestra) brat)* 'Assume I(make sister(work sister)brother)'. Here is the derivation of this axiom.

(1)	S	
(2)	MdS'	rule (1)
(3)	$((PsT)\,(Ca'T))$	rules (2), (4)
(4)	$((Ps\dot{T})\,((Ca''S')\,\dot{T}))$	rules (7), (12)
(5)	$((Ps\dot{T})\,(((CaT)\,S'')\,\dot{T}))$	rules (8), (2)
(6)	$((Ps\dot{T})\,(((Ca\dot{T})\,(P_aT))\,\dot{T}))$	rules (5.1), (12)
(7)	$((Ps\dot{T})\,(((Ca\dot{T})\,(P_a\dot{T}))\,\dot{T}))$	rules (5.2), (12)
(8)	$((Ps\dot{T}^1)\,(((Ca\dot{T}^{2\prime})\,(\dot{P}_a\dot{T}^{3\prime}))\,\dot{T}^4))$	rule (13).

By omitting the superfluous parentheses we obtain the desired axiom.

We shall give the derivation of one more axiom which is interesting from the point of view of a possibility for the recursive generation of causative constructions

$$PsT^1\,(CaT^{2\prime}\,(CaT^{3\prime\prime}\,(P_aT^{4\prime\prime})\,T^{5\prime})\,T^6).$$

This axiom correponds to phrases such as *Ja polagaju, čto otec velel bratu, čtoby brat zastavil sestru, čtoby sestra učilas* 'I assume that father told brother that brother make sister that sister study/I assume that father told brother to make sister study'. In a hydrid language this phrase is written:

polagat' ja (*velet' brat* (*zastavit' sestra* (*učit'sja sestra*) *brat otec*). 'Assume I (tell brother(make sister(study sister) brother) father)'.

Below is the derivation of an axiom with a dual causative embedding:

(1)	S	
(2)	(MdS')	rule (1)
(3)	$((PsT)(Ca'T))$	rules (4), (2)
(4)	$((Ps\dot{T})((Ca''S')\,\dot{T}))$	rules (12), (7)
(5)	$((Ps\dot{T})((Ca''(Ca'T))\,\dot{T}))$	rule (2)
(6)	$((Ps\dot{T})((Ca''((Ca''S')\,\dot{T}))\,\dot{T}))$	rules (7), (12)
(7)	$((Ps\dot{T})(((CaT)(((CaT)\,S'')\,\dot{T}))\,\dot{T}))$	rules (8), (2)
(8)	$((Ps\dot{T})(((Ca\dot{T})(((Ca\dot{T})(P_xT))\,\dot{T}))\,\dot{T}))$	rules (5.1), (12)
(9)	$(Ps\dot{T})(((Ca\dot{T})(((Ca\dot{T})(P_aT))\,\dot{T}))\,\dot{T}))$	rules (5.2), (12)
(10)	$((Ps\dot{T}^1)(((Ca\dot{T}^{2'})(((Ca\dot{T}^{3''})(\dot{P}_aT^4))\,\dot{T}^{5'}))\,\dot{T}^{6''}))$	
		rule (13).

When we remove the parentheses the tenth line assumes the form of the desired axiom.

The axioms whose derivation has been shown above are paired with far from elementary natural language phrases. As we have seen, these are sentences complicated by coordination or subordination. At the same time, from the point of view of the genotype language all of these structures are simple, since they contain nothing but pure predicate structures.

It must be noted that the axioms considered above only correspond exactly to phrases of a hybrid language. Natural language phrases paired with them correspond only approximately. More exact genotype analogues of these phrases are obtained by applying semantic derivation rules to the axioms. These rules will be examined in the next section of the present chapter.

12. SEMANTIC RULES

Let us turn to the semantic rules. It must be kept in mind that all of the semantic rules given below, except the reduction rules, are reciprocal, i.e., if $A \Rightarrow B$ occurs, then $B \Rightarrow A$ also occurs.

As for the reduction rules, they are reciprocal only at the level of interpreting terms as pronouns. For example, if we reduce the sentence *Mal'ciki čitajut knigu* 'The boys read the book' and *Čitajut knigu* '(They) read the book'', the reduced sentence can only be transformed back into the sentence *Kto-to čitaet knigu* 'Someone reads the book'.

The Semantic rules can be applied both to axioms and to derived structures obtained through the preceding application of the semantic rules. A non-axiom to which a semantic rules is applied is called an intermediate structure. The necessity of obtaining intermediate structures depends on the fact that many axioms correspond to non-grammatical phrases of natural language. The intermediate structures also correspond to non-grammatical phrases of natural language.

Besides combinatory operators, which will be used in the semantic rules, we shall introduce operators of the group H, which have the following categorial characteristics

$$\Delta\Delta\beta\beta\Delta\alpha\beta H_1$$

$$\Delta\Delta\beta\Delta\alpha\beta\Delta\alpha\Delta\alpha\beta H_2$$

$$\Delta\Delta\alpha\Delta\beta\beta\Delta\alpha\Delta\alpha\beta H_3$$

$$\Delta\Delta\alpha\Delta\beta\Delta\alpha\beta\Delta\alpha\Delta\alpha\Delta\alpha\beta H_4.$$

A role of the operators of the group H consists in the deproposition or nominalization of embedded sentences. H_1 transforms an embedded sentence functioning as the argument of the one-place predicate $P_\beta S$ into a noun phrase, H_2 and H_3 nominalize embedded sentences functioning as one of the arguments of two-place predicates. H_2 operates on predicates of the type $P_{\beta\alpha}ST$, and H_3 operates on predicates such as $P_{\alpha\beta}TS$. H_4 transforms middle arguments – sentences in three-place predicates of the type $P_{\alpha\beta\alpha}TST$ – into noun phrases.

In addition, we introduce the semion $\Delta\beta\Delta\alpha\beta$, Cp, which functions as an analogue of desemanticized copulative verbs such as *delat'* 'do'. *okazyvat'* 'exert', *proizvodit'* 'produce', *vypolnjat'* 'perform'.

12.1. *Rules with combinatory operators*

(1) Argument conversion rule

$$F_n T^1 \dots T^i \dots T^k \dots T^n \rightarrow Cv_{ik}F_n T^1 \dots T^k \dots T^i \dots T^n.$$

(2) Identical argument fusion rule

$$F_2 XX \rightarrow WF_2 X.$$

(3) Function composition rule

$$F(GX) \rightarrow BFGX.$$

(4) Confluence rule

$$FX(GX) \rightarrow LFGX.$$

(5) Fictive argument introduction rule

$$F_n X^1 \ldots X^i X^j \ldots X^n \rightarrow K_{(i)} F_n X^1 \ldots X^i X^{i+1} X^j \ldots X^n.$$

(6) Identification rule

$$X \rightarrow JX.$$

(7) Argument and function role transposition rule

$$FX \rightarrow UXF.$$

(8) Argument elimination rule

$$F_n X^1 \ldots X^k X^i X^j \ldots X^n \rightarrow E_i F_n X^1 \ldots X^n X^j \ldots X_n.$$

12.2 *Special rules*

(9) Deproposition rules

(9.1) $P_\beta S \rightarrow H^1 P_\beta (R_\alpha S)$

(9.2) $P_{\beta\alpha} ST \rightarrow H^2 P_{\beta\alpha} (R_\alpha S) T$

(9.3) $P_{\alpha\beta} TS \rightarrow H^3 P_{\alpha\beta} T (R_\alpha S)$

(9.4) $P_{\alpha\beta\alpha} TST \rightarrow H^4 P_{\alpha\beta\alpha} T (R_\alpha S) T.$

(10) Coordination rules

(10.1) $CS^1 S^2 \rightarrow CS^2 S^1$

(10.2) $C (P^1 T^1) (P^1 T^2) \rightarrow P^1 (CT^1 T^2)$

(10.3) $C (P^1 T^1) (P^2 T^1) \rightarrow (CP^1 P^2) T^1.$

(11) Alternation rules

(11.1) $AS^1 S^2 \rightarrow AS^2 S^1$

(11.2) $A (P^1 T^1) (P^1 T^2) \rightarrow P^1 (AT^1 T^2)$

(11.3) $A (P^1 T^1) (P^2 T^1) \rightarrow (AP^1 P^2) T^1.$

(12) Relativization rules

(12.1) $C (P^1 T_1^1) (P^2 T^1) \rightarrow P^2 (R_{\alpha'} (P^1 T^1)) T^1$

(12.2) $Im (P^1 T^1) (P^2 T^1) \rightarrow P^2 (R_{\alpha'} (P^1 T^1)) T^1.$

(13) Pronominalization rules

(13.1) $P^1 T^1 (P^2 T^1) \rightarrow P^1 T^1 (P^2 T_{pr}^1)$

(13.2) $\begin{Bmatrix} C \\ Im \\ A \\ Lc \end{Bmatrix} (P^1 T^1) (P^2 T^2) \rightarrow \begin{Bmatrix} C \\ Im \\ A \\ Lc \end{Bmatrix} (P^1 T^1) (P^2 T_{pr}^1)$

(13.3) $P^1 (R_{\alpha'} (P^2 T^1)) T^1 \rightarrow P (R_{\alpha'} (P^2 T_{rl}^1)) T^1.$

(14) Interrogative sentence rule

$$QT^1\,(PT^2T^3) \rightarrow \begin{Bmatrix} QT^1\,(PT_Q^2T^3) \\ QT^1\,(PT^2T_Q^3) \end{Bmatrix}.$$

(15) Copulative predicate introduction rule

$$PT \rightarrow Cp\,(PT^1)\,T^1.$$

(16) Rules for transforming two-place predicates into three-place predicates

(16.1) $B\,(LCa)\,HbT_0^1T_f^2T_a^3 \rightarrow P_{ofa}T_0^1T_f^2T_a^3$

(16.2) $B\,(LCa)\,P_{oi}T_0^1T_i^2T_a^3 \rightarrow P_{oia}T_0^1T_i^2T_a^3.$

(17) Rule connecting Es and Hb

$$HbT_0^1T_f^2 \rightarrow EsT_f^2T_0^1.$$

(18) Noun phrase substitution rule

$$R_\alpha\,(PT) \rightarrow (R_{\alpha'}P)\,T.$$

12.3 *Notes*

The first group of rules, i.e., those with an application of combinatory operators, need no explanations, since they have been treated in detail in the section on combinatory operators.

Rule (9), or the deproposition rule, functions as an analogue of the process by which an embedded sentence is nominalized. Dependeing on the nature of the predicate structure, either H^1 or H^2 or H^3 or H^4 is applied. The application of the group H involves the appearance of the relator R_α as the operator of the embedded sentence.

R_α functions in this cases as an analogue of various nominalizators, specifically, the conjunctions *čto* 'that', *kak* 'how, that', *čtoby* 'that, so that', etc. In natural language rule (9.2), for example, looks like: *Ja slyšu* 'I hear': *on poet* 'he sings' → *Ja slyšu kak on poet* 'I hear him singing'. Rule (9.3): *Ja polagaju* 'I assume': *vy ošibaetes'* 'you are mistaken' *Ja polagaju čto vy ošibaetes'* 'I assume that you are mistaken'.

The rules under (10), or the coordination rules, show its commutativity, e.g. *Otec spit, a mat' čitatet* 'Father is sleeping and mother is reading' → *Mat' čitaet, a otec spit* 'Mother is reading and father is sleeping' (10.1). Moreover, the coordination rules show that it is possible to obtain sentences with homogeneous sentence parts from compound sentences which contain identical predicates (10.2) and identical terms (10.3).

Rules (11) show that the alternator has the same properties as the coordinator.

The rules under (12), i.e., the relativization rules, show how conjunctor structures, specifically, coordination and implication, are transformed into relative sentences. In accordance with rule (12) the coordinator block $C(P'T')$ is transformed into the analogue of a relative sentence $R_{\alpha'}(P'T')$. $R_{\alpha'}$ is the relator and indicates that the predicate structure in this instance becomes the operator of the term $R_{\alpha'}(P^1T^1)$.

Rule (12.2) shows similar transformations on the implicative block $Im(P^1T^1)$. Transformation (12.1) can be illustrated as *Prišla devuška* 'A girl came' *i devuška zvonila* 'the girl rang, and the girl called' → *Prišla devuška, kotoraja zvonila* 'There came a girl who called'. (The word *kotoroja* is obtained by applying the pronominalization rule (13.3).) Rule (12.2) corresponds to transformations of the type *Esli deti bezdel'ničajut, to deti šaljat* 'If children are idle then children are naughty' → *Deti, kotorye bezdel'ničajut, šaljat* 'Children that are idle are naughty, get into mischief' (*kotorye* is also a result of pronominalization).

Rules (13), i.e., the pronominalization rules, have to do with transformations of identical terms in the main and embedded clauses or clauses joined by a conjunctor. Thus, (13.1) corresponds to transformations such as *Sestra uverena: sestra ošiblas'* 'Sister is sure: sister has made a mistake' → *Sestra uverena: ona Ošiblas'* 'Sister is sure: she has made a mistake'. Rule (13.2) can be interpreted, for example, as *Esli brat pridet, to brat pomožet* 'If brother comes, then brother will help' → *Esli brat pridet, to on pomožet* 'If brother comes he will help'. The index *pr* on the term *T* indicates that the term is pronominalized. Rule (13.3) shows how a term contained in a relative construction and identical with one of the terms of the main clause is then substituted by a relative pronoun, designated T_{rl}, e.g. *Bežit čelovek, čelovek opozdal* 'A man is running, a man is late' → *Bežit čelovek, kotoryj opozdal* 'The man who is late is running'.

Rule 14, or the rule for interrogative sentences, shows how a general question is transformed into a special one. One of the terms of the embedded clause is replaced by an interrogative word, e.g.: *Ja sprašivaju: brat živet v Moskve?* 'I ask: does the brother live in Moscow?' → *Ja sprašivaju: kto živet v Moskve?* 'I ask: who lives in Moscow?', or *Ja sprašivaju, gde živet brat?* 'I ask where the brother lives'. The interrogative word is written T_Q.

Rule (15), or the copulative predicate introduction rule, is a transformation of the pure situation *PT* into one of the arguments of the two-place copulative predicate *Cp*, whose second argument is the term identical with the term of the embedded clause. The application of rule (15) obtains an intermediate structure which has no grammatical interpretation in Russian: *Mal'čik rabotaet* 'The boy works' → **Mal'cki delaet, mal'cik rabotaet* 'The boy does, the boy works'. To be able to obtain the genotype analogue of the correct sentence *Mal'cik vypolnjaet rabotu* 'The boy does, performs the work', it is necessary to apply a series of semantic derivation rules. See below, p. 327.

Rules (16), or the rules for transforming two-place predicates into three-place predicates, stand somewhat apart from the other rules, because the left-hand part of the rule is a derived predicate structure obtained by successively applying several combinatory operators. The derivation of such structures will be shown below on p. 331.

The meaning of rule (16.1) consists in explaining how three-place constructions with the instrumental case are obtained from similar structures:

Ja kauziruju topor, topor rubit derevo 'I cause the axe, the axe chops the tree' → *Ja rublju derevo toporom* 'I chop the tree with an axe'. Cp. the derivation on p. 331.

Rule (17) displays the converse dependency existing between predicates of the type *byt'* 'to be' and *imet'* 'to have, own'. For example, *Brat imeet dom* 'Brother has, owns a house' → *U brata est' dom* 'Brother has a house'.

The last rule, (18), models the transformations of noun phrases such as *mal'čik čitaet* 'the boy is reading' into *čitajuscij mal'čik* 'the reading boy'. Such a transformation is necessary as an intermediate step in the formation of nominalizations of the type *čtenie mal'čika* 'the boy's reading'. Nominalization derivation will be given in the appropriate place. See p. 326.

13. EXAMPLES OF SEMANTIC RULES

Semantic rules are applied to semantic axioms, parts of axioms, derivative structures and parts of derivative structures.

To better illustrate them, the rules will be given in the genotype, a hybrid and the Russian languages. See Table I.

For the sake of simplicity we shall omit the ordinal numeration of terms. Thus, for example, instead of $MtT^1(P_{oa}T_o^2T_a^3)$ we shall write $MtT(P_{oa}T_oT_a)$. When necessary, coreferential terms or predicates will be denoted with identical numerical indices (instead of apostrophes as we agreed above). See Table I.

14. EXAMPLES OF SEMANTIC DERIVATIONS

In this chapter we shall examine some individual examples of how derived structures are obtained from base structures (i.e., axioms) with the help of the semantic rules presented above. We will show the derivation of structures which are derivative from the point of view of any generative grammar. These are infinitive, participial and verbal adverbial constructions, constructions with the anticipatory 'it' in English, copulative structures and certain others.

TABLE I

Rule number	Example of rule application	Example of interpretation in hybrid language	Example of interpretation in natural language
(1)	$P_{oa}T_oT_a \rightarrow Cv_oP_{oa}T_oT_a$	Читать$_{oa}$книга$_o$мальчик$_a$ → Cv$_o$читать$_{oa}$книга$_o$мальчик$_a$	Мальчик читает книгу → Мальчик читает книгу
	$P_{oa}T_oT_a \rightarrow Cv_{12}P_{oa}T_aT_o$	Читать$_{oa}$книга$_o$мальчик$_a$ → Cv$_{12}$читать$_{oa}$мальчик$_a$книга$_o$	Мальчик читает книгу → Книга читается мальчиком
	$\dot{P}_{foa}T_fT_oT_a \rightarrow Cv_o\dot{P}_{foa}T_fT_oT_a$	Давать$_{foa}$сестра$_f$деньги$_o$брат$_a$ → Cv$_o$давать$_{foa}$сестра$_f$деньги$_o$брат$_a$	Брат дает деньги сестре → Брат дает деньги сестре
	$\dot{P}_{foa}T_fT_oT_a \rightarrow Cv_{23}\dot{P}_{foa}T_fT_aT_o$	Давать$_{foa}$сестра$_f$деньги$_o$ → брат$_a$ Cv$_{23}$давать$_{foa}$сестра$_f$брат$_a$деньги$_o$	Брат дает деньги сестре → Деньги даются братом сестре
(1)	$P_{foa}T_fT_oT_a \rightarrow Cv_{12}P_{foa}T_oT_fT_a$	Давать$_{foa}$сестра$_f$деньги$_o$ брат$_a$ → Cv$_{12}$давать$_{foa}$деньги$_o$сестра$_f$брат$_a$	Брат дает деньги сестре → Брат снабжает сестру деньгами
	$P_{foa}T_fT_oT_a \rightarrow Cv_{13}P_{foa}T_aT_oT_f$	Давать$_{foa}$сестра$_f$деньги$_o$брат$_a$ → Cv$_{13}$давать$_{foa}$брат$_a$деньги$_o$сестра$_f$	Брат дает деньги сестре → Брат снабжает сестру деньгами
(2)	$\dot{P}_{fa}\dot{T}_fT_{a^1} \rightarrow WP_{fa}T_{f,a^1}$	Умывать$_{fa}$отец$_f$отец$_a$ → W умывать$_{fa}$отец$_f$, a	*Отец умывает отца → Отец умывается
	$BIg\dot{P}_a\dot{T}_a^1\dot{T}_{a^1} \rightarrow W(BIg\dot{P}_a)\dot{T}_a$	В начать читать$_a$он$_a$он$_a$ → W(В начать читать$_a$)он$_a$	*Он, он начал читать → Он начал читать
(3)	$Cv_{12}VI(\dot{P}_aT_{a^1}) T_f^2 \rightarrow B(Cv_{12}VI) \dot{P}_aT_a^1T_f^2$	Cv$_{12}$ want (smoke$_a$you$_a$) I$_f$ → B(Cv$_{12}$want) smoke$_a$ you$_a$I$_f$	* I want, you smoke → I want you to smoke
	$Cv_{12}Mt(\dot{P}_aT_{a^1}) T_f^2 \rightarrow B(Cv_{12}Mt) \dot{P}_aT_a^1T_f^2$	Cv$_{12}$know (paint$_a$he$_a$) I$_f$ → B(Cv$_{12}$know) paint$_a$he$_a$I$_f$	I know he paints → I know him to paint
(3)	$E_oNg(\dot{P}_f\dot{I}_f) \rightarrow B(E_oNg) \dot{P}_f\dot{I}_f$	E$_o$неверно(спать$_f$он$_f$) → B(E$_o$не)спать$_f$он$_f$	*неверно, он спит → он не спит

Table I (continued)

Rule number	Example of rule application	Example of interpretation in hybrid language	Example of interpretation in natural language
	$E_oPs(\dot{P}_a\dot{T}_a) \rightarrow B(E_oPs)\,\dot{P}_a\dot{T}_a$	E_oвероятно(работать$_a$он$_a$) $\rightarrow$ $B(E_o$должен)работать$_a$он$_a$	Вероятно, он работает $\rightarrow$ Он должен работать
	$Ig(\dot{P}_a\dot{T}_a{}^1)\,\dot{T}_a{}^1 \rightarrow BIg\dot{P}_a\dot{T}_a{}^1\dot{T}_a{}^1$	Начать(читать$_a$он$_a$)он$_a$ $\rightarrow$ начать читать он$_a$он$_a$	*начал, он читает $\rightarrow$ *он, он начал читать
(4)	$VI\dot{T}_f{}^1(\dot{P}_a\dot{T}_a{}^1) \rightarrow LVI\dot{P}_a\dot{T}_{f,\,a}$	Хотеть я$_f{}^1$ (курить$_a$я$_a{}^1$) $\rightarrow$ L хотеть курить$_a$я$_{f,\,a}$	*Я хочу, я курю $\rightarrow$ я хочу курить
	$Ca\dot{T}_f(\dot{P}_a\dot{T}_a{}^1)\,\dot{T}_a{}^2 \rightarrow LCa\dot{P}_a\dot{T}_{f,\,a}{}^1\dot{T}_a{}^2$	Велеть$_f$ба мальчик (гулять$_{ba}$мальчик$_a$) мать$_a \rightarrow$ велеть$_{fba}$гулять$_a$мальчик$_{f,\,a}$ мать$_a$	*Мать велит мальчик, Мальчик гуляет $\rightarrow$ Мать велит мальчику гулять
(5)	$FiI\dot{T}_f(\dot{P}_a\dot{T}_a) \rightarrow K_2FiI\dot{T}_f(\dot{P}_a\dot{T}_a)\,T_\phi$	seem I_f(come$_a$he$_a$) $\rightarrow K_2$seem I_f(come$_a$he$_a$) it	* I seem he will come $\rightarrow$ It seems to me he will come
(7)	$H^2Pr((R_\alpha\cdot\dot{P}_a)\,\dot{T}_a)\,\dot{T}_f \rightarrow H^2Pr(U\dot{T}_a(R_\alpha\cdot\dot{P}_a))\,\dot{T}_f$	H_2слышать$((R_\alpha\cdot$петь)птица$_a$я$_f \rightarrow$ H_2слышать$(U$ птица$(R_\alpha$петь$_a$))я	Слышу поющую птицу $\rightarrow$ Слышу пение птицы
(8)	$\dot{P}_o\dot{T}_o \rightarrow E_o\dot{P}_o$	Дуть$_o$ветер$_o \rightarrow$ ДУТЬ$_{(o)}$	Ветер дует $\rightarrow$ Дует
	$\dot{P}_{oa}\dot{T}_o\dot{T}_a \rightarrow E_o\dot{P}_{oa}\dot{T}_o$	Читать$_{oa}$книга$_o$мальчик$_a \rightarrow$ читать$_{(o)a}$ мальчик$_a$	Мальчик читает книгу $\rightarrow$ Мальчик читает
	$\dot{P}_{oa}\dot{T}_o\dot{T}_a \rightarrow E_l\dot{P}_{oa}\dot{T}_o$	Читать$_{oa}$книга$_o$мальчик$_a \rightarrow$ читать$_{(o)a}$ книга$_o$	Мальчик читает книгу $\rightarrow$ Книгу читают
	$\dot{P}_{foa}\dot{T}_f\dot{T}_o\dot{T}_a \rightarrow E_o\dot{P}_{foa}\dot{T}_o\dot{T}_a$ [a]	Приносить$_{foa}$сестра$_f$книга$_o$брат$_a \rightarrow$ E_oприносить$_{(f)oa}$книга$_o$брат$_a$	Брат приносит сестре книгу $\rightarrow$ Брат приносит книгу

[a] In the tables below the dots on terminal semions are omitted because they are obvious.

Table I (continued)

Rule number	Example of rule application	Example of interpretation in hybrid language	Example of interpretation in natural language
	$DbT(P_oT_o{}^2) \rightarrow E_oDb(P_oT_o)$	Сомневаться он (идти$_o$дождь$_o$) → E_oсомнительно(идти$_o$дождь$_o$)	*Он сомневается, идет дождь → *Сомнительно, идет дождь
	$(QT^1)(P_{oa}T_o{}^2T_a{}^3) \rightarrow E_oQ(P_{oa}T_o{}^2T_a{}^3)$	Спрашивать она (писать$_{oa}$книга$_o$она$_a$) → E_oспрашивается (писать$_{oa}$книга$_o$она$_a$)	Она спрашивает: пишет он книгу? → Спрашивается, пишет ли он книгу
(9.1)	$E_oPs(P_fT_f) \rightarrow E_oH^1Ps(R_\alpha(P_fT_f))$	Возможно(отдыхать$_f$он$_f$) → E_oH^1 Возможно(R_α(отдыхать$_f$он$_f$)	Возможно, он отдыхает → Возможно, что он отдыхает
(9.2)	$MtT_f(P_aT_a) \rightarrow H^2MtT_f(R_\alpha(P_aT_a))$	Знать дети$_f$ (приехать$_a$отец$_a$) → H^2знать дети$_f$ (R_α(приехать$_a$отец$_a$)	Дети знают, отец приехал → Дети знают, что отец приехал
(9.3)	$EmT_f(P_aT_a) \rightarrow H^2EmT_f(R_\alpha(P_aT_a))$	Сердить$_{a\text{я}f}$(спорить он$_a$) → H^2сердить$_{a\text{я}f}$(R_α(спорить$_a$она$_a$)	Меня сердит, он спорит → Меня сердит то, что он спорит
(9.4)	$CaT_f{}^1(P_aT_a{}^1)T_a{}^2 \rightarrow H^4CaT_f{}^1(R_\alpha(P_aT_a{}^1)T_a{}^2$	Велеть$_{fa}$мальчик$_f$ (гулять$_a$мальчик$_a$) мать$_a$ → H^3велеть$_{fa}$мальчик$_f$(R_α(гулять$_a$мальчик$_a$)) мать$_a$	Мать велит мальчику, мальчик гуляет → Мать велит мальчику, чтобы мальчик гулял
(10.1)	$C(P_aT_a{}^1)(P_{oa}T_oT_a{}^2) \rightarrow C(P_{oa}T_oT_a)(P_aT_a)$	C(гулять$_a$брат$_a$) (читать$_{oa}$книга$_o$сестра$_a$) → C(читать$_{oa}$книга$_o$сестра$_a$) (гулять$_a$брат$_a$)	Сестра читает книгу, а брат гуляет → Брат гуляет, а сестра читает книгу
(10.2)	$C(P_aT_a{}^1)P_a{}^1T_a{}^2) \rightarrow P_a{}^1(CT_a{}^1T_a{}^2)$	C(работать$_a$сын$_a$) (работать$_a$отец$_a$) → работать$_a$(C сын$_a$отец$_a$)	Отец работает и сын работает → Отец и сын работают

Table I (continued)

Rule number	Example of rule application	Example of interpretation in hybrid language	Example of interpretation in natural language
(10.3)	$C(P_o{}^1 T_o{}^1)(P_o{}^2 T^1) \rightarrow CP_o{}^1 P_o{}^2 T^1$	$C(\text{таять}_o\text{снег}_o)(\text{падать}_o\text{снег}_o) \rightarrow$ $C(\text{таять}_o\text{падать}_o)\text{снег}_o$	Снег падает, и снег тает $\rightarrow$ Снег падает и тает
(11.1)	$A(P_{1a}T T_a)(P_{oa}T_o T_a) \rightarrow A(P_{oa}T_o T_a)(P_{1a}T T_a)$	$A(\text{пойти}_{1a}\text{театр}_1\text{Я}_a)(\text{читать}_{oa}\text{книга}_o\text{Я}_a) \rightarrow$ $A(\text{читать}_{oa}\text{книга}_o\text{Я}_a)(\text{пойти}_{1a}\text{театр}_1\text{Я}_a)$	Или я пойду в театр, или я буду читать книгу $\rightarrow$ Или я буду читать книгу, или я пойду в театр
(11.2)	$A(P_a{}^1 T_a{}^1)(P_a{}^1 T_a{}^1) \rightarrow P_a{}^1(A T_a{}^1 T_a{}^2)$	$A(\text{работать}_a\text{отец}_a)(\text{работать}_a\text{сын}_a) \rightarrow$ $\text{работать}_a(A\text{отец}_a\text{сын}_a)$	Или отец работает, или сын работает $\rightarrow$ Отец или сын работает
(11.3)	$A(P^1 T^1)(P^2 T^1) \rightarrow (A P^1 P^2) T^1$	$A(\text{петь}_a\text{девочка}_a)(\text{танцевать}_a\text{девочка}_a) \rightarrow$ $(A\text{петь}_a\text{танцевать}_a)\text{девочка}_a$	То девочка поет, то девочка танцует $\rightarrow$ девочка поет, то танцует
(12.1)	$C(P_f T_f)(P_a T_a) \rightarrow P_f(R_\alpha(P_a T_a{}^1)) T_f{}^1$	$C(\text{уставать}_f\text{человек}_f)(\text{бегать}_a\text{человек}_a) \rightarrow \text{уставать}_f(R_\alpha(\text{бегать}_a\text{человек}_a))$ человек_f	Человек бегает и человек устает $\rightarrow$ человек (человек бегает)устает
(12.2)	$Im(P_a T_a)(P_f T_f) \rightarrow P_f(R_\alpha(P_a T_a)) T_f$	$Im(\text{бегать}_a\text{человек}_a)(\text{уставать}_f \text{человек}_f) \rightarrow \text{уставать}_f(R_{\alpha'}$ $(\text{бегать}_a\text{человек}_a))\text{человек}_f$	Если человек бегает, то человек устает $\rightarrow$ человек, человек бегает, устает
(13.1)	$H^2 Aff T_f{}^1(R_\alpha(P_{oa}T_o T_a{}^1)) \rightarrow H^2 Aff T_f{}^1(R_\alpha(P_{oa}T_o T_{pr}{}^1))$	$\text{Утверждать мальчик}_f{}^1(\text{делать}_{oa}$ $\text{уроки}_o\text{мальчик}_a{}^1) \rightarrow \text{утверждать}$ $\text{мальчик}_f{}^1(\text{делать}_{oa}\text{уроки}_o\text{он}_a{}^1)$	Мальчик утверждает, что мальчик делает уроки $\rightarrow$ мальчик утверждает, что он делает уроки
(13.2)	$Im(P_a T_a{}^1)(P_f T_f{}^1) \rightarrow Im(P_a T_a)(P_f T_{pr})$	$Im(\text{бегать}_a\text{человек}_a{}^1)(\text{уставать}_f$ $\text{человек}_a{}^1) \rightarrow Im(\text{бегать}_a\text{человек}_a{}^1)$ $(\text{уставать}_f\text{он}_a{}^1)$	Если человек бегает, то человек устает $\rightarrow$ если человек бегает, то он устает

Table I (continued)

Rule number	Example of rule application	Example of interpretation in hybrid language	Example of interpretation in natural language
(13.1)	$H^4CaT_f^1(R_\alpha(P_aT_a^1))\,T_a^2 \rightarrow$ $H^4CaT_f^1(R_\alpha(P_aT_{gr}))\,T_a^2$	H^3велеть$_{fa}$ мальчик$_f$ (R_α(гулять$_a$ мальчик$_\alpha$))мать$_a \rightarrow H^3$велеть мальчик$_\alpha$ (R_{α}(гулять он$_\alpha$))	Мать велела мальчику, чтобы мальчик гулял $\rightarrow$ мать велела мальчику, чтобы он гулял
(13.3)	$P_f(R_\alpha(P_aT_a^1))\,T_f^1 \rightarrow P_f(R_\alpha(P_aT_a^{r1}))\,T_f^1$	Уставать$_f$ (R_α (бегать$_a$человек$_\alpha$)) человек$_\alpha \rightarrow$ уставать$_f$ (R_α (бегать$_a$ который$_\alpha$))человек$_f$	*Человек, человек бегает, устает $\rightarrow$ человек, который бегает, устает
(13.3)	$P_{of}(R_\alpha(P_{tf}T_1T_f))\,T_oT_f \rightarrow$ $P_{of}(R_\alpha(P_{tf}T_{gr}^1T_f^2))\,T_o^1T_f^3$	Видеть$_{of}$(жить$_{tf}$дом$_1$вы$_f$)дом$_o^1$я$_f \rightarrow$ видеть$_{of}$(жить$_{tf}$который$_1$вы$_f$)я$_f$	Я вижу дом, в доме живете вы $\rightarrow$ Я вижу дом, в котором вы живете
(14)	$QT_f(P_{tf}T_1T_f) \rightarrow QT_f(P_{tf}T_aT_f)$	Спросить я$_f$(жить$_{tf}$Москва$_1$вы$_f$) $\rightarrow$ спросить я$_f$ (жить$_{tf}$Москва$_a$вы$_f$)	Я спросил, вы живете в Москве $\rightarrow$ Я спросил где вы живете
(15)	$P_aT_a \rightarrow C_p(P_aT_a^1)\,T_a^1$	Работать$_a$мальчик$_a$делать$_a \rightarrow$ (работать$_a$мальчик$_a$)мальчик$_a$	Мальчик работает $\rightarrow$ *Мальчик делает, мальчик работает
(15)	$P_{fa}T_fT_a \rightarrow C_p(P_{fa}T_fT_a^1)\,T_a^1$	Влиять$_{fa}$читатель$_a$писатель$_a \rightarrow$ оказывать$_a$(влиять$_{fa}$читатель$_f$ писатель$_a$) писатель$_a$	Писатель влияет на читателей $\rightarrow$ *Писатель оказывает писатель влияет на читателей
(17)	$HbT_oT_f \rightarrow EsT_fT_o$	Иметь дом брат $\rightarrow$ есть дом брат	Брат имеет дом $\rightarrow$ У брата есть дом
(18)	$H^2P_2(R_\alpha(P_aT_a))\,T_f \rightarrow H^2P_2(R_\alpha{}^1P_a)\,T_aT_f$	Слышать (R_α(петь$_a$птица$_a$))я$_f \rightarrow$ слышать(R_α(петь$_a$)птица$_a$)я$_f$	Я слышу, что поет птица $\rightarrow$ Я слышу поющую птицу

TABLE II

Derivation of participial constructions

Line of derivation	Semantic rule	Genotype language	Hybrid language	Natural language
1.	Axiom	$C(P_{oa}T_oT_a{}^1)\,(P_fT_f{}^1)$	$C(\text{читать}_{oa}\text{книга}_o\text{девочка}_a{}^1)$ (улыбается_f девочка$_f$)	Девочка улыбается, и девочка читает книгу
2.	Relativization	$P_f(R_\alpha(P_{oa}T_oT_a{}^1)\,T_f{}^1$	$\text{Улыбаться}_f(R_\alpha(\text{читать}_{oa}$ книга$_o$девочка$_a{}^1$) девочка$_f{}^1$	Девочка, девочка читает книгу, улыбается
3.	Argument elimination	$P_f(R_\alpha(E_1P_{oa}T_o{}^1))\,T_f{}^1$	$\text{Улыбаться}(\text{читать}_o{}_{(a)}$книга$_o)$ девочка$_f$	Девочка, читающая книгу, улыбается

The derivations of derived structures from axioms will be given in the form of a column consisting of the lines of the derivation. The axiom is written on the first line, the result of the application of the first rule is on the second, of the second rule on the third, etc. The derivation is given in the genotype language and is illustrated in a hybrid Russian or English language. A sentence of natural language is matched to each sentence of the hybrid language.

We shall begin with the derivation of participial constructions, relative clauses and verbal adverbial constructions. All of these are derived from conjunctor axioms – coordinative and locative. In the tables of derivations (Tables I–IV) the modal operator $AffT$ is omitted for the sake of simplicity. The axiom $AffT(C(P_{oa}T_oT_a^1)(P_fT_f^1))$ is written in an abbreviated form as $C(P_{oa}T_oT_a^1)(P_fT_f^1)$. The axiom $AffT(Lc(P_{oa}T_oT_a)(P_fT_f))$ is written $Lc(P_{oa}T_oT_a^1)(P_fT_f^1)$.

It can be seen from Table II that sentences containing participles are obtained from coordinator structures (line 1) by transforming one of the sentences connected by a coordinator into an operator on the term of the other sentence (line 2) identical with one of the terms of the first sentence. Then, the identical term is eliminated (line 3) in the sentence which is the operator to the term. The relator $R_{\alpha'}$ which indicates that the sentence $P_{oa}T_oT_a$ is an operator of the term T_f^1, is transformed after the elimination of T_a^1 into an operator of the predicate $R_{\alpha'}(E_1P_{oa}T^1)$. The latter is interpreted as a participial construction.

If instead of applying the argument elimination rule after the relativization rule we apply the pronominalization rule, we obtain a sentence with a subordinate relative construction rather than a participial phrase.

On line 3 of Table III we apply a rule to pronominalize a term of an embedded sentence which is identical with one of the terms of the main sentence. In this case T_a^1 is pronominalized, which is identical with T_f^1. T_{rl} is the analogue of relative prounouns such as *kotoryj* 'which' *čej* 'whose', *kto* 'who'.

A comparison of the derivations in Tables II and III shows that two ways are possible from the axioms after applying the relativization rule – to participial constructions and to relative subordinate sentences. Thus, in our system these two grammatical synonyms are not necessarily obtained from each other, but independently, from the same base structure (axioms), and passing by the same intermediate structure.

Verbal adverbial constructions are derived from the same axioms as participial constructions. The difference is that a coordinator device is used in the derivation of participial constructions, and the conjunctor Lc, which functions as an analogue of temporal conjunctions, is used to derive verbal adverbial constructions. In the first step of the derivation we perform elimination of the closing term of the sentence, which has Lc for an operator. As a

TABLE III
Derivation of relative clauses

Line of derivation	Semantic rule	Genotype language	Hybrid language	Natural language
1.	Axiom	$C(P_{oa}T_oT_a{}^1)(P_fT_f{}^1)$	(Читать$_{oa}$книга$_o$девочка$_a{}^1$)(улыбаться$_f$девочка$_f{}^1$)	Девочка улыбается и девочка читает книгу
2.	Relativization	$P_f(R_{\alpha'}(P_{oa}T_oT_a)\,T_f$	Улыбаться$(R_{\alpha'}$(читать$_{oa}$книга$_o$девочка$_a{}^1$)девочка$_f{}^1$	Девочка, девочка читает книгу, улыбается
3.	Pronominalization	$P_f(R_{\alpha'}(P_{oa}T_oT_{r1}{}^1)\,T_f{}^1$	Улыбаться$(R_{\alpha'}$(читать$_{oa}$книга$_o$который$_a$)девочка$_f$	Девочка, которая читает книгу, улыбается

result of this step an intermediate structure is generated which has no grammatical interpretation in natural language (line 2). In the third step of derivation the operator B composes the operator Lc and the predicate $E_1P_{oa}T_o$. $BLc(E_1P_{oa})T_o$ is interpreted as a verbal adverbial construction that is an operator in relation to the second sentence $(P_fT_f^1)$. The derivation of the verbal adverbial construction could be completed here, since an analogue of a grammatical phrase of Russian has been obtained. The next derivational step – the repeated application of the operator B composes the function $BLc(E_1P_{oa})T_o$ with the predicate of the sentence P_f. As a result we obtain an analogue of verbal adverbial construction belonging to the predicate P_f. The same Russian phrase is matched to the derivational structure on line 4, but the internal structure of these phrases is different, and this difference is shown on lines 3 and 4 of the derivation.

If instead of deleting the argument of the initial base structure we apply the pronominalization rule, we will obtain the genotype analogue of a compound sentence with a temporal subordinate clause:

$Lc(P_{oa}T_oT_a{}^1)\,(P_f\mathbf{T}_{f^{1pr}})$	(*čitat'* 'read' *kniga* 'book' *devočka*$_a$ 'girl') (*ulybat'sja*$_f$ 'smile' *ona*$_f$ 'she')	While the girl reads the book she is smiling

From the same axiom, its coordinator variant, we can obtain two more grammatical synonyms by applying another rule:

$(C(P_{oa}T_o)\,P_f{}^1)\,T_{a,f}{}^1$	(*C*(*čitat'* 'read' *kniga*$_o$ 'book') *ulybat'sja*$_f$ 'smile') *devočka*$_{a,f}$ 'girl'	The girl is smiling and reading the book
$C(P_{ff}T_f)\,(P_{oa}T_oT_a)$	*C*(*ulybat'sja*$_f$ 'smile' *devočka*$_f$ 'girl') (*čitat'*$_{oa}$ 'read' *kniga*$_o$ 'book' *devočka*$_o$ 'girl')	*The girl reads the book and the girl smiles

The last phrase can be made grammatical by applying the pronominalization rule:

Devočka čitaet knigu, i ona ulybaetsja 'The girl is reading the book and she is smiling'.

Infinitive constructions. Subjectival and objectival infinitive constructions can be derived from variants of the same axiom, for example, from an axiom with volative modality. Axiom variants differ by the fact that an axiom variant with identical terms in the main and embedded clauses underlies a subjective infinitive, e.g. $VlT_f^1(P_aT_a^1)$, while an axiom variant without identical terms underlies an objective infinitive, e.g. $VlT_f(P_aT_a)$.

Subjective infinitives are derived in two steps by applying the confluentor, which fuses the functions *Vl xotet'* 'to want' and P_a *kurit'* 'to smoke' on the

TABLE IV

Derivation of verbal adverbial constructions

Line of derivation	Semantic rule	Genotype language	Hybrid language	Natural language
1.	Axiom	$Lc(P_{oa}T_oT_a^1)(P_fT_f^1)$	$Lc(\text{читать}_{oa}\text{книга}_o\text{девочка}_a)$ $(\text{улыбаться}_f\text{девочка}_f)$	*В то время как девочка читает книгу, девочка улыбается *В то время как девочка читает
2.	Argument deletion	$Lc(E_1P_{oa}T_o)(P_fT_f^1)$	$(Lc(\text{читать}_{o(a)}\text{книга}_o)$ $(\text{улыбаться}_f$ $\text{девочка}_f)$	книгу, девочка улыбается
3.	Compositor application	$BLc(E_1P_{oa})T_o(P_fT_f^1)$	$BLc(E_1\text{читать}_{o(a)})\text{книга}_o$ $(\text{улыбаться}_f$ $\text{девочка}_f)$	Девочка улыбается, читая книгу
4.	Compositor application	$B(BLc(E_1P_{oa})T_o)P_fT_f^1$	$B(BLc\ E_1\text{читать}_{o(a)})\text{книга}_o$ $\text{улыбаться}_f\text{девочка}_f$	Девочка улыбается, читая книгу

identical arguments T_f^1 and T_a^1 into one complex function $LVlP_a$. The derivation of a subjective infinitive is shown in Table V.

Objectival infinitives, whose derivation is shown in Table VI, are obtained in three steps. First the conversion operator Cv_{12}, which makes T_f and the embedded clause P_aT_a change places, is applied. Then the compositor B performs the composition of the complex function $(Cv_{12}Vl)$ and the predicate P_a.

The complex functions $LVlP_a$ and $B(Cv_{12}Vl)P_a$ are interpreted as combinations of finite verbs with an infinitive. In the case of subjective infinitives the term $T_{f,a}$ functions as an argument of the complex function. The joining of the case indices on T shows that this is simultaneously an argument of a state and an action. In the case of objectival infinitives the complex func-

TABLE V

Derivation of subjectival infinitives

1. Axiom	$VlT_f^1(P_aT_a^1)$	Хотеть я$_f$ (курить$_a$я$_a$)	* Я хочу, я курю
2. Operation of the confluentor	$LVlP_aT_{f,a}$	хотеть курить я$_{f,a}$	Я хочу курить

TABLE VI

Derivation of objectival infinitives

1. Axiom	$VlT_f(P_aT_a)$	Want I$_f$(paint$_a$he$_a$)	* Want I, he paints
2. Operation of conversion operator	$Cv_{12}Vl(P_aT_a)\,T_f$	Cv_{12}want(paint$_a$he$_a$) I$_f$	* I wants he paints
3. Operation of the compositor B	$B(Cv_{12}Vl)\,P_aT_aT_f$	$B(Cv_{12}$ want)paint$_a$he$_a$I$_f$	I want him to paint

tion has two arguments. In interpreting the last line of the derivation in Table V we 'break' the complex function *want to paint* in between its arguments: *I want him to paint.*

The derivation of objectival infinitives is illustrated with English examples, since constructions with objectival infinitives with volative verbs are not realized in Russian.

Nominalization. Abstract deverbative nouns of the type *penie* 'singing', *čtenie* 'reading' *beg* 'running' are obtained from embedded clauses within the system of an applicative grammar. A possible derivation is proposed in Table VII. The derivation is performed in five derivational steps. The deproposition operator H^2, which nominalizes the sentence P_aT_a is applied to the axiom containing an embedded clause, for example, $AffT(Pr(P_aT_o)T_f)$.

If we interpret P_aT_a as *Poet ptica* 'A bird is singing', then $R_\alpha(P_aT_a)$ can be interpreted as... *čto poet ptica* 'that a bird is singing'. In the third step. according to the rule for substituting noun phrases, the complex $R_\alpha(P_aT_a)$ is replaced by the complex $(R_{\alpha''}P_a)T_a$. The latter can be interpreted as *pojuščaja ptica* 'the singing bird'. The application of the operator U in the next step accomplishes a switch in the roles of the functions $(R_{\alpha''}P_a)$ *pojuščaja* 'singing' and the argument T_a *ptica* 'bird'. The resultant complex $UT_a(R_{\alpha''}P_a)$ is interpreted as a nominalization of the phrase *penie ptic* 'the singing of the birds'. If we then eliminate T_a, we obtain an analogue to the abstract noun *penie* 'singing'. See Table VII. A similar series of derivational steps can be applied to any other axiom, e.g. $MtT(P_aT_a)$. Let us show one more time the derivation of analogues of abstract nouns, for example, the analogue of words such as *priezd* 'arrival'. The derivation will be shown in the form of a column:

(1) $Mt\dot{T}(\dot{P}_a\dot{T}_a)$

(2) $H^3Mt\dot{T}R_\alpha(\dot{P}_a\dot{T}_a)$

(3) $H^3Mt\dot{T}(R_{\alpha'}\dot{P}_a)\dot{T}_a$

(4) $H^3Mt\dot{T}(U\dot{T}_a(R_{\alpha''}\dot{P}_a))$

(5) $H^3Mt\dot{T}(EU(R_{\alpha''}\dot{P}_a))$.

If we interpret the first line, i.e., the axiom, as *Ja znaju, priezžaet otec* 'I know father is coming', then the second, after applying the appropriate deproposition operator, here H^3, can be interpreted as *Ja znaju, cto priezžaet otec* 'I know that father is coming'. In the third step the analogue of the phrase *čto priezžaet otec* 'that father is coming' is replaced with the analogue of the participial construction *priezžajuščij otec* 'coming father'. The third line corresponds approximately to the phrase *Ja znaju o priezžajuščem otce* 'I know about the coming father'. A change in the roles of the argument T_a *otec* 'father' and the function *priezžajuščij* 'coming' generates the analogue of the noun phrase *priezd otca* 'father's arrival'. The fourth line is therefore interpreted as a phrase with a nominalized object *Ja znaju o priezde otca* 'I know about father's arrival'. The argument $EU(R_{\alpha''}P_a)$ which is interpreted as a deverbative noun, remains after T_a has been eliminated, and the whole fifth line corresponds to the phrase *Ja znaju o priezde* 'I know about the arrival'. See also Table VII.

Copulative predicates. A similar series of derivational steps is applied to derive sentences with copulative predicates such as *Čelovek vypolnjaet rabotu* 'The man does the work', *Pisatel' okazyvaet vlijanie na čitatelej* 'The writer exerts influence on the readers'. Let us consider the derivation of the analogue of the second sentence. See Table VIII.

We will take the axiom $Fi\dot{T}(\dot{P}_{fa}\dot{T}_f\dot{T}_a)$, which can be interpreted with the phrase *Mne predstavljaetsja: pisatel' vlijaet na čitatelej* 'I imagine, it seems to

TABLE VII
Nominalization derivation

1. Axiom	$A_{ff}T(Pr(P_aT_a)\ T_f)$	Утверждать я (слышать (петь$_а$птица$_a$)он$_f$)	Я утверждаю: он слышит: поет птица
2. Deproposition of embedded clause, operation of H^2	$A_{ff}T(H^2Pr(R_\alpha(P_aT_a))\ T_f)$	Утверждать я (H^2слышать (R_α(петь$_а$птица$_a$))он$_f$)	Я утверждаю: он слышит, что поет птица
3. Substitution of NP by participial construction	$A_{ff}T(H^2Pr((R_\alpha \cdot P_a)\ T_a)\ T_f)$	Утверждать я (H^2слышать ((R_αпеть)птица$_a$)он$_f$)	Я утверждаю: он слышит поющую птицу
4. Argument and function role change	$A_{ff}T(H^2Pr(UT_a(R_\alpha \cdot P_a))\ T_f)$	Утверждать я (H^2слышать (Uптица (R_αпеть))он$_f$)	Я утверждаю: он слышит пение птиц
5. Term elimination	$A_{ff}T(H^2Pr(E_0U(R_\alpha \cdot P_a))\ T_f)$	Утверждать я (H^2слышать $E_1U(R_\alpha \cdot P_a)$ (R_αпеть))	Я утверждаю: он слышит пение

TABLE VIII

1. Axiom	$FiT(P_{fa}T_fT_a)$	Казаться я (влиять$_{fa}$читатель$_f$ писатель$_a$)	Мне кажется, писатель влияет на читателей
2. Introduction of copulative predicate	$...Cp(P_{fa}T_fT_a^1) T_a^1$	...оказывать(влиять$_{fa}$читатель$_f$ писатель$_f$)писатель$_a$	писатель оказывает, писатель влияет на читателей
3. Nominalization of embedded clause	$...H^2Cp(R_\alpha(P_{fa}T_fT_a)) T_a$	...H^2 оказывать(R_α(влиять$_{fa}$ читатель$_f$писатель$_a$))писатель	писатель оказывает, что писатель влияет на читателей
4. Substitution of noun phrase	$...H^2Cp((R_{\alpha'}(P_{fa}T_f)) T_a^1) T_a^1$	...H^2оказывать((R_α(влиять$_{fa}$читатель$_f$)) писатель)писатель$_a$	писатель оказывает, писатель, влияющий на читателей
5. Change of argument and function roles	$H^2Cp(UT_a^1(R_{\alpha'}(P_{fa}T_f))) T_a$	...H^2оказывать($UT_a(R_\alpha$(влиять$_{fa}$ читатель$_f$))) писатель$_a$	*Писатель оказывает, влияние писателя на читателей
6. Term elimination	$...H^2Cp(E_oU(R_{\alpha'}(P_{fa}T_f))) T_a$	...H^2 оказывать($E_oU(R_{\alpha'}$(влиять читатель$_f$))) писатель$_a$	Писатель оказывает влияние на читателей

me: the writer influences the readers'. Since the modal operator ($Fi\dot{T}$) does not participate in what follows, we will omit it beginning with the second line of Table VIII. However, we assume the presence of this operator on each line of the derivation. The second step of the derivation consists in introducing the two-place copulative predicate Cp after the modal operator FiT. The introduction of Cp is accompanied by a doubling of T_a. The predicate Cp now has two arguments – ($P_{f_a}T_fT_a$) and T_a. In the third step we apply the operator H^2, which causes nominalization of the following embedded clause. A part of the complex ($R_\alpha(P_{f_a}T_fT_a)$) is interpreted as *čto pisatel vlijaet na čitatelej* 'that the writer influences the readers'. This noun phrase is then replaced by the participial construction ($R_{\alpha'}(P_{f_a}T_f))T_a$. The latter phrase is interpreted as *vlijajusčij na čitatelej pisatel'* 'influencing the readers-writer'. Switching the roles of the function ($R_{\alpha'}(P_{f_a}T_f)$) and the argument T_a on the fifth line generates the analogue of the noun phrase *vlijanie pisatelja na čitatelej* 'influence of the writer on the readers'. The elimination of T_a leaves *vlijanie na čitatelej* 'influence on the readers'. The sixth line of the derivation corresponds to the desired phrase.

Constructions with a false argument. The anticipatory 'it' in English is one possible interpretation of a false argument. For an example, let us consider the generation of the analogue of impersonal passive constructions such as *It is known that John robbed the bank*. The corresponding genotype complex is obtained in five derivational steps from the axiom $MtT(P_{oa}T_oT_a)$. See the derivation in Table IX. The operator H^3 is applied to the axiom on the second line of the derivation, causing the nominalization of the embedded clause. *John robbed the bank* is transformed into *that John robbed the bank*. The application of the operator K_1 then introduces a false argument into the second place after the subject of the modal operator. The introduction of the false argument into the second place after Mt generates an intermediate structure which is not interpreted in English. The application of the conversion operator Cv_{23}, which makes the argument T_ϕ and the argument ($R_\alpha(P_{oa}T_oT_a)$) switch places, makes the sentence grammatical, if a little cumbersome: *It is known by me that John robbed the bank*. Eliminating the first term, which corresponds to a personal pronoun, produces the desired analogue of an impersonal passive construction.

The derivation of other passive constructions corresponding to the phrase *I know John robbed the bank*, specifically, such constructions as *John robbed the bank is known (by me), John is known (by me) to rob the bank,* may be obtained by applying different derivation rules.

If we consider the derivation of impersonal passive constructions outside the system of derivation of other passive constructions, we can omit the step on which the conversion operator Cv_{23} is applied and introduce the false

TABLE IX

1. Axiom	$MtT(P_{oa}T_oT_a)$	Know I $(rob_{oa}bank_oJohn_a)$	I know John robbed the bank
2. Deproposition	$H^3MtT(R_\alpha(P_{oa}T_oT_a))$	H^3know I $(R_\alpha(rob\ bank\ John))$	I know that John robbed the bank
3. Introduction of fictive argument	$K_1(H^3Mt)TT_\phi(R_\alpha(P_{oa}T_oT_o))$	$K_1(H^3$know) I it $R_\alpha(rob_{oa}bank_oJohn_a)$	I know it that John robbed the bank
4. Argument conversion	$Cv_{23}(K_1(H^3Mt))T(R_\alpha(P_{oa}T_oT_a))T_\phi$	$Cv_{23}(K_1(H^3$know)) I $(R_\alpha(rob_{oa}bank_oJohn)$ it	It is known by me that John robbed the bank
5. Term elimination	$E_o(Cv_{23}(K_1(H^3Mt)))(R_\alpha(P_{oa}T_oT_a))T_\phi$	$E_o(Cv_{23}(K_1(H^3$know)))(R_\alpha(P_{oa}T_oT_a))$ it	It is known that John robbed the bank

argument T_ϕ directly into the place of the final term. To do this we would have to apply not the operator K_1, but the operator K_2, which indicates that the new argument is introduced into the third place after the predicate. The predicate Mt would then have to be interpreted from the very beginning with the passive verb form *is known*, and MtT would be interpreted as *is known to me* or *by me*. The derivation would then be one step shorter, and the fourth line would look like $K_2(H^3Mt)T(R_\alpha(P_{oa}T_oT_a)T_\phi$.

Such a series of operations, however, removes impersonal passive constructions from the class of other passive constructions obtained from the corresponding active constructions by means of the conversion operator. In addition, this assumes a relation of equal derivability between *knows* and *is known*, which seems to us to be less justified than the relation of successive derivability *knows* → *is known*.

The derivation of three-place predicates. Three-place predicates are obtained from causative constructions with specific embedded clauses. This embedded clause has as its predicate a verb *Hb imet', vladet'* 'have, own'. If we take, for example, $DbT(CaT_f(HbT_oT_f)T_a)$ as the initial axiom, and interpret its embedded part as *Brat kauziruet sestru, sestra imeet den' gi* 'Brother causes sister, sister has money', then in the second step the confluention operator L fuses the predicates *Ca kauzirovat'* 'cause' and (HbT_o) *imet' den' gi* 'to have money'. The complex predicate $LCa (HbT_o)$ is interpreted as a combination *kauzirovat' den' gi imet* 'cause to have money'. In the third step the compositor B composes the predicate (LCa) and Hb. The new complex predicate $B(LCa)Hb$ is already a three-place predicate with the arguments $T_oT_fT_a$.

On the last line of the derivation the predicate $B(LCa)Hb$ is replaced by the predicate P_{ofa}, which is interpreted with such verbs as *snabžat'* 'supply', *obespečivat'* 'provide'. By continuing this derivation we could obtain, by means of the conversion operator, analogues of the phrases *Brat daet den'gi sestre* 'Brother gives money to sister', *Sestra polučaet den'gi ot brata* 'Sister receives money from brother' and others. The derivation of three-place predicates from two-place predicates is shown in Table X.

15. ON GRAMMATICAL SYNONYMY

As has been shown in the preceding section and in the section illustrating the derivation rules, it is often possible to derive different derivative structures from a single axiom. The various derivative structures obtained from one and the same axiom model grammatical synonymy, that is, the phrases are synonymous to each other and to the axiom. Thus, for example, it was shown above how from a single axiom with a coordinator were obtained compound

TABLE X

The derivation of three place predicates

1. Axiom	$Db\hat{T}(Ca\hat{T}_f^1(Hb\hat{T}_o\hat{T}_f^1)\,\hat{T}_a)$	Сомневаться я$_f$ (каузировать сестра$_f$ (иметь$_{oa}$деньги$_o$сестра$_f$) брата$_a$)	Я сомневаюсь, брат каузирует сестру, сестра имеет деньги
2. Confluention	$Db\hat{T}(LCa(Hb\hat{T}_o)\,\hat{T}_f)\,\hat{T}_a)$	Сомневаться я$_f$(L каузировать (иметь$_{fo}$ деньги$_{io}$)сестра$_f$) брата$_a$)	Я сомневаюсь, брат каузирует сестру иметь деньги
3. Composition	$Db\hat{T}(\hat{P}_{ofa}\hat{T}_o\hat{T}_f\hat{T}_a)$	Сомневаться (каузировать иметь$_{oof}$ деньги$_o$ сестра$_f$ брата$_a$)	Я сомневаюсь: брат снаб-жает сестру деньгами
4. Predicate substitutions rule (16.1)	$Db\hat{T}(\hat{B}(LCa)\,Hb\hat{T}_o\hat{T}_f\hat{T}_a)$	Сомневаться я$_f$ (снабжать$_{ofa}BL$ деньги$_{io}$ сестра$_f$ брата$_a$)	Я сомневаюсь: брат снаб-жает сестру деньгами

sentences, sentences with subordinate relative clauses, participial constructions and with homogeneous sentence parts. We shall attempt to show as
graphically as possible the grammatical field of synonyms obtained from a
single axiom by applying various derivation rules.

Let us take as our base the axiom (or rather, a part of the axiom)
$C(P_{oa}\dot{T}_o\dot{T}_a^1)(\dot{P}_f\dot{T}_f^1)$ and show, with the help of a table and a tree, how we
obtain a field of grammatical synonyms. We shall number the Russian
sentences that can be corresponded to the derived structures obtained from
this axiom:

The axiom: *Devočka ulybaetsja, i devočka čitaet knigu* 'The girl is smiling
and the girl is reading a book'

(1)   *Devočka ulybaetsja, i ona čitaet knigu*
       'The girl is smiling, and she is reading a book'

(2)   *Devočka čitaet knigu, i ona ulybaetsja*
       'The girl is reading a book, and she is smiling'

(3)   *Devočka ulybaetsja i čitaet knigu*
       'The girl is smiling and reading a book'

(4)   *Devocka, kotoraja čitaet knigu, ulybaetsja*
       'The girl who is reading a book is smiling'

(5)   *Devočka, čitajuscaja knigu, ulybaetsja*
       'The girl reading a book is smiling'

The numbers of the above sentences are given horizontally in Table XI,
and the numbers of the derivation rules are listed vertically. Where the lines
and columns cross there are numbers indicating in what order a given rule

TABLE XI

Derivation rule	Sentence synonyms	(1)	(2)	(3)	(4)	(5)
Pronominalization	13.2	1	2			
Pronominalization	13.3				2	
Transposition of arguments with coordinator	10.1		1			
Joining of predicates with the coordinator	10.3			1		
Relativization	12.1				1	1
Argument elimination	8					2

is to be applied. The information contained in the table can also be presented in the form of a tree:

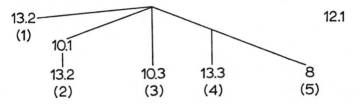

The root of the tree designates the axiom. The nodes are designated by rules applied to the axiom or to the intermediate structures. The number of the sentence, the grammatical synonym, is indicated in the final step of the derivation.

Soviet Academy of Sciences, Moscow

JU. S. MARTEM'JANOV

VALENCY–JUNCTION–EMPHASIS RELATIONS AS A LANGUAGE FOR TEXT DESCRIPTION

In order to obtain a statical description of the coherent segments which constitute a sentence, a special language is needed, all expressions of which are explicit, that is, have a clear and unambiguous structure. One means of creating a sufficiently abundant set of expressions about which it is known *of what* and *how* they are built is a calculus, i.e., a system which permits us to perform certain operations on a set of given initial expressions, through which process other expressions are derived from the original ones (accordingly, the operations themselves are called rules of 'derivation' or 'inference'). This system will be said to be a grammar.

The grammar we need will be constructed gradually – from the most simple system, or valency grammar, to a more complex one, such as a valency – junction grammar and finally, a valency – junction–emphasis grammar (VAJUNEM–grammar).

This grammar corresponds in its form to the categorial component of a generative grammar as understood in (Chomsky, 1965). In its linguistic content the VAJUNEM–grammar is oriented towards describing the external 'statutes' of a statement as it is found in a natural text, including such things as *junction* (as used in (Jespersen, 1924), *adjunct*, *emphasis*, etc., and the corresponding categories are described in more detail than in (Chomsky, 1965). On The other hand, the categories which characterize the internal constitution of a statement – for example, modality, tense (Aux), the predicate-nominal complex (P) – are not distinguished in our grammar; the necessary differentiation must come from a special 'internal' grammar not described here[1].

1. 1st SYSTEM: THE VALENCY GRAMMAR

1.1. *Preliminary Remarks*

A valency grammar is intended to give the most primary, most abstract, possible description of the relationships existing between such words as verbs, adjectives, prepositions, conjunctions, etc., on the one hand, which are declared to be 'valents' (valenty) with a various number of valences (valentnosti) – and the segments of various kinds which 'complete' the appropriate valences, and are called 'complements', also in the broadest sense. The terms

---

[1] A very general presentation of an 'internal' grammar is given in Dorofeev and Martem'-yanov (1969), and Martem'yanov and Mouchanov (1967).

F. Kiefer (ed.), Trends in Soviet Theoretical Linguistics, 335–388. All Rights Reserved.
Copyright © 1973 by D. Reidel Publishing Company, Dordrecht-Holland.

'valent' (or 'valent word'), 'valence' (or 'valent group'), are chosen to emphasize, on the one hand, that the corresponding categories are not identical with the 'surface' parts of speech (verb, adjective, conjunction, etc.), and, on the other hand, to prohibit any kind of associations with the notion of predicates, since this category, together with quantifiers, copulas, etc., belongs to an 'internal' grammar which introduces further differentiations.

Special attention is paid to the category of incomplete valent group 'applicatives', which embodies the property of a whole series of constructions (the prepositional, conjunctive, non-finite verbal detached group and the detached adjective), and prognosticating weakly one of their complements, the left or non-contract right substantive for prepositions and conjunctions, the modified complement (opredeljaemoe) for non-finite verbs and adjectives. Another general feature of these groups is their capability of functioning as adverbials with an adjacent valent group.

1.2. *Formation Rules*

(I) $V^{(n)} \to C^0, \ldots, C^{n-1} \; \overline{V}$

(II) $V^{(n)} \to C^1, \ldots, C^{n-1} \; \overline{V}^{(0)}$

(III) $P \to V^{(n)} \cdot P.$

1.3. *Initial Categories*

V^n or V	*valent*; unit having a valence; *n*-number of valences (e.g. *otdal* (gave, handed over) – V^3, *otložil* (set aside, postpone) – V^3).
$V^{(n)}$	*valent group*; a valent all of whose valences are completed.
$C^0, C^1, \ldots, C^{n-1}$	*Complements*; units which complete the valences of a valent within the srtucture of a valent group; $C^1, \ldots, C^{n-1}$ are here *transitive* complements differentiated by their upper indices: C^1 is the direct transitive complement, $C^2, \ldots, C^{n-1}$ are indirect transitive complements (cf. *otdat' drugu* (to give to a friend) (C^2) *dolg*, debt (C^1); *otložit' progulku* (postpone a walk) (C^1) *na god* (for a year((C^2)). C^0 is the applicative complement of which all valents have no more than one (cf. *Ja(I)* (C^0) *otdal* (gave, returned) (V^3) *drugu* ((my) friend) (C^2) *dolg* (the debt) (C^1); *druz'ja* (the friends) (C^0) *otložili progulky* (postponed their walk) (C^1) *na god* (for a year) (C^2); etc.)
C^i	a *certain complement*, a general designation for any complement.

V^0 an *applicative*; a valent group for which all valences, except the applicative one, are completed, e.g., *otdat'* (return) (V^0) *drugu* (friends) (C^2) *dolg* (debt) (C^1); *na* (for) (V^0) *den'* (day) (C^1); *čtoby* (in order to) (V^0) *otlozit' progulku* (postpone the walk) (C^1).

P   a *component* of a valent group; generalized designation for the valent and the complements of the group.

1.4. *Comments*

(1) Rules (I)–(II) allow the valence $V^{(n)}$ to be represented in a more explicit form, through its components V and C^i, in accordance with the definition of $V^{(n)}$, V and C^i (see above). The relations between the components of a valence are designated with an arc (dužka) whose start (⌐) and finish (¬) terminuses are differentiated; the start terminus corresponds to the valent, the finish to its complements; for the sake of uniformity, all complements are shown to the left of their valents.

(2) Rule III reveals the possible categorial content of a component (i.e., a valent or a complement); its internal category: the internal category of a component, can be a group $V^{(n)}$ which is further expandable according to rules I–II. The internal category of a component is indicated with the sign of conjunction (.) to the left of the symbol for the component itself, which in this case is considered to be the external category of the component. Categories which are connected through conjunction constitute a *complex* (compleks).

(3) The replacement of the general complement symbol C^i by a particular individual symbol C^0, C^1, ..., C^{n-1} and the replacement of P by V or C^i are absent from the rules, although they are implied:

     (A) $C^i \rightarrow C^0/C^1/.../C^{n-1}$

     (B) $P \rightarrow C^i/V$.

The set of valence categories and the rules for forming valence expressions in the aggregate will be known below as a *grammar of a valence language* or a *valence grammar*.

The expressions – the initial expressions and those derived according to the rules of a valence grammar – constitute *valence language*. Expressions such as the following, for example, should appear among the expressions of this language:

(1) C^0 C^1 V^0 . C^1 V^0 . C^1 V

(2) C^1 C^1 V^0 . C^2 V^0 . C^0 C^1 V^0 . C^1 V^0 . C V . C^1 V

Expression (1), for example, can be derived as follows (the left and right parts of the rule used are in italics)

$$V^{(2)} \to C^0 \quad C^1 \quad V \qquad \text{(Rule (I), Step 1)}$$

$$C^0 \quad C^1 \quad V \to C^0 \quad V^{(2)} \quad . \quad C^1 \quad V \qquad \text{(Rule (III + B) Step 2)}$$

$$C^0 \quad V^{(2)} \quad . \quad C^1 \quad V \to C^0 \quad C^1 \quad V^0 \quad . \quad C^1 \quad V \qquad \text{(Rule (II) Step 3)}$$

$$C^0 \quad C^1 \quad V^0 \quad . \quad C^1 \quad V \to C^0 \quad V^{(2)} \quad . \quad C^1 \quad V^0 \quad . \quad C^1 \quad V \qquad \text{(Rule (III + B) Step 4)}$$

And finally:

$$C^0 \quad V^{(2)} \quad . \quad C^1 \quad V^0 \quad . \quad C^1 \quad V \to C^0 \quad C^1 \quad V^0 \quad . \quad C^1 \quad V^0 \quad . \quad C^1 \quad V$$

$$\text{(Rule (II) Step 5)}$$

(2) is derived in a similar manner.

The expressions of the valence language, i.e., the category– and complex-trees obtained according to the rules of the valence grammar, constitute the stock of resources for an *explicit, integral,* and *coherent* description of a certain aspect of the phrases of a natural language (see the examples below).

We call this description *explicit* because the expressions used have an absolutely clear and unambiguous structure which corresponds to a sufficiently simple grammar.

This description is *integral* insofar as the expression contrasted to a given phrase is contrasted to *each* segment of the phrase by its individual categories (or their complexes): from the phrase as a whole to its successively smaller word-groups – right down to its individual words (for the fact that the word itself in such a description can correspond to a whole word-group, see below in connection with the valency-junction grammar).

Finally, the description is *coherent*, since each category (or complex of categories) which is contrasted to an individual segment of a phrase is a component of some coherent expression, by which means an individual segment of a phrase is united with all its remaining segments.

Thanks to the explicitness, integrity, and coherence of the proposed descriptions, it becomes possible to show concretely the similarities and differences between the structures of phrases. For example, the phrase *Druz'ja byli vynuždeny otložit'progulku* (The friends were forced to postpone their walk) can be described by contrasting it to expression (1) (see p. 337); here the individual categories or their complexes are contrasted to each word of the phrase; the words of the phrase are arranged in the order required by the rigorous structure of the valence expression:

Druz'ja (The friends) C^0 ⌉
progulku (walk) C^1 ⌉
otložit' (postpone) V^0 ⌊ . C^1 ⌉
vynuždeny (forced) V^0 ⌊ . C^1 ⌐
byli (were) V ⌊

Expression (2) (see p. 337) can be selected to describe the structure of the phrase: *Otložit'progulku na god – značit otkazat'sja ot nee okončatel'no* (To postpone the walk for a year means giving it up for good).

Progulku (walk) C^1 ⌉
god (year) C^1 ⌉
na (for) V^0 ⌊ . C^2 ⌐
otložit' (postpone) V^0 ⌊ C^0 ⌉
nee (it) C^1 ⌉
ot (from) V^0 ⌊ . C^1 ⌉
otkazat'sja (give up, relinquish) V^0 ⌊ . C ⌉
okončatel'no (finally, for good) V ⌊ . C^1 ⌐
značit (means) V ⌊

If we compare the descriptions obtained with each other, i.e., the expressions (1) and (2) (of which it is known how and of what they are constructed) contrasted with the phrases, it is easy to determine where the structures of the phrases themselves are similar and where they differ. It is obvious that they both represent complete groups of bivalent words, and that the transitive complements (C^1) of these words are equally expanded into full valent groups (cf. *vynuždeny otložit'* (forced to postpone)...and *otkazat'sja ot nee okončatel' no* (give it up for good)); it is easy to see from the differences (if, of course, we disregard the lexical divergences) that the transitive complement in the second phrase has a greater depth than that in the first (is expanded in three steps rather than two), not to mention the applicative complement (C^0): it is not expanded at all in the first phrase (*druz'ja* (friends) – C^0).

2. THE LINGUISTIC BASIS OF THE VALENCE GRAMMAR

(1) *The category of valent* is a generalization of the particular categories differentiated in syntax such as:

(a) The FINITE VERB (V_{fin}), whose complements (C^i) have the form of objects and/or subjects: Druz'ja (C^0) *otložili* (V^2) progulku (C^1) (The friends (C^0) *postponed* (V^2) the walk (C^1); druz'jam (C^0) *prišlos'* (V^2) otložit' progulku (The friends (C^0) *had to* (V^2) postpone the walk);

(b) The ADJECTIVE (A), including the participle (Part.), whose complements have the form of objects and/or a determinatum: *sovmestnaja* (V^1) progulka (C) (*common* (V^1) walk (C)); *otložennaja* (V^2) druz'jami (C^0) progulka (C^1) (the walk (C^1) *postponed* (V^2) by the friends (C^0); Čelovek (C^0) *vnimatel'nyj* (V^2) k okružajuščim (C^2) (a man (C^0) *considerate* (V^2) to those around him (C^2);

(c) The ADVERB (Adv.), the complement of which usually functions as a determinatum: rabotat' (C) *sovmestno* (V^1); (*to work* (C) *together* (V^1)); *vnimatel'no* (V^1) otnosit'sja (C) k okružajuščim (to treat (C) one's associates *considerately*) (V^1);

(d) The PREPOSITION (Prep.), one of the complements of which (the transitive one) has the form of an introduced (subordinated) word, and the other one (the applicative) can function as a determinatum, can have some other function, or can be entirely absent: Progulki (C^0) *dlja* (V^2) otdyxajuščix (C^1) (Walks (C^0) *for* (V^2) the holiday-makers (C^1)); Kniga (C^0) *o* (V^2) priklju-čenijax (C^1) (A book (C^0) *on* (V^2) adventure (C^1); Progulka otložili (C^0) *iz-za* (V^2) doždja (They postponed (C^0) the walk *because of* (V^2) the rain);

(e) The CONJUNCTION (Conj.), one of the complements of which (the transitive one) has the form of a clause introduced by the conjunction, and the other (the applicative one) does not have a fixed form and position, and can be lacking: *Kogda* (V^2) sosedi otkazalis' ot sovmestnoj progulki (C^1), druz'ja otpravilis' odni (C^0) (*When* (V^2) the neighbors declined a walk (C^1) with them, the friends set off alone (C^0); Ja znaju, *čto* (V^1) gorod budet (C^1) (I know *that* (V^1) there shall be a city).

Certain PARENTHETICAL WORDS; the complement of a parenthetical word is always the sentence into which the parenthetical word is inserted: Druz'ja, verojatno (V^1), otložili progulku (The friends, *most likely* (V^1), postponed their walk).

The examples enumerated above suffice to show that for all the variety in the parts of speech (of, for example, Russian) and in the ways of forming their complements, they are all valents, since they all require the presence of other words or groups.

We can cite even further considerations which speak in favor of combining these word classes. The words for the parts of speech mentioned above are *equally capable* of assuming the form of complements to other valents, cf.

Valent word	Complement form
Guljaju (I walk) (finite verb)	*Progulka*
sovmestnyj (joint, common) (Adj.)	*sovmestnost'* ('jointness')
sovmestno (jointly, together) (Adv.)	*sovemstnost'*
vozle (by, near) (Prep.)	*blizost'* (nearness, proximity)
esli (if) (Conj.)	*uslovie* (condition)

For example: predpočitaju (I prefer) (V) *progulku* (C^1), *blizost'* (C^1). *sovmestnost'* (C^1).

The words of these classes *behave very similarly* in relation to the speech operations of *junction* and *emphasis* (see below Sections 3, 4).

The generalized category of a valent, which ignores the specific differences between the parts of speech, allows us to make a uniform description of segments belonging to various parts of speech – ti is sufficient that they have a constant valence characterization. Cf. the segments *blagodarja* (thanks to, thanking), *sleduja* (following, *načinaja* (beginning, from), etc., which can be both verbs and prepositions; *verno* (true, most likely), *estestvenno* (naturally, of course), which are adverbs and parenthetical words. Cf. also the numerous examples of conversion (homonymy of parts of speech) in English and French.

Finally, to obtain the next classification of word-forms, for example, to accurately describe the similarities and differences between a finite verb and an adjective (participle), an adjective and an adverb, an adverb and a parenthetical word, it is necessary that all those different word-forms be first included in one universal class.

(2) *The introduction of a single category of complement* – C^i – *into the valance grammar* conforms to the linguistic fact that in the majority of cases, any word or group of words which appears in a coherent phrase serves to specify the content of some other word of this phrase, that is, in a case where this other word is seen to be valent, functions as its complement (see the examples above, p. x).

(3) *Rule I, which reveals the structure of a full valent group*, does not specify whether one or another complement is a dependent actant of the valent or the dominant determinatum thereof. The arcs show the relationships, but do not distinguish the dominant and dependent members:

otložit' (V) progulku (C^1) and otložennaja (V) progulka (C^1).

This neutralization is in accordance with the attempt to single out the relationship of complement to valent as a fundamental relationship between words, thus getting away from more superficial differences of the dominance–dependence type. Such differences will be introduced later in the valence–junction grammar (see below Section 3).

(4) *The differentiation of two types of complements for a valent* (in accordance with its valences) – the applicative complement (C^0) and the transitive complement(s) $C^1,..., C^{n-1}$ – is based on the linguistic fact that one of the complements of a word (or various forms of the same word) does not appear in speech as regularly and obligatorily as the other(s). The regularly appearing complements have a definite form and/or are arranged relative to their

valent in a definite way (in Russian usually after it). Cf.: ctložit' (V) *progulku* (C^1); prišlos' (V) *otložit'* (C^1); k (V) *okružajuščim* (C^1); vnimatel'nyj (V) *k okružajuščim* (C^2); kogda (V) *sosedi otkazalis'* (C^1), etc.

These complements are called transitive because of the definiteness of their arrangement and/or form – by analogy with the transitive objects of verbs.

The second type is made up of complements which appear with their valents (with their individual forms) very irregularly, and generally have neither a constant form, nor a fixed place relative to the valent. It is these complements, which sharply differ from the transitive ones in both regularity of formation and arrangement, which we have called APPLICATIVES. Cf. the irregularity in form and appearance of the applicative complement with various word-forms of the verbal valent:

FINITE: *Druz'ja* (C^0) OTLOŽILI probulku (C^1) (The *friends* (C^0) POST-PONED their walk (C^1), but: *Druz'jam* (C^0) PRIŠLOS' otložit' (C^1) (The *friends* (C^0) HAD to postpone (C^1) (indefiniteness of the applicative complement *form*);

PARTICIPIAL: *Druz'ja* (C^0), OTLOŽIVŠIE progulku (C^1) (*The friends* (C^0) WHO HAD POSTPONED their walk (C^1)), but OTLOŽIV ŠIE progulku (C^1) *druz'ja* (C^0) (indefiniteness of place); OTLOŽNAJA na god (C^2) *progulka* (C^0) (*The walk* (C^0) POSTPONED for a year (C^2)), but OTLOŽENNAJA na god (C^2), éta progulka (C^0) ne sostojalas' voobšče (POSTPONED for a year (C^2), this walk (C^0) didn't take place at all) (shift of applicative complement to neighboring sentence);

ADVERBIAL PARTICIPLE: OTLOŽIV progulku (C^1) na god (C^2), *druz'ja* (C^0) otkazalis' ot nee sovsem (HAVING POSTPONED the walk (C^1) for a year (C^2), *the friends* (C^0) gave up the idea altogether) (shift to neighboring sentence);

INDEFINITE: OTLOŽIT' progulku (C^1) na god (C^2) – značit otkazat'sja ot nee sovsem (To POSTPONE the walk (C^1) for a year (C^2) would mean giving it up altogether (applicative complement absent); *Druz'jam* prišlos' OTLOŽIT' progulku (C^1) na god (C^2) (*The friends* were forced TO POSTPONE their walk (C^1) for a year (C^2)) (absence of immediate relation with the applicative complement).

Cf. the irregularity of the C^0 for valent-*adjectives*: VNIMATEL'NYJ k okružajuš čim, *ětot čelovek* (C^0) sniskal ljubov' sosluživcev (CONSIDERATE of his associates, *this man* (C^0) won the liking of his colleagues) (shift to neighboring sentence).

Cf. also the preposition: On napisal *knigu* (C^0) *o* priključenijx (C^1) (He wrote *a book* (C^0) *about* adventures (C^1)), but O priključenijax (C^1) napisano mnogo khig (Many books have been written *about* adventures (C^1)) (in the second case the applicative complement is lacking for the preposition, because the preposition itself (*o*-about, on) is simply a form of government with the word *napisana* (written)); Vot *ručka* (C^0) OT čemodana (C^1) (Here is the *handle* (C^0) FROM the suitcase (C^1)), but OT čemodana (C^1) otorvalas' *ručka* (*The handle* has been ripped OFF the *suitcase* (C^1)); *Progulku otložili* (C^0) *iz-za* doždja (C^1) (*They postponed the walk* (C^0) BECAUSE OF the rain (C^1)), but: IZ-ZA doždja (C^1) *progulku otložili* (C^0) (BECAUSE OF the rain (C^1) *the walk was postponed* (C^0) (indefiniteness in the position of the applicative complement relative to the valent).

(5) Rule II, which allows us to consider a valence group without an applicative complement as regular, that is, which permits an applicative valence to be left incomplete for a valent $V^{(n)}$, is recognized as reflecting the irregularity in the appearance of the applicative complement for the valents as this was pointed out above.

A special category of applicative (V^0) is introduced to designate valents with an imcomplete applicative valence.

$$
\begin{array}{llll}
\text{Druz'jam} & C^0 & \quad \text{progulku} & C^1 \\
\text{progulku} & C^1 & \quad \text{god} & C^1 \\
\text{otložit'} & V^0 \quad . \quad C^1 & \quad \text{na} & V^0 \quad . \quad C^2 \\
\hline
\text{prišlos'} & V^1 & \quad \text{otloživ} & V^0 \\
\end{array}
$$

$$
\begin{array}{llll}
 & & \text{druz'ja} & C^0 \\
\text{doždja} & C^1 & \text{nee} & C^1 \\
\text{iz-za} & V^0 & \text{ot} & V^0 \quad . \quad C^2 \\
\hline
\text{progulku} & C^1 & \text{otkazalis'} & V \quad . \quad C \\
\text{otložit'} & V^0 \quad . \quad C^1 & \text{okončatel'no} & V \\
\hline
\text{prišlos'} & V^0 \\
\end{array}
$$

(6) *The category of applicative* can be contrasted to such externally heterogeneous constructions as verbal adverb groups, detached adjectival groups, detached noun-apposition groups, prepositional or conjunctive groups, etc., when these constructions are adjacent to a full valence group within a phrase; for example:

Otloživ progulku na god (V^0), *druz'ja otkazalis' ot nee sovsem* ($V^{(n)}$),
Otložennaja na god (V^0), *progulka ne sostojalas' vovse* ($V^{(n)}$),
Inžener po obrazovaniju (V^0), *on ne umel rešat' čisto-matematičeskie zadači* ($V^{(n)}$).

(*An engineer by education* (V^0), he was unable to solve purely mathematical problems ($V^{(n)}$)).

Iz-za svoego inženernogo obrazovanija (V^0), *on ne umel rešat' čisto matematičeskie zadači* ($V^{(n)}$) (*Because of his engineer's education* (V^0), he was unable to solve purely mathematical problems ($V^{(n)}$);

U nego (V^0) *vsegda veselo* ($V^{(n)}$) (*At his place* (lit. *by him* (V^0) it's always lively); *Esli druz'ja otložili progulku na god* (V^0), to oni otkazalis' ot nee sovsem ($V^{(n)}$) (*If the friends have postponed their walk for a year* (V^0), then they have given up the idea altogether ($V^{(n)}$).

An applicative, if a full valence group in the phrase corresponds to its unexpanded complement, will be called an annex (anneks).

It is easy to see that the proposed formal generalization is justified in respect to content: the annex usually functions in the phrase as an adverbial for a valence group adjacent to it.

(7) *By means of the categories of the full valence group, and the applicative* it is possible to describe precisely the difference between certain uses of one and the same word or group, e.g., between uses of a preposition such as: Petrov *u* Ivanova (Petrov is *at* Ivanov's), *U* Ivanova ukrali den'gi (Money was stolen *from* Ivanov), *U* Ivanova slučilos' nesčast'e (Ivanov *had* an accident).

U in the first phrase is a valent, all of whose valences have been completed:

Petrov	C^0
Ivanova	C^1
u	V

U in the second phrase is an applicative, a transitive complement to the valent *ukrali* (stolen, stole), and consequently, is *not* an annex:

Ivanova	C			
u	V^0	.	C^2	
den'gi			C^1	
ukrali			V^0	

Finally, in the third phrase *u* is an applicative neighboring on a full valence group and is therefore an annex:

Ivanova	C
u	V^0
nesčast'e	C^0
slučilos'	V

(8) *In introducing the generalizing category of component* (P) *for the complements* C^i *and the valent* V, we wanted to emphasize that in spite of the variety of which they fulfill in the organization of the external structure of a valence group (rules I–II), these components can just as easily have their own internal structure. In fact, rule III shows that any component of valence group V, or C^i can in turn represent a full valence group; the latter can be further expanded according to rules I or II (see also below on junction).

Thus, the structure of the phrase *Ja znaju – gorod budet* (I know there shall be a city):

$$
\begin{array}{ll}
\text{Ja} & C^0 \\
\text{gorod} \quad C^0 \\
\text{budet} \quad V \\
\text{znaju} & V_k
\end{array}
\quad . \quad
\begin{array}{l}
C^1 \\
V_k
\end{array}
$$

is the result of the consecutive expansion:

$$
\begin{array}{ll}
V_k^{(n)} \to C^0 \quad C^1 \quad V^k & \text{Rule I} \\
\quad\Downarrow & \\
C^1 \to V_1^{(n)} . C^1 & \text{Rule III + B} \\
\quad\Downarrow & \\
V_1^{(n)} \to C^0 \quad V_1 & \text{Rule I}
\end{array}
\Bigg\} = C^0 \quad C^0 \quad V_1 . C^1 \quad V^k,
$$

where the internal valence group $V^{(n)}$, obtained with rule III, is further expanded according to rule I, and changes into the full group *gorod budet*. (This expansion is not optimal – see p. 353.)

$$
\begin{array}{lll}
\text{Druz'jan} & & C^0 \\
\text{progulka} & & C^1 \\
\text{den'} & C^1 & C^2 \\
\text{na} & V_m^0 & V_1^0 \\
\text{otložit'} & & \\
\text{prišlos} & & V_k
\end{array}
. \quad C^1
$$

The structure of the phrase Druz'jam prišlos' otložit' progulku na den'. is in contrast constructed in such a way that the internal valence groups $V_1^{(n)}$ and $V_m^{(n)}$ obtained with rule III are then expanded according to rule II and transformed into applicatives (the infinitive group V_1^0 and the prepositional group V_m^0):

$$
\begin{array}{ll}
V_k^{(n)} \to C^0 \quad C^1 \quad V_k & \text{Rule I} \\
\quad\Downarrow & \\
C^1 \to V_1^{(n)} \quad . \quad C^1 & \text{Rule III + B} \\
\quad\Downarrow & \\
V_1^{(n)} \to C^1 \quad C^2 \quad V_1^0 & \text{Rule II} \\
\quad\Downarrow & \\
C^2 \to V_m^{(n)} \quad . \quad C^2 & \text{Rule III + B} \\
\quad\Downarrow & \\
V_m^{(n)} \to C^1 \quad V_m^0 & \text{Rule II}
\end{array}
\Bigg\} =
$$

$$
= C^0 \quad C^1 \quad C^1 \quad V_m^0 \quad . \quad C^2 \quad V_1^0 \quad . \quad C^1 \quad V_k
$$

(9) *The possibility of expanding the internal valence group obtained with rule III not only in the form of a full group (with rule I), but also in the form of an applicative (with rule II)* once again emphasizes the essential nature of the applicative category. An applicative can function as the internal structure of some component of an external valence group. Cf.:

$$\text{U Ivanova } (V^0 \quad . \quad C^2) \text{ ukrali } (V^2) \text{ den'gi } (C^1).$$

The expressions of the valence language allow us, on the one hand, to describe a very large number of conceivable natural phrases, as can be seen from the examples cited earlier. This can in particular be attributed to the sufficient degree of abstractness that the few categories which form the basis for a valence grammar possess.

On the other hand, a description made with the help of an artificial language is convenient in that it is easy to judge from the grammar of such a language just how adequate it is for describing all conceivable natural sentences. Thus, the valence language is clearly inadequate for the description of all natural sentences, since it is impossible to derive in its grammar the expressions necessary, for example, to be able to differentiate between the following two intuitively different phrases: (a) ljubovat'sja *krasotoj* (V) *lužajki* (c) (to admire *the beauty* (V) *of the lawn* (C)), (b) ljubovat'sja *krasivoj* (V) *lužajkoj* (C) (to admire the *beautiful* (V) *lawn* (C)). If *krasota* (beauty) and *krasivoj* (beautiful) are in an identical way valence words (see above, p. 341), then we are forced to give a single expression to both phrases:

(a)

lužajki	C ⌉		
krasotoj	V_k ⌊⌉	.	C^1 ⌉
ljubovat'sja			V_1^0 ⌊⌉

(b)

lužajkoj	C ⌉		
krasivoj	V_k ⌊⌉	.	C^1 ⌉
ljubovat'sja			V_1^0 ⌊⌉

which obviously levels the differences between them: the structure of phrase (b) is reduced to the structure of phrase (a).

Furthermore, both of these phrases have a quality in common, namely, that the *whole world-group* (a) *krasotoj lužajki* or (b) *krasivoj lužajkoj* should in each case function as the complement (C^1) to the valent 'ljubovat'sja', and not the individual words *krasotoj* or *krasivoj*; at the same time, category C^1 is compared in the valence expressions to just these separate words, and we have nowhere agreed to have the internal category V_k with C^1 ($V_k . C^1$) designate the whole valence group, that is, V and its complement.

Both of these examples indicate that the valence grammar must be expanded.

3. 2ND SYSTEM: A VALENCY-JUNCTIVE GRAMMAR

The junctive (in the sense described by Jespersen, 1924) 'superstructure' over

a valence expression makes it possible to (a) describe the immediate relations not only between individual words, but also between whole word-
groups, cof. (dolgo ljubovat'sja – long admire/admire for a long time) V
(krasivoj lužajkoj – the beautiful lawn) C^1 and (b) specify just which word of
such a word group is its representative ('node') within a particular immediate
relation, cf.: (dolgo *ljubovat'sja*) V (krasivoj *lužajkoj*) C^1 or (dolgo *ljubovat'sja*)
V (*krasotoj* lužajki). Valence-junction expressions are close in meaning to
the SSG language (see Gladky, 1969).

(Additional) rules of formation

(IV) $V^{(n)}$. $P \rightarrow V^{(n)}$. W-JUNC . P

(V) $V^{(n)}$. W'-JUNC $\rightarrow V^{(n)}$. W-adj   W'-J

Categories (in addition to those given earlier):

W – a generalized designation for some ELEMENT of the valence group $V^{(n)}$,
either the category of valent V, its immediate or indirect (oposredovan-
noe) complement C^i, or, finally, the category of the valence group $V^{(n)}$
as a whole; it is this last feature which distinguishes the concept of an element (W) from the concept of a component (P), which is a proper part
of the valence group.

$V^{(n)}$. W-JUNC . P – W-JUCNTION OVER THE VALENCE GROUP $V^{(n)}$, OR A
JUNCTION OVER $V^{(n)}$ WITH RESPECT TO ITS ELEMENT W, or with *node* W;
this is a method of specifying what element of the valence group $V^{(n)}$
the external category P is related to (see above p. 336) when it is assigned
to the valence group as a whole. Accordingly, if the phrases (a) *ljubovat'-
sja krasotoj lužajki* and (b) *ljubovat'sja krasivoj lužajkoj* cannot be distinguished by means of the valence language (see above, p. 346), using
a junction we can give them two different expressions:

lužajki   C
krasotoj   V   . *V-junc* . C^1
ljubovat'sja   V

lužajkoj   C
krasivoj   V   . *C-junc* . C^1
ljubovat'sja   V

W-J – W-JUNCT (junkt), or a JUNCT OF SOME VALENCE GROUP IN RESPECT TO
ELEMENT W of this group; element W of group $V^{(n)}$ is designated as the
representative for the whole group to which the external category of this
group should be directly related; example: in the phrase ljubovat'sja
krasivoj lužajkoj the word *lužajkoj* is on the one hand a complement (C)

of the valence word *krasivoj* (V^1), and on the other hand, it is precisely *lužajkoj*, but already as the representative of the whole first valence group (its junct in relation to C), to which the external category belongs – the complement (C^1) with the valent ljubovat'sja (V^2): (lužajkoj

(C) krasivoj (V^1)) *lužajkoj* (C-J . C^1) ljubovst'sja (V^2), that is, 'ljubovat'sja toj lužajkoj (C-J), kotoraja (est') krasivaja lužajka' (admire that lawn (C-J) which is a beautiful lawn). Cf. ljubovat'sja krasotoj lužajki, where the valence word *krasota* (V^1) is the C-junction:

(lužajki (C) krasotoj (V^1)) *krasotoj* (V-J . C^1) ljubovat'ska (V^2).

$V^{(n)}$. W-adj – $V^{(n)}$ as W-ADJUNCT, or $V^{(n)}$ IN THE CAPACITY OF ADJUNCT ATTACHED TO W, or with *node* W; this signifies the fact that a valence group $V^{(n)}$ receives an external category only through its own element W, which should be repeated as the representative of this whole group (see above); in other words, W-adj is a preliminary external category for $V^{(n)}$, signifying that the basic external category of this group is indicated in its nodal element W, which is repeated as the W-junct of the whole group. The example cited above looks like this in its complete form: lužajkoj (C) krasivoj (V . C-adj) lužajkoj (C-J . C^1) ljubovat'sja (V^2), i.e., 'ljubovat'sja toj lužajkoj (C-J), kotoraja est' krasivaja lužajka';

cf.: lužajki (C) krasotoj (V. V-adj) krasotoj (V-J . C^1) ljubovat'sja (V^2), i.e., 'ljubovat'sja toj krasotoj (V-J), kotoraja est' krasota lužajki'.

3.1. *Comments*

(1) Rule IV shows that any full valence group, if it comprises the inner content of component P (valent or complement) of some other valence group, can be subjected to the operation of 'junction' with respect to any of its elements. Caregory P here remains the external category of the whole junction.

(2) Rule V reveals the essence of a junction: the valence group $V^{(n)}$ receives a preliminary external category, W-adjunct, and should attach itself to the repeated appearance of its element W, where W functions as the representative of the whole valence group, that is, as junct W-J. It is understood that the external category P, which is left outside the parentheses' of rule IV, is after expansion transferred to the junct:

$$V^{(n)} \quad . \quad \text{W-adj} \quad \text{W-J} \quad . \quad P$$

(3) The replacement of the general symbol W by its occasional meanings

C^i, V, V^0 or $V^{(n)}$ is implied; these substitutions should be uniform for all the appearances of symbol W in a given expression which are supplied with the index (').

This expanded file of categories and rules of formation is called below a *valence-junction grammar*.

Among the expressions which are derivable in the system of the valence-junction grammar, the following obviously appear:

(3)   C   V . C-adj   C-J . C'   V

(4)   C   V . V-adj   V-J . C'   V

which are descriptions of the phrases ljubovat'sja krasivoj lužajkoj and ljubovat'sja krasotoj lužajki, respectively.

From our treatment of rules IV–V it is possible to derive two conclusions:

(A) An expression constituting a junction also contains some valence group.

(B) If there is more than one valence group within a single regular valence-junction expression, then all of them but one must be junctions.

3.2. *The Linguistic Basis for the Junction Grammar*

(1) *Rule V makes it possible to repeat element W of some valence group* $V^{(n)}$ *as a junction, and only as such allows it to have in addition any external category, regardless of what category this element had within the first valence group.*

This conditional allowance is brought forth to describe the linguistic fact that a single word in an actual phrase can function as many components, i.e., as complements to various valence words:

dolgoždannuju (V) voskresnuju (V) *progulku* ($C_{,1}$ C_2, C_3) otložili (V)
(the long-awaited (V)
Sunday (V) *walk* (C_1, C_2, C_3) was postponed (V)),

or as a complement in relation to one word and as a valent in relation to another:

voskresnuju progulku (C) okončatel'no (V) *otložili* (C, V).

The interrelations between these various functions for one word cannot be described in the form of a complex V. P, i.e,. as an unity of external and internal categories. These different functions for a given word are independent of each other: each of them designates separetaly a special valence relationship of the given word to one or another of the other words of the phrase, and all of these functions are thereby EXTERNAL categories of the word in question.

A natural way of describing the relations existing between the external categories of a single word is to:

(2) contrast the individual appearance of a word in the appropriate valence group to a special external category of this word. For example, for the phrase otložit' dolgoždannuju voskresnuju progulku, the word *progulku* is presented in the form of three appearances:

Progulku	C_1	1st appearance, as a complement to the valence
voskresnuju	V	'voskresnuju',
progulku	C_2	2nd appearance, as a complement to the valence
dolgoždannuju	V	'dolgoždannuju',
progulku	C_3	3rd appearance, as a complement to the valence
otložit'	V^0	'otložit''.

(3) indicate the identity of these various appearances. The significance of rule V consists in the identification of each successive appearance of word X with its preceding appearance; this identification is attained, firstly, through the relation between the complex W-J . P (in our example C-J . C) ascribed to word X in some not-first appearance, and category W-adj (C-adj) assigned to word Y, which is valent for word X in its preceding appearance; secondly, through the symbol (in our case C) attached with Y, since this symbol is a precise 'address', which points beyond Y to the sought-after word X in its preceding appearance; cf.:

X=progulku	C_1		
Y=voskresnuju	V	. C_1-adj	indentification 1
X=progulku		C_1-J	. C_2
Y=dolgoždannuju		V	. C_2-adj identifica-
X=progulku			C_2-J C_3 tion 2
Y=otložit'			$V^{(0)}$

The identity of the last appearance of the word with its preceding one should be understood conditionally. We are in reality speaking of the identity of the last appearance of word X (C_{i+1}) not only with word X of the preceding appearance (C_i), but also with the whole preceding valence group in which X appears; word X in its last appearance (C_{i+1}) designates, in effect, not only itself, but itself in the capacity of a JUNCTION of the whole preceding group (C_i-J . C_{i+1}), i.e., the whole preceding adjunct valence group (C_i V . C_i-adj), which thereby makes it possible for the valence-junction language to establish the relations existing between whole word-groups. Cf.

(otložit') V (dolgoždannuju voskresnuju progulku) C_i V . C_i-adj C_i-J . C_{i+1}.
Permitting the 'multiplication' of a single word proves to be a very
convenient way of conditionally designating all of the more extended word-
groups, however unnatural this might seem at first glance. And, vice versa,
the single appearance of determinata words in the phrases of a natural
language should be treated as an ordinary example of omission (ellipsis).
These omissions, which have been legitimatized by the traditions of natural
language, should be expanded in an explicit language.

It is well to add here that the convention accepted in syntactic descriptions
of treating attributive relationships as non-valent cannot be considered
successful in either form[2] or content. We think that the attributive relationship does not absolutely differ from the valent one, but does so only 'privativ-
ly', that is, includes it, differing in an additional feature – the junction relation, cf.

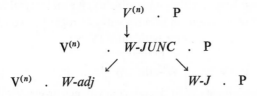

(4) *Rules IV-V, which make it possible to multiply the appearances of one and
the same word in various functions,* simultaneously establish a fixed order of
appearances: its appearance in a valence group constituting the inner content
of some component (P) is considered to come first, and an appearance to
which an external category (component P itself) is ascribed follows:

$$V^{(n)} \ . \ P$$
$$\downarrow$$
$$V^{(n)} \quad . \quad W\text{-}JUNC \ . \ P$$
$$\swarrow \qquad\qquad \searrow$$
$$V^{(n)} \ . \ W\text{-}adj \qquad\qquad W\text{-}J \ . \ P$$

This arrangement of appearances should reflect an intuitively perceptible
linguistic reality: the various functions of a single word in a phrase are in fact
not simultaneous, but occur in a definite sequence: thus, in the phrase
dolgoždannuju voskresnuju progulku otložil', it is clear that it was not the
'walk' (progulka) in general that was long-*awaited* (dolgoždannaja), but the
'Sunday walk' (voskresnaja progulka), and then is postponed not just 'the
walk', and not even 'the Sunday walk', but 'the Sunday walk' which was in
addition 'long-awaited'. This sequence of functions is shown by repeating the

---

[2] Cf. cases where a single word has two 'masters' in a phrase of the type:
among *those* the people trust.

word *progulka* in the form of a junction representing an ever more complicated content – due to the next junctured valence group. Cf.:

progulku C_1 ⌉
voskresnuju   V ⌊⌋ . C-adj ⌉
progulku $C\text{-}J_2$ ⌊⌋ . C ⌉
dolgoždannuju V^0 ⌊⌋ . C-adj ⌉
progulku $C\text{-}J_3$ ⌊⌋ . C^1 ⌉
otložili V^0 ⌊⌋

Cf. also the phrases (a) Progulku okončatel'no otložili, and (b) Progulku otložili okončatel'no. In the first instance the word *otložili* at first functions as a complement to the valent *okončatel'no* and then, as a junction (not just *otložili* but *okončatel'no otložili*), functions as a valent for *progulku*. In the second case, in contrast, the word *otložili* first functions as a valent to *progulku*, and only then, as the junction of the whole valence group ('progulko-otloženie') becomes a complement of the valent *okončatel'no*.

(a)   (b)
progulku C' ⌉   progulku C' ⌉
otložili C ⌉   otložili V^0 ⌊⌋ . V-adj ⌉
okončatel'no V ⌊⌋ . C-adj ⌉   otložili   V-J ⌊⌋ . C ⌉
otložili $C\text{-}J$ ⌊⌋ . V^0 ⌊⌋ okončatel'no   V ⌊⌋

Accordingly, if in phrase (a) the adverb *okončatel'no* is an adjunct, in phrase (b) it is an independent valent.

(5) *The abbreviated designation W, which names any element of an internal valence group from a junction*, makes it possible to give an integral representation of the structure of junctions in general without regard to concrete types of junctions, namely, in accordance with rules IV–V:

$$V^{(n)} \quad . \quad P{\to}V^{(n)} \quad . \quad W'\text{-adj.} \quad \overline{W'\text{-J}} \quad . \quad P,$$

i.e. "some one of the elements W in the internal valence group $V^{(n)}$ should be repeated as the representative of this whole group (junction W-J) in order to take on the external category P, which was originally assigned to the whole valence group."

This generalization is in fact legitimate, since in such a formulation all the intuitively similar constructions which are called attributive have the same junction structure, whether this construction consists of 'adjective + noun' (*dolgoždannaja voskresnaja progulka*), 'noun + attributive dependent clause' (*progulka, kotoruju dolgo ždali*), or 'adverb in pre-position + verb' (*okončatel' no otložilj*). The generalization is expecially attractive in that it helps us to see the same junction structure even in constructions which are uasally sharply distinguished from attributive clauses, namely, object clauses introduced with the conjunction *čto* (that) (including subject clauses): Ja slyšal, *čto on poet* (I heard *him singing*); *Čto volki žadnyvsjakij znaet* (lit. *That wolves are greedy* – everyone knows); Čto volki žadny, vsem izvestno (That wolves are greedy is well-known/known to all).

It is obvious first of all that all completive clauses have any rate the structure $V^{(n)}$. P, that is, they are full valent groups to which some external category is attributed, namely, the complement category: $V^{(n)}$. C. In the second place, since we have agreed to understand by element W of group $V^{(n)}$ not only the individual components of the group (V or C^i), but also the entire valence group $V^{(n)}$ taken as a whole, a completive clause can, in a more expanded form, have a shape which exactly corresponds to a junction structure:

$$V^{(n)} \quad . \quad V^{(n)}\text{-adj} \quad V^{(n)}\text{-J} \quad . \quad C^1 \quad V$$

Volki   žadny (tot fakt, čto) volki žadny vsjjakij znaet

Or, in a detailed description:

Vsjakij					C^0
volki	C^0				
žadny	V		.	$V^{(n)}$-adj	
(čto) volki žadny				$V^{(n)}$-J	. C^1
znaet					V

Cf. also: Čto volki žadny, vsem izvestno:

volki	C^0			
žadny	V	.	$V^{(n)}$-adj	
(čto) volki žadny			$V^{(n)}$-J	. C^0
vsem				C^1
izvestno				V

The subject clause of the last example differs from a completive clause in a detail as minor as the external category C^0 instead of C^1; in other respects a subject clause is also a junction with the junction $V^{(n)}$-J.

(6) *The generalized nature of element W in the expression $V^{(n)}$. W-adj* also consists in the fact that is it possible to understand W not only as an immediate, but also as any oblique complement to the valent V^n from $V^{(n)}$, that is, as a complement to a complement of V^n etc. Allowing this takes into account natural-language constructions of the form: Lužajka, *č'ej* krasotoj my ljubovalis', kišela zmejami (The meadow *whose* beauty we admired was

crawling with snakes).

My		C^0	
lužajka (č'ej)	C^*		
krasotoj	V	. V-adj	
krasotoj	V-J	. C^1	
ljubovalis'		V . C^*-adj	
lužajka		C^*-J . C^0	
zmejami			C^1
kišela			V

Cf.: Lužajka, kotoroj my ljubovalis'..., where W is an immediate complement to valent V.

my	C^0	
lužajka (kotoroj)	C^1	
ljubovalis'	V . C^1-adj	
lužajka	C^1-J . C^0	

(7) The introduction of the generalizing category W does not exclude, but on the contrary, presupposes the concretization of this category, thanks to which the particular types of junction expressions which reflect the diversity of the corresponding constructions of natural language are 'denumerated'. Some of the particular forms of juncture are menioned here:

(I) $\quad W = C^i : V^{(n)} . C^i\text{-adj} \quad C^i\text{-J} . P,$

i.e., from the internal valence group $V^{(n)}$, the complement (C^i) is chosen as its representative to assume the external category (P).

A concrete junction such as this can serve to describe the attributive constructions:

– 'adjective or attributive clause + noun': *voskresnaja progulka, dolgoždannaja progulka; progulka, kotoruju dolgo ždali;*

– 'subordinate clause with an indefinite pronoun': *(to) čto on poet* ((that) which he sings); *(tot) kto prišel* (person) who came);

– or also to represent the structure of the combination 'pre-positional adverb + verb': *dolgo ždat', okončatel'no otkazatisja, postojanno kurit,* (smoke constantly).

Examples: *Dolgoždannuju progulku prišlos'otložit'*

Progulku	C^1		
dolgoždannuju	V . C^1-adj		
progulku		C^1-J . C^1	
otložit'		V . C^1	
prišlos'			V

Emu prišloz' *dolgo ždat'* priema (He had to wait a long time to be received)

```
Emu                                          C⁰ ⊐
priema                          C¹ ⊐           |
ždat'         C ⊐                |             |
dolgo         V ⌐⌐  .  C-adj ⊐   |             |
ždat'                   C-J ⌐⌐ . V⁰ ⌐⌐ . C¹ ⊐
prišlos'                                     V ⌐⌐
```

Progulka, *kotoruju vse dolgo ždali*, sorvalas'

```
Progulka                        C¹ ⊐
vse                             C⁰ ⊐
ždali         C ⊐                 |
dolgo         V ⌐⌐  C-adj ⊐       |
ždali              C-J ⌐⌐ . V ⌐⌐ . C'-adj ⊐
progulka                            C -J ⌐⌐ . C⁰ ⊐
sorvalas'                                    V ⌐⌐
```

Ja slyšu, *čtó on poet* (I hear *what he is singing*):

```
Ja                                      C⁰ ⊐
on               C⁰ ⊐                     |
čtó              C¹ ⊐                     |
poet             V ⌐⌐  C¹-adj ⊐           |
čtó                    C¹-J ⌐⌐ . C' ⊐
slyšu                             V ⌐⌐
```

Druz'ja *okončatel'no otkazalis'* ot progulki:

```
Druz'ja                                 C⁰ ⊐
progulki              C' ⊐                |
ot                    V⁰ ⌐⌐  .  C² ⊐
otkazalis'      C ⊐               |
okončatel'no    V ⌐⌐ . C-adj ⊐    |
otkazalis'             C-J ⌐⌐ . V ⌐⌐
```

The external category (P) of a junction does not at all depend on its internal category W, and can be anything, e.g.:

— a complement to an external valent:

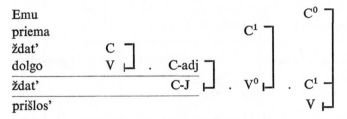

otložit' (V) *dolgoždannuju progulku* (C-J . C̄)

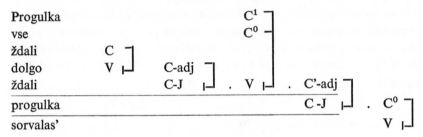

prišlos' (V) *dolgo ždat'* (C-J . C̲)

– and/or the valent for the external complements:

dolgo ždat'(C-J . $\underline{V}$) priema (C′)

Druz'ja (C⁰) okončatel'no otkazalis'(C-J . $\underline{V}$) ot (C²) progulki

(II) $W = \underline{V} : V^{(n)}$.   V-adj   V-J   .   P

that is, valent (V) of the internal valence group with the external category P is chosen as the representative of this group.

This type of junction is used to describe a construction where the principal valent (the predicate) of some sentence proves to be a complement of an external valent, whether that be an anticipatory verb or a post-positional adverb. For example: Ja slyšal (V), *kak* on *poet* (V-J . C¹) (I heard him singing):

```
Ja                                            C⁰ ⌐
on                    C⁰ ⌐
poet                  V  ⌐⌐  . V-adj ⌐
(kak) poet                 V-J  ⌐⌐  . C  ─
─────────────────────────────────────
slyšal                               V ⌐⌐
```

Ot progulki oni *otkazalis'* (V-J C) okončatel'no (V)

```
Oni                            C⁰ ⌐
progulki              C′ ⌐
ot                    V⁰ ⌐⌐  C² ─
otkazalis'                     V ⌐⌐  . V-adj ⌐
otkazalis'                          V-J ⌐⌐  . C ⌐
─────────────────────────────────────────
okončatel'no                                V ⌐
```

It is to this type of junction (cf. above, p. 355) that belong the speech constructions such as: (a) *Ivanov kak student* zasluživaet pooščrenija (*Ivanov, as a student*, deserves encouragement); (b) *Ivanov* ograničen *v pravax* (*Ivanov is limited in his rights/Ivanov's rights* are restricted); (c) *On* pedagogue *po prizvaniju* (*He is a pedagogue by vocation*). An intelligent structural interpretation consists in the fact that the words in italics introduced by the collocations *kak* (=in the capacity of), or the prepositions *v* and *po* constitute a junction with the grammatical subject of the phrase, and jointly as junctive function as complements of the predicate:

(a)   *Those 'student qualities'* which Ivanov possesses deserve encouragement.

(b)   *The rights* which Ivanov enjoys are limited.

(c) *The vocation* belonging to him is that of a pedagogue.

(d) *On* porazil vsex *svoim peniem* (*He* surprised everyone *with his singing*) 'To kak on poet porarilo vsex' (*How he sang* surprised everyone).

Cf. in a formal description:

(a)

Ivanov	C
student	V
student (kak)	V-adj · V-J
pooščrenija	C⁰
zasluživaet	C¹ · V

$$\text{Ivanov} \quad \text{C}$$
$$\text{student} \quad \text{V} \quad . \quad \text{V-adj}$$
$$\text{student (kak)} \quad \text{V-J} \quad . \quad \text{C}^0$$
$$\text{pooščrenija} \qquad\qquad \text{C}^1$$
$$\text{zasluživaet} \qquad\qquad \text{V}$$

(b)

$$\text{Ivanov} \quad \text{C}$$
$$\text{pravax} \quad \text{V} \quad . \quad \text{V-adj}$$
$$\text{pravax (v)} \quad \text{V-J} \quad . \quad \text{C}$$
$$\text{ograničen} \qquad\qquad \text{V}$$

(c)

$$\text{On} \quad \text{C}$$
$$\text{prizvaniju} \quad \text{V} \quad . \quad \text{V-adj}$$
$$\text{prizvaniju (po)} \quad \text{V-J} \quad . \quad \text{C}$$
$$\text{pedagog} \qquad\qquad \text{V}$$

(d)

$$\text{On (svoim)} \quad \text{C}$$
$$\text{peniem} \quad \text{V} \quad . \quad \text{V-adj}$$
$$\text{peniem} \quad \text{V-J} \quad . \quad \text{C}^0$$
$$\text{vsex} \qquad\qquad \text{C}'$$
$$\text{porazil} \qquad\qquad \text{V}$$

(III) $W = V^{(n)} \; : \; V^{(n)} \; . \; V^{(n)}\text{-adj} \quad V^{(n)}\text{-J} \; . \; \text{P}$

i.e., the valence group taken as a whole is the representative of the internal valence group with the external category P.

The completive clauses with the conjunction *čto* cited above (p. 353) are examples of this kind of concrete junction. We see, in fact, that these clauses are individual occurrences of junction, and their intuitively perceptible peculiarity in comparison with the two preceding cases (I and II) can evidently be explained by the fact that it is not an individual component (C^i or V) of an internal valence group with an external category which functions as its representative, but the internal group taken as a whole ($V^{(n)}$).

(8) *Precisely differentiating for a single word two external categories*, one of which, (W), is related to the internal valence group, and the second of which, (P), is related to the external group, cf.:

otložit' (V) dolgoždannuju (V) *progulku* (*W*-J . P),

makes it possible to establish a logical hierarchy of differences in the classification, of, for example, attributive constructions. Obviously, the most superficial feature of classification will be the character of category P, in accordance with which these constructions will prove to be either predicative (V) or completive (C^i); the complements can further be divided into subclasses with respect to the concrete type of complement – C^0, C', C^{n-1}, i.e., applicative complements ('subjectives'), direct-objectives (C'), etc.; finally, further division within the obtained subclasses should be based on the meaning of the internal category W: cf. cases I, II, and III above.

Thus, the subordinate clauses in the phrases:

(a)	(Ja slyšu,) *čtó on poet*	$= C^1$-J . C^1
(b)	(Mne slyšno,) *čt on poet*	$= C^1$-J . C^0
(c)	(Ja znaju,) *čto on poet*	$= V^{(n)}$-J . C
(d)	(Mne izvestno,) *čto on poet*	$= V^{(n)}$-J . C^0
(e)	(Ja slyšu,) *kak on poet*	$= V$-J . C^1
(f)	(Mne slyšno,) *kak on poet*	$= V$-J . C^0

belong to the class of external completives, where (a), (c) and (e) are transitive completives (C^1) and (b), (d) and (f) are applicative completives ('subjectives'-C^0). Within the subclasses (a), (c), (e): (a) belongs to the class of completive-junctural sentences (C'-J), since *čtó on poet* is a junct with regard to the complement to the internal valent *poet*; (c) belongs to the class of global-junctural sentences ($V^{(n)}$-J), since *čto on poet* is a junct of the group $V^{(n)}$ taken as a whole; (e) belongs to the class of valence-junctural sentences (V-J), since 'kak on poet' is a junct of the valent of the group. We find an analogous division within the subclasses (b), (d), and (f).

(9) *Analysing the structure of a junction into its member parts*:

$$V^{(n)} \quad . \quad \text{W-adj} \quad \text{W-J} \quad . \quad P$$

we can give an unambiguous and structurally determined (COHERENT, cf. p. 338) interpretation of the functional role of the linguistic means which make up the junction in natural speech. To illustrate this, let us dwell for a moment on some of these means.

The conjunctive word 'kotoryj' (which, that, who) (in all its word-forms) is used to form junctions when the central word W of a junction functions as the object in both the inner adjunctive and outer valency groups (i.e., $W = C^i$ and $P = C^j$). The conjunctive word here is first of all a REPRESENTATIVE of the NODAL WORD in the inner valency group. Secondly, through its inflected ending it indicates the role of the nodal word in relation to the valent of THE INNER GROUP; the ending of the nodal word itself indicates the role of the nodal word in relation to the outer VALENCY GROUP. Thirdly, the conjunctive word *'kotoryj'* functions as A MARKER OF THE ADJUNCTION W-adj in the inner valency group.

This triple role of the conjunctive word in forming junctive structures can be shown within parentheses opposite its category in descriptions of appropriate phrases:

Progulka, kotoruju vse ždali, sorvalas',
'The outing which everyone had waited for fell through'

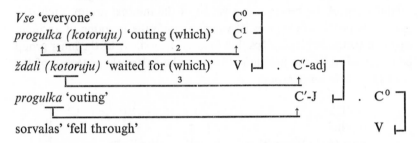

(the numbers on the lines correspond to the three functions of the conjunctive word enumerated above).

The conjunctive word čto (kto) (stressed) 'what, who' differs from *kotoryj* by the fact that together with the three functions given above, it can also designate the nodal word IN THE ROLE OF COMPLEMENT to the outer valent.

Cf. *Ja slyšu, čtó on poet*, 'I hear *what* he is singing':

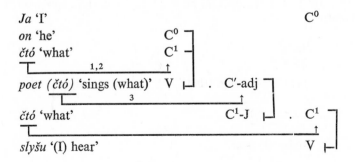

The conjunction čto (unstressed) 'that' functions mainly as a MARKER of AD-JUNCTION in the whole complete valency group (a sentence) which it introduces; since *čto* designates global junction, i.e., the whole inner valency group is a junct, the first and second functions disappear; on the other hand, similar to the conjunctive word *čtó*, the conjuction *čto* indicates that the group it introduces is a COMPLEMENT to the *outer* valent (4).

Ja znaju, čto on poet 'I know that he is singing'

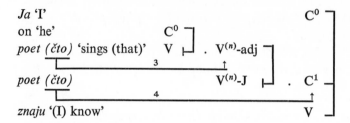

The conjunctive word kak (unstressed) 'that' is used to form a junction when the nodal word of the junction is a valent of the internal group. Thus, the conjunctive word *kak*: (1) gives its valency group the meaning of an inner group or an ADJUNCT; (2) specifies that namely the VALENT of the inner group is the nodal word of the junction; (3) gives the valent the category of the junct of the whole inner group.

```
Ja 'I'                                              C⁰ ┐
on 'he'                           C⁰ ┐                 │
poet (kak) 'sings (that)'   V └┘  . V-adj ┐            │
   └─────────────────1,2──────────────┘↑  │           │
poet (kak)                          V-J └┘ . C¹ ┘      │
   └─────────────3───────────────────┘↑               │
slyšu '(I) hear'                                    V └┘
```

The noun category (pénie ← poet) 'singing ← sings' fulfills only the last func-tion for the valent word, giving it the character of a JUNCT. Cf.: Ja slyšu, *kak* on *poet*, (lit.): 'I hear how/that he is singing' = Ja slyšu ego *penie* 'I hear his singing':

```
Ja 'I'                                              C⁰
on 'he'                           C⁰ ┐
poet (kak) 'sings (that)'   V └┘  . V-adj ┐
   └─────────────────1,2──────────────┘↑  │
poet (kak)                          V-J └┘ . C¹ ┐
   └─────────────3───────────────────┘↑        │
slyšu '(I) hear'                                V └┘
```

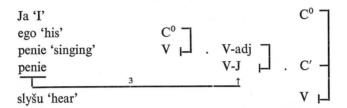

In contrast to the empty word *kak*, however, the nominal form of the valent is ambiguous: it can equally well denote not only *valent* junct (V-J), but also a GLOBAL junct ($V^{(n)}$-J), i.e., it can be an occasional synonym of the conjunction *čto* (see above). Cf. Ja slyšu *penie* 'I hear (the) *singing*' = Ja slyšu, *kak* kto-to poet 'I hear somebody singing (*how* somebody is singing)' and Ja slyšu, *čto* kto-to poet 'I hear somebody singing (*that* somebody is singing)'.

(a)   Ja 'I' C^0 ⌐
        penie $V^{(n)}$.   V-adj ⌐
        penie 'singing'   V-J ⌐_⌐ . C^1 ─
        ⌐_____↑
        slyšu 'hear'   V ⌐_⌐

(b)   Ja 'I' C^0 ⌐
        penie 'singing' $V^{(n)}$. $V^{(n)}$-J ⌐
        penie $V^{(n)}$-J ⌐_⌐ . C^1 ─
        ⌐_____↑
        slyšu 'hear'   V ⌐_⌐

The category of the adjective (and participle) plays only two roles in the formation of a junction – (1) for its own stem it is the MARKER OF THE INNER GROUP (adjunct) and (2) it indicates that the nodal (dominant) word is also a component of this inner (adjunctive) group; as for a more precise indicatioin of the role of the nodal word in relation to the stem of the adjective, it is often lacking (and is determined in a special way). Cf.: *Ožidavšajasja* progulka sorvalas' 'The *awaited* outing fell through':

Progulka 'outing' C^i ⌐
        ⌐_____2_____↑
        ⌐
ožidavšajasja 'which was awaited'   V ⌐_⌐ . C^i-adj ⌐
        ⌐_____1_____↑
progulka C^i-J ⌐_⌐ . C^0⌐
sorvalas' 'fell through'   V ⌐_⌐

(where C^1 can be both C^0 and C^1).

Cf.: *Spičečnaja* fabrika zakryta 'The match factory is closed':

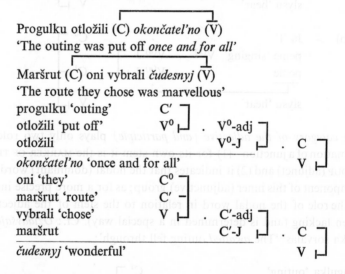

fabrika 'factory'   P′
spičečnaja 'match'   P″   .   P′-adj
                   1
fabrika   P′-J   .   C′
zakryta 'closed'   V

(where P′ = C or V, and P″ = V or C, respectively).

By comparing the analyzed structure of a junction with the natural language means which express it, we can establish that these means are of two kinds:

EXPLICIT means, which are empty words (*kotoryj, čtó, čto, kak*) or forms (nouns, adjectives) with the nodal word or within the inner group of the junction;

IMPLICIT means of expression, which consist in the very fact that there is a special valency group for A WORD WHICH IS ALREADY INCLUDED in some (inner) valency group. Adverbs and adjectives in post-position, when they are outer valents of a phrase, belong to the latter kind, cf.

Progulku otložili (C) *okončatel'no* (V)
'The outing was put off *once and for all*'

Maršrut (C) oni vybrali *čudesnyj* (V)
'The route they chose was marvellous'

progulku 'outing'   C′
otložili 'put off'   V⁰   .   V⁰-adj
otložili   V⁰-J   .   C
okončatel'no 'once and for all'   V
oni 'they'   C⁰
maršrut 'route'   C′
vybrali 'chose'   V   .   C′-adj
maršrut   C′-J   .   C
čudesnyj 'wonderful'   V

(10) *Statement A on the necessity of a base valency relation* (see above, p. 349) means for a natural language that of two linguistic items, if they make up a junction, one is obligatorily either ITSELF the valent, or CONTAINS the valent, or IMPLIES some omitted valent word. This presumed base valency relation can be described with various degrees of approximation.

Thus, the junction *knigi Tolstogo* 'the books of Tolstoj' or *snežnye veršiny* 'snowy peaks', whose base valency groups are undetermined, can be described in three approximations:

(1)

knigi 'books'	P'		veršiny 'peaks'	P'
Tolstogo 'Tolstoj's'	P''/P'-adj		snežnye 'snowy'	P''/P'-adj
knigi	P'-J		veršiny	P'-J

where P'-P'' designates an undetermined component of the base valency relation – V or C^i.

Determining the valency word – even if this is done in a negative way – makes it possible to show a valency relation correct to the difference between the valent and a complement:

(2)

knigi 'books'	C^i	.	C^i-adj
Tolstogo 'Tolstoj's'	V	.	C^i-adj
knigi			C^i-J
veršiny 'peaks'	C^i		
snežnye 'snowy'	V	.	C^i-adj
veršiny			C^i-J

Finally, using what we know about the actual relations connecting the objects 'knigi' and 'Tolstoj', 'veršiny' and 'sneg', the base valency relation can be shown in an even more exact manner:

(3)

$$\text{Tolstogo 'of Tolstoj'} = \begin{cases} \text{knigi 'books'} & C^0 \\ \text{Tolstoj(mu) '(to) Tolstoj'} & C^2 \\ \text{prinadležat 'belong'} & V \quad C^0\text{-adj} \\ \text{knigi} & C^0\text{-J} \end{cases}$$

(=knigi, priuadležaščie Tolstomu 'books belonging to Tolstoj')

$$\text{snežnye 'snowy'} = \begin{cases} \text{veršiny} & C^0 \\ \text{sneg(om) '(with) snow'} & C^2 \\ \text{pokryty 'covered'} & V \quad . \quad C^0\text{-adj} \\ \text{veršiny} & C^0\text{-J} \end{cases}$$

(=veršiny, pokrytye snegom 'peaks covered with snow').

Thus, the importance of assertion A for linguistic description lies in the fact it allows to make use of indirect facts; on the basis of the facts that (a) some group is a junction and (b) one of the two elements of this junction is explicitly not the valent word, we can draw the conclusion that the second word is either itself the valent or it contains the valent in its semantic structure (snežnye 'snowy'=pokrytye snegom 'covered with snow'; Tolstogo

'Tolstoj's, of Tolstoy'=prinadležat Tolstomu 'belong to Tolstoj'; fabrika 'factory'=to, gde proizvodjat nečto 'a place where things are produced', etc.).

On the other hand, it is not mentioned in assertion A which of the elements of the junction should become the valent of the base group; in a case where all the elements of the junction are capable of being valents, therefore, all alternative interpretations must be admitted. For example, two alternative interpretations are possible for the combination ego 'his' (=prinadležaščij 'belonging to' V^2 emu 'him' C^2)+beg 'run, running':

(1)   beg 'run'   C ⌐
        ego 'his'   V ⌐⌐ .   C-adj ⌐
        beg   C-J   ⌐⌐

=beg, prinadležaščij emu 'the run belonging to him'.

(2)   ego 'his'   C ⌐
        beg 'run'   V ⌐⌐ .   V-adj ⌐
        beg   V-J   ⌐⌐

=to, kak on bežit 'how he runs'.

Similarly, for the combination spičečnaja fabrika 'match factory', where spišečnaja 'match'=svjazannyj 'connected' (V) so spičkami (C^2) 'with matches',

fabrika 'factory'=to, gde proizvodjat 'where something is produced' (V):

        fabrika 'factory'   C ⌐
        spičečnaja 'match'   V ⌐⌐ .   C-adj ⌐
        fabrika   C-J   ⌐⌐

=fabrika, svjazannaja so spičkami, 'factory connected with matches'.

(2)   spičečnaja 'match'   C ⌐
        fabrika (to, gde
        proizvodjat, 'place
        where is produced')   V ⌐⌐   V-adj ⌐
        fabrika   V-J   ⌐⌐

=fabrika, gde prizvodjat spički, 'factory where matches are produced'.

In a clearly formulated alternative it is easy to determine what information is sufficient to be able to make a choice in favor of the second, more natural interpretations: it is obvious that the adjective ego 'his' (or any other adjective) is a valent conditionally, that is, it can be considered to be the valent only on the condition that there are no other aspirants to this role: as, for example, in the combinations *ego knigi 'his book', ego karandaš 'his pencil', snežnye veršiny 'snowy peaks'*; in any other case some other valent word must be considered to be the valent of the group: ego 'his' (C) *beg 'run'* (V) to, kak on bežit 'how he runs'; snežnye 'snow' (C) *zanosy 'drifts'* (V) = tot fakt, čto nečto zaneseno snegom 'the fact that something is drifted, bound with snow'.

Thus, it is not at all obligatory that the JUNCTIVES, i.e., the forms which make up the junction, adjectives (ego, snežnye, spičečnyj) or the genitive case of nouns (Tolstogo), be base valents of this junction: all that is important is that if there is a junction there must also be a base valency relation; with respect to the distribution of roles within this relation, an adjective or a word form in the genitive can aspire to the role of valent only TOGETHER with other elements of the junction. That we are compelled to consider junctives to be the valents when we lack sufficient information is another matter.

(11) *Statement B on the obligatoriness of a junction in an expanded valent group* (see above, p. 349), which says that of two interrelated valent groups one must constitute a junction, makes it possible to explain, on the one hand, the intuitively felt semantic identity of phrases such as:

(1)   (a) Ja znaju – gorod budet
          'I know – there shall be a city',
      (b) Ja znaju, čto gorod budet
          'I know that there shall be a city'.

(2)   (a) On poet izumitel'no
          'He sings amazingly',
      (b) To, kak on poet (ego penie), izumitel'no
          'The way that he sings (his singing) is amazing'.

(3)   (a) Maršrut oni vybrali čudesnyj
          'The route they chose was marvellous',
      (b) Maršrut, kotoryj oni vybrali – čudesnyj
          'The route they chose was marvellous'.

and on the other hand, the clearly sensed ambiguity of phrases:

(4)   On napisal povest' o priključenijax

is either

      (a) Povest', kotoruju on napisal – o priključenijax (posvjaščena priključenijam),
          'The story he has written is about adventures (devoted to adventures),

or

    (b) On napisal priključenčeskuju povest'
        'He has written an adventure story'.

(5)   Ivanov ne ljubil ženščin

is either

    (a) To, čto Ivanov ljubil ženščin – lož' (=u hego ne byle romanovs
        ženščinami)
        'That Ivanov loved women is false (=he had no love affairs
        with women),

or

    (b) Ivanov čuvstvoval neprijazn' k ženščinam
        'Ivanov felt enmity towards women.

The identity of the pairs (1)–(3) above can easily be explained by the fact that in spite of the external differences between the corresponding phrases of each pair, they can be assigned a single valency-junctive expression:

(1)   Ja 'I' C^0
        gorod 'city' C^0
        budet 'there shall be'   V . $V^{(n)}$-adj
        budet $V^{(n)}$-J . C'
        znaju 'know'   V

        Ja 'I' C^0
        gorod 'city' C^0
        budet 'there shall be'   V . $V^{(n)}$-adj
        (čto) budet '(that) there
        shall be $V^{(n)}$-J . C'
        znaju 'know'   V

(2)   On 'he' C^0
        poet 'sings'   V . V-adj
        poet   V-J . C
        izumitel'no 'amazingly'   V

        On 'he' C^0
        poet 'sings'   V . V-adj
        (to kak) poet 'the way
        that he sings'   V-J . C
        izumitel'no 'amazingly'   V

(3)   Oni 'they' C^0
        maršrut 'route' C^1
        vybrali 'chose'   V . C'-adj
        maršrut C'-J . C
        čudesnyj 'marvellous'   V

Oni	C^0		
maršrut			
(kotoryj) 'which'	C'		
vybrali	V	. C'-adj	
maršrut		C'-J	. C
čudesnyj			V

If the junction for the second phrase of each pair is chosen with regard for the categorial meaning of the empty words (*čto, to kak, kotoryj*), in the first phrases the choice of junction is based directly on the assertion (B) about its obligatoriness in phrases with coherent valency groups; in the phrases given here, it was most natural to assign the junction to the word *budet* there shall be" in phrase (1), to the word *poet* 'sings' in phrase (2), and to the word *vybrali* 'chose' in phrase (3), respectively, rather than the reverse.

Ambiguous (in terms of the valency-junctive grammar) interpretations of a singl phrase, on the other hand, can be explained by the fact that it is actually possible to assign the phrase two different valency-junctive expressions:

(4) (a) on 'he' C^0
         povest' 'story' C^1
         napisal 'wrote' V . C^1-adj
         povest' C^1-J   . C^0
         priključenijax 'adventures' C'
         o 'about' V

(= povest', kotoruju on napisal, – o priključenijax 'the story which he wrote is about adventures, i.e., posvjaščena priključenijam 'devoted to adventures')

(b)   On 'he' C^0
         povest' 'story' C^0
         priključenijax 'adventures' C^1
         o 'about' V . C^0-adj
         povest C^0-J   . C'
         napisal 'wrote' V

(= on napisal povest'-c-priključenijax 'he wrote a story of adventure' i.e., priključenčeskuju povest' 'an adventure story')

(5) (a) Ivanov C^0
         ženščin 'women' C^1
         ljubil 'loved' V . $V^{(2)}$-adj
         ljubil $V^{(2)}$-J   . C
         ne 'not' V

(= to, čte Ivanov ljubil ženščin – lož' 'that Ivanov loved women is false')

(b) Ivanov

ženščin 'women'

ljubil 'loved'

ne 'not'

ljubil

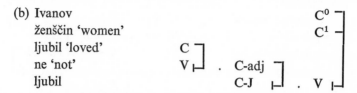

(= Ivanov ne-ljubil ženščin 'Ivanov disliked women', i.e., čuvstvoval ne-prijazn' k ženščinam 'felt enmity towards women').

(12) It is appropriate to remark here that the facility with which we allow (and mix) both interpretations directly corresponds to the *simplicity of the transition from one of the valency-junctive expressions (a) to the other (b)*: it is sufficient to 'open' the junction over one of the two valent groups and 'close' the junction over the other. In speech this 'closure' can be rendered by the unity of the intonation with which the corresponding valent group is pronounced: cf.

(4)   On *napisal povest'*/o priključenijax,

(= *povest', kotoruju on napisal* – o priključenijax 'the story which he wrote is about adventures'),

and

On napisal/*povest o priključenijax,*

(= on napisal *priključenčeskuju povest'* 'he wrote an adventure story'),

(5)   Ivanov *ne ljubil* ženščin,

(= Ivanov čuvstvoval neprijazn' k ženščinam 'Ivanov felt enmity towards women'),

and

Ivanov ne *ljubil ženščin*

(= to, čto Ivanov ljubil ženščin – lož' 'that Ivanov loved women is false').

The valency-junctive language, although it is stronger than the valency language, still does not have a power of discrimination sufficient to be able to distinguish fully any structures. To describe such natural phrases as *Ljubovalis' oni krasivoj lužajkoj* (a), 'They admired the beautiful lawn' and *Oni ljubovalis' krasivoj lužajkoj* (b), it has only one expression, i.e., phrase (a) with its EMPHATIC structure is indistinguishable from phrase (b), which has no emphasis.

4. 3RD SYSTEM: A VALENCY-JUNCTIVE-EMPHASIS GRAMMAR

The purpose of the emphasis 'superstructure' on a valency-junctive grammar is to provide a means for describing the 'emphasis' or 'logical emphasis' of one or another element of a valency group: cf. *ljubovalir'* oni *krasivoj lužajkoj* ('beautiful lawn' emphasized), *krasivoj lužakoj oni ljubovalis'* ('admired' emphasized), etc.

4.1. Rules of Formation

(VI) $\quad V^{(n)} \to V^{(n)}$. W-EMPH.

(VII) $\quad V^{(n)}$. W'-EMPH $\to V^{(n)}$. $\tilde{W}'$-JUNC . $\overline{C^E \quad W^1\text{-}V^E}$.

4.2. Categories (in Addition to the Previous Ones)

$V^{(n)}$. W-EMPH – W-EMPHASIS over $V^{(n)}$ or THE EMPHASIS on THE ELEMENT W FROM $V^{(n)}$; the designation for the operation of 'emphasis' (mise en relief) of the element W from the complete valency group $V^{(n)}$.

$\tilde{W}$ – W-FICTIVE; the designation of the appearance of element W in the group $V^{(n)}$ when an empty (indefinite) content corresponds to this element; for example: $\tilde{C}^0 =$ 'something', $\tilde{C}^2 =$ 'to something', $\tilde{V} =$ 'some property', $\tilde{V}^0 =$ 'at some time', or 'somewhere' or 'for some reason', $\tilde{V}^{(n)} =$ 'something occurs', etc.

$W\text{-}V^E$ – W-SUPERVALENT; the designation of an element W from a group $V^{(n)}$ as a valent meaning 'to be W', 'have the meaning W' and with one free valency.

C^E – C-SUPERCOMPLEMENT; the designation for a complement to a supervalent.

4.3. Commentary

(1) Rule VI allows any full valency group to undergo the 'emphasis' operation on any of its elements W, i.e., any of its elements may be 'underlined' ('emphasized').

(2) Rule VII reveals the essence of emphasis: the emphasized element W' is first substituted by its fictive $\tilde{W}'$ (that is, is deprived of its definite content), and the whole valency group is transformed into a junction with respect to this fictive ($=$ 'that something', 'that certain property...') so that it can again obtain its full definite content using the supervalency... $\overline{C^E \quad W\text{-}V^E}$. We mean here that the left-hand part of the emphatic structure $V^{(n)}$. $\tilde{W}$-JUNG . C^E is then expanded, like any junction, in accordance with rule V, and that the right-hand part $W\text{-}V^E$, like any valency component (P), can, in accordance with rule III, have as its content a whole valency group: $W\text{-}V^E \to V^{(n)}$. $W\text{-}V^E$.

The left-hand part – the super-complement of the emphatic structure – we shall also call the TOPIC OF EMPHASIS or simply THE TOPIC, and the right-hand part – the supervalent – will be said to be the EMPHASIS COMMENT or simply THE COMMENT.

The complete set of categories and rules of inference below will be said to be a valency-junctive-emphasis grammar or a VAJUNEM-grammar, just as the expressions generated by this grammar will be known as VAJUNEM-expressions, and their complete set will be a VAJUNEM language.

Among the expressions of the VAJUNEM language we should in particular find:

$$C^0 \quad \tilde{C}^1 \quad V \ . \ \tilde{C}^1\text{-adj} \quad \tilde{C}^1\text{-J} \ . \ C^E \quad C \quad V \ . \ C\text{-adj} \quad C\text{-J} \ . \ C^1\text{-}V^E \qquad (4)$$

which constitutes the structure of phrase (a) *Ljubovaliz' oni krasivoj lužajkoj*, 'what they admired was a beautiful lawn' with the emphasis on 'beautiful lawn'. Expression (4) clearly distinguishes the structure of this emphatic phrase from that of phrase (b) *Oni ljubovalis' krasivoj lužajkoj*, where there is no emphasis. Compare:

(a)

Oni 'they'	C^0	
–	$\tilde{C}^1$	
ljubovalis' 'admired'	V . $\tilde{C}^1$-adj	
–	$\tilde{C}^1$-J . C^E	
lužajkoj 'lawn'	C	
karsivoj 'beautiful'	V . C-adj	
lužajkoj	C-J . C^1-V^E	

= to nečto, čem oni ljubovalis', est': krasivoj lužajkoj 'that something which they admired was: the beautiful lawn'.

(b)

Oni	C^0
lužajkoj	C
krasivoj	V . V-adj
lužajkoj	C-J . C^1
ljubovalis'	V

= oni ljubovalis' krasivoj lužajkoj 'they admired the beautiful lawn'.

Rules VI–VII mean that emphasis – or supervalency – always presupposes some base valency relation. In other words, if a given expression is an emphasis over $V^{(n)}$, the comment of the emphasis is also related to the topic by a valency relation.

5. THE LINGUISTIC BASIS OF THE EMPHASIS GRAMMAR

(1) *Emphasis, or supervalency, as was shown in rule VII, is regarded as a special kind of valency relation...* C^E W-$\overline{V}^E$. Supervalency differs from ordinary valency relations, i.e., the connection between a valent and its complement, in that:

(a) its components – the supercomplement and supervalent – are a result of the 'splitting' of one and the same element into two 'states': an EMPTY CATEGORY devoid of any definite content, or, what amounts to the same thing, with an indefinite content $\tilde{W}$, on the one hand, and the same category filled by the CONCRETE CONTENT W, on the other.

(b) the essence of the relationship between them consists in the concretization of the 'empty' category $\tilde{W}$ through giving it a definite content, and, conversely, in putting a given definite content into a special, earlier given category W.

Thus, the supervalency

$$V^{(n)} \ . \ \tilde{W}'\text{-JUNC} \ . \ C^E \ W'\text{-}\overline{V}^E$$

is only a form for showing the transition between two states of the same element W' from $V^{(n)}$ – from the 'empty' state $\tilde{W}'$ to its filled state W'-V^E. Cf.:

To nečto, čem my ljubovalis', est' lužajka

$$V^{(n)} \ . \ W'\text{-JUNC} \ . \ C^E \ W'\text{-}V^E$$

'that something which we admired was the lawn'.

We shall henceforth consider this transition to be the essence of emphasis.

This interpretation of emphasis is directly oriented towards a representation of the structure of natural phases such as: *Ljubovalis' oni krasivoj lužajkoj* 'what they admired was the beautiful lawn (emphasized)' or *Otlo žit prišlos' voskresnuju progulku* 'Whas had to be postponed was the Sunday outing'. To illustrate this point, let us take some variants of a phrase with an identical emphasis.

(1) *Čto (Ŵ')* prišlos' otložit' – tak eto *voskresnuju progulku* (W') '*What* had to be postponed was the *Sunday outing*',

(2) Prišlos' otložit' ne *čto-nibud' (Ŵ')*, a *voskresnuju progulku* 'It was not just *anything* that had to be postponed, but the *Sunday outing*',

(3) Prišlos' otložit' – *(Ŵ')* imenno *voskresnuju progulku* (W') 'It was the *Sunday outing* that had to be postponed',

(4)   Prišlos' otložit' *(W̃')* *voskresnuju progulku* (W') 'It was necessary to postpone the *Sunday outing*',

(5)   Otložit' prišlos' – *(W̃')* – *voskresnuju progulku* (W') 'The *Sunday outing* had to be postponed'.

It is easy to show that these phrases fit similarly into the structure of an emphasis (supervalent) relation:

<table>
<tr><td>(3)–(5)</td><td>(2)</td></tr>
<tr><td>–</td><td>čto-nibud' 'anything'</td></tr>
<tr><td>otložit' 'postpone'</td><td>otložit'</td></tr>
<tr><td>prišlos' 'had to'</td><td>prišlos'</td></tr>
<tr><td>–</td><td>(ne) čto-nibud' '(not) anyting'</td></tr>
<tr><td>progulku 'outing'</td><td>progulku</td></tr>
<tr><td>voskresnuju 'Sunday'</td><td>voskresnuju</td></tr>
<tr><td>(imenno) 'exactly,
namely'</td><td></td></tr>
<tr><td>progulku</td><td>(a) progulku '(but) the outing'</td></tr>
</table>

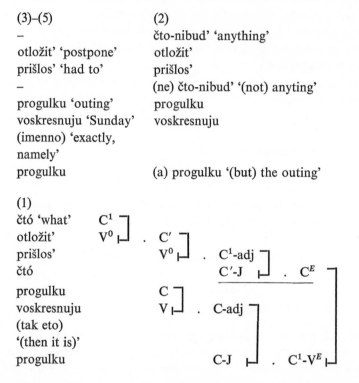

(1)
čtó 'what'	C^1
otložit'	V^0
prišlos'	
čtó	
progulku	
voskresnuju	
(tak eto)	
'(then it is)'	
progulku	

Note. We must first of all note that the 'emptiness' of the element W (in this particular example – C) can be expressed: positively, as the PRESENCE OF AN INDEFINITE CONTENT, as in phrases (1)–(2) with an indefinite pronoun; negatively, as the ABSENCE OF A DEFINITE CONTENT, as in phrases (3)–(5). The essence of the emphatic structure of these phrases remains unchanged. Secondly, we must take into account the fact that the substance of emphasis is not connected with any sort of linguistic device – the means for expressing emphasis (in Russian) are quite varied and can be lexical (1–3), intonational (4) or related to word order (5).

A comparison of the above phrases with their 'base' non-emphatic phrase Prišlos' otložit' voskresnuju progulku 'It was necessary to postpone the

Sunday outing' provides us with yet another chance to see that the difference between ordinary (according to rule I) and emphatic expansions (according to rules VI–VII) can be reduced to the fact that one of the elements of the base phrase (progulku 'outing') 'splits' and functions first as an 'empty space' (for example, in the form of 'čto' (what, that) 'ne-čto-nibud', (not just anything, but), etc.) and then, with the help of special means (e.g., the collocation 'tak éto' (then it is)), is given a concrete content. But it is just this operation that is established by rule VII.

(2) *The supercomplement – or the topic of emphasis – has the form of a junction with respect to the empty element W.* This is done by analogy with the general assumption (rule IV) according to which all valency groups, if they are complements of an outer valency relation (in our case the super-valency $W\text{-}V^E$), must have the form of junctions. The assumption 'by analogy' is fully substantiated linguistically, since in natural languages the topic of emphasis often 'copies' even the external form of the junction. Cf.:

> *Čto prišlos' otložit'* – tak ete voskresnuju progulku
>
> '*What had to be postponed* (this) was the Sunday outing',
>
> *Vinovnikom (=tot kte vinoven v) avarii* okazalsja streločnik
>
> 'The one who was responsible for the crash was the switchman',
>
> *Ce qui m'inquiète* – c'est le retard des amis.

(3) *The supervalent – or the emphasis comment – has a complex structure:* besides the index W', which repeats the category of the empty element of the topic (this will be treated specifically below), it also includes the symbol V^E. The introduction of this formal symbol of valency, determined first of all by the internal demands of the structure of an artificial language (to represent the emphasis relation as a particular instance of the valency relation), also has an immediate concrete linguistic reason: in natural languages the emphasis comment is often introduced by a formal valency marker – the copula and its analogues.

Cf. the examples given above: Vinovnikom avarii *okazalsja* streločnik 'The one responsible for the crash *proved to be* the switchman'. Čto prišlos' otložit', *tak éto* voskresnuju progulku 'What had to be postponed *was* the Sunday outing'. Ce qui m'inquiète – *c'est* le retard des amis.

(4) *The symbol W' in the combination $W'\text{-}V^E$ (=to be W') acts as a categorizer*: it indicates that its content should have the same category as the empty content $\tilde{W}'$, which is included in the valency group $V^{(n)}$. In other words, the category W' from $W'\text{-}V^E$ means that its content enters (together with, or more exactly, by means of the relation of supervalency with $\tilde{W}'$) into an ordinary valency relation with the base group $V^{(n)}$, the same relation

that $\tilde{W}$ enters:

$$(W'...) \quad \overline{V^{(n)}} \quad . \quad W'\text{-JUNC} \quad . \quad C^E \quad W'\text{-}V^E$$

In postulating a double role for the content which corresponds to the category W' in emphasis structures we want to reflect the actual duality of the emphasized element X in natural speech:

(a) it is an emphasis comment, that which is stated and emphasized (not simply anything, but X; NAMELY X);

(b) it is (or enters through the emphasis relation) in a valency relation within the base valency group; this is clearly visible in Russian constructions, where a word of the base group is emphasized.

Cf. Čto prišlos' otložit' (V^0) 'What had to be postponed' (V^0 requires the accusative), tak éto voskresnuju *progulku* (C^1) 'was the Sunday outing' (C' is in the accusative).

It is important to stress, however, that in theory the base valency relation of an emphasized element of speech exists (or is established) not apart from the emphasis, but BY MEANS OF IT; this can be clearly observed in an example of categories which have no morphological form in the given natural language:

$$Ce \ qui \ (C^0) \ m'inquiète \ (V) \ c'est \ le \ retard \ des \ amis \ (C^0\text{-}V^E).$$

The group *le rètard des amis* receives the base category C^0 (of the subject) to the valent *m'inquiète* through the emphasis relation which connects this group with the 'empty' item *ce qui*, which already has the category C^0.

(5) *According to general rule III, a full valent group can constitute the content of the supervalent W-V^E,* since the latter is a particular instance of a valent and consequently a component of the (super-) valency group. In an expanded emphatic structure we thereby distinguish, besides (a) the external emphasis relation:

$$...W'\text{-}J \quad . \quad C^E \quad W'\text{-}V^E,$$

and (b) the base valency relation, which connects the emphasized element with the base valency group

$$(\tilde{W}'...) \overline{V^{(n)}} \quad . \quad \tilde{W}'\text{-adj} \ \tilde{W}\text{-}J \quad . \quad C^E \quad W'\text{-}V^E$$

also (c) the inner categorial content of the emphasized element:

$$...\text{W-J} \quad . \quad \overline{C^E \quad \underline{V^{(n)}} \quad . \quad \text{W}'\text{-}\overline{V^E}}$$

Here, as has already been stated above, the valency relation (b) between W' and the base valency relation is completely determined by the 'empty' category $\tilde{W}'$. We add now that it does not at all depend on the inner categorial content of $\text{W}'(= \underline{V^{(n)}} \ . \ \text{W}')$.

The linguistic significance of this independence consists in the fact that the comment of emphasis can be an element which externally – with respect to the base valency group – functions as a complement, for example, but with respect to its internal categorial structure is a valent or an entire valency group, and vice versa. Cf.: (a) Prišlos' druz'jam/progulku otložit' 'The friends had to postpone their outing', where the object of the emphasis *progulku otložit'* is a complement to the outer valent *prišlos'* and with respect to its internal structure is a valency group (applicative); (b) Otložit' prlgulku/druz'jam prišlos', where the emphasis comment *druz'jam prišlos'* 'the friends had to' is externally a member of the base valency group, but with respect to its internal structure is a full valency group:

(a)

Druz'jam 'friends'	C^0		
–	$\check{C}'$		
prišlos' 'had to'	V	$\check{C}'\text{-adj}$	
		$\check{C}'\text{-J}$	$. \quad C^E$
progulku 'outing'	C'		
otložit' 'postpone'	V^0	$. \quad C'\text{-}V^E$	

(b)

progulku	C^0		
otložit'	V^0	$. \quad C$	
–		$\tilde{V}'$	$. \quad \tilde{V}'\text{-adj}$
–			$\tilde{V}'\text{-J} \quad . \quad C^E$
druz'jam		C^0	
prišlos'		$*V$	$. \quad V'\text{-}V^E$

Note: In the structure of phrase (b) the comment of the emphasis, according to the general rule for expanding valency groups (I), should in its complete form be shown as:

$$
\begin{array}{ll}
\text{Druz'jam} & \text{C}^0 \\
\text{progulku} & \text{C} \\
\text{otložit'} & \text{V}^0 \quad . \quad \text{C} \\
\text{prišlos'} & \text{V}
\end{array}
$$

To avoid repeating segments already represented in full in the topic, however, we shall henceforth agree to delete them from the comment and mark the deletion with an asterisk, as was done in the example with phrase (b). In other words, we shall observe the RULES OF ANAPHORIC AGREEMENT:

$$
\begin{aligned}
& V^{(n)'} \quad . \quad \tilde{W}''\text{-JUNC} \quad . \quad C^E \ V^{(n)'} \quad . \quad W''\text{-}V^E \rightarrow \\
& \rightarrow V^{(n)'} \quad . \quad \tilde{W}''\text{-JUNC} \quad . \quad C^E \ *V^{(n)'} \quad . \quad W''\text{-}V^E,
\end{aligned}
$$

where $*V^{(n)}$ designates the valency group $V^{(n)}$ with the deletion of all the elements which constitute the expansion of the element W'' from the same group $V^{(n)'}$ represented in the topic.

It can easily be seen that the elements deleted from the comment can be reconstructed with no difficulty by means of the element $\tilde{W}''$, with which W'' is connected by the emphasis relation.

(6) *The generalized meaning of the category W* makes it possible, as in the case of a junction, to show the characteristic features of emphatic structures in general, independently of the special role of the emphasized element in the base valency group, which is what has been done above. In addition, the generalization of W is of interest, as always, at its extreme: since a whole base valency group in its entirely can function as W, this means that the whole base group can be the emphasis comment; it is sufficient that it be given in the form of two states: an indefinite ($\tilde{W}$) and a specific (W).

It is a fact that natural speech creates phrases with global emphasis, and in just the way the general structure of emphasis demands. The phrase *druz'jam prišlos' otložit' progulku* 'the friends had to postpone the outing', which is *per se* without emphasis, becomes global-emphatic in the form: *Slučilos' tak, čto druz'jam prišloś otložit' progulku* 'As it turned out, the friends had to postpone the outing'. The collocation *slučilos' tak, čto* is nothing other than an 'empty' designation of the whole event, i.e., the indefinite category $\tilde{V}^{(n)}$, and the following full phrase is thus the second, specific state of the element $W = V^{(n)}$.

$$
\begin{array}{ll}
\text{Slučilos' (tak) 'as it} & \tilde{V}^{(n)} \quad . \quad \tilde{V}^{(n)}\text{-adj} \quad . \\
\text{turned out'} & \tilde{V}^{(n)}\text{-J} \quad . \quad C^E \\
\text{druz'jam 'friends'} & C^0 \\
\text{prugulku 'outing'} & C' \\
\text{otložit' 'postpone'} & V^0 \quad . \quad C' \\
\text{prišlos' 'had to'} & V \quad . \quad V^{(n)}\text{-}V^E
\end{array}
$$

=to nečto, čto slučilos', est': druz'jam prišlos' otložit' progulku 'the something that happened was: the friends had to postpone their outing'.

(7) *By assigning the category $\tilde{W}$ all possible particular meanings*, we can obtain expressions which correspond to the particular cases of emphasis in natural speech. Almost all of the more common types of emphasis have already been given and illustrated above, namely:

(A) $\tilde{W} = \tilde{C}^i : V^{(n)}$. $\tilde{C}^i$-JUNC . C^E C^i-V^E.

Čto prišlos' otložit' 'what had to be posponed' (...$\tilde{C}$'-JUNC . C^E)-tak éto voskresnuju progulku 'was the Sunday outing' (C'-V^E). Vinovnikom avarii 'the one who was responsible for the crash' (...$\tilde{C}^0$-JUNC . C^E) okazalsja streločnik 'turned out to be the switchman' (C^0-V^E).
Prišlos' druz'jam (...$\tilde{C}$'-JUNC . C^E) 'the friends had to' progulku otložit' 'postpone the outing' (C'-V^E).

(B) $\tilde{W} = \tilde{V} : V^{(n)}$. $\tilde{V}$-JUNC . C^E V-V^E.

Progulku 'the outing' (...$\tilde{V}$-JUNC . C^E) druz'jam prišlos' otložit' (V-V^E).

(C) $\tilde{W} = \tilde{V}^{(n)} : V^{(n)}$. $\tilde{V}^{(n)}$-JUNC . C^E $V^{(n)}$-V^E.

Slučilos' tak 'as it turned out' (...$\tilde{V}^{(n)}$-JUNC . C^E), čto druz'jam prišlos' otložit' progulku 'the friends had to postpone the outing' ($V^{(n)}$-V^E).

In addition to the possibilities already mentioned, we should note a particular case where we are concerned with specific elements of an expanded group containing an applicative-annex V^0 with a full valency group $V^{(n)}$ as its C^1-complement.

(D) $\tilde{W} = \tilde{V}^0 : V^0$. $\tilde{V}^0$-JUNC . C^E V^0-V^E.

Druz'jam prišlos' otložit' progulku 'The friends had to postpone the outing (...$\tilde{V}^0$-JUNC . C^E) iz-za doždja 'because of the rain' (V^0-V^E).

Druz'jam 'friends'	C^0					
progulku 'outing'	C'					
otložit' 'postpone'	V^0	. C'				
prišlos' 'had to'	V	. C^1				
–		$\tilde{V}^0$	. $\tilde{V}^0$-adj			
–			$\tilde{V}^0$-J	. C^E		
doždja 'rain'			C'			
iz-za 'because of'			V^0	. V^0-V^E		

=to, počemu druz'jam prišlos' otložit' progulku, est': iz-za doždja 'the reason why the friends had to postpone the outing was: because of the rain'.

(8) *With respect to its structure, emphasis nearly resembles an expanded valency group with a junction as a complement.* Cf.

$$V_i^{(n)} \quad . \quad \tilde{W}'\text{-JUNC} \quad . \quad \overline{C^E \quad W'\text{-}V^E} \qquad \text{(emphasis)}$$

$$V_i^{(n)} \quad . \quad W\text{-JUNC} \quad . \quad C \; \overline{V_k} \qquad \text{(valency)}$$

The difference between these structures is determined by whether or not the element W is fictitious; in the first case the valent V_k is automatically a concretization of this fictive; that is, it acquires the external form of the supervalent V^E (to be): $V_k \rightarrow V_k\text{-}V^E$.

This theoretical proximity and, under the given conditions, the possibility of an direct shift from an expanded valency structure to an emphatic one allows us to explain the ambiguous interpretation of phrases such as:

(1)   *Kačestvo* vypolnenija zakaza otlićnoe 'The *quality* of the filling of the order is excellent'.

(2)   *Osobennost'* marśruta, kotoryj oni vybrali – riskovannost' 'A *feature* of the route which they have chosen is its riskiness'.

where the element W (underlined) is lexically a typical fictive. The first interpretation possible for these phrases is the usual valency one, where the lexical content of the element W is ignored:

```
Zakaza        C ⌉
vypolnenija   V ⌊⌡  . V-adj ⌉
vypolnenija        V-J  ⌊⌡ . C ⌉
kaćestvo                 V' ⌊⌡ . V'-adj ⌉
kaćestvo                       V'-J ⌊⌡ . C ⌉
otli ćnoe                               V" ⌊⌡
```

Secondly, if we take into account the fictive meaning expressed by the element V' these phrases reveal a typical emphatic structure with the emphasis on the valent V", which also proves to be a concretization of the fictive V' (in the form V"-V^E=to be V").

```
(1)  Zakaza        C ⌉
     vypolnenija   V ⌊⌡  . V-adj ⌉  .
     vypolnenija        V-J  ⌊⌡ . C ⌉
     kaćestvo                 Ṽ' ⌊⌡ . Ṽ'-adj ⌉
     kaćestvo                       Ṽ'-J ⌊⌡ . C^E ⌉
     otlićnoe                                 V"-V^E ⌊⌡
```

$= to$, *kak* vypolnen zakaz, – est': otlično '*The way in which* the order has been filled is: excellent!'

Cf. the possibility of an ambiguous interpretation of phrase (2) (see diagram on next page).

The emphatic interpretation must of course be regarded as the more adequate, since it also takes into account the lexical expression of the fictiveness of the element W.

(9) *The interpretation of emphasis as a gradual, two-step introduction of the element W* makes it possible to assume that the return to the base valency group can be attained through the reverse fusion of the two states of the element into a single element:

$$V^{(n)} \quad . \quad \tilde{W}'\text{-JUNC} \quad . \quad C^E \quad W'\text{-}\overline{V}^E$$
$$\searrow \qquad \swarrow$$
$$V^{(n)} \quad (W)$$

Such an inverse operation generallly means an important change in the structure of the group $V^{(n)}$, since what is involved is a rejection of emphasis. This change, however, can be ignored if the structure of the original emphatic group differs minimally from the base valency structure, namely, when ONE AND THE SAME ELEMENT is OUTERMOST in both the emphatic and base groups; such a thing is possible if this element is the outer valent of the base group or the base group in its entirety.

(I)
(a) $C^i \quad \overline{\tilde{V}}' \quad . \quad \tilde{V}'\text{-JUNC} \quad . \quad C^E \quad V'\text{-}\overline{V}^E$ (group with emphasis on the valent V')

$$\searrow \qquad \swarrow$$

(b) $\qquad\qquad\qquad C^i \quad V'$ (base group with the valent V')

(II)
(a) $\tilde{V}^{(n)} \quad . \quad \tilde{V}^{(n)}\text{-JUNC} \quad . \quad C^E \quad V^{(n)}\text{-}\overline{V}^E$ (group with global emphasis on $V^{(n)}$)

$$\searrow \qquad \swarrow$$

(b) $\qquad\qquad\qquad V^{(n)} \quad (V^{(n)})$ (the base group $V^{(n)}$)

Under the condition mentioned above, the difference between cases (a) and (b) amounts to the fact that the same element – a valent or a group – is introduced either *in two steps* (the empty category ($\tilde{V}'$ or $\tilde{V}^{(n)}$) + its concretćization ($V'\text{-}V^E$ or $V^{(n)}\text{-}V^E$); cf. (a): *To, kak* vypolnen zakaz ($\tilde{V}'$), est': OT-LIĆNO ($V'\text{-}V^E$) '*The way in which* the order has been filled is: EXCELLENT' or *To, čto slučilos*' ($\tilde{V}^{(n)}$, est': DRUZ'JAM PRIŠLOS' OTLOŽIT' PROGULKU ($V^{(n)}\text{-}V^E$) 'What happened was: the friends had to postpone the outing') or *in one step* (the category which immediately has a concrete content (V' or $V^{(n)}$); cf. (b):

Oni 'they'
marśruta 'route'
vybrali 'have chosen'
marśruta
osobennost' 'feature'
osobennost'
riskovannost' 'riskiness'

$$
\begin{array}{l}
C^0 \\
C' \quad . \quad C'\text{-adj} \\
V \qquad \quad C'\text{-J} \quad . \quad C \\
\qquad\qquad\qquad\qquad V \quad . \quad V'\text{-adj} \\
\qquad\qquad\qquad\qquad\qquad V'\text{-J} \quad . \quad C \\
\qquad\qquad\qquad\qquad\qquad\qquad\qquad V' \\
\qquad\qquad\qquad\qquad\qquad\qquad\qquad V \\
\textit{or:} \quad \hat{V} \quad . \quad \hat{V}'\text{-adj} \\
\qquad\qquad\qquad\quad \hat{V}'\text{-J} \quad . \quad C^E \\
\qquad\qquad\qquad\qquad\qquad\qquad V''\text{-}V^E
\end{array}
$$

= *to, kakov* marśrut, kotoryj oni vybrali, – est': riskovannyj '*what* the route they have chosen *is like* is: risky'.

Zakaz vypolnen OTLIĆNO (V') 'The order was filled PERFECTLY'; Druz'jam priš-los' otložit' progulku ($V^{(n)}$). In other words, the difference consists in the fact that in cases (a) the topic and assertion are more clearly de limited than in (b).

The transitions I and II will be called below emphasis REDUCTION RULES, abbreviated TR–I (transformation rule I) and TR–II.

By asserting the proximity of an emphatic structure and the base valency structure under special conditions, we make it possible to:

(a) clearly distinguish between an emphatic structure and the base structure in certain subtle border cases, e.g., *vypolnenie zakaza – otlićnoe* 'the filling of the order is perfect' (emphasis) and *zakaz vypolnen otlićno* 'the order has been filled perfectly' (base valency);

(b) reveal with precision the cases where the reduction of an emphatic structure to the base structure will not result in a serious distortion of meaning, e.g., show the conditions under which the emphasis reduction rules can be applied.

Thus, the emphatic structures in the following phrases can be reduced without any special distortions in their meanings:

(1) (a) Vypolnenie zakaza – otlićnoe 'The filling of the order is perfect',
     Vypolnen zakaz otlićno 'The order has been filled perfectly',
     Kaćestvo vypolnenija zakaza – otlićnoe 'The quality of the filling of the order is perfect',

reduced to the base valency structure:

     (b) Zakaz vypolnen otlićno 'The order has been filled perfectly'.

(Cf. also the diagrams on next page.)
Cf. also:

(2) (a) Ee poćerk krasiv 'Her handwriting is beautiful',
     (b) Ona pišet krasivo 'She writes beautifully';
(3) (a) Osobennost' marśruta, kotoryj oni vybrali – riskovannost' 'A feature of the route they have chosen is its riskiness',
     (b) Marśrut, kotoryj oni vybrali – riskovannyj; Marśrut oni vybrali riskovannyj 'The route they have chosen is risky'.

It is well to note that externally, on the surface level, the abbreviation of an emphatic structure to the base valency structure can be expressed:
– in a 'normalization' of the word order:

$$\overset{2}{\text{Vypolnen}}\ \overset{1}{\text{zakaz}}\ \text{otlićno} \rightarrow \overset{1}{\text{Zakaz}}\ \overset{2}{\text{vypolnen}}\ \text{otli ćno},$$

$$\overset{1}{\text{'The order}}\ \overset{2}{\text{has been}}\ \text{filled perfectly'};$$

EMPHATIC STRUCTURE

$$\overset{C}{V}\left[\quad\overset{V\text{-adj}}{V\text{-J}}\left[\quad\overset{\hat{V}}{\hat{C}}\left[\quad\overset{\hat{V}\text{-adj}}{\hat{V}\text{-J}}\left[\quad\overset{C^E}{V\text{-}V^E}\right.\right.\right.\right.$$

Zakaz 'order'	Zakaza	Zakaza
vypolnen 'filled'	vypolnenie	vypolnenija
vypolnen	vypolnenie	vypolnenija
–	–	kačestvo 'quality'
–	–	kačestvo
otlično 'perfectly'	otličnoe	otlično

VALENCY STRUCTURE

$$\overset{C}{V}\left[\quad\overset{V\text{-adj}}{V\text{-J}}\left[\quad\overset{C}{V}\right.\right.$$

Zakaz	
vypolnen	
vypolnen	
tolično	

– in the rejection of special words or word-forms which include a pronominal, fictive meaning:

> Vypoln*enie* 'filling' ($=to$, *kak* vypolneno '*the way in which* something is filled)
>
> Zakaz *vypolnen* otlično 'The order has been filled perfectly';
>
> Ee *poćerk* ($=to$, *kak* ona pišet '*how* she writes') krasiv 'Her *handwriting* is beautiful';
>
> Ona *pišet* krasivo 'Whe *writes* beautifully';

– in the rejection of lexemes which have an exclusively fictive meaning (see above, p. 378):

> *Kaćestvo* ($=to$, *kak* '*how*') vypolnenija zakaza – otlično 'The *quality* of the filling of the order is perfect';
>
> Zakaz *vypolnen* otlično 'The order *has been filled* perfectly'.

Note: Of course, this reduction presumes the IDENTITY (reduction to a single SEMEME) of different word-forms (vypolnenie 'filling' – vypolnen 'filled'), words (po ćerk 'handwriting' – pišet 'writes') and word-groups (kaćestvo vypolnenija 'quality of filling' – vypolnen 'filled').

(10) *General rule VI allows any full valency group to be submitted to emphasis*. In particular, an emphatic valency group with emphasis on some element W can undergo emphasis repeatedly.

– either (A) with respect to some other of its OWN (immediate or mediated) elements (W″):

$$
\left. \begin{array}{l}
V^{(n)} \quad . \quad \tilde{W}'\text{-JUNC-}C^{E} \quad \overline{W'\text{-}V^{E}} \\
\Downarrow \\
V^{(n)} \quad . \quad \tilde{W}''\text{-JUNC} \quad . \quad C^{E} \quad \overline{W''\text{-}V^{E}}
\end{array} \right\} =
$$

$$
= V^{(n)} \quad . \quad \tilde{W}''\text{-JUNC} \quad . \quad C^{E} \quad \overline{W''\text{-}V^{E}} \quad . \quad \tilde{W}'\text{-JUNC} \quad . \quad C^{E} \quad \overline{W'\text{-}V^{E}},
$$

– or (B) with respect to some element (W″) of the INNER valency GROUP which is possible for the SUPERVALENT (according to rule III, see p. 336):

$$
\left. \begin{array}{l}
V^{(n)}_{k} \quad . \quad W'\text{-JUNC} \quad . \quad \overline{C^{E} \; V^{(n)}_{1} \quad . \quad W\text{-}V^{E}} \\
\Downarrow \\
V^{(n)}_{1} \quad . \quad W''\text{-JUNC} \quad . \quad \overline{C^{E} \quad W''\text{-}V^{E}}
\end{array} \right\} =
$$

$$
= V^{(n)}_{k} \quad . \quad W'\text{-JUNC} \quad . \quad \overline{C^{E} \; V^{(n)}_{1} \quad . \quad W''\text{-JUNC} \quad . \quad \overline{C^{E} \; W''\text{-}V^{E}} \quad . \quad W'\text{-}V^{E}}
$$

Thanks to the fact that we are allowed to do this, we obtain 'many layered' emphatic structures with an internal emphasis on the TOPIC (case A) on the COMMENT (case B), or on the topic and the comment at the same time.

The admission of structures with internal emphases is fully justifiable linguistically. For example, by means of such structures we are enabled to describe adequately the differences existing between phrases (a) and (b) in the following examples.

(1) (a) *voskresnuju progulku* (weak rise in tone) druz'jam priślos' otložit', The *Sunday outing*, the friends had to postpone it';
    (b) Progulku *voskrésnuju* (sharp rise in tone) druz'jam priślos' otložit', 'It was the *Sunday* outing the friends had to postpone';
(2) (a) *Progulku* (weak rise in tone) druz'jam priślos' otložit';
    (b) Čto kasaetsja *progulki* (sharp rise in tone), to durz'jam priślos' ee otložit' 'As for the *outing*, the friends had to postpone it';
(3) (a) Progulku druz'jam priślos' *okončatel'no* (weak stress) otložit', 'The friends had to postpone the outing once and for all';
    (b) Progulku druz'jam priślos' otložit' *okončátel'no* (strong stress).

In example (1) both sentences are emphatic, with the emphasis on *druz'jam priślos' otlorit'* 'the friends had to postpone'. Moreover, in phrase (b) the TOPIC of the first (or EXTERNAL) emphasis receives special emphasi – namely, its element *voskresnuju* 'Sunday': progulku *ne kakuju-nibud'* a voskresnuju 'not JUST ANY outing, but the SUNDAY outing'.

(1a)

progulku 'outing'	C ⌐					
voskresnuju 'Sunday'	V ⌐⌐	C-adj ⌐				
progulku		C-J ⌐⌐ .	C' ⌐			
–			Ṽ' ⌐⌐ .	V'-adj ⌐		
–				V'-J ⌐⌐ .	C^E ⌐	
druz'jam 'friends'				C^0		
otložit' 'postpone'			*V^0 .	C' ⌐		
priślos' 'had to'				V ⌐⌐ .	$V'-V^E$ ⌐⌐	

= *To, čto sdelali* s voskresnoj progulkoj, *est'*: druz'jam priślos' (ee) otložit' '*What was done* with the Sunday outing *was*: the friends had to postpone it' (For Example (1b) see next page.)

Example (2) is interesting because the topic, which consists of one word and does not constitute a full valency group, something which is absolutely necessary for emphasis (see rule VI), undergoes emphasis. However, as soon as the difference of phrase (b) from phrase (a) in example (2) is completely analagous to the difference of phrase (b) from (a) in example (1), we have to assume that the means for expressing this difference must also be similar: phrase (2b) should be a valency group, namely:
– in contrast to phrase (2a), which means 'what happened with the outing

(1b)

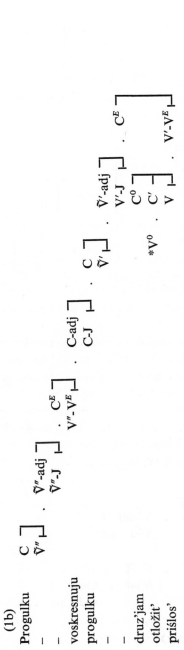

Progulku
—
—
voskresnuju
progulku
—
druz'jam
otložit'
prišlos'

=*To, čto sdelali s progulkoj* NE KAKOJ-NIBUD', A VOSKRESNOI, *est'*: druz'jam prišlos' (ee) otložit' '*What was done with the outing,* NOT JUST ANY outing, but the SUNDAY outing, *was*: the friends had to postpone it', was: the friends had to postpone it', phrase (2b) should mean: 'what happened, not WITH JUST ANYTHING, BUT WITH THE OUTING, was: the friends had to postpone it'. Cf:

Progulku 'outing' C'
− $\tilde{V}'$. $\tilde{V}'$-adj
− $\tilde{V}'$-U . C^E
durz'jam 'friends' C^0
otložit' 'postpone' $*V^0$. C'
prišlos' 'had to' V . V'-V^E

(2b)
− $\tilde{C}'$
− $\tilde{V}'$. $\tilde{C}'$-adj
− C'-J . C^E
progulku C'-V^E . C'
− $\tilde{V}'$. $\tilde{V}'$-adj
− $\tilde{V}'$-J . C^E
druz'jam C^0
otložit' $*V^0$. C'
prišlos' (to) V . V' . V^E

In example (3), phrase (b) differs from (a) in the additional internal emphasis on the COMMENT, with respect to the word *okončatel'no* 'finally, once and for all'. Cf.:

(3a) Progulku druz'jam prišlos' okon čatel'no (weak stress) otložit' = 'To, čto slu čilos's progulkoj, est': druz'jam prišlos' ee okon čatel'no otložit'' 'What happened with the outing was: the friends had to postpone it once and for all' (*okončatel'no otložit'* 'postpone once and for all' is a junction).

(3b) Progulku druz'jam prišlos' otložit' *okon čatel'no* (strong stress) = 'To, čto slučilos' s progulkoj, est': druz'jam prišlos' ee otložit' NE KAK-NIBUD', A OKONČATEL'NO 'What happened with the outing was: the friends had to postpone it, NOT JUST ANY WAY, but FINALLY'.

(3a)
Progulku C'
− $\tilde{V}'$. $\tilde{V}'$-adj
− $\tilde{V}'$-J C^E
druz'jam C^0
otložit' $*V^0$. C
okon čatel'no V . C-adj
otložit' C-J . C
prišlos' V . V'-V^E

(For Example (3b) see next page.)

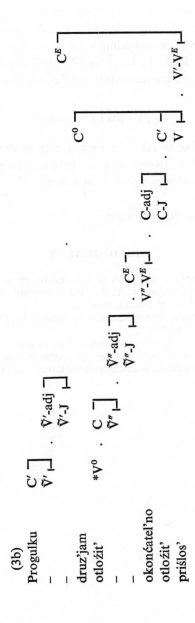

The intralinguistic means used to signal inner emphasis can be very subtle, e.g., in Russian a rise in tone or intensity of accent:

(1a) *Voskresnuju* (weak rise in tone) progulku druz'jam prišlos' otložit';

(1b) *Voskrésnuju* (sharp rise in tone) progulku druz'jam prišlos' otložit'.

(2a) *Progulku* (weak rise in tone) druz'jam prišlos' otložit';

(2b) *Progulku* (sharp rise in tone) durz'jam prišlos' otložit'.

(3a) Progulku druz'jam prišlos' *okončatel'no* (weak stress) otložit';

(3b) Progulku druz'jam prišlos' *okončatel'no* (strong stress) otložit'.

It can easily be seen that these 'subtle' intonational-accentual means signal inner emphasis on the corresponding word of the topic (1b, 2b) or the comment (3b), i.e., they form the same 'two-layered' emphatic structure as are found in phrases where the intonation is reinforced by more 'visible' lexical and syntactic devices.

ACKNOWLEDGEMENT

The author would like to take this opportunity to express his gratitude to A. V. Gladkij and V. V. Ivanov, who read the first manuscript of this paper and made a number of very valuable comments.

State Pedagogical Institute, Moscow

BIBLIOGRAPHY

Chomsky, N., 1965, *Aspects of the Theory of Syntax*, MIT Press.
Dorofeev, G. V. and Martem'yanov, Y. S., 1969, *Logičesnij vyled i lyjavl'enije sv'azej meždu predloženijami b tekste*, No. 12, Moskva.
Gladkij, A. V., 1969, 'O sposobah opisanija sintansičeskoj' struktury predloženija', *Computational Linguistics* 7, Budapest.
Jespersen, O., 1924, *The Philosophy of Grammar*, Copenhagen.
Martem'yanov, Y. and Mouchanov, Y., 1967, *Une notation sémantique et ses implications linguistiques*, 2ième Conférence Internationale sur le traitement automatique des langues, Grenoble.

L. N. IORDANSKAJA

TENTATIVE LEXICOGRAPHIC DEFINITIONS FOR A GROUP OF RUSSIAN WORDS DENOTING EMOTIONS*

I

1. The object of this study is to suggest such lexicographic definitions for a group of Russian words as would satisfy the fundamental requirement of present-day semantics, that of standardizing the semantic description of language units. In the final analysis, this requirement means that to describe meaning a formalized language must be developed, with a dictionary and syntax of its own, and the meaning of all significant units of the natural language, including words, must be represented in terms of this artificial language which could be called 'semantic language'. The development of a semantic language is a very complex problem, however, and its solution is still a long way off. The above requirement therefore, is understood here only as a demand for maximum uniformity in the formulations used in the definitions. Since the words at issue are semantically homogeneous (they all denote emotions of the same type), the question about the general form of the definitions for these words has arisen. We consider the answer to this question to be our principal task. So far as the definitions themselves are concerned, many of them may probably be refined.**

The majority of the words used in the right parts of the definitions given

* Originally published in *Machine Translation and Applied Linguistics* (ed. by V. Ju. Rozencvejg), Athenäum Verlag, 1973, by permission of Språkförlaget Skriptor, Copyright © 1972, Skriptor, Stockholm. This paper has been revised for the present volume. (*Editor's note.*)

** We would like to make the following two important comments on the English translation of this article:

(1) The reader should be warned against extending the definitions of Russian words described below to their English translations. The meanings of words which designate emotions are extremely complex and specific in different languages. For this reason, even when the most apt English equivalent of a Russian word has been found, it is still impossible to be certain (without special semantic research) that the senses of the Russian and English words fully coincide. Moreover, it often happens that such 'felicitious' equivalents simply do not exist, so the English translations of Russian words for emotions may be very approximate.

(2) The author has chosen a certain fragment of Russian as the language in which the definitions are written. Here, in the English version of the article, the majority of the definitions (the right-hand side of them – that which is called the *definiens*) are given immediately in their 'English form'. Omission of the 'Russian' definitions here is possible for the following reason. The meanings of the Russian words used in the definitions are for the most part rather simple, and, consequently, nearly universal. We can hope, therefore, that these words have close enough English equivalents.

F. Kiefer (ed.), Trends in Soviet Theoretical Linguistics, 389–410. All Rights Reserved.
Copyright © 1973 by D. Reidel Publishing Company, Dordrecht-Holland.

below (i.e. in *definiens*) have a nonelementary character, that is they themselves need definitions. These non-elementary words, however, have meanings such that their definitions clearly should not include the words denoting emotion defined here. Thus, we eliminate the possibility of a situation arising in which the name of an emotion is defined by means of a word which is defined by means of the name of the emotion (a vicious circle).

As for the substantive aspect of our definitions, we have tried to follow the principle that the definitions should be adequate to the words defined (in contrast, for example, to Bendix's principle of 'minimal definition' [12]). The adequacy principle is understood in conformity with [6] and [9] as follows: all the semantic components necessary for the complete description of the meaning of a particular word in a particular sense should be present in the definition, and there should be no superfluous components[1]; when such a definition is substituted into a text instead of the word defined (in the sense under consideration), the meaning of the text does not change[2]. Of course, our orientation towards definition adequacy does not mean that we have succeeded in all cases in suggesting adequate definitions. One of the means of refining definitions is to broaden the range of the words under examination (only 38 words are described here).

In the process of our work we have drawn fisrt of all on materials from dictionaries of modern Russian [1–4] in an attempt to utilize the informal aspect of the definitions for the words we are interested in and to analyze the numerous examples of the textual usages for these words. Z. E. Aleksandrova's *Dictionary of Russian Synonyms* (1968), which shows the relationships between words with respect to their greater or lesser semantic proximity, was also used. Moreover, the device of constructing expressions containing the word to be defined was extensively used: the admissibility/inadmissibility of such an expression indirectly points to the presence (absence) of a certain component in the meaning of the word in question. Acquaintance with the philosophico-ethical words of Spinoza (*Ethics*) and Descartes ("Passions

---

[1] Example of an inadequate definition: in all mono-lingual dictionaries of modern Russian *stydit'sja* (be ashamed of) is defined as 'ispytyvat' styd' (to experience shame), and the word *styd* (shame) as 'čuvstvo smuščenija, raskajanija ot soznanija predosuditel'nosti postupka' (feeling of embarrassment, repentance from the realization of the reprehensibility of one's acting). Such a definition does not take account of all the usages possible for the words in question; cf. *stydit'sja svoej bednosti* (be ashamed of one's poverty)/ *svoego budničnogo vida* (one's everyday appearance)/*svoego bol'šogo rosta* (one's great height) (and not only the reprehensibility of an act)/*grubosti načal'nika* (the rudeness of one's superior)/*ètoj zatej xozjaina* (this venture of the landlord) (and not only one's own actions, as is given to understand by the component 'raskajanie' (repentance) in the defination cited.

[2] The possible stylistic deviance of the result of the substitution is irrelevant for our purposes.

de l'âme"), where definitions of various emotions are given which are in fact lexicographic definitions of the respective words[3], and with certain text-books in Psychology containing a classification of emotions, was also useful for our purposes.

2. 38 words were chosen among words denoting emotions. All of these words designate emotional states rather than emotional attitudes (cf. the division of emotions into experiences and stable emotional attitudes made in psychology textbooks). This means that we shall study words of the type *radost'* (joy), *ogorčenie* (grief), *gnev* (rage), *strax* (fright), *udivlenie* (surprise), and exclude from consideration words of the type *ljubov'* (love), *nenavist'* (hate), *uvaženie* (respect), *prezrenie* (contempt), *simpatija* (sympathy), *doverie* (trust), etc.

The definitions given below belong to one of two types: (a) 'basic' definitions, where the emotion is described independently of other emotions; (b) derived definitions, where the emotion under analysis is described by reference to another emotion.

Let us consider the general form of the basic definitions (derived definitions may be mostly reduced to basic definitions). Attempting to meet the requirement of definition adequacy means, in essence, allowing as fully and precisely as possible for the intuition of the speakers in respect to a given word. This intuition is reflected in one way or another in explanatory dictionaries, and for this reason one should treat the materials of these dictionaries very attentively. The definitions in explanatory dictionaries of modern Russian for the words we are interested in usually connect the internal characteristics of an emotion with an indication as to its cause (for example, *gordost'* (pride) – 'čuvstvo udovletvorenija ot soznanija prevosxodstva ('feeling of satisfaction arising from an awareness of superiority'), *dosada* (vexation) – 'ogorčenie' neudovol'stvie, razdraženie, vyzvannoe čem-libo' (chagrin, dissatisfaction, annoyance, caused by something) etc. In our opinion, the definitions of the words under consideration should include just these two parts: *an internal description of the emotional state and the reason for its occurrence*. The question as to exactly which internal attributes of the emotional states should be considered basic is very complicated. Three characteristics are used here: (1) 'an aroused' state, which simply designates the presence of *emotion*, in contrast to a 'quiet' state of the emotional system; (2) positive (pleasant)/negative (unpleasant) state (if a state is positive or negative, it follows that it is 'aroused'; in the definitions therefore, the expressions 'positive state', 'negative state' will be used instead of the expressions 'positive-aroused/negative-aroused states'); (3) active state (re-

---

[3] Cf. remarks in [10], pp. 7–8, on the essentially linguistic nature of the Aristotle's definitions for a number of concepts.

quiring manifestation in behaviour)/passive state. For example, *udivlenie* (surprise) is simply an 'aroused' state, *vosxiščenie* (delight, rapture) a positive state, *ogorčenie* (grief) a passive-negative state, *gnev* (anger, rage) an active-negative state. Obviously, it is impossible to obtain the necessary differentiation of the meanings of the words under study through these characteristics. As for a more differentiated and precise system of attributes of emotional states, it seems to us that the semantics of these words does not suggest such a system [4]. The necessary differentiation can be obtained thanks to the second, principal part of the definitions, where the cause for the occurrence of a described emotion is indicated. Such a cause is always *a particular evaluation* [5] *of the emotion of some event*, that is, an aggregate of opinions on this event, its evaluation from the point of view of its desirability, and, for active states, a definite wish in connection with this event. Thus, this evaluation is the core of the definition, the part which is sufficient to specify the meanings of the words described. As an example of definition: *A ogorčaetsja iz-za B* (*A* is grieved because of *B*) = '*A* experiences a passive-negative emotional state caused by the fact that: (a) *A* is sure of the realization of the event *B*, (b) *B* is undesirable for *A*'.

We will now touch upon yet another complex problem which is related to the general form of our definitions. *Ogorčenie* (grief), *gore* (sorrow), *otčajanie* (despair), *obida* (insult), *styd* (shame), *raskajanie* (repentance), *strax* (fright), *trevoga* (anxiety), etc., are passive-negative states. Although all the appropriate corresponding meanings are differentiated thanks to the 'evaluation' part of the definitions, it is intuitively wrong that these meanings are identical according to the type of the state. Since, as was said above, we see no possibility of matching various state characteristics against all these meanings, we propose another alternative, which will be demonstrated by the following definition. *A ogorčaetsja iz-za B* = '*A* experiences a passive-negative emotional state such as is usually caused about in an average person *i* through the following evaluation he makes of some event *j*: (a) *i* is sure of the realization of event *j*, (b) *j* is undesirable for *i*: the state is caused in *A* by the evaluation on the part of *A* of the event *B*'. A definition of this kind manages to capture the specific properties of the emotional state defined although these properties are described not in terms of some new internal characteristics of emotional

---

[4] Note that the existence of such a system in physiology or psychology has no relationship to semantics. Cf. Weinreich on this point: "For even if we had neurological specifications of, say, the emotions, the semantic description of emotion terms could be continued independently..." ([14], p. 29).

[5] In accordance with the definition adequacy principle, the redundancy of the first part of a definition does not follow from the fact that the 'evaluative' part is sufficient for differentiating the definitions. For the critique of the 'minimal definition' principle, see [13].

states (other than characteristics (1) – (3) on page 391), but through reference to the conditions typical for the advent of the given state[6]. From the theoretical point of view, such definitions seem to us to be more precise than the definitions of the type cited in the first paragraph on p. 392. Definitions such as these, however, are extremely bulky and difficult to read. In the list of definitions below we have neglected this precision in favor of greater clarity, all the more so as for one to allow for this precision it is sufficient to reformulate all the definitions in the identical manner.

We shall make a few more comments concerning the structure of the definitions.

(1) Although the discussion above dealt with the definitions of individual words, the left part of the definitions always contains more than one word. The point is that names of emotions are predicate words, and in this instance it is the predicate expressions that must be *definienda*. In a predicate expression, besides the predicate word, there appear symbols of variables corresponding to the semantic 'places', or valencies, of this predicate (for example, *A ogorčaetsja iz-za B*). If a semantic 'place' can not be expressed in Russian with a syntactic object of the word in question (never or when another syntactic object is present), a conventional object is chosen, which is then enclosed in brackets: for example, *A v èkstaze [ot B]* (*A* is in ecstasy over *B*). The introduction of such a conventional object makes clear the underlying semantic structure of the corresponding predicate word.

(2) It should be noted that the object of evaluation in definitions of words designating emotional experiences is always an event (emotions-experiences are reactions to events), in contrast to words which designate an emotional attitude, where the object of evaluation is any fact of reality, an event, a property, a physical object, etc., cf. *On doverjaet ètomu čeloveku* (He trusts this person), *On ljubit èti stixi* (He likes this poem). Under certain conditions, however, the meaning of an experience changes into the meaning of an attitude, e.g., *Ja bojus' tigrov* (I am afraid of tigers), *Ja udivljajus' takim ljudjam* (I am amazed by such people), *Ja vosxiščajus' drevnej živopis'ju* (I admire ancient painting). We do not take up usages such as these in our definitions because we assume that they should be accounted for by regular semantic transformation rules. As for expressions of the type *Ja obradovalsja drugu* (My friend made me glad) or *Ja ispugalsja tigra* (I was frightened by

---

[6] Definitions of the form: $X =$ 'an emotional state of type Y such as is caused by conditions Z' diverge from the classical form of a definition, where the meaning of a word is described in terms of its constituent meanings; the meaning of a word is represented here in a more complex manner. A definition of a similar type can be found in the paper [15] (p. 46): English *to be afraid* = 'to feel the way a man feels who is awaiting something unpleasant' (the feeling is described through the conditions typical for its advent but without any of its internal characteristics).

the tiger), they are semantically elliptic, that is, they are abbreviations of the expressions *Ja obradovalsja prixodu/priezdu druga* (I was gladdened by the arrival of my friend) and *Ja ispugalsja pojavlenija/pryžka/ ... tigra* (I was frightened by the appearance/jump/ ... of the tiger).

(3) It can appear that instead of the expression '*A* uveren v osuščestvlenii sobytija *B*' (*A* is sure of the realization of the event *B*), one should simply write 'imeet mesto sobytie *B*' (event *B* takes place). However, the first expression emphasizes the generally known fact that emotions have a particularly subjective character: for a specific emotion to appear (and accordingly, to use the name of this emotion), it is not the real occurrence of the event that is important, but only the person's certainty that it has or will take place. One can *vozmuščat'sja* (be indignant) not only at an event which has taken place in his presence, but also at a future event, if one is certain it will occur, or at an event which is thought to have occurred but in reality has not.

(4) There are no temporal indications in the general form of the 'basic' definitions. The following two conventions are adopted in this regard.

The absence of temporal indications in expressions designating an opinion (desire) of person *A* about event *B* (i.e., in the expressions '*A* uveren...' (*A* is sure...), '*A* sčitaet...' (*A* believes...). '*B* želatel'no...' (*B* is desirable...), '*A* želaet...' (*A* wants...), shows that the time interval during which the given opinion takes place includes the moment of 'feeling'. For example, *radost'* (joy, gladness) is aroused by a person's certainty in the realization of some event *B* that is pleasant for him; this evaluation takes place during the very moment of joy. If the moment of the evaluation of event *B* does not coincide with the moment t_0 of feeling, this will be specially noted. For example, *udivlenie* (surprise) contains the component 'until t_0 *A* believed that the realization of event *B* was unlikely'.

The absence of indications as to the moment of event *B*'s realization means that this moment is immaterial. *B* can occur both in the past (the moment of feeling is the present) and in the future. In all definitions but two the time of event *B*'s realization is of no significance: it is possible to *radovat'sja* (be glad), *udivljat'sja* (be surprised), *serdit'sja* (be angry), *bojat'sja* (be afraid), *nadejat'sja* (hope), because of past and future events (cf. *Radovat'sja polučeniju pis'ma/blizkomu priezdu druga* (be glad to have received a letter/that a friend is coming soon); *nadejat'sja na to, čto ona sdast ekzameny/čto ona sdala ekzameny* (hope she will pass / has passed her exams)). The time of *B*'s realization is important in but two definitions: one can *raskaivat'sja* and *ispytyvat' ugryzenija sovesti* (repent and experience the pangs of remorse) only because of an event which has already occurred, and respective definitions contain the corresponding temporal indications.

3. It was stated above that the diversity the definitions display is connect-

ed with differences in evaluations on the part of a person A – the subject of an emotion – of event B or its participants. All the evaluations used in the definitions are listed below. Evaluations which are close in content are combined under one heading (a slanted line divides expressions that are not encountered simultaneously; expressions which are not obligatory for the given component, but are found in at least one definition, are enclosed in parentheses).

(1) A believes that the realization/non-realization of event B is 100% probable/highly probable/probable/unlikely. The expression 'A is sure of the (non)realization of event B' will be used instead of 'A believes that the (non)-realization of event B is 100% probable'.

(2) Event B / person A / person C is (very) desirable / (very) undesirable for A (because of B). By 'desirable for A' is meant not only what corresponds to the 'current' desires of person A, but also what corresponds to his constant, potential desires (specifically, such is the desire to come into contact with a thing which suits our tastes; whatever pleases us, is desirable for us). The expression 'person A/C is desirable/undesirable for A because of B' means that the person in question pleases *(nravitsja)* / does not please the subject of the emotion in respect of some action B performed by this person.

The reader should be reminded that, in the absence of any time indications, this evaluation refers to the moment of feeling.

(3) A believes that event B is (in some respect) (very) good/(very) bad. Here, in contrast to (2), A evaluates B not from the point of view of his desires and tastes, but more objectively.

(4) A believes (i) that persons D believe that event B is very good/very bad, and (ii) that A is desirable/undesirable for D because of B.

(5) A believes that actions B are immoral/unjust in relation to A.

(6) A believes that he should not have performed actions B.

(7) A believes that event B is (the greater) evil (for person A/C).

(8) A believes that event B contradicts the fundamental principles of private and social life.

(9) A believes that the person C is close to him.
By 'close' we mean that in some way or other A identifies himself with C.

(10) A believes that not-B is important for A to the highest degree.

(11) A believes that it is impossible to cause not-B.

(12) A believes that he is not capable of counteracting B.

(13) A wants to manifest in his behaviour that B is undesirable for A / A wants to counteract event B or its recurrence / A wants to do something to person C in order to counteract event B or its recurrence.

As for the 'derived' definitions, they include, in addition to references to some emotion, semantic components indicating:

(1) the intensity of the emotion (e.g. *A izumljaetsja B* (*A* is amazed at *B*) is '*A* is very surprised at *B*'); for the expansion of derived definitions which include indications of the intensity of the basic emotion, see p. 400;

(2) the cause of an emotion (e.g., *zloradstvo* (malignant joy) is 'joy caused by an event which is an evil to someone else');

(3) the consequence of an emotion (the components 'loss of selfcontrol', 'loss of the capability of understanding', e.g., *èkstaz* (ecstasy) is 'to be overjoyed so that it causes to lose selfcontrol'), *ošelomlen* (stunned) – 'to be surprised so that it causes to lose the capability of understanding';

(4) the specific character of the 'place' (valency) of the predicate designated in the name of the emotion used in the definition (*A zaviduet C v B* (*A* envies *C* in *B*) ='*A* is annoyed at *X*, where *X* is *A*'s lack of fact *B*, which *A* wants to have, and *C*'s possession of fact *B*').

The set of distinctive semantic components for a particular group of words can differ from language to language. The peculiarities of a particular language may also find expression in the fact a certain meaningful combination of components can be rendered by a single word in the given language and cannot be so rendered in another language. For certain meanings not expressible in Russian by single words there exist stereotyped combinations, e.g., *prijatnoe/neprijatnoe udivlenie* (pleasant/unpleasant surprise) or *čuvstvo oblegčenija* (feeling of relief); the meaning of the latter expression differs from the meaning of the word *razočarovanie* (disappointment, disillusionment) only in the type of the state – positive rather than negative – and the undesirability of that which has failed to be realized (from the subject's point of view). If there is no appropriate stereotype combination, the meaning is expressed descriptively. For example, *ot otčajanija on poterjal vsjakuju vlast' nad soboj* (out of despair he completely lost control of himself) (meaning 'despair causing loss of self-control').

4. The definitions of the words treated here correspond to the following model of man's spiritual constitution.

(1) The human personality (its 'spiritual side') is a complex mechanism consisting of numerous interacting systems, specifically, the systems of reason, memory, will, self-control, desires, and emotions (see [6] and [11]). Although the system of emotions (the emotional system) and the system of desires are closely connected with each other and together make up what is called the 'soul', these systems differ in the following respect: feelings or emotions are usually reactions of the soul to events, whereas desires are a kind of 'demands' which the soul imposes on reality (cf. the analogous difference between sensations – reactions of the body – and needs – 'demands' of the body).

(2) The emotional system consists of two components, one of which is

connected with 'momentary' feelings, and the other, with 'lasting' ones. The difference between momentary and lasting feelings corresponds to the difference remarked in psychology between emotional experiences and lasting emotional attitudes (see above, p. 391). Since lasting feelings are not treated here, the word 'feeling/emotion' will hereafter be used to designate only momentary feelings, and the expression 'emotional system' will denote only the system of momentary feelings. The fact that a person experiences a particular feeling means that his emotional system finds itself in an 'aroused' state.

(3) The internal structure of the emotional system is unknown[7], and consequently we do not know just which states of the components of the system build up a particular emotional state. We suggest here that the important characteristics of emotional states are *arousal* (vozbuždennost), positiveness/negativity and activeness/passivity. Accordingly, feelings are described through the type of an emotional state and also through the conditions under which they arise. These conditions are an evaluation by the subject of the feeling of some event. Differences of emotions are determined by differences in evaluations and types of emotional states.

(4) The evaluation a person makes of an event can include a set of opinions about the event, its evaluation from the point of view of desirability (whether this event corresponds to the 'current' or 'potential' desires of the subject of the feeling), and a definite desire which has arisen in connection with this event. Thus, the states of the emotional system are closely connected with the functioning of other systems, in particular the system of reason and that of desires.

(5) The reverse dependency also exists: emotional states influence the states of other systems, in particular the systems of reason and self-control, which sometimes causes a loss of the capability of understanding, cf. *ošelomlen* (stunned) or a loss of selfcontrol, cf. *ekstaz* (ecstacy), *panika* (panic).

(6) In works on philosophical ethics (in particular those mentioned above by Descartes and Spinoza) and in works on psychology a question has often been discussed that of which feelings are primary, i.e. such that all other feelings can be considered nuances thereof. Obviously, this question is closely connected with emotion classification. We have undertaken to classify feelings from the point of view of the semantics of the corresponding Russian words. Six groups were obtained, called tentatively as follows: RADOST' (joy, gladness), OGORČENIE, (grief, chagrin), GNEV (rage, anger), NADEŽDA (hope), STRAX (fear), UDIVLENIE (surprise). These results

---

[7] Note again that the model we are describing is a generalization of lexicographic definitions. The statement that "the internal structure of the emotional system is unknown", therefore, means here that this structure cannot be inferred from the semantics of the words under consideration.

are shown in Table I. There it is shown which semantic components are characteristic for each group. It should be noted that these components are not always explicitly present in the definitions of the corresponding words; when they are not, however, they can easily be inferred from the components which are present.

As can be seen from the table, the groups are contrasted with regard to the following three features related to the 'evaluative' part of the definitions: (i) the probability evaluation of event B (according to which the group UDIVLENIE, the groups NADEŽDA-STRAX and the groups RADOST'-OGORČENIE-GNEV are contrasted), (ii) the desirability/undesirability of event B for person A (this feature differentiates the NADEŽDA group from the STRAX group and the RADOST' group from the OGORČENIE-GNEV groups), (iii) the presence/absence of some desire which has arisen in connection with event B (this differentiates the *ogorčenie* group – a passive reaction to something undesirable – from the *gnev* group – an active reaction to something undesirable or unpleasant).

II

The words investigated and their definitions are divided among the six groups indicated above.

RADOST' (Joy)

(1) *A raduetsja B (A* is glad of *B*)=A experiences a positive emotional state caused by the fact that:

   (a) A is sure of the realization of event B.

   (b) B is very desirable for A.

(2) *A vosxiščaetsja B (A* is delighted by/at *B*)=A experiences a positive emotional state caused by the fact that:

   (a) A is sure of the realization of event B,

   (b) A believes that B is in some respect very good.

Thus, vosxiščenie (admiration, delight) implies a more objective evaluation of the event than does *radost'* (joy); in other words, *radost'* is a more 'personal' feeling which arises due to the fact that the subject of the feeling is closely involved (due to something very desirable or pleasant for him). Cf. the different meanings of the statements *On vosxiščaetsja ètoj replikoj* (He is delighted with this remark) (='He believes that it is very good') and *On raduetsja ètoj replike* (He is glad of this remark/This remark makes him glad) ('It was very desirable for him', for example, because the remark led the conversation in the direction he wanted; here it is possible that he does not consider the remark itself very good). As a comparison of these state-

TABLE I

A's expectancy with respect to the event B desirability/undesirability of the event B for the person A		A is sure that event B is going to take place	A believes that event B is probable	A is sure that B will/will not take place, at t_0 A considered B to be/not to be improbable
B is desirable for A		RADOST' radovat'sja vosxiščat'sja byt' v vostorge byt' v èkstaze gordit'sja zloradstvovat'	NADEŽDA nadejat'sja	UDIVLENIE udivljat'sja izumljat'sja byt' ošelomlennym ispytyvat' razočarovanie
B is undesirable for A	That A has definite desires for B is not true	OGORČENIE ogorčat'sja byt' v gore byt' v otčajanii ispytyvat' sostradanie ispytyvat' žalost' sočuvstvovat' obižat'sja stydit'sja raskaivat'sja ispytyvat' ugr-zenija sovesti byt' v užase	STRAX ispytyvat' strax bojat'sja ispugat'sja byt' v panike bespokoit'sja trevožit'sja	
	A has definite desires for B	GNEV dosadovat' serdit'sja zlit'sja byt' v bešenstve byt' v jarosti vozmuščat'sja negodovat' gnevat'sja zavidovat' revnovat'		

ments shows, *radost'* does not at all imply *vosxiščenie*; *vosxiščenie* usually implies some (possibly weak) *radost'*, since contact with anything very good is in general desirable. It should be emphasized that either side of a generally speaking bad event can *vosxiščat'* (delight/cause admiration) (see the expression 'in some respect' above). For example, *On vosxiščaetsja tem, s kakim artistizmom ona lžet* (He is delighted by/admires her artistry in lying).

(3) *A – v vostorge ot B* (*A* is overjoyed by/enraptured with *B*) = *A očen' raduetsja B ili očen' vosxiščaetsja B* (*A* is very glad of *B* or is delighted with *B*).

For example, *Trudno opisat', v kakom ja byl vostorge, kogda ponjal, čto spasen* (It is difficult to describe how overjoyed I was when I understood that I was saved) where *vostorg* is *bol'šaja radost'* (great joy); *Ja v vostorge ot étoj knigi* (I am enraptured with/overjoyed with this book) where *vostorg* is *sil'noe vosxiščenie* (strong delight).

When a derived definition is expanded, that is, when the name of a feeling (here *raduetsja* and *vosxiščaetsja*) is replaced by its definition, the component which designates the intensity of feeling should be assigned, firstly, to the state, and secondly, to those elements of the evaluation for which it is relevant: *A – v vostorge ot B* (*A* is overjoyed by *B*) = *A očen' raduetsja B ili očen' vosxiščaetsja B* (*A* is very glad at *B* or is very much delighted with *B*:) = *A* experiences an intense positive emotional state caused by the fact that: (a) *A* is sure of the realization of event *B*, (b) *B* is extremely (*očen'-očen'*) desirable for *A* or *A* believes that *B* is in some respect extremely good. The expressions **A očen' uveren...* (*A* is very sure...) or **A uveren v bol'šom osuščestvlenii sobytija B* (*A* is sure of the considerable realization of event *B*) are meaningless, so that the component (a) is not supplemented by an indication of intensity.

(4) *A – v èkstaze [ot B]* (*A* is in ecstasy [over *B*]) = *A – v takom bol'šom vostorge ot B...* (*A* is so delighted with *B* that this causes him to lose self-control.)

(5) *A zloradstvuet [po povodu B u C]* (*A* gloats [because *B* happens to *C*]) = = *A* is glad of *B*, which is caused by the fact that *B* is an evil to *C*.

(6) *A gorditsja pered D (sobytiem) B (lica) A/C* (*A* is proud before *D* of (event) *B* of (person) *A/C*) = *A* experiences a positive emotional state caused by the fact that:

(a) *A* is sure of the realization of event *B*, the subject of which is *A* or person *C*, whom *A* believes to be close to himself,

(b) *A* believes that *B* is very good,

(c) *B* is very desirable for *A*,

(d) *A* is desirable for *A* because of *B*,

(e) *A* believes (i) that persons *D* (*D* can coincide with *A*) believe that *B* is very good and (ii) *A* is desirable for *D* because of *B*.

Component (c) is introduced because people *gordjatsja* (are proud of/ take pride in) that good which is very dear to them. Although the feeling *gordost'* (pride) usually includes the awareness that others approve of you, one can often be proud of that for which one approves of oneself, cf. *Robinzon Kruzo gordilsja svoej lodkoj* (Robinson Crusoe was proud of his boat – *pered soboj*, since Robinson lived in total isolation); for this reason it is noted in the definition that *D* can coincide with *A*. Examples: $\underset{D}{On}$ $\overset{A}{gordilsja}$ $\underset{B}{pered}$ $\underset{C}{tovariščami}$ $\underset{C}{krasotoj}$ $\underset{B}{dočeri}/svoej$ $kollekciej$ (He bragged to his comrades about the beauty of his daughter / He bragged about / showed off his collection); *On gordilsja, čto vyderžal éto ispytanie* (He prided himself on having stood this test); *A ja gordilsja mež druzej podrugoj vetrenoj moej* (And among my friends I boasted of my frivolous sweetheart).

OGORČENIE (grief, chagrin)

(7) *A ogorčaetsja iz-za B* (*A* is grieved due to *B*) = *A* experiences a passive-negative emotional state caused by the fact that:

(a) *A* is sure of the realization of event *B*,

(b) *B* is undesirable for *A*.

Ogorčat'sja (to grieve/be chagrined) is a 'broad' antonym to *radovat'sja* (to be glad of): in *radovat'sja* '*B* is *very* desirable for *A*', whereas in the corresponding component of *ogorčat'sja* 'very' is absent.

(8) *A – v gore iz-za B* (*A* is distressed because of *B*) = *A* experiences a passive-negative state caused by the fact that:

(a) *A* is sure of the realization of event *B*,

(b) *B* is very undesirable for *A*,

(c) *A* believes that not-*B* is important for *A* to the highest degree

Byt' v gore (to be distressed (by, at)) is a 'narrow' antonym to *radovat'sja* (it has a component which is absent from *radovat'sja*).

(9) *A – v otčajanii ot B* (*A* is driven to despair by *B*) = *A* experiences a passive-negative emotional state caused by the fact that:

(a) *A* is sure of the realization of event *B*,

(b) *B* is very undesirable for *A*,

(c) *A* believes that not-*B* is important for *A* to the highest degree,

(d) *A* believes that it is impossible to cause not-*B*.

Thus, *otčajanie* (despair) is formed from *gore* (distress) and *beznadežnost'* (hopelessness).

(10) *A ispytyvaet žalost' k C [po povodu B]* (*A* feels pity towards *C* [because of *B*]) = *A* is grieved *(ogorčaetsja)* because of *B*, and this is caused by the fact that *A* believes that *B* is an evil for *C*.

Žalost' (pity, compassion) is an antonym to *zloradstvo* (malignant joy).

(11) *A ispytyvaet sostradanie k C* [*po povodu B*] (*A* feels compassion, commiseration for *C* because of *B*)=*A* is grieved *(ogorčaetsja)* because of *B*, and this is caused by the fact that *A* believes that *B* causes *C* to suffer.

Sostradanie is a 'narrow' antonym to *zloradstvo* (the component '*B* causes *C* to suffer' corresponds to a special case of the situation designated by the component '*B* is an evil for *C*').

(12) *A sočuvstvuet C* [*v svjazi s B*] (*A* symphathizes with *C* [in connection with *B*])=*A* is grieved because of *B*, and this is caused by the fact that *A* believes that *B* is unpleasant for *C*. *Sočuvstvovat'* (to sympathize) is a 'narrow' antonym to *zloradstvovat'*.

(13) *A styditsja pered S za B* [(*lica*) *A/C*] (*A* is ashamed/feels shame before *D* because of *B* of (person)*A/C*]=*A* experiences a passive-negative emotional state caused by the fact that:

(a) *A* is sure of the realization of event *B*, the subject of which is *A* or person *C*, whom *A* believes to be close to himself,

(b) *A* believes that *B* is very bad,

(c) *B* is very undesirable for *A*,

(d) *A* is undesirable for *A* because of *B*,

(e) *A* believes (i) that persons *D* (*D* can coincide with *A*) believe that *B* is very bad, and (ii) *A* is undesirable for *D* because of *B*.

Component (d) means that *A* is objectionable to himself in because of *B*. *Stydit' sja* (to be ashamed) is an antonym to *gordit'sja* (to be proud of).

Examples: *Prikazčik, stydjas' za menja i moej zatei, otošel v storonu* (The sales clerk, embarrassed by me and my little joke, turned away from me); *Oṇ stydilis' pered novym čelovekom grubosti svoego načal'nika* (The rudeness of their boss embarrassed them in front of the new man), *Ona stydilas' svoego proisxoždenija* (She was ashamed of her origins), *On ustydilsja ètoj svoej mysli* (He was shamed by this thought of his) (here the subject of the feeling judges himself – *D* coincides with *A*).

(14) *A ispytyvaet ugryzenija sovesti iz-za B* (*A* experiences pangs of remorse because of *B*)=*A* experiences a passive-negative emotional state caused by the fact that:

(a) *A* performed actions *B* before the moment t_0 of feeling,

(b) *A* believes that actions *B* are immoral,

(c) *A* is undesirable for *A* because of *B*.

Obviously, one *ispytyvajet ugryzenija sovesti* (feels pangs of remorse) and *raskaivajetsja* (repents; see below) in an already completed act, and, since the subject of the act is the subject of the feeling, it is difficult to imagine a situation where the subject of the feeling is sure that he has committed some act, while in fact the act did not take place (emotional states are after all determined by the conditions under which they arise in a normal person in a normal general state). The beginning of the 'evaluative' part of the definition, therefore, can be abbreviated: instead of '*A* is sure of the realization of event *B*, the subject of which is person *A*, in moment t_1 which precedes moment t_0' we can write '*A* performed actions *B* before t_0'.

(15) *A raskaivaetsja v B* (*A* repents of *B*) = *A* experiences a passive-negative emotional state caused by the fact that:

(a) *A* performed actions *B* before t_0,

(b) *A* believes that he should not have performed actions *B*.

Let us compare the meanings of the last three words. *Stydit'sja* differs from *raskaivat' sja* and *ispytyvat' ugryzenija sovesti* in the following respects: (1) One can *raskaivat'sja* (repent) and *ugryzat'sja* (to feel pangs of remorse) only due to an act, deed, behaviour, but one can *stydit'sja* (be ashamed) of an act, incapability of doing something, an external flaw or deficiency, etc., that is, of or by anything bad that 'belongs' to the subject of the feeling; (2) *raskajanie* (repentance) and *ugryzenija sovesti* (remorse) are felt only on account of *one's own* actions, but is possible *stydit'sja* (to be ashamed) of something that pertains to someone close to you, but not to yourself, cf. *stydit'sja postupka syna* (be ashamed of one's son's behaviour); (3) There is a 'social' component in *stydit'sja* ('*A* believes that persons *D* believe that *B* is very bad...'), but this component is absent from *ugryzat'sja* and *raskaivat'sja*. *Stydit'sja* is connected with *ugryzat'sja* with regard to the presence of the component '*A* is undesirable for *A* because of *B*', and together these two words are opposed to the word *raskaivat'sja* (the component signifying that the subject of the feeling is unpleasant to himself is not contained in 'raskajanie', since it is possible to repent of something good as well as of something bad. See the example below). Finally, *raskajante* differs from *ugryzenija sovesti* in that one *ugryzaetsja* (is remorseful) only due to a *bad* act, whereas it is possible *raskaivat'sja* (regret) even a good act. Cf. *On raskaivalsja i v tom, čto poprežnemu sčital xorošim* (He regretted also that which he, as before, considered good) – *vo vsej svoej byloj dejatel'nosti* (the whole of his former activity): although he continues to consider this activity good, for some reason he now thinks that it was wrong of him to occupy himself with it.

(16) *A obižaetsja na C za B* (*A* takes offence at/resents *C* for *B*) = *A* experiences a passive-negative emotional state caused by the fact that:

(a) *A* is sure of the realization of event *B*, the subject of which is person *C*, and the object, person *A*,

(b) *A* believes that actions *B* are unjust in relation to *A*,

(c) *C* is undesirable to *A* because of *B*.

(17) *A –v užase ot B* (*A* is horrified by *B*) = *A* experiences a passive-negative

emotional state caused by the fact that:

(a) *A* is sure of the realization of event *B*,
(b) *A* believes that *B* is the greater evil.

Thus, *užas* (horror, terror) is an emotional shock resulting from an encounter with something monstrous. In such a situation a person is very often gripped by a strong fear, which explains the very common definition of the word *užas* as a 'sil'nyj strax' (strong fear). At the same time, there are a number of important differences in the meanings of these words: *strax* (fear) is connected with an expectation of something bad, *užas* (horror, terror) is a reaction to something already in existence; *strax* is an especially 'personal' feeling: a person expects something bad for himself or for those dear to him, while *užas* is a reaction to something monstrous which may or may not concern the subject of the feeling. We will cite some examples that show the differences in meaning between *užas* and *strax*. *Zrelišče kazni navodit užas na vsjakogo čeloveka* (The sight of an execution would horrify anyone); *Mat' prišla v užas ot besporjadka, carivšego v komnate* (Mother was horrified by the mess in the room); *On v užase ot neobrazovannosti našego pokolenija* (He is horrified by the lack of education in our generation); *Nexljudov byl pogloščen užasom pered tem, čto sdelala s soboj Maslova* (Nexljudov was overwhelmed with horror when he was confronted with what Maslova had done to herself).

GNEV (Anger, Wrath)

The words of this group share the following feature: they designate an active-negative emotional state that demands external expression, a surface outlet, discharge. The definitions of the words of this group, therefore, contain a component designating a desire on the part of the subject of the feeling to manifest his dissatisfaction. All of the words of this group are divided into two subgroups according to the presence/absence of the component '*A* believes that *B* contradicts the fundamental principles of private and social life'; on the one hand, 'noble' emotions arising due to 'lofty' reasons – *vozmuščenie* (indignation), *negodovanie* (indignation), *gnev* (wrath), on the other, *dosada* (vexation, annoyance), *serdit'sja* (to be angry), *zlit'sja* (be irritated), *bešenstvo* (frenzy), *jarost'* (fury), *zavist'* (envy), *revnost'* (jealousy). Cf. *Narody mira vyražajut svoe negodovanie/vozmuščenie/gnev* (The peoples of the world express their indignation/wrath) but not *dosada, zlost', bešenstvo, jarost', zavist', revnost'*. It is no coincidence that, as is pointed out in the *Dictionary of Russian Synonyms* (1968), the words of the first subgroup are inapplicable (in a serious usage) to animals. A further division of words is possible with regard to the presence/absence of a component designating the desire of the subject of the feeling to do something to some person. Thus, *gnev* contains a desire to affect a person guilty of some event which is undesirable for *A*, while *vozmuščenie* and *negodovanie* do not necessarily have to do with concrete persons: he who is indignant wants to counteract an event that is undesirable for him, and does not necessarily have a definite person in mind. *Serdit'sja, zlost', bešenstvo, jarost'* – are all feelings directed against a concrete person (in the sense indicated above), while *dosada* can arise due to undesirable circumstances (bad weather, lack of influence on social life, etc.) and does not generally contain a desire to do something to anyone. *Zavist'* and *revnost'* are special cases of *dosada* such that the presence of a specific person is always assumed (or even two persons, as is the case with *revnost'*). The other, more specific semantic differences of these words can be found from their definitions.

(18) *A dosaduet na B* (*A* is annoyed by *B*) = *A* experiences an active-negative emotional state caused by the fact that:

(a) *A* is sure of the realization of event *B*,

(b) *B* is undesirable to *A*,

(c) *A* wants to manifest in his behaviour that *B* is undesirable to *A*.

Thus, *dosada* differs from *ogorčenie* in the activeness of the negative reaction to that which is undesirable and in the desire conditioned by this active character to express one's dissatisfaction. Cf. *Vtajne on dosadoval na to, čto ne imel bol'še nikakogo vlijanija* (He was secretly irritated by the fact that he no longer had any influence) in such a situation it would also be possible *ogorčat'sja* (to be chagrined/distressed i.e., react to it passively).

(19) *A serditsja na B za C* (*A* is angry at/with *B* because of *C*) = *A* experiences an active-negative emotional state caused by the fact that:

(a) *A* is sure of the realization of event *B*, the subject of which is person *C* (*C* can coincide with *A*),

(b) *B* is undesirable to *A*,

(c) *C* is undesirable to *A* because of *B*,

(d) *A* wants to do something to *C* in order to counteract event *B* or its recurrence.

Cf. *serdit'sja na sebja* (be angry with oneself) – *C* coincides with *A*.

(20) *A zlitsja na C za B* (*A* is mad at *C* because of *B*) = *A* is very angry with *C* because of *B*. There is a stylistic difference between *serdit'sja* and *zlit 'sja*: *tilz'sja* is more colloquial.

(21)–(22) *A – v bešenstve/v jarosti po povodu B (lica) C* (*A* is in a frenzy/a fury due to *B* of person *C*) = *A* is so angry with *C* because of *B* that this anger causes *A* to lose his self-control or causes him great difficulties in keeping it.

(23–24) *A vozmuščaetsja B; A negoduet po povodu B* (*A* is indignant on account of *B*) = *A* experiences an active-negative emotional state caused by the fact that:

(a) *A* is sure of the realization of event *B*,

(b) *B* is undesirable to *A*,

(c) *A* believes that *B* contradicts the fundamental principles of private and social life,

(d) *A* wants to counteract event *B* or its recurrence.

(25) *A gnevaetsja na C za B* (*A* is angry/wrathful with *C* on account of *B*) = *A* experiences an active-negative emotional state caused by the fact that:

(a) *A* is sure of the realization of event *B*, the subject of which is person *C*,

(b) *B* is undesirable to *A*,

(c) *A* believes that *C* contradicts the fundamental principles of private and social life,

(d) *C* is undesirable for *A* because of *B*,

(e) *A* wants to do something to *C* in order to counteract event *B* or its recurrence.

(26) *A zaviduet C v B* (*A* envies *C* (in) *B*) = *A* is annoyed by his lack of fact *B*, which *A* wants to have, and by *C*'s possession of fact *B*.

For example: *On zaviduet talantu Sergeja* (He envies Sergej his talent), *U vas na juge sejčas vesna, i ja zaviduju vam* (You're having spring down south just now, and I envy you).

(27) *A revnuet B k C* (*A* is jealous of *C*'s having *B*) = *A* is annoyed because *C* has fact *B*, which *A* wants to have all to himself.

For example, *Vrači revnovali drug k drugu: každyj sčital, čto tol'ko emu dolžna prinadležat' zasluga iscelit' bol' nogo* (The doctors were jealous of each other: each thought that the credit for healing the patient should go to him only). Fact *B* is very often a definite person, cf. *Grafinja xodila za besprestanno ubegavšim ot nee Petej, revnuja ego k Nataše* (The Countess, jealous of Nataša, watched over Petja, who was continually running away from her). The adverb *revnivo* (jealously) also means a desire to possess something exclusively, cf. *Stariki revnivo xranjat ètu tajnu* (The old men jealously guard this secret).

It can be seen that the definitions of the words *zavidovat'* and *revnovat'* are very close to each other. It is interesting that in Polish there is a word which is used to designate both *zavist'* (envy) and *revnost'* (jealousy) – *zazdrość*. '*A* is annoyed because *C* has fact *B*, which *A* wants to have' is a part common to the meanings of *zavist'* and *revnost'*. It can be seen that this is also the meaning of the word *zazdrość*. In contrast to Polish, Russian differentiates this situation with regard to two features: (1) *A* does not have fact *B* (*zavist'*)/it is unimportant whether *A* has fact *B* or not (*revnost'*); (2) *A* wants that *only A* would have fact *B* (*revnost'*)/*A* does not necessarily have such a desire (*zavist'*).

NADEŽDA (Hope)

(28) *A nadeetsja na B* (*A* hopes that *B*) = *A* experiences a positive emotional state caused by the fact that:

(a) *A* believes that the realization of event *B* is highly probable,

(b) *B* is desirable for *A*.

Note that it is possible *nadejat'sja* (to hope) or *bojat'sja* (to be afraid) not only for a future event, but for a supposed past event: *Ja vse-taki nadejus', čto on menja ponjal* (Still, I hope he understood me). The expressions *A nadeetsja na B/čto B* (*A* hopes for *B*/that *B*) and *A boitsja B/čto B* (*A* is afraid of *B*/that *B*) are often used to mean only *A*'s evaluation of event *B* (*A* believes that the realization of *B* is highly probable and *B* is desirable/undesirable to *A*), without implying the corresponding emotion (see [15], p. 46). There is an interesting case of antonymy connected with *nadejat'sja*: this word is antonymous to two words – *otčaivat'sja* (to despair) and *bojat'sja* (to be afraid); compare the opposite meanings of the expressions *Nadejus', čto ona priedet* (I hope she will come) and *Bojus', čto ona priedet* (I'm afraid she's coming), and the following examples of contrast in the corresponding nouns: *Budem strax in adeždu delit'*... (We will share our hopes and fears); *Suščestvujut položenija, pri kotoryx strax i nadežda slivajutsja voedino* (There are situations where hope and fear merge into one/become one); *Rodnye deti vnušajut emu ne nadeždu, a strax* (His own children fill him not with hope, but with fear). *Nadejat'sja* contrasts with the word *otčaivat'sja* with respect to the first component of the evaluation (cf. in *otčajani* (despair): '*A* believes that it is impossible to cause some event') and to the word *bojat'sja* with respect to the second component (see *strax* below).

STRAX (Fear)

(29)–(30) *A ispytyvaet strax pered B [za A/C]* (*A* experiences fear when faced with *B* [for *A/C*]); *A boitsja, čto B [slučitsja c A/C]* (*A* is afraid that *B* [will happen to *A/C*]) = *A* experiences a passive-negative emotional state caused by the fact that:

(a) *A* believes that the realization of event *B* is highly probable,

(b) *A* believes that *B* is an evil to *A* or to person *C*, whom *A* believes to be close to himself,

(c) *A* believes that he is not capable of counteracting event *B*.

Thus, *strax* (fear) contains not only an expectation of some kind of harm for oneself, but also an awareness of one's own weakness. Examples: *Ego terzal strax za druga* (He was tormented by fear for his friend); *Ne strax pered smert'ju zastavil menja ne prinjat' vaš vyzov* (It was not the fear of death that forced me to decline your challenge).

Very often expressions with the words *strax, bojat'sja, ispugat'sja* (to take fright), *bespokoit'sja* (to worry, be anxious) are elliptic: the object of these words is often not the name of the event that is immediately feared, as in *bojat'sja gneva otca* (to fear paternal wrath), but the name of the subject of this event: *bojat'sja otca* (to fear one's father).

(31) *A ispugalsja B [za A/C]* (*A* was frightened by *B* [for *A/C*])=the perfective aspect of *bojat'sja* (=*zabojat'sja*).

Thus, the definition proper of the word *ispugat'sja* coincides with the definition of the word *bojat'sja*. The difference in meaning between these words is purely aspectual. Here it is necessary to note the following. The definitions of the verbs described here, with the exception of the verb *ispugat'sja*, reflect the usages of these verbs in the imperfective aspect. The word *ispugat'sja* is distinguished in this respect because it is a suppletive form of the perfective aspect which has a special root, in distinction, for example, to *obradovat'sja, udivit'sja, zabespokoit'sja, zabojat'sja*. A separate problem which is not discussed here is that concerning the changes occurring in the definitions when the imperfective aspect is replaced by the perfective.

(32) *A – v panike iz-za B* (*A* is panic-striken because of *B*) = *A* is so frightened by *B* that this causes him to lose his self-control.

Thus, there is an aspectual distinction between *byt' v panike* and *bojat'sja* (*byt' v panike* is defined through *ispugat'sja*).

(33)–(34) *A bespokoitsja/trevožitsja, čto B [slučitsja s A/C]* (*A* is uneasy/ alarmed [lest *B* happen to *A/C*]) = *A* experiences a passive-negative emotional state caused by the fact that:

(a) *A* believes that the realization of event *B* is probable,

(b) *A* believes that *B* is an evil to *A* or to person *C*, whom *A* believes to be close to himself,

(c) *A* believes that he is not capable of counteracting event *B*.

Thus, there is less certainty of the realization of the undesirable event in *bespokojstvo* (worry, uneasiness) and *trevoga* (anxiety, alarm) than in *strax* (cf. the first component).

UDIVLENIE (Surprise)

(35) *A udivljaetsja B* (*A* is surprised at/by *B*)=*A* experiences an 'aroused' emotional state caused by the fact that:

(a) *A* is either sure of the realization of event *B* or believes that the realization of *B* is highly probable,

(b) before t_0 *A* believed that the realization of event *B* was unlikely.

It is possible to be *surprised* not only at an event which has happened, but also by an event of whose future realization *A* is sure (or which he considers highly probable). For example, *Ja udivljajus' tomu, čto kniga, po-*

vidimomu, vse-taki vyjdet (I am surprised that the book will probably be published anyway).

(36) *A izumljaetsja B* (*A* is amazed by *B*)=*A* is very surprised by *B*.

(37) *A ošelomlen B* (*A* is stunned by *B*)=*A* is so strongly amazed by *B* that this causes him to lose capability of understanding.

(38) *A ispytyvaet razočarovanie [po povodu B]* (*A* experiences disappointment [on account of *B*])=*A* experiences a passive-negative emotional state caused by the fact that:

(a) *A* is either sure in the non-realization of event *B*, or believes that the non-realization of event *B* is highly probable,

(b) before t_0 *A* was sure of the realization of event *B*,

(c) before t_0 and at t_0 event *B* was very desirable for *A*.

For example, *On nadejalsja vstretit'ee tam, i uznav, čto ona ne pridet, ispytal ostroe razočarovanie* (He had hoped to meet her there, and when he found out that she wasn't going to come, he felt a sharp disappointment). As for expressions of the type *razočarovat'sja v rabote/druge/žizni* (be disillusioned in one's work/friend/life), they designate not the experience of the subject of the feeling, but his emotional relationship to his work, friend, life: earlier he thought well of them, now he thinks ill.

ACKNOWLEDGEMENTS

My thanks go to numerous persons who have helped me with the present paper. It could not certainly be written without many helpful discussions I have had with my colleagues J. D. Apresjan, N.N. Leont'eva, J. A. Mel'čuk, and A. K. Žolkovskij; I tried to account for a lot of their considerations so generously put at my disposal. I have also profited much from remarks and comments made on this paper by members of the Machine Translation Laboratory Staff (at M. Thorez Institute).

State Pedagogical Institute, Moscow

BIBLIOGRAPHY

[1] *Slovar' Sovremennogo Russkogo Literaturnogo Jazyka*, AN S.S.S.R., 17 Vols.
[2] *Slovar' Russkogo Jazyka*, AN S.S.S.R., 4 Vols.
[3] *Tolkovyj Slovar' Russkogo Jazyka*, D. N. Ušakov (ed.), 4 Vols.
[4] *Slovar, Russkogo Jazyka*, S. I. Ožegov (ed.).
[5] Aleksandrova, Z. E., *Slovar' Sinonimov Russkogo Jazyka*, Moscow, 1968.
[6] Apresyan, Ju. D., *Tolkovanie Leksičeskix Značenij Kak Problema Teoretičeskoj Semantiki*, Izvestija AN S.S.S.R., Serija literatury i jazyka, 1969, Vol. 28, No. 1, 11–23.
[7] Apresyan, Ju. D., *O Jazyke Dlja Opisanija Značenij Slov*, Izvestija AN S.S.S.R., Serija literatury i jazyka, 1969, Vol. 28, No. 5, 415–428.

[8] Loulin, Dž., Ličnost' 'Oldos', *Zarubežnaja Radioelektronika*, 1969, No. 1.
[9] Mel'čuk, I. A., *Ob Opredelenii Bolšej/men'šej Smyslovoj Složnosti Pri Slovoobrazo-vatel'nyx Otnošenijax*, Izvestija AN S.S.S.R., Serija literatury i jazyka, 1969, Vol. 28, No. 2, pp. 126–135.
[10] *Mašinnyj Perevod i Prikladnaja Lingvistika*, Vol. 8, Moscow, 1964.
[11] Ščeglov, Ju. K., *Dve Gruppy Slov Russkogo Jazyka*, Mašinnyj perevod i prikladnaja lingvistika, Vol. 8., Moscow, 1964, pp. 50–66.
[12] Bendix, E. H., *Componential Analysis of General Vocabulary: The Semantic Structure of a Set of Verbs in English, Hindi, and Japanese*, Mouton and Co., The Hague, 1966.
[13] Fillmore, C. J., Review of Edvard Herman Bendix *Componential Analysis of General Vocabulary: The Semantic Structure of a Set of Verbs in English, Hindi, and Japanese*, Working Papers in Linguistics (Technical Report 68-3. The Ohio State University), No. 2, 1968, pp. 30–64.
[14] Weinreich, U., 'Lexicographic Definition in Descriptive Semantics'. In 'Problems of Lexicography' (ed. by J. W. Householder, Jr., and Sol Saporta) (=IUPAL, No. 21), 1962, pp. 25–43.
[15] Wierzbicka, A., *Negation – A Study in the Deep Grammar*, MIT Press, March, 1967.

JU. D. APRESJAN, I. A. MEL'ČUK, AND A. K. ŽOLKOVSKIJ

MATERIALS FOR AN EXPLANATORY COMBINATORY DICTIONARY OF MODERN RUSSIAN

The present publication contains almost no new dictionary entries. Most of the words included in it have been described in Issue 4 of the *Experimental and Applied Linguistics Problems Group* (*EALPG*), Preprints (Ju. D. Apresjan, A. K. Žolkovskij, and I. A. Mel'čuk: 1970, '11 Dictionary Entries in an Explanatory-Combinatory Dictionary of Russian', Russian language Institute, U.S.S.R. Academy of Sciences, M.). All these entries, however, have been re-edited to reflect the results of two basic types of alterations made on the earlier variant.

First, the authors have attempted to take into account both the critical remarks they have received after and as a result of the publication of the preprint and the experience accumulated during this time from work done on the definitions of other words; a great many refinements have been introduced, definitions have been altered, etc.; the entries PRISNIT'SJA 'dream', ZASYPAT' 'fall asleep' (impf.), ZASNUT' 'fall asleep' (perf.) have been added to the semantic field of *son* 'sleep'. (The experimental, working nature of the preprints was specifically foreseen when the preliminary *EALPG* publications were planned, and constitutes the distinctive feature of this series).

Secondly, the proposed dictionary entries differ essentially from those in the earlier variant with respect to the means through which they have been organized. A comparison of the published dictionary entries performed by T. Ja. Kazavčinskaja and A. K. Polivanova revealed a large number of inconsistencies, vagueness, and contradictions in the means used to record the information. A. K. Polivanova (together with I. A. Mel'čuk and A. K. Žolkovskij) is presently developing an *Instruction for Compilers* which aims at regulating notational systems and which will be published as a preprint. The present publication will attempt to provide the compilers with model entries written in accordance with the Instruction which can in some sense serve as a substitute for it until it is published. With this aim in view the dictionary entries have been supplied with notes explaining the notational devices and the new lexical functions. The notes will be found at the end of all the dictionary entries; there are no references to the notes in the main body of the text, but the notes themselves carry indications of the pages to which they refer.

(N.B.: the reader should not consider the entry variants here to be

F. Kiefer (ed.), Trends in Soviet Theoretical Linguistics, 411–438. *All Rights Reserved.*
Copyright © *1973 by D. Reidel Publishing Company, Dordrecht-Holland.*

definitive. A number of problems of organization (e.g., how periods are to be used for demarcation purposes) have not yet been solved.)

METÉL/', *i*, fem.:	'snowstorm' Bad weather (nepogoda[1]) – a strong wind which shifts great quantities of snow in the air $[=S_0(\text{Magn} \leftarrow mesti \text{ II } 2, \text{ lit.}:$ 'sweep')].
	Connotation: rapid flight of many small objects.
	[*ognennaja metel'* 'fire-storm, hail of bullets'; *Pux zakružilsja beloj metel'ju* 'The down swirled like a snowstorm'].
	Cf. SNEGOPAD 'snowfall'; POZ'OMKA 'drifting snow, ground wind'.
Syn:	folklore *metelica* 'snowstorm'.
Syn$_c$:	*v juga, purga* 'blizzard'.
Gener:	*nepogoda* 'bad weather'.
A_0:	*metel'nyj* 'snowstorm-'.
Adv_0:	*v* [~] 'at the time of [snowstorm]'.
V_0:	Magn ← *mesti* II 2 'to sweep, to storm'.
Magn:	*sil'naja* 'strong', colloq. *strašnaja, užasnaja, žutkaja,...* 'terrible, awful, dreadful' // *buran* 'snowstorm (said of storms on the steppes)', *snežnaja burja* 'snowstorm'.
IncepPredMagn:	*razygryvat'sja (vovsju), razgulivat'sja (vovsju)* 'break out, break loose (in full force)'.
IncepPredPlus:	*usilivat'sja* 'grow, become stronger'.
IncepPredMinus or IncepPredAntiMagn:	*oslabevat'* 'weaken, grow weaker, become quiet'.
Loc_{in}:	*v* [*i*] 'in'.
$Func_0$:	*mesti* 'to storm', *byt'* 'there is'.
$IncepFunc_0$:	*podnimat'sja/podymat'sja* 'rise, start up', *načinat'sja* 'begin'.
$ProxIncepFunc_0$[2]:	*sobirat'sja* 'gather', *nadvigat'sja* 'approach'.
$ContFunc_0$:	*(vse) ne unimat'sja,* 'refuse to calm down' *prodolžat'sja* 'continue'.

---

[1] Bad weather (*nepogoda*) – cloudy, with precipitation or wind which hampers normal vital human activities.

[2] Prox is a new lexical function meaning ≈ 'be close to' (usually a part of complex functions), thus, $ProxIncepFunc_0$ (*vojna* 'war') = *nadvigat'sja* 'approach'.

$\mathrm{FinFunc_0}$:   *stixat'* 'quiet down', *unimat'sja* 'calm down', *uleč'sja* 'subside', *prekraščat'sja* 'abate', *kon-čat'sja* 'end'.

$\mathrm{Func_0 + Magn}$:   *buševat'* 'rage'.[3]

$\mathrm{PerfIncepFunc_0 + Magn}$:   *razygrat'sja (vovsju), razguljat'sja (vovsju)* 'break loose (in full force)', *razbusevat'sja (vovsju)* 'rage, come into (full) fury'.

$\mathrm{PerfIncepFunc_0 + frequent}$:   *zarjadit'*[4] | M. − pl.

$\mathrm{Involv \xrightarrow{2} X}$[4]:   *guljat'* [$\mathrm{Loc_{in}}/po\ S = X$] | S is the name of a part of the landscape 'move [about $S = X$]'.

$\mathrm{IncepInvolv \xrightarrow{2} X}$[5]:   *naletat'* | $D_2 = \emptyset$ 'fly, swoop down upon'.

$F_k = $ at an intermediate point of X's route

$\mathrm{IncepInvolv \xrightarrow{2} X}$:   *zastigat'* [$S_{\mathrm{acc}} = X$] 'catch, intercept [$S = X$]'.

$\mathrm{Conv_{21}}(F_k)$:[6]   *popadat'* [$v \sim$] 'land in, encounter [a snowstorm]'.

---

[3] A notation in the form '$F_1 + F_2$' [a *conjunction* of the lexical functions F_1 and F_2] should be interpreted as: $F_1(F_2(C_0) + C_0)$. In the corresponding part of the deep-syntax tree, F_1 and F_2 are connected with C_0 *separately* (by means of the dependency arrows which correspond to these lexical functions). Hence, the notation $\mathrm{Func_0 + Magn}$ (*metel'* 'snowstorm') has the tree

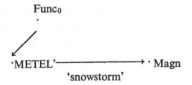

$\mathrm{Func_0}$

·METEL' —————————→ · Magn
'snowstorm'

in contrast to, say, $\mathrm{IncepOper_1}$ [a *composition* of lexical functions]: $\mathrm{Incep} \xrightarrow{1} \mathrm{Oper_1} \xrightarrow{2} C_0$

[4] $C_0 \xleftarrow{1} \mathrm{Involv} \xrightarrow{2} X \approx C_0 \xleftarrow{1}$ 'influence, have an effect on' $\xrightarrow{2} X$; Involv thereby always introduces an additional variable – 'who/what is influenced', which is not included among the participants of the situation described by the key-word. Thus, the situation 'metel'' 'snowstorm' does not presuppose any participants; hence, '*čelovek, zastignutyj metel'ju*' 'man caught in a snowstorm' is a new participant, i.e., a participant of a new situation

[5] 'Involv (*metel'* 'snowstorm')'. 'IncepInvolv $\xrightarrow{2} X$: *naletat'* | $D_2 = \emptyset$, 'fly, swoop down upon'. Here D_2 means 'D_2 of the word *naletat'*'. In general, such symbols as M_1, D_1 and the like placed after a vertical line refer to the word which comes immediately before this line or to the group of words to the left of the line up to the nearest semi-colon. (Cf. the notation for $\mathrm{Adv_{1A}}$, $\mathrm{Loc_{in}}$ and not $\mathrm{Adv_2}$ on p. 431.)

[6] In the notation '$F_k = \ldots$' the symbol F_k is used to denote, within the given dictionary entry, the complex function standing to the right of the equation.

$F_1 = \text{Involv} \xrightarrow{2} X$ and
cover X with snow[7]:   *zametat'* II 1a, *zanosit'* II 1a $[S_{acc}(snegom)]$
'cover, block $[S(\text{with snow})]$'.[8]

$\text{Conv}_{\theta 21}(F_1)$:[8]   *zametat'* II 1b, *zanosit'* II 1b $[S_{acc} \sim 'ju]//$
zametat' II 1c, *zanosit'* II 1c $[S_{acc}]$.

$S_3' \text{Result}(F_1)$:   *(snežnyj) zanos* '(snow) drift' | usually pl. $[D_2$
is the (proposed) route, way].[9]

become invisible because
of $\text{Conv}_{21}\text{Involv}$:   *tonut'* $[v \sim i]$ 'sink, disappear' [in the snow-
storm].

$A_2\text{Involv}$: $v\ [\sim/\sim i]$ 'in [the snowstorm]'.

Son: *vyt', zavyvat'* 'howl'.

when there are many: $s\ [-jami]$ with '[snowstorms]'//rare *metelistyj*
'stormy'.

Za oknom metel' 'There is a snowstorm outside'. *Uže s utra sobiralas'metel'*;
k dvum časam ona razygralas' vovsju 'A snowstorm had been gathering ever
since morning; by two o'clock it was in full force'. *Nastupila sneznaja zima
s meteljami i zanosami* 'A snowy winter set in with blizzards and drifts'. *Na
perevale nas zastigla metel'* 'A snowstorm caught us in the pass' = ...*my
popali v metel'* '...we were caught in a snowstorm'. *Kogda my podnjalis' na
pereval, tam guljala metel'* 'When we climbed the pass, there was a snowstorm (in progress) there' = ...*naletela metel'* 'A snowstorm swooped down'.
Zamela metel' dorožki, zaporošila 'A snowstorm has covered and powdered
the paths' (popular song), *'N'ju-Jork v metel''* 'New York (plunged) in
blizzard' (caption to newspaper picture). *On šagnul za porog i srazu potonul v
meteli* 'He stepped over the threshold and immediately disappeared in the
snowstorm'. *I opjat'my v meteli, A ona vse metet...* 'And again we're in a
snowstorm, and it keeps on storming/blows and blows...' (B. Pasternak).

---

[7] F_1 is assumed to have three actants: the first is C_0, the second the one introduced by
Involv ('that which is blocked, snowed under'), and the third is 'that which covers'; in this
particular case the last actant is always *sneg* 'snow', so that $S_3\text{Result}(F_1) \approx$ 'the snow with
which the road is covered as a result of the drift'.

[8] The symbol θ (assigned to the Conv's) designates an impersonal subject (which calls
for agreement of the predicate in the neuter gender). The transition from F_1 to $\text{Conv}_{\theta 21}(F_1)$
here corresponds to a transition of the type *Metel' (A) zamela dorogu (B)* 'A snowstorm
(A) blocked the road (B)' $\approx$ *Dorogu (B) zamelo metel'ju (A)* 'The road (B) has been
blocked by a snowstorm (A)', In general:

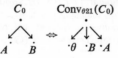

[9] S_i' means: 'S_i or S_0'; the order of the places in S_i' coincides with the order of the places
in S_0, unlike the ordinary S_i, whose place order is 'displaced'.

SNEGOPAD 'snowfall' – fall of snow, usually heavy [//S_0Func$_0$ (*sneg* 'snow' +Magn)].

POZ'OMKA 'ground wind with snow' – snow swept from the ground and moved by the wind close to its surface, or such a wind itself [differs from *metel'* in that there is no snowfall and no snow at the level of a man's face].

SNEŽNAJA BURJA 'snowstorm, blizzard' – Magn +*metel'*.

BURAN 'blizzard' – a heavy snowstorm, usually in a large open space.

V'JUGA 'blizzard' – a snowstorm with whirling snow [circle-shaped shifts of snow dominate].

PURGA 'blizzard' – a snowstorm with violent gusts of wind and (usually) biting, stinging snow [snow is moved horizontally].

PRISN | IT'SJA, *jús', íš'sja*, Perf (snit'sja) 'to dream'

> MU[10] like that of SNIT'SJA

Mne prisnilas' bol'šaja lestnica 'I dreamed of a large staircase'; *Petru prisnilos', čto on kupalsja v okeanie* 'Petr dreamed that he was swimming in the ocean'; *Koške prisnilos', kak ona rodila kotjat* 'The cat dreamed about how she was having kittens'.

Syn: bookish *prigrezit'sja* 'dream (be lost in a reverie)'.
Gener: *predstavit'sja, prividet'sja vo sne* 'appear to somebody while sleeping'.

Ja tebe pozvonila, potomu čto ty mne segodnja prisnilsja 'I called you because I dreamed of you last night'.

• *I (VO SNE) NE PRISNIT'SJA.* Perf(*i (vo sne) ne snit'sja*) 'that you couldn't even dream of', used only in the future tense or in the subjunctive mood. See *SNIT'SJA*. *Maša pobyvala v takix peredrjagax, čto tebe i (vo sne) ne prisnitsja!* 'Maša has been in scrapes you couldn't even possibly dream of, imagine' ⟨=*kakie tebe i (vo sne) ne prisnjatsja!*⟩.

Impossible! **Emy takoe i (vo sne) ne prisnilos'.*

SN | IT'SJA, *jús', íš'sja*, imperf. *X-u snitsja Y* 'X dreams of Y (Y comes to X in a dream)' = in the consciousness of X, who is sleeping (*spit*[1] 1a), there takes place a process resembling the perception of Y which X does not perceive with his sense organs.

Mne snilas' ty 'I dreamed of you, saw you in a dream'; *Na starosti let*

---

[10] MU = model' upravlenija 'pattern of government'.

snjatsja molodye gody 'In our old age we dream of our younger years.'[11] *Petru snilos', čto on letal* 'Petr dreamed that he was flying'; *Mne snilos', kak ty menja vstrečal* 'I dreamed that you met me'.

1 = X [who/what is perceived]	2 = Y [who is the sleeper]
(1) S_{nom}	
(2) *čto* 'that' SENTENCE	
(3) *kak* 'how, that' SENTENCE	S_{dat}
(4) SENTENCE	obligatory

Syn:	bookish *grezit'sja* 'dream'.
Conv$_{21}$:	bookish *grezit'* 'dream'.
Gener:	*predstavljat'sja, videt'sja vo sne* 'appear to somebody while sleeping'.
S_1:	*son* II 1, *snovidenie* 'dream'.
Magn^{temp}:	*vsju noč'* 'all night'.
Perf:	*prisnit'sja* 'to dream'.

Vsju-to nočen'ku mne spat' bylo nevmoč', Raskrasavec-barin snilsja mne vsju noč' 'I couldn't sleep the whole night through, I dreamed all night of the handsome gentleman' (Russian folk song). *I snilas' mne dolina Dagestana* 'And I dreamed of a valley in Dagestan' (M. Ju. Lermontov). *Mne snilos', čto ko mne na provody. Šli po lesu vy drug za družkoj* 'I dreamed that you came through the forest one after the other to see me off' (B. Pasternak). *Mne snitsja: iz rebjat ja vzjat v nauku k ispolinu* 'I dream: as a child I am chosen by a giant as his pupil' (B. Pasternak).

• I (VO SNE) NE SNIT'SJA, colloq. *X Y-u i (vo sne) ne snitsja* 'Y couldn't even dream of X' = X, often desirable for Y, is so unusual for Y that Y cannot even imagine X. Cf. NEOBYCAJNYJ 'unusual', UDIVLJAT'SJA 'be surprised', VOOBRAŽAT' 'imagine'; MEČTAT' 'dream of'.

   Podobnye rezul'taty emu i (vo sne) ne snilis'! 'He couldn't even dream of such results!'

SNOVIDÉNI | E, *ja*, usually pl., neuter (bookish). *Snovidenie Y-a ob X-e* = *son* II 1 *Y-a ob X-e* 'Y's dream about X'

---

[11] It is assumed that there is always a second actant in the deep-syntax structure of the verb *snit'sja* 'to dream'; in the given instance, it is the conventional symbol with the signifié ≈ 'anyone'.

1 = X [who/what is dreamed about]	2 = Y [who is the dreamer]
	(1) S_{gen} (2) A_{poss}

snovidenija pacienta 'the patient's dreams', *moi ⟨Juriny⟩ snovidenija* 'my [Jurij's] dreams'

Syn:	*son* II 1 'dream'.
AntiBon:	*tjaželye* 'gloomy' [something unpleasant is dreamed].
Caus:	*vyzyvat'* [~*ja u* S_{gen}] 'provoke, cause, call forth [somebody's dreams]'.

explain what *S* means: *tolkovat'* [~*ja*] 'interpret [somebody's dreams]'.

'*Tolkovanie snovidenij*' 'The Interpretation of Dreams' (a book by S. Freud). *Ty v snoviden'jax mne javljalsja...* 'You appeared to me in dreams' (A. S. Puškin). *Marixuana v nebol'šix dozax vyzyvaet u ispytuemyx krasočnye snovidenija* 'Marijuana in small doses causes colorful dreams in the subjects'.

• PRIJATNYX SNOVIDENIJ! 'Pleasant dreams!' The speaker wishes the listener a good sleep. See SPAT'1 1a, 'to sleep'.

SP | AT'¹, *lju, iš'*, past *al, alá, aló,* imperf. 1a. *X spit* '*X* sleeps, is sleeping' = *X* is resting, with all systems of his organism switched off to the highest degree attainable without adverse effects to the organism [usually almost motionless, eyes closed, relaxed muscles, a partially switched-off consciousness, etc; one of the basic periods in the daily or yearly cycle of vital activities].

1 = X [who is resting]
S_{nom}

Petr spit 'Petr is sleeping, sleeps'.

Syn:	archaic bookish *počivat'* 'sleep, rest', colloq. child. *baj-baj* 'bye-bye', *bain'ki, spatki* 'sleepy-bye', pop. *zadavat' xrapaka ⟨=xrapovickogo⟩* 'saw some logs', pop. vulg. *dryxnut'* 'snooze', low middle-class euphemism *otdyxat'* 2 'rest',
Syn∩:	*dremat'* 'doze, nod', slang *kemarit', prikornut'* 'nestle down, have a nap'.

not to S: F_k = not to S when S is necessary:	bookish *bodrstvovat'* 'keep awake'.

ne smykat' glaz [not of the moment of speech] 'not get a wink of sleep'; *byt'* $\langle$ = *provesti* $\rangle$ *bez sna* [S_{acc}] 'be $\langle$ = pass $\rangle$ without sleeping [S]'.

$F_{k \supset}$:   *byt' na nogax* [S_{acc}] 'be on one's feet [S]' *ne ložit'sja* [S_{acc}] 'not go to bed [S]'.

S is a time-interval which includes the normal sleeping period.

$A_0(F_k)$:   *bessonnyj* 'sleepless' | G is usually the name of an interval of time.[12]

S_0:   *son* I 1a, rare *span'e* 'sleep'.

$S_{0 \subset}$:   *spjačka* 1 'hibernation' [of some animals].

person S_1:   *spjaščij* 'sleeper, he who is sleeping'.

Son(S_1)[13]:   *xrapet'* 'to snore'.

room $S_{\text{loc-usual}}$:   *spal'nja, spal'naja komnata* 'bedroom'; archaic *dortuar'* '(dortoir) dormitory'.

$S_{\text{loc-instr-usual}}$:   *krovat'* 'bed', *kojka* 'cot'; *kreslo-krovat'* 'arm-chair-bed', *divan-krovat'* 'sofa-bed'; *ležanka* 'stove-couch'; *topčan* 'trestle bed'; *kolybel'* 'cradle'; *nary* 'bunk', *polka* 2 [in a train] 'berth'; *lavka* 2 [in a hut] 'bench'; *peč'* [in a hut] 'stove'.

$S_{\text{loc-instr-med-usual}}$:   *postel'* 'bed'.

$S_{\text{instr-med-usual}}$:   *spal'nyj mešok*, colloq. *spal'nik* 'sleeping bag'.

$S_{\text{med-usual}}$:   bookish *postel'nye* $\langle$ = *spal'nye* $\rangle$ *prinadležnosti* 'bedclothes', *postel'2* 'bed'.

S_0PredAble$_{1 \subset}$:   *son* I 1b 'sleep'.

Conv$_{01}$PredAble$_1$:   *spat'sja* [S_{dat}] | with *ne* 'not' or an evaluatory adverb [such as *xorošo* 'well', *ploxo* 'poorly', *kak* 'how']. (Found in expressions like *mne ne spit'sja* 'I don't feel like sleeping, I can't get to sleep' and *Xoroso špitsja pod utro* 'Sleep is

---

[12] $G(X)$ is a word that governs X syntactically – the so-called (syntactic) 'master' of the word X.

[13] The index (usual under various S's (e.g., S_1 or S_{loc}, etc.)) indicates, in reference to an object, that this is the name of an article which is especially intended for the corresponding purpose; if it refers to a person it is the name of a profession, i.e., the person can thus be named only if he performs the corresponding function in his professional capacity.

sound, you sleep well, soundly, towards morning'. – [Translator's note].)

$Magn_{[switched\ off]}$:[14]

kak mertvyj ⟨ubityj⟩ 'like the dead', bez zadnix nog 'beat, worn out' [usually of the moment of speech – as a result of fatigue, lack of sleep, etc.]; kak surok 'like a log', (tak cto [$S_{acc/gen} = X$]) ne dobudiš'sja 'so that it is impossible to wake somebody', ([pri S_{loc}, nad S_{instr}, okolo $S_{gen} = X$]) xot' iz pusek streljaj ⟨=pali⟩ [usually not of the moment of speech] 'you could shoot a cannon next to somebody (he wouldn't wake up)'.

$Magn_{[switched\ off]}$ [+]Bon:

krepko 'soundly'; kak mladenec 'like a baby', snom pravednika ⟨archaic pravednyx⟩ [soundly and peacefully] 'the sleep of the righteous'

$Magn_{[switched\ off]}$
[+]Bon and the speaker thinks this is inappropriate:

//razospat'sja 'oversleep'.

$AntiMagn_{[switched\ off]}$:

čutko 'lightly' [with a minimal switching off of the organs of perception – so that the sleeper is ready to respond to a possible interference] //dremat' [be half-asleep] 'doze, nod'.

$F = AntiMagn_{[switched\ off]}$
[+]AntiBon:

nespokojno, bespokojno 'restlessly' [the sleeper tosses and turns, moans in his sleep, wakes up often].

$Excess^{motor}$ (body)
$- Sympt_2 (F_k + S)$:[15]

//voročat'sja (s boku na bok) (vo sne) 'toss and turn (from one side to the other) (while sleeping)'; voročat'sja, metat'sja (vo sne) 'toss and turn, move about restlessly (while sleeping)'.

---

[14] The indices under Magn, Fact and Real indicate the definition component to which the corresponding function refers. Thus $Magn_{[switched\ off]}$ from SPAT' 1a 'to sleep' means: 'the systems of the organism are completely switched off'. (Cf. $Fact_{[rest]}$, p. 429).

[15] LF's of the type $Excess^{motor}$ (body) – $Sympt_2$ (sleep restlessly) have been introduced to describe a great many expressions which designate the physical symptoms of certain physical or emotional states of a human being (for example, voročat'sja s boku na bok 'toss and turn from side to side' is a symptom of restless sleep, ne deržat'sja na nogax 'be on one's last legs' and klevat' nosom 'to nod' are symptoms of a strong desire to sleep, pokrasnet' ot styda 'blush with shame', dyxanie perexvatyvaet ot gneva 'anger is suffocating somebody, nogi podkaxivajutsja ot straxa 'one's legs buckle with fear', vytaraščit' glaza ot udivlenija 'one's eyes goggle out with surprise', etc.) Physical changes which are symptoms of something can often be represented by indicating two things:

Excess (*speech*)
— $\text{Sympt}_2(F_k+S)$:

//*stonat'* 'moan', *kričat'* 'shout', *bredit'* 'rave, babble' (*vo sne*) '(while sleeping)'.

Bon:

tixo 'quietly', *mirno* 'peacefully', *spokojno* 'calmly', *bezmjatežno* 'tranquilly'; *sladko* (*prjamo*) *žalko budit'* 'sweetly' (it's a (downright) pity to wake (somebody) up)') ⟨*tak sladko, čto žalko budit'* 'so sweetly, that it's a pity to wake (somebody) up'⟩ [tranquilly, with an expression of innocent bliss on the face or in the pose of the sleeper].

Bon+Ver:

xorošo 'well' ⟨*prekrasno*,... 'wonderfully'⟩// *slavno ja* ⟨*my*⟩ *pospal* (*i*)! 'I⟨we⟩ slept marvellously!'.

AntiBon+AntiVer:

ploxo 'poorly' ⟨*užasno* 'terribly', *otvratitel'no*, ... 'disgustingly, vilely'⟩.

too much Magn^{temp}:

//*zaspat'sja; perespat'*[16] 'oversleep' ['too much' for the organism M_1].

S_1 (too much Magn^{temp} S) or S_1 (to like to S.):

sonja 'sleepyhead'.

---

the nature of the change and the part (or system) of the organism that is undergoing the change: Excess (*body*), Excess (*speech*), Excess (*eyes*), etc. The following types of physical changes have been distinguished: Excess – the extraordinary functioning of X; Degrad – a stoppage in the functioning of X; Obstr – a difficulty in the functioning of X. 'Symptomatic' LF's, unlike those treated earlier, are *two-argument* functions. As is apparent from the notation of these LF's, one argument is the name of the place of the change, and the other is the name of the symptomized phenomenon. For example, Degrad^{vertic}-Sympt for the arguments *golova* 'head' and *očen' xotet'sja spat'* 'to want very much to sleep' is expressed with the word-group *klevat' nosom* 'to nod'; for the arguments *nogi* 'legs' and *ocen' xotet'sja spat'* 'to want very much to sleep' it is expressed by *ne deržat'sja na nogax* 'be on one's last legs'; and for the arguments *nogi* 'legs' and *strax* 'fear' – by *nogi podkašivajutsja (ot straxa)* 'one's legs buckle (from fear)'.

The number index on the symbol 'Sympt' has been introduced to characterize the syntactic structure of 'symptomatic' expressions. The index consists of the following signs: θ, $\emptyset$, 1, 2, 3. The *positions* of the signs correspond to the *syntactic* actants: the first, second, third, and fourth positions correspond to the first, second, third, and fourth actants, respectively. The *numbers* designate *semantic* actants, i.e., the participants of the symptomized situation: 1 is 'the place of change', 2 is the 'person', 3 is 'that which is symptomized'. The signs θ and $\emptyset$, which are used only in the first position, designate the absence of a subject (the first syntactic actant) corresponding to any kind of semantic actant: θ means that the subject is absent altogether, $\emptyset$ indicates that there is a subject, but that it is included in the expression of the LF itself. For example, the expression *on ne deržalsja na nogax* 'he was on his last legs' is defined as Degrad^{vertic} (*nogi* 'legs') – Sympt$_{21}$ (Magn + *xotet'sja spat'* 'to want to sleep'): 2 in the first position means that the first object (the second syntactic actant) designates the place of change.

[16] *Perespat'$_2$* = 'spend the night with (a woman)'.

Adv_1:   vo sne 'in one's sleep, while sleeping, asleep'.

not Adv_1:   bez sna 'without sleep'.

Adv_1 +not completely: v polysne; skvoz' son 'half asleep, sleepily' | G is a verb of perception or speech.

Incep: //zasypát'[1] [17] 'fall asleep'.

$Incep_n$:   //zabyvat'sja 'doze, drop off'.

Fin   //prosypat'sja, archaic probuždat'sja 'wake up'.

$F_1 = Fin_n$:   //vstavat' 2, podymat'sja 2 [getting out of bed] 'arise, get up'

$Imper(F_1)$:   //pod''em! 'reveille!' | usually in the army, in hospitals, camps, etc.

Adv_1 (not completely Perf Fin):   so sna, sprosonok, sproson'ja 'half-awake, sleepily'.

Caus: //usypljat 'lull'; bajukat', ubajukivat' 'lull, rock-a-bye' [usually by means of singing, rocking etc.] | M_2 is usually a child.

medicine S_{med}Caus: snotvornoe 'soporific'; archaic pop. sonnyj porosok 'sleeping powders', archaic folklore sonnoe zel'e 'sleeping potion.'

Liqu: //budit', archaic probuzdat' 'awaken, wake somebody up'.

$Liqu_n$:   //podymat' 'get somebody up'.

clock $S_{instr-usual}$Liqu: budil'nik 'alarm-clock'.

Perm: davat [~at'] 'let [sleep]'.

Prepar: klast'([~at']);ukladyvat'([~at']), 'put [to bed, to sleep]' M_2 is usually a child.

$Prepar_1$:   itti [~at'] 'go' [to bed)]lozit'sja ([~at']) 'go to· bed, to sleep]', ukladyvat'sja ([~at]) 'lie down, go to bed' // pop. (i) na bokovuju 'hit the hay' | used as a syntactic equivalent of the infinitive.

$ImperPrepar_1$:   v postel! '(get) to bed!'.

Imper: báju-báju, báju-baj, baj-baj, bájuski-bajú 'lull-abye, go to sleep' | usually to children; otboj! 'taps, lights out!' | usually in the army, hospitals, etc.

F_m=to feel that one's body needs: xotet' [~at'] 'want [to sleep], be sleepy'.

---

[17] Zasýpat'[2] [vysypát'sja, etc. are derivatives from the verb sýpat' 'to sprinkle'].

$F_n = \text{Conv}_{21}(F_m)$:

$S_{0\cap}(F_n)$:

$A_{2\text{-actual}}(F_n)$:

characteristic of a sleepy
person 1:
$A_{2\text{-usual}}(F_n)$:
characteristic of a
drowsy person:

$\text{Degrad}^{\text{motor}}$ (*opened eyelids*)
-$\text{Sympt}_{\theta 2}(\text{Magn}+F_n)$:

to try $\text{Liqu}_1 \text{Degrad}^{\text{motor}}$
(*opened eyelids*) –
$\text{Sympt}_2(\text{Magn}+F_n)$:
$\text{Degrad}^{\text{vertic}}$(*feet*) –
$\text{Sympt}_{21}(\text{Magn}+F_n)$:

$\text{Obstr}^{\text{vertic}}$(*feet*) –
$\text{Sympt}_{21}(\text{Magn}+F_n)$:

$\text{Degrad}^{\text{vertic}}$(*head*) –
$\text{Sympt}_2(\text{Magn}+F_n)$:
$\text{Degrad}^{\text{vertic}}$(*head*) –
$\text{Sympt}_{12}(\text{Magn}+F_n)$:

$\text{Excess}^{\text{incep}}$ – Sympt_2
$(\text{Magn}+F_n)$:

to breathe deeply and slowly
in a particular way –
$\text{Sympt}_2(\text{Magn}+F_n)$:
to try $\text{AntiReal}_2^{\text{I}}(F_n)$:

$\text{Real}_2^{\text{II}}(F_n)$

xotet'sja [~*at'* S_{dat} | 'feel like, want (to sleep),
be sleepy'.

son I 7b 'sleep'; *sonlivost'* 'sleepiness'.

vo vlasti [*sna*] 'in the grip of [sleep]' // *sonnyj* 1
'sleepy'.

sonnyj 2 [*golos, glaza*] 'sleepy [voice, eyes]'.
sonlivyj 1 'drowsy'.

sonlivyj 2 [*vyraženie lica, lico, golos...*]
'drowsy [facial expression, face, voice]....

// *veki tjazelejut* ⟨*nalivajutsja svincom*⟩ [*u*
S_{gen}] 'one's eyelids become heavy, become
leaden', *glaza slipajutsja* [*u* S_{gen}] 'one's eyes
want to stick together, one can hardly keep
one's eyes open'.

// *teret'* (*sebe*) *glaza* 'rub one's eyes'.

// *ne deržat'sja* [*na* ~*ax*] 'be unable to keep [on
one's legs]', *valit'sja* [*s* ~] 'be falling [off one's
feet]'.

// *ele deržat'sja* ⟨*stojat'*⟩ [*na* ~*ax*] 'be on one's
last legs, be ready to drop'.

// *klevat' nosom* 'to nod, begin to doze'.

// [~*a u* S_{gen}] *padat' na grud'* '[one's head]
sinks, drops to one's chest.

// *spat' na xodu, stoja* 'sleep standing up';
(*prjamo* ⟨*prosto*⟩) *zasypat'*[1] 'drop right off'.

// *zevat'* 'to yawn'.
// *borot'sja so snom* 'fight sleep, try to stay
awake'.

// *vysypát'sja* ; *otsypát'sja* 'get a good sleep,

sleep enough, make up for lost sleep' [to satisfy an intense need for sleep caused by lack of sleep].

Incompletely $\text{Real}_2^{\text{II}}(F_n)$:
Continue to *S.* until
$\text{Real}_2^{\text{II}}(F_n)$ or until a fixed
time:

|| *nedosypát'*[1] 'not sleep enough'.

|| *dosypát'* 'finish sleeping, sleep out, sleep until...'

S. during the time *T*:

|| *prospat'* $[S_{\text{acc}} = T]$ 'sleep (through) $[S = T]$'.

S. during the short time interval *T*:

|| *pospat'* $[S_{\text{acc}} = T]$, colloq. *sosnut'* 'sleep a little, have a nap'.

to miss U as a result of sleeping

|| *prospat'*2 $[S_{\text{acc}} = U]$ 'sleep through $[S = U]$'.

become sober up as a result of sleeping:

|| *prospat'sja* 'sleep off'.

by the looks of *X* it is obvious that he has just slept:

X-zaspannyj 1 '*X* is, looks sleepy'.

Excess $^{t^o}$ (*body*) –
Sympt$_2$ (*has just slept*):

|| *byt' teplym so sna* 'has just awakened'.

to have been *S.* for a long time:

videt' desjatyj son 'be fast asleep, lit. see one's tenth dream'.

S. with no shelter above:

pod otkrytym nebom 'under the stars, in the open'.

immediately before *S.*:

pered snom, na son grjaduščij 'before sleeping, at bedtime'.

be $\text{Loc}^{\text{in}} + Y$ with the aim of *S.* there:

nocevat' $[\text{Loc}_{\text{in}} + Y]$ 'stay for the night $\text{Loc}_{\text{in}} + Y$'

Standard greetings in connection with sleep.

Before going to bed, in the evening: *Spokojnoj noci!* 'Good night!', more seldom *Prijatnyx sovidenij!* 'Pleasant dreams!'.

After waking up: *Kak spal(i)?, Kak spalos'?* 'How did you sleep, did you have a good sleep?'.

Sleeping poses.

S. razmetavsis' 'toss about in one's sleep'; *svernuvsis' kalačikom* ⟨*komočkom, v komoček*⟩ sleep 'rolled up in a ball, hunched up'; *na spine* 'on one's back', *na živote* 'on one's stomach', *na boku* 'on one's side'; *nakryvšis'* ⟨*zavernuvšis'*⟩*s golovoj* 'covered, bundled up'.

Special times for sleeping during the day.

In institutions for children: *mertvyj čas* 'nap-time'. In hospitals, sanatoriums, etc.: *tixij čas* 'rest hour'. In Latin countries, during the hot part of the day after lunch: *siesta* 'siesta'.

A sleeping person can see *sny II 1* 'dreams'. Sleep can be induced artificially: *snotvornym* 'through a soporific' or *gipnozom* 'by hypnosis'.

Pathologically prolonged sleep is called *letargija* 'lethargy'; the pathological condition manifesting itself in the performance of various actions while asleep is *somnambulizm* 'somnambulism', *lunatizm* 'somnambulism, sleepwalking'; the serious illness caused by the bite of the African tse-tse fly and characterized by prolonged sleep is known as *sonnaja bolezn'* 'sleeping sickness'. The method of teaching sleeping subjects is known as *gipnopedija* 'hypnopedia, sleep-learning'.

Vsju noc' emu ne davali spat' razgovory za stenoj 'The talking on the other side of the wall kept him from sleeping all night'; *on metalsja vorocalsja s boku na bok, no tak i ne somknul glaz* 'He tossed and turned from side to side, but he couldn't get a wink of sleep'; *Mne pora otdyxat' – ja uže troe sutok na nogax* ⟨=*ne ložilsja, bez sna*⟩ 'I have to rest – I've been on my feet for three days and nights now ⟨=haven't gone to bed, have been without sleep⟩'. – *Kolja u nas užasnyj sonja: kak razospitsja, tak ego ne dobudiš'sja* 'Our Kolja is a terrible sleepyhead: once he's fast asleep, you can't wake him up': *spit bez zadnix nog, xot' iz pusek streljaj* 'Sleeps like the dead – you couldn't wake him with a cannon'. *A Mašen'ka spit očen' čutko – prosypaetsja ot ljubogo šoroxa* 'But Masen'ka is a light sleeper – she wakes up from the least little noise'. – *Deti, nemedlenno idite spat'* ⟨*v postel'!*⟩! 'Children, go to sleep right now ⟨get to bed⟩!' *Xotja on vsjačeski borolsja so snom, on to i delo kleval nosom* 'Although he did his best to stay awake ⟨to fight off sleep⟩ now and again he dozed off ⟨nodded⟩'.

• SPAT' I VIDET' 'sleep and see'. // Magn (*xotet'* 'to want'). *LAVRY Y-a NE DAJUT SPAT' X-u* '*Y*'s laurels won't let *X* sleep' = *X* envies *Y*'s successes very much. See ZAVIDOVAT' 'to envy'.

NE DAVAT' SPAT' 'Not let sleep'. // Magn (*volnovat'* 'excite, disturb').

(1f) *X spit* '*X* sleeps, is sleeping' = a rather large, inanimate *X*, for which motion and noises are normal, is in the evening, at night or early in the morning quiet and motionless, as if sleeping

---

MU is the same as for SPAT'[1] 1a.

M_1 is usually a whole landscape or a large part of it [*gorod* 'city', *more* 'sea', *port* 'port', *gory* 'mountains', *les* 'forest', ...].

More spit 'The sea is sleeping'

S_0:	*Son I* 1c 'sleep'.
A_1(almost S):	*sonnyj* 3 'sleepy'.
Epit:[18]	*tixo* 'quietly', *mirno* 'peacefully', *spokojno* 'calmly', *bezmjatežno* 'tranquilly'.
Incep:	// *zasypát'* *I* 1b 'go to sleep, fall asleep'.
Fin:	// *prosyp'át'sja* , *probuždat'sja* 'wake up'.
Liqu:	// *budit'*, *propuzdat'* wake up, awaken.

Derevnja ešče spala: ni odin dymok ne podymalsja nad kryšami 'The village was still sleeping: there wasn't a single wisp of smoke over the rooftops. *Gornye veršiny Spjat vo t'me nočnoj, Sonnye doliny Polny svežej mgloj* 'The mountaintops sleep in the darkness of the night, The sleepy valleys are filled with fresh haze' [M.Ju. Lermontov].

(2a) *X spit* '*X* sleeps, is sleeping, is asleep' = *X* is idle or careless when he should act or pay attention – as if sleeping[1] 1a.

> MU is the same as for SPAT'[1] 1a.

M_1 is a person or a group of persons

Evropa spit 'Europe is asleep', *Jura spit* [*na urokax*] 'Jura sleeps [during his lessons]'.

Syn_c:	colloq. *zevat'2* 'gape', *rotozejnicat'* 'loaf around', *xlopat' ušami* 'listen without understanding', lit. 'bat one's ears', *lovit'* 〈*sčitat'*〉 *voron* 〈*galok*〉' dawdle, loaf about', lit. 'count crows'.
Anti:	*byt' načeku* 〈*nastorože*〉 'be alert, on one's guard'; *ne dremat'*, archaic *bdet'* 'stay awake, vigilant'.
S_1Anti:	archaic *nedremljuščee* 〈*nedremánnoe*〉 *oko, nedremljuščij glaz* 'vigilant, watchful eye'.
A_1Anti:	*bditel'nyj* 'vigilant', *vnimatel'nyj* 'attentive', *nedremljuscij* 'watchful'.
MagnAnti:	*burlit'* 'seethe' [be energetically active].

---

[18] Epit is an 'empty attribute'; a standard epithet with C_0 that repeats a part of its meaning. Cf. Epit (*spuskat'sja* 'descend') = *vniz* 'down', Epit (*opyt* 'experience') = *imejuščijsja*, 'that somebody has'.

S_0:   *son I* 2 'sleep', *spjačka* 2 'hibernation'. [19]

A_1:   *sonnyj* 4 'sleepy'.

Incep: // *zasypát'* 'fall asleep'.

Fin: // *prosypát'sja*[1] 'wake up'; *probuzdat'sja* 'awake', *vskolyx-*
                           nut'sja 'stir', *prixodit' v dvizenie* 'start up, begin to move' |
                           M_1 are mainly countries or social groupings, etc.

miss as a result
of sleeping: // *prospat' 2* 'oversleep, sleep through', *promorgat'*, *proze-*
                           vat', *proxlopat'*, *provoronit'* 'miss, let slip'.

*Nu, dolgo ešče vaš glavk spat' budet? Davno pora ekskavatory otgružat', a vy
i ne čuxaetes'!* [from a telephone conversation] 'Well how much longer does
your head office up there plan on sleeping, anyway? Those steam-shovels
should have been sent out a long time ago, and you haven't so much as
wiggled a finger!'.

(2b) Not $Fact_1^I$ (X) [$X = $*čuvstvo II* 'emotion', *sovest'* 'conscience', *razum*
'reason', *sila* 'strength',... – a faculty or organ of intellectual or spiritual
activity].

$1 = X$ [that which does not $Fact_1^I$]	$2 = M_1(X)$ [whose faculty or organ]
S_{nom}	v 'in' S_{loc}

Čuvstva (poka) spjat v nej 'Her emotions are (still) sleeping ⟨slumbering,
dormant⟩ within her'.

$Syn_\cap$:   *dremat'* 2 'doze, slumber'.

Fin: // *prosypát'sja* , *probuždát'sja* [v S_{loc}] [$=IncepFact_1^I$ (X)] 'awaken
              [in S]'.

Liqu: // *probuždat'*, *budit'* [$S_{acc} v$ S_{loc}] 'awaken, arouse [S in S], [$=$Caus
              $Fact_1^I$ (X)].

[19] For SPAT'[1] 2b the definition is a conventional one, i.e., in the form of a lexical function;
moreover, the lexical function F (in this case: not Fact[I]) refers not to any specific word
(cf. *son* 'sleep' $= S_0(spat'$ 'to sleep')), but to a variable X. In other words, the given word
C_0 (here *spat'*[1] 2b) is the lexical function F for all the words (for all X's) where in dictionary
entries C_0 is given as a value of the lexical function F. In the commentary to the definition
a type of these X's is given, since in this particular case they make up a closed group with
a common semantic element (unlike, say, a group of words for which Oper[1] is *vesti* 'lead,
bring').
    The actant structure in this particular case is determined by the relation: X *spit v*
$Y - e$ 'X sleeps in Y' $= X$, which belongs to Y, does not Fact [1].

Vaš um ozloblen, a sovest' spit 'Your mind is embittered, and your conscience is asleep'

(2c) Temporarily not $Func_1$ (X) or temporarily $AntiMagnFunc_1$ (X) [X is an emotion or emotional experience].

$1 = X$ [that which does not $Func_1$]	$2 = M_1(X)$ [whose emotion or emotional experience]
S_{nom}	(1) v 'in' S_{loc} (2) *v grudi* ⟨*serdce, duše*⟩ 'in the breast ⟨heart, soul⟩' S_{gen}

Nenavist' (*poka*) *spit v Maše* ⟨*v Mašinoj grudi,…*⟩ 'Hate is (still) sleeping within Maša ⟨in Maša's breast⟩'.

PerfIncep:

|| *Usnut'* 'fall asleep'.

Fin.

|| (*vnov', opjat'*) *prosypat'sja[1]*, *probuždat'sja* '(again, anew) awake'.

Magn(X) + Fin:

|| *s novoj siloj prosypát'sja*, *probuždat'sja* 'awake with new force'.

Liqu:

|| *probuždat', budit'* [S_{acc}] 'awaken, arouse [S].'

[v S_{loc} 'in S' *v grudi* ⟨*serdce, duše*⟩ S_{gen} 'in the breast ⟨heart, soul,…⟩ of S'].

(3) elevated X *spit v Y-e* 'X is sleeping in Y' = X is dead and his body is in Y, where it will always be, as if sleeping[1] 1a.

(N.B: this word is used in limited contexts the nature of which is not quite clear.)

$1 = X$ [whose body]	$2 = Y$ [where it is located]
S_{nom}	$Loc_{in}S$

(1) $D_1 \neq Q$ [S is not used in indefinite personal constructions].[20]

[20] Q is the symbol of the so-called indefinite personal subject, meaning 'some people'; cf. the German *man*, French *on*, etc.

(2) $D_2 \neq \emptyset$ [except for formulas of the type: *Spi spokojno, dorogoj tova-rišč!* 'Sleep peacefully, dear comrade!'].

Syn: elevated *pokoit'sja* 2 'repose'; *ležat'* [$Loc_{in}S$] 'lie' [$Loc_{in}S$].
Syn_c: *byt' poxoronen* [$Loc_{in}S$] 'be buried' [$Loc_{in}S$].
S_0:   *son I* 3 'sleep'.
S_1:   *pokojnik* 'the deceased'.
S_2:   *mogila* 'grave'
Bon: *mirno, spokojno* 'peacefully, quietly'.

Mertvyj, v grobe mirno spi, Žizn'ju pol'zujsja, živusčij! 'May the dead sleep peacefully in their graves and the living make the most of life!'

SP | AT'^2, *lju, iš'*, past *al, alá, aló*, imperf. *X spit s Y* '*X* sleeps, is sleeping with *Y*' = *X* and *Y* have sexual intercourse in normal conditions; not the moment of speech. (Cf. POLOVAJA ŽIZN' 'sexual life'.)

1 = X [who has intercourse]	2 = Y [with whom intercourse is had]
S_{nom}	*s* 'with' $S_{instr\ obligatory}$

M_1, M_2 are people.

On s nej spit 'He sleeps with her'.
Syn: *žit'^2* 'live'.
S_0:   *(polovaja) svjaz'* '(sexual) relationship'.
$SingS_0$:   *(polovye) snoženija* '(sexual) intercourse', bookish *soitie* 'coition', med. *koitus* 'coitus'.
S_{loc}:   *postel'3* 'bed'.
Sing: *perespat'* 'sleep over with, spend the night with'.

SON, *sna, sn\u00fd*, masc. I 1a. no. pl. S_0 (*spat'^1* 1a 'to sleep') 'sleep'.

1 = X [who is sleeping]
(1) S_{gen} (2) A_{poss}

son Petra 'Petr's sleep', *Mašin son* 'Maša's sleep'.

V_0:

Figur:

S_{loc}:

$\text{Magn}_{\text{[switched off]}}$:

$\text{Magn} + \text{Bon}_{\text{[switched off]}}$:

$\text{AntiMagn}_{\text{[switched off]}}$:

$\text{AntiMagn}_{\text{[switched off]}} +$
Anti Bon:

Bon:

AntiVer + AntiBon:

Loc_{in}:

Oper_1:

IncepOper_1:

$\text{IncepOper}_1 +$
$\text{Magn}_{\text{['switched off']}}$:

$\text{IncepOper}_1 + \text{AntiVer}$:

FinOper_1:

LiquFunc_0:

hinder LiquFunc_0:

Func_1:

(not) IncepFunc_1:

Fact_1 ['rest']:

$F_k = \text{Conv}_{012}$ (to feel the physical need of S):

---

spat'[1]*Ia* 'sleep'.

ob'jat'ja [~*a*] 'embrace [of sleep] | *S* has no dependent words // *ob'jat'ja Morfeja* 'Morpheus' embrace'.

lože 'couch, bed'.

besprobudnyj 'heavy, deep'. *mertvyj* lit, 'dead'.

krepkij 'sound', *glubokij* 'deep', *bogatyrskij* 'sound, lit. heroic'.

čutkij 'light'.

nespokojnyj 'restless', *bespokojnyj* 'troubled'.

legkij 'light', *tixij* 'quiet', *mirnyj* 'peaceful', *spokojnyj* 'calm'. *bezmjatežnyj* 'tranquil'; *sladkij* 'sweet' [of the moment of speech].

tjaželyj 'uneasy, troubled' [giving no rest, unrefreshing].

vo [~*e*] 'in [one's sleep]'. ⎫ *S* must have
spat' [~*om*] 'to sleep [a, ⎬ an attribute,
the sleep]'. ⎪ usually one
zasypát' [~*om*] 'fall asleep'. ⎭ of its LF.

pogružat'sja [*v*~] 'sink, plunge [into a slumber]'.

zabyvat'sja [~ −*om*] 'doze, drop off' | it is desirable to have an attribute with *S*, generally one of its LF.

bookish *probuždat'sja* [*ot (o)* ~*a*] 'awaken [from sleep]'.

narušat' 'disturb', *preryvat'* 'interrupt', *trevožit'* 'disturb, bother', *spugnut'* 'frighten' [~] | $D_1(S) \neq \emptyset$.

oxranjat' 'protect', *stereč* 'guard', *storožit'* 'watch over' elevated *lelejat'* 'cherish, foster' [~] | M_1 is a person.

bookish *posetit'* [S_{acc}] 'visit [*S*]'.

(ne) idti (ne) prixodit' [*k* S_{dat}] '(not) come [to *S*]'.

osvežat' [S_{acc}] 'to refresh [*S*]'.

klonit' [$S_{acc}v$~⟨*ko* ~*u*⟩], lit. 'drive, incline [*S* towards sleep]'.

Magn(F_k):   *neuderžimo* 'irresistibly'.
the sleep which comes
during the morning hours
of the normal S time: *utrennij* 'morning sleep'.

On spal očen' čutkim snom, prosypajas' ot ljubogo moego dviženija 'He slept very lightly (a very light sleep), waking up at my every movement'. *Ja ešče ne uspel opustit' golovu na podušku, kak uže pogruzilsja v glubokij son* 'My head hadn't even touched the pillow and already I sank into a deep sleep'. *Deva totčas umolkla, Son ego legkij leleja* 'The maid immediately fell silent to cherish his light sleep' [A. S. Puškin]. *Byvalo, ves' večer neuderžimo klonit v son, a ljažeš' – i son ne idet* 'Sometimes you'd feel irresistibly drowsy all evening, but if you lay down, you couldn't get to sleep ⟨sleep wouldn't come⟩'. *Liš' pod utro on zabylsja tjaželym snom* 'It wasn't until towards morning that he dropped off into an uneasy sleep'. *Utrennij son osobenno polezen* 'Morning sleep is especially healthy'.

(1b) no pl. The physical ability or need to sleep (*spat'*[1] 1a). [$= S_0$PredAble$_1$ (*spat'*[1] 1a) or S_0 (feel the need to sleep[1] 1a)].

> MU is the same as for SON I 1a 'sleep', but the corresponding actant is not expressed syntactically.

Except for the examples specified below, S. has no subordinate words.
Syn: *sonlivost'* 'sleepiness, drowsiness'.
Anti: *bessonica* 'insomnia'.
Ver: *normalnyj* 'normal', *zdorovyj* 'healthy' [not of the moment of speech].
FinOper$_1$:   *poterjat'* [~] 'lose [one's sleep]' *lisit'sja* [~*a*] 'be deprived of [sleep]'.
Func$_1$:   *byt'* [*u* S_{gen}] 'have' S must have an attribute – an LF of S or of *son I 1a* 'sleep'.
Func$_1$+AntiVer: *byt' narušen* [*u* S_{gen}] 'be disturbed'.
Magn not Func$_1$:   [~*a u* S_{gen}] *ne byt' ni v odnom glazu* 'not feel at all like sleeping' | usually in the present.
FinFunc$_1$:   *propadat'* [*u* S_{gen}] 'vanish'.
instantly PerfFinFunc$_1$:   [~*a* (*u* S_{gen})] *kak ne byvalo* 'not a trace [of sleep] remained, [sleep] vanished without a trace'.
CausFunc$_1$:   *navevat'* [~*na* 'evoke S_{acc}] lit. cast [sleep onto S]' | M_1 is information, activity or its results [*razgovor* 'conversation', *muzyka* 'music', *melodija* 'melody'].

instantly PerfLiquFunc$_1$:	[*u S*$_{gen}$] *kak rukoj snimat'* 'vanish as if by magic' | *M*$_1$ is not a person; usually impersonal.
Liqu$_{(1)}$Func$_1$:	*gnat', progonjat* [$\sim$ *ot S*$_{gen}$] 'drive away [sleep from *S*]'.
Liqu$_1$Func$_1$:	*strjaxivat'* [*s sebja* $\sim$] 'shake [sleep] off [oneself]'.
try AntiReal$_1$:	*borot'sja* [*so* $\sim$ *om*] 'fight, struggle with, against [sleep]'.
Fact$_1$:	*odolevat'* 'overcome', *smorit'* 'vanquish' [*S*$_{acc}$]; poetic *smežit'* [*S*$_{dat}$] *resnicy* ⟨*veki, veždy*⟩ 'shut somebody's lashes ⟨eyelids⟩'.

U nego očen' čutkij son, ego budit malejšee dviženie 'He sleeps very lightly – the least noise wakes him up'. *Naprasno ja gnal ot sebja son; menja vse ravno odolevala zevota* 'I tried in vain to drive my sleepiness away; I was seized by a yawn anyway'; *nakonec, ja vypil kofe – i sna kak ne byvalo* ⟨= *i son kak rukoj snjalo*⟩ 'Finally, I drank some coffee, and my sleepiness vanished without a trace' ⟨it disappeared as if by magic⟩'. — *Kak živeš'? – Borjus': do obeda s golodom, posle obeda so snom* 'How's it going? It's a struggle – with hunger before dinner and with sleep afterwards' [current joke].

(1c) No pl. S_0 (*spat'*[1] 1b 'to sleep').

> MU is the same as for SON I 1a 'sleep'

Son morja 'the sleep of the sea', *ego son* 'its sleep'.

Syn$_⊃$:	*pokoj* 'rest, peace', *tišina* 'quiet, silence'.
A$_1$:	*ob'jatyj* [$\sim$ *om*] 'embraced, enveloped [by sleep]'.
Oper$_1$:	*byt' ob'jat* [$\sim$ *om*] 'to be embraced [by sleep]'.
IncepOper$_1$:	*pogružat'sja* [*v* $\sim$] 'sink [into sleep]'.
FinOper$_1$:	*probuždat'sja* [*ot (o)* $\sim$ *a*] 'awake from [sleep]'.
LiquFunc$_0$:	*narušat'* 'disturb', *trevožit'* 'bother' [$\sim$ *S*$_{gen}$].

Ob'jata Sevil'ja I mrakom, i snom 'Seville is enveloped by darkness and sleep' [A. S. Puškin]. *Ničto ne narušalo son gornyx veršin* 'Nothing disturbed the slumber of the mountain peaks'.

(2) no pl. S_0 (*spat'*[1] 2b 'to sleep').

> MU is the same as for SON I 1a

D$_1$ is not a person.

[*tysjaceletnij*] *son Azii* '[the thousand-year] slumber of Asia'.

Syn: 　　　　　　　*spjačka 2* 'dormancy'.

Syn⊐: 　　　　　　*apatija* 'apathy'.

Magn^{intens}: 　　　*besprobudnyj* 'deep', *mertvyj* 'heavy'.

Magn^{temp}: 　　　　*mnogoletnij* 'many years long', *stoletnyj* 'hundred-year', *vekovoj* 'age long, lasting for ages', *mnogovekovoj* 'century-old, ancient', *tysjaceletnij* 'thousand-year'.

Oper$_1$: 　　　　　　*spat'* [~*om*] 'to sleep [a, the sleep]' | *S* must have an attribute, usually Magn.

IncepOper$_1$: 　　　*pogružat'sja* [*v* ~] 'sink [into slumber]'.

FinOper$_1$: 　　　　*očnut'sja* 'come to', *probuždat'sja* 'awake', poetic archaic *vosprjanut'* [*ot(o)* ~*a*] 'arise [from sleep]'.

CausFunc$_1$: 　　　*nagonjat'* [~ *na* S_{acc}] 'make [somebody sleep]' [sleep is caused by boredom] | *S* is a person.

Rossija vsprjanet oto sna! 'Russia shall arise from her slumber!' [A. S. Puškin]. *Svoimi lekcijami on sposoben* ⟨=*ego lekcii sposobny*⟩ *nagnat' son na ljubuju auditoriju* 'He can put any audience to sleep with his lectures ⟨=his lectures are capable of putting any audience to sleep⟩'.

(3) no pl. S_0 (*spat'*^{1} 3 'to sleep').

1 = X [whose body]	2 = Y [where it is located]
(1) S_{gen}	
(2) $A_{poss\ obligatory}$	

Epit is obligatory with *S*.

večnyj son Petra 'the eternal sleep of Peter', *ee večnyj son* 'her eternal sleep'.

Epit: 　　　　　　　*večnyj* 'eternal', *poslednij* 'last', archaic *mogil'nyj* 'sepulchral'; poetic ~ *mogily* 'of the grave' | $D_1(S)=\emptyset$.

Oper$_1$: 　　　　　　*spat'* '[~*om* (Loc$_{in}$ *S*)]' 'to sleep [(Loc$_{in}$ *S*)]'

PerfIncepOper$_1$: 　　*usnut'*, archaic elevated *(o)počit'* [~*om*] 'fall asleep'.

F_k=make noise or create disorder near the place of burial – as if LiquFunc$_0$: 　　*narušat'* 'disturb', *trevožit'* 'bother' [~],

as if not Perm F_k: 　　　*sterreč'* 'guard', *storožit* 'watch over' [~].

I volny finskie ne budut Trevozit' vecnyj son Petra 'And the Finnish waves shall not disturb Peter's eternal slumber' [A. S. Puškin]. *Tri sosny nad mogiloj steregut poslednij son poeta* 'Three pine trees over his grave watch over the poet's final slumber'.

II.1. S_1 (*snit'sja* 'to dream'). (Cf. GALLIUCINACIJA 'hallucination'.)

$1 = Y$ [who/what is dreamed (about)]	$2 = X$ [who is dreaming]
(1) Sentence (2) (colloq.) *pro* S_{gen} 'about S' (3) (colloq.) *o* S_{loc} 'about S'	(1) S_{gen} (2) A_{poss}

[... *rasskazal mne užasnyj*] *son (Vasilija): v pole stojali viselicy, i na nix kačalis' trupy:* 'told me about Vasilij's horrible dream: there were gallows in the field with corpses dangling from them'; *Kolin son* ⟨ = *Son Koli*⟩ *pro Marinu* ⟨*o poezdke s Marinoj v Pariz*⟩ 'Kolja's dream about Marina ⟨about his trip to Paris with Marina⟩'; '*Son Popova*' '*Popov's Dream*' [name of a poem by A. K. Tolstoj]

Syn:	*snovidenie* 'dream'.
Syn$_\cap$:	*grezy* 1 'dreams, reverie'.
Anti$_\cap$:	*jav'* 'reality'.
Gener:	*videnie* 'vision' │ usually in pl.
Figur:	*carstvo* [~*ov*] 'world of dreams' S is in pl.
IncepOper$_2$(Figur):	*unosit'sja* [*v carstvo* ~*ov*] 'be carried away into a dream world'.
V_0:	*snit'sja* 'dream'.
Bon:	*xorošij* 'good', *čudnyj* 'wonderful'.
AntiBon:	*ploxoj* 'bad', *durnoj* 'bad'; *strašnyj* 'terrible', *užasnyj* 'horrible', *žutkij* 'awful', *košmarnyj* 'nightmarish'// *košmar* 'nightmare'.
Adv$_{1A}$:	*vo* [~*e*] 'in [one's sleep]' │ $M_1(G) = M_2(S)$.
Loc$_{in}$:	*vo* [~*e*] 'in [one's sleep]' │ $D_2(S) = \emptyset$, 'be only a dream'.
not Adv$_2$:	*bez* [~*ov*] 'without, [sleep]-less' │ $D_1(S) = \emptyset$.
Copul = Oper$_1$:	*byt'* [*tol'ko* ⟨ = *liš'*⟩~] │ $D_1 = to$, *èto*, 'this' [*Uvy, èto byl liš' son,...* 'Alas, it was but a dream']; *byt'* [~*om*] 'to be [a dream]'.
Oper$_2$:	*videt'* [~] 'see [a dream]'.

$Func_2$:

$Func_2 + AntiBon +$
$Magn^{intens}$:

$Labor_{12}$:

$Labor_{21}$:
$Magn(Labor_{21})$:
$F_k = Fact_0$ (S as a prediction of the future):
$Perf(F_k)$:

$A_1(Perf(F_k)$ or should $F_k)$:
believe that Ss can F_k:
$F_1 =$ explain what a S
means:
book – $S_{instr}(F_1)$:

snit'sja [S_{dat}] 'to dream'; *byvat'* [*u* S_{gen}] '[somebody] has dreams'.

mucit' [S_{acc}] 'torment [S]'.

javljat'sja [$S_{dat}vo \sim e$] 'appear [to somebody in his sleep]' | D_1 is a living being; *prividet'sja* [$S_{dat}vo \sim e$] 'appear [to somebody in his sleep]'.

videt' [$S_{acc}vo \sim e$] 'see [something in a dream]'.
kak najavu 'as if one were awake'.

sbyvat'sja 'come true'.
[$\sim$] *v ruku* 'has come true' | only present tense; the phrase is a complete utterance.
veščij 'oracular', *proročeskij* 'prophetic'.
verit' [*v* $\sim y$] 'believe [in dreams]' | in pl.

tolkovat' [$\sim$] 'interpret [a dream]'.
//archaic *sonnik* 'dream-book'.

Mne snitsja, snitsja, snitsja, Mne snitsja čudnyj son: Šikarnaja devica Evangel' skix vremen 'I dream, I dream, I dream a marvellous dream: An elegant maiden from gospel times' [A. A. Arxangel'skij]. *Est' son* [=*son II 1*] *takoj, ne spiš, a tol'ko snitsja, Čto žaždeš' sna* [=*son I 1a*] 'There is a kind of dream [*son II 1*] where you don't actually sleep but only dream that you hunger for sleep [*son I 1a*]' [B. L. Pasternak]. *Včera vo sne ja dolgo razgovarival s Vami* 'I spoke for a long while with you in a dream yesterday'. *Agrippina zadremala, snačala pomnja skvoz' dremu, gde ona, potom zasnula gluboko i vo sne uvidela, čto budto fotografiruet kogo-to.* 'Agrippina nodded... first she remembered through her drowsiness where she was, then she fell into a deep sleep and dreamed she was photographing someone' [*Novyj mir* 10, 1971].

• VO SNE I NAJAVU 'in one's sleep and in one's waking hours, asleep and awake'. Dupl (*postojanno* 'constantly').[21]

(2a) mostly pl. *Son X-a = mečta X-a* 'X's dream = X's day-dream, vision, dream [of something in the future, unrealized, etc.]' – as if *son II 1*.

[21] Dupl is a lexical function. If Dupl$(X) = Y$, then 'X' $\approx$ 'Y', and

$$Y = Z_1 \cdot \overset{6}{\to} \cdot \text{ and } \cdot \overset{2}{\to} \cdot Z_2,$$

where Z_1 and Z_2 are antonyms or synonyms.

$1 = Y$ [what the dream (*mečta*) is about]	$2 = X$ [who (*mečtaet*)] dreams
	(1) S_{gen} (2) A_{poss}

[*Zolotye*] *sny celovecestva* '[The golden] dreams of mankind'; *ee*⟨*Verin*⟩ *volšebnyj son* 'Her ⟨Vera's⟩ enchanted dream'.

Syn⊃:   *mečta* 'dream, vision'.
Syn∩:   *illjuzija* 'illusion', *miraž* 'mirage'.
Anti∩:   *jav'* 'reality, real life', *real'naja* 'real' ⟨*grubaja* 'coarse', *žestokaja* 'cruel', *surovaja* 'harsh'⟩ *dejstvitel'nost'* 'reality', *grubaja* 'coarse' ⟨*surovaja* 'harsh'⟩ *real'nost'* 'reality'.
Bon: *prekrasnyj* 'wonderful', *zolotoj* 'golden', *volšebnyj* 'enchanted', *divnyj* 'marvellous'.
Fact₀: *sbyvat'sja* 'come true'.
CausFunc₂: bookish *navevat'* ~*s* [dat] 'evoke' [a dream in somebody]'.

Čest' bezumcu, kotoryj naveet Čelovecestvu son-zolotoj 'Honor the madman who gives mankind a golden dream' [P. Béranger].

(2b) no pl. *Son X-a* 'X's dream' = X which is improbable, ephemeral or transient – as if *son* II 1.

$1 = X$ [that which is unlikely]
S_{gen}

(1) M_1 is not a physical object.
(2) D_1 is undesirable if S has no attribute.
(3) D_1 is obligatory if $G(S) \neq \mathrm{LF}(S)$.

[*Košmarnyj*] *son fašizma* [*otošel v prošloe*] '[The nightmarish] dream of Fascism [has receded into the past, is a part of the past]'.
   Impossible: *ego ⟨*naš*⟩ *son* 'his (our) dream', *son čertoga 'dream of the palace'.
   Undesirable: ⁇*Son fašizma otošel v prošloe* 'The dream of Fascism has

receded into the past', ?*Košmarnyj son otošel v prošloe* 'The nightmarish dream has receded into the past'.

Syn∩:   *skazka* 2 'tale, fairy tale', *miraž* 'mirage'.

A_1 = Adv₁: *kak* ⟨bookish *točno*⟩ [~] 'like, just like [a dream]', *kak* [*vo* ~*e*] 'as if [in a dream]'.

Bon: *zolotoj* 'golden', *volšebnyj* 'enchanted', *čudesnyj* 'wondrous'.

AntiBon: *durnoj* 'bad', *tjaželyj* 'troubled', *strašnyj* 'terrible', *žutkij* 'awful', *košmarnyj* 'nightmarish'⟩.

Oper₁: *byt'* [~] 'be [a dream]', *byt'* [*kak* ~] 'be like [a dream]', *byt' poxož* [*na* ~] 'resemble [a dream]', *byt'* [*kak vo* ~*e*] 'be [as in a dream]'.

Ja navsegda soxranju v pamjati volšebnyj son etix mesjacev 'I shall always remember the enchanting dream of these months'. *'Zizn' est' son'* 'La vida es sueña' – *Life is a Dream* [play by Calderón]. *Isčezli junye zabavy, Kak son, kak utrennij tuman* 'The amusements of youth have all disappeared like a dream, like the morning fog' [A. S. Puškin].

ZASYPÁ|T' [22], *ju, eš', jut*, imperf. I 1a. 'to fall asleep'//Incep (*spat'*[1] 1a 'to sleep').

$1 = X$
[who sleeps]

S_{nom}

Petr zasypaet 'Petr is falling asleep'.

Anti: *prosypát'sja* 'awake', bookish *probuždat'sja*.

MagnPredAble₁: *legko* 'easily' ⟨*xorošo* 'well'⟩, *bystro* 'quickly', *mgnovenno* 'instantly' ~*t'*.

AntiMagnPredAble₁: *ploxo* 'poorly' ⟨*s trudom* 'with difficulty'⟩ ~*t'*.

Perf: *zasnut'* 1a, *usnut'* 1a 'fall asleep'.

LF Caus, medicine S_{med} Caus and Imper – the same as for *spat'*[1] 1a.

(1b) *zasypaet* 'X is falling asleep' – It is obvious from X's appearance that his body needs (to) sleep [≈Sympt (Magn⁻⁵ *xotet' spat'*[1] 1a 'want to sleep'].

---

[22] ZASYPAT'² is from *sypat'* 'to sprinkle', cf. ZASY'PAT'².

$1 = X$
[who wants to sleep]
S_{nom}

Rebenok (prjamo) zasypaet 'The baby is going (right) to sleep'.

Magn: *prosto* 'simply', *prjamo* 'straight, right', *(prjamo) na xodu* '(right)' on one's feet'.

Ne mogu rabotat' – prosto zasypáju 'I can't work – I simply drop off, want to go to sleep'.

(1c) // Incep *(spat'*[1] *1b)*.

$1 = X$
[what/who is sleeping]
S_{nom}

Gory zasypajut 'The mountains go to sleep, are dozing'.

M_1 is usually a whole landscape or a large part of it [*gorod* 'city', *more* 'sea', *port* 'port', *gory* 'mountains', *les* 'forest', ...].
Syn$_\cap$: *zamirat'* 'die down, come to a standstill', *cepenet'* 'freeze, become torpid'.
Anti: *prosypát'sja* 'awake', *probuždat'sja*.
Epit: *tixo* 'quietly'.
Perf: *zasnut'* 1c, *usnut'* 1b 'fall asleep'.

(2) // Incep *(spat'*[1] *2a* 'to sleep').

$1 = X$
[who is sleeping]
S_{nom}

M_1 is a person or group of persons.

Auditorija zasypaet 'The audience is falling asleep'.
Anti: *prosypát'sja*[1], *probuždat'sja* 'awake'; *prixodit' v dviženie* 'begin to move, stir'.
Perf: *zasnut'* 'fall asleep'.

X zasypáet '*X* drops off to sleep, goes to sleep' = *X* is dying little by little, non-violently – as if going to sleep[1] Ia, not of the moment of speech.

$$1 = X$$
[who is dying]

$$S_{nom}$$

(1) M_1 is either a fish or a human being.

(2) If M_1 is a human being: (a) Z. must be used with *naveki, navsegda* 'forever' or *čtoby bol'še (nikogda) ne prosypat'sja ⟨prosnut'sja⟩* 'never again to awake', (b) *zasypat'* is generally used in the perf. aspect [*zasnut'*]

Perf: *zasnut', usnut'* 'fall asleep'.
A_1Perf: *snulyj* 'sleepy' | M_1 is a fish.

ZASN | UT', *ú, es'* perf (*zasypát'*[1] I, II) 'to fall asleep'.

> MU is the same as for ZASYPÁT'[1] I, II respectively

Epit: *tixo* 'quietly'.
Magn[intens]:   *krepko* 'soundly', *kak ubityj* 'like the dead' | from *spat'*[1] Ia 'to sleep'.

Liza zasnula prjamo v kresle. 'Liza fell asleep right there in the armchair'. *My stojali s toboj U zasnuvšej reki* 'You and I stood on the bank of the sleeping river' [romance by P. I. Cajkovskij]. *Lektora ne smuščalo to, čto polovina studentov davno zasnula* 'The lecturer was not bothered by the fact that half of the students had fallen asleep a long time ago'. *5 Marta 1653 g. velikij učenyj tixo zasnul naveki nad svoej rukopis'ju* 'On March 5, 1653 the great scholar quietly went to sleep forever over his manuscript'.

State Pedagogical Institute, Moscow

FOUNDATIONS OF LANGUAGE

SUPPLEMENTARY SERIES

Edited by Morris Halle, Peter Hartmann,
K. Kunjunni Raja, Benson Mates, J. F. Staal,
Pieter A. Verburg, and John W. M. Verhaar

SOLE DISTRIBUTORS IN THE U.S.A. AND CANADA:
Volumes 1–12: Humanities Press / New York